AA

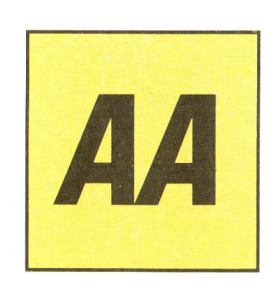

MOTORISTS ATLAS OF GREAT BRITAIN

Produced by the Cartographic Department,
Publications Division of the Automobile Association

Based on the Ordnance Survey maps, with the permission of the Controller of HM Stationery Office. Crown Copyright reserved. The Ordnance Survey is not responsible for the accuracy of the National Grid in this production.

The contents of this book are believed correct at the time of printing. Nevertheless, the publisher can accept no responsibility for errors or omissions, or for changes in the details given.

© The Automobile Association 1984   58133
 First edition Nov 1977
 Second edition Nov 1978
 Third edition Mar 1980
 Fourth edition Nov 1981
 Fifth edition Mar 1984

All rights reserved. No part of this publication may be reproduced, stored in a retrieval system, or transmitted in any form or by any means — electronic, mechanical, photocopying, recording or otherwise, unless the permission of the publisher has been given beforehand.

Published by the Automobile Association,
Fanum House, Basingstoke, Hampshire RG21 2EA

Printed and bound in Great Britain by
Purnell and Sons (Book Production) Ltd.,
Member of the BPCC Group, Paulton, Bristol

ISBN 0 86145 227 5

CONTENTS

Emergency Driving *4-18*
Emergency Situations 4-5
Mechanical Failures 6-7
Emergency Problem 8-9
Preparation for
Emergencies 10-11
Skidding 12-13
Skid Pans 14-15
Emergency Quiz 16-17
Emergency Toolkit 18

Journey Planning *20*

Route Planning Maps 20-25
Sign Language 26
Grasp the Grid 27

Legend 28
Key to Map Pages 1

Road Maps *2-67*
Mileage Chart 68

Index to Road Maps 69-100

Emergency Situations

An unexpected situation demanding immediate action can happen to any driver at any time. A great deal can be done to prevent a situation catching a driver unawares, and it is also possible to learn how to handle such a situation safely.

AVOIDING EMERGENCIES
There are some basic rules which should govern everyone's driving. If these are followed properly, few situations should develop unexpectedly.

Keep alert Driving is a task which demands full concentration. If you are being distracted, perhaps by children or pets in the car, you should stop and try to minimise the distraction. You should not drive if you feel tired, ill or unable to concentrate properly. Always expect the unexpected.

Drive within your capabilities
Recognise that many factors such as your age will affect your reactions and also your eyesight, so adjust your driving accordingly. Gear your driving to the changing weather conditions.

Anticipate developments Good and thorough observation of everything that is going on all around will enable you to anticipate a situation before it develops. Feet, noticed under a parked vehicle, should warn you of the hitherto unseen presence of a pedestrian. One of the children fighting on the pavement may run in the road in front of you. A ball rolling into the road will probably be followed by a child. Any suspicion that another road user is acting dangerously or is

At all costs a head-on collision must be avoided. The overtaking car is committed to a dangerous manoeuvre, so the blue car, approaching from the opposite direction, has to brake firmly in a straight line. When speed is reduced, the driver closely inspects the verge and then steers into it to avoid collision

Potential hazards: a parked ice-cream van (above), and (right) slow-moving farm vehicles

in trouble should prompt you to slow down and give him plenty of room. Keep asking yourself what you would do if someone around you did something unexpected.

Know your car A well-maintained car should behave predictably in response to your handling, and you should be thoroughly familiar with what it will do under different conditions. The car will, of course, behave differently when it is fully laden with passengers and luggage, compared with its performance when you are driving on your own. You should also know how it will behave in response to sudden action on your part. Lack of knowledge or experience of your car's capabilities can severely hamper your reactions in an emergency.

Avoid head-on collisions A head-on collision, particularly with another moving vehicle, and even at slow speeds, will usually cause a great deal of injury and damage. If a collision is inevitable it is always preferable to try and make it a sideways scrape, or to drive obliquely on to a soft verge or through a hedge. Do not risk turning your car over, however. In every emergency situation you have a choice. Always try to minimise the danger to car passengers and other road users, before protecting the car.

COPING WITH AN EMERGENCY

An emergency can happen at any time, so always be prepared. Careful observation and considerate driving should prevent you being taken by surprise. In spite of these precautions, you may nevertheless be presented with a situation demanding emergency action. Every situation is different, of course, but there are several points to remember in every case which should enable you to minimise the risk.

The red car pulls out in front of the blue car, which is travelling at speed. There is not time for the blue car to stop, so it brakes in a straight line for as long as possible, but retains steering control by not allowing the wheels to lock

Do not brake too hard The instinctive reaction to an emergency is to brake hard. In some cases, however, it may be better to accelerate out of trouble. If braking is called for, apply the brakes firmly and in a straight line. Do not swerve while braking, and do not allow the wheels to lock up. If they do so, release the brakes at once, then re-apply them more sensitively. This allows you to be able to steer out of trouble to some extent. Brake progressively rather than harshly and give the vehicle behind as much time as possible to react to your brake lights so that he will not run into the back of you. When the road surface is not dry or even, braking should always be carried out more carefully to ensure adhesion of all the tyres. If this adhesion is lost the car will get out of control, and you will no longer be able to minimise the effects of the emergency on yourself or others.

Warn other road users Generally, other road users will be unaware that an emergency is developing, so sound your horn to warn them.

Never give up Keep control of your car all the time. This will usually turn an emergency into a problem you have managed to solve.

5

Mechanical Failures

Not all emergencies are produced by the behaviour of other road users. Some of them are caused by a failure of one or more of the mechanical components on a car, although this is less likely to happen if the car is properly maintained. Should a failure occur unexpectedly, the most important consideration is to retain control of the car. Let other road users know that something is wrong by sounding the horn and switching on the lights, then check the mirrors, indicate and move to the side of the road.

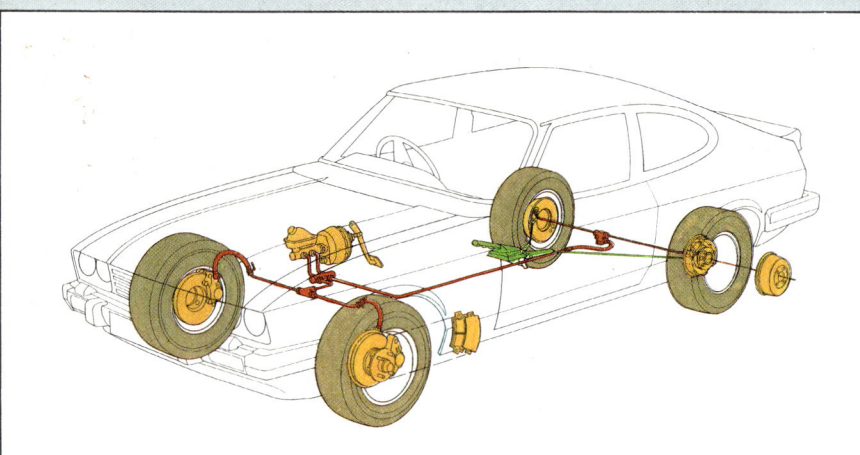

BRAKE FAILURE
Most modern cars have dual braking circuits so complete brake failure is unlikely. If one circuit fails, perhaps due to a break in the hydraulic pressure line, the other will usually be sufficient, although less effective.

In the event of complete brake failure slow down using the handbrake and changing down quickly through the gears. Attempts to change gear too quickly or over-harsh use of the handbrake can make the car unstable, however.

As the speed drops gently ease the car to the side of the road and stop. Should there be insufficient time to stop using handbrake and gears, it may be necessary to scrape the side of your vehicle against walls or banks.

The brakes may become ineffective if they get wet after you have driven through a ford or a flood. Dry them by applying the brakes gently for a short distance whilst the car is moving at moderate speed. A leaking oil seal can also drastically reduce braking efficiency.

If the brakes get too hot they can also lose their effectiveness. This could happen, for example, when descending a long hill in top gear. The brake fluid may partially vaporise and the pedal would sink to the floor with little effect on the brakes. Pumping the pedal rapidly up and down frequently restores braking power.

Should the brake pads get so hot that they 'fade', there will be no feeling of sponginess when the brake pedal is applied. A short stop usually allows them to recover, but they should be checked at the soonest opportunity.

BURST TYRE
If a front tyre bursts, there will be a strong pull to one side. This must be controlled by deliberate and jerk-free counter-steering to retain a straight course. A rear tyre burst may provoke a tail slide, which again, requires restrained, smooth steering correction. In either case do not change gear, but take your feet off the accelerator and clutch pedals, then brake gently and bring the car to a standstill. Use a hard shoulder if possible, but do not attempt to stop the car on a soft verge. A firm base will be required when jacking up the car to change the wheel.

The essentials of tyre maintenance are to keep the correct tyre pressures, to ensure that the treads are adequate and that there are no cuts or bulges in the side walls.

STEERING FAILURE
It is very rare indeed for steering to fail without some warning, such as an increase in steering wheel movement, or steering 'wander' when attempting to keep a straight line. As soon as any of these symptoms are detected, the system should be checked by a fully qualified mechanic.

A sudden jolt to badly worn steering joints could cause them to part, resulting in steering loss. On no account try to crash stop but brake gently and progressively.

LOOSE WHEEL
Warnings of a wheel becoming loose are 'clanking' noises and unusual handling. If these symptoms occur, slow down gently and stop. If the cause is loose wheel nuts, tighten them, then drive gently to the nearest garage where a competent mechanic can check the wheel, its nuts and bolts, wheel bearings and allied parts.

If the wheel comes off suddenly and without any warning, the car will drop at the corner affected. It will pull strongly to one side and this must be countered by firm steering and gentle, progressive braking to bring the car to a halt and prevent it slewing.

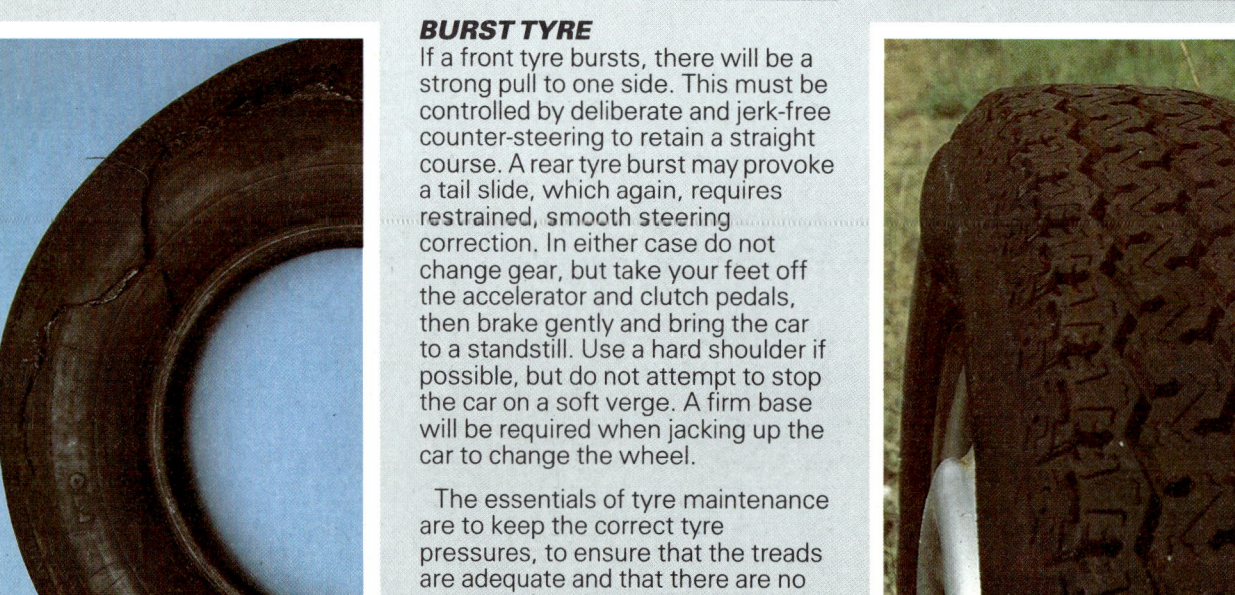

SUSPENSION FAILURES

Although suspension failures are relatively rare, calm, deliberate control will prevent an accident if failure should occur. Coil springs are least prone to failure. Hydrolastic and Hydrogas units usually give some indication before they fail completely, but should a leaf spring break, it may puncture a tyre or it could sever a hydraulic pressure line.

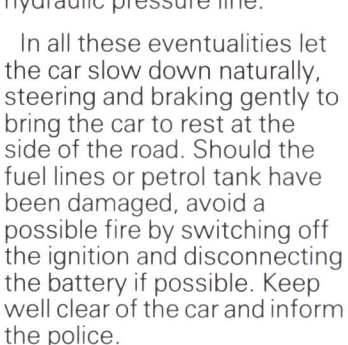

In all these eventualities let the car slow down naturally, steering and braking gently to bring the car to rest at the side of the road. Should the fuel lines or petrol tank have been damaged, avoid a possible fire by switching off the ignition and disconnecting the battery if possible. Keep well clear of the car and inform the police.

ENGINE FAILURE

A frequent cause of an engine faltering is lack of fuel, usually the result of an empty tank rather than a carburettor fault. If, when the engine splutters, a quick change into a lower gear does not jerk the engine into life again, change into neutral and use the momentum of the car to move to the side of the road in order to stop. Under damp conditions a neglected ignition system can produce the same effects.

Engine seizure is another matter and is often due to overheating because of a broken fan belt or lack of coolant. Increasingly poor engine response will be felt when the car slows progressively at the same throttle opening on level ground.

If the engine seizes up completely the driving wheels will lock up. De-clutch immediately and move the gear lever into neutral so that the car can move under its own momentum. Check the mirrors, signal and move to the side of the road, without cutting in front of another vehicle.

BONNET FLIES UP

This is only a problem with bonnets which open from the front of the car. There is no need to panic if this should occur. Steer on the same course, brake progressively, signal and move carefully to stop at the side of the road.

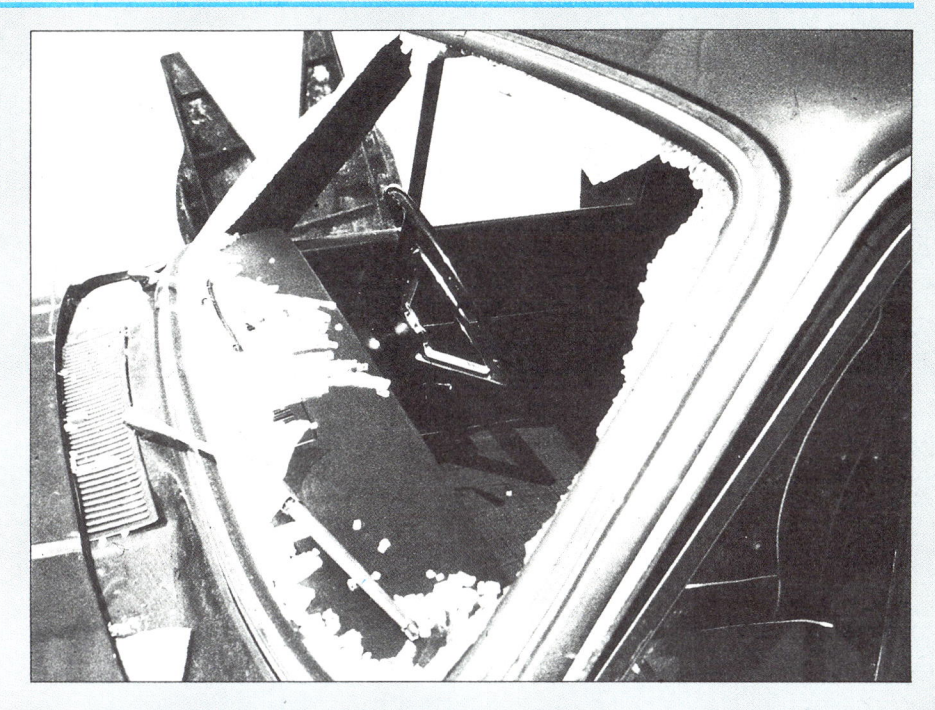

Toughened windscreen

WINDSCREEN SHATTERS

Laminated windscreens present little problem as they remain transparent even after an impact by a stone causing nothing more than a star-shaped scar. Toughened glass screens usually incorporate a zone in front of the driver which gives fair visibility.

When the windscreen shatters do not punch a hole through it immediately. Check your mirrors, signal, move gently to the side of the road and stop when it is safe to do so. Remove as much of the broken glass as possible by pushing it out onto a sheet of newspaper on the bonnet. Do not push the glass into the car interior.

A temporary windscreen will allow you to proceed safely, but if you do not have one you can still drive, although with great care and at a low speed. In that eventuality make sure that all the glass fragments have been removed from the windscreen surround.

Impact on laminated windscreen

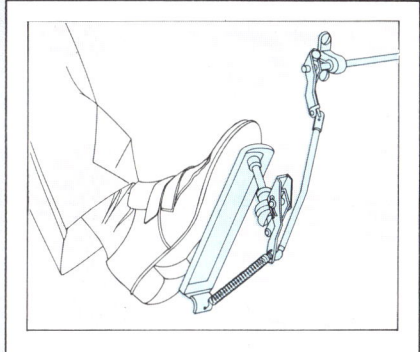

ACCELERATOR STICKS DOWN

A first reaction to this problem is to try to get a toe under the pedal and lift it. In many cases, however, the cause is a broken throttle return spring and the pedal stays down. The appropriate action is to check mirrors, move the gear lever into neutral, then signal left. Switch off the ignition, but do not withdraw the ignition key as this can lock the steering, then coast to the side of the road, and stop.

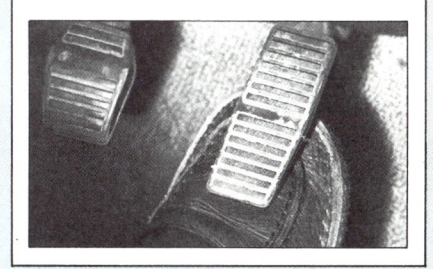

MAINTENANCE SAVES EMERGENCIES

A check of the tyres, brakes and steering at the start of every journey, plus regular maintenance and the immediate replacement of any suspect components would prevent most of the emergencies described here from taking place.

Emergency Problem

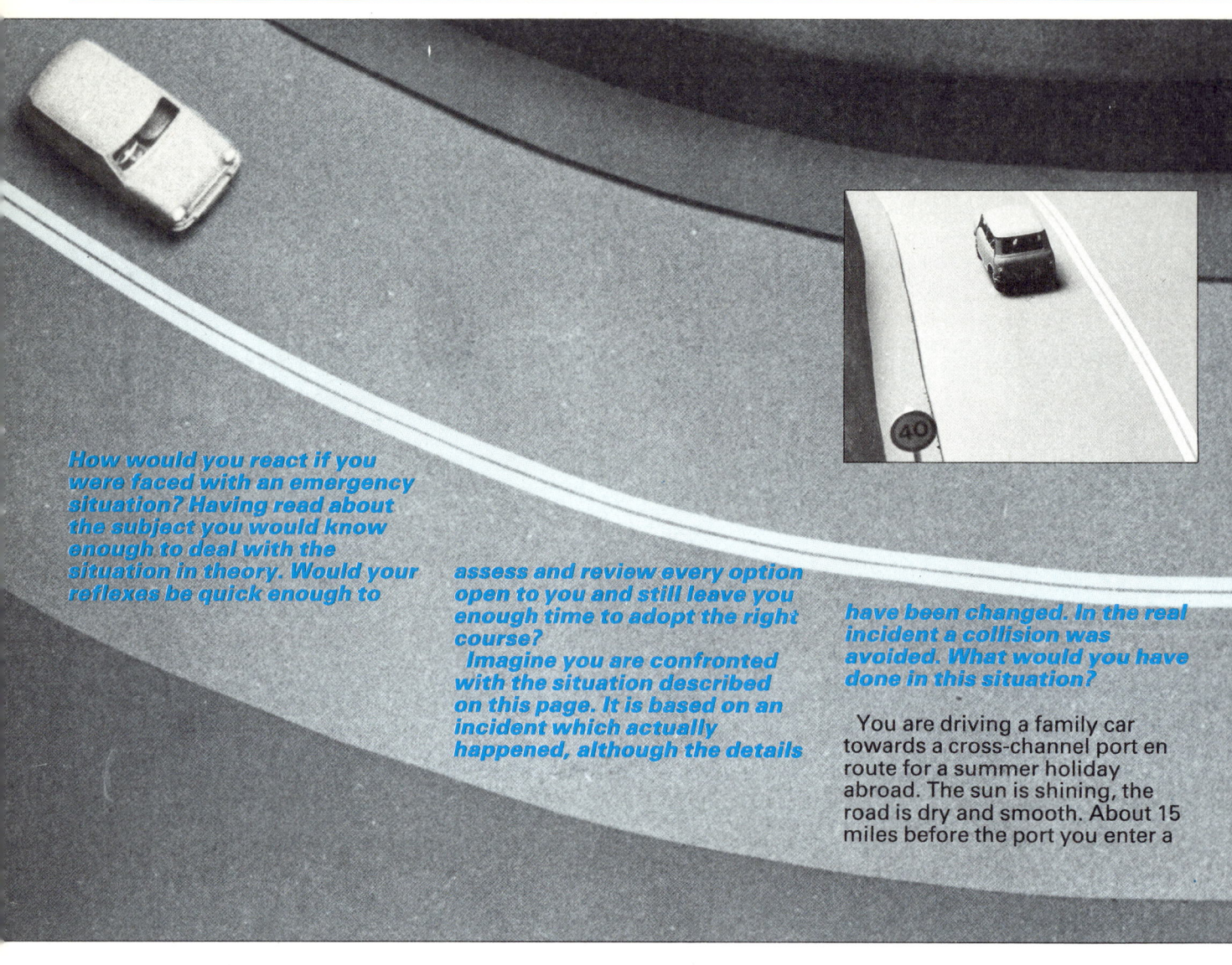

How would you react if you were faced with an emergency situation? Having read about the subject you would know enough to deal with the situation in theory. Would your reflexes be quick enough to assess and review every option open to you and still leave you enough time to adopt the right course?

Imagine you are confronted with the situation described on this page. It is based on an incident which actually happened, although the details have been changed. In the real incident a collision was avoided. What would you have done in this situation?

You are driving a family car towards a cross-channel port en route for a summer holiday abroad. The sun is shining, the road is dry and smooth. About 15 miles before the port you enter a

WHAT WOULD YOU DO?
a Freeze up completely
b Brake hard
c Swerve to the right
d Swerve to the left
e Brake firmly and swerve out of the way at the last moment when you see where the other driver moves.

a It will be too late to avoid a head-on collision if you do not react instantly. Suppose both cars are travelling at 35mph, the closing speed is 70mph or about 34 yards a second. When the two cars are 50 yards apart, there are about 1½ seconds in which to take positive avoiding action.

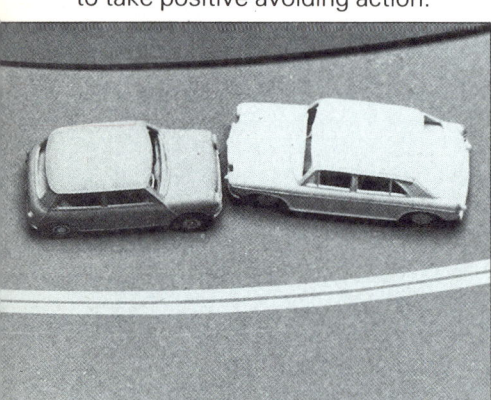

b Panic braking will lock up the front wheels and the car will slide straight on with no steering control at all, or the rear end may break away and the car will slew. It would be impossible to swerve out of the way at any point if this particular course of action was taken.

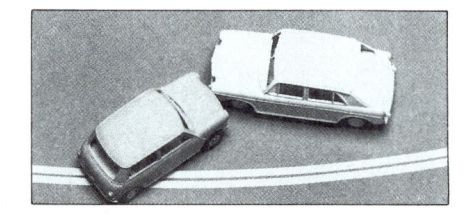

c A sudden swerve to the right can easily result in loss of control. If the back wheels start to slide there will be a collision.

d A sudden swerve to the left could also result in a loss of control. In this case it would also have resulted in a head-on collision. The oncoming car was, indeed, French. He had just come off a cross-channel ferry and had not yet oriented himself to driving on the left hand side of the road.

The fact that the driver made no attempt to return to the correct side of the road even after your horn warning confirms that this is so and also that he believes he is perfectly in the right. In fact, his reaction to the situation is to behave as he would have done at home, and he swerves to his right, (your left) and into the kerb. If you had swerved left, you would certainly have hit him.

Approaching the bend at 35 mph visibility is restricted to 50 yards. At first all seems clear

Suddenly an oncoming car is seen approaching on the wrong side of the road

When the cars first see each other 1½ seconds are left for avoiding action

built-up area. The speed restriction is 40mph, the road has two wide lanes bordered by normal width pavement and kerbing, with fences beyond.

Driving at a safe 35mph you approach a left hand bend. Buildings on your left restrict forward vision to around 50 yards. You have taken up a position to the left of the centre line in order to obtain the best view through the bend. On entering the bend you find an oncoming car driving directly towards you on your side of the road.

You sound your horn to alert the other driver. Generally, you will have been driving with sufficient care and anticipation to avoid an accident, but in this case the other driver makes no attempt to steer his car back to his own side of the road. In the first split-second you notice that it carries a French registration plate.

Initially, brake firmly in a straight line

e The correct response is to get your speed right down while keeping firm control of the car.

Knowing you were near a port would, in any case, have forewarned you to expect some cars to be on the wrong side of the road. You will have been driving with the appropriate degree of caution when this incident arose and have been prepared to react quickly if necessary. Firstly, avoid any kind of panic reaction. Brake firmly in a straight line, but not so hard that you lock the wheels and lose control. At this point the other driver begins his turn towards your left. With your speed now much reduced, and steering under control, you turn your car to the right, towards the centre of the road, thus avoiding contact. A careful study of the situation as it developed while remaining firmly in control of the car, enabled you to react quickly but without panic. Pull over to the side of the road in order to regain your composure.

Steer right when you see what the other car does

Preparation for Emergencies

Everyone can prepare themselves to cope with emergencies. Each time you go out in a car, whether as the driver or not, you should observe and study the road in order to anticipate what will develop. Accurate anticipation often prevents emergencies. Keep asking yourself what you would do if the situation ahead of you changed suddenly and dramatically.

You should take every opportunity to practise and improve your car control. This should not be done on a public road but on a specialised training area, skid-pan, or on a disused airfield.

Several specialist courses are available in advanced and high speed driving and these are extremely useful as a start towards preparing yourself to deal with emergencies. A most valuable feature of these courses is that they reveal any weaknesses or bad habits in your driving, enabling you to overcome them. After that, continue to practise the relevant techniques.

ANTICIPATION AND CONTROL

Most emergency situations can be prevented by good observation and intelligent anticipation. Careful reading of the road scene and gentle car handling should ensure that you enter each situation at the right speed and in perfect control.

BRAKING

The general rules about braking, whether in an emergency situation or not are:

1. Brake in plenty of time.
2. Brake firmly only when travelling in a straight line.
3. Vary the brake pressure according to the condition of the road surface.

When preparing to handle a possible future emergency situation, an important aspect of car control to practise is braking from speed. You should know just how hard you can brake in your car without locking the wheels and losing steering control.

Practise, off the public roads, driving at a series of different speeds, then slowing the car down in a straight line by adjusting the braking pressures. When you have mastered control at one speed try a slightly higher one.

Once you can control the braking of your car from speed, start gently swerving to one side while braking and keeping steering control at all times. This will increase your confidence in your own driving ability and will help you to react positively to emergencies.

Reading the road well ahead enables you to spot hold-ups such as lorries turning in good time, so you can avoid braking harshly

Sharp observation is needed when driving in busy streets to spot the pedestrians stepping into the road, as well as other hazards.

When following a large vehicle, particularly on a narrow road, keep a safe distance and when possible look along its nearside

The parked van actually conceals some road works, as the observant driver will have noted from the warning sign ahead

Observing the road beyond the lorry would have given you advance warning of the parked car

Seeing the broken-down lorry in plenty of time helps you make an early lane change, minimising disruption to traffic flow

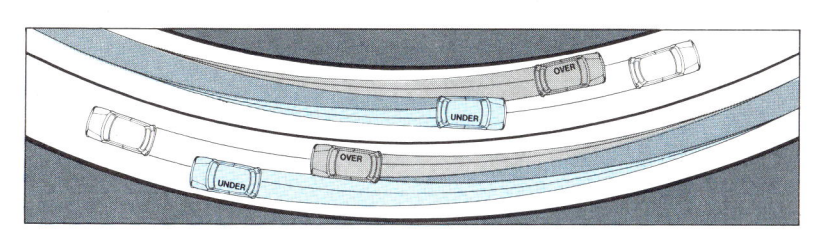

UNDER-STEER
A small degree of understeering characteristics are designed into most modern cars. This gives them stability in a straight line at speed, under crosswind conditions and also when cornering.

The front of the car tends to run wider than the curve of the bend and this must be countered by greater movement of the steering in the direction of the bend.

OVER-STEER
The behaviour of an over-steering car on a bend is the opposite of one with understeer. The car tends to turn in towards the bend, because the centrifugal force moves the rear of the car outwards. This requires a steering correction in order to maintain control. An oversteering car will not have the inherent stability of an understeering one in gusty crosswinds, and will need constant steering correction. Correction will also be required on roads with pronounced changes in road cambers.

As the speed at which a bend is taken is increased, so the steering characteristics of a car will change. One which normally has a degree of understeer will, at high speed on a corner, develop neutral steer and then change to over-steer. This transition should, ideally, be progressive and predictable. If it takes place too rapidly it can be unexpected and dangerous.

CAR CARE
However proficient the driver in coping with an emergency, it is essential that the car behaves and responds reliably and as expected. This is only achieved if it is maintained in good condition.

Great stress will be thrown on the brakes, tyres, steering and hydraulic dampers in dealing with an emergency, and these should always be kept in first class condition. The driving exercises above will indicate whether any of them is deficient.

Brakes If these are not working at full efficiency, it will take you longer to stop. Have the brakes and brake fluid levels checked regularly and do not wait to replace friction linings until they are worn down.

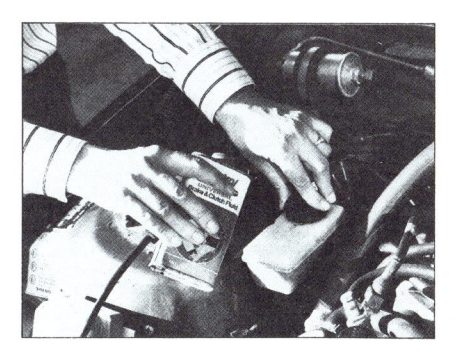

Tyres The steering response can be critically affected by the wrong, or incorrectly inflated, tyre. Tyre pressures should be checked regularly, and tyres inspected for signs of over- or under-inflation.

Hydraulic dampers Weak dampers can cause the car to pitch badly with an increased tendency to roll. This can seriously affect braking and steering, particularly in an emergency situation.

Windscreen A clean windscreen free from smears will aid observation and visibility, particularly if an emergency should arise. Good windscreen wipers and an effective screen wash are also important.

Headlights Properly adjusted headlights will maximise your own vision when driving at night, and also minimise dazzle to others.

Seat belts Make sure your seat belts work properly, and, if you have children, install approved safety restraints to the back seat. Front seat passengers must now wear seat belts, by law.

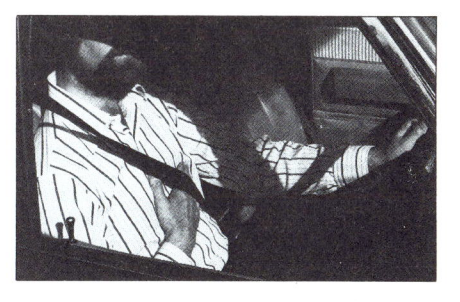

Parcel shelf Keep the rear parcel shelf free from loose objects which could fly forward during a collision, into the necks of the driver or passengers. Even light objects can be dangerous if propelled with enough force.

Roll-over bar If driving an open car have a roll-over bar fitted. If a car without one turns over, the occupants have no protection.

Skidding

No good driver should ever find his car skidding unintentionally. A skid is usually the result of poor observation, too high a speed, harsh use of the controls or a badly-maintained car. Knowing how to control a skid is essential, however, since even a good driver may skid sometime.

TYRE GRIP
A skid is caused when a tyre loses its grip on the road surface and starts sliding instead of rolling. As soon as this happens, control of the car is lost. The area of contact between tyre and road is very small, no bigger than a size 9 shoe. It is critical that this small area remains effective.

The tread of the tyre is an important factor in retaining grip, particularly if the road is not dry. Water on the road surface is dispelled by the channels and slots of the tread pattern so that the tyre can grip on the road surface proper.

FOUR WHEEL SKID
When harsh braking locks all four wheels and the car skids, the only way to regain control is to release the brakes and then re-apply them more gently, remembering to take into account the condition of the roads. This allows the tyres to roll again and re-establish their grip on the road. If the steering is not straight ahead, it is important to straighten up before trying to get back on course.

Skid control is not taught to learner drivers, and for many people the first skid will be a completely unexpected experience. The most important consideration is not to panic. Look in the direction you want to go, not where you appear to be going. The next thing to remember is not to over-correct a skid. It is better to let the car sort itself out than to induce a secondary skid by over-correction. Most modern cars respond very quickly to even a slight steering correction. Radial ply tyres react in a fraction of the time that cross-plies used to do, at a fraction of the steering input formerly required.

SUSPENSION AND STEERING
The design of the car's suspension and steering are inter-related and have important effects upon its handling.

Worn dampers cause unsteady cornering, a bumpy ride when on the move and unpleasant dipping movement when braking. The tyres may not be kept in sufficiently close contact with the road surface and skidding is much more likely to occur. Badly misaligned steering geometry can also increase the risks of skidding, especially in adverse conditions.

ROAD SURFACES
A good appreciation of the nature of the road surface and its camber is an important aspect of skid prevention. In fine weather, dust or gravel on the surface can dramatically reduce tyre adhesion, as can mud on country roads. Light rain on roads which have been dry for some time causes a potentially dangerous situation. The rain water can mix with the oily and rubber deposits which are lying on the road surface to form a very slippery surface for the tyres, and a mixture which could block up the tyre tread.

Rain on the road surface will obviously reduce tyre adhesion. Autumn and winter bring their own skid hazards to road surfaces. Fallen leaves in the autumn produce a very slippery surface.

Top row: The four pictures in this sequence demonstrate a spin resulting from an uncorrected rear-wheel skid

Bottom row: These pictures show how a rear-wheel skid, induced by insensitive control of the steering, is corrected by applying opposite lock, effectively negating the car's tail-heavy momentum

ROAD OBSERVATION
Accurate reading of the road ahead and to the side will prevent most skids, particularly in adverse weather. Judging the severity of an approaching bend is not always easy, but the line of the roadside hedge in the distance can provide an indication. Do not always trust the line of telegraph posts, however, as these can sometimes cut straight across a field, while the road bends in a different direction.

SMOOTH HANDLING
Skids can be induced or made worse by harsh or sudden braking, harsh acceleration, jerky steering and excessive speed. If the car handling were carried out more smoothly and with greater delicacy, the risks of skidding would be halved. Too heavy a grip on the steering wheel is sometimes a cause of harsh car handling.

WHEELSPIN
The definition of a skid, in which the grip of the tyre on the road surface is lost, could include wheelspin, with which most drivers are familiar. It is usually caused by harsh use of the accelerator, and can only be cured by easing off. Continuing to press the accelerator will not increase the chances of regaining traction.

FRONT WHEEL SKID
The car tends to travel straight on in this type of skid despite the direction in which the driver is trying to steer. It is usually brought on by harsh acceleration into a corner, when the front wheels lose their grip. It may seem as though the steering has failed, but do not attempt to apply more steering lock. The first thing to do is to take your foot off the accelerator. Then straighten up the front wheels, so that they can start rotating again. Once grip has been restored steer gently in the direction you wish to take.

This steering correction must be applied very briefly and very gently. Over-correction could result in a rear wheel skid which will be very difficult to control. On no account apply the brakes.

FRONT WHEEL DRIVE CARS
When a front wheel drive car gets into a front wheel skid, do not take your foot off the accelerator suddenly, as this would have the effect of braking. Reduce the acceleration, but keep a light pressure. Continue to steer into the corner until the car regains its course, then gently start to increase the acceleration.

REAR WHEEL SKID
When driving too fast round a corner or bend, the rear of the car may break away and cause a rear wheel skid. The commonly-stated advice is 'steer into the skid', but this is not always easy to interpret.

Modern radial ply tyres and recent types of suspension system are extremely quick to respond to a skid. They can react a great deal more quickly than most drivers will be able to. Steel-braced tyres generate a self-straightening effect very much more quickly than older generation tyres, particularly cross plies. For the same steering correction, steel-braced tyres will develop up to three times the sideways guidance force that cross ply tyres used to do. This sideways guidance force restores straight line running.

Because of these developments in tyre technology, it is now frequently the best course of action to take your foot off the accelerator (do not touch the brake or clutch pedals). Apply only very slight steering correction for a short time, very quickly but not jerkily. Do not attempt to steer into the skid for any length of time since this could provoke a dangerous aggravation of the skid. As soon as possible return to a neutral steering position.

A major danger with this type of skid is over-reaction, resulting in excessive correction of the initial skid. A secondary skid is set up, often worse than the first one, and this again could provide excessive steering response. The result can easily be a 'sawing' motion of the steering wheel, rapidly leading to loss of control.

It is not necessary to grip the steering wheel more tightly than usual during skid control. A light but firm handhold is preferable, and allows the car's course, once it starts to skid, to be corrected quickly and accurately without nearly so much risk of over-correction.

Skid Pans

Practice at recognising a skid and learning to control it can only be gained on a skid-pan. This is a specially prepared area, set away from public roads, where members of the public may learn about skids.

Unfortunately there are not many skid-pans in existence, partly because they are so expensive to run and seldom attract sufficient support. Their value, however, cannot be over-estimated.

The skid-pan is coated with special compounds to facilitate skidding

SKID-PAN CONSTRUCTION
The surface of a skid-pan is usually designed to give minimum tyre grip, especially when the surface is wet, as it normally will be. In some cases, in addition to water, the surface will have been specially treated to deliberately induce slipperiness.

It is often the case that you do not use your own car, but one which is supplied. This may be fitted with 'slick' tyres which have no tread at all, so skids will happen at low speed. Occasionally, after completing a course of instruction, you may be encouraged to take your own car on to the skid-pan to discover its own particular skid characteristics.

INSTRUCTION
Different arrangements are made at every skid-pan. In some cases the sessions last several hours and include lectures and demonstrations. In others, the sessions are one hour or less. The use of the skid-pan may be linked to a course on better driving run by the Local Authority. The qualified instructors may come from the Police, the Institute of Advanced Motorists or be Approved Driving Instructors. Details of current opening times, charges, how the courses are organised, the use of your own car, etc., are best obtained from your local Road Safety Officer.

RECOGNISING A SKID
One of the advantages of a skid-pan is that it teaches you what the onset of a skid feels like. This is particularly valuable if you have not experienced it before. Failing to recognise that a skid is developing, and thus reacting to it too slowly or too abruptly are common causes of loss of control in a skid. It is important to recognise it quickly and to respond smoothly and in good time.

In some ways a skid-pan gives an artificial idea of what a skid is like. The treated surface means that a skid is induced at a relatively low speed. In addition, however, you will be expecting a skid to occur on a skid-pan. Some skid-pans have one area treated differently from the rest to make things less predictable. This will teach you how to cope with differing degrees of adhesion.

Familiarity with the sensation of skidding, achieved through practice on a skid-pan, is the first step to avoiding the panic over-reaction which so often occurs. The results of over-correction of a skid will become apparent at an early stage and you can then learn to appreciate how effective the strategy is of

Practising cornering on a skid-pan

By avoiding a front wheel skid it is found that control is retained through the bend

A rear wheel skid is provoked (below). Skid-pan practice will enable it to be controlled

making only the minimum necessary steering corrections, taking the feet off all the pedals and letting the tyres correct the skid.

Another important benefit of skid-pan experience is that you learn to recognise the point at which control has been regained. Just as you will feel when tyre to road grip becomes marginal, that is when a skid is about to happen, so you will be able to tell that you have regained control. Skid-pan practice will accustom you to the feeling of skids of different types.

SKID PRACTICE

A skid-pan provides an opportunity to keep practising a particular type of skid until it is familiar and understood. In most real life situations, however, events will happen much more quickly for loss of tyre grip will occur at higher speeds.

A front wheel skid can be provoked by turning the steering wheel and braking hard. The front wheels will lock and steering control will be lost. By releasing the brakes, some steering control will be restored and you can practise trying to keep to a proper steering line.

A rear wheel skid can be provoked simply by going a little too fast round the skid-pan circuit. It can also be induced at a moderate speed by turning the steering wheel, pulling the handbrake on briefly and then releasing it. This will lock the rear wheels while retaining front wheel grip, and the rear of the car will slew. Take your foot off the accelerator, do not touch the brake or clutch pedals, apply any necessary steering correction, then return the steering to a neutral position until control of the car is regained.

A more advanced driver can use the skid-pan to make the basic manoeuvre from which to engineer more problems, allowing the driver to improve his skill further. It is possible, for example, to learn the knack of sliding the car from lock to lock under complete control, while maintaining speed by keeping the foot on the throttle.

Emergency Quiz

It may be easy to feel that the essentials of skid control are understood after reading about them in a book. Experience on the road is very different, and can be assisted by practice gained on a skid-pan. One way to check whether you would do the right thing if you were involved in a skid is to try the quiz on this page. Although the answers are given here, try to work out your own answer before reading them.

1 What are the factors that could cause a skid?

2 Which pedal must you not press when you have got into a skid?

3 Which pedal would you press in a car with a manual gear box if you get into a skid?

4 In the event of a rear wheel skid on a left hand bend with the car sliding to your right, in which direction would you turn the steering wheel?

5 What effect do weak shock absorbers have on road adhesion?

6 Under what road conditions are you most likely to skid?

7 What should you do if, when braking for a bend, your front wheels lock up?

8 In a similar situation what should you do if the front wheels start to skid outwards towards the crown of the road?

9 What is a secondary skid and how is it caused?

10 Is a front-wheel-drive car more prone to front wheel skidding than either a front engine rear-wheel-drive car or a rear engine car?

11 What should you do if a front-wheel drive car gets into a front wheel skid?

12 How would you deliberately induce a skid on a skid-pan?

13 What is the most important aspect of skid-pan practice?

14 What is done to some skid-pans to give them varying degrees of adhesion?

15 Which tyres, radials or cross-plies, have better cornering power?

16 Why do bald or badly-worn tyres lose adhesion on wet roads?

17 Apart from bald tyres, what other tyre conditions contribute to skids?

18 What tyres should you fit to your car to minimise the chance of any form of skid?

19 What is the essence of skid prevention for a driver?

20 In the event of getting into a skid what is the first requirement of the driver?

ANSWERS

1 Poor driving involving perhaps driving too fast, insufficiently good observation of the road ahead or harsh use of controls.

2 The brake pedal. Applying the brakes in a skid will tend to lock up the wheels, making it even more difficult to regain control. Control is only regained when the tyres are in rolling contact with the road surface. The best strategy when in a skid is not to press any of the pedals at all.

3 It has sometimes been suggested that depressing the clutch may help, but as stated in the answer to question 2, it is better not to press any of the pedals. You may get into another skid when you let in the clutch.

4 Any movement of the steering wheel must be carried out as soon as the slide is detected, and then with great care. In this case, steer slightly to the right, enough to 'catch' the slide, then return the steering to a neutral position. Do not steer too far to the right, or keep the steering in that position for more than a very short time or the car will start to slide to the left.

5 Weak shock absorbers allow the wheels to bounce excessively on the road surface. This means that road contact is poorly maintained, resulting in reduced tyre-to-road adhesion. They will also cause imbalance in the car's handling.

6 Under almost any road condition if you are inattentive. In general terms, anything on the road surface which is loose such as gravel, anything which will provide a film between the tyre and the road, such as rain or ice, increases the risk of skidding. Particularly hazardous is light rain after a long dry spell. This spreads a film of water over a surface covered with an oily, rubber deposit and the road becomes extremely slippery.

7 Release the brakes for a fraction of a second to regain steering control, then re-apply them more sensitively.

8 Release the accelerator and straighten up the steering so that, for a very short time you are steering in the direction of the skid. Once steering control has been regained continue your course round the corner. Do not brake under any circumstances.

9 A secondary skid is caused by over-correcting the first skid, either by applying too harsh a steering correction or continuing it for too long. The result is to make the car go from one skid to another on the other side, the second usually more difficult to control than the first.

10 The idea that all front-wheel-drive cars have superior road-holding to other cars is not borne out in practice.

11 You should ease off the accelerator smoothly, but not completely. A small amount of power should still be applied to the front wheels. Otherwise, removal of the power can have a braking effect which could result in the rear of the car breaking away.

12 There are several ways of doing this. Driving too fast into a curve will provoke a skid, so will steering into a curve and braking hard or steering left or right and pulling very hard on the handbrake.

13 To get used to the feeling of the car's loss of adhesion. Once you can recognise the onset of a skid you will be able to react quickly and smoothly enough to control it before it goes too far. Practice in dealing with the different types of skid is also most important.

14 Certain sections of the skid-pan may be treated with a liquid having a low co-efficient of friction or may have a permanent special surface treatment which simulates a greasy patch offering less adhesion than other parts.

15 Radial ply tyres have better cornering performance as a built-in feature.

16 The tread of a tyre dispels the water lying on the road so that the tyre can grip on the surface below. When the tread is very thin or absent, the tyre cannot make such good contact with the road surface even at low speeds. At high speeds the tyre may 'float' off the surface and aquaplane.

17 Underinflated tyres distort excessively when cornering and this reduces their grip on the road surface. Unevenly worn tyres offer reduced tyre to road grip. Unequal pressure distribution side to side can also promote the onset of a skid.

18 In most cases you should fit the tyres recommended by your car's manufacturer, but you should seek the advice of a tyre specialist before changing to anything very different.

19 To read the road well ahead, to be at the right speed and in the right gear for every situation, especially when cornering. You should always bear in mind the road surface conditions at the time, whether the road is dry, or covered in rain, mud or ice.

20 The first requirement is not to panic. If you can think quickly and clearly and recognise the type of skid involved you are well on the way to taking the correct action. Remembering that modern car and tyre design is such that a great deal of the correction will be carried out automatically by the car itself without active participation of the driver, you should try to make any steering correction precisely and smoothly. This is better than reacting suddenly and losing complete control of the vehicle.

Emergency Toolkit

A KIT OF GET-YOU-HOME TOOLS AND MATERIALS
A lot of the bits and pieces that AA patrols use for the strictly get-you-home repairs are bits of jetsam which people would throw away as useless. Or they are forgotten items that you or your passenger carry around (perhaps for that rainy day that has now arrived), gathering fluff in the bottom of a handbag or briefcase. This is an aspect of car repair that Baden-Powell would have loved, for the techniques and materials used are little removed from the native wit and cunning methods of the great Scout leader.

This kit is a shortlist of some of the materials which can make all the difference between reaching your destination half an hour late or spending hours on a cold wet night in a fruitless and depressing quest for the right part.

You can split the emergency kit into the sort of emergency items useful for a multitude of problems — those that could profitably be considered as a part of any comprehensive tool-kit — and those which may eventually and unexpectedly prove invaluable.

One very important item is baling (soft, galvanised-iron) wire. Talking among AA patrols it is possible to compile a list of up to 50 uses for this relatively cheap and widely available material.

PTFE plumbers' tape can be made to pack out worn threads, but it should be used with discretion. Because it has not mechanical strength, it should not be employed on steering suspension units or on load-bearing components.

A get-you-home tool-kit is also a very individual thing. The items in it are those that you can foresee a need for when they first come to hand — odd screws and bolts found at the roadside or in a forgotten corner of the garage are examples. Then there are items invaluable in certain emergencies — a bottle of nail varnish and a handbag mirror, for example.

Some of the proprietary products you would do well to carry have many uses around the home. Fast-setting epoxy-resin adhesives are every handyman's stand-by for speedy repairs, and the superglue type of adhesive works on parts that cannot be tackled with epoxy resin (nylon, for example).

A small magnet is not only useful to clip papers to any metallic part of the facia, it can be a boon for retrieving parts from inaccessible recesses, or perhaps to magnetise a screwdriver so that small screws can be replaced in awkward areas. You can, incidentally, also use a magnet to check if filler has been used on suspect body repairs.

An aerosol lubricant will not only rid an ignition system of damp, it will also take the squeak out of noisy door hinges. The beauty of this is that its flexible outlet tube can reach inaccessible areas.

Above all, remember that there is an art to successful emergency repairs that is just as exacting as the proper use of conventional tools, techniques and materials. Study some of the tried and trusted remedies of the AA patrols and you will soon find that when you are in a fix, a careful search will often turn up something that you are able to use to get you on your way — something that perhaps even the AA's experts have never dreamed of.

A FIRST AID KIT FOR THE CAR

ESSENTIALS

Fire extinguisher
Torch or lantern
Tow rope
Jump leads
Soft iron wire
PVC insulating tape
Fast-setting epoxy-resin adhesive and/or superglue
Aerosol water-repellent lubricant
Selection of hose clips
Selection of nuts and bolts
Radiator sealant
Small magnet
Length of insulated wire or flex

WORTHWHILE EXTRAS

PTFE plumbers' tape
Lengths of hose in various sizes
Epoxy-resin filler
Exhaust sealing cement
Wet-or-dry abrasive paper
Pieces of copper pipe (sizes from ½in (13mm) internal diameter up)
Handbag mirror
Sheet of gasket cork
Selection of washers
Thick polythene sheeting
Inner tube patches and tube of rubber solution
Strong elastic bands
Stout cord

ROAD MAPS

JOURNEY PLANNING

The maps and Charts at the beginning of this atlas are designed to help you plan your journey with ease and economy.

If your destination is a town or village whose location you do not know, you should turn to the index section at the back of the book and find the place name you require. The name is followed by a page number and a National Grid reference. Turn to the atlas page indicated and, using the National Grid reference supplied, you can locate the place concerned.

A full explanation of the National Grid is given on page 27.

Having located your destination in the main atlas, find the nearest large town, which also appears on the Route Planning Maps, pages 20 to 25. These maps show the principal routes throughout Britain and a basic route can be planned from them. A more detailed route can then be worked out from the main atlas, taking note of the road numbers and route directions. These notes can then be used on the journey, minimising the need to stop to consult the atlas. Remember that, in general, motorways are quicker and more economical than other routes because you can maintain a more consistent speed and avoid traffic delays. If you cannot use a motorway, the primary route system should be considered. These roads are coloured green on the maps and are signposted in green on the roads. Page 26 shows you the style and colour of the different types of road signs you can expect to come across on your journey.

It should be remembered that the shortest route is not necessarily the quickest, and primary routes tend to take you around towns rather than through their centres, thus avoiding delays caused by traffic lights, one way systems, etc. It is always a good idea to keep an alternative route in your mind should the road you are planning to use be the source of some delay, such as road works.

If you have a radio in your car, it is worth listening to traffic reports during the journey. Frequent bulletins are issued by national and local radio stations on road conditions, local hold-ups, etc., and these can be of great assistance to the drivers in avoiding delays. This will be especially valuable if you are catching a ferry or have to keep an urgent appointment. Alteration to your route could save you from missing a boat or aeroplane. Always leave plenty of time for your journey.

On a particularly long journey allow extra time for short rest breaks. A tired driver is a hazard to himself and other road users, and the extra time spent during the journey will help ensure a safe arrival at your destination. The motorist may find it both more convenient and less tiring to take advantage of the British Rail Motorail service. The cost of transporting a car and a family of four by rail is between 10 and 20% higher than travelling by road, but there may be considerable gains in travelling time, and savings in vehicle wear and tear.

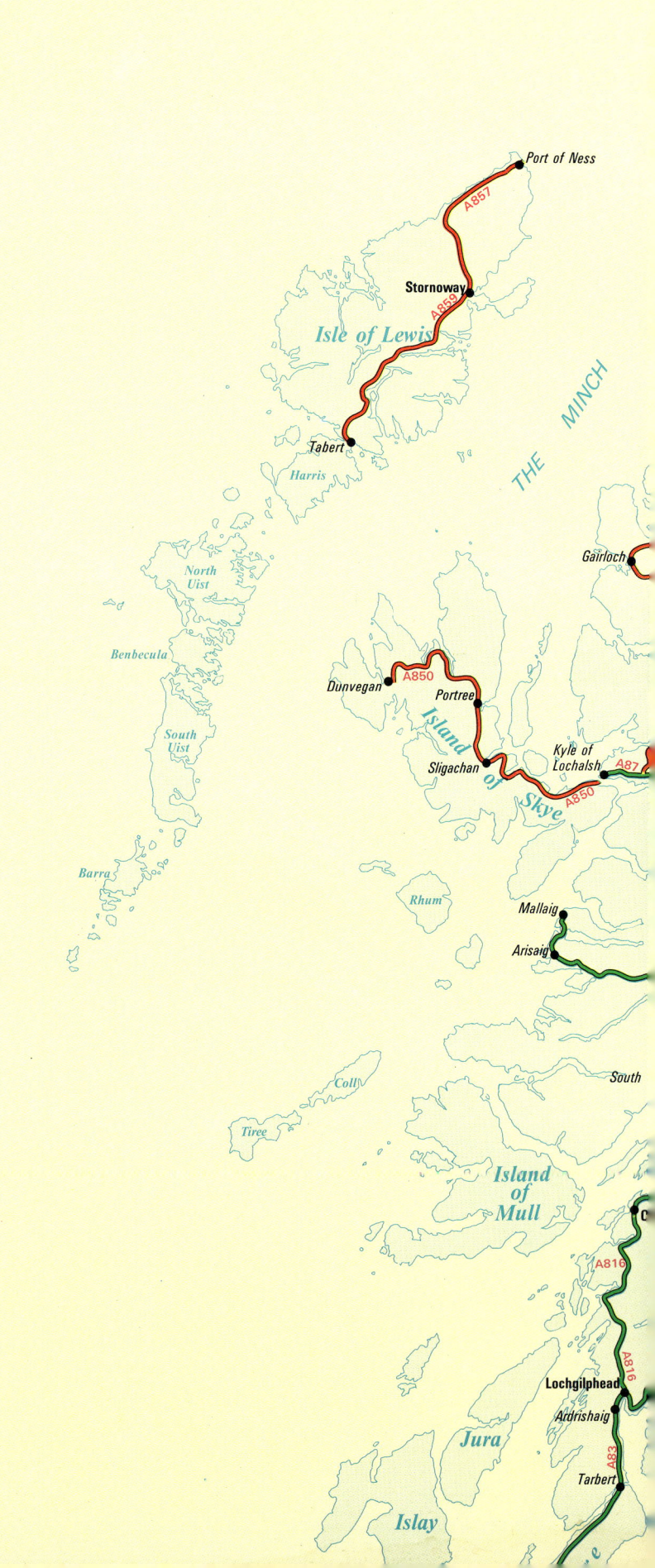

ROUTE PLANNING MAPS

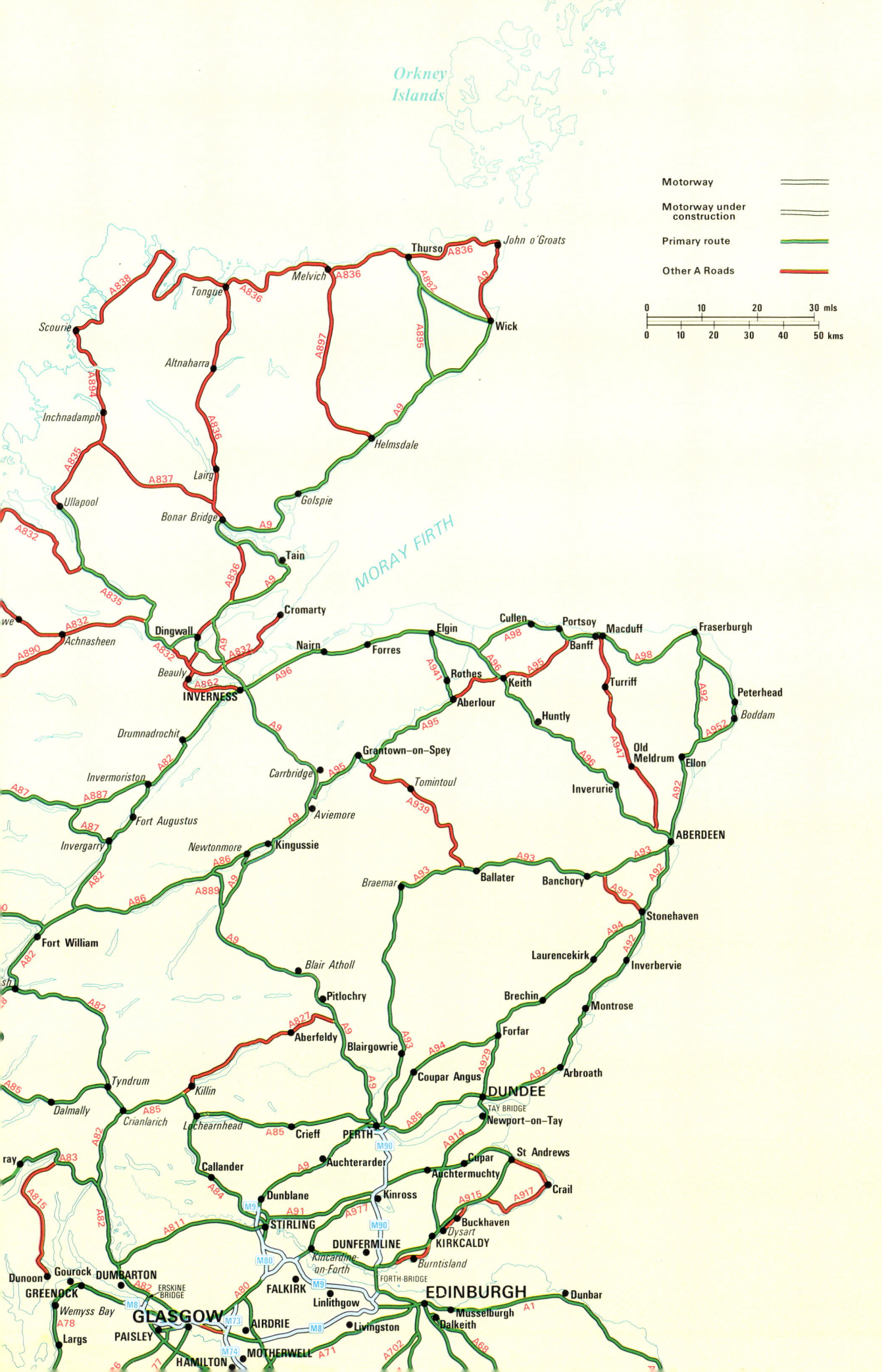

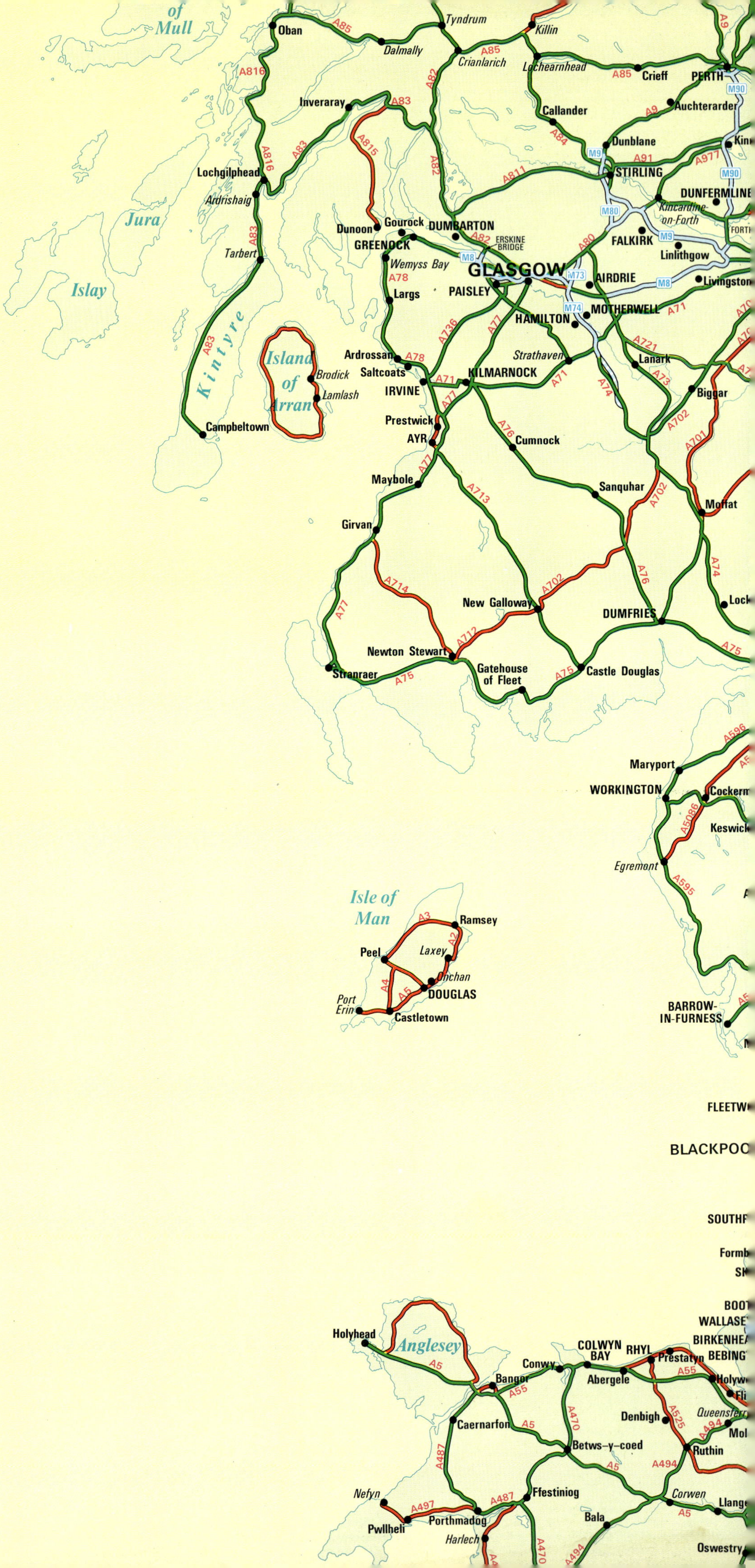

of Mull
Oban
A85
Tyndrum
Killin
Dalmally
A85
Crianlarich
Lochearnhead
A85
Crieff
PERTH
A9
M90
A816
Inveraray
A83
A82
Callander
A9
Auchterarder
A815
A84
Dunblane
Lochgilphead
A816
A83
M9
A91
A977
Ardrishaig
A82
A811
STIRLING
M90
DUNFERMLINE
Kincardine-on-Forth
Jura
Dunoon
Gourock
DUMBARTON
M80
GREENOCK
A82
ERSKINE BRIDGE
A80
FALKIRK
M9
Tarbert
A83
M8
Wemyss Bay
Linlithgow
Islay
GLASGOW
M73
AIRDRIE
A78
M8
Livingston
Largs
PAISLEY
M74
MOTHERWELL
A71
HAMILTON
Kintyre
A736
A77
Island of Arran
Ardrossan
A78
Strathaven
A721
Brodick
Saltcoats
KILMARNOCK
Lanark
A83
IRVINE
A71
A71
A73
Lamlash
A77
A74
Biggar
Prestwick
AYR
A76
Cumnock
A702
Campbeltown
A701
A77
Maybole
A713
Sanquhar
A702
Moffat
Girvan
A76
A74
A714
A702
A77
New Galloway
DUMFRIES
A712
Newton Stewart
A75
Gatehouse of Fleet
A75
Castle Douglas
Stranraer
A75
A596
Maryport
WORKINGTON
Cockerm
A5086
Keswick
Egremont
A595
Isle of Man
A3
Ramsey
A2
Peel
Laxey
Onchan
A4
A5
DOUGLAS
Port Erin
Castletown
BARROW-IN-FURNESS
FLEETW
BLACKPOO
SOUTHP
Formb
BOOT
WALLASE
BIRKENHE
Holyhead
Anglesey
COLWYN BAY
RHYL
Prestatyn
BEBING
A5
Conwy
Bangor
A55
Abergele
A55
Holyw
A55
A470
Denbigh
A525
Queensferr
Caernarfon
A5
A494
Mol
Betws-y-coed
Ruthin
A487
A5
A494
Nefyn
Ffestiniog
Corwen
A497
A487
A5
Llang
Pwllheli
Porthmadog
Bala
Harlech
A470
A494
Oswestry

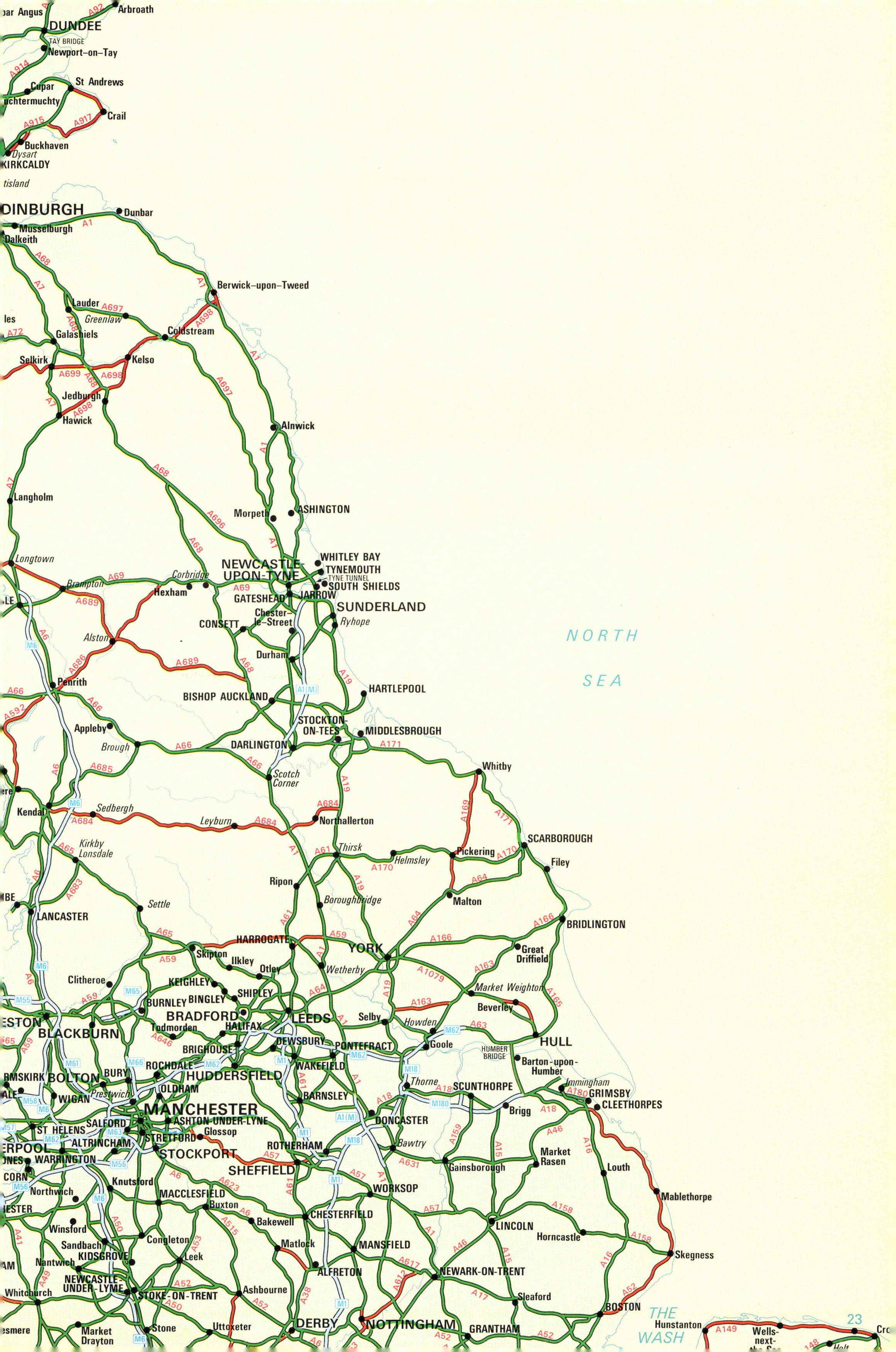
Arbroath
DUNDEE
TAY BRIDGE
Newport-on-Tay
Cupar
St Andrews
Crail
Buckhaven
Dysart
KIRKCALDY
Dunbar
Musselburgh
Dalkeith
Berwick-upon-Tweed
Lauder
Greenlaw
Galashiels
Coldstream
Selkirk
Kelso
Jedburgh
Hawick
Alnwick
Langholm
Morpeth
ASHINGTON
Longtown
WHITLEY BAY
NEWCASTLE-UPON-TYNE
TYNEMOUTH
TYNE TUNNEL
SOUTH SHIELDS
Brampton
Corbridge
Hexham
GATESHEAD
JARROW
SUNDERLAND
Ryhope
CONSETT
Chester-le-Street
Alston
Durham
NORTH SEA
Penrith
HARTLEPOOL
BISHOP AUCKLAND
Appleby
STOCKTON-ON-TEES
MIDDLESBROUGH
Brough
DARLINGTON
Whitby
Scotch Corner
Kendal
Sedbergh
Leyburn
Northallerton
SCARBOROUGH
Kirkby Lonsdale
Thirsk
Helmsley
Pickering
Filey
Ripon
Malton
Boroughbridge
LANCASTER
Settle
BRIDLINGTON
HARROGATE
Skipton
YORK
Great Driffield
Ilkley
Otley
Wetherby
Clitheroe
KEIGHLEY
BINGLEY
SHIPLEY
Market Weighton
BURNLEY
BRADFORD
LEEDS
Selby
Howden
Beverley
BLACKBURN
Todmorden
HALIFAX
HULL
BRIGHOUSE
DEWSBURY
PONTEFRACT
Goole
HUMBER BRIDGE
Barton-upon-Humber
ROCHDALE
BURY
HUDDERSFIELD
WAKEFIELD
BOLTON
Thorne
SCUNTHORPE
Immingham
GRIMSBY
CLEETHORPES
WIGAN
Prestwich
OLDHAM
BARNSLEY
MANCHESTER
Brigg
ST HELENS
SALFORD
ASHTON-UNDER-LYNE
DONCASTER
Glossop
ALTRINCHAM
STRETFORD
ROTHERHAM
Bawtry
Market Rasen
WARRINGTON
STOCKPORT
SHEFFIELD
Gainsborough
Louth
Knutsford
Northwich
MACCLESFIELD
WORKSOP
Mablethorpe
Buxton
Bakewell
CHESTERFIELD
Winsford
LINCOLN
Horncastle
Congleton
Sandbach
KIDSGROVE
Leek
Matlock
MANSFIELD
Skegness
Nantwich
ALFRETON
NEWARK-ON-TRENT
NEWCASTLE-UNDER-LYME
STOKE-ON-TRENT
Ashbourne
Sleaford
Whitchurch
BOSTON
THE WASH
Hunstanton
Wells-next-
Market Drayton
Stone
Uttoxeter
DERBY
NOTTINGHAM
GRANTHAM

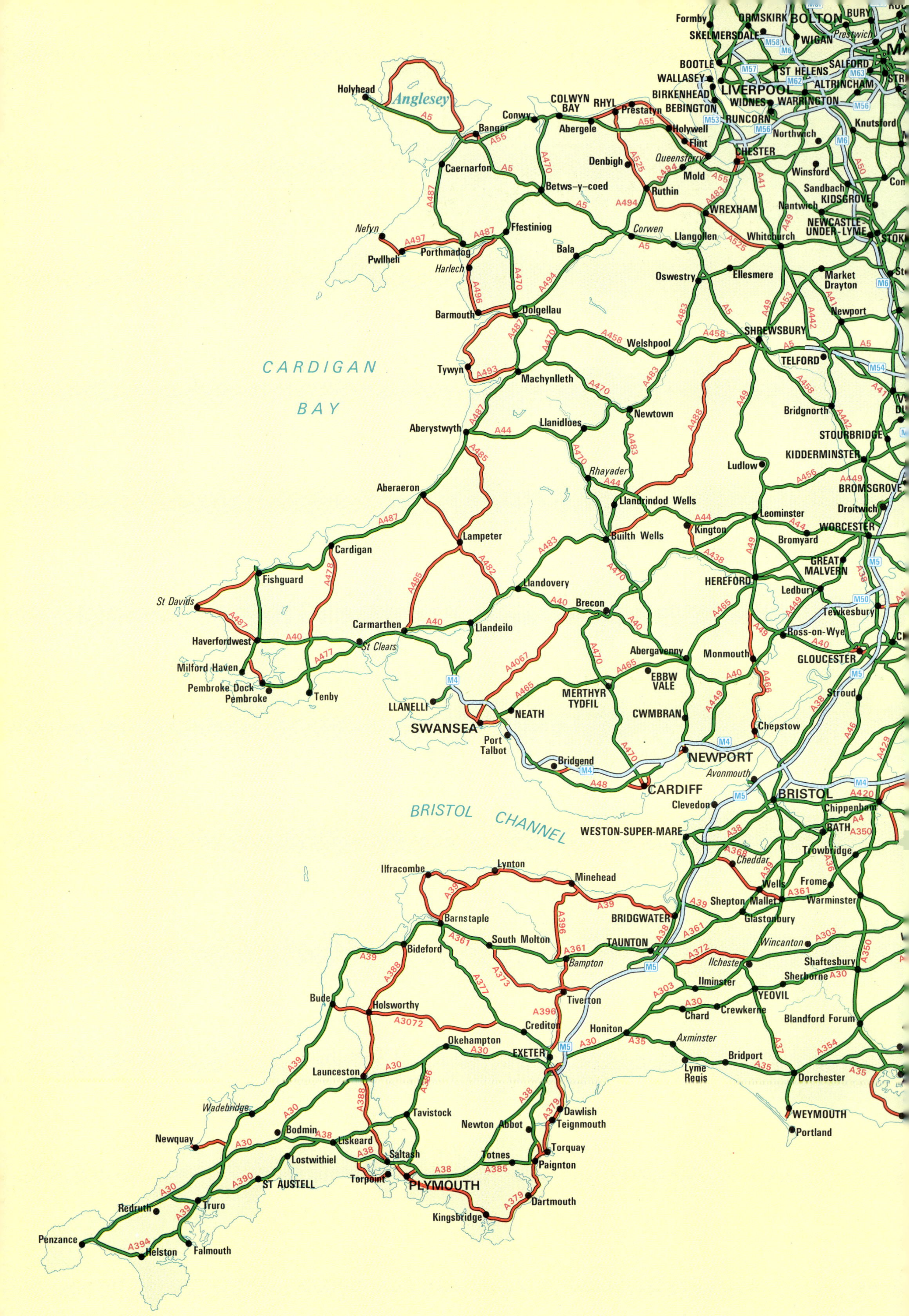

Formby
ORMSKIRK
BOLTON
BURY
SKELMERSDALE
WIGAN
Prestwich
BOOTLE
ST HELENS
SALFORD
WALLASEY
LIVERPOOL
ALTRINCHAM
BIRKENHEAD
WIDNES
WARRINGTON
BEBINGTON
RUNCORN
Knutsford
Northwich
CHESTER
Holyhead
Anglesey
COLWYN BAY
RHYL
Prestatyn
Conwy
Abergele
Holywell
Flint
Bangor
Denbigh
Queensferry
Caernarfon
Mold
Winsford
Betws-y-coed
Ruthin
Sandbach
KIDSGROVE
WREXHAM
Nantwich
NEWCASTLE-UNDER-LYME
Nefyn
Ffestiniog
Corwen
Llangollen
Whitchurch
Pwllheli
Porthmadog
Bala
Harlech
Oswestry
Ellesmere
Market Drayton
Barmouth
Dolgellau
Newport
SHREWSBURY
Welshpool
TELFORD
CARDIGAN
BAY
Tywyn
Machynlleth
Newtown
Bridgnorth
STOURBRIDGE
Aberystwyth
Llanidloes
KIDDERMINSTER
Ludlow
Rhayader
BROMSGROVE
Aberaeron
Llandrindod Wells
Droitwich
Leominster
Kington
WORCESTER
Lampeter
Builth Wells
Bromyard
Cardigan
GREAT MALVERN
Fishguard
Llandovery
HEREFORD
Ledbury
St Davids
Brecon
Tewkesbury
Carmarthen
Llandeilo
Ross-on-Wye
Haverfordwest
St Clears
Abergavenny
Monmouth
GLOUCESTER
Milford Haven
EBBW VALE
Pembroke Dock
Pembroke
Tenby
MERTHYR TYDFIL
Stroud
LLANELLI
NEATH
CWMBRAN
SWANSEA
Chepstow
Port Talbot
Bridgend
NEWPORT
Avonmouth
CARDIFF
BRISTOL
Chippenham
Clevedon
BATH
BRISTOL
CHANNEL
WESTON-SUPER-MARE
Trowbridge
Cheddar
Ilfracombe
Lynton
Minehead
Wells
Frome
Shepton Mallet
Warminster
BRIDGWATER
Barnstaple
Glastonbury
South Molton
TAUNTON
Wincanton
Bideford
Bampton
Ilchester
Shaftesbury
Ilminster
Sherborne
Bude
Holsworthy
Tiverton
YEOVIL
Chard
Crewkerne
Crediton
Blandford Forum
Okehampton
Honiton
Axminster
EXETER
Bridport
Launceston
Lyme Regis
Dorchester
Wadebridge
Dawlish
Teignmouth
WEYMOUTH
Tavistock
Newton Abbot
Portland
Newquay
Bodmin
Liskeard
Torquay
Lostwithiel
Saltash
Totnes
Paignton
ST AUSTELL
Torpoint
PLYMOUTH
Redruth
Truro
Dartmouth
Kingsbridge
Penzance
Helston
Falmouth

Humber
Thorne
SCUNTHORPE
Immingham
GRIMSBY
CLEETHORPES
BARNSLEY
DONCASTER
Brigg
Glossop
ROTHERHAM
Bawtry
Market Rasen
SHEFFIELD
Gainsborough
Louth
WORKSOP
Mablethorpe
Buxton
Bakewell
CHESTERFIELD
LINCOLN
Horncastle
Matlock
MANSFIELD
Skegness
ALFRETON
NEWARK-ON-TRENT
Ashbourne
Sleaford
BOSTON
THE WASH
Uttoxeter
DERBY
NOTTINGHAM
GRANTHAM
Hunstanton
Wells-next-the-Sea
Sheringham
Cromer
Holt
BURTON UPON TRENT
LOUGHBOROUGH
Fakenham
North Walsham
Melton Mowbray
Bourne
Spalding
KING'S LYNN
Lichfield
Ashby-de-la-Zouch
Tamworth
Oakham
Stamford
Wisbech
Swaffham
Dereham
NORWICH
Acle
Caister-on-Sea
GREAT YARMOUTH
LEICESTER
Uppingham
PETERBOROUGH
Downham Market
HINCKLEY
March
Attleborough
NUNEATON
Market Harborough
CORBY
Chatteris
Bungay
LOWESTOFT
Beccles
COVENTRY
KETTERING
Ely
Thetford
Diss
LEAMINGTON SPA
Huntingdon
Warwick
Daventry
NORTHAMPTON
Newmarket
BURY ST EDMUNDS
Saxmundham
Stratford-upon-Avon
St Neots
CAMBRIDGE
Towcester
BEDFORD
Haverhill
Biggleswade
IPSWICH
BANBURY
MILTON KEYNES
Ampthill
Royston
Sudbury
Brackley
Baldock
Felixstowe
Chipping Norton
Leighton Buzzard
HITCHIN
Halstead
Harwich
Stow-on-the-Wold
Bicester
STEVENAGE
BISHOP'S STORTFORD
LUTON
DUNSTABLE
Puckeridge
Braintree
COLCHESTER
Great Dunmow
Witney
AYLESBURY
Ware
Hertford
HARPENDEN
OXFORD
CLACTON-ON-SEA
Thame
HARLOW
Hatfield
ST ALBANS
EPPING
CHELMSFORD
Abingdon
HIGH WYCOMBE
Amersham
WATFORD
Faringdon
BRENTWOOD
Beaconsfield
Northolt
Tottenham
MAIDENHEAD
SOUTHEND-ON-SEA
Dagenham
SLOUGH
EALING
LONDON
READING
WINDSOR
DARTFORD TUNNEL
Tilbury
NEWBURY
HEATHROW AIRPORT
KINGSTON-UPON-THAMES
DARTFORD
GRAVESEND
Sheerness
Hungerford
STAINES
Swanley
Bromley
ROCHESTER
GILLINGHAM
MARGATE
CHERTSEY
CROYDON
Orpington
CHATHAM
Faversham
RAMSGATE
EPSOM
Wrotham
BASINGSTOKE
LEATHERHEAD
CANTERBURY
Sandwich
REIGATE
SEVENOAKS
MAIDSTONE
DEAL
Andover
GUILDFORD
FARNHAM
DORKING
Redhill
TONBRIDGE
Alton
East Grinstead
ASHFORD
Stockbridge
Sutton Scotney
Gatwick
CRAWLEY
TUNBRIDGE WELLS
DOVER
SALISBURY
WINCHESTER
Liphook
FOLKESTONE
Hythe
HORSHAM
Romsey
Petersfield
Midhurst
New Romney
EASTLEIGH
Rye
SOUTHAMPTON
Uckfield
Lyndhurst
FAREHAM
CHICHESTER
Arundel
Lewes
HASTINGS
HOVE
BRIGHTON
BEXHILL-ON-SEA
Minster
PORTSMOUTH
WORTHING
BOGNOR REGIS
EASTBOURNE
Cowes
CHRISTCHURCH
RYDE
Freshwater
Newport
Isle of Wight
Sandown
Shanklin

SIGN LANGUAGE

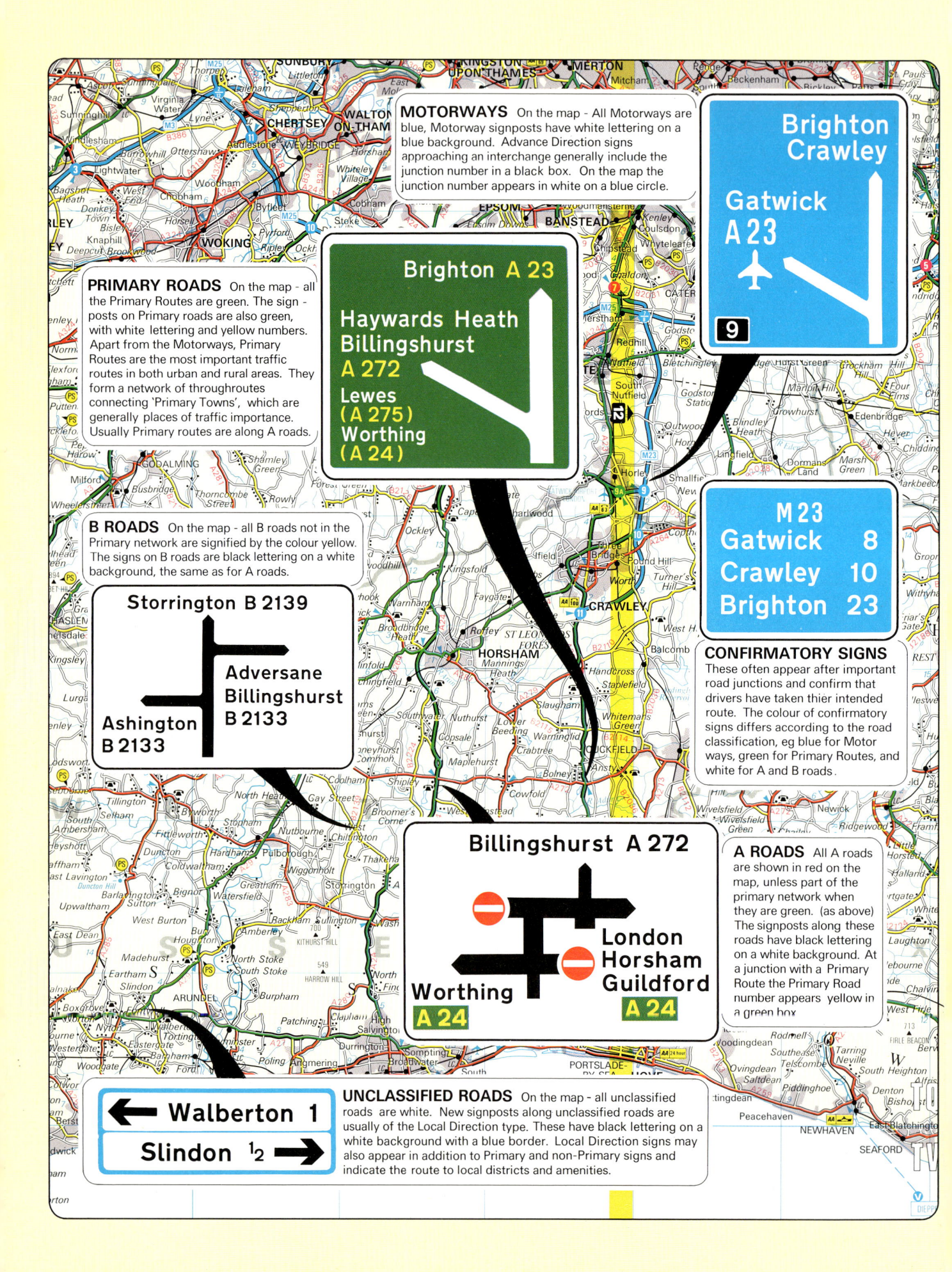

MOTORWAYS On the map - All Motorways are blue, Motorway signposts have white lettering on a blue background. Advance Direction signs approaching an interchange generally include the junction number in a black box. On the map the junction number appears in white on a blue circle.

PRIMARY ROADS On the map - all the Primary Routes are green. The signposts on Primary roads are also green, with white lettering and yellow numbers. Apart from the Motorways, Primary Routes are the most important traffic routes in both urban and rural areas. They form a network of throughroutes connecting 'Primary Towns', which are generally places of traffic importance. Usually Primary routes are along A roads.

B ROADS On the map - all B roads not in the Primary network are signified by the colour yellow. The signs on B roads are black lettering on a white background, the same as for A roads.

CONFIRMATORY SIGNS These often appear after important road junctions and confirm that drivers have taken thier intended route. The colour of confirmatory signs differs according to the road classification, eg blue for Motor ways, green for Primary Routes, and white for A and B roads.

A ROADS All A roads are shown in red on the map, unless part of the primary network when they are green. (as above) The signposts along these roads have black lettering on a white background. At a junction with a Primary Route the Primary Road number appears yellow in a green box.

UNCLASSIFIED ROADS On the map - all unclassified roads are white. New signposts along unclassified roads are usually of the Local Direction type. These have black lettering on a white background with a blue border. Local Direction signs may also appear in addition to Primary and non-Primary signs and indicate the route to local districts and amenities.

26

GRASP THE GRID

Indexing System & The National Grid.

To locate a place in the atlas, first check the index at the back of the book, eg:

Weyhill (Hants)	10	SU 3146
Weymouth (Dorset)	8	SY 6778
Whaddon (Bucks)	18	SP 8034

Using Weymouth as our example - this is the reference given in the index - 8 SY 6778

8 This is the number of the page on which Weymouth lies.

SY These first two letters show the major relevant area in which Weymouth is situated. They relate to an area labelled SY which is bound by heavy lines numbered in all cases O. (It can be seen that Poole lies in the next area labelled SZ).

67 The first set of numbers refer to the thin blue grid lines labelled along the bottom of the page. The 6 relates to the line of that number while the 7 is an estimated 7/10ths of the division between the 6 and 7.

78 The second set of figures refer to the numbers on the side of the page, the 7 relates to the line of that number, whereas the 8 is approximately 8/10ths of the division between 7 and 8.

If a line is drawn, from 67 vertically and from 78 horizontally, Weymouth should lie where the two intersect. Further examples of references given in the index, to the following appropriate towns may be checked against their locations in the map sample above:

Dorchester	8 SY 6890
Poole	8 SZ 0190
Swanage	8 SZ 0278
Wareham	8 SY 9287
Wool	8 SY 8486

It may be noted that, in every instance, it is the first set of figures after the area letters that applies to the number along the bottom of the grid. Therefore the second set will relate to the figures up the side of the page.

The National Grid

The National Grid provides a reference system common to maps of all scales. The country is divided into major grid squares (100kmsq), which are outlined on the map by heavy blue lines and each is designated two letters (eg SY) as its reference code. Each of these squares is then sub-divided into 100 10km sq, thus forming a finer grid which is numbered from 0 to 9, west to east, and south to north within each of the major lettered squares.
Thus each location can be referred to by first, two letters; showing the 100km square in which it lies, then a set of figures representing co-ordinates within the forementioned square, which gives precise location.

27

LEGEND

AUTOSTRADA	AUTOBAHN		MOTORWAY	AUTOROUTE
N. di autostrade	Autobahn mit nummer	M3	Motorway with number	Autoroute avec numéro
Nodo stradale con e senza numeri	Anschlusstellen mit und ohne Nummern	5	Junctions with and without numbers	Echangeurs avec et sans numéros
Nodo stradale con entràte ed uscite limitate	Anschlusstellen mit beschränkten Auf- oder Abfahrten	7	Junctions with limited entries or exits	Echangeurs aux entrées ou sorties restreintes
Area di servizio	Tankstelle mit Raststätte	S	Service area	Aire de service
Autostrada e Snodo i costruzione	Im Bau befindliche Autobahn und Anschlusstelle		Motorway & Junction under construction	Autoroute et Echangeur en construction
STRADE	**STRASSEN**		**ROADS**	**ROUTES**
Rotta primaria	Hauptverbindungsstrasse	A9	Primary route	Route primaire
Altre strade A	Andere A Strasse	A129	Other A roads	Autres routes A
Strade Classe B	Strasse der Klasse B	B2137	B Roads	Routes catégorie B
Non-classificate	Nicht klassifizierte Strasse		Unclassified	Non classifiée
Corsia a due piste	Strasse mit getrennten Fahrbahnen	A7	Dual Carriageway	Double chaussée
In construzione	Im Bau befindliche Strasse		Under construction	En construction
Scozia : strade strette con aree di passaggio Scotland	Schottland: enge Strasse mit Uberholstellen		Scotland: narrow roads with passing places.	L'Écosse: Route étroite avec lieu de déplacement
SERVIZI AA DI SOCCORSO E DI INFORMAZIONI	**AA-PANNEN-UND INFORMATIONSDIENST**		**AA BREAKDOWN & INFORMATION SERVICES**	**SERVICES AA DEPANNAGE ET DE RENSEIGNEMENT**
Centro di servizio (24 ore ☎)	AA Dienststelle (24 stunden ☎)	AA 24 hour	AA Centre (24 hours ☎)	Centre AA (24 heures ☎)
Centro di servizio (ore di lavoro normali)	AA Dienststelle (übliche bürostunden)	AA	AA Centre (normal office hours)	Centre AA (heures d'ouverture normales)
Centro di servizio autostrada	AA Autobahndienststelle	AA info	AA Motorway Information Centre	Centre AA - renseignement d'autoroute
Centro di servizio strada	AA Strassendienststelle	AA 13	AA Road Service Centre	Centre AA - service de route
Centro di servizio porto	AA Hafendienststelle	AA	AA Port Service Centre	Centre AA - service de porte
Telefoni AA & RAC	AA und RAC Telefonzellen	☎	AA & RAC telephones	Téléphones AA & RAC
Telefoni PTT in aree isolate	Öffentliche Telefonzellen in abgelegenen Gebieten (PO)	☎	PO telephones in isolated areas	Téléphones PTT dans endroits isolés
Area di pic-nic	Picknickplatz	PS	Picnic site	Terrain de Pique-nique
Punti di vista AA	AA-Aussichtspunkt	Bembridge Viewpoint	AA viewpoint	Points de vue AA
Inclinazione (la freccia indica in pendio)	Steigung (Pfeile weisen bergab)		Steep gradient (arrows point downhill)	Côte (la flèche est dirigée vers le bas)
Pedaggio Strada	Gebührenpflichtige Strasse	Toll	Road toll	Péage de route
Passaggio a livello	Bahnübergang	LC	Level crossing	Passage à niveau
Traghetto veicoli (Gran Bretagna)	Autofähre (Grossbritannien)	V	Vehicle ferry (Gt Britain)	Bac pour véhicules (Grande-Bretagne)
Traghetto veicoli (continentale)	Autofähre (Kontinent)	CALAIS V	Vehicle ferry (continental)	Bac pour véhicules (Continental)
Aeroporto	Flughafen	✈	Airport	Aéroport
Area urbana Villaggio	Stadtgebiet Dorf		Urban area Village	Zone urbaine Village
Confine nazionale	Nationale Grenze		National boundary	Frontière nationale
Confine di contea	Grafschaftsgrenze		County boundary	Frontière provinciale
Distanza in mille fra simboli	Entfernung zwischen Zeichen in Meilen	2	Distance in miles between symbols	Distance en milles entre symboles
A.S.M. in piedi	Ortshöhe nach Füssen	2525 ▲	Spot height in feet	Altitude en pieds anglais
Fiume e lago	Fluss und See		River and lake	Rivière et lac
Numeri di pagine di seguito	Hinweiszahlen für Anschlusskarten	13	Overlaps and numbers of continuing pages	Chiffres de guide pour cartes voisines

Scale 5 miles to 1 inch 1: 316,800

0 1 2 3 4 5 10 15 20 miles

0 1 2 3 4 5 10 15 20 25 30 kilometres

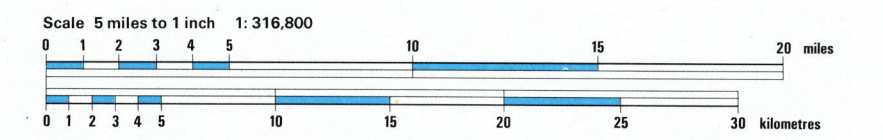

KEY TO MAP PAGES

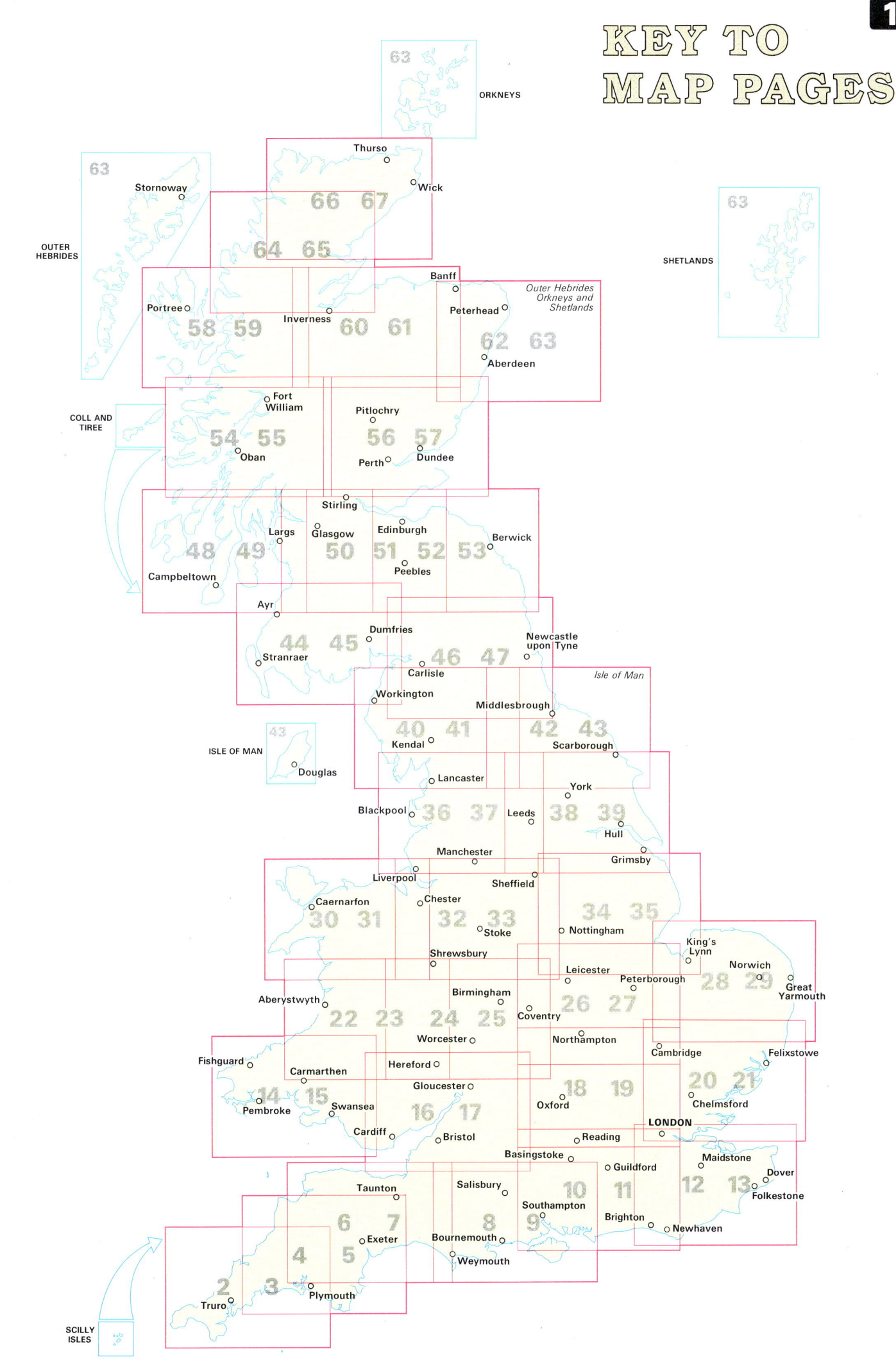

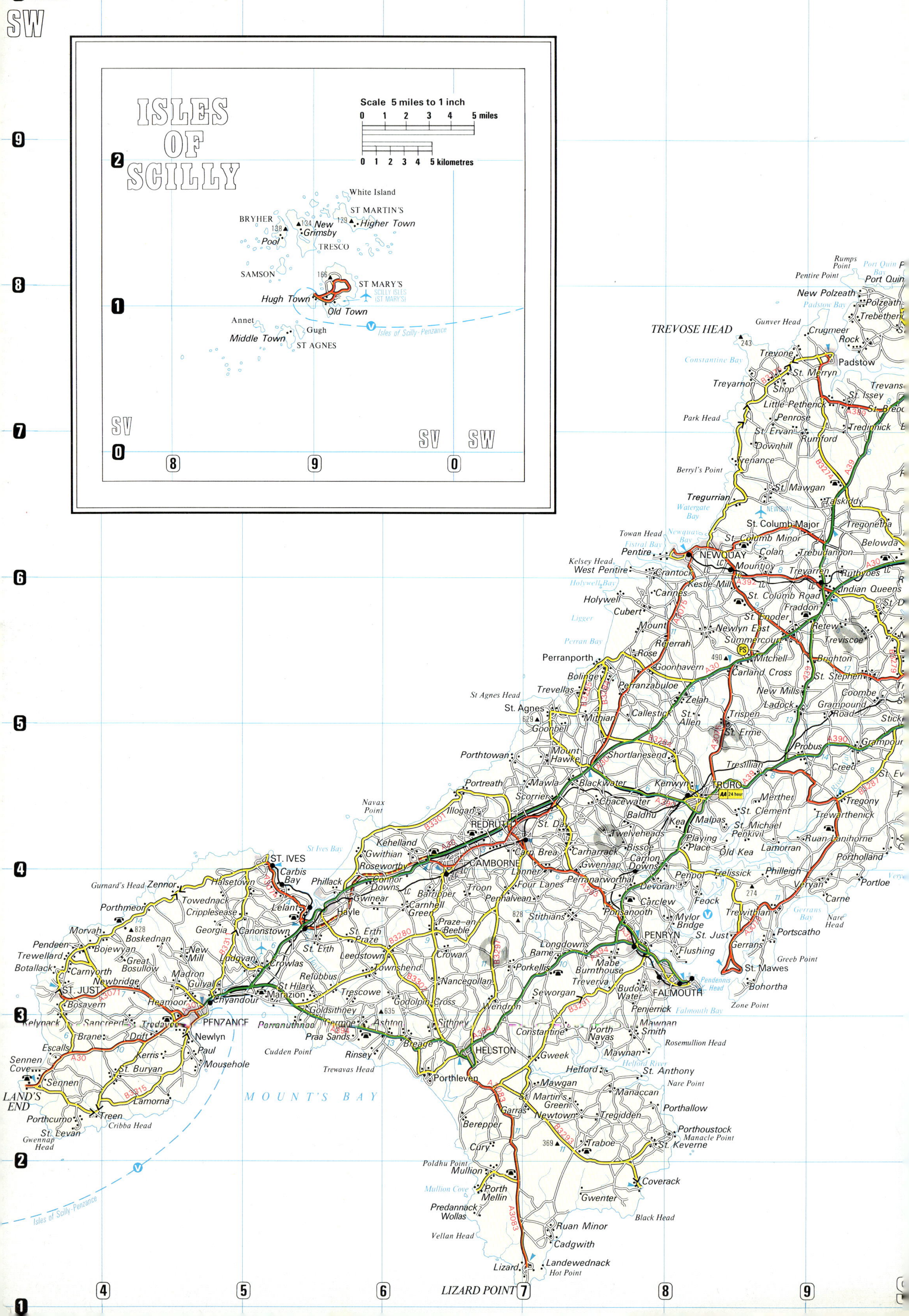
SW
ISLES OF SCILLY
Scale 5 miles to 1 inch
0 1 2 3 4 5 miles
0 1 2 3 4 5 kilometres
White Island
ST MARTIN'S
BRYHER
New Grimsby
Higher Town
Pool
TRESCO
SAMSON
ST MARY'S
Hugh Town
Old Town
SCILLY ISLES (ST MARY'S)
Annet
Gugh
Middle Town
ST AGNES
Isles of Scilly-Penzance
SV
SW
TREVOSE HEAD
Rumps Point
Port Quin Bay
Port Quin
Pentire Point
New Polzeath
Polzeath
Padstow Bay
Trebetherick
Gunver Head
Crugmeer
Rock
Constantine Bay
Trevone
Padstow
St. Merryn
Treyarnon
Shop
Trevans
St. Issey
Little Petherick
Park Head
Penrose
Tredinnick
St. Ervan
Rumford
Downhill
Trenance
Berryl's Point
St. Mawgan
Tregurrian
Watergate Bay
Talskiddy
St. Columb Major
Tregonetha
Towan Head
Fistral Bay
Newquay Bay
St. Columb Minor
Belowda
Pentire
NEWQUAY
Colan
Trebudannon
Kelsey Head
West Pentire
Crantock
Mountjoy
Trevarren
Ruthvoes
Holywell Bay
Kestle Mill
Indian Queens
Holywell
St. Columb Road
Cubert
Fraddon
Ligger
St. Enoder
Mount
Newlyn East
Retew
Perran Bay
Rejerrah
Summercourt
Treviscoe
Rose
Perranporth
Mitchell
Brighton
Goonhavern
Carland Cross
St. Stephen
Bolingey
Trevellas
Perranzabuloe
New Mills
Coombe
St Agnes Head
Zelah
Ladock
Grampound Road
St. Agnes
Callestick
St. Allen
Trispen
Goonbell
Mithian
St. Erme
Grampound
Probus
Mount Hawke
Shortlanesend
Porthtowan
Tresillian
Creed
Blackwater
Kenwyn
TRURO
Portreath
Mawla
Scorrier
Chacewater
Merther
Tregony
Illogan
St. Clement
Trewarthenick
Navax Point
REDRUTH
St. Day
Baldhu
Kea
Malpas
St. Michael Penkivil
St Ives Bay
Kehelland
Twelveheads
Playing Place
Ruan Lanihorne
Gwithian
Carn Brea
Carharrack
Bissoe
Old Kea
Lamorran
ST. IVES
Roseworthy
CAMBORNE
Lanner
Gwennap
Carnon Downs
Portholland
Carbis Bay
Connor Downs
Four Lanes
Perranarworthal
Penpol
Trelissick
Philleigh
Gurnard's Head
Zennor
Halsetown
Phillack
Barripper
Troon
Devoran
Veryan
Portloe
Towednack
Gwinear
Penhalvean
Carclew
Feock
Carne
Porthmeor
Lelant
Hayle
Carnhell Green
Stithians
Ponsanooth
Mylor Bridge
Trewithian
Cripplesease
St. Erth Praze
Praze-an-Beeble
Gerrans Bay
Nare Head
Morvah
Georgia
Canonstown
PENRYN
St. Just
Portscatho
Pendeen
Boskednan
Bojewyan
St. Erth
Crowan
Longdowns
Flushing
Gerrans
Trewellard
New Mill
Ludgvan
Leedstown
Rame
Greeb Point
Botallack
Great Bosullow
Crowlas
Townshend
Porkellis
Mabe Burnthouse
St. Mawes
Carnyorth
Madron
Relubbus
Nancegollan
Treverva
Pendennis Head
Newbridge
Gulval
St Hilary
Budock Water
FALMOUTH
Bohortha
ST. JUST
Heamoor
Marazion
Trescowe
Godolphin Cross
Seworgan
Bosavern
Chyandour
Goldsithney
Penjerrick
Falmouth Bay
Zone Point
Kelynack
Sancreed
Trodavoe
PENZANCE
Perranuthnoe
Germoe
Ashton
Sithney
Wendron
Mawnan Smith
Brane
Drift
Newlyn
Praa Sands
Constantine
Port Navas
Escalls
Paul
Cudden Point
Rinsey
Breage
HELSTON
Mawnan
Rosemullion Head
Sennen Cove
Kerris
Mousehole
Gweek
Helford River
St. Buryan
Trewavas Head
Porthleven
Helford
St. Anthony
Sennen
Mawgan
Nare Point
LAND'S END
Lamorna
MOUNT'S BAY
St. Martin's Green
Manaccan
Porthcurno
Treen
Garras
Newtown
Tregidden
Porthallow
St. Levan
Cribba Head
Berepper
Porthoustock
Gwennap Head
Manacle Point
Cury
Traboe
St. Keverne
Poldhu Point
Mullion
Coverack
Mullion Cove
Porth Mellin
Gwenter
Predannack Wollas
Black Head
Ruan Minor
Vellan Head
Cadgwith
Landewednack
Lizard
Hot Point
LIZARD POINT
A30
A39
A392
A3075
A390
A3076
A3078
A394
A3083
A3071
A3074
B3301
B3274
B3276
B3280
B3302
B3297
B3311
B3315
B3293
B3291
B3284
B3287
AA 24 hour

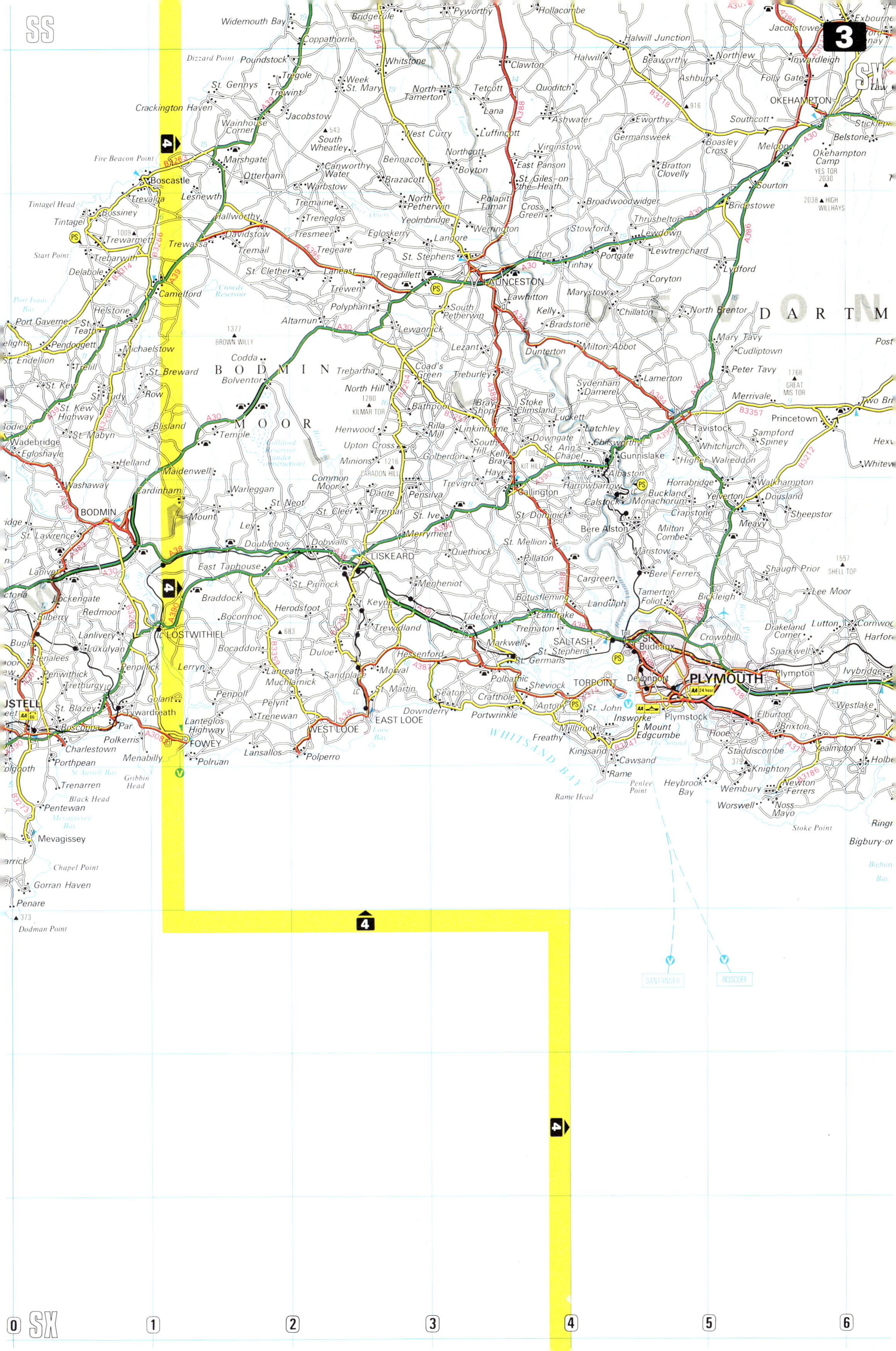

SS
SX
3
4
Widemouth Bay
Bridgerule
Pyworthy
Hollacombe
Halwill Junction
Jacobstowe
Exbourne
Coppathorne
Dizzard Point
Poundstock
Whitstone
Clawton
Halwill
Beaworthy
Northlew
Inwardleigh
Tregole
St. Gennys
Week St. Mary
North Tamerton
Tetcott
Quoditch
Ashbury
Folly Gate
Trewint
Crackington Haven
Jacobstow
Lana
Ashwater
Eworthy
OKEHAMPTON
Southcott
Wainhouse Corner
South Wheatley
West Curry
Luffincott
Germansweek
Sticklepath
Virginstow
Boasley Cross
Belstone
Northcott
Meldon
Okehampton Camp
Fire Beacon Point
Marshgate
Canworthy Water
Bennacott
Boyton
East Panson
Bratton Clovelly
Boscastle
Otterham
Warbstow
Brazacott
St. Giles-on-the-Heath
Sourton
YES TOR
2030
Trevalga
Lesnewth
Tremaine
North Petherwin
Polapit Tamar
Broadwoodwidger
Bridestowe
HIGH WILLHAYS
Tintagel Head
Bossiney
Cross Green
2038
Tintagel
Hallworthy
Treneglos
Yeolmbridge
Thrushelton
Werrington
Davidstow
Tresmeer
Egloskerry
Stowford
Lewdown
Trewarmett
Langore
Trewassa
Tremail
Tregeare
Lewtrenchard
Start Point
Trebarwith
St. Stephens
Lifton
Portgate
St. Clether
Laneast
Tinhay
Delabole
Tregadillett
Lydford
LAUNCESTON
Coryton
Camelford
Trewen
Port Isaac Bay
Crowdy Reservoir
Lawhitton
Marystow
South Petherwin
Helstone
Polyphant
Kelly
Chillaton
North Brentor
Port Gaverne
St. Teath
Altarnun
Bradstone
Lewannick
DEVON
DARTMOOR
Pendoggett
1377
BROWN WILLY
Mary Tavy
St. Endellion
Michaelstow
Lezant
Dunterton
Milton Abbot
Cudliptown
Post
Codda
Coad's Green
Trelill
St. Breward
BODMIN MOOR
Trebartha
Treburley
Sydenham Damerel
Peter Tavy
St. Kew
Bolventor
North Hill
Lamerton
1768
GREAT MIS TOR
Merrivale
Two Bridges
St. Tudy
Row
1280
KILMAR TOR
Bathpool
Bray Shop
Stoke Climsland
St. Kew Highway
Luckett
Princetown
Blisland
Temple
Rilla Mill
Linkinhorne
Latchley
Tavistock
Henwood
Sampford Spiney
Wadebridge
St. Mabyn
Downgate
Egloshayle
Upton Cross
South Hill
St. Ann's Chapel
Chilsworthy
Whitchurch
Colliford Reservoir (under construction)
Kelly Bray
1094
KIT HILL
Gunnislake
Higher Walreddon
Helland
Minions
1216
CARADON HILL
Golberdon
Whiteworks
Maidenwell
Hayes
Albaston
Horrabridge
Walkhampton
Washaway
Cardinham
Common Moor
Trevigro
Harrowbarrow
Buckland Monachorum
Callington
Yelverton
Dousland
Warleggan
Darite
Pensilva
Calstock
BODMIN
St. Neot
St. Cleer
Crapstone
Sheepstor
Tremar
St. Ive
St. Dominick
Mount
Meavy
Ley
Milton Combe
St. Lawrence
Bere Alston
Merrymeet
Doublebois
Dobwalls
St. Mellion
Maristow
1557
SHELL TOP
Quethiock
LISKEARD
Pillaton
Lanivet
East Taphouse
Bere Ferrers
Shaugh Prior
St. Pinnock
Menheniot
Cargreen
Lee Moor
Lockengate
Braddock
Tamerton Foliot
Botusfleming
Landulph
Bickleigh
St. Keyne
Redmoor
Herodsfoot
Boconnoc
Landrake
Tideford
Drakeland Corner
Lutton
Cornwood
Bilberry
683
Trewidland
Trematon
Lanlivery
LOSTWITHIEL
Harford
Bugle
SALTASH
Crownhill
Luxulyan
Bocaddon
Markwell
St. Budeaux
Stenalees
Duloe
Hessenford
St. Stephens
St. Germans
Sparkwell
Lerryn
Penwithick
Penpillick
Ivybridge
Lanreath
Morval
Devonport
PLYMOUTH
Plympton
Trethurgy
Muchlarnick
Sandplace
Polbathic
Sheviock
TORPOINT
Golant
St. Martin
Seaton
Crafthole
St. John
Westlake
St. Blazey
Tywardreath
Penpoll
Pelynt
Downderry
Antony
Elburton
Lanteglos Highway
Trenewan
EAST LOOE
Portwrinkle
Insworke
Plymstock
Par
WEST LOOE
Mount Edgcumbe
Boscoppa
Looe Bay
Hooe
Brixton
Polkerris
FOWEY
WHITSAND BAY
Freathy
Millbrook
Yealmpton
Charlestown
Kingsand
Staddiscombe
Holbeton
Menabilly
Polruan
Lansallos
Polperro
Cawsand
The Sound
379
Porthpean
Gribbin Head
St Austell Bay
Knighton
Trenarren
Rame
Penlee Point
Heybrook Bay
Newton Ferrers
Black Head
Wembury
Pentewan
Rame Head
Worswell
Noss Mayo
Mevagissey Bay
Stoke Point
Ringmore
Mevagissey
Bigbury-on-Sea
Chapel Point
Bigbury Bay
Gorran Haven
Penare
373
Dodman Point
SANTANDER
ROSCOFF
0
1
2
3
4
5
6

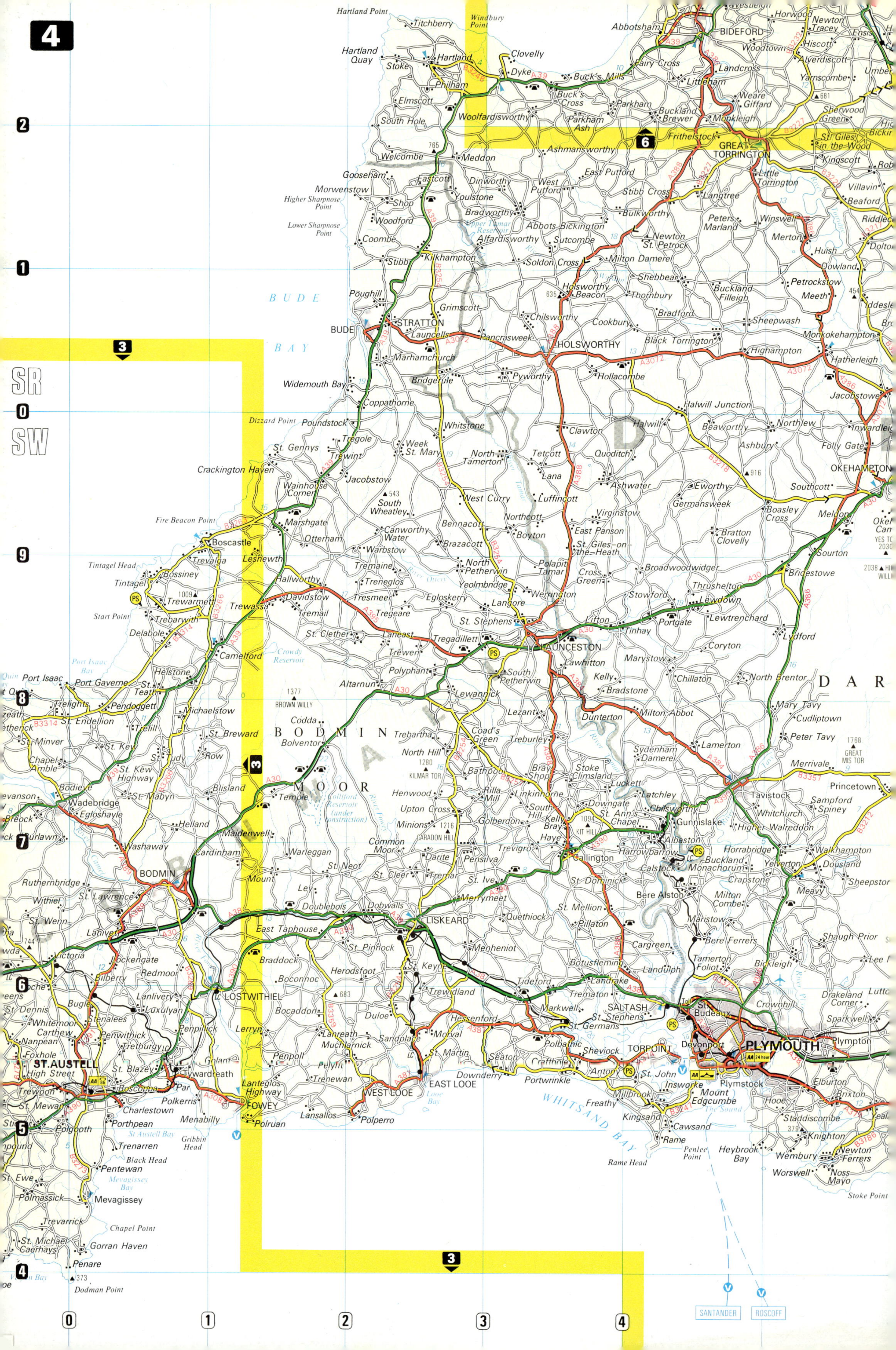

4
Hartland Point
Windbury Point
Titchberry
Hartland Quay
Stoke
Hartland
Clovelly
Dyke
Buck's Mills
Abbotsham
BIDEFORD
Fairy Cross
Littleham
Landcross
Woodtown
Horwood
Newton Tracey
Hiscott
Alverdiscott
Yarnscombe
Philham
Elmscott
South Hole
Woolfardisworthy
Buck's Cross
Parkham
Parkham Ash
Buckland Brewer
Monkleigh
Weare Giffard
Frithelstock
GREAT TORRINGTON
St. Giles in the Wood
Sherwood Green
Kingscott
Welcombe
Meddon
Ashmansworthy
East Putford
Little Torrington
Villavin
Beaford
Gooseham
Eastcott
Dinworthy
West Putford
Stibb Cross
Langtree
Morwenstow
Higher Sharpnose Point
Shop
Woodford
Lower Sharpnose Point
Coombe
Stibb
Kilkhampton
Youlstone
Bradworthy
Upper Tamar Reservoir
Alfardisworthy
Abbots Bickington
Sutcombe
Bulkworthy
Peters Marland
Winswell
Merton
Huish
Dowland
Newton St. Petrock
Soldon Cross
Milton Damerel
Shebbear
Petrockstow
Holsworthy Beacon
Thornbury
Buckland Filleigh
Meeth
BUDE
Poughill
Grimscott
Bradford
Sheepwash
STRATTON
Launcells
Chilsworthy
Cookbury
BUDE BAY
Pancrasweek
HOLSWORTHY
Black Torrington
Monkokehampton
Marhamchurch
Highampton
Hatherleigh
Bridgerule
Pyworthy
Hollacombe
Widemouth Bay
Jacobstowe
Coppathorne
Halwill Junction
Dizzard Point
Poundstock
Whitstone
Clawton
Halwill
Beaworthy
Northlew
Inwardleigh
St. Gennys
Tregole
Week St. Mary
North Tamerton
Tetcott
Quoditch
Ashbury
Folly Gate
Trewint
Lana
OKEHAMPTON
Crackington Haven
Jacobstow
Ashwater
Eworthy
Southcott
Wainhouse Corner
South Wheatley
West Curry
Luffincott
Germansweek
Boasley Cross
Meldon
Fire Beacon Point
Marshgate
Northcott
Virginstow
Bennacott
Canworthy Water
Boyton
East Panson
Bratton Clovelly
Boscastle
Otterham
Brazacott
St. Giles-on-the-Heath
Sourton
Trevalga
Lesnewth
Warbstow
Tintagel Head
Tremaine
North Petherwin
Polapit Tamar
Broadwoodwidger
Bridestowe
Tintagel
Bossiney
Hallworthy
Treneglos
Yeolmbridge
Cross Green
Thrushelton
Trewarmett
Davidstow
Tresmeer
Egloskerry
Werrington
Stowford
Lewdown
Start Point
Trebarwith
Trewassa
Tremail
Tregeare
Langore
Lewtrenchard
Delabole
St. Clether
Laneast
St. Stephens
Lifton
Portgate
Lydford
Camelford
Crowdy Reservoir
Tregadillett
Trewen
LAUNCESTON
Tinhay
Coryton
Port Isaac Bay
Port Isaac
Helstone
Polyphant
South Petherwin
Lawhitton
Marystow
Port Gaverne
St. Teath
Altarnun
Lewannick
Kelly
Chillaton
North Brentor
Trelights
Pendoggett
BROWN WILLY
Bradstone
Mary Tavy
Michaelstow
Codda
Lezant
Dunterton
Milton Abbot
Cudliptown
St. Endellion
Trelill
St. Breward
BODMIN
Bolventor
Trebartha
Coad's Green
Treburley
Peter Tavy
St. Minver
St. Kew
North Hill
Sydenham Damerel
Lamerton
GREAT MIS TOR
Chapel Amble
St. Tudy
Row
KILMAR TOR
Bathpool
Bray Shop
Stoke Climsland
Luckett
Merrivale
St. Kew Highway
Blisland
MOOR
Latchley
Princetown
Bodieve
Temple
Henwood
Rilla Mill
Linkinhorne
Chilsworthy
Tavistock
Wadebridge
St. Mabyn
Colliford Reservoir (under construction)
Upton Cross
South Hill
Downgate
St. Ann's Chapel
Gunnislake
Whitchurch
Sampford Spiney
Egloshayle
Helland
Minions
Golberdon
Kelly Bray
KIT HILL
Higher Walreddon
Maidenwell
Haye
Albaston
Washaway
Cardinham
Common Moor
Darite
Pensilva
Trevigro
Callington
Harrowbarrow
Horrabridge
Walkhampton
Warleggan
Buckland Monachorum
Yelverton
Dousland
Mount
St. Neot
St. Cleer
Tremar
Calstock
Ruthernbridge
St. Ive
St. Dominick
Crapstone
Sheepstor
Ley
Bere Alston
Meavy
St. Lawrence
Withiel
Doublebois
Dobwalls
Merrymeet
St. Mellion
Milton Combe
Quethiock
St. Wenn
LISKEARD
Pillaton
Maristow
Lanivet
East Taphouse
St. Pinnock
Menheniot
Cargreen
Bere Ferrers
Shaugh Prior
Victoria
Lockengate
Braddock
St. Keyne
Botusfleming
Tamerton Foliot
Bickleigh
Lee Moor
Redmoor
Boconnoc
Herodsfoot
Landulph
Bilberry
Tideford
Landrake
Bugle
Lanlivery
Luxulyan
LOSTWITHIEL
Trewidland
Trematon
Drakeland Corner
St. Dennis
Stenalees
Bocaddon
Duloe
Hessenford
Markwell
SALTASH
St. Budeaux
Crownhill
Sparkwell
Whitemoor
Carthew
Penwithick
Penpillick
Lerryn
Lanreath
Sandplace
Morval
St. Stephens
St. Germans
Nanpean
Trethurgy
Muchlarnick
St. Martin
Polbathic
Sheviock
TORPOINT
Devonport
PLYMOUTH
Plympton
Foxhole
Golant
Penpoll
Pelynt
Seaton
Crafthole
Antony
ST. AUSTELL
St. Blazey
Tywardreath
High Street
Par
Lanteglos Highway
Trenewan
EAST LOOE
Downderry
Portwrinkle
St. John
Insworke
Plymstock
Elburton
Trewoon
Boscoppa
Polkerris
FOWEY
WEST LOOE
Looe Bay
WHITSAND BAY
Freathy
Millbrook
Mount Edgcumbe
Hooe
Brixton
St. Mewan
Charlestown
Menabilly
Polruan
Lansallos
Polperro
Kingsand
The Sound
Staddiscombe
Porthpean
St Austell Bay
Gribbin Head
Polgooth
Cawsand
Rame
Knighton
Trenarren
Black Head
Penlee Point
Rame Head
Heybrook Bay
Wembury
Newton Ferrers
Pentewan
Mevagissey Bay
Worswell
Noss Mayo
St. Ewe
Polmassick
Mevagissey
Stoke Point
Trevarrick
Chapel Point
St. Michael Caerhays
Gorran Haven
Penare
Dodman Point
SANTANDER
ROSCOFF
DAR
SR
SW
2
1
0
9
8
7
6
5
4
3

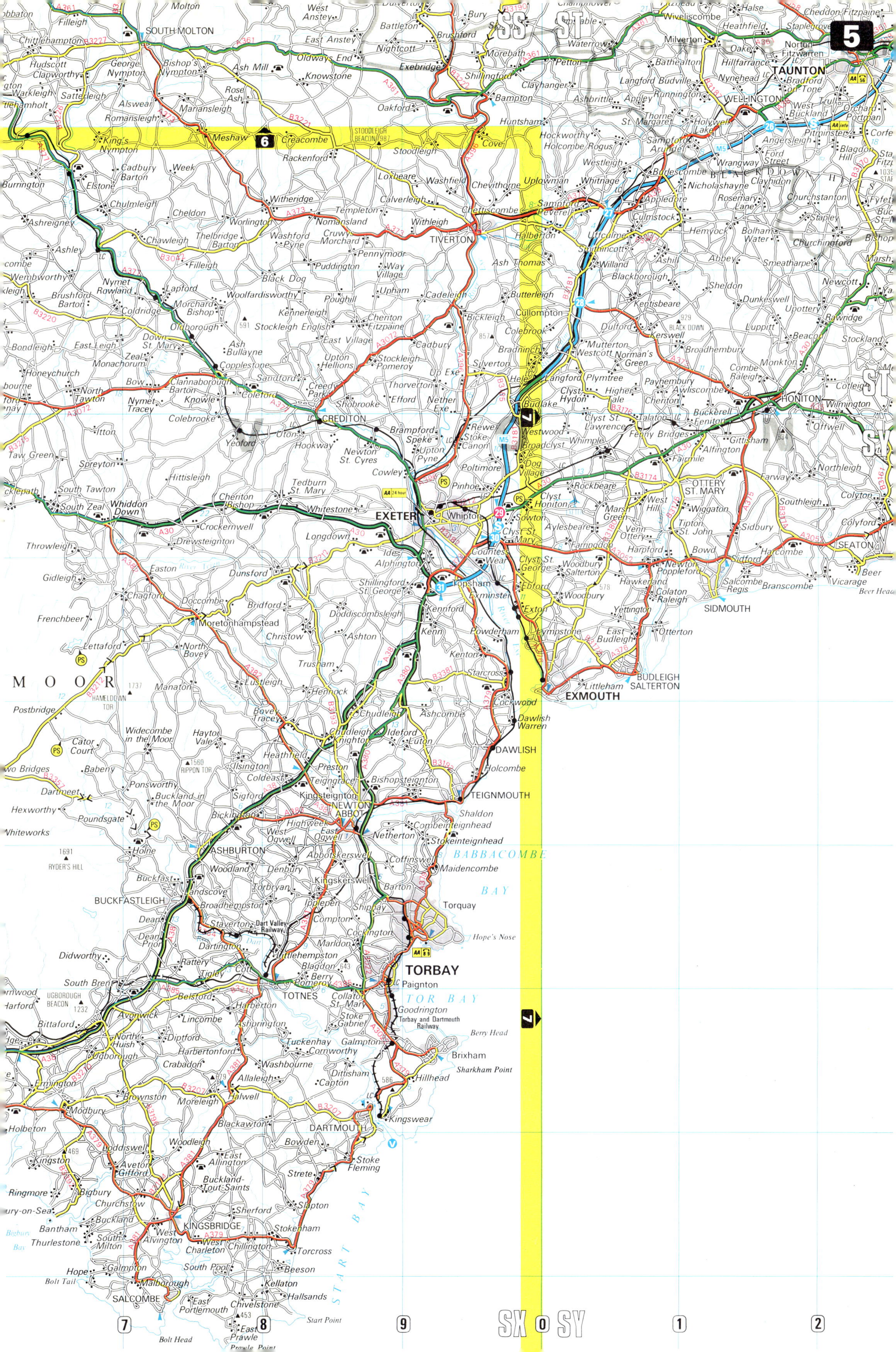

5
SOUTH MOLTON
TAUNTON
WELLINGTON
TIVERTON
Meshaw
6
Creacombe
CREDITON
EXETER
Whipton
Topsham
HONITON
OTTERY ST. MARY
SIDMOUTH
SEATON
EXMOUTH
BUDLEIGH SALTERTON
DAWLISH
TEIGNMOUTH
NEWTON ABBOT
Kingsteignton
ASHBURTON
BUCKFASTLEIGH
TOTNES
Torquay
TORBAY
Paignton
Brixham
DARTMOUTH
Kingswear
KINGSBRIDGE
SALCOMBE
Moretonhampstead
Chagford
Cullompton
Bampton
Chudleigh
Bovey Tracey
Modbury
Cove
Halberton
Sampford Peverell
BABBACOMBE BAY
TOR BAY
START BAY
Berry Head
Start Point
Bolt Head
Prawle Point
Hope's Nose
Sharkham Point
Dart Valley Railway
Torbay and Dartmouth Railway
MOOR
SS
ST
SX
SY
7
8
9
0
1
2

6

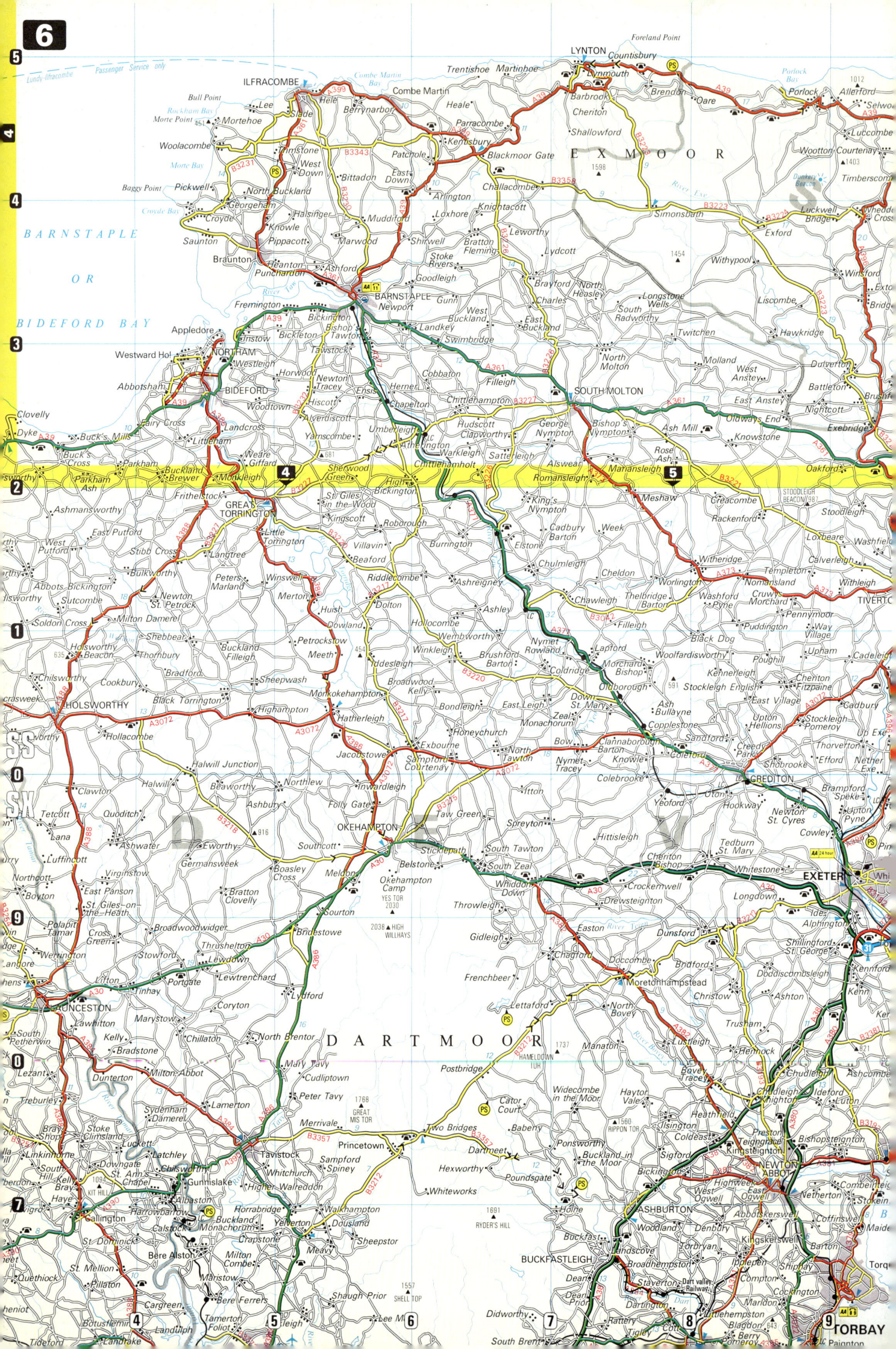

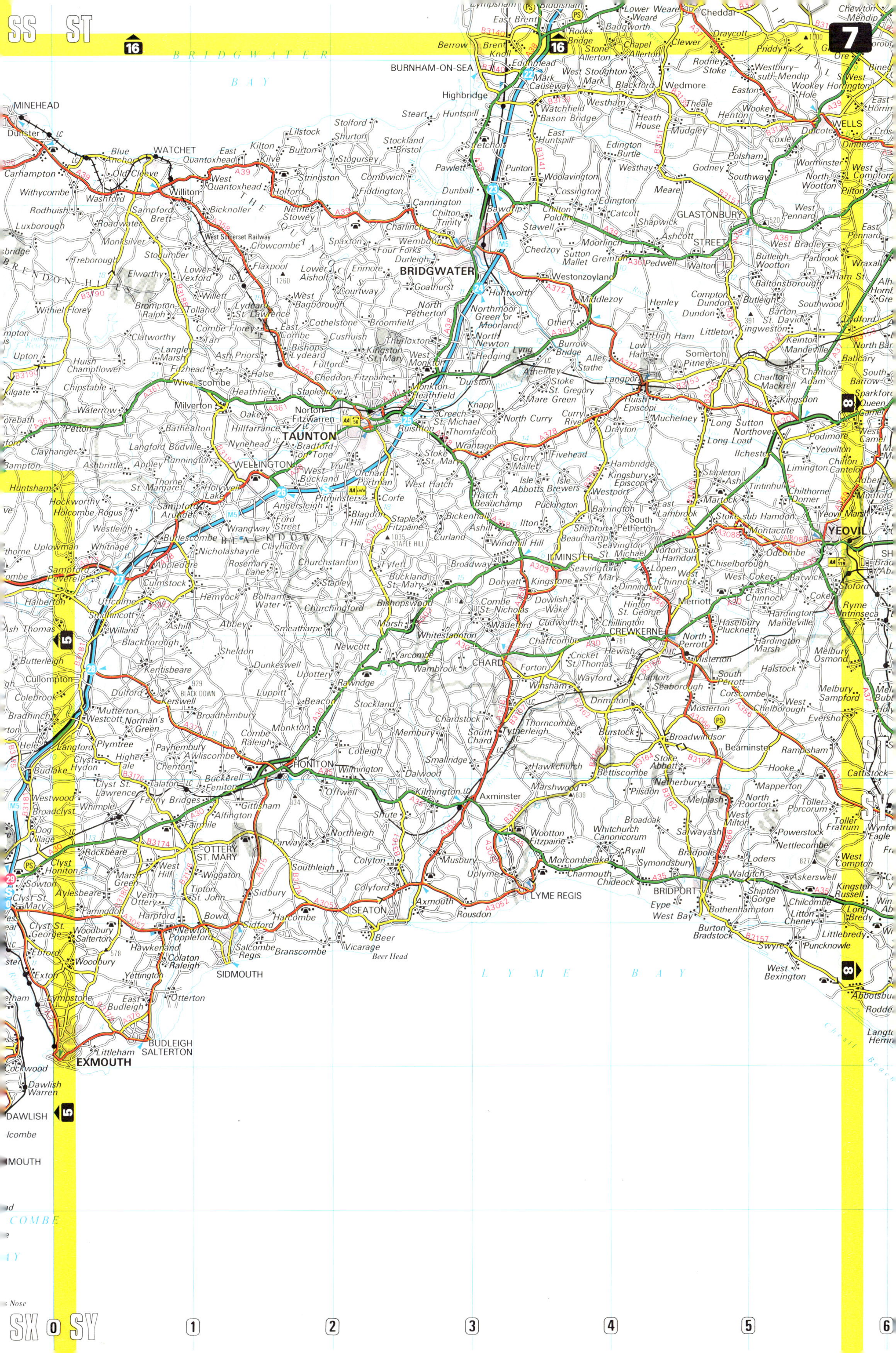

7
SS
ST
16
BRIDGWATER
BAY
BURNHAM-ON-SEA
Berrow
Brent Knoll
East Brent
Edithmead
Highbridge
Mark Causeway
West Stoughton
Watchfield
Bason Bridge
East Huntspill
Rooks Bridge
Stone Allerton
Chapel Allerton
Badgworth
Lower Weare
Weare
Cheddar
Draycott
Clewer
Wedmore
Rodney Stoke
Westbury-sub-Mendip
Wookey Hole
Priddy
Chewton Mendip
Easton
Theale
Blackford
Westham
Heath House
Mudgley
Henton
Wookey
WELLS
Dulcote
Coxley
Polsham
Godney
Southway
Worminster
North Wootton
West Compton
Pilton
West Pennard
East Pennard
GLASTONBURY
STREET
Meare
Westhay
Edington Burtle
MINEHEAD
Dunster
Carhampton
WATCHET
Blue Anchor
Old Cleeve
Williton
East Quantoxhead
West Quantoxhead
Kilton
Kilve
Lilstock
Stolford
Shurton
Stogursey
Burton
Stockland Bristol
Steart
Huntspill
Pawlett
Puriton
Dunball
Combwich
Fiddington
Cannington
Chilton Trinity
Stringston
Holford
Nether Stowey
Bicknoller
Withycombe
Washford
Rodhuish
Luxborough
Sampford Brett
Roadwater
Monksilver
Stogumber
Treborough
BRENDON HILLS
Elworthy
Withiel Florey
Brompton Ralph
Lower Vexford
Willett
Lydeard St. Lawrence
Tolland
Crowcombe
Flaxpool
West Bagborough
Lower Aisholt
Enmore
Spaxton
Charlinch
Wembdon
Four Forks
BRIDGWATER
Goathurst
Courtway
North Petherton
Cothelstone
Broomfield
East Combe
Combe Florey
Bishops Lydeard
Cushuish
Thurloxton
Kingston St. Mary
West Monkton
Clatworthy
Tarr
Ash Priors
Langley Marsh
Fitzhead
Huish Champflower
Upton
Chipstable
Wiveliscombe
Halse
Fulford
Cheddon Fitzpaine
Heathfield
Staplegrove
Milverton
Waterrow
Oake
Norton Fitzwarren
Hillfarrance
TAUNTON
Bathealton
Petton
Langford Budville
Nynehead
Bradford-on-Tone
Clayhanger
Ashbrittle
Appley
Runnington
WELLINGTON
Thorne St. Margaret
Holywell Lake
West Buckland
Trull
Orchard Portman
Pitminster
Corfe
Angersleigh
Huntsham
Hockworthy
Holcombe Rogus
Sampford Arundel
Wrangway
Ford Street
Westleigh
Burlescombe
BLACKDOWN HILLS
Nicholashayne
Whitnage
Uplowman
Appledore
Sampford Peverell
Clayhidon
Rosemary Lane
Churchstanton
Culmstock
Halberton
Uffculme
Smithincott
Hemyock
Bolham Water
Stapley
Churchingford
Willand
Ashill
Abbey
Smeatharpe
Blackborough
Sheldon
Butterleigh
Cullompton
Kentisbeare
Dunkeswell
Upottery
Colebrook
Bradninch
Dulford
Kerswell
BLACK DOWN
Luppitt
Mutterton
Westcott
Norman's Green
Broadhembury
Hele
Langford
Plymtree
Payhembury
Combe Raleigh
Monkton
HONITON
Clyst Hydon
Higher Tale
Awliscombe
Cheriton
Buckerell
Feniton
Budlake
Talaton
Clyst St. Lawrence
Fenny Bridges
Whimple
Westwood
Broadclyst
Gittisham
Alfington
Fairmile
Dog Village
Rockbeare
OTTERY ST. MARY
West Hill
Clyst Honiton
Sowton
Aylesbeare
Marsh Green
Venn Ottery
Tipton St. John
Wiggaton
Clyst St. Mary
Farringdon
Harpford
Bowd
Sidbury
Clyst St. George
Woodbury Salterton
Newton Poppleford
Sidford
Ebford
Woodbury
Hawkerland
Colaton Raleigh
Salcombe Regis
SIDMOUTH
Exton
Yettington
Lympstone
East Budleigh
Otterton
BUDLEIGH SALTERTON
Littleham
EXMOUTH
Cockwood
Dawlish Warren
DAWLISH
5
Staple Fitzpaine
STAPLE HILL
Curland
Blagdon Hill
West Hatch
Hatch Beauchamp
Bickenhall
Ashill
Fyfett
Buckland St. Mary
Broadway
Bishopswood
Whitestaunton
Donyatt
Combe St. Nicholas
Wadeford
Dowlish Wake
Cudworth
Chaffcombe
CHARD
Yarcombe
Wambrook
Marsh
Newcott
Rawridge
Beacon
Stockland
Chardstock
South Chard
Tytherleigh
Thorncombe
Forton
Winsham
Membury
Cotleigh
Smallridge
Dalwood
Wilmington
Offwell
Kilmington
Axminster
Shute
Northleigh
Farway
Southleigh
Colyton
Colyford
SEATON
Beer
Beer Head
Branscombe
Vicarage
Axmouth
Musbury
Uplyme
Rousdon
LYME REGIS
LYME BAY
Hawkchurch
Marshwood
Wootton Fitzpaine
Morcombelake
Charmouth
Chideock
Bettiscombe
Pilsdon
Broadoak
Whitchurch Canonicorum
Ryall
Symondsbury
BRIDPORT
Eype
West Bay
Bothenhampton
Burton Bradstock
Shipton Gorge
Swyre
West Bexington
Puncknowle
Litton Cheney
Chilcombe
Askerswell
Kingston Russell
Littlebredy
Long Bredy
Abbotsbury
Loders
Powerstock
Nettlecombe
West Compton
West Milton
North Poorton
Mapperton
Toller Porcorum
Toller Fratrum
Wynford Eagle
Melplash
Salwayash
Bradpole
Netherbury
Stoke Abbott
Broadwindsor
Beaminster
Hooke
Cattistock
Rampisham
Evershot
Mosterton
Drimpton
Burstock
Seaborough
Clapton
Misterton
South Perrott
Corscombe
Chelborough
Halstock
Melbury Osmond
Melbury Sampford
Hardington Marsh
Hardington Mandeville
North Perrott
Haselbury Plucknett
Merriott
East Chinnock
West Chinnock
Chiselborough
West Coker
Coker
Odcombe
Montacute
Norton sub Hamdon
Stoke sub Hamdon
Lopen
Dinnington
Hinton St. George
Chillington
CREWKERNE
Hewish
Cricket St. Thomas
Wayford
Seavington St. Michael
Seavington St. Mary
Kingstone
ILMINSTER
Ilton
Windmill Hill
Shepton Beauchamp
South Petherton
Barrington
Puckington
Isle Abbotts
Isle Brewers
Curry Mallet
Fivehead
Hambridge
Kingsbury Episcopi
Westport
East Lambrook
Martock
Ash
Stapleton
Tintinhull
Chilthorne Domer
YEOVIL
Yeovil Marsh
Ilchester
Limington
Yeovilton
Long Load
Long Sutton
Northover
Podimore
Drayton
Muchelney
Huish Episcopi
Langport
Curry Rivel
North Curry
Wrantage
Thornfalcon
Stoke St. Mary
Creech St. Michael
Ruishton
Monkton Heathfield
Durston
Knapp
Stoke St. Gregory
Mare Green
Athelney
Burrow Bridge
Aller
Stathe
Lyng
Hedging
North Newton
Northmoor Green or Moorland
Huntworth
Bawdrip
Chilton Polden
Cossington
Woolavington
Stawell
Chedzoy
Edington
Catcott
Shapwick
Moorlinch
Sutton Mallet
Greinton
Pedwell
Ashcott
Walton
Westonzoyland
Middlezoy
Othery
Henley
Compton Dundon
Dundon
Butleigh
Butleigh Wootton
Baltonsborough
Parbrook
West Bradley
Barton St. David
Kingweston
Littleton
High Ham
Low Ham
Somerton
Pitney
Charlton Mackrell
Charlton Adam
Kingsdon
Keinton Mandeville
Babcary
Lydford
Southwood
North Barrow
South Barrow
Sparkford
Queen Camel
West Camel
Mudford
Ryme Intrinseca
Yetminster
8
SX
SY
0
1
2
3
4
5
6

SALISBURY PLAIN
WILTSHIRE
DORSET
CRANBORNE CHASE
PURBECK
WESTBURY
WARMINSTER
FROME
SHEPTON MALLET
WELLS
Bruton
Castle Cary
Wincanton
Gillingham
SHAFTESBURY
Mere
Zeals
Amesbury
Shrewton
Wylye
Wilton
SALISBURY
Quidhampton
Laverstock
Britford
Downton
Fordingbridge
Ringwood
Cranborne
Verwood
Wimborne St Giles
Sixpenny Handley
Tollard Royal
Tisbury
Hindon
Fonthill Bishop
Chilmark
Teffont Magna
Fovant
Broad Chalke
Bishopstone
Ebbesbourne Wake
Alvediston
Bowerchalke
Donhead St Mary
Donhead St Andrew
Semley
Motcombe
Stalbridge
Sturminster Newton
Milborne Port
SHERBORNE
Yeovil
Yetminster
Henstridge
Templecombe
Sandford Orcas
Marnhull
Hazelbury Bryan
Child Okeford
Shillingstone
BLANDFORD FORUM
Bryanston
Pimperne
Tarrant Hinton
Tarrant Gunville
Tarrant Keyneston
Tarrant Rushton
Spetisbury
Sturminster Marshall
WIMBORNE MINSTER
Colehill
Ferndown
Stapehill
West Moors
St Ives
St Leonards
Parley Cross
Hurn
Kinson
Broadstone
Corfe Mullen
Lytchett Matravers
Lytchett Minster
Upton
Hamworthy
POOLE
Parkstone
Branksome
Westbourne
Boscombe
Pokesdown
Southbourne
BOURNEMOUTH
Canford Cliffs
Sandbanks
Brownsea Island
POOLE BAY
Studland
Studland Bay
The Foreland or Handfast Point
Swanage Bay
SWANAGE
Durlston Bay
DURLSTON HEAD
Langton Matravers
Worth Matravers
Kingston
Corfe Castle
Church Knowle
Steeple
Kimmeridge
ST ALDHELM'S OR ST ALBAN'S HEAD
Tyneham
West Lulworth
East Lulworth
Lulworth Cove
Wool
Bovington Camp
Stoborough
WAREHAM
Sandford
Holton Heath
Bere Regis
Milborne St Andrew
Puddletown
Tolpuddle
Affpuddle
Briantspuddle
Charminster
DORCHESTER
Martinstown
Winterborne Herringston
Broadmayne
Warmwell
Owermoigne
Poxwell
Osmington
Osmington Mills
Preston
Upwey
Broadwey
WEYMOUTH
WEYMOUTH BAY
Wyke Regis
Chickerell
Charlestown
Abbotsbury
Portesham
Chesil Beach
FORTUNESWELL
West Bay
Grove
Easton
Weston
Southwell
BILL OF PORTLAND
GUERNSEY JERSEY
CHERBOURG summer only
Cerne Abbas
Maiden Newton
Frampton
Piddletrenthide
Piddlehinton
Buckland Newton
Minterne Magna
Sydling St Nicholas
Milton Abbas
Winterborne Whitechurch
Winterborne Kingston
Winterborne Stickland
Okeford Fitzpaine
Fifehead Neville
Lydlinch
Bishop's Caundle
Longburton
Leigh
Melbury Bubb
Holywell
Chetnole
Evershot
Frome St Quintin
ST SU
SY 0 SZ
17
7
10
6 7 8 9 1 2
5 4 3 2 1 0 9 8 7
A303 A30 A350 A36 A354 A35 A31 A338 A37 A352 A357 A351 A348
BEACON HILL 303
AA 24 hour

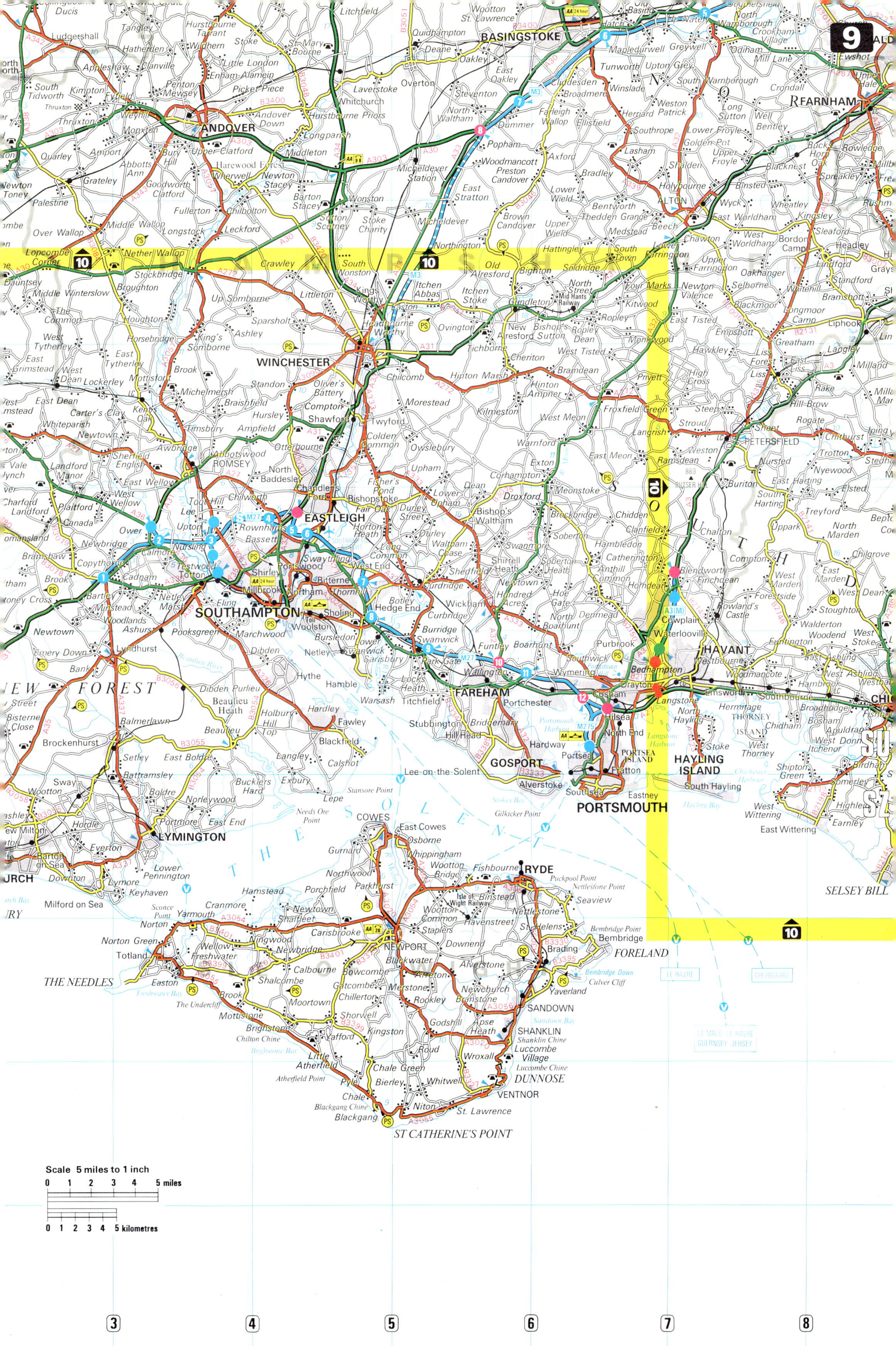
BASINGSTOKE
ANDOVER
FARNHAM
ALTON
WINCHESTER
ROMSEY
EASTLEIGH
SOUTHAMPTON
FAREHAM
GOSPORT
PORTSMOUTH
HAVANT
HAYLING ISLAND
PETERSFIELD
LYMINGTON
NEW FOREST
THE SOLENT
COWES
RYDE
NEWPORT
SANDOWN
SHANKLIN
VENTNOR
DUNNOSE
FORELAND
THE NEEDLES
ST CATHERINE'S POINT
SELSEY BILL
ISLE OF WIGHT
HAMPSHIRE
SOUTH DOWNS
Stockbridge
Lyndhurst
Totton
Hythe
Fawley
Bishop's Waltham
Wickham
Cosham
Emsworth
Waterlooville
Yarmouth
Totland
Freshwater
East Cowes
Brading
Bembridge
Lee-on-the-Solent
Milford on Sea
Scale 5 miles to 1 inch
0 1 2 3 4 5 miles
0 1 2 3 4 5 kilometres
10
3
4
5
6
7
8

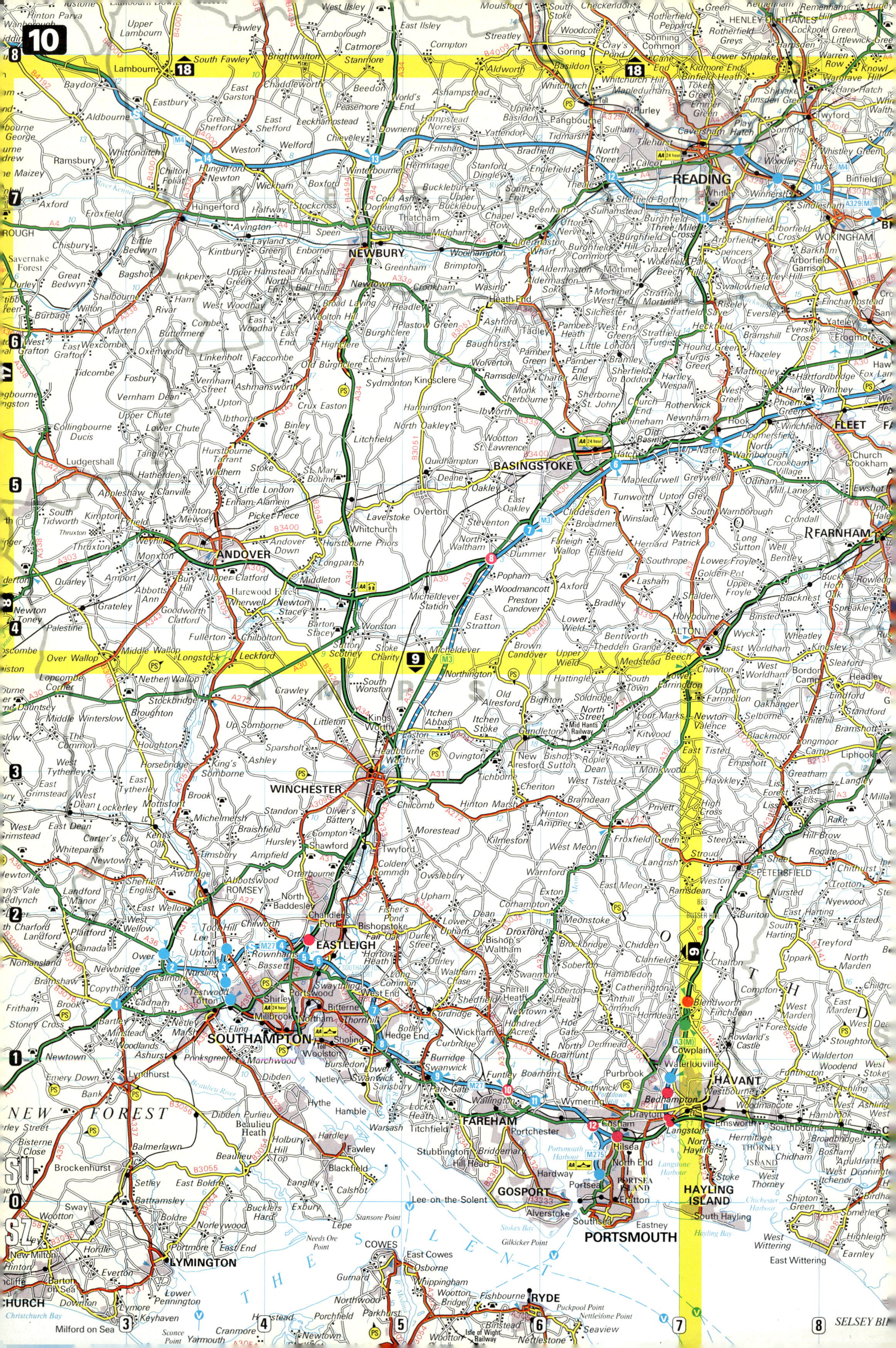
10
18
9
17
SU
SZ
READING
NEWBURY
BASINGSTOKE
ANDOVER
WINCHESTER
EASTLEIGH
SOUTHAMPTON
FAREHAM
GOSPORT
PORTSMOUTH
HAVANT
HAYLING ISLAND
LYMINGTON
FLEET
FARNHAM
WOKINGHAM
ALTON
PETERSFIELD
ROMSEY
RYDE
COWES
NEW FOREST
THE SOLENT
Hungerford
Lambourn
Thatcham
Kingsclere
Whitchurch
Overton
Stockbridge
Alresford
Bishop's Waltham
Lyndhurst
Hythe
Totton
Waterlooville
Emsworth
Milford on Sea
New Milton
Lee-on-the-Solent
Alverstoke
Southsea
Eastney
Fawley
Brockenhurst
Beaulieu
Yarmouth
Seaview
Mid Hants Railway
Isle of Wight Railway
Hayling Bay
Stokes Bay
Chichester Harbour
Langstone Harbour
Portsmouth Harbour
SELSEY BI

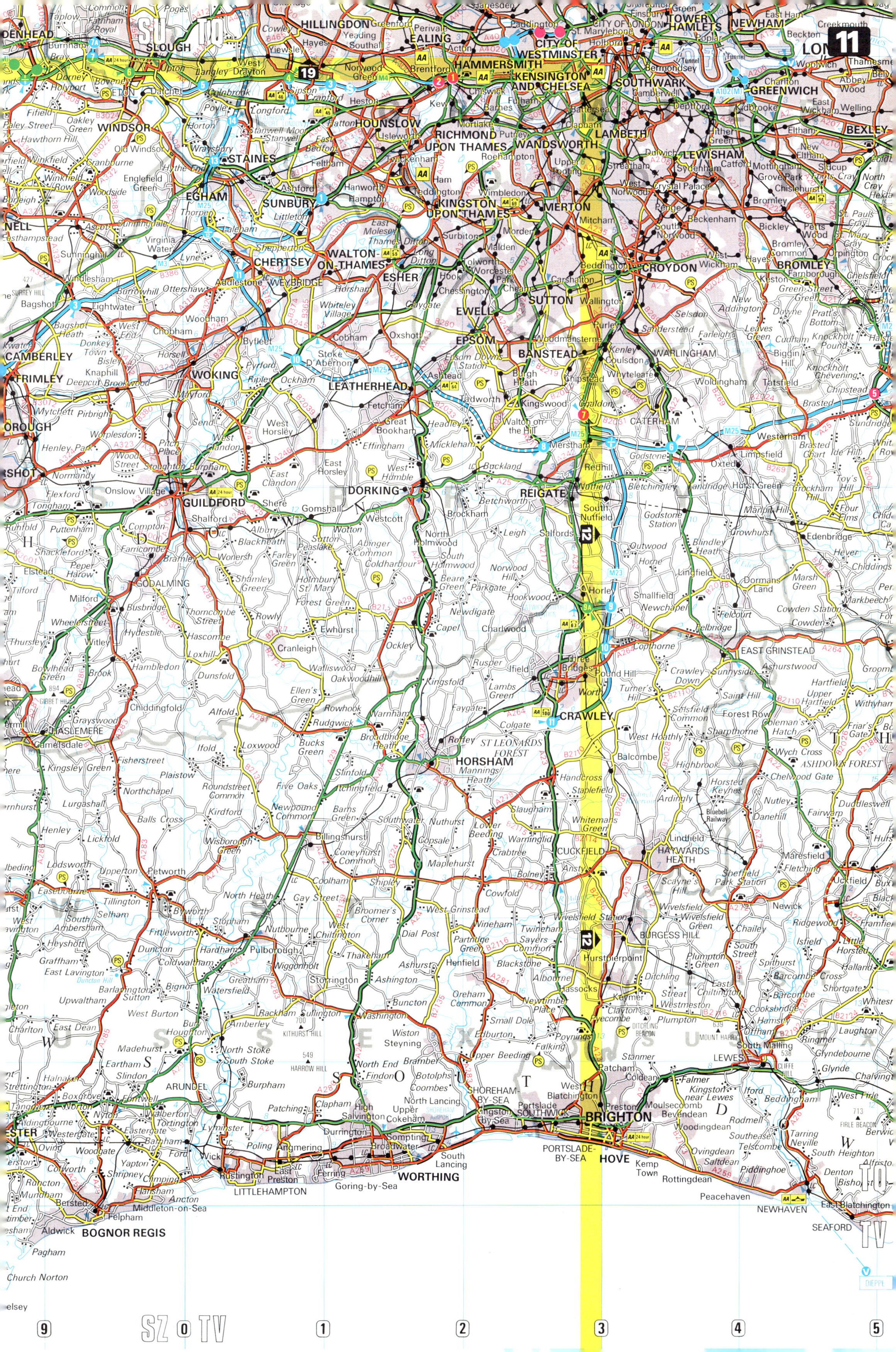

11
19
12
SU
TQ
SZ
TV
HILLINGDON
EALING
CITY OF WESTMINSTER
CITY OF LONDON
TOWER HAMLETS
NEWHAM
SLOUGH
HAMMERSMITH
KENSINGTON AND CHELSEA
SOUTHWARK
GREENWICH
WINDSOR
HOUNSLOW
RICHMOND UPON THAMES
WANDSWORTH
LAMBETH
BEXLEY
LEWISHAM
STAINES
EGHAM
SUNBURY
KINGSTON UPON THAMES
MERTON
CHERTSEY
WALTON-ON-THAMES
ESHER
WEYBRIDGE
CROYDON
BROMLEY
SUTTON
EWELL
EPSOM
BANSTEAD
CAMBERLEY
FRIMLEY
WOKING
LEATHERHEAD
WARLINGHAM
CATERHAM
GUILDFORD
DORKING
REIGATE
GODALMING
HASLEMERE
EAST GRINSTEAD
CRAWLEY
HORSHAM
ST LEONARDS FOREST
ASHDOWN FOREST
CUCKFIELD
HAYWARDS HEATH
BURGESS HILL
ARUNDEL
SHOREHAM-BY-SEA
SOUTHWICK
PORTSLADE-BY-SEA
BRIGHTON
HOVE
LEWES
WORTHING
LITTLEHAMPTON
BOGNOR REGIS
NEWHAVEN
SEAFORD
Peacehaven
Rottingdean
Steyning
Petworth
Pulborough
Billingshurst
Henfield
Hurstpierpoint
Redhill
Oxted
Edenbridge
9
0
1
2
3
4
5

LONDON
CITY OF WESTMINSTER
HAMMERSMITH
KENSINGTON AND CHELSEA
SOUTHWARK
LAMBETH
LEWISHAM
GREENWICH
TOWER HAMLETS
ISLINGTON
CAMDEN
NEWHAM
BARKING
WANDSWORTH
RICHMOND
MERTON
SUTTON
CROYDON
BROMLEY
BEXLEY
DARTFORD
GRAYS
TILBURY
NORTHFLEET
GRAVESEND
CANVEY ISLAND
ROCHESTER
GILLINGHAM
CHATHAM
MAIDSTONE
SEVENOAKS
TONBRIDGE
ROYAL TUNBRIDGE WELLS
EPSOM
BANSTEAD
REIGATE
CATERHAM
CRAWLEY
HORSHAM
EAST GRINSTEAD
ASHDOWN FOREST
HAYWARDS HEATH
CUCKFIELD
BURGESS HILL
LEWES
BRIGHTON
HOVE
PORTSLADE-BY-SEA
SHOREHAM-BY-SEA
NEWHAVEN
SEAFORD
EASTBOURNE
BEACHY HEAD
BEXHILL
Pevensey Bay
Langney Point
THE WEALD
SOUTH DOWNS
DIEPPE
TQ
TV

SOUTHEND
-ON-SEA
Westcliff-on-Sea
Thorpe Bay
Shoeburyness
TQ
TR
21
VLISSINGEN (FLUSHING)
Allhallows
ISLE OF GRAIN
Grain
Wallend
SHEERNESS
Halfway Houses
Minster
Warden Point
Queenborough
Warden
Eastchurch
Leysdown-on-Sea
ISLE OF SHEPPEY
ELMLEY ISLAND
ISLE OF HARTY
Iwade
Lower Halstow
Bobbing
Milton Regis
SITTINGBOURNE
Conyer
Uplees
Newington
Borden
Bapchild
Teynham
Oare
Tunstall
Rodmersham
Graveney
Goodnestone
Oad Street
Highsted
FAVERSHAM
Preston
Bredgar
Lynsted
Ospringe
Bicknor
Milstead
Doddington
Newnham
Wormshill
Frinsted
Eastling
Throwley
Hollingbourne
Wichling
West Street
Leaveland
Harrietsham
Stalisfield Green
Warren Street
Lenham
Lenham Heath
Boughton Malherbe
Charing
Grafty Green
Charing Heath
Egerton
The Forstal
Westwell Leacon
Westwell
Little Chart
Pluckley
Hothfield
Pluckley Station
Headcorn
Smarden
Maltman's Hill
ASHFORD
Kennington
Haffenden Quarter
Bethersden
Great Chart
Standen
High Halden
Kingsnorth
Shadoxhurst
Redbrook Street
St. Michaels
Woodchurch
Orlestone
TENTERDEN
Kenardington
Leigh Green
Reading Street
Rolvenden Layne
Small Hythe
Appledore
ISLE OF OXNEY
Wittersham
Stone
Brookland
Four Oaks
Peasmarsh
Iden
Beckley
Rye Foreign
Playden
East Guldeford
RYE
Udimore
Rye Harbour
Winchelsea
Icklesham
Winchelsea Beach
Pett
Cliff End
Fairlight
Ore
HASTINGS
WHITSTABLE
Swalecliffe
Seasalter
Chestfield
Yorkletts
Dargate
Hernhill
Dunkirk
Boughton Street
Sheldwich
Selling
Badlesmere
Shottenden
Molash
Godmersham
Challock Lees
Bilting
Boughton Aluph
Boughton Lees
Wye
Brook
Chilham
Old Wives Lees
Chartham Hatch
Harbledown
Chartham
Blean
Honey Hill
Hales Place
Broadoak
Tyler Hill
Sturry
Fordwich
CANTERBURY
Thanington
Patrixbourne
Littlebourne
Bekesbourne
Nackington
Bridge
Lower Hardres
Petham
Upper Hardres Court
Kingston
Sole Street
Waltham
Crundale
Hassell Street
Elmsted Court
Stelling Minnis
Bossingham
Derringstone
Barham
Lyminge Forest
Rhodes Minnis
Hastingleigh
Hinxhill
Willesborough
Brabourne
Brabourne Lees
Lymbridge Green
Sevington
Mersham
Smeeth
Cheeseman's Green
Sellindge
Aldington
Bonnington
Stanford
Stowting
Postling
Beachborough
Etchinghill
Newington
Paddlesworth
Lyminge
Elham
Acrise Place
Denton
Wootton
Swingfield Minnis
Densole
Hawkinge
Capel le Ferne
FOLKESTONE
Sandgate
Saltwood
HYTHE
Lympne
Bilsington
Ruckinge
Hamstreet
Warehorne
Snave
Burmarsh
ROMNEY MARSH
Newchurch
St. Mary in the Marsh
Dymchurch
St. Mary's Bay
Ivychurch
Snargate
Brenzett
Old Romney
NEW ROMNEY
Littlestone-on-Sea
Greatstone-on-Sea
WALLAND MARSH
LYDD
Denge Marsh
Camber
Lydd-on-Sea
DUNGENESS
Romney Hythe & Dymchurch Light Railway
HERNE BAY
Reculver
Herne
Hillborough
Broomfield
St. Nicholas at Wade
Boyden Gate
Chislet
Hoath
Upstreet
Hersden
Grove
Westbere
Stodmarsh
Sarre
West Stourmouth
East Stourmouth
Westmarsh
Monkton
Minster
Preston
Elmstone
Hoaden
Wickhambreaux
Ickham
Wingham
Ash
Marshborough
Staple
Goodnestone
Adisham
Bishopsbourne
Aylesham
Chillenden
Nonington
Womenswold
Easole Street
Barfreston
Eythorne
Woolage Green
Shepherdswell or Sibertswold
Elvington
Coldred
Lydden
Temple Ewell
Ewell Minnis
Alkham
Buckland
West Hougham
DOVER
Whitfield
Guston
East Langdon
West Langdon
St. Margaret's at Cliffe
West Cliffe
SOUTH FORELAND
Ringwould
Kingsdown
Ripple
Sutton
East Studdal
Tilmanstone
Northbourne
Betteshanger
Knowlton
Eastry
Ham
Worth
Woodnesborough
SANDWICH
Great Stonar
Sholden
DEAL
Great Mongeham
Walmer
MARGATE
Westgate on Sea
Birchington
Acol
St. Peter's
NORTH FORELAND
BROADSTAIRS
RAMSGATE
Cliffsend
Long Nose Spit
Foreness Point
White Ness
DUNKERQUE (OUEST)
CALAIS BOULOGNE
ZEEBRUGGE OOSTENDE DUNKERQUE (OUEST) CALAIS BOULOGNE
OOSTENDE CALAIS BOULOGNE
STRAIT OF DOVER
M2
M20
A2
A20
A28
A249
A252
A253
A256
A257
A258
A259
A262
A268
A299
A260
B2231
B2068
B2067
B2070
B2080
B2082
TR
TW
9
TV
0
TW
1
2
3
4

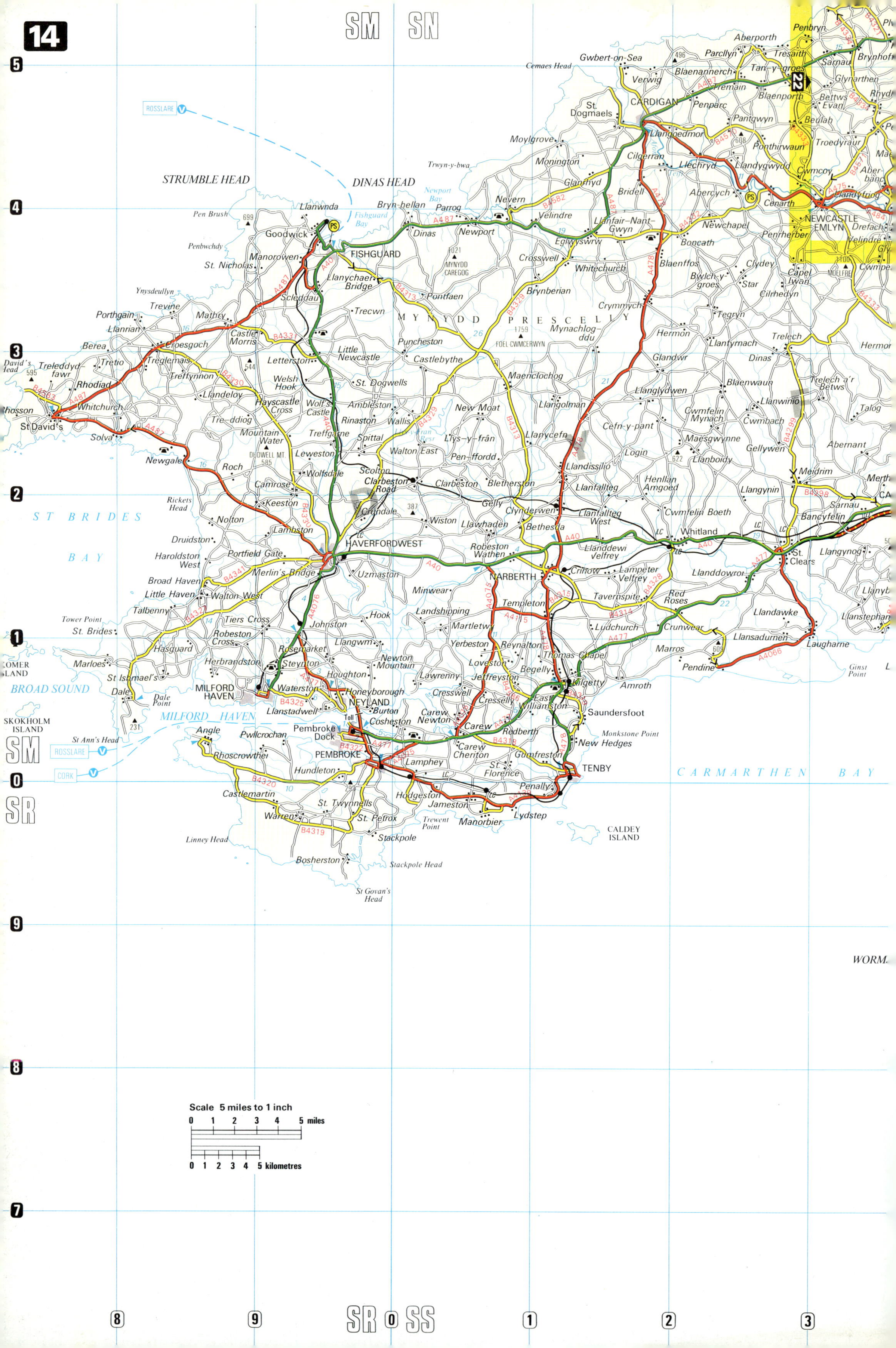
SM SN
STRUMBLE HEAD
DINAS HEAD
Cemaes Head
Gwbert-on-Sea
Aberporth
Penbryn
Parcllyn
Tresaith
Tan-y-groes
Sarnau
Brynhoffnant
Verwig
Blaenannerch
Tremain
Glynarthen
Rhydlewis
CARDIGAN
Penparc
Blaenporth
Bettws Evan
St. Dogmaels
Beulah
Pantgwyn
Llangoedmor
Troedyraur
Moylgrove
Cilgerran
Ponthirwaun
Monington
Llechryd
Llandygwydd
Cwmcoy
Aber-banc
Trwyn-y-bwa
Glanrhyd
Bridell
Abercych
Cenarth
Llandyfriog
Newport Bay
Nevern
NEWCASTLE EMLYN
Drefach
Velindre
Llanfair-Nant-Gwyn
Newchapel
Penrherber
Llanwnda
Bryn-henllan
Parrog
Pen Brush
699
Fishguard Bay
Goodwick
Dinas
Newport
Eglwyswrw
Boncath
Penbwchdy
FISHGUARD
1021
MYNYDD CAREGOG
Crosswell
Whitechurch
Blaenffos
Clydey
Capel Iwan
St. Nicholas
Manorowen
Llanychaer Bridge
Pontfaen
Brynberian
Bwlch-y-groes
Star
Cilrhedyn
Ynysdeullyn
Scleddau
Crymmych
Trevine
Porthgain
Mathry
Trecwn
MYNYDD PRESCELLY
Tegryn
Llanrian
Castle Morris
1759
FOEL CWMCERWYN
Mynachlog-ddu
Hermon
Trelech
Berea
Croesgoch
Puncheston
Llanfyrnach
Tretio
Treglemais
544
Little Newcastle
Castlebythe
Glandwr
Dinas
St David's Head
595
Treleddyd-fawr
Letterston
Rhodiad
Treffynnon
St. Dogwells
Maenclochog
Blaenwaun
Trelech a'r Betws
Welsh Hook
Llanglydwen
Llandeloy
Hayscastle Cross
Wolf's Castle
Ambleston
Llangolman
Cwmfelin Mynach
Llanwinio
Talog
Whitchurch
New Moat
Rinaston
Wallis
Cefn-y-pant
Cwmbach
Porthclais
St David's
Tre-ddiog
Llys-y-frân Resr
Solva
Mountain Water
Treffgarne
Spittal
Llys-y-frân
Llanycefn
Maesgwynne
Abernant
Gellywen
Pen-ffordd
Logan
Walton East
622
Llanboidy
Newgale
Leweston
Wolfsdale
Scolton
Llandissilio
DUDWELL MT.
585
Roch
Clarbeston Road
Clarbeston
Bletherston
Henllan Amgoed
Meidrim
Llanfallteg
Camrose
Llangynin
Rickets Head
Keeston
Gelly
Clynderwen
Llanfallteg West
Cwmfelin Boeth
Sarnau
387
Crundale
ST BRIDES BAY
Nolton
Wiston
Llawhaden
Bancyfelin
Bethesda
Whitland
Lambston
Druidston
HAVERFORDWEST
Robeston Wathen
Llanddewi Velfrey
St. Clears
Llangynog
Haroldston West
Portfield Gate
Crinow
Lampeter Velfrey
Merlin's Bridge
Uzmaston
NARBERTH
Llanddowror
Broad Haven
Minwear
Little Haven
Walton West
Templeton
Tavernspite
Red Roses
Llanybri
Talbenny
Landshipping
Hook
Llandawke
Llanstephan
Tower Point
Tiers Cross
Johnston
Martletwy
Ludchurch
Crunwear
St. Brides
Robeston Cross
Llangwm
Yerbeston
Reynalton
Llansadurnen
Laugharne
Hasguard
Rosemarket
Thomas Chapel
Marros
608
Marloes
Newton Mountain
Loveston
Begelly
SKOMER ISLAND
Herbrandston
Steynton
Houghton
Lawrenny
Jeffreyston
Pendine
Ginst Point
BROAD SOUND
St. Ishmael's
Kilgetty
Amroth
MILFORD HAVEN
Waterston
Honeyborough
Cresswell
Cresselly
Dale
Dale Point
NEYLAND
Burton
East Williamston
Saundersfoot
SKOKHOLM ISLAND
231
MILFORD HAVEN
Llanstadwell
Toll
Cosheston
Carew Newton
Carew
Redberth
Monkstone Point
Angle
Pwllcrochan
Pembroke Dock
St. Ann's Head
ROSSLARE
New Hedges
Rhoscrowther
PEMBROKE
Carew Cheriton
Gumfreston
TENBY
CORK
Hundleton
Lamphey
St. Florence
CARMARTHEN BAY
Castlemartin
Hodgeston
Penally
Jameston
St. Twynnells
Warren
St. Petrox
Trewent Point
Manorbier
Lydstep
CALDEY ISLAND
Linney Head
Stackpole
Bosherston
Stackpole Head
St Govan's Head
WORM.
ROSSLARE
A487
A40
A478
A484
A475
A477
A4076
A4075
A4115
A4066
A4139
A4075
B4582
B4332
B4313
B4329
B4331
B4330
B4583
B4341
B4327
B4325
B4320
B4319
B4318
B4314
B4316
B4328
B4298
B4299
B4333
B4570
B4333
B4334
B4321
22
PS
LC
5
4
3
2
1
0
9
8
7
SR
SM
8
9
SR 0 SS
1
2
3
Scale 5 miles to 1 inch
0 1 2 3 4 5 miles
0 1 2 3 4 5 kilometres

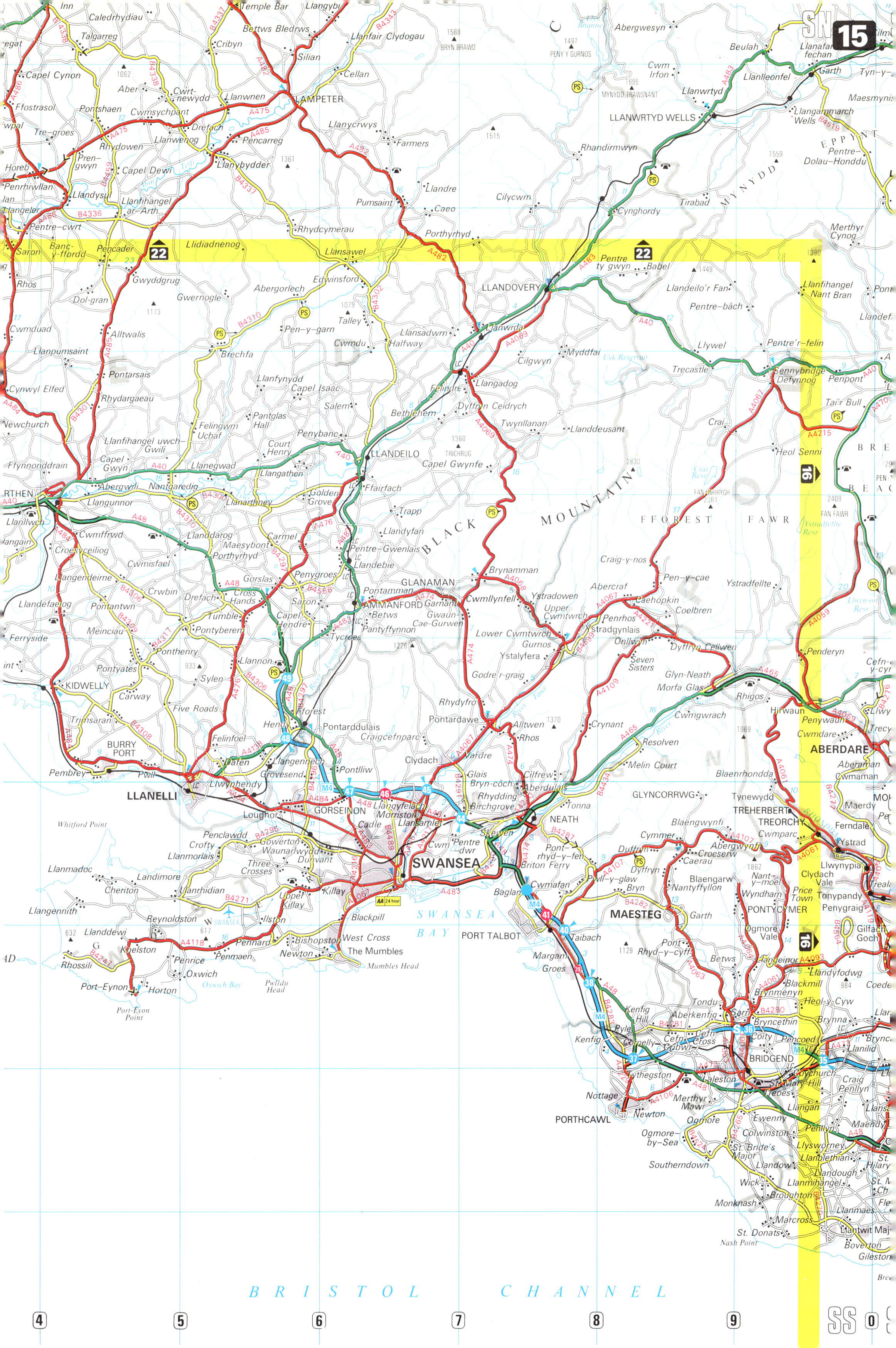

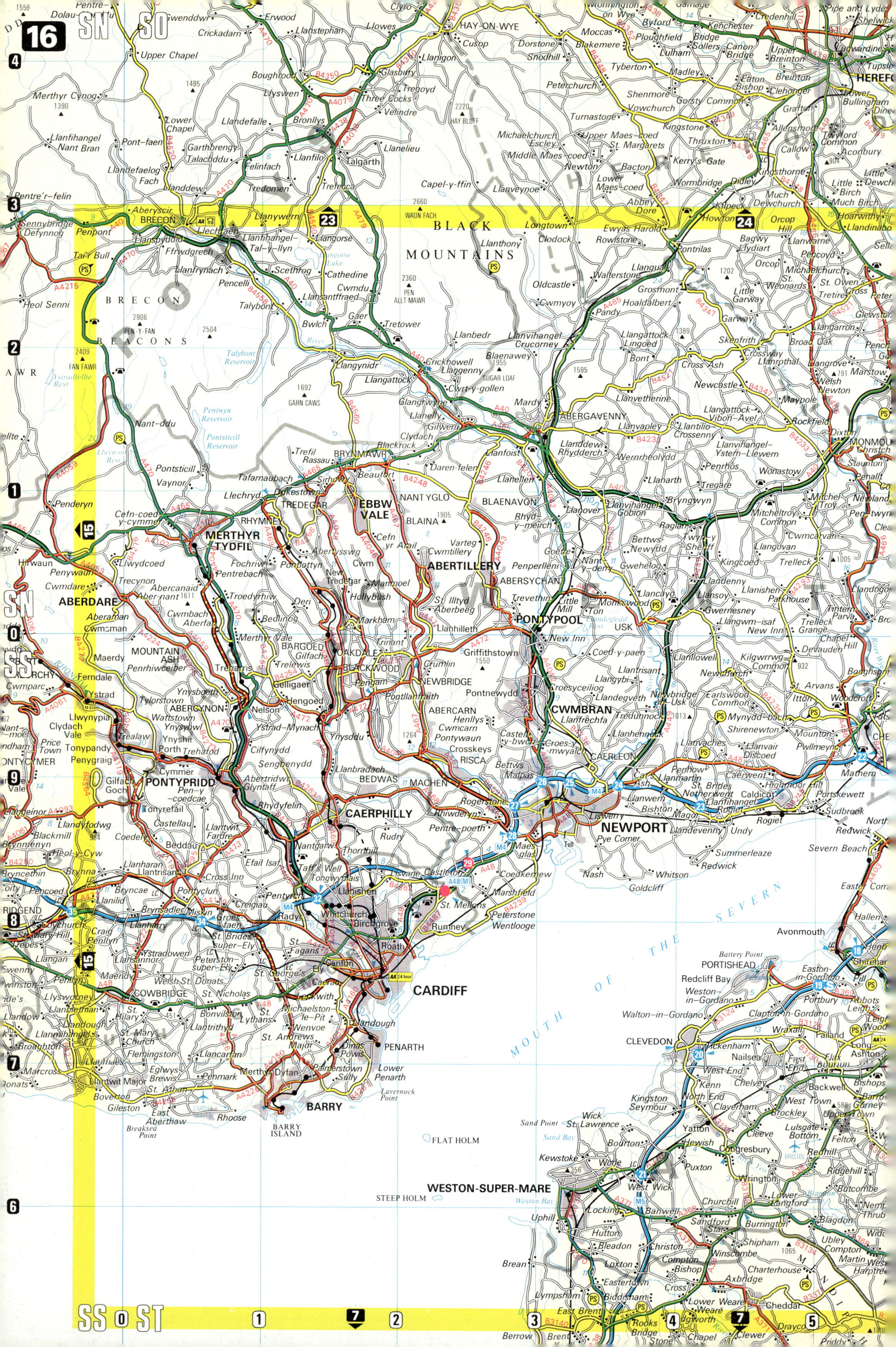

CHELTENHAM
GLOUCESTER
TEWKESBURY
LEDBURY
ROSS-ON-WYE
STROUD
NAILSWORTH
CIRENCESTER
MALMESBURY
SWINDON
CHIPPENHAM
CALNE
MELKSHAM
DEVIZES
BATH
BRISTOL
KINGSWOOD
MANGOTSFIELD
KEYNSHAM
BRADFORD-ON-AVON
TROWBRIDGE
RADSTOCK
MIDSOMER NORTON
WESTBURY
MARLBOROUGH
Tetbury
Wotton-under-Edge
Dursley
Chipping Sodbury
Yate
Thornbury
Berkeley
Lydney
Newent
Mitcheldean
Cinderford
Winchcombe
Northleach
Fairford
Lechlade
Cricklade
Wootton Bassett
Corsham
Pewsey
Broadway
Chipping Campden
Moreton-in-Marsh
Stow-the-Wold
Bishop's Cleeve
Painswick
Minchinhampton
Upton upon Severn
Malvern Wells
Little Malvern
FOREST OF DEAN
SO
SP
ST
SU
24
25
8
10
18

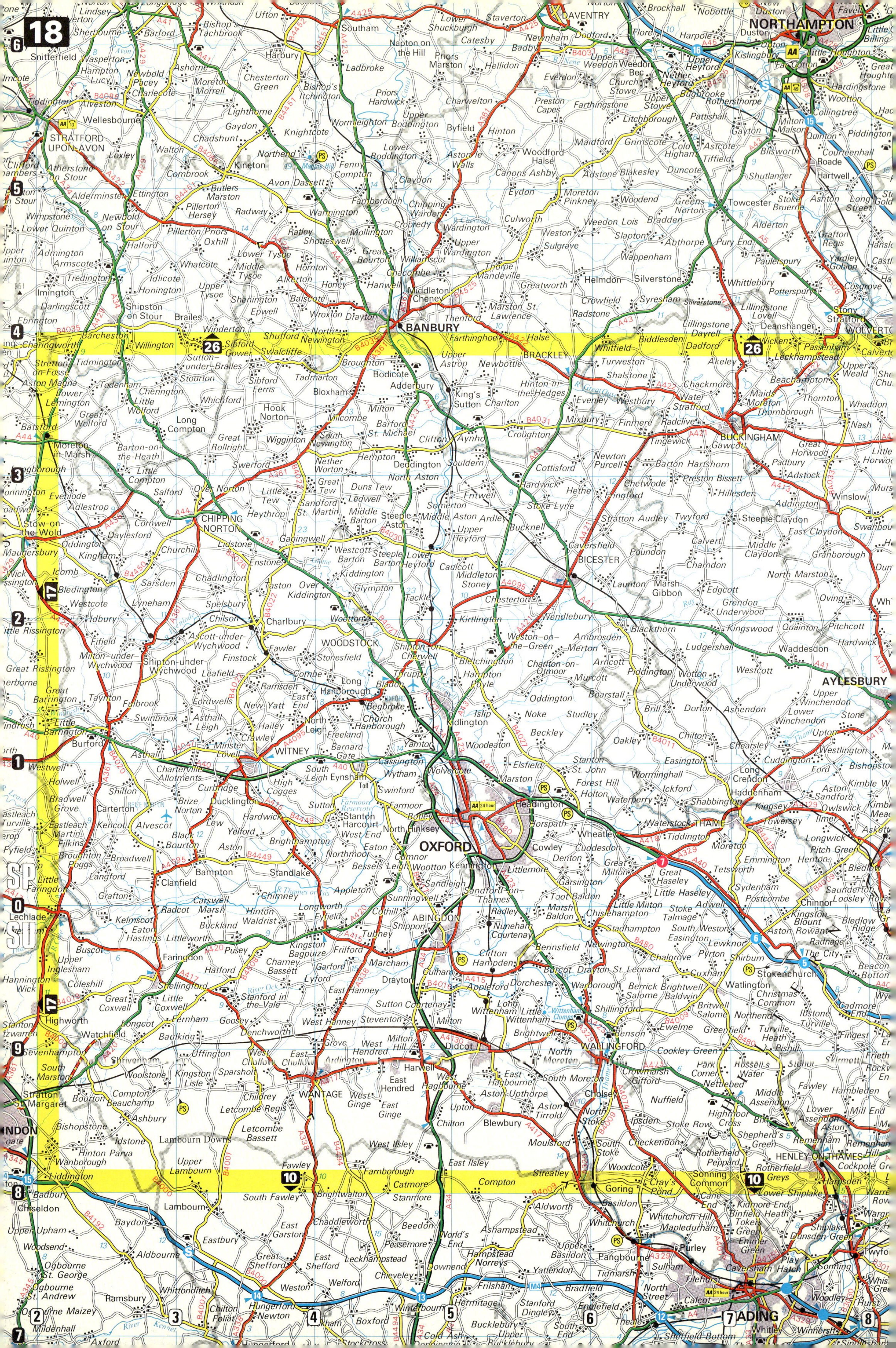

19
SP
TL
SU
TQ
BEDFORD
MILTON KEYNES
NEWPORT PAGNELL
CAMBRIDGE
ST NEOTS
SANDY
BIGGLESWADE
ROYSTON
LETCHWORTH
BALDOCK
HITCHIN
STEVENAGE
LUTON
DUNSTABLE
LEIGHTON BUZZARD
HARPENDEN
WELWYN GARDEN CITY
HERTFORD
HODDESDON
HARLOW
ST.ALBANS
HEMEL HEMPSTEAD
TRING
CHESHAM
WATFORD
RICKMANSWORTH
BUSHEY
POTTERS BAR
CHESHUNT
ENFIELD
BARNET
HARROW
HIGH WYCOMBE
BEACONSFIELD
MAIDENHEAD
SLOUGH
WINDSOR
STAINES
HOUNSLOW
EALING
HILLINGDON
BRENT
CAMDEN
ISLINGTON
HACKNEY
HARINGEY
WALTHAM FOREST
REDBRIDGE
TOWER HAMLETS
NEWHAM
CITY OF WESTMINSTER
HAMMERSMITH
KENSINGTON AND CHELSEA
SOUTHWARK
LAMBETH
WANDSWORTH
LEWISHAM
GREENWICH
RICHMOND UPON THAMES
KINGSTON
THE THREE HUNDREDS OF AYLESBURY

20

TL
TM
BURY ST.EDMUNDS
STOWMARKET
29
IPSWICH
WOODBRIDGE
FELIXSTOWE
HARWICH
COLCHESTER
WIVENHOE
BRIGHTLINGSEA
MERSEA ISLAND
WEST MERSEA
CLACTON-ON-SEA
FRINTON-ON-SEA
WALTON ON THE NAZE
ALDEBURGH
LEISTON
SAXMUNDHAM
Framlingham
Hadleigh
Manningtree
Mistley
Dedham
Tiptree
Tollesbury
Bradwell-on-Sea
Southminster
BURNHAM-ON-CROUCH
FOULNESS ISLAND
SOUTHEND -ON-SEA
Shoeburyness
SHEERNESS
Rochford
Great Wakering
River Blackwater
River Stour
River Orwell
Holland-on-Sea
Jaywick
St Osyth Marsh
Colne Point
The Naze
Orford
Orford Ness
Rendlesham Forest
Tunstall Forest
Sudbourne
Snape
Woodbridge
Martlesham
Kesgrave
Nacton
Shotley Gate
Trimley Heath
Old Felixstowe
ZEEBRUGGE
OSLO ESBJERG HAMBURG BREMERHAVEN HOEK VAN HOLLAND GOTEBORG
VLISSINGEN (FLUSHING)
Scale 5 miles to 1 inch
0 1 2 3 4 5 miles
0 1 2 3 4 5 kilometres
TM
TR
13
TQ
TR
9
0
1
2
3
4
5

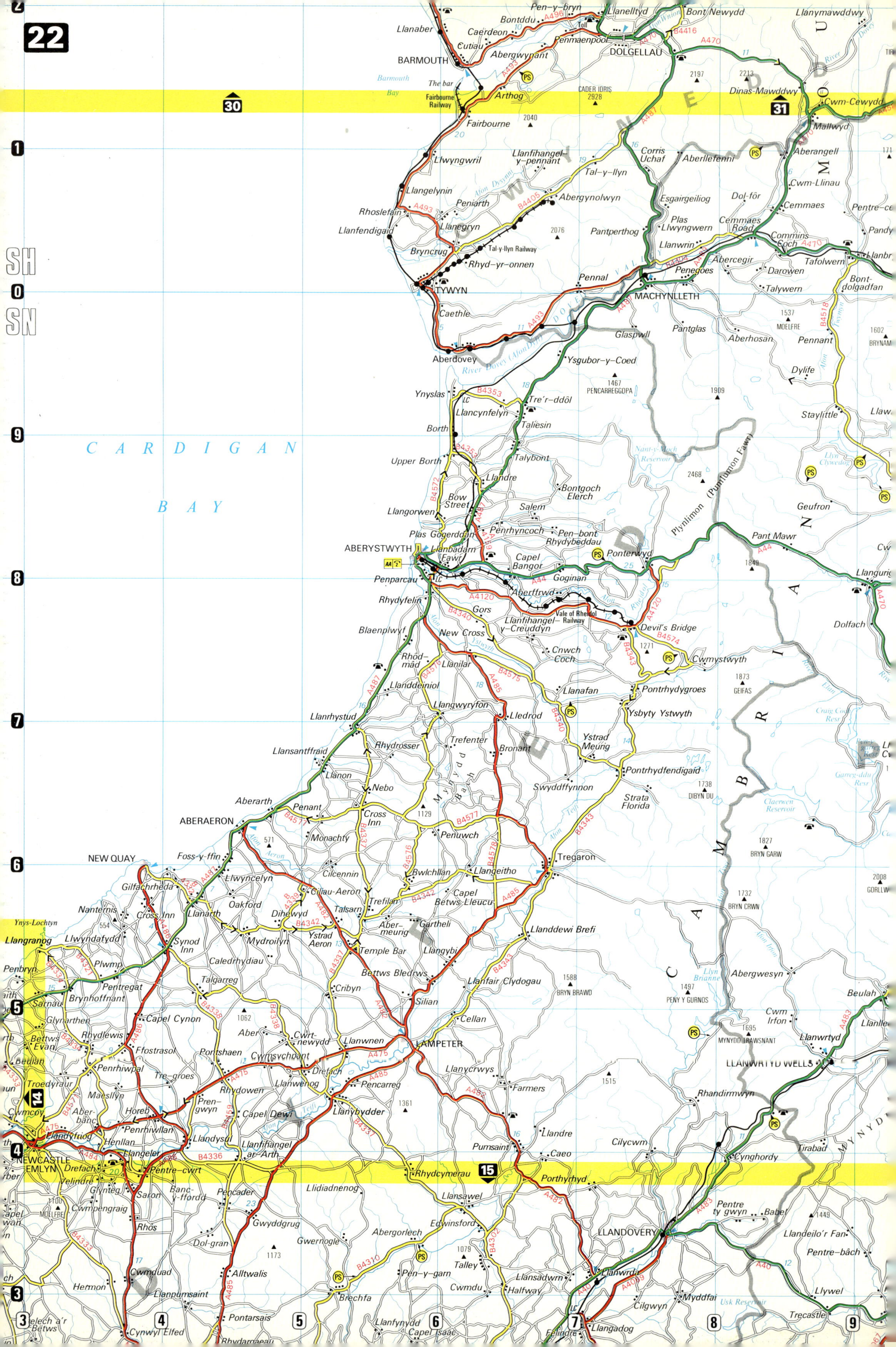
CARDIGAN BAY
Barmouth Bay
SH
SN
30
31
14
15
Llanaber
BARMOUTH
Caerdeon
Cutiau
Bontddu
Pen-y-bryn
Llanelltyd
Bont Newydd
Llanymawddwy
Penmaenpool
DOLGELLAU
Abergwynant
Arthog
The bar
Fairbourne Railway
Fairbourne
CADER IDRIS
2928
Dinas-Mawddwy
Cwm-Cewydd
Mallwyd
Llwyngwril
Llanfihangel-y-pennant
Tal-y-llyn
Corris Uchaf
Aberllefenni
Aberangell
Llangelynin
Peniarth
Abergynolwyn
Cwm-Llinau
Rhoslefain
Llanegryn
Esgairgeiliog
Dol-fôr
Cemmaes
Llanfendigaid
Plas Llwyngwern
Cemmaes Road
Pantperthog
Commins Coch
Bryncrug
Tal-y-llyn Railway
Llanwrin
Rhyd-yr-onnen
Abercegir
Darowen
Tafolwern
TYWYN
Pennal
Penegoes
MACHYNLLETH
Talywern
Bont-dolgadfan
Caethle
Pantglas
MOELFRE
Aberhosan
Pennant
Glaspwll
Aberdovey
River Dovey (Afon Dyfi)
Ysgubor-y-Coed
Dylife
PENCARREGGOPA
Ynyslas
Tre'r-ddôl
Llancynfelyn
Staylittle
Taliesin
Borth
Nant-y-Moch Reservoir
Upper Borth
Talybont
Llandre
Bontgoch Elerch
Plynlimon (Pumlumon Fawr)
Bow Street
Salem
Geufron
Llangorwen
Penrhyncoch
Pen-bont Rhydybeddau
Plas Gogerddan
Pant Mawr
ABERYSTWYTH
Llanbadarn Fawr
Capel Bangor
Ponterwyd
Penparcau
Goginan
Aberffrwd
Rhydyfelin
Vale of Rheidol Railway
Gors
Llanfihangel-y-Creuddyn
Devil's Bridge
Blaenplwyf
New Cross
Dolfach
Cnwch Coch
Rhod-mâd
Llanilar
Cwmystwyth
Llanddeiniol
Llanafan
Pontrhydygroes
GEIFAS
Llanrhystud
Llangwyryfon
Lledrod
Ysbyty Ystwyth
Trefenter
Ystrad Meurig
Llansantffraid
Rhydrosser
Bronant
Pontrhydfendigaid
Llanon
Nebo
Swyddffynnon
DIBYN DU
Strata Florida
Aberarth
Penant
Cross Inn
ABERAERON
Monachty
Penuwch
Claerwen Reservoir
NEW QUAY
Foss-y-ffin
Tregaron
BRYN GARW
Gilfachrheda
Llwyncelyn
Cilcennin
Bwlchllan
Llangeitho
GORLLWYN
Oakford
Cilliau-Aeron
Capel Betws Lleucu
Nanternis
Cross Inn
Llanarth
Dihewyd
Talsarn
Trefilan
BRYN CRWN
Ynys-Lochtyn
Llangranog
Llwyndafydd
Synod Inn
Mydroilyn
Ystrad Aeron
Aber-meurig
Gartheli
Llanddewi Brefi
Penbryn
Plwmp
Caledrhydiau
Temple Bar
Llangybi
Pentregat
Talgarreg
Bettws Bledrws
Abergwesyn
Sarnau
Brynhoffnant
Cribyn
Llanfair Clydogau
BRYN BRAWD
PENY Y GURNOS
Llyn Brianne
Beulah
Glynarthen
Capel Cynon
Silian
Cellan
Cwm Irfon
Bettws Evan
Rhydlewis
Aber
Cwrt-newydd
Llanwnen
LAMPETER
MYNYDD TRAWSNANT
Llanwrtyd
Ffostrasol
Pontshaen
Cwmsychpant
Beulah
Penrhiwpal
Tre-groes
Drefach
Llanycrwys
LLANWRTYD WELLS
Troedyraur
Llanwenog
Pencarreg
Farmers
Maesllyn
Rhydowen
Rhandirmwyn
Aber-banc
Prengwyn
Capel Dewi
Llanybydder
Cwmcoy
Horeb
Penrhiwllan
Llandre
Llandyfriog
Henllan
Llandysul
Llanfihangel-ar-Arth
Pumsaint
Caeo
Cilycwm
Tirabad
NEWCASTLE EMLYN
Llangeler
Cynghordy
Drefach
Pentre-cwrt
Rhydcymerau
Porthyrhyd
Velindre
Glynteg
Saron
Banc-y-ffordd
Pencader
Llidiadnenog
Llansawel
Cwmpengraig
MOELFRE
Pentre ty gwyn
Babel
Rhos
Gwyddgrug
Edwinsford
Abergorlech
Llandeilo'r Fan
LLANDOVERY
Dol-gran
Gwernogle
Pentre-bâch
Cwmduad
Alltwalis
Talley
Llansadwrn
Pen-y-garn
Llanwrda
Llywel
Hermon
Llanpumsaint
Cwmdu
Halfway
Brechfa
Cilgwyn
Myddfai
Usk Reservoir
Trecastle
Pontarsais
Llanfynydd
Capel Isaac
Cynwyl Elfed
Rhydargaeau
Felindre
Llangadog
Llanwrtyd Wells
GWYNEDD
DYFED
CAMBRIAN MOUNTAINS
A496
A470
A493
A487
B4405
A44
A4120
B4340
B4574
B4343
A485
B4575
B4576
B4577
B4342
B4337
A482
A486
A475
B4336
B4338
B4333
A484
A483
A40
A4069
B4302
B4310
B4353
B4572
B4416
B4518

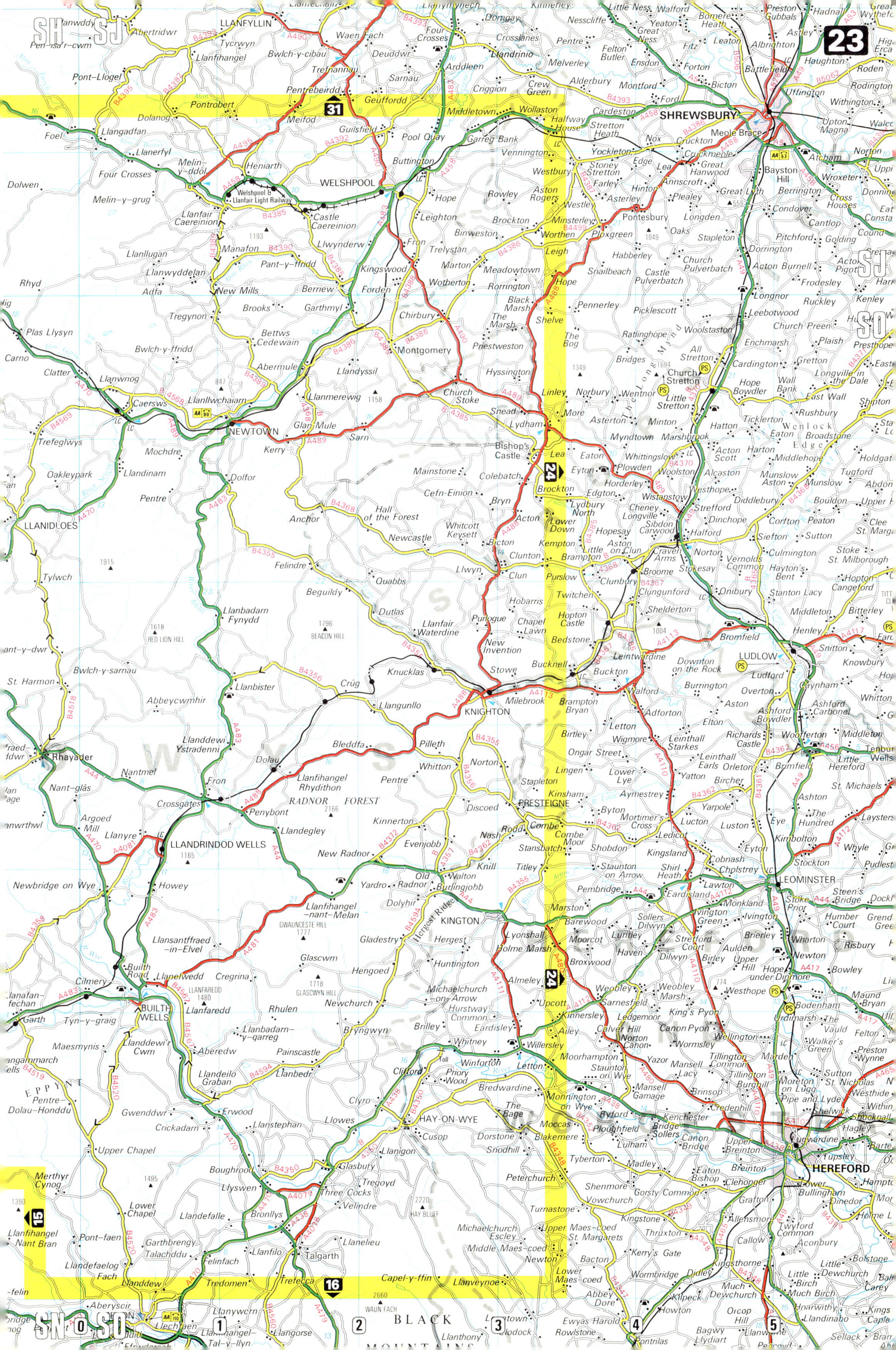

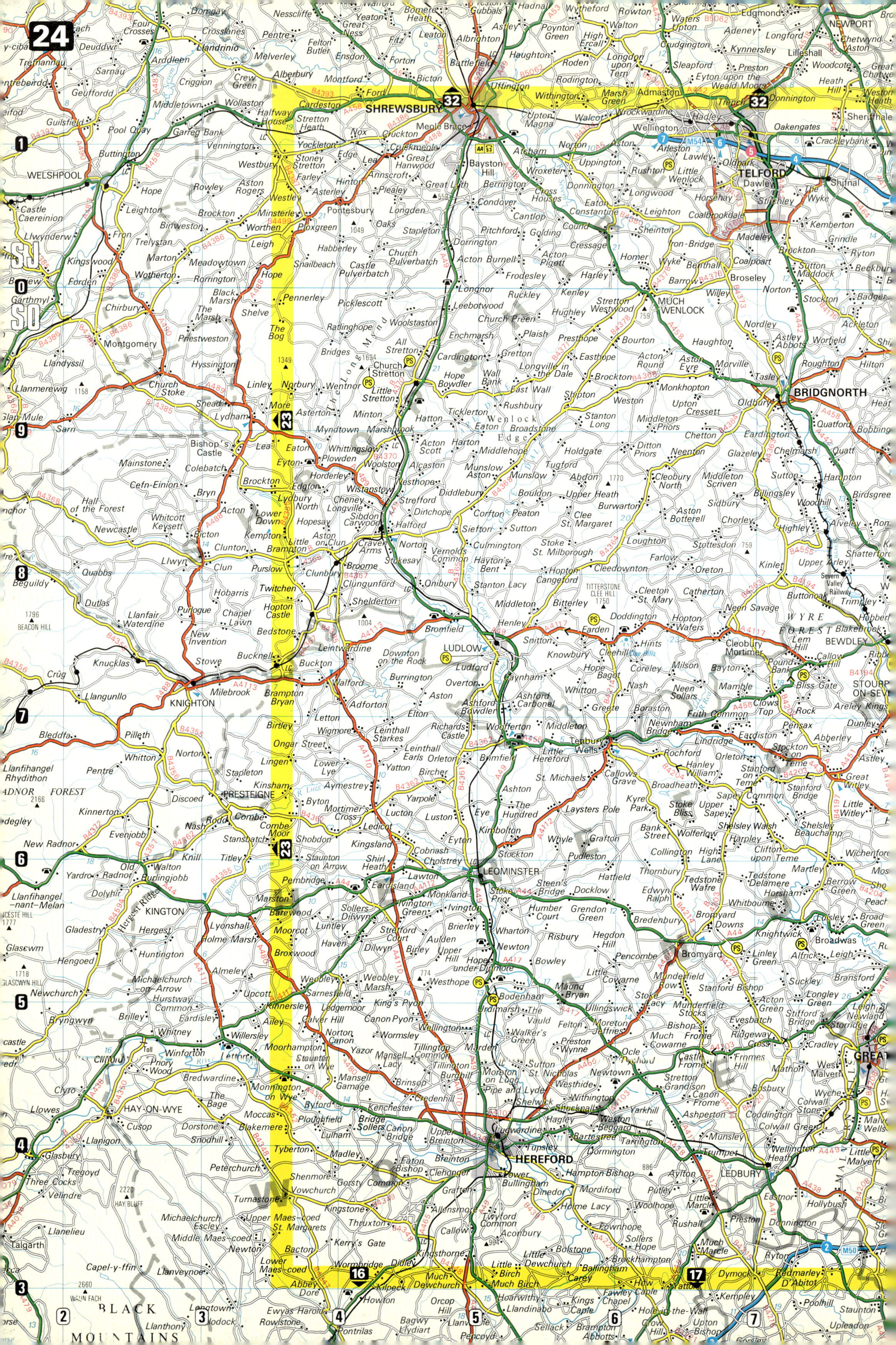
SHREWSBURY
TELFORD
BRIDGNORTH
WELSHPOOL
Montgomery
MUCH WENLOCK
LUDLOW
KNIGHTON
PRESTEIGNE
KINGTON
LEOMINSTER
HAY-ON-WYE
HEREFORD
LEDBURY
Bromyard
BEWDLEY
Cleobury Mortimer
Tenbury Wells
Church Stretton
Bishop's Castle
Craven Arms
Wellington
Oakengates
Shifnal
Madeley
Dawley
Broseley
Newport
Pontesbury
Minsterley
Clun
Leintwardine
Weobley
Pembridge
Bodenham
Fownhope
Much Birch
Dymock
SJ
SO
BLACK MOUNTAINS
RADNOR FOREST
WYRE FOREST
Severn Valley Railway
TITTERSTONE CLEE HILL 1750
BEACON HILL
HAY BLUFF
32
23
16
17

25
33
26
17
CANNOCK
LICHFIELD
BROWNHILLS
TAMWORTH
ALDRIDGE
WOLVERHAMPTON
WALSALL
SUTTON COLDFIELD
WEST BROMWICH
DUDLEY
WARLEY
BIRMINGHAM
HALESOWEN
STOURBRIDGE
SOLIHULL
KIDDERMINSTER
BROMSGROVE
REDDITCH
DROITWICH
WORCESTER
EVESHAM
STRATFORD-UPON-AVON
WARWICK
ROYAL LEAMINGTON SPA
KENILWORTH
COVENTRY
NUNEATON
BEDWORTH
HINCKLEY
TEWKESBURY
CHIPPING CAMPDEN
SHIPSTON ON STOUR
MORETON-IN-MARSH
CHIPPING NORTON
ASHBY-DE-LA-ZOUCH
SJ SK
SO SP
1
2
3
4
9

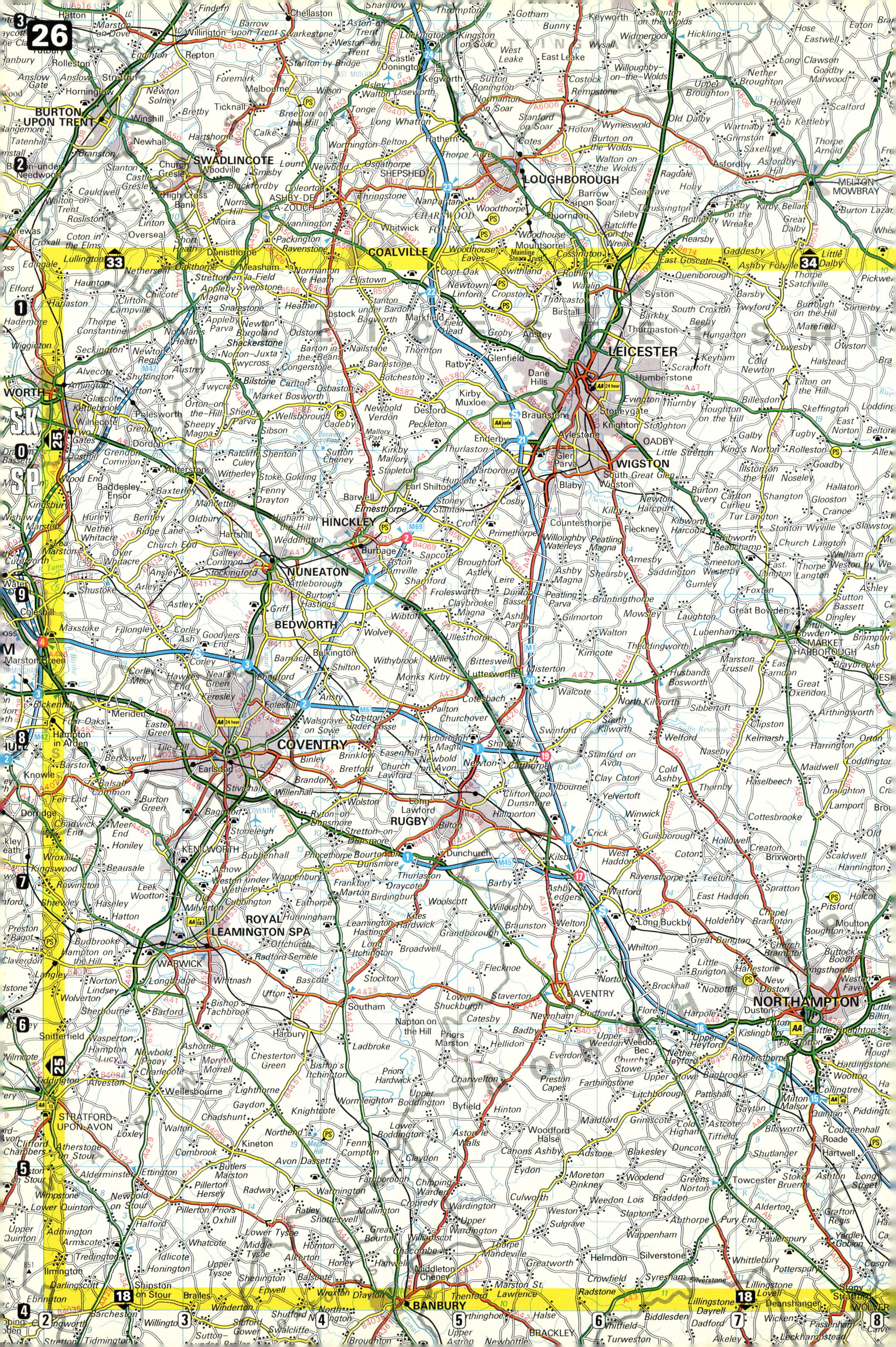
BURTON UPON TRENT
SWADLINCOTE
ASHBY-DE-LA-ZOUCH
COALVILLE
LOUGHBOROUGH
SHEPSHED
MELTON MOWBRAY
LEICESTER
WIGSTON
OADBY
HINCKLEY
NUNEATON
BEDWORTH
COVENTRY
RUGBY
KENILWORTH
ROYAL LEAMINGTON SPA
WARWICK
STRATFORD UPON-AVON
DAVENTRY
NORTHAMPTON
MARKET HARBOROUGH
BANBURY
BRACKLEY
Castle Donington
Kegworth
Melbourne
Repton
Measham
Ibstock
Markfield
Anstey
Birstall
Syston
Thurmaston
Mountsorrel
Quorndon
Earl Shilton
Lutterworth
Atherstone
Polesworth
Coleshill
Kingsbury
Meriden
Southam
Kineton
Shipston on Stour
Wellesbourne
Towcester
Long Buckby
Husbands Bosworth
Kibworth Harcourt
Fleckney
Blaby
Enderby
Narborough
Shenstone
Sheepy Magna
Market Bosworth
Desford
Ratby
Groby
Glenfield
Braunstone
Kirby Muxloe
Cosby
Broughton Astley
Ullesthorpe
Dunchurch
Hillmorton
Kilsby
Crick
Welford
Naseby
Guilsborough
Brixworth
Moulton
Kislingbury
Bugbrooke
Weedon Bec
Blisworth
Roade
Hartwell
Byfield
Fenny Compton
Cropredy
Middleton Cheney
Lullington
Gaddesby
Queniborough
Ashby Folville
Little Dalby
33
34
25
18
M1
M6
M42
M45
M69
A5
A45
A47
A46
A427

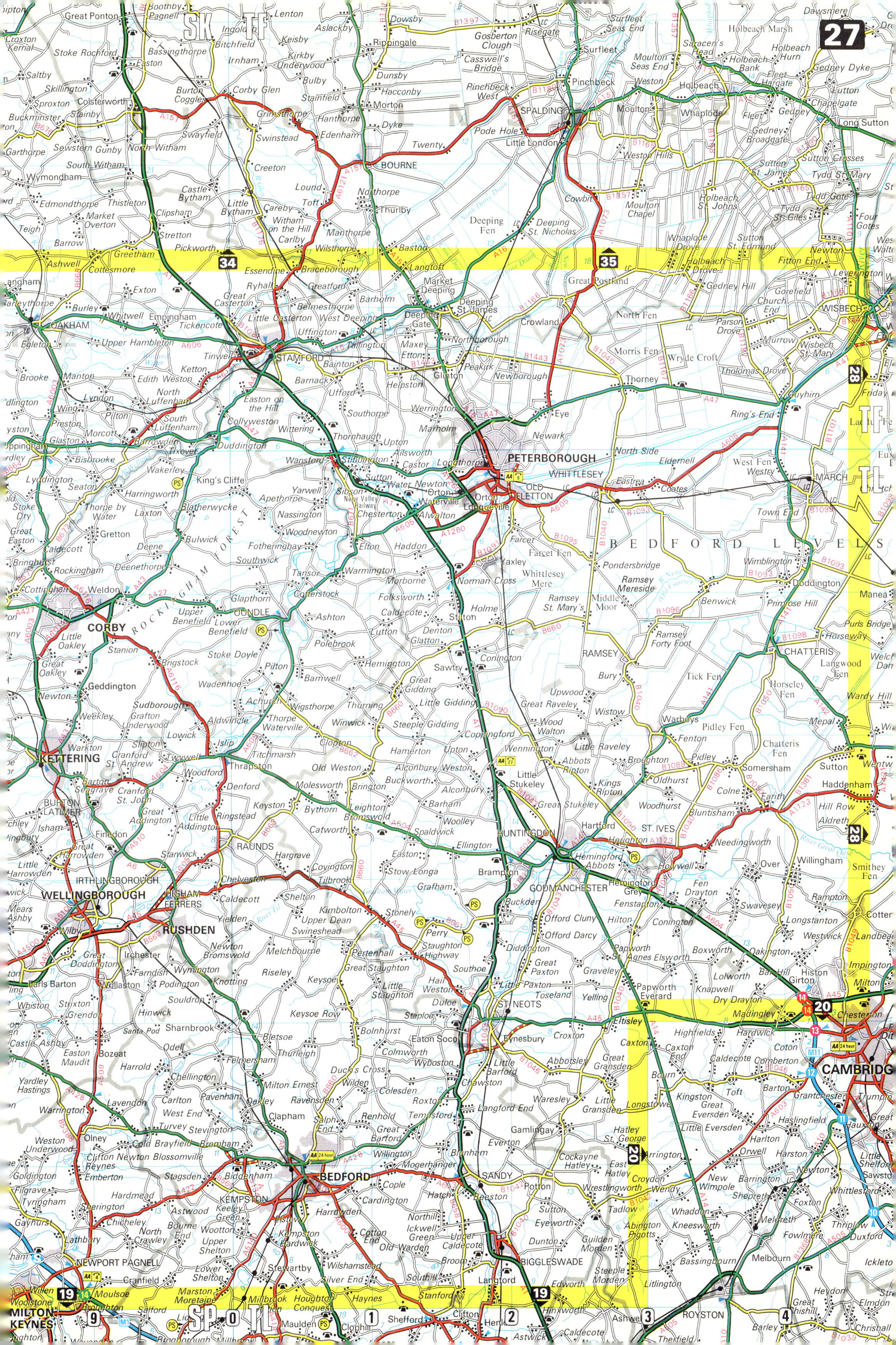
SK
TF
Great Ponton
Boothby Pagnell
Lenton
Ingoldsby
Aslackby
Dowsby
Rippingale
Gosberton Clough
Risegate
Surfleet
Surfleet Seas End
Saracen's Head
Holbeach Marsh
Holbeach Hurn
Dawsmere
Gedney Dyke
Croxton Kerrial
Stoke Rochford
Bassingthorpe
Bitchfield
Keisby
Kirkby Underwood
Irnham
Casswell's Bridge
Pinchbeck
Moulton Seas End
Holbeach Bank
Fleet Hargate
Lutton
Saltby
Skillington
Colsterworth
Easton
Burton Coggles
Corby Glen
Bulby
Dunsby
Hacconby
Pinchbeck West
Weston
Holbeach
Long Sutton
Sproxton
Buckminster
Stainby
Grimsthorpe
Stainfield
Morton
Hanthorpe
SPALDING
Moulton
Whaplode
Fleet
Gedney
Chapelgate
Swayfield
Swinstead
Dyke
Edenham
Pode Hole
Little London
Gedney Broadgate
Garthorpe
Sewstern
Gunby
North Witham
Twenty
Weston Hills
Sutton Crosses
South Witham
Creeton
BOURNE
Sutton St. James
Tydd St. Mary
Wymondham
Castle Bytham
Lound
Northorpe
Cowbit
Tydd Gote
Edmondthorpe
Thistleton
Toft
Thurlby
Holbeach St. Johns
Tydd St. Giles
Little Bytham
Careby
Moulton Chapel
Market Overton
Clipsham
Witham on the Hill
Deeping Fen
Deeping St. Nicholas
Four Gotes
Teigh
Stretton
Carlby
Manthorpe
Whaplode Drove
Sutton St. Edmund
Barrow
Pickworth
Wilsthorpe
Baston
Newton
Ashwell
Greetham
34
35
Cottesmore
Essendine
Braceborough
Langtoft
Holbeach Drove
Fitton End
Leverington
Langham
Market Deeping
Great Postland
Gedney Hill
Gorefield
Exton
Ryhall
Greatford
Church End
Barleythorpe
Burley
Whitwell
Empingham
Great Casterton
Barholm
Deeping St. James
North Fen
WISBECH
OAKHAM
Tickencote
Little Casterton
Belmesthorpe
West Deeping
Deeping Gate
Crowland
Parson Drove
Egleton
Upper Hambleton
Uffington
Tallington
Northborough
Murrow
Wisbech St. Mary
Tinwell
STAMFORD
Maxey
Etton
Morris Fen
Wryde Croft
Ketton
Bainton
Peakirk
Thomas Drove
Brooke
Manton
Edith Weston
Barnack
Helpston
Glinton
Newborough
Thorney
28
North Luffenham
Ufford
Guyhirn
Lyndon
Easton on the Hill
Southorpe
Werrington
Eye
Ring's End
Wing
Pilton
South Luffenham
Collyweston
Wittering
Marholm
Newark
Preston
Morcott
Thornhaugh
Upton
Glaston
Barrowden
Duddington
Ailsworth
Uppingham
Tixover
Bisbrooke
Wansford
Stibbington
Castor
Longthorpe
PETERBOROUGH
North Side
Eldernell
West Fen
Westry
MARCH
Wakerley
King's Cliffe
Sutton
Water Newton
WHITTLESEY
Eastrea
Coates
Lyddington
Seaton
Harringworth
Yarwell
Orton
OLD FLETTON
Nene Valley Railway
Waterville
Longueville
Stoke Dry
Thorpe by Water
Laxton
Blatherwycke
Apethorpe
Nassington
Sibson
Chesterton
Alwalton
Town End
Great Easton
Gretton
Woodnewton
Farcet
Farcet Fen
BEDFORD LEVELS
Caldecott
Deene
Bulwick
Fotheringhay
Elton
Haddon
Yaxley
Pondersbridge
Wimblington
Rockingham
Deenethorpe
Southwick
Tansor
Warmington
Whittlesey Mere
Ramsey Mereside
Doddington
Cottingham
Weldon
Cotterstock
Morborne
Norman Cross
Benwick
Primrose Hill
Manea
Glapthorn
OUNDLE
Folksworth
Ramsey St. Mary's
Middle Moor
Upper Benefield
Lower Benefield
Caldecote
Holme
CORBY
ROCKINGHAM FOREST
Ashton
Stilton
Ramsey Forty Foot
Purls Bridge
Little Oakley
Stanion
Polebrook
Denton
Lutton
Glatton
CHATTERIS
Horseway
Great Oakley
Brigstock
Stoke Doyle
Conington
RAMSEY
Langwood Fen
Geddington
Pilton
Hemington
Sawtry
Bury
Tick Fen
Wadenhoe
Barnwell
Great Gidding
Upwood
Horseley Fen
Wardy Hill
Newton
Sudborough
Achurch
Wigsthorpe
Thurning
Little Gidding
Great Raveley
Wistow
Mepal
Weekley
Grafton Underwood
Aldwincle
Thorpe Waterville
Winwick
Steeple Gidding
Wood Walton
Warboys
Pidley Fen
Lowick
Islip
Clopton
Coppingford
Fenton
Chatteris Fen
Warkton
Slipton
Titchmarsh
Hamerton
Upton
Wennington
Little Raveley
Somersham
KETTERING
Cranford St. Andrew
Twywell
Thrapston
Old Weston
Alconbury Weston
Abbots Ripton
Broughton
Pidley
Sutton
Barton Seagrave
Woodford
Denford
Molesworth
Brington
Buckworth
Alconbury
Little Stukeley
Kings Ripton
Oldhurst
Colne
Earith
Haddenham
Burton Latimer
Cranford St. John
Keyston
Bythorn
Leighton Bromswold
Barham
Great Stukeley
Woodhurst
Bluntisham
Hill Row
Isham
Great Addington
Little Addington
Ringstead
Catworth
Spaldwick
Woolley
HUNTINGDON
Hartford
ST. IVES
Aldreth
Finedon
RAUNDS
Ellington
Houghton
Needingworth
Great Harrowden
Stanwick
Hargrave
Easton
Hemingford Abbots
Holywell
Willingham
Little Harrowden
IRTHLINGBOROUGH
Covington
Stow Longa
Brampton
Over
Smithey Fen
Chelveston
Tilbrook
GODMANCHESTER
Hemingford Grey
Fen Drayton
WELLINGBOROUGH
HIGHAM FERRERS
Caldecott
Shelton
Grafham
Buckden
Fenstanton
Swavesey
Rampton
Mears Ashby
Kimbolton
Stonely
Hilton
Longstanton
Cottenham
Wilby
RUSHDEN
Yielden
Upper Dean
Perry
Offord Cluny
Conington
Westwick
Landbeach
Great Doddington
Irchester
Newton Bromswold
Melchbourne
Swineshead
Pertenhall
Staughton Highway
Offord Darcy
Papworth St. Agnes
Elsworth
Boxworth
Oakington
Impington
Earls Barton
Farndish
Wymington
Great Staughton
Southoe
Diddington
Great Paxton
Graveley
Lolworth
Bar Hill
Histon
Girton
Milton
Wollaston
Podington
Knotting
Riseley
Keysoe
Little Staughton
Hail Weston
Little Paxton
Toseland
Yelling
Papworth Everard
Knapwell
Dry Drayton
Whiston
Strixton
Souldrop
Duloe
ST. NEOTS
Madingley
20
Chesterton
Grendon
Hinwick
Keysoe Row
Staploe
Eltisley
Castle Ashby
Sharnbrook
Santa Pod
Bletsoe
Bolnhurst
Eaton Socon
Eynesbury
Croxton
Caxton
Highfields
Hardwick
Coton
CAMBRIDGE
Easton Maudit
Bozeat
Odell
Thurleigh
Colmworth
Wyboston
Little Barford
Abbotsley
Great Gransden
Caxton End
Caldecote
Comberton
Harrold
Felmersham
Duck's Cross
Wilden
Chawston
Bourn
Toft
Barton
Yardley Hastings
Chellington
Milton Ernest
Ravensden
Colesden
Roxton
Waresley
Little Gransden
Longstowe
Kingston
Great Eversden
Grantchester
Trumpington
Lavendon
Carlton
Pavenham
Oakley
Renhold
Tempsford
Langford End
Little Eversden
Haslingfield
Warrington
West End
Turvey
Stevington
Clapham
Salph End
Great Barford
Gamlingay
Hatley St. George
Harlton
Great Shelford
Weston Underwood
Olney
Cold Brayfield
Bromham
Willington
Blunham
Everton
Cockayne Hatley
Arrington
Orwell
Harston
Little Shelford
Clifton Reynes
Newton Blossomville
Mogerhanger
East Hatley
Emberton
Stagsden
Biddenham
BEDFORD
Cople
SANDY
Potton
Croydon
New Wimpole
Barrington
Newton
Sawston
Goldington
Filgrave
Hardmead
KEMPSTON
Cardington
Hatch
Beeston
Wrestlingworth
Wendy
Shepreth
Whittlesford
Tyringham
Sherington
Astwood
Kempston
Elstow
Harrowden
Northill
Sutton
Tadlow
Whaddon
Foxton
Gayhurst
Chicheley
Bourne End
Keeley Green
Wootton
Kempston Hardwick
Cotton End
Ickwell Green
Upper Caldecote
Eyeworth
Abington Pigotts
Kneesworth
Meldreth
Thriplow
Lathbury
North Crawley
Upper Shelton
Old Warden
Dunton
Guilden Morden
Fowlmere
Duxford
NEWPORT PAGNELL
Stewartby
Wilshamstead
Broom
BIGGLESWADE
Bassingbourn
Melbourn
Ickleton
Cranfield
Lower Shelton
Silver End
Southill
Langford
Steeple Morden
Litlington
Willen
Woolstone
19
Moulsoe
Salford
Marston Moretaine
Millbrook
Houghton Conquest
Haynes
Stanford
Edworth
Hinxworth
Heydon
Great Chishill
Elmdon
MILTON KEYNES
Broughton
SP
TL
Maulden
Clophill
Shefford
Clifton
Henlow
Astwick
Caldecote
Ashwell
ROYSTON
Therfield
Barley
Chrishall
24 hour
A1
A6
A14
A45
A47
A428
A421
A43
A605
M1
M11

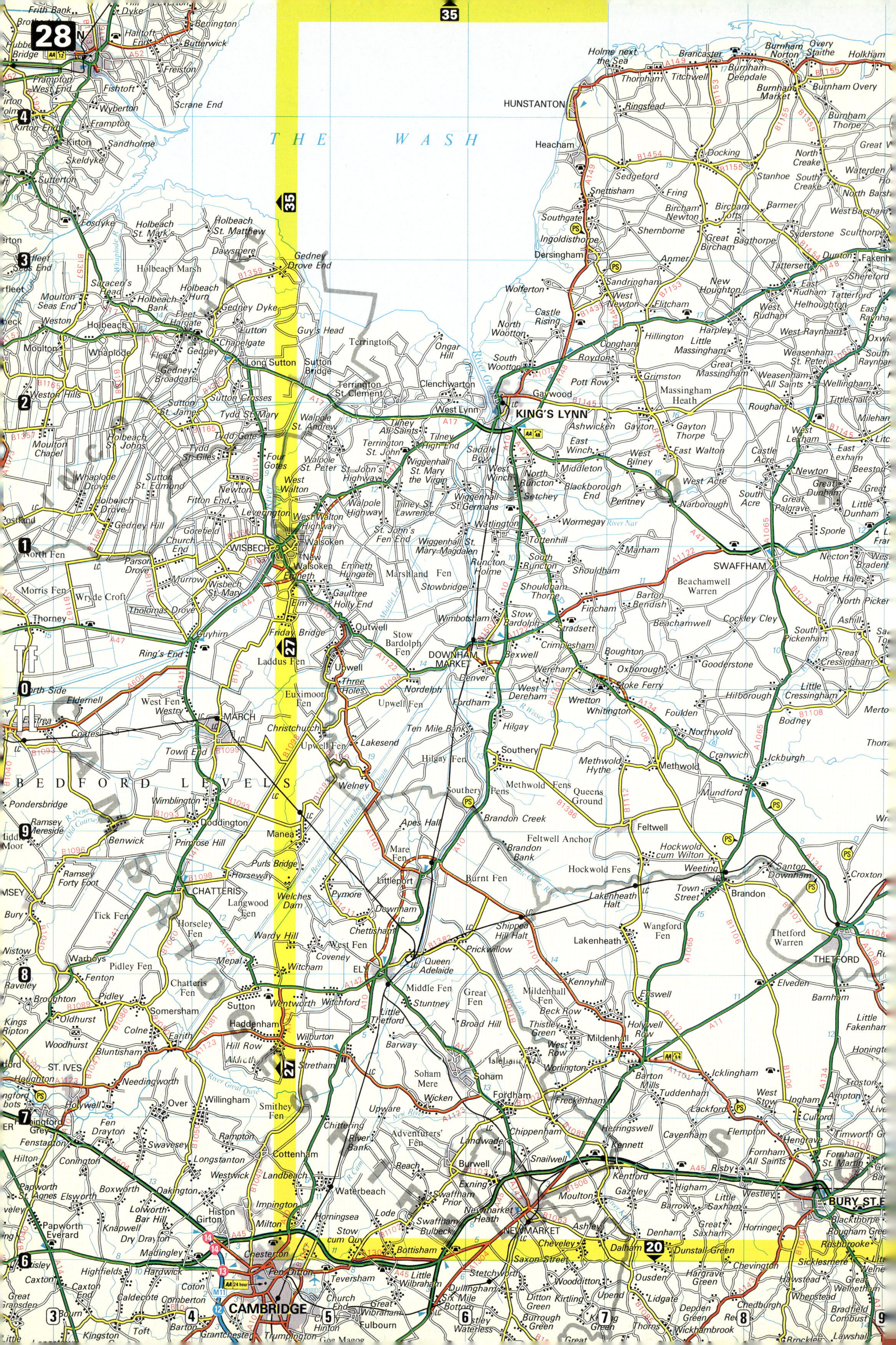

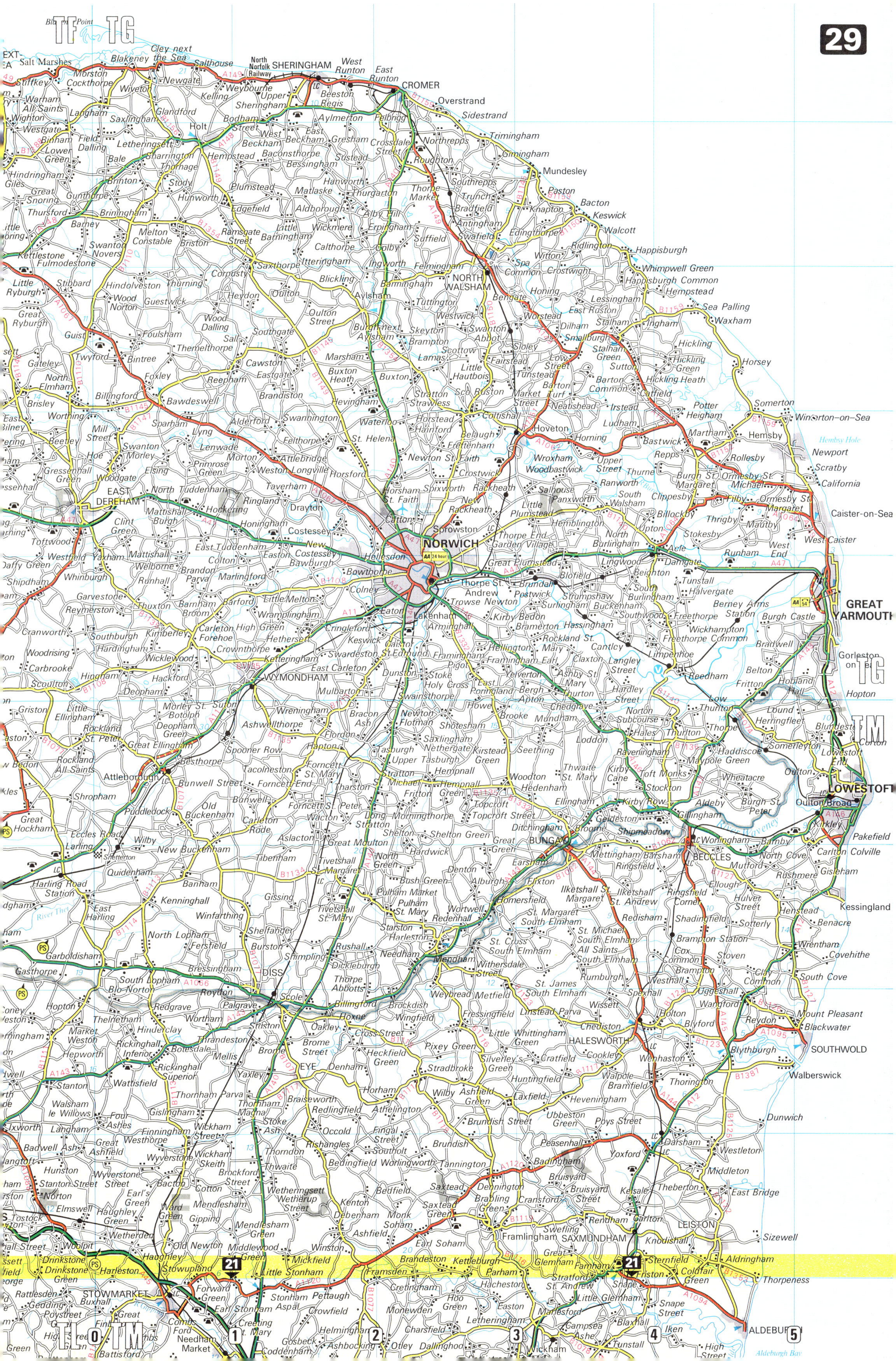

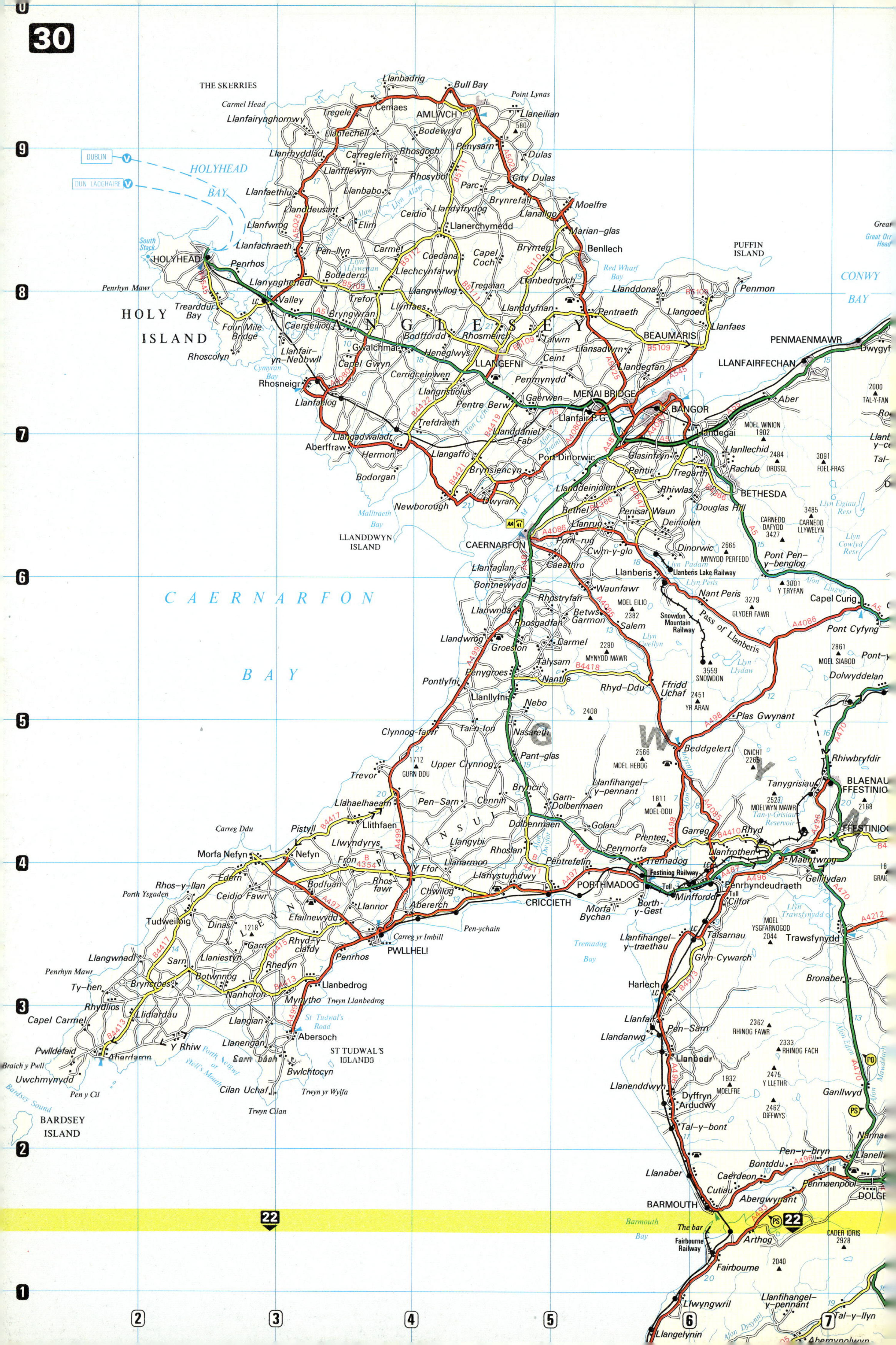
THE SKERRIES
Carmel Head
Llanbadrig
Bull Bay
Point Lynas
Cemaes
AMLWCH
Llaneilian
Tregele
Llanfairynghornwy
Llanfechell
Bodewryd
580
Penysarn
Dulas
DUBLIN
DUN LAOGHAIRE
HOLYHEAD BAY
Llanrhyddlad
Carreglefn
Rhosgoch
Llanfflewyn
Rhosybol
City Dulas
Parc
Llanfaethlu
Llanbabo
Llyn Alaw
Brynrefail
Moelfre
Llanddeusant
Llandyfrydog
Ceidio
Llanallgo
Llanfwrog
Elim
Llanerchymedd
Marian-glas
South Stack
Llanfachraeth
Pen-llyn
Carmel
Coedana
Capel Coch
Brynteg
Benllech
PUFFIN ISLAND
HOLYHEAD
Penrhos
Llyn Llywenan
Lechcynfarwy
Red Wharf Bay
Penrhyn Mawr
Llanynghenedl
Bodedern
Tregaian
Llanbedrgoch
CONWY BAY
Valley
Trefor
Llangwyllog
Llanddona
Penmon
Trearddur Bay
Llynfaes
Llanddyfnan
Pentraeth
Llangoed
HOLY ISLAND
Bryngwran
Caergeiliog
ANGLESEY
Llanfaes
Four Mile Bridge
Bodffordd
Rhosmeirch
Talwrn
BEAUMARIS
PENMAENMAWR
Dwygyf
Gwalchmai
Heneglwys
Llansadwrn
Rhoscolyn
Llanfair-yn-Neubwll
LLANGEFNI
Ceint
LLANFAIRFECHAN
Cymyran Bay
Capel Gwyn
Llandegfan
Cerrigceinwen
Penmynydd
Rhosneigr
Llangristiolus
MENAI BRIDGE
Aber
2000 TAL-Y-FAN
Llanfaelog
Gaerwen
Pentre Berw
BANGOR
Trefdraeth
Afon Cefni
Llanfair P.G.
MOEL WNION 1902
Llandegai
Llangadwaladr
Llanddaniel Fab
Afon Braint
Aberffraw
Port Dinorwic
Llanllechid
Hermon
Llangaffo
Glasinfryn
2484 DROSGL
3091 FOEL-FRAS
Rachub
Bodorgan
Brynsiencyn
Pentir
Tregarth
Llanddeiniolen
Rhiwlas
BETHESDA
Newborough
Dwyran
MENAI STRAIT
Bethel
Penisar Waun
Douglas Hill
Llyn Eigiau Resr
Malltraeth Bay
Llanrug
Deiniolen
3485 CARNEDD DAFYDD
CARNEDD LLYWELYN
3427
LLANDDWYN ISLAND
CAERNARFON
Pont-rug
Dinorwic
2665 MYNYDD PERFEDD
Llyn Cowlyd Resr
Cwm-y-glo
Llyn Padarn
Pont Pen-y-benglog
Llanfaglan
Caeathro
Llanberis
Llanberis Lake Railway
Llyn Peris
3001 Y TRYFAN
Bontnewydd
Waunfawr
Nant Peris
Capel Curig
CAERNARFON BAY
Rhostryfan
MOEL EILIO 2382
3279 GLYDER FAWR
Llanwnda
Betws Garmon
Snowdon Mountain Railway
Pass of Llanberis
Pont Cyfyng
Rhosgadfan
Salem
Llandwrog
Llyn Cwellyn
Carmel
Groeslon
2290 MYNYDD MAWR
2861 MOEL SIABOD
Talysarn
Llyn Llydaw
Pont-y
Penygroes
Nantlle
3559 SNOWDON
Dolwyddelan
Pontlyfni
Rhyd-Ddu
Ffridd Uchaf
Llanllyfni
Nebo
2451 YR ARAN
2408
Plas Gwynant
Clynnog-fawr
Tai-n-lon
Nasareth
GWYNEDD
Beddgelert
CNICHT 2265
Pant-glas
2566 MOEL HEBOG
Rhiwbryfdir
1712 GURN DDU
Upper Clynnog
Afon Glaslyn
Trevor
Llanfihangel-y-pennant
Tanygrisiau
BLAENAU FFESTINIOG
Bryncir
2527 MOELWYN MAWR
Tan-y-Grisiau Reservoir
2168
Llanaelhaearn
Garn-Dolbenmaen
1811 MOEL-DDU
Pen-Sarn
Cennin
Dolbenmaen
Golan
Garreg
Rhyd
FFESTINIOG
Carreg Ddu
Pistyll
Llithfaen
Llwyndyrys
Llangybi
Afon Dwyfor
Prenteg
Morfa Nefyn
Nefyn
Rhoslan
Penmorfa
Llanfrothen
Fron
Llanarmon
Pentrefelin
Tremadog
Maentwrog
Rhos-y-llan
Edern
Rhos fawr
Y Ffor
Llanystumdwy
Festiniog Railway
Gellilydan
Porth Ysgaden
Bodfuan
Chwilog
PORTHMADOG
Penrhyndeudraeth
Ceidio Fawr
Llannor
Abererch
CRICCIETH
Toll
Minffordd
Cilfor
Tudweiliog
Dinas
Efailnewydd
Morfa Bychan
Borth-y-Gest
Llyn Trawsfynydd
1218
Carreg yr Imbill
Pen-ychain
Llanfihangel-y-traethau
MOEL YSGFARNOGOD 2044
Trawsfynydd
Garn
Rhyd-y-clafdy
Talsarnau
Llangwnadl
Llaniestyn
PWLLHELI
Penrhos
Tremadog Bay
Glyn-Cywarch
Sarn
Penrhyn Mawr
Rhedyn
Bronaber
Ty-hen
Bryncroes
Botwnnog
Llanbedrog
Harlech
Nanhoron
Mynytho
Trwyn Llanbedrog
Rhydlios
Capel Carmel
Lidiardau
Llangian
St Tudwal's Road
Llanfair
Pen-Sarn
2362 RHINOG FAWR
Abersoch
Llandanwg
2333 RHINOG FACH
Pwlldefaid
Y Rhiw
Llanengan
ST TUDWAL'S ISLANDS
Afon Eden
Aberdaron
Porth Neigwl or Hell's Mouth
Sarn Bach
Llanbedr
Braich y Pwll
Bwlchtocyn
2475 Y LLETHR
Uwchmynydd
1932 MOELFRE
Llanenddwyn
Ganllwyd
Pen y Cil
Cilan Uchaf
Trwyn yr Wylfa
Dyffryn Ardudwy
Bardsey Sound
2462 DIFFWYS
Trwyn Cilan
BARDSEY ISLAND
Tal-y-bont
Pen-y-bryn
Bontddu
Llanaber
Caerdeon
Cutiau
Penmaenpool
DOLGE
BARMOUTH
Abergwynant
Barmouth Bay
The bar
Arthog
CADER IDRIS 2928
Fairbourne Railway
2040
Fairbourne
Llwyngwril
Llanfihangel-y-pennant
Tal-y-llyn
Llangelynin
Afon Dysynni
Abergynolwyn
22

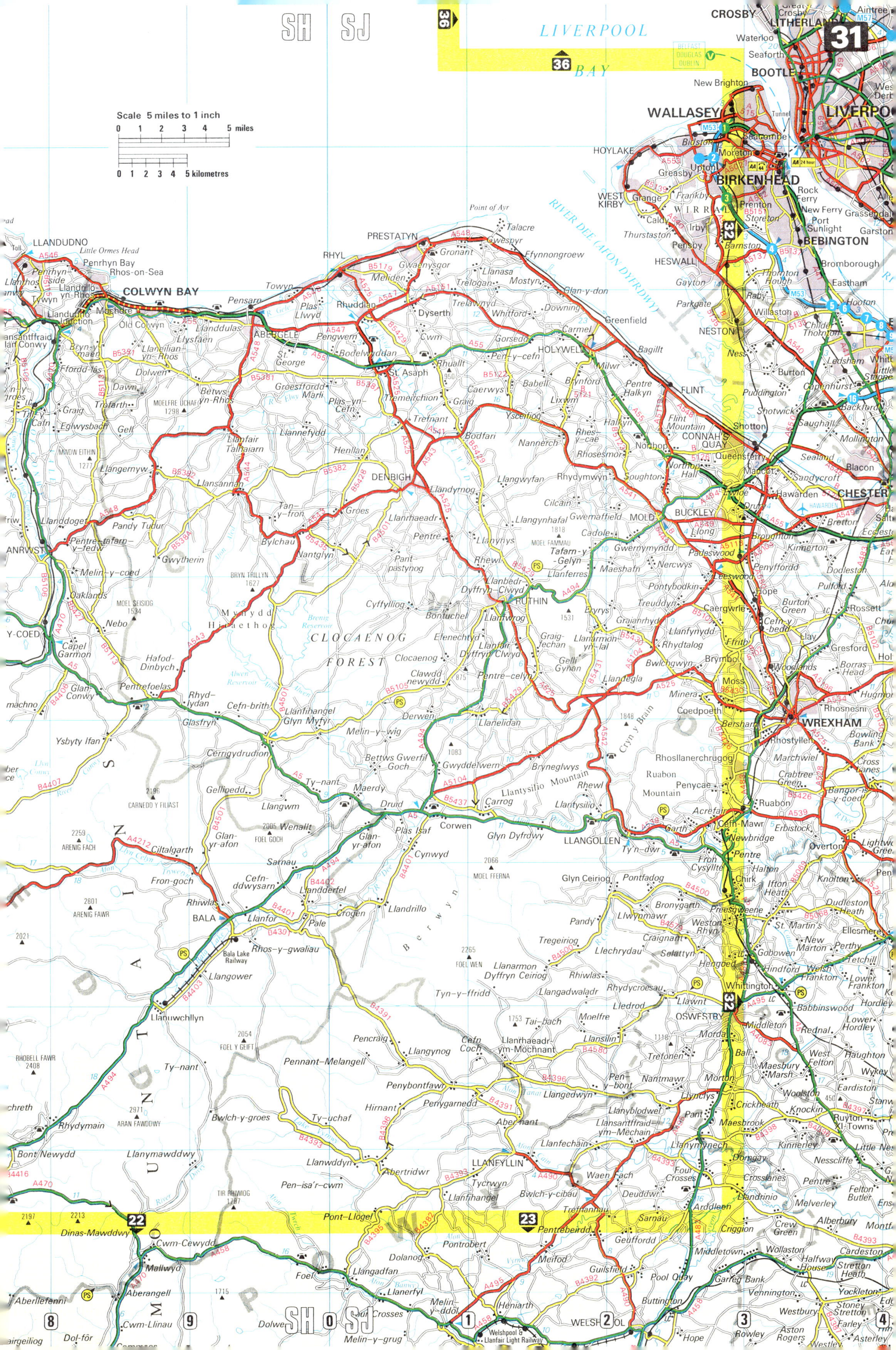
SH SJ
36
LIVERPOOL
BAY
31
Scale 5 miles to 1 inch
0 1 2 3 4 5 miles
0 1 2 3 4 5 kilometres
CROSBY
LITHERLAND
Waterloo
Seaforth
BOOTLE
New Brighton
WALLASEY
LIVERPOOL
HOYLAKE
Seacombe
Moreton
Upton
Greasby
BIRKENHEAD
Rock Ferry
New Ferry
Port Sunlight
BEBINGTON
WEST KIRBY
Grange
Frankby
WIRRAL
Prenton
Storeton
Irby
Caldy
Thurstaston
Pensby
Barnston
HESWALL
Bromborough
Eastham
Gayton
Thornton Hough
Raby
Willaston
Hooton
Parkgate
NESTON
Ness
Childer Thornton
Ledsham
Burton
Puddington
Capenhurst
Shotwick
Backford
Saughall
Mollington
Sealand
Blacon
Sandycroft
Hawarden
CHESTER
Bretton
Broughton
Kinnerton
Dodleston
Pulford
Rossett
Gresford
Borras Head
WREXHAM
Rhosnesni
Bowling Bank
Marchwiel
Cross Lanes
Bangor-is-y-coed
Crabtree Green
Erbistock
Overton
Knolton
Dudleston Heath
Ellesmere
St. Martin's
Perthy
Gobowen
Hindford
Welsh Frankton
Lower Frankton
Whittington
Babbinswood
Hordley
Middleton
Rednal
West Felton
Haughton
Wykey
Maesbury Marsh
Woolston
Knockin
Eardiston
Ruyton-XI-Towns
Kinnerley
Nesscliffe
Pentre
Felton Butler
Melverley
Alberbury
Crew Green
Wollaston
Halfway House
Stretton Heath
Cardeston
Vennington
Westbury
Yockleton
Stoney Stretton
Farley
Aston Rogers
Asterley
Rowley
Hope
LLANDUDNO
Little Ormes Head
Penrhyn Bay
Rhos-on-Sea
COLWYN BAY
Old Colwyn
Llanddulas
Llysfaen
ABERGELE
Towyn
Pensarn
St. George
Llanelian-yn-Rhos
Dolwen
Bryn-y-maen
Betws-yn-Rhos
Dawn
Trofarth
Groesffordd Marli
MOELFRE UCHAF 1298
Llanfair Talhaiarn
Llannefydd
Llangernyw
Gell
Eglwysbach
Graig
Llansannan
Henllan
Llanddoget
Pandy Tudur
Gwytherin
Tan-y-fron
Bylchau
Nantglyn
LLANRWST
Melin-y-coed
Oaklands
Nebo
Capel Garmon
Hafod-Dinbych
Pentrefoelas
Rhyd-lydan
Cefn-brith
Glan Conwy
Ysbyty Ifan
Glasfryn
Cerrigydrudion
Mynydd Hiraethog
BRYN TRILLYN 1627
MOEL SEISIOG 1534
Brenig Reservoir
Alwen Reservoir
CLOCAENOG FOREST
Clocaenog
Cyffylliog
Bontuchel
Clawdd-newydd
Llanfihangel Glyn Myfyr
Derwen
Melin-y-wig
Bettws Gwerfil Goch
Gwyddelwern
Maerdy
Ty-nant
Druid
Corwen
Glyn Dyfrdwy
Cynwyd
Llandrillo
Gellioedd
Llangwm
Glan-yr-afon
Sarnau
Cefn-ddwysarn
Llandderfel
Crogen
Frongoch
Ciltalgarth
ARENIG FACH
ARENIG FAWR
Rhiwlas
BALA
Llanfor
Pale
Rhos-y-gwaliau
Bala Lake Railway
Llangower
Llanuwchllyn
FOEL Y GEIFT 2054
RHOBELL FAWR 2408
Ty-nant
ARAN FAWDDWY 2971
Rhydymain
Bwlch-y-groes
Bont Newydd
Llanymawddwy
Dinas-Mawddwy
Cwm-Cewydd
Mallwyd
Aberangell
Aberllefenni
Cwm-Llinau
Dol-fôr
22
PRESTATYN
RHYL
Gronant
Gwaenysgor
Meliden
Talacre
Point of Ayr
Gwespyr
Ffynnongroew
Llanasa
Trelogan
Mostyn
Glan-y-don
Rhuddlan
Dyserth
Trelawnyd
Whitford
Downing
Pengwern
Bodelwyddan
Cwm
Gorsedd
HOLYWELL
Carmel
Greenfield
Bagillt
St Asaph
Rhuallt
Pen-y-cefn
Milwr
Brynford
Babell
Caerwys
Trefnant
Tremeirchion
Plas-yn-Cefn
Bodfari
Lixwm
Halkyn
Rhes-y-cae
Pentre Halkyn
FLINT
Flint Mountain
CONNAH'S QUAY
Shotton
Queensferry
Mancot
Northop
Northop Hall
Nannerch
Rhosesmor
Soughton
DENBIGH
Llandyrnog
Llangwyfan
Rhydymwyn
Cilcain
Llangynhafal
Gwernaffield
MOLD
BUCKLEY
Ewloe
Llanrhaeadr
Pentre
Llanynys
Rhewl
MOEL FAMMAU 1818
Tafarn-y-Gelyn
Cadole
Gwernymynydd
Nercwys
Padeswood
Penyffordd
Leeswood
Pontybodkin
Treuddyn
Hope
Caergwrle
Cefn-y-bedd
Llanbedr-Dyffryn-Clwyd
RUTHIN
Llanferres
Maeshafn
Llanfwrog
Efenechtyd
Llanfair Dyffryn Clwyd
Graig-fechan
Eryrys
Graianrhyd
Llanarmon-yn-Ial
Llanfynydd
Rhydtalog
Ffrith
Brymbo
Bwlchgwyn
Gelli Gynan
Pentre-celyn
Llandegla
Minera
Moss
Coedpoeth
Bersham
Rhostyllen
Llanelidan
Cryn y Brain
Rhosllanerchrugog
Ruabon Mountain
Penycae
Ruabon
Bryneglwys
Llantysilio Mountain
Llantysilio
Rhewl
Carrog
LLANGOLLEN
Acrefair
Garth
Cefn-Mawr
Newbridge
Ty'n-dwr
Froncysyllte
Pentre
Chirk
Halton
Glyn Ceiriog
Pontfadog
Bronygarth
Llwynmawr
Preesgweene
Weston Rhyn
Pandy
MOEL FFERNA
Berwyn
FOEL WEN
Tregeiriog
Llechrydau
Llanarmon Dyffryn Ceiriog
Rhiwlas
Selattyn
Craignant
Hengoed
Llangadwaladr
Rhydycroesau
Llawnt
OSWESTRY
Morda
Tyn-y-ffridd
Lledrod
Moelfre
Tai-bach
Llansilin
Trefonen
Pencraig
Llangynog
Cefn Coch
Llanrhaeadr-ym-Mochnant
Pennant-Melangell
Penybontfawr
Pen-y-bont
Nantmawr
Morton
Llangedwyn
Llynclys
Pant
Crickheath
Maesbrook
Hirnant
Penygarnedd
Llanyblodwel
Llansantffraid-ym-Mechain
Ty-uchaf
Abernant
Llanfechain
Llanymynech
Domgay
Llanwddyn
Abertridwr
LLANFYLLIN
Waen Fach
Four Crosses
Crosslanes
Pen-isa'r-cwm
Tycrwyn
Llanfihangel
Bwlch-y-cibau
Deuddwr
Llandrinio
Pont-Llogel
Trefnannau
Sarnau
Ardleen
Criggion
23
Pentrebeirdd
Geuffordd
Middletown
Pontrobert
Meifod
Dolanog
Llangadfan
Guilsfield
Pool Quay
Garreg Bank
Foel
Llanerfyl
Melin-y-ddol
Heniarth
Buttington
WELSHPOOL
Welshpool & Llanfair Light Railway
Melin-y-grug
SH SJ
1
2
3
4
8
9
32

BELFAST DOUGLAS DUBLIN
CROSBY
LITHERLAND
KIRKBY
BOOTLE
ST HELENS
NEWTON-LE-WILLOWS
ECCLES
SALFORD
URMSTON
STRETFORD
WALLASEY
LIVERPOOL
BIRKENHEAD
WARRINGTON
SALE
ALTRINCHAM
WIDNES
BEBINGTON
RUNCORN
RIVER MERSEY
ELLESMERE PORT
FLINT
KNUTSFORD
WILMSLOW
NORTHWICH
CONNAH'S QUAY
CHESTER
WINSFORD
MIDDLEWICH
MOLD
BUCKLEY
SANDBACH
ALSAGER
CREWE
NANTWICH
WREXHAM
Ruabon
Whitchurch
OSWESTRY
MARKET DRAYTON
Ellesmere
NEWPORT
SHREWSBURY
TELFORD
Wellington
M53
M56
M6
M62
M54
36
31
23
24

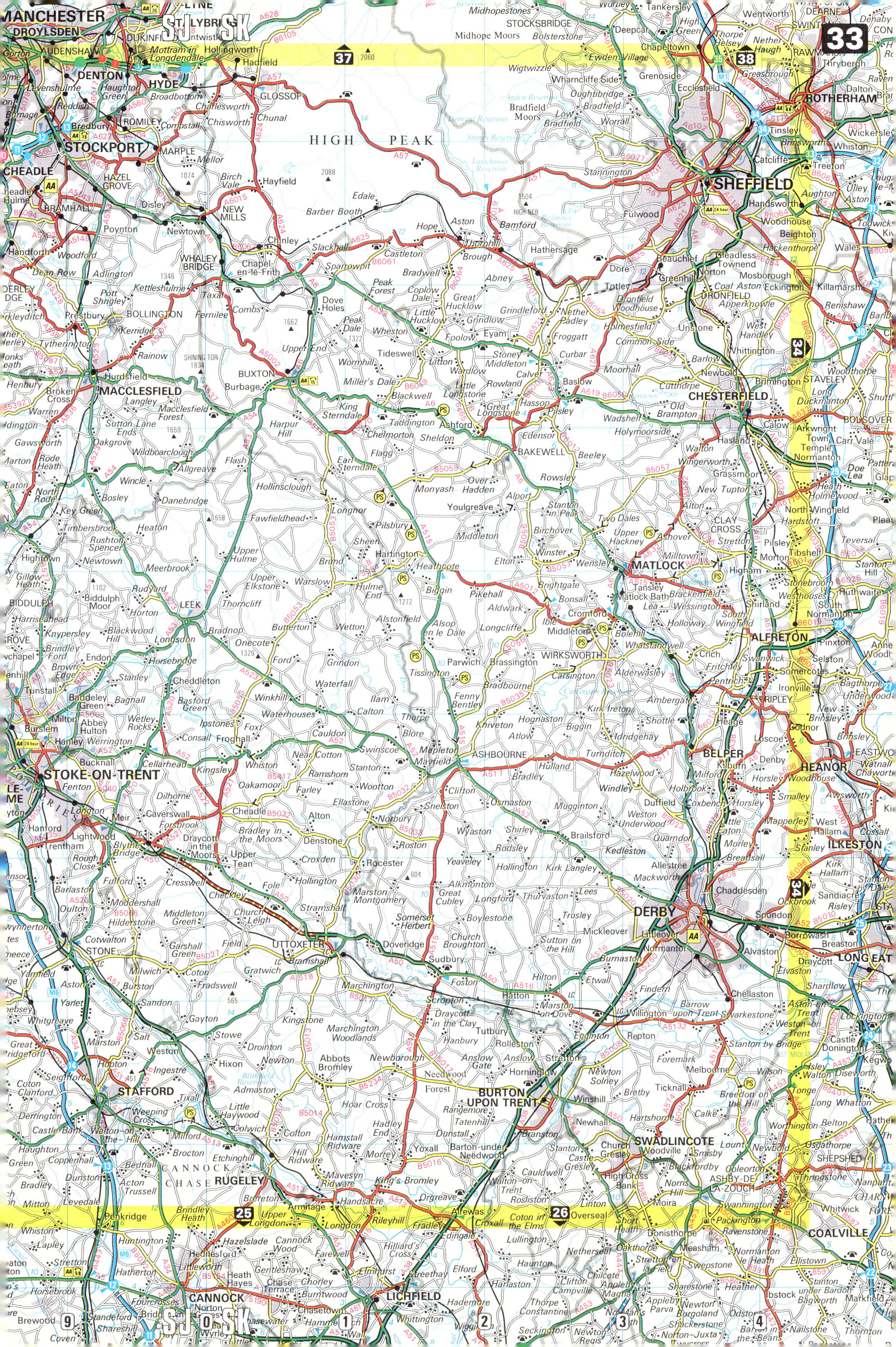

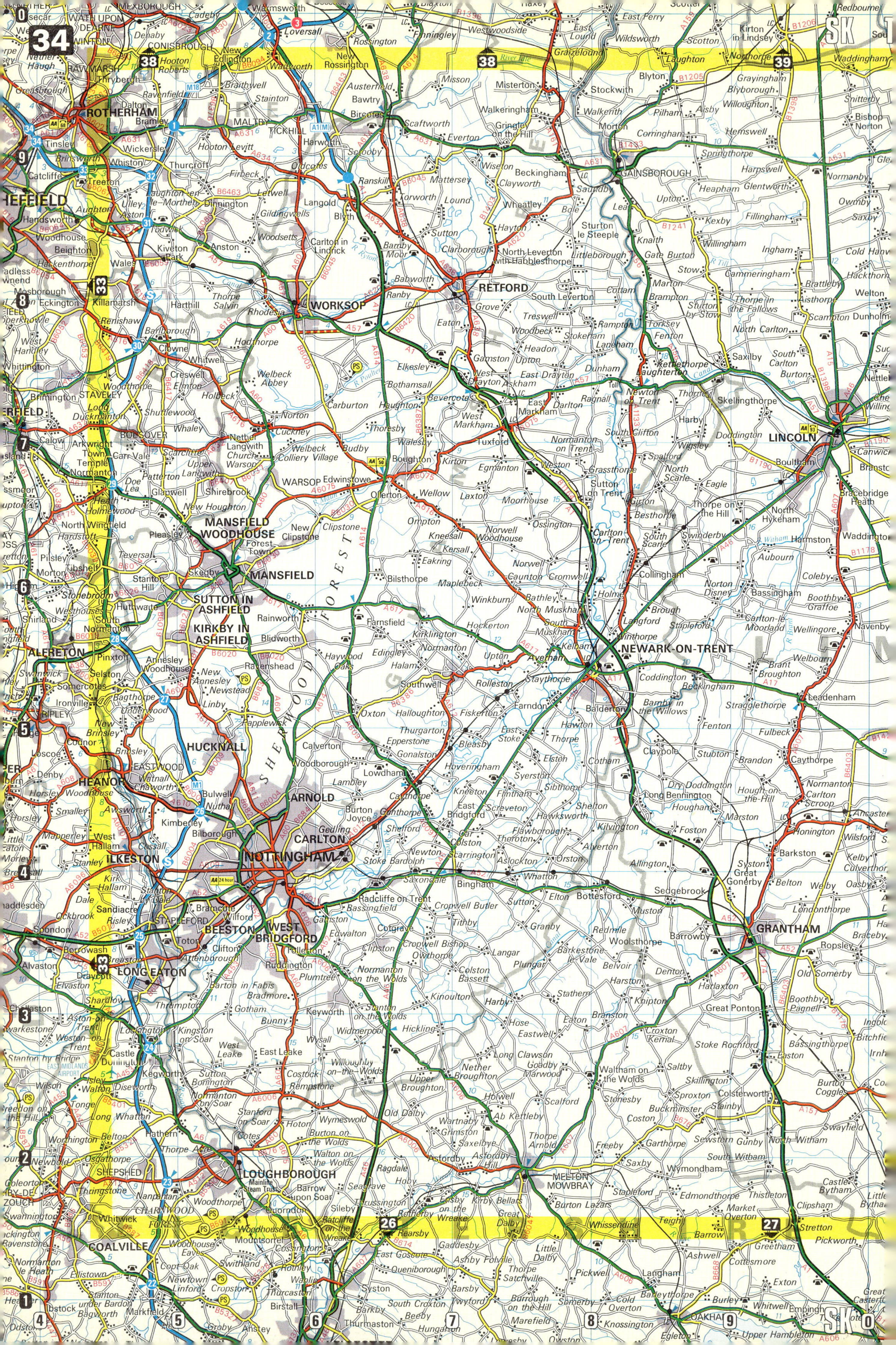
34
SK
38
38
39
33
26
27
ROTHERHAM
SHEFFIELD
WORKSOP
RETFORD
GAINSBOROUGH
LINCOLN
MANSFIELD WOODHOUSE
MANSFIELD
SUTTON IN ASHFIELD
KIRKBY IN ASHFIELD
ALFRETON
RIPLEY
HUCKNALL
HEANOR
ARNOLD
CARLTON
NOTTINGHAM
ILKESTON
BEESTON
WEST BRIDGFORD
LONG EATON
NEWARK-ON-TRENT
GRANTHAM
LOUGHBOROUGH
MELTON MOWBRAY
COALVILLE
STAVELEY
SHERWOOD FOREST

35

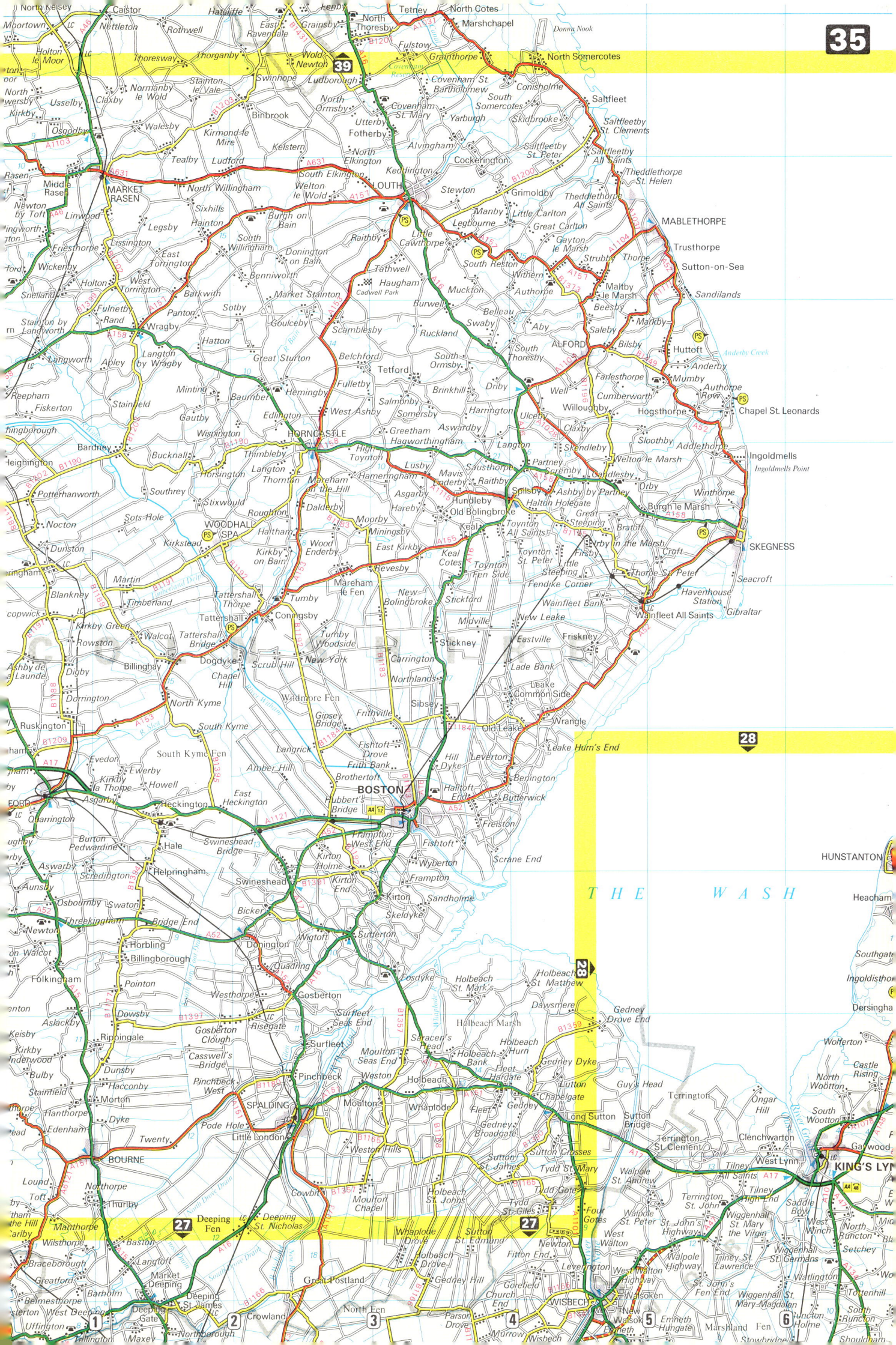

MORECAMBE BAY
BARROW-IN-FURNESS
ULVERSTON
Askam in Furness
DALTON-IN-FURNESS
GRANGE-OVER-SANDS
CARNFORTH
MORECAMBE
HEYSHAM
LANCASTER
Kirkby Lonsdale
Bentham
FLEETWOOD
CLEVELEYS
THORNTON
POULTON-LE-FYLDE
BLACKPOOL
LYTHAM ST ANNE'S
St Anne's
KIRKHAM
PRESTON
LONGRIDGE
BLACKBURN
DARWEN
LEYLAND
CHORLEY
SOUTHPORT
ORMSKIRK
SKELMERSDALE
WIGAN
BOLTON
FARNWORTH
ATHERTON
LEIGH
FORMBY
MAGHULL
KIRKBY
CROSBY
LITHERLAND
BOOTLE
LIVERPOOL
WALLASEY
ST HELENS
NEWTON-LE-WILLOWS
ECCLES
LIVERPOOL BAY
Forest of Bowland
Scale 5 miles to 1 inch
0 1 2 3 4 5 miles
0 1 2 3 4 5 kilometres
DOUGLAS
DOUGLAS Summer only
DUBLIN
BELFAST
SD
SJ
40
31
32

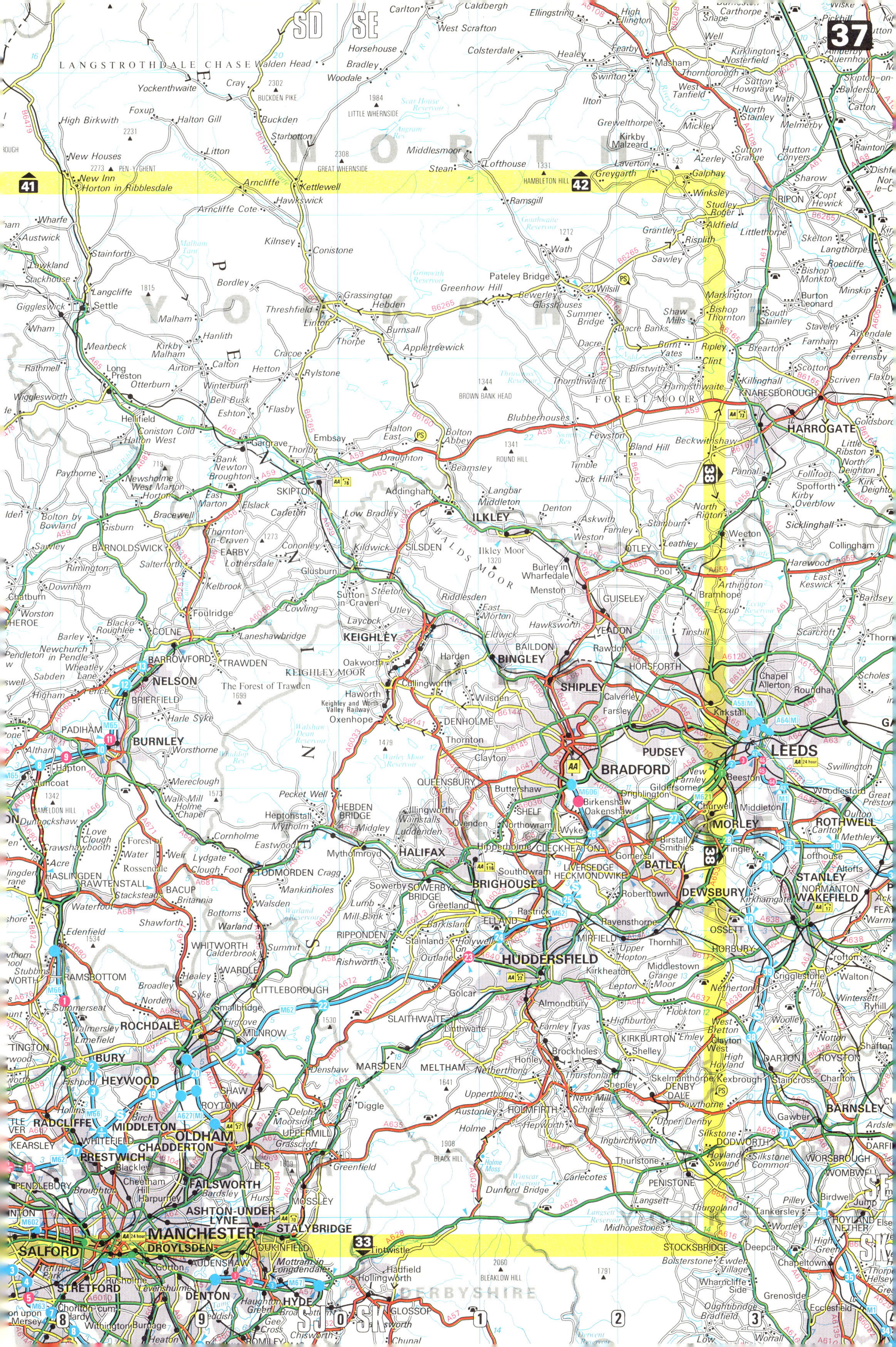

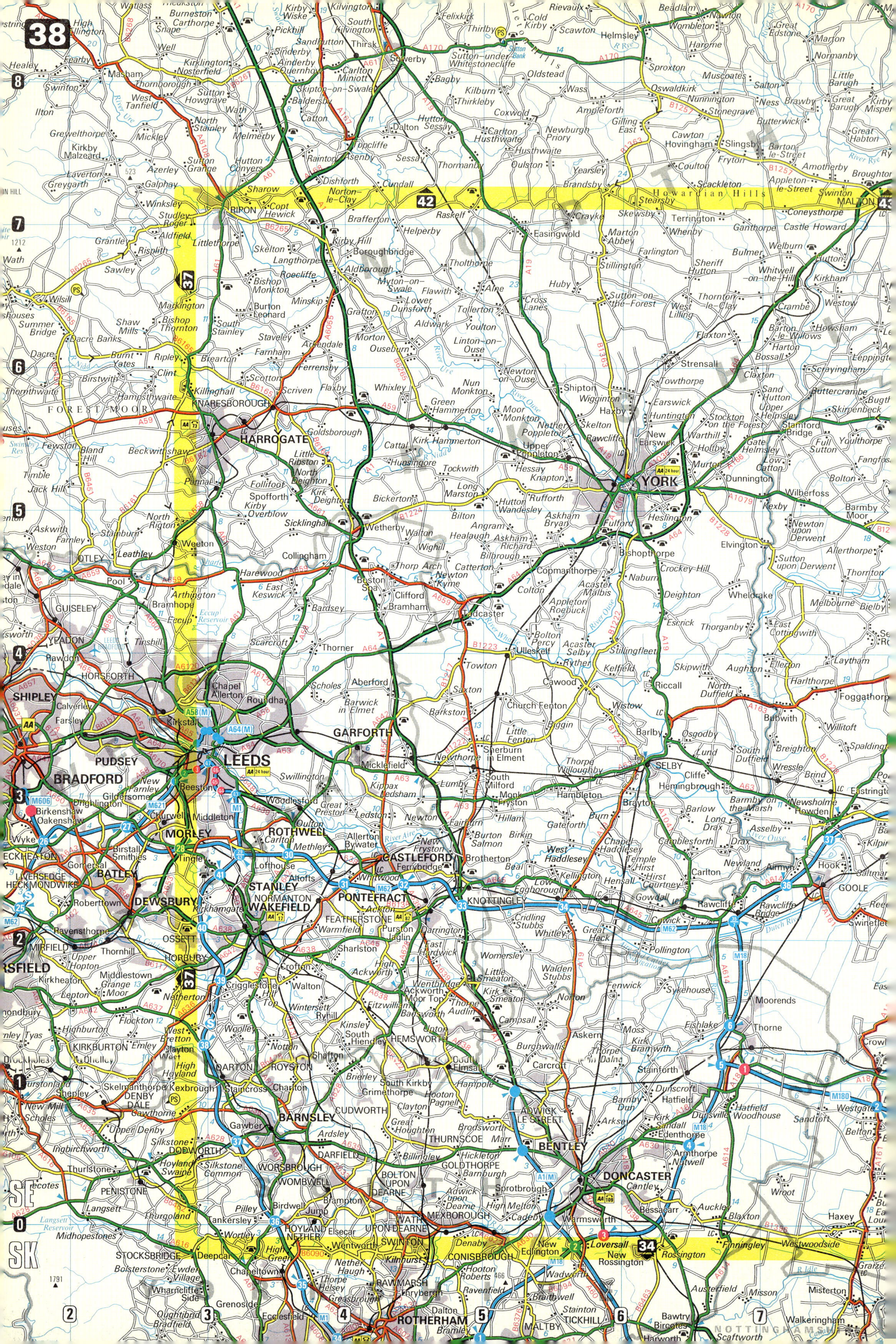

Osgodby
Cayton Bay
Eastfield
Irton
Seamer
Cayton
Thornton Dale
Wilton
Ebberston
Snainton
Wykeham
Allerston
Brompton
The Wyke
Gristhorpe
Lebberston
THE CARRS
Yedingham
Willerby
Flixton
Folkton
FILEY
Filey Bay
Staxton
Muston
River Derwent
Sherburn
Ganton
Hunmanby
Knapton
East Heslerton
Scampston
West Heslerton
Reighton
Fordon
Speeton
Rillington
Wintringham
Wold Newton
Crab Rocks
Malton
Thorpe Bassett
Foxholes
Burton Fleming
Bempton
FLAMBOROUGH HEAD
Scagglethorpe
Weaverthorpe
Butterwick
Grindale
Flamborough
Settrington
West Lutton
Helperthorpe
Thwing
Sewerby
North Grimston
Boynton
Rudston
BRIDLINGTON BAY
Duggleby
Kirby Grindalythe
Langtoft
BRIDLINGTON
Wharram le Street
Carnaby
Hilderthorpe
Sledmere
THE WOLDS
Kilham
Haisthorpe
Burton Agnes
Thixendale
Ruston Parva
Fraisthorpe
Harpham
Fimber
Lowthorpe
Kirby Underdale
Garton-on-the-Wolds
Gransmoor
Fridaythorpe
Wetwang
Nafferton
Barmston
GREAT DRIFFIELD
Great Kelk
Lissett
Ulrome
Wansford
Huggate
Tibthorpe
Foston on the Wolds
Skipsea
Kirkburn
Skerne
Beeford
Great Givendale
Brigham
North Dalton
North Frodingham
Millington
Bainton
Dunnington
Hutton Cranswick
Rotsea
Warter
Middleton-on-the-Wolds
Hempholme
Bewholme
Kilnwick
Watton
Atwick
Pocklington
Nunburnholme
Holme on the Wolds
Lund
Beswick
Burshill
HORNSEA
Brandesburton
Seaton
Burnby
Lockington
Aike
Hornsea Mere
Leven
Siggleshorne
Rolston
Londesborough
South Dalton
Scorborough
Catwick
Goxhill
Mappleton
Arram
Goodmanham
Routh
Long Riston
Rise
Great Hatfield
Everingham
Etton
Leconfield
Cherry Burton
Tickton
Withernwick
Market Weighton
Molescroft
BEVERLEY
New Ellerby
Bishop Burton
Meaux
West Newton
Holme upon Spalding Moor
Sancton
South Skirlaugh
Aldbrough
Woodmansey
Ellerby
North Cliffe
Walkington
Wawne
Newbald
Bentley
Thearne
Coniston
Flinton
Garton
South Cliffe
High Hunsley
Dunswell
Swine
Ganstead
Hotham
Skidby
COTTINGHAM
Sproatley
Humbleton
Little Weighton
Sutton-on-Hull
Lelley
Owstwick
Tunstall
North Cave
Rowley
Bilton
Elstronwick
Sandholme
Riplingham
South Cave
Willerby
Preston
Burton Pidsea
Roos
Newport
Marfleet
HEDON
Gilberdyke
Staddlethorpe
Brantingham
Kirk Ella
Swanland
KINGSTON UPON HULL
Waxholme
Rimswell
Ellerker
Elloughton
Welton
Anlaby
Burstwick
Thorngumbald
WITHERNSEA
Halsham
Broomfleet
Brough
HESSLE
Paull
Hollym
Blacktoft
Faxfleet
North Ferriby
Keyingham
Winestead
Whitton
New Holland
Ottringham
Holmpton
Ousefleet
Alkborough
BARTON-UPON-HUMBER
Barrow upon Humber
Patrington
Out Newton
Whitgift
Read's Island
Goxhill
Welwick
Skeffling
West Halton
Winteringham
South Ferriby
Fockerby
Coleby
East Halton
Sunk Island
Easington
Garthorpe
Thealby
Winterton
Horkstow
Thornton Curtis
Burton upon Stather
North Killingholme
Immingham Dock
Luddington
Normanby
Roxby
Saxby All Saints
Barnham
Wootton
South Killingholme
Kilnsea
Amcotts
Flixborough
Appleby
Bonby
Ulceby
Immingham
RIVER HUMBER
Low Santon
Worlaby
Croxton
Habrough
Gunness
Crosby
Elsham
Kirmington
Brocklesby
Stallingborough
GRIMSBY
SPURN HEAD
SCUNTHORPE
Melton Ross
Healing
ROTTERDAM (EUROPOORT)
ZEEBRUGGE
Burringham
Barnetby le Wold
Keelby
Great Coates
CLEETHORPES
Broughton
Wrawby
Great Limber
Aylesby
Ashby
Bottesford
Bigby
Riby
Laceby
Scartho
Yaddlethorpe
BRIGG
Searby
Bradley
Humberston
Butterwick
Messingham
Scawby
Howsham
Grasby
Irby upon Humber
Waltham
New Waltham
Manton
Cadney
Swallow
Barnoldby le Beck
Holton le Clay
Scotterthorpe
Hibaldstow
Caistor
Cabourne
Brigsley
Tetney Lock
Susworth
Scotter
North Kelsey
Cuxwold
Beelsby
Ashby cum Fenby
North Cotes
Owston Ferry
Tetney
East Ferry
Redbourne
Nettleton
Hatcliffe
Grainsby
Marshchapel
Scotton
Kirton in Lindsey
South Kelsey
Moortown
Rothwell
East Ravendale
North Thoresby
Fulstow
Grainthorpe
Wildsworth
Northorpe
Holton le Moor
Thorganby
Wold Newton
Laughton
Waddingham
Thornton le Moor
Thoresway
Swinhope
Ludborough
Covenham St Bartholomew
Covenham St Mary
Conisholme
Blyton
Grayingham
North Owersby
Normanby le Wold
Stainton le Vale
Utterby
South Somercotes
Saltfleet
Blyborough
Snitterby
Claxby
Binbrook
North Ormsby
Pilham
Aisby
Bishop Norton
Osgodby
Walesby
Yarburgh
Skidbrook
TA
TF
SE
SK

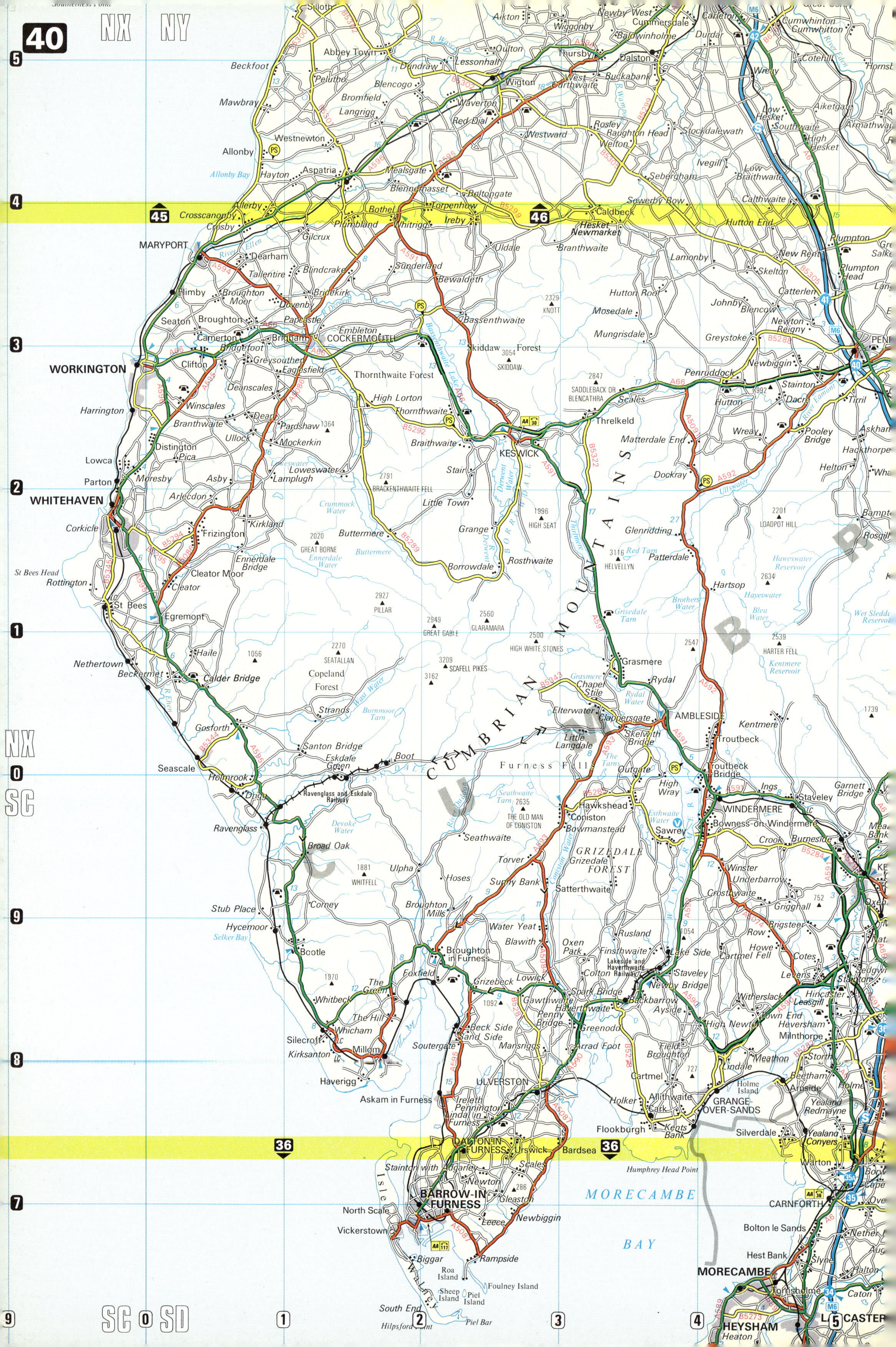

NX
NY
SC
SD
45
46
36
Silloth
Abbey Town
Beckfoot
Mawbray
Allonby
Allonby Bay
Westnewton
Hayton
Aspatria
Allerby
Crosscanonby
Crosby
MARYPORT
Dearham
Tallentire
Flimby
Broughton Moor
Seaton
Broughton
Camerton
WORKINGTON
Harrington
Distington
Lowca
Parton
Moresby
WHITEHAVEN
Corkickle
St Bees Head
Rottington
St Bees
Egremont
Cleator Moor
Cleator
Frizington
Nethertown
Beckermet
Calder Bridge
Gosforth
Seascale
Holmrook
Drigg
Ravenglass
Ravenglass and Eskdale Railway
Eskdale Green
Boot
Santon Bridge
Broad Oak
Stub Place
Hycemoor
Selker Bay
Bootle
Corney
Whitbeck
Whicham
Silecroft
Kirksanton
Millom
Haverigg
Askam in Furness
Broughton in Furness
Foxfield
Ulpha
Seathwaite
Torver
Coniston
Hawkshead
Sawrey
Grizedale Forest
Satterthwaite
Lowick
Greenodd
ULVERSTON
Dalton-in-Furness
Urswick
Bardsea
BARROW-IN-FURNESS
North Scale
Vickerstown
Isle of Walney
Biggar
Roa Island
Foulney Island
Piel Island
Sheep Island
South End
Hilpsford Point
Piel Bar
Rampside
Newbiggin
Leece
Gleaston
Flookburgh
Cark
Allithwaite
Cartmel
GRANGE-OVER-SANDS
Holme Island
Humphrey Head Point
MORECAMBE BAY
Silverdale
Arnside
Carnforth
Warton
Bolton le Sands
Hest Bank
MORECAMBE
HEYSHAM
Heaton
Torrisholme
LANCASTER
Caton
Slyne
Yealand Redmayne
Yealand Conyers
Beetham
Milnthorpe
Heversham
Levens
Witherslack
Lindale
Newby Bridge
Lake Side
Staveley
WINDERMERE
Bowness-on-Windermere
Crook
Burneside
Troutbeck
Troutbeck Bridge
AMBLESIDE
Rydal
Grasmere
Skelwith Bridge
Clappersgate
Elterwater
Chapel Stile
Little Langdale
Kentmere
Kentmere Reservoir
Harter Fell
Patterdale
Glenridding
Hartsop
Brothers Water
Haweswater Reservoir
Ullswater
Pooley Bridge
Dockray
Matterdale End
Threlkeld
Scales
Penruddock
Stainton
Dacre
Greystoke
Mungrisdale
Mosedale
Hutton Roof
KESWICK
Derwent Water
Borrowdale
Rosthwaite
Grange
Buttermere
Crummock Water
Loweswater
Lamplugh
Ennerdale Water
Ennerdale Bridge
Great Gable
Scafell Pikes
Glaramara
Pillar
Great Borne
Helvellyn
Skiddaw
Skiddaw Forest
Saddleback or Blencathra
Knott
Bassenthwaite
Bassenthwaite Lake
Thornthwaite Forest
Thornthwaite
Braithwaite
High Lorton
COCKERMOUTH
Embleton
Brigham
Papcastle
Dovenby
Bridekirk
Blindcrake
Gilcrux
Plumbland
Bothel
Torpenhow
Ireby
Uldale
Caldbeck
Hesket Newmarket
Sebergham
Wigton
Waverton
Dundraw
Thursby
Dalston
Carleton
Wreay
Calthwaite
Hutton End
Plumpton
Skelton
Catterlen
Blencow
Newton Reigny
PENRITH
Wast Water
Copeland Forest
Seatallan
Burnmoor Tarn
Devoke Water
Whitfell
Seathwaite Tarn
The Old Man of Coniston
Coniston Water
Esthwaite Water
Furness Fells
CUMBRIAN MOUNTAINS
CUMBRIA
Holker
Field Broughton
Cartmel Fell
Crosthwaite
Winster
Underbarrow
Brigsteer
Grizebeck
Gawthwaite
Penny Bridge
Haverthwaite
Backbarrow
Lakeside and Haverthwaite Railway
High Wray
Outgate
Rusland
Oxen Park
Colton
Water Yeat
Blawith
Spark Bridge

41
NORTHUMBERLAND
NY
NZ
Slaggyford
Ninebanks
Sinderhope
Shotley Bridge
STANLEY
Blanchland
Edmondbyers
CONSETT
Castleside
Muggleswick
Hunstanworth
Healeyfield
Iveston
Knitsley
Lanchester
Cumrew
Newbiggin
Croglin
Ayle
Alston
Carr Shield
Allenheads
Coalcleugh
Bayles
Scale Houses
Renwick
Gilderdale Forest
Leadgate
Nenthead
Rookhope
Waskerley
Butsfield
Cornsay
Satley
Quebec
Esh Winning
Waterhouses
East Hedley
Kirkoswald
Garrigill
Cornriggs
Cowshill
Crawleyside
BOLT'S LAW
COLLIER LAW
Gamblesby
Glassonby
46
47
Burnhope Reservoir
Ireshopeburn
Westgate
Eastgate
Stanhope
TOW LAW
Wolsingham
Sunniside
Melmerby
St. John's Chapel
Daddry Shield
Frosterley
Thornley
CROOK
Billy Row
Little Salkeld
Hunsonby
ROUND HILL
Hill End
River Wear
Winskill
Ousby
CROSS FELL
River Tees
Skirwith
Kirkland
Milburn Forest
Harwood
St. John's
Fir Tree
Howden-le-Wear
Blencarn
CHAPELFELL TOP
Witton le Wear
Culgaith
Milburn
Cow Green Res.
Langdon Beck
Low Redford
Bedburn
Hamsterley
Witton Park
Temple Sowerby
Newbiggin
Dufton Fell
Forest
HAMSTERLEY FOREST
High Etherley
St. Helen Auckland
Knock
Newbiggin
Holwick
Middleton in Teesdale
Woodland
Morley
Butterknowle
Melkinthorpe
Kirkby Thore
Dufton
Bowbank
Mickleton
Eggleston
Copley
Evenwood
Cliburn
Long Marton
Thringarth
Cockfield
Morland
Bolton
Brampton
Crackenthorpe
Romaldkirk
Wackerfield
Great Strickland
Kings Meaburn
APPLEBY
Murton
Kinninvie
Hilton
Newby
Colby
Hilton
Lune Forest
Grassholme
Hunderthwaite
Staindrop
Ingleton
Little Strickland
Sleagill
Great Ormside
Selset Reservoir
Hury
Cotherstone
Stainton
Langton
Headlam
Lartington
Cleatlam
Reagill
Maulds Meaburn
Sandford
Warcop
Balderhead Reservoir
Little Newsham
Gainford
Startforth
BARNARD CASTLE
Winston
Drybeck
Hillbeck
North Stainmore
DEEP DALE
Piercebridge
Crosby Ravensworth
Brough
Boldron
Whorlton
Ovington
Great Asby
Great Musgrave
Bowes
Greta Bridge
Caldwell
Brough Sowerby
Brignall
Hutton Magna
Forcett
Kaber
MOUDY MEA
Stainmore Forest
Scargill
West Layton
East Layton
Soulby
Barningham
Newsham
Crosby Garrett
Winton
Hartley
Waitby
Kirkby Stephen
Orton
Raisbeck
NORTHBOUND TRAFFIC ONLY
Nateby
CLEASBY HILL
Dalton
Gayles
Ravensworth
Kirby Hill
Whashton
Kelleth
Newbiggin-on-Lune
Whaw
Gilling West
Tebay
Ravenstonedale
Langthwaite
Washfold
Skeeby
West Stonesdale
GREAT PINSEAT
Outhgill
Keld
Skelton
Marske
Hudswell
River Swale
Thwaite
Gunnerside
Muker
Feetham
Kearton
Healaugh
Reeth
Marrick
Low Row
Grinton
Downholme
Crackpot
Stainton
Catterick Camp
GREAT SHUNNER FELL
THE CALF
LAMBRIGG FELL
Cautley
Cotterdale
Barden
East Hauxwell
Hunton
Constable Burton
New Hutton
Sedbergh
Garsdale Head
River Ure
High Shaw
Hardrow
Sedbusk
Askrigg
Newbiggin
Castle Bolton
Bellerby
Preston-under-Scar
Leyburn
SOUTHBOUND TRAFFIC ONLY
Millthrop
Woodhall
Redmire
Hawes
Bainbridge
Carperby
Swinithwaite
Wensley
Harmby
Finghall
Spennithorne
Old Hutton
Killington
River Dee
Burtersett
Thornton Rust
Aysgarth
West Witton
Middleham
Gawthrop
Lea Yeat
Dent
Countersett
Thoralby
Agglethorpe
Coverham
Middleton
CALF TOP
Stone House
Stalling Busk
West Burton
Newbiggin
Melmerby
East Witton
Carlton
Caldbergh
Ellingstring
Deepdale
Mansergh
West Scrafton
Barbon
WHERNSIDE
Horsehouse
Colsterdale
Healey
Lupton
Kearstwick
LANGSTROTHDALE CHASE
Walden Head
Bradley
Woodale
Casterton
Kirkby Lonsdale
Cray
BUCKDEN PIKE
Yockenthwaite
LITTLE WHERNSIDE
Scar House Reservoir
Ilton
Chapel le Dale
Whittington
Cowan Bridge
High Birkwith
Foxup
Halton Gill
Buckden
Angram Res.
Newton
Nether Burrow
Ireby
Westhouse
Starbotton
Tunstall
36
INGLEBOROUGH HILL
New Houses
Litton
37
GREAT WHERNSIDE
Middlesmoor
Cantsfield
Skirwith
PEN-Y-GHENT
Stean
Lofthouse
HAMBLETON HILL
Arkholme
Burton in Lonsdale
Ingleton
New Inn
Horton in Ribblesdale
Arncliffe
Kettlewell
Melling
Wennington
Lower Bentham
High Bentham
Newby
Hawkswick
Ramsgill
Arncliffe Cote
Hornby
Clapham
Wharfe
Gouthwaite Reservoir
Wray
Austwick
Malham Tarn
Kilnsey
Conistone
Wath
Stainforth
Keasden
Lawkland
Claughton
Stackhouse
Langcliffe
Bordley
Grimwith Reservoir
Pateley Bridge
Lowgill
Eldroth
Grassington
Hebden
Greenhow Hill
Bewerley
Glasshouses
Giggleswick
Settle
Salter
Threshfield
SD
SE
Summer Bridge
Crossgill
Thrushgill
Malham
Burnsall
Wham
Hanlith
Mearbeck
Kirkby Malham
Appletreewick
6
7
8
9
0
1
42

42

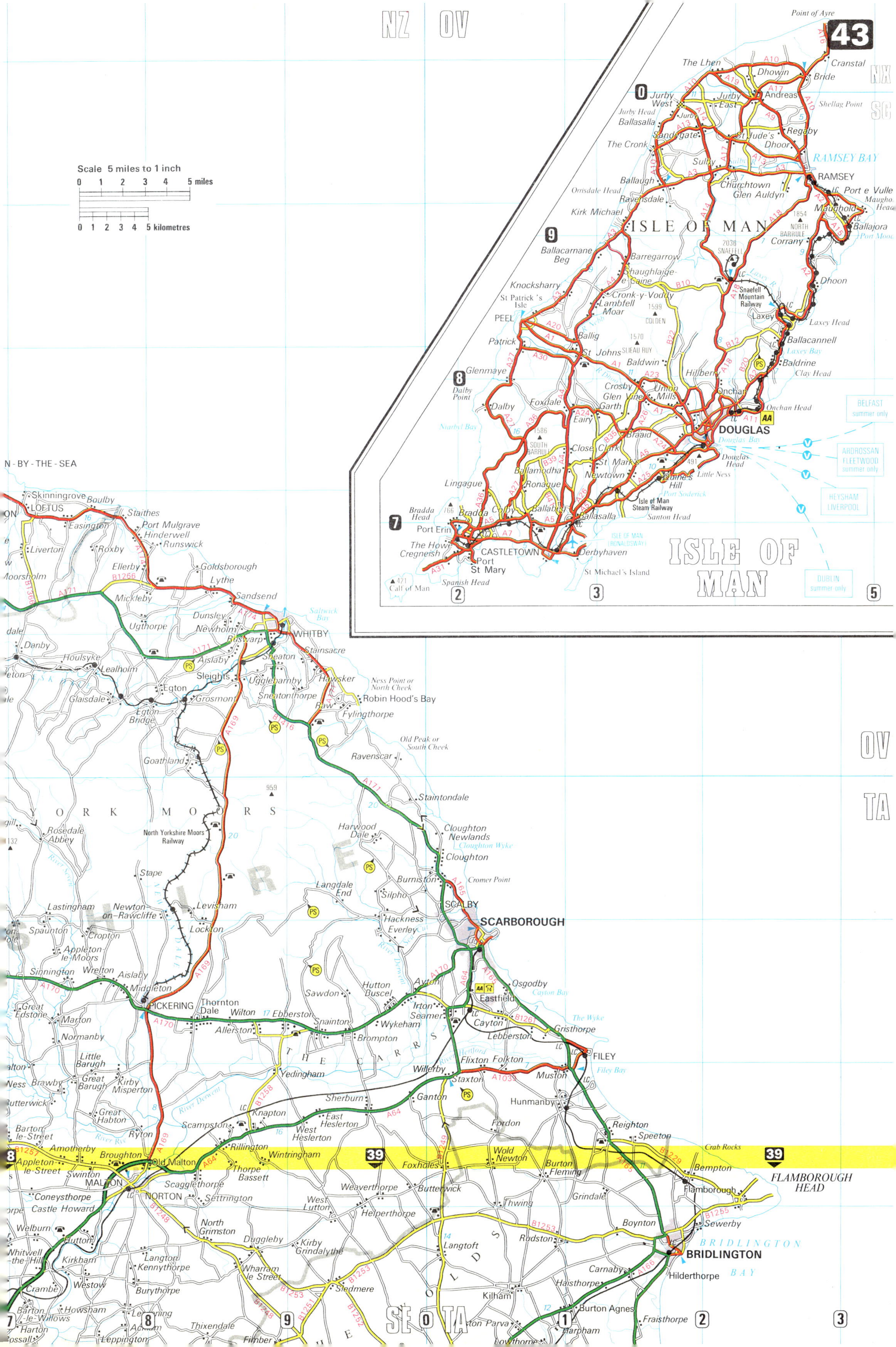

NZ
OV
Scale 5 miles to 1 inch
0 1 2 3 4 5 miles
0 1 2 3 4 5 kilometres
ISLE OF MAN
Point of Ayre
Cranstal
The Lhen
Dhowin
Bride
Jurby West
Jurby East
Andreas
Shellag Point
Jurby Head
Ballasalla
Sandygate
St Jude's
Regaby
The Cronk
Dhoor
Sulby
RAMSEY BAY
RAMSEY
Ballaugh
Churchtown
Glen Auldyn
Port e Vullen
Maughold Head
Orrisdale Head
Ravensdale
Maughold
Kirk Michael
1854 NORTH BARRULE
Ballajora
Corrany
Port Mooar
Ballacarnane Beg
Barregarrow
2036 SNAEFELL
Shaughlaige-e-Caine
Dhoon
Knocksharry
Cronk-y-Voddy
Snaefell Mountain Railway
St Patrick's Isle
Lambfell Moar
1599 COLDEN
Laxey
Laxey Head
PEEL
Ballig
1570 SLIEAU RUY
Ballacannell
Patrick
St Johns
Laxey Bay
Baldwin
Baldrine
Glenmaye
Clay Head
Dalby Point
Crosby
Hillberry
Union Mills
Glen Vine
Onchan
Garth
Onchan Head
Dalby
Foxdale
Eairy
DOUGLAS
Douglas Bay
Niarbyl Bay
1586 SOUTH BARRULE
Braaid
Close Clark
Douglas Head
Ballamodha
St Marks
Little Ness
Newtown
Lingague
Ronague
Quine's Hill
Port Soderick
Bradda Head
Bradda
Colby
Ballabeg
Isle of Man Steam Railway
Ballasalla
Santon Head
Port Erin
The Howe
CASTLETOWN
Derbyhaven
Cregneish
Port St Mary
St Michael's Island
Calf of Man
Spanish Head
BELFAST summer only
ARDROSSAN FLEETWOOD summer only
HEYSHAM LIVERPOOL
DUBLIN summer only
NX
SC
N-BY-THE-SEA
Skinningrove
Boulby
LOFTUS
Staithes
Easington
Port Mulgrave
Hinderwell
Runswick
Liverton
Roxby
Goldsborough
Ellerby
Lythe
Moorsholm
Sandsend
Mickleby
Dunsley
Saltwick Bay
Ugthorpe
Newholm
WHITBY
Danby
Ruswarp
Stainsacre
Houlsyke
Aislaby
Sneaton
Lealholm
Sleights
Hawsker
Ness Point or North Cheek
Egton
Ugglebarnby
Robin Hood's Bay
Glaisdale
Grosmont
Sneatonthorpe
Raw
Fylingthorpe
Egton Bridge
Old Peak or South Cheek
Goathland
Ravenscar
959
Staintondale
YORK MOORS
Rosedale Abbey
North Yorkshire Moors Railway
Harwood Dale
Cloughton Newlands
Cloughton Wyke
Cloughton
Stape
Burniston
Cromer Point
Langdale End
Silpho
Lastingham
Newton-on-Rawcliffe
Levisham
SCALBY
Hackness
SCARBOROUGH
Spaunton
Lockton
Everley
Cropton
Appleton-le-Moors
Sinnington
Wrelton
Aislaby
Middleton
Osgodby
Cayton Bay
Hutton Buscel
Ayton
Sawdon
Eastfield
Great Edstone
PICKERING
Thornton Dale
Irton
Seamer
Marton
Wilton
Ebberston
Snainton
Cayton
The Wyke
Allerston
Wykeham
Lebberston
Gristhorpe
Normanby
Brompton
THE CARRS
FILEY
Little Barugh
Filey Bay
Yedingham
Willerby
Flixton
Folkton
Muston
Great Barugh
Brawby
Kirby Misperton
Staxton
Butterwick
Sherburn
Ganton
Hunmanby
Great Habton
Knapton
East Heslerton
Barton-le-Street
Scampston
West Heslerton
Fordon
Reighton
Ryton
Speeton
Amotherby
Rillington
Crab Rocks
Appleton-le-Street
Broughton
Old Malton
Wintringham
Wold Newton
Burton Fleming
Bempton
Swinton
Thorpe Bassett
Foxholes
MALTON
Scagglethorpe
FLAMBOROUGH HEAD
NORTON
Flamborough
Coneysthorpe
Settrington
Weaverthorpe
Butterwick
Grindale
Castle Howard
West Lutton
Helperthorpe
Thwing
Welburn
Sewerby
North Grimston
Boynton
Hutton
Duggleby
Kirby Grindalythe
Rudston
BRIDLINGTON BAY
Whitwell-on-the-Hill
Kirkham
Langton
Langtoft
BRIDLINGTON
Kennythorpe
Wharram le Street
Carnaby
Hilderthorpe
Westow
Burythorpe
Crambe
Sledmere
Haisthorpe
Kilham
Barton-le-Willows
Howsham
Burton Agnes
Harton
Leavening
Acklam
Thixendale
Fraisthorpe
Rudston Parva
Harpham
Leppington
Fimber
Lowthorpe
WOLDS
39
SE
TA

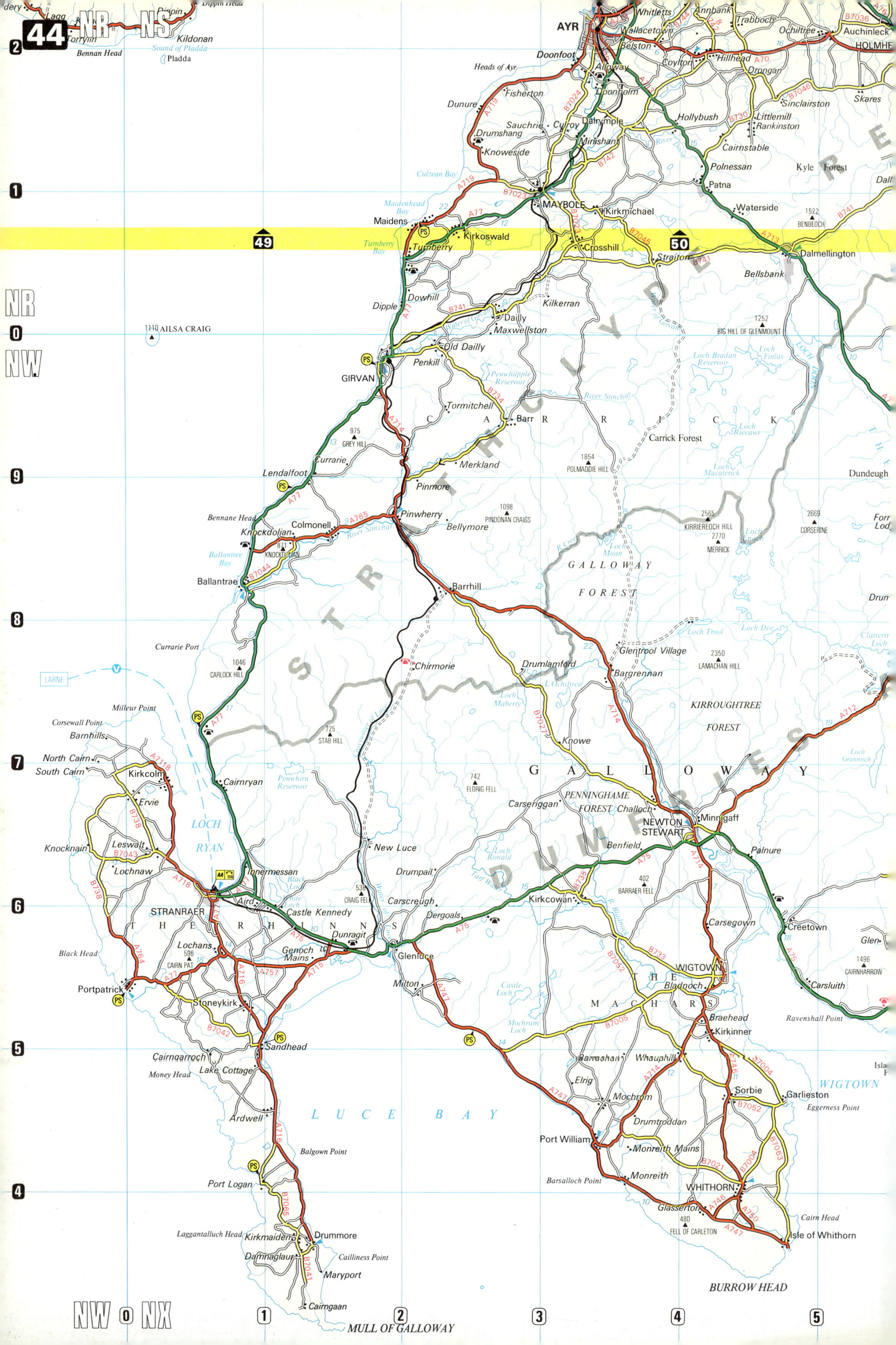
NR
NS
Lagg
Torrylin
Kildonan
Bennan Head
Sound of Pladda
Pladda
Dippin Head
AYR
Whitletts
Annbank
Trabboch
Ochiltree
Auchinleck
HOLMHEAD
Wallacetown
Belston
Coylton
Hillhead
Drongan
Doonfoot
Heads of Ayr
Alloway
Doonholm
Fisherton
Dunure
Sinclairston
Skares
Hollybush
Littlemill
Rankinston
Sauchrie
Culroy
Dalrymple
Drumshang
Minishant
Cairnstable
Knoweside
Polnessan
Kyle Forest
Culzean Bay
Patna
MAYBOLE
Kirkmichael
Waterside
1522 BENBEOCH
Maidenhead Bay
Maidens
Kirkoswald
Turnberry
Turnberry Bay
Crosshill
Straiton
Dalmellington
Bellsbank
49
50
Dowhill
Kilkerran
Dipple
Dailly
Maxwellston
1110 AILSA CRAIG
1252 BIG HILL OF GLENMOUNT
Old Dailly
GIRVAN
Penkill
Penwhapple Reservoir
Loch Bradan Reservoir
Loch Finlas
Loch Doon
River Stinchar
Tormitchell
Barr
CARRICK
Carrick Forest
975 GREY HILL
Loch Riecawr
Currarie
Merkland
1854 POLMADDIE HILL
Loch Macaterick
Lendalfoot
Pinmore
Dundeugh
Pinwherry
1098 PINDONAN CRAIGS
2565 KIRRIEREOCH HILL
2669 CORSERINE
Bennane Head
Colmonell
Bellymore
2770 MERRICK
Loch Enoch
Knockdolian
871 KNOCKDOLIAN
Ballantrae Bay
Loch Moan
GALLOWAY FOREST
Ballantrae
Barrhill
STRATHCLYDE
Loch Trool
Loch Dee
Clatteringshaws Loch
Currarie Port
Glentrool Village
2350 LAMACHAN HILL
1046 CARLOCK HILL
LARNE
Chirmorie
Drumlamford
Bargrennan
Milleur Point
L. Ochiltree
Loch Maberry
KIRROUGHTREE FOREST
Corsewall Point
Barnhills
725 STAB HILL
Knowe
North Cairn
South Cairn
Kirkcolm
Cairnryan
Penwhirn Reservoir
742 ELDRIG FELL
GALLOWAY
Loch Grannoch
Ervie
LOCH RYAN
PENNINGHAME FOREST
Carseriggan
Challoch
NEWTON STEWART
Minnigaff
Knocknain
Leswalt
New Luce
Benfield
Palnure
Lochnaw
Innermessan
Drumpail
Loch Ronald
DUMFRIES
STRANRAER
Aird
Castle Kennedy
538 CRAIG FELL
Carscreugh
Kirkcowan
402 BARRAER FELL
Creetown
THE RHINNS
Dergoals
Carsegowan
Black Head
Lochans
596 CAIRN PAT
Dunragit
Genoch Mains
Glenluce
WIGTOWN
Glen
1496 CAIRNHARROW
Portpatrick
Milton
Castle Loch
Bladnoch
Carsluith
Stoneykirk
THE MACHARS
Ravenshall Point
Mochrum Loch
Braehead
Kirkinner
Sandhead
Cairngarroch
Lake Cottage
Money Head
Barrachan
Whauphill
Elrig
Mochrum
Sorbie
Garlieston
WIGTOWN BAY
Eggerness Point
LUCE BAY
Ardwell
Drumtroddan
Balgown Point
Port William
Monreith Mains
Port Logan
Barsalloch Point
Monreith
WHITHORN
Glasserton
480 FELL OF CARLETON
Cairn Head
Isle of Whithorn
Laggantalluch Head
Kirkmaiden
Drummore
Damnaglaur
Cailliness Point
Maryport
BURROW HEAD
Cairngaan
MULL OF GALLOWAY
NW 0 NX
NR 0 NW
1 2 3 4 5

Lugar
Cronberry
Logan
CUMNOCK
Dalblair
Netherthird
Fingland
Pathhead
Mansfield
New Cumnock
Afton Bridgend
Bankglen
Burnside
Kirkland
Kirkconnell
Crawick
SANQUHAR
Ulzieside
Mennock
Wanlockhead
Leadhills
LOWTHER HILLS
Abington
Kirkton
Crawford
Elvanfoot
Water Meetings
TEWSGILL HILL
CLYDE LAW
GREEN LOWTHER
THIRSTANE HILL
KIRKLAND HILL
NS
NT
Glenbreck
Meggethead
Talla Linnfoots
Talla Reservoir
Fruid Reservoir
WHITE COOMB
HART FELL
BROAD LAW
Nether Howecleuch
Ericstane
Granton
Bridgend
GALLOW HILL
MOFFAT
Dumcrieff
LOCH FELL
ESKDALE
50
51
BLACKCRAIG HILL
BALLENCLEUCH LAW
Afton Reservoir
Enterkinfoot
Durisdeer
Enoch
Earshaig
Kinnelhead
Beattock
Poldean
Marchbankwood
Laverhay
Holestane
CAIRNKINNA HILL
BELLYBOUGHT HILL
COLT HILL
Big Corlae
AIRNSMORE OF CARSPHAIRN
Carsphairn
Auchenbrack
Carronbridge
Locherben
Gatelawbridge
Benbuie
Burnhead
Penpont
Thornhill
FOREST OF AE
Loshwood
Newton
Keir Mill
Tynron
St Ann's
GREAT HILL
Closeburn
Johnstonebridge
Dinwoodie Mains
Boreland
Knowehead
Moniaive
Kirkland
Keir Hills
Blackacre
Ae Village
Parkgate
Nethermill
Templand
GALLOWAY
REGION
BOGRIE HILL
Dunscore
Dalswinton
Duncow
LOCHMABEN
Amisfield Town
Kirkton
Tinwald
LOCKERBIE
Earlstoun Loch
Garroch
Glenlee
Bogue
St. John's Town of Dalry
STEILSTON HILL
Holywood
Locharbriggs
Torthorwald
Hightae
Castlemilk
Balmaclellan
NEW GALLOWAY
Corsock
Craig
Terregles
Shawhead
Collin
DUMFRIES
Racks
Middlebie
Dalton
Ecclefechan
Cargenbridge
Crocketford or Ninemile Bar
Lochfoot
Cargen
Kingholm Quay
Mouswald
Carrutherstown
CAIRN EDWARD FOREST
Drumrash
Parton
Mossdale
Mabie
Milton
Springholm
Kirkpatrick Durham
Beeswing
Glencaple
Bankend
Clarencefield
Brydekirk
Old Bridge of Urr
Crossmichael
Kirkgunzeon
Kirkconnel
Ruthwell
Clarebrand
Haugh of Urr
New Abbey
Cummertrees
Powfoot
Blackshaw
Laurieston
LAURIESTON FOREST
Townhead of Greenlaw
LONG FELL
Loch Kindar
Overton
Bowness-on-Solway
CASTLE DOUGLAS
CRIFFEL
GLENGAP FOREST
BENGRAY
Bridge of Dee
Miefield
Rhonehouse or Kelton Hill
Gelston
DALBEATTIE
Kirkbean
Carsethorn
Cardurnock
Anthorn
SOLWAY FIRTH
Ringford
DALBEATTIE FOREST
Caulkerbush
GATEHOUSE OF FLEET
Palnackie
Twynholm
Skinburness
Southerness
Southerness Point
Tongland
BENGAIRN
Kippford or Scaur
Colvend
Rockcliffe
Silloth
Girthon
Sandgreen
KIRKCUDBRIGHT
Auchencairn
Auchencairn Bay
Hestan Island
Balcary Point
Abbey Town
Knockbrex
Borgue
St Mary's Isle
Kirkcarswell
Beckfoot
Pelutho
Dundrannan
Rascarrel
Blencogo
Mawbray
Bromfield
Langrigg
Borness
Townhead
Orroland
Ross
Netherlaw
Balmae
WALL HILL
Abbey Head
Westnewton
Little Ross
Allonby
Allonby Bay
Hayton
Aspatria
Mealsgate
40
Allerby
Crosscanonby
Crosby
Bothel
Plumbland
Gilcrux
MARYPORT
Dearham
Tallentire
Blindcrake
Flimby
Broughton Moor
Bridekirk
Dovenby
Papcastle
Broughton
Brigham
Camerton
Embleton
COCKERMOUTH
NX
NY
6
7
8
9
0
1
2
46

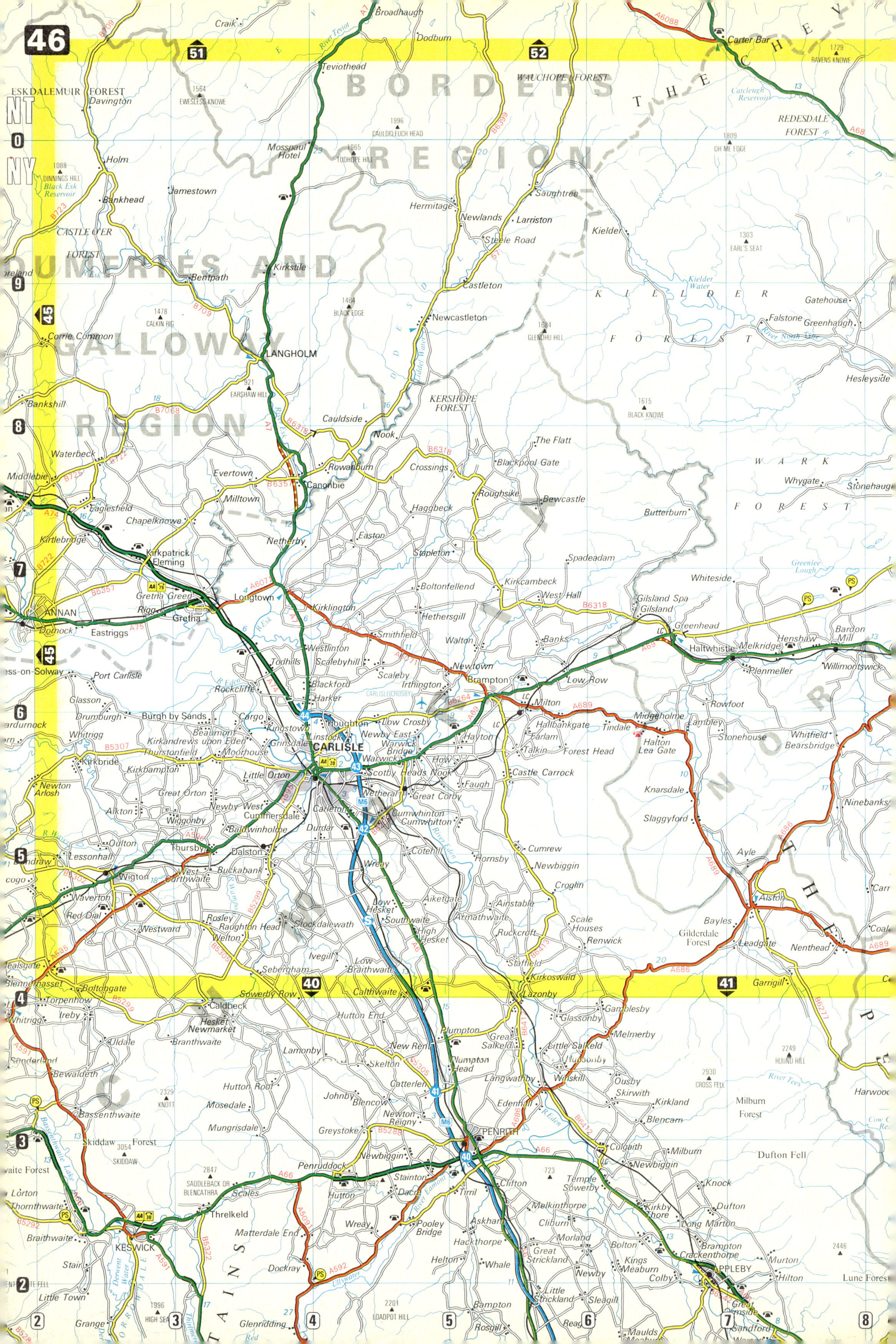
51
52
40
41
45
BORDERS REGION
DUMFRIES AND GALLOWAY REGION
THE CHEVIOTS
KIELDER FOREST
WARK FOREST
NORTHUMBERLAND
ESKDALEMUIR FOREST
WAUCHOPE FOREST
REDESDALE FOREST
KERSHOPE FOREST
CASTLE O'ER FOREST
Carter Bar
Broadhaugh
Dodburn
Craik
Teviothead
Davington
Mosspaul Hotel
Holm
Bankhead
Jamestown
Hermitage
Newlands
Larriston
Saughtree
Steele Road
Kielder
Castleton
Newcastleton
Bentpath
Kirkstile
LANGHOLM
Corrie Common
Bankshill
Cauldside
Nook
Canonbie
Rowanburn
Crossings
The Flatt
Blackpool Gate
Roughsike
Bewcastle
Butterburn
Gatehouse
Falstone
Greenhaugh
Hesleyside
Whygate
Stonehaugh
Waterbeck
Middlebie
Evertown
Milltown
Eaglesfield
Chapelknowe
Kirtlebridge
Kirkpatrick Fleming
Netherby
Easton
Haggbeck
Stapleton
Spadeadam
Kirkcambeck
West Hall
Boltonfellend
Longtown
Gretna Green
Gretna
Rigg
ANNAN
Dornock
Eastriggs
Kirklington
Hethersgill
Smithfield
Walton
Banks
Gilsland Spa
Gilsland
Greenhead
Haltwhistle
Melkridge
Henshaw
Bardon Mill
Willimontswick
Plenmeller
Whiteside
Westlinton
Todhills
Scaleby
Scalebyhill
Blackford
Harker
Rockcliffe
Port Carlisle
Glasson
Drumburgh
Burgh by Sands
Cargo
Kingstown
Beaumont
Kirkandrews upon Eden
Grinsdale
Houghton
Linstock
Low Crosby
Newby East
Irthington
Newtown
Brampton
Low Row
Milton
Hallbankgate
Farlam
Talkin
Tindale
Midgeholme
Halton Lea Gate
Lambley
Rowfoot
Stonehouse
Whitfield
Bearsbridge
CARLISLE
Warwick Bridge
Hayton
How
Heads Nook
Scotby
Wetheral
Faugh
Great Corby
Castle Carrock
Forest Head
Knarsdale
Slaggyford
Ninebanks
Whitrigg
Thurstonfield
Moorhouse
Kirkbride
Kirkbampton
Little Orton
Newton Arlosh
Great Orton
Alkton
Newby West
Wiggonby
Cummersdale
Carleton
Durdar
Cumwhinton
Cumwhitton
Baldwinholme
Oulton
Lessonhall
Thursby
Dalston
Cotehill
Wigton
West Curthwaite
Buckabank
Wreay
Hornsby
Cumrew
Newbiggin
Croglin
Ayle
Alston
Waverton
Red Dial
Westward
Rosley
Raughton Head
Welton
Stockdalewath
Low Hesket
Southwaite
High Hesket
Aiketgate
Armathwaite
Ainstable
Ruckcroft
Scale Houses
Renwick
Bayles
Gilderdale Forest
Leadgate
Nenthead
Ivegill
Low Braithwaite
Sebergham
Staffield
Kirkoswald
Lazonby
Garrigill
Sowerby Row
Calthwaite
Boltongate
Torpenhow
Ireby
Caldbeck
Hesket Newmarket
Hutton End
Plumpton
Great Salkeld
Little Salkeld
Glassonby
Gamblesby
Melmerby
Uldale
Branthwaite
Lamonby
Skelton
New Rent
Plumpton Head
Langwathby
Winskill
Hunsonby
Ousby
Skirwith
Kirkland
Blencarn
Milburn Forest
Bewaldeth
Hutton Roof
Mosedale
Mungrisdale
Johnby
Blencow
Catterlen
Newton Reigny
Edenhall
Bassenthwaite
Skiddaw Forest
Greystoke
Newbiggin
PENRITH
Culgaith
Milburn
Dufton Fell
Penruddock
Stainton
Dacre
Hutton
Tirril
Clifton
Temple Sowerby
Knock
Dufton
Scales
Threlkeld
KESWICK
Braithwaite
Stair
Thornthwaite
Matterdale End
Wreay
Pooley Bridge
Askham
Hackthorpe
Melkinthorpe
Cliburn
Morland
Great Strickland
Kirkby Thore
Long Marton
Brampton
Crackenthorpe
APPLEBY
Bolton
Kings Meaburn
Colby
Murton
Hilton
Lune Forest
Dockray
Helton
Whale
Newby
Little Strickland
Sleagill
Bampton
Rosgill
Great Ormside
Sandford
Little Town
Grange
Glenridding
Ullswater
Maulds Meaburn
Bassenthwaite Lake
Derwent Water
Thirlmere
Kielder Water
River Eden
River Eamont
River Tees
River Teviot
Liddel Water
Black Esk Reservoir
Catcleugh Reservoir
Greenlee Lough
1564 EWESLESS KNOWE
1996 CAULDCLEUCH HEAD
1865 TODHOPE HILL
1088 DINNINGS HILL
1809 OH ME EDGE
1729 RAVENS KNOWE
1303 EARL'S SEAT
1478 CALKIN RIG
1484 BLACK EDGE
1684 GLENDHU HILL
921 EARSHAW HILL
1615 BLACK KNOWE
2249 HOUND HILL
2930 CROSS FELL
2329 KNOTT
3054 SKIDDAW
2847 SADDLEBACK OR BLENCATHRA
723
992
2446
1996 HIGH SEAT
2201 LOADPOT HILL
NT
NY
A7
A6088
A68
A74
A75
A69
A689
A686
A595
A591
A66
A6
A592
A5091
B6399
B709
B723
B7068
B6318
B6357
B6264
B5307
B5299
B5305
B5288
B6412
B6413
B6277
B5292
B5322
B6263
M6

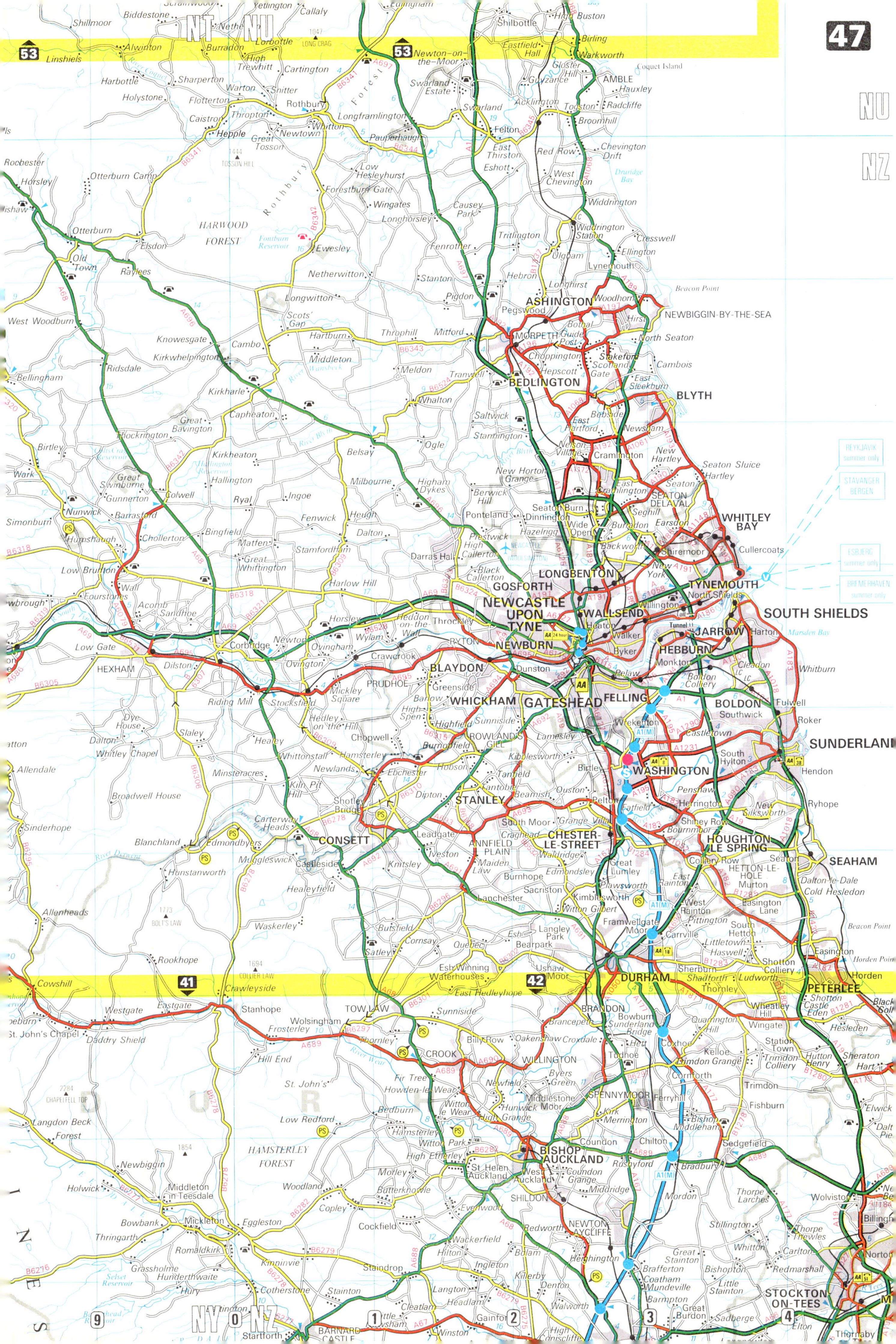

53
Linshiels
Alwinton
NT
NU
Rothbury
ASHINGTON
NEWBIGGIN-BY-THE-SEA
MORPETH
BEDLINGTON
BLYTH
Cramlington
WHITLEY BAY
TYNEMOUTH
SOUTH SHIELDS
LONGBENTON
GOSFORTH
NEWCASTLE UPON TYNE
WALLSEND
JARROW
HEBBURN
NEWBURN
BLAYDON
WHICKHAM
GATESHEAD
FELLING
BOLDON
SUNDERLAND
WASHINGTON
STANLEY
CONSETT
CHESTER-LE-STREET
HOUGHTON LE SPRING
SEAHAM
HEXHAM
Corbridge
PRUDHOE
DURHAM
PETERLEE
41
42
Stanhope
CROOK
WILLINGTON
SPENNYMOOR
BISHOP AUCKLAND
SHILDON
NEWTON AYCLIFFE
STOCKTON ON-TEES
BARNARD CASTLE
Middleton in Teesdale
HAMSTERLEY FOREST
HARWOOD FOREST
NY
NZ
1
2
3
4
9

48

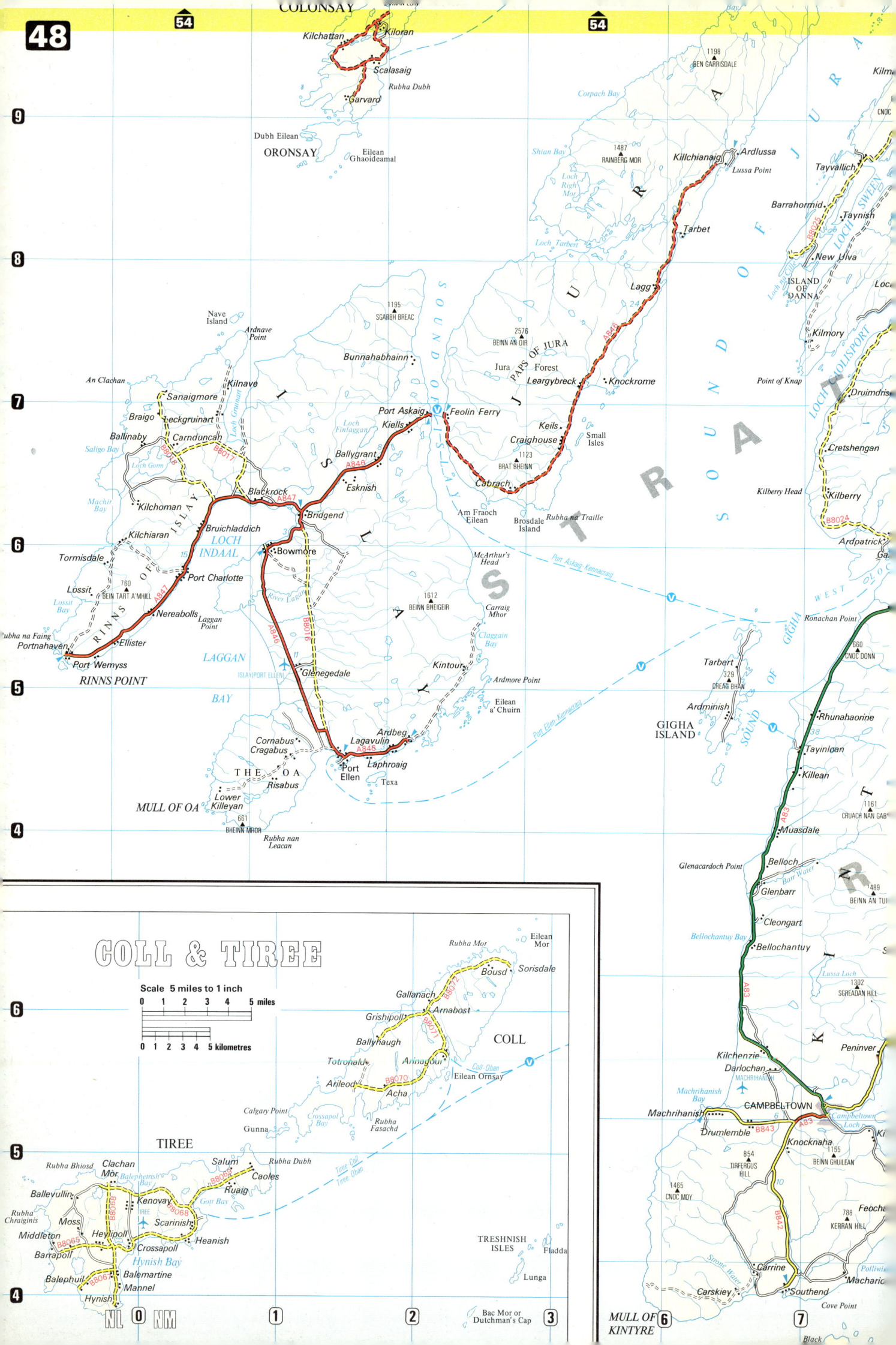

COLONSAY
Kilchattan · Kiloran
Scalasaig
Garvard
Rubha Dubh

ORONSAY
Dubh Eilean
Eilean Ghaoideamal

Corpach Bay
1198
BEN GARRISDALE
Shian Bay
1487
RAINBERG MOR
Killchianaig · Ardlussa
Lussa Point
Tayvallich
Barrahormid
Taynish
Loch Tarben
New Ulva
ISLAND OF DANNA
Lagg
Kilmory
Point of Knap
Druimdris

Nave Island
Ardnave Point
1195
SGARBH BREAC
2576
BEINN AN OIR
PAPS OF JURA Forest
Leargybreck
Knockrome
Cretshengan

An Clachan · Kilnave
Sanaigmore
Braigo · Leckgruinart
Ballinaby · Carnduncah
Saligo Bay
Loch Gorm
B8018
Loch Gruinart
Bunnahabhainn
Port Askaig · Feolin Ferry
Kiells
Ballygrant
Esknish
Keils
Craighouse
Small Isles
1123
BRAT BHEINN
Cabrach
Kilberry Head
Kilberry
B8024
Ardpatrick

Machir Bay
Kilchoman
Blackrock
A847
Bridgend
Bruichladdich
LOCH INDAAL
Bowmore
Am Fraoch Eilean
Brosdale Island
Rubha na Traille

Tormisdale
Lossit
Lossit Bay
760 BEIN TART A'MHILL
Port Charlotte
RINNS OF ISLAY
Nereabolls
Ellister
Portnahaven · Port Wemyss
RINNS POINT
Laggan Point
River Laggan
B8016
A846
I S L A Y
1612
BEINN BHEIGEIR
McArthur's Head
Port Askaig-Kennacraig
Carraig Mhor
Claggain Bay
Kintour
Ardmore Point
Eilean a' Chuirn
Tarbert
329 CREAG BHAN
Ardminish
GIGHA ISLAND
Ronachan Point
660 CNOC DONN

LAGGAN BAY
ISLAY PORT ELLEN
Glenegedale
Cornabus Cragabus
THE OA
Risabus
MULL OF OA
Lower Killeyan
661 BHEINN MHOR
Rubha nan Leacan
Lagavulin · Ardbeg
Port Ellen · Laphroaig
Texa
Port Ellen-Kennacraig
Rhunahaorine
Tayinloan
Killean
1161 CRUACH NAN GAB
Muasdale
Glenacardoch Point
Belloch
Barr Water
Glenbarr
1489 BEINN AN TUI
Cleongart
Bellochantuy Bay
Bellochantuy

COLL & TIREE
Scale 5 miles to 1 inch
0 1 2 3 4 5 miles
0 1 2 3 4 5 kilometres

Rubha Mor · Eilean Mor
Bousd · Sorisdale
Gallanach
Grishipoll · Arnabost
B8071
Ballyhaugh
COLL
Totronald · Arinagour
Arileod · Acha
Eilean Ornsay
B8070
Calf of Oban
Calgary Point
Gunna
Crossapol Bay
Rubha Fasachd
Tiree-Coll
Tiree-Oban

TIREE
Rubha Bhiosd · Clachan Mor
Balephetrish Bay
Salum · Rubha Dubh
Caoles
Ballevullin
Kenovay
B8068
Ruaig
Moss
Scarinish
Gott Bay
Rubha Chraiginis
Middleton · Heylipoll
B8069
Crossapoll
Heanish
Barrapoll
Balephuil · Balemartine
Hynish Bay
Mannel
Hynish

TRESHNISH ISLES
Fladda
Lunga
Bac Mor or Dutchman's Cap

Lussa Loch
1302 SGREADAN HILL
Peninver
Kilchenzie · Darlochan
Machrihanish
Machrihanish Bay
CAMPBELTOWN
Campbeltown Loch
Drumlemble
B843
Knocknaha
854 TIRFERGUS HILL
1155 BEINN GHUILEAN
1465 CNOC MOY
788 KERRAN HILL
Feocha
Carrine
Carskiey
MULL OF KINTYRE
Southend
Cove Point

54
55
NR NS
MINARD
Tullochgorm
Kilmichael
Bridgend
Cairnbaan
Lochgair
Asknish
LOCHGILPHEAD
Carrick
Port Ann
Castleton
Ardrishaig
Lephinmore
Dunans
Conchra
1666
CRUACH AN LOCHAIN
GLENBRANTER
BEINN BHEULA
LOCH ECK
FOREST
Largiemore
Otter Ferry
Clachan of Glendaruel
Balliemore
1972
SGORACH MOR
2178
BEINN RUADH
Ardentinny
BENMORE FOREST
Kilmun
Strone
HOLY LOCH
Clachaig
Sandbank
Ardnadam
Hunters Quay
Kirn
DUNOON
GOUROCK
GREENOCK
PORT GLASGOW
1044
CRUACH BRENFIELD
1530
1503
CRUACH NAN CAORACH
2005
CRUACH NAN CAPULL
Kilfinan
Kilfinan Bay
1488
BEINN BHREAC
Achahoish
Erines
1843
SLIABH GAOIL
Melldalloch
Port Driseach
Tighnabruich
Colintraive
Altgaltraig
Kames
Millhouse
Portavadie
KYLES OF BUTE
LOCH STRIVEN
Bullwood
1057
BEINN RUADH
Dunan
Innellan
Toward
Toward Point
913
WINDY HILL
680
CNOC NA CARRAIGE
St Colmac
Port Bannatyne
Bogany Point
ROTHESAY
Ascog
Kerrycroy
Upper Scoulag
Straad
Ardlamont Point
Tarbert
West Tarbert
Rhu
1383
CNOC A' BHAILE SHIOS
Kennacraig
Whitehouse
1612
CNOC NA MEINE
Glenrisdell
Skipness
Skipness Point
Claonaig
INCHMARNOCK
Ardscalpsie Point
Kingarth
Kilchattan Bay
Kilchattan
Garroch
GREAT CUMBRAE ISLAND
MILLPORT
LITTLE CUMBRAE ISLAND
The Tan
Fairlie Roads
886
FUAR LARACH
SOUND OF BUTE
Cock of Arran
Crossaig
Lochranza
Catacol
1057
TORR NEAD AN EOIN
Mid Thundergay
Mid Sannox
Corrie
Pirnmill
Cour
Sunadale
Grogport
Imachar
2868
GOAT FELL
ISLAND OF ARRAN
Balliekine
749
BEINN LOCHAIN
Dougurie
Carradale
Carradale Point
Machrie Bay
Auchagallon
Glencloy
Brodick
Brodick Bay
Strathwhillan
Clauchlands Point
Tormore
1649
BEINN BHREAC
Ballymichael
Lamlash
Lamlash Bay
Margnaheglish
HOLY ISLAND
Torbeg
Shiskine
Drumadoon Point
Drumadoon Bay
Blackwaterfoot
Kilpatrick
Kingscross
1503
TIGHVEIN
Knockenkelly
Whiting Bay
Brown Head
737
CNOC REAMHAR
Bennecarrigan
Largymore
Largybeg
Dippin
Dippin Head
Sliddery
Lagg
Kilmory
Torrylin
Kildonan
Bennan Head
Sound of Pladda
Pladda
Ugadale
KILBRANNAN SOUND
FIRTH OF CLYDE
CLYDE REGION
Brodick-Ardrossan
Portincaple
Garelochhead
2339
BEINN CHAORACH
Strone
Coulport
Shandon
Rahane
Ardpeaton
Clynder
Rosneath
COVE
KILCREGGAN
Rhu
HELENSBURGH
Craigendoran
Luss
Inchlonaig
Aldochlay
Inchmurrin
Arden
Balloch
Alexandria
Renton
Cardross
Colgrain
Jamestown
Bonhill
Bellsmyre
Larkfield
Braeside
Inverkip
Gryfe Reservoirs
Bardrainney
Langbank
Garvock
Kilmacolm
Bishopton
Wemyss Bay
Upper Skelmorlie
Skelmorlie
Bridge of Weir
Quarrier's Homes
Ranfurly
Brookfield
Kilbarchan
Knock Castle
Routenburn
LARGS
1586
IRISH LAW
Lochwinnoch
Howwood
Whitehill
Fairlie
Kilbirnie
Beith
Gateside
Glengarnock
Barrmill
The Den
Highfield
Drakemyre
Burnhouse
Portencross
West Kilbride
Dalry
Seamill
Auchentiber
Dalgarven
KILWINNING
Montgreenan
ARDROSSAN
SALTCOATS
STEVENSTON
Cunninghamhead
IRVINE
Knockentiber
Springside
Dreghorn
Crosshouse
Drybridge
Gatehead
Irvine Bay
Dundonald
Barassie
Bogend
TROON
Symington
Rosemount
Monkton
PRESTWICK
New Prestwick
St Quivox
Whitletts
AYR
Wallacetown
Belston
Doonfoot
Heads of Ayr
Alloway
Doonholm
Fisherton
Dunure
Culroy
Dalrymple
Sauchrie
Drumshang
Minishant
Knoweside
Culzean Bay
Maidenhead Bay
Maidens
MAYBOLE
Kirkmichael
Kirkoswald
Turnberry
Turnberry Bay
Crosshill
Straiton
DOUGLAS Summer only
50
44
8
9
NR 0 NS
1
2
3
4

55
56
44
45
49
ROWARDENNAN FOREST
LOCH LOMOND
CENTRAL
KILPATRICK HILLS
CAMPSIE FELLS
Kilsyth Hills
CARRON VALLEY FOREST
Carron Valley Reservoir
STRATHCLYDE
WHITELEE FOREST
Kyle Forest
LOWTHER HILLS
BRIDGE OF ALLAN
ALVA
TILLICOULTRY
STIRLING
Cambuskenneth
Tullibody
ALLOA
St. Ninians
Bannockburn
Plean
Cowie
DUNIPACE
Larbert
Stenhousemuir
FALKIRK
Denny
Bonnybridge
Grangemouth
KILSYTH
CUMBERNAULD
Croy
Condorrat
Kippen
Arnprior
Buchlyvie
Gargunnock
Balfron
Killearn
Fintry
Drymen
Gartmore
Dalmary
Luss
Aldochlay
Balmaha
Milton
Buchanan Smithy
Gartocharn
Croftamie
Arden
HELENSBURGH
Craigendoran
Balloch
Jamestown
Bonhill
Alexandria
Renton
Cardross
GREENOCK
PORT GLASGOW
DUMBARTON
Bowling
Duntocher
Old Kilpatrick
Langbank
Bishopton
ERSKINE
Inchinnan
RENFREW
CLYDEBANK
Yoker
MILNGAVIE
BEARSDEN
Drumchapel
Blanefield
Strathblane
Lennoxtown
Milton of Campsie
Torrance
Balmore
Bardowie
Bishopbriggs
Lenzie
KIRKINTILLOCH
Auchinloch
Stepps
Lumloch
Muirhead
Moodiesburn
Chryston
Gartcosh
Glenboig
Annathill
Riggend
Greengairs
Longriggend
Slamannan
Avonbridge
Caldercruix
Plains
Airdriehill
AIRDRIE
Coatdyke
Calderbank
Chapelhall
Salsburgh
Kirk of Shotts
Shotts
Harthill
Whitburn
GLASGOW
Springburn
Partick
Govan
Pollokshields
Shettleston
Baillieston
RUTHERGLEN
Cathcart
Pollokshaws
Thornliebank
Nitshill
BARRHEAD
Clarkston
Busby
Newton Mearns
Carmunnock
Cambuslang
Flemington
Uddingston
Bothwell
Viewpark
Bellshill
Mossend
Newarthill
New Stevenston
Holytown
Carfin
Cleland
MOTHERWELL
Craigneuk
WISHAW
Waterloo
Overtown
Newmains
Allanton
Stane
Hartwood
COATBRIDGE
Old Monkland
Carmyle
Newton
Stonefield
Blantyre
High Blantyre
Nerston
EAST KILBRIDE
HAMILTON
Meikle Earnock
Quarter
Larkhall
Millheugh
Limekilnburn
Chapelton
Glassford
Strathaven
Stonehouse
Netherburn
Dalserf
Rosebank
Crossford
Braidwood
Carluke
Castlehill
Law
Kirkfieldbank
Hazelbank
Lanark
Sandford
Blackwood
Kirkmuirhill
Auchenheath
Brocketsbrae
Lesmahagow
Auchlochan
Stockbriggs
Coalburn
Braehead
Happendon
Douglas
Douglas Water
Uddington
Rigside
Glespin
Glenbuck
Carmacoup
Muirkirk
Smallburn
Netherwood
Kames
Crawfordjohn
Abington
Leadhills
Wanlockhead
Fingland
Kirkland
Kirkconnell
Sanquhar
Crawick
Mennock
Kilmacolm
Bridge of Weir
Quarrier's Homes
Houston
Ranfurly
Brookfield
Kilbarchan
Linwood
PAISLEY
JOHNSTONE
Elderslie
Milliken Park
Howwood
Glenburn
Neilston
Uplawmoor
Lochwinnoch
Kilbirnie
Beith
Gateside
Lugton
Halket
Barrmill
The Den
Highfield
Burnhouse
Dalry
Dunlop
Gabroc Hill
Fullwood
STEWARTON
Kilmaurs
Fenwick
Waterside
Moscow
Eaglesham
Auldhouse
Waterfoot
Netherplace
Thorntonhall
Jackton
Rogerton
KILWINNING
Montgreenan
Cunninghamhead
STEVENSTON
IRVINE
Dreghorn
Springside
Knockentiber
Crosshouse
KILMARNOCK
Hurlford
NEWMILNS
DARVEL
GREENHOLM
GALSTON
Drumclog
Caldermill
Sornhill
Middleyard
Gatehead
Riccarton
Earlston
Shortlees
Dundonald
Barassie
Loans
TROON
Symington
Bogend
Craigie
Rosemount
Monkton
PRESTWICK
New Prestwick
St Quivox
Whitletts
AYR
Wallacetown
Belston
Doonfoot
Alloway
Coylton
Annbank
Mossblown
Tarbolton
Failford
Mauchline
Catrine
Sorn
Auchmillan
Millburn
Mossgiel
Stair
Trabboch
Ochiltree
Auchinleck
Sinclairston
Hillhead
Drongan
HOLMHEAD
CUMNOCK
Netherthird
Lugar
Logan
Cronberry
Dalblair
Limmerhaugh
Skares
Littlemill
Rankinston
Hollybush
Cairnstable
Polnessan
Patna
Dalrymple
Minishant
Culroy
Sauchrie
Fisherton
Doonholm
MAYBOLE
Kirkmichael
Crosshill
Straiton
Waterside
Dalmellington
Dalleagles
Burnside
Bankglen
New Cumnock
Pathhead
Mansfield
Afton Bridge
Doon
Irvine Bay
River Forth
River Carron
River Clyde
River Ayr
River Nith
River Doon
1898 BEINN BHREAC
560 DRUM OF CLASHMORE
2339 BEINN CHAORACH
1678 STRONEND
1897 EARL'S SEAT
1487 TOMTAIN
1084 BALLAGEICH HILL
927 WHITELEE HILL
1099 MILL RIG
1711 NUTBERRY HILL
1286 AUCHENSAUGH HILL
1945 CAIRN TABLE
1675 KIRKLAND HILL
2403 GREEN LOWTHER
1912 THIRSTANE HILL
1522 BENBEOCH
1866 ENOCH HILL
2298 BLACKCRAIG HILL
1029 HARE HILL
M8
M9
M73
M74
M80
M898
A82
A811
A809
A81
A803
A80
A8
A89
A71
A77
A76
A70
A73
A74
A78
A70
A713
A723
A726
A737
A760
A719
A759
A758
A735
A736
B8031
B822
B818
B835
B821
AA 24 hour
1
2
3
4
5
6
7
8
9
3
4
5
6
7
8
9

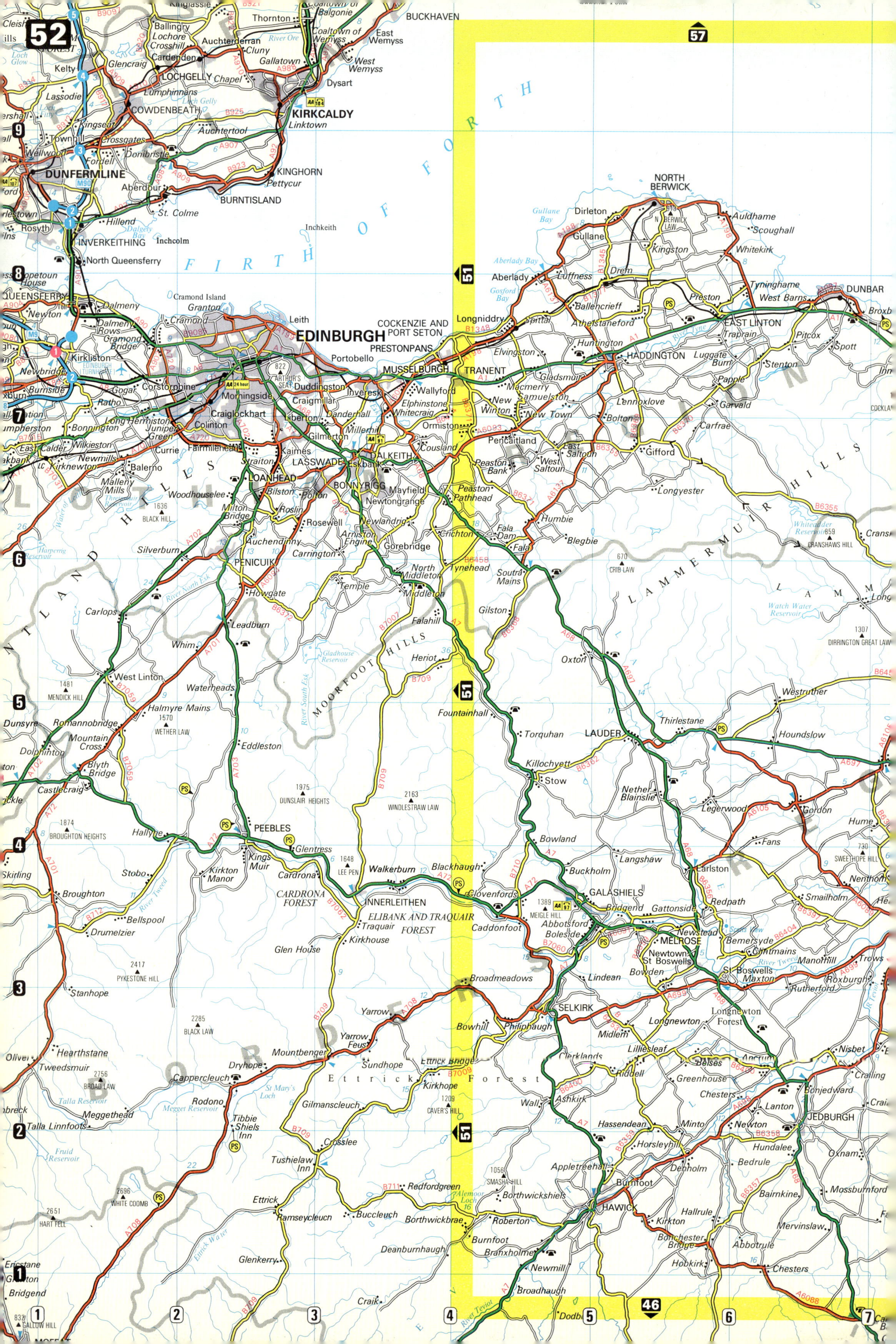
52
57
51
46
BUCKHAVEN
Thornton
Ballingry
Lochore
Crosshill
Auchterderran
Cardenden
Cluny
Coaltown of Balgonie
Coaltown of Wemyss
East Wemyss
West Wemyss
Dysart
Gallatown
Kelty
Glencraig
LOCHGELLY
Chapel
Lumphinnans
Lassodie
COWDENBEATH
KIRKCALDY
Linktown
Kingseat
Auchtertool
Townhill
Crossgates
Wellwood
Donibristle
Fordell
DUNFERMLINE
KINGHORN
Pettycur
Aberdour
BURNTISLAND
St. Colme
Hillend
Rosyth
INVERKEITHING
Inchcolm
Inchkeith
North Queensferry
FIRTH OF FORTH
QUEENSFERRY
Dalmeny
Newton
Cramond Island
Granton
Cramond
Leith
EDINBURGH
Portobello
COCKENZIE AND PORT SETON
PRESTONPANS
Kirkliston
Newbridge
Burnside
Ratho
Gogar
Corstorphine
Morningside
Duddingston
Craigmillar
Craiglockhart
Colinton
Liberton
Inveresk
MUSSELBURGH
TRANENT
Wallyford
Elphinstone
Whitecraig
Dandernall
Millerhill
Ormiston
Gilmerton
DALKEITH
Eskbank
LASSWADE
Kaimes
Fairmilehead
Straiton
LOANHEAD
Bonnington
Long Hermiston
Juniper Green
Currie
Wilkieston
East Calder
Kirknewton
Newmills
Balerno
Malleny Mills
Woodhouselee
Bilston
Roslin
Milton Bridge
BONNYRIGG
Polton
Mayfield
Newtongrange
Rosewell
Newlandrig
Arniston Engine
Gorebridge
Carrington
Auchendinny
PENICUIK
Silverburn
Temple
Howgate
North Middleton
Middleton
Crichton
Tynehead
Carlops
Leadburn
Whim
Falahill
Heriot
MOORFOOT HILLS
PENTLAND HILLS
West Linton
Waterheads
Halmyre Mains
Romannobridge
Mountain Cross
Blyth Bridge
Dolphinton
Castlecraig
Eddleston
Dunsyre
PEEBLES
Glentress
Kings Muir
Kirkton Manor
Cardrona
CARDRONA FOREST
Walkerburn
INNERLEITHEN
ELIBANK AND TRAQUAIR FOREST
Traquair
Kirkhouse
Glen House
Hallyne
Stobo
Broughton
Bellspool
Drumelzier
Stanhope
Hearthstane
Tweedsmuir
Talla Linnfoots
Meggethead
Cappercleuch
Rodono
Dryhope
Tibbie Shiels Inn
Mountbenger
Yarrow
Yarrow Feus
Sundhope
Ettrick Forest
Gilmanscleuch
Crosslee
Tushielaw Inn
Ettrick
Ramseycleuch
Buccleuch
Redfordgreen
Borthwickbrae
Glenkerry
Craik
Deanburnhope
Longniddry
Aberlady
Aberlady Bay
Gosford Bay
Gullane Bay
Dirleton
Gullane
NORTH BERWICK
Auldhame
Scoughall
Whitekirk
Kingston
Drem
Luffness
Ballencrieff
Athelstaneford
Spittal
Preston
Tyninghame
West Barns
DUNBAR
EAST LINTON
Traprain
Pitcox
Spott
Stenton
Luggate Burn
Pappie
HADDINGTON
Huntington
Elvingston
Gladsmuir
Macmerry
Samuelston
New Winton
New Town
Lennoxlove
Bolton
Garvald
Carfrae
Pencaitland
East Saltoun
West Saltoun
Gifford
Peaston Bank
Peaston
Pathhead
Cousland
Longyester
Humbie
Blegbie
Fala Dam
Fala
Soutra Mains
Gilston
LAMMERMUIR HILLS
Oxton
Fountainhall
Torquhan
LAUDER
Thirlestane
Westruther
Houndslow
Killochyett
Stow
Nether Blainslie
Legerwood
Gordon
Hume
Bowland
Langshaw
Earlston
Buckholm
GALASHIELS
Clovenfords
Caddonfoot
Abbotsford
Boleside
Bridgend
Gattonside
Redpath
Smailholm
Newstead
MELROSE
Newtown St Boswells
Bemersyde
Clintmains
Bowden
Lindean
St Boswells
Maxton
Mannerhill
Rutherford
Roxburgh
Broadmeadows
SELKIRK
Bowhill
Philiphaugh
Midlem
Longnewton
Longnewton Forest
Lilliesleaf
Clerklands
Riddell
Belses
Ancrum
Nisbet
Greenhouse
Chesters
Bonjedward
Crailing
Ashkirk
Wall
Lanton
JEDBURGH
Hassendean
Minto
Newton
Horsleyhill
Hundalee
Denholm
Oxnam
Appletreehall
Bedrule
Burnfoot
Bairnkine
Mossburnford
HAWICK
Kirkton
Hallrule
Mervinslaw
Bonchester Bridge
Abbotrule
Hobkirk
Chesters
Borthwickshiels
Roberton
Burnfoot
Branxholme
Newmill
Broadhaugh
Ettrick Bridge
Kirkhope
Gollvlow Hill
Elibank
Edmonstone
Smithfield
River Tweed
River Teviot
Talla Reservoir
Megget Reservoir
Fruid Reservoir
St Mary's Loch
Gladhouse Reservoir
Whiteadder Reservoir
Watch Water Reservoir
1636 BLACK HILL
1481 MENDICK HILL
1570 WETHER LAW
1975 DUNSLAIR HEIGHTS
2163 WINDLESTRAW LAW
1874 BROUGHTON HEIGHTS
1648 LEE PEN
2417 PYKESTONE HILL
2285 BLACK LAW
2756 BROAD LAW
2696 WHITE COOMB
2651 HART FELL
1209 CAVER'S HILL
1056 SMASHA HILL
1389 MEIGLE HILL
670 CRIB LAW
859 CRANSHAWS HILL
1307 DIRRINGTON GREAT LAW
730 SWEETHOPE HILL
832 GALLOW HILL
Ericstane
Bridgend
Olliver
Skirling
1
2
3
4
5
6
7
8
9

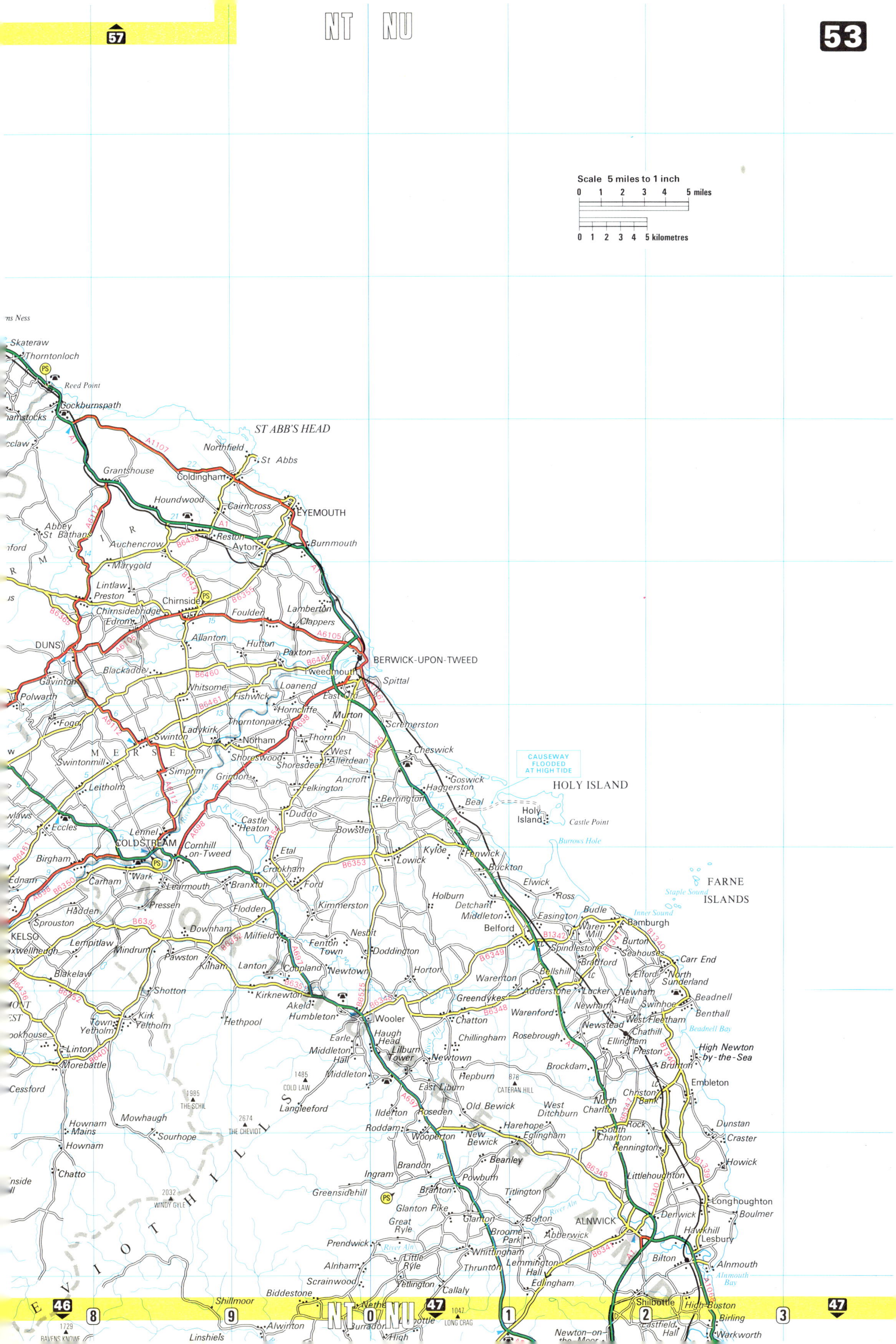
57
NT
NU
Scale 5 miles to 1 inch
0 1 2 3 4 5 miles
0 1 2 3 4 5 kilometres
Skateraw
Thorntonloch
Reed Point
Cockburnspath
ST ABB'S HEAD
Northfield
St Abbs
Grantshouse
Coldingham
Houndwood
Cairncross
EYEMOUTH
Abbey St Bathans
Reston
Auchencrow
Ayton
Burnmouth
Marygold
Lintlaw
Preston
Chirnside
Chirnsidebridge
Edrom
Foulden
Lamberton
Clappers
DUNS
Allanton
Hutton
Paxton
BERWICK-UPON-TWEED
Blackadder
Tweedmouth
Spittal
Gavinton
Whitsome
Loanend
Polwarth
Fishwick
East Ord
Horncliffe
Murton
Fogo
Ladykirk
Thorntonpark
Scremerston
Swinton
Norham
Thornton
Cheswick
Swintonmill
MERSE
Shoreswood
Shoresdean
West Allerdean
Goswick
Simprim
Grindon
Ancroft
Haggerston
CAUSEWAY FLOODED AT HIGH TIDE
HOLY ISLAND
Leitholm
Felkington
Berrington
Beal
Holy Island
Castle Point
Duddo
Eccles
Castle Heaton
Bowsden
Burrows Hole
Lennel
COLDSTREAM
Cornhill on-Tweed
Etal
Kyloe
Fenwick
Birgham
Lowick
Buckton
FARNE ISLANDS
Wark
Crookham
Ednam
Carham
Learmouth
Branxton
Ford
Elwick
Staple Sound
Ross
Holburn
Detchant
Hadden
Pressen
Kimmerston
Middleton
Inner Sound
Flodden
Budle
Sprouston
Easington
Bamburgh
Belford
KELSO
Downham
Milfield
Nesbit
Waren Mill
Burton
Lempitlaw
Mindrum
Fenton Town
Doddington
Spindlestone
Seahouses
Carr End
Pawston
Bradford
Kilham
Lanton
Coupland
Newtown
Horton
Elford
North Sunderland
Blakelaw
Warenton
Bellshill
Adderstone
Lucker
Newham Hall
Beadnell
Shotton
Kirknewton
Greendykes
Newham
Swinhoe
Akeld
Chatton
Warenford
West Fleetham
Benthall
Kirk Yetholm
Town Yetholm
Humbleton
Wooler
Hethpool
Newstead
Chathill
Beadnell Bay
Haugh Head
Chillingham
Rosebrough
Ellingham
Linton
Earle
High Newton -by-the-Sea
Middleton Hall
Lilburn Tower
Newtown
Preston
Morebattle
Brockdam
Brunton
1485 COLD LAW
Middleton
Hepburn
876 CATERAN HILL
Embleton
Cessford
1985 THE SCHIL
East Lilburn
North Charlton
Christon Bank
Langleeford
Old Bewick
West Ditchburn
Ilderton
Roseden
Mowhaugh
2674 THE CHEVIOT
Hownam Mains
Roddam
New Bewick
Harehope
Rock
Dunstan
Sourhope
Wooperton
Eglingham
South Charlton
Craster
Hownam
Rennington
Brandon
Beanley
Howick
Chatto
Ingram
Powburn
Littlehoughton
Greensidehill
Branton
Titlington
Longhoughton
2032 WINDY GYLE
Glanton Pike
Boulmer
Great Ryle
Glanton
Bolton
ALNWICK
Denwick
CHEVIOT HILLS
Broome Park
Abberwick
Hawkhill
Prendwick
River Aln
Lesbury
Whittingham
Bilton
Little Ryle
Lemmington Hall
Alnham
Thrunton
Alnmouth
Alnmouth Bay
Scrainwood
Edlingham
Yetlington
Callaly
Biddlestone
Shillmoor
Shilbottle
High Buston
Alwinton
Netherton
Birling
Linshiels
Burradon
High
1047 LONG CRAG
Newton-on-the-Moor
Eastfield Hall
Warkworth
1729 RAVENS KNOWE
46
47
8
9
0
1
2
3

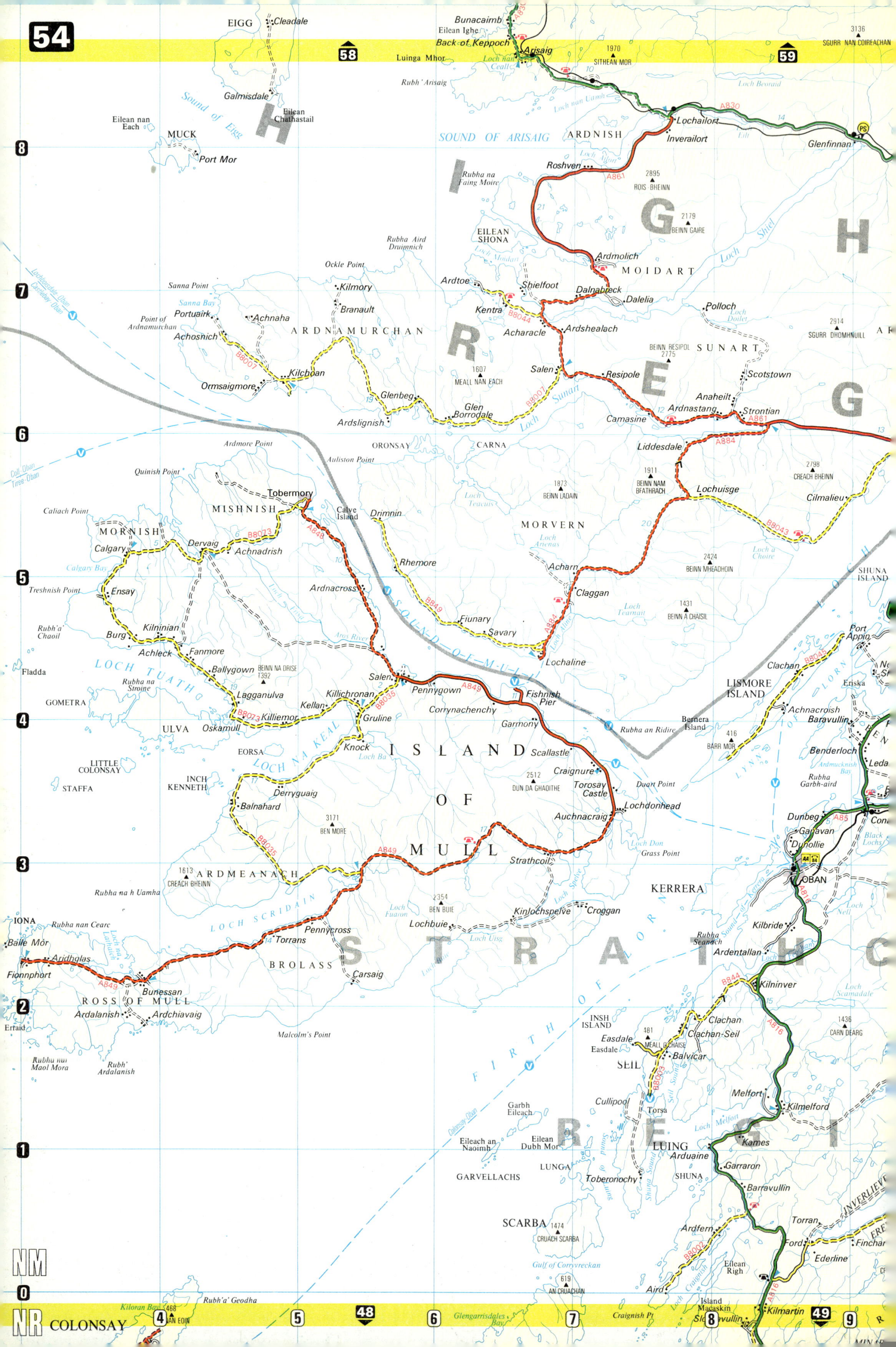

58
59
48
49
EIGG
Cleadale
Bunacaimb
Eilean Ighe
Back of Keppoch
Arisaig
Loch nan Ceall
Luinga Mhor
Rubh' Arisaig
1970
SITHEAN MOR
3136
SGURR NAN COIREACHAN
Loch Beoraid
Loch nan Uamh
A830
Lochailort
Inverailort
Glenfinnan
Galmisdale
Sound of Eigg
Eilean Chathastail
Eilean nan Each
MUCK
Port Mor
SOUND OF ARISAIG
ARDNISH
Roshven
Loch Ailort
A861
Rubha na Faing Moire
2895
ROIS BHEINN
2179
BEINN GAIRE
Loch Shiel
EILEAN SHONA
Loch Moidart
Ardmolich
MOIDART
Rubha Aird Druimnich
Ockle Point
Sanna Point
Sanna Bay
Kilmory
Ardtoe
Shielfoot
Dalnabreck
Dalelia
Point of Ardnamurchan
Portuairk
Achnaha
Branault
Kentra
B8044
Polloch
Loch Doilet
Achosnich
ARDNAMURCHAN
Acharacle
Ardshealach
2914
SGURR DHOMHNUILL
BEINN RESIPOL
2775
SUNART
B8007
Kilchoan
Ormsaigmore
1607
MEALL NAN EACH
Salen
Resipole
Scotstown
Glenbeg
Glen Borrodale
Loch Sunart
Anaheilt
Ardnastang
Strontian
Ardslignish
Camasine
A861
Ardmore Point
ORONSAY
CARNA
Liddesdale
A884
Auliston Point
Quinish Point
1873
BEINN LADAIN
1911
BEINN NAM BHATHRACH
2798
CREACH BHEINN
Lochuisge
Cilmalieu
Loch Teacuis
Tobermory
Caliach Point
MISHNISH
Calve Island
Drimnin
MORVERN
Loch Arienas
B8043
MORNISH
Dervaig
B8073
Achnadrish
Calgary
A848
Calgary Bay
Rhemore
2424
BEINN MHEADHOIN
Loch a' Choire
SHUNA ISLAND
Acharn
Treshnish Point
Ensay
Ardnacross
Claggan
Loch Frisa
SOUND OF MULL
B849
Loch Tearnait
1431
BEINN A' CHAISIL
Rubh' a' Chaoil
Burg
Kilninian
Fiunary
Savary
Port Appin
Achleck
Fanmore
Aros River
Lochaline
Clachan
Fladda
LOCH TUATH
Ballygown
BEINN NA DRISE
1392
Salen
Pennygown
A849
Fishnish Pier
LISMORE ISLAND
Eriska
Rubha na Stroine
GOMETRA
Lagganulva
Kellan
Killichronan
B8035
Corrynachenchy
Achnacroish
Baravullin
Killiemor
Oskamull
ULVA
Gruline
Garmony
Rubha an Ridire
Bernera Island
416
BARR MOR
EORSA
Knock
Loch Ba
ISLAND OF MULL
Scallastle
Benderloch
LITTLE COLONSAY
LOCH NA KEAL
Craignure
Ardmucknish Bay
STAFFA
INCH KENNETH
2512
DUN DA GHAOITHE
Torosay Castle
Duart Point
Rubha Garbh-aird
Derryguaig
Balnahard
Lochdonhead
Auchnacraig
Dunbeg
A85
Ganavan
Dunollie
3171
BEN MORE
Loch Don
Grass Point
Black Lochs
A849
Strathcoil
OBAN
1613
CREACH BHEINN
ARDMEANACH
KERRERA
Rubha na h Uamha
2354
BEN BUIE
Loch Spelve
Loch Feochan
Kilbride
A816
IONA
Rubha nan Cearc
Loch Fuaron
Kinlochspelve
Croggan
LOCH SCRIDAIN
Lochbuie
Loch Uisg
Baile Mòr
Pennycross
Torrans
Loch na Lathaich
Rubha Seanach
Ardentallan
Ardchglas
Fionnphort
BROLASS
Carsaig
FIRTH OF LORN
B844
Kilninver
Loch Scamadale
Bunessan
ROSS OF MULL
Ardalanish
Ardchiavaig
Clachan
1436
CARN DEARG
Erraid
INSH ISLAND
Easdale
481
MEALL A' CHAISE
Clachan-Seil
Malcolm's Point
Balvicar
SEIL
Rubha nan Maol Mora
Rubh' Ardalanish
B8003
Seil Sound
Melfort
Kilmelford
Cullipool
Torsa
Garbh Eileach
Colonsay-Oban
Loch Melfort
Eileach an Naoimh
Eilean Dubh Mor
LUING
Kames
Arduaine
LUNGA
Garraron
GARVELLACHS
Toberonochy
SHUNA
Shuna Sound
Barravullin
Torran
INVERLIEVER
SCARBA
1474
CRUACH SCARBA
Ardfern
Ford
Fincharn
Ederline
B8002
Gulf of Corryvreckan
Eilean Righ
619
AN CRUACHAN
Loch Craignish
Aird
NM
0
NR
Rubh' a' Geodha
Kiloran Bay
468
CARN EOIN
COLONSAY
Glengarrisdale Bay
Craignish Pt
Island Macaskin
Slockavullin
Kilmartin
8
7
6
5
4
3
2
1
4
5
6
7
8
9
HIGHLAND REGION
STRATHCLYDE REGION

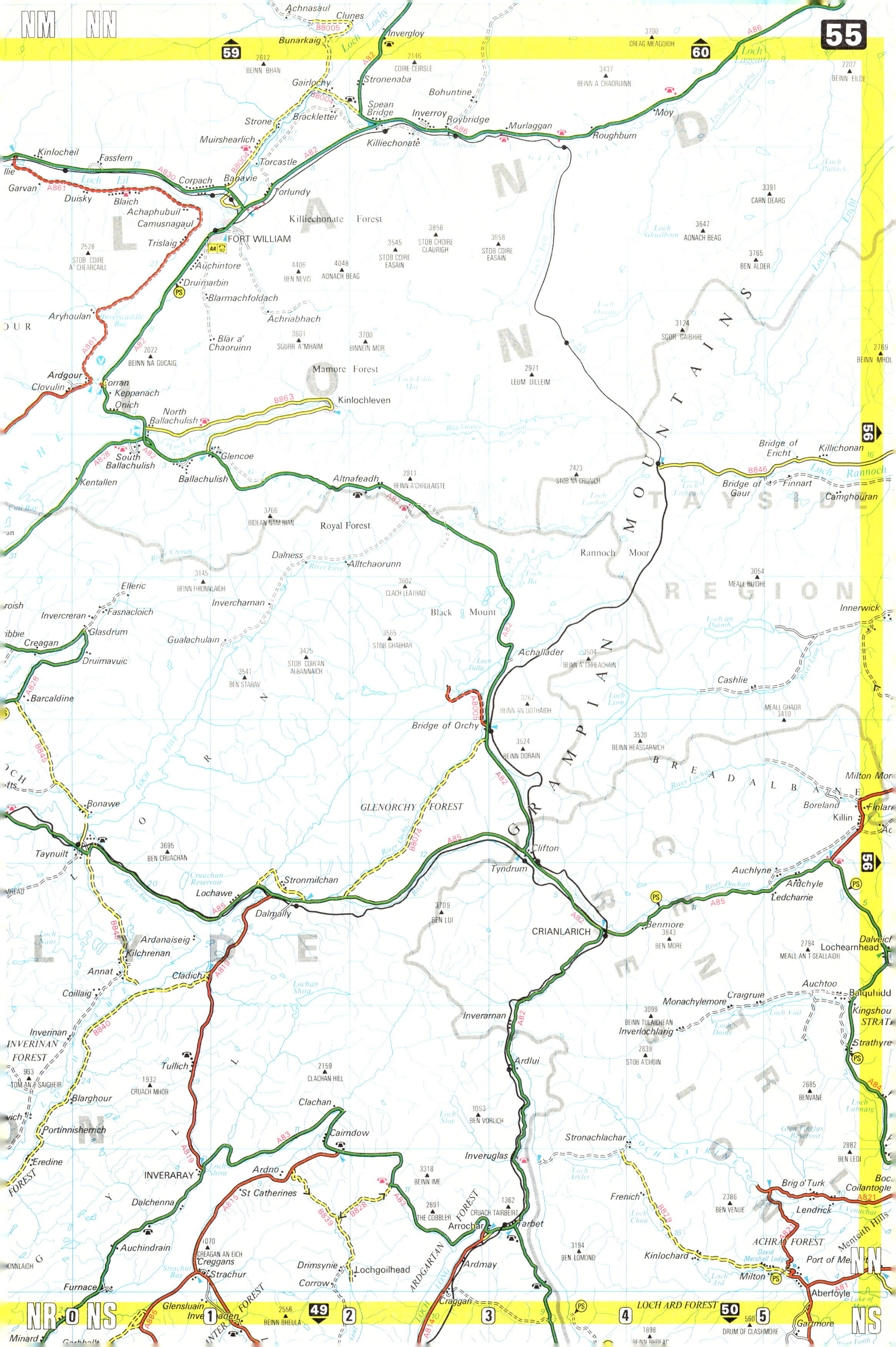
NM
NN
59
60
56
49
50
NR
NS
0
1
2
3
4
5
Achnasaul
Clunes
B8005
Loch Lochy
Invergloy
Bunarkaig
2612
BEINN BHAN
2146
COIRE CEIRSLE
3700
CREAG MEAGOIDH
A86
Loch Laggan
2207
BEINN EILDE
3437
BEINN A CHAORUINN
Gairlochy
Stronenaba
Bohuntine
Spean Bridge
B8004
Brackletter
Strone
Inverroy
Roybridge
Murlaggan
Moy
Roughburn
Muirshearlich
Killiechonate
Kinlocheil
Fassfern
Torcastle
A830
Corpach
Banavie
Loch Eil
Garvan
A861
Duisky
Blaich
Torlundy
Achaphubuil
Camusnagaul
Killiechonate Forest
3391
CARN DEARG
Loch Ghuilbinn
3647
AONACH BEAG
Trislaig
FORT WILLIAM
3856
STOB CHOIRE CLAURIGH
3545
STOB COIRE EASAIN
3658
STOB COIRE EASAIN
3765
BEN ALDER
2528
STOB COIRE A' CHEARCAILL
Auchintore
4406
BEN NEVIS
4048
AONACH BEAG
Druimarbin
Blarmachfoldach
Achriabhach
Aryhoulan
3601
SGURR A' MHAIM
3700
BINNEIN MOR
3124
SGOR GAIBHRE
Blàr a' Chaoruinn
2022
BEINN NA GUCAIG
A82
2769
BEINN MHOL
Mamore Forest
Ardgour
Clovulin
Corran
Keppanach
Onich
2971
LEUM UILLEIM
B863
Kinlochleven
North Ballachulish
Blackwater Reservoir
MOUNTAINS
A828
South Ballachulish
Glencoe
Bridge of Ericht
Killichonan
Kentallen
Ballachulish
Altnafeadh
2911
BEINN A'CHRULAISTE
2423
STOB NA CRUAICH
B846
Loch Rannoch
Bridge of Gaur
Finnart
Camghouran
TAYSIDE
3766
BIDEAN NAM BIAN
Royal Forest
Dalness
Alltchaorunn
Rannoch Moor
3145
BEINN FHIONNLAIDH
3602
CLACH LEATHAD
3054
MEALL BUIDHE
REGION
Elleric
Invercharnan
Invercreran
Fasnacloich
Black Mount
Innerwick
Glasdrum
Creagan
Gualachulain
Achallader
3504
BEINN A' CHREACHAIN
Druimavuic
3425
STOB COIR'AN ALBANNAICH
3565
STOB GHABHAR
3541
BEN STARAV
Cashlie
Loch Tulla
Barcaldine
3267
BEINN AN DOTHAIDH
MEALL GHAOR 3410
A8005
Bridge of Orchy
3524
BEINN DORAIN
3530
BEINN HEASGARNICH
B845
BREADALBANE
GRAMPIAN
Milton Mor
Bonawe
GLENORCHY FOREST
B8074
Boreland
Killin
Finlar
3695
BEN CRUACHAN
Taynuilt
A85
Clifton
Tyndrum
Auchlyne
Ardchyle
Ledcharrie
Cruachan Reservoir
Stronmilchan
Lochawe
Dalmally
3709
BEN LUI
River Dochart
Benmore
CRIANLARICH
3843
BEN MORE
Ardanaiseig
Kilchrenan
2794
MEALL AN T-SEALLAIDH
Lochearnhead
Dalveich
Annat
Cladich
A819
Coillaig
Lochan Shira
Auchtoo
Balquhidd
Monachylemore
Craigruie
Kingshou
Inverarnan
3099
BEINN TULAICHEAN
Inverlochlarig
Loch Voil
Loch Doine
Inverinan
INVERINAN FOREST
2839
STOB A'CHOIN
Strathyre
993
TOM AN T-SAIGHEIR
Tullich
1932
CRUACH MHOR
2159
CLACHAN HILL
Ardlui
2685
BENVANE
Blarghour
Clachan
3093
BEN VORLICH
Loch Sloy
Loch Lubnaig
Portinnisherrich
Cairndow
Stronachlachar
Glen Finglas Reservoir
A83
Eredine
INVERARAY
Loch Shira
Ardno
Inveruglas
Loch Katrine
2882
BEN LEDI
3318
BEINN IME
Loch Arklet
Brig o' Turk
Coilantogle
Dalchenna
St Catherines
B839
B828
2891
THE COBBLER
1362
CRUACH TAIRBEIRT
Frenich
B829
2386
BEN VENUE
A821
Lendrick
Arrochar
Tarbet
ARDGARTAN FOREST
Loch Chon
ACHRAY FOREST
Menteith Hills
Auchindrain
1070
CREAGAN AN EICH
Creggans
Strachur
Drimsynie
Lochgoilhead
Ardmay
3194
BEN LOMOND
Kinlochard
David Marshall Lodge
Port of Me
Corrow
Milton
Loch Ard
Aberfoyle
Furnace
A81
Glensluain
Inverchaden
Craggan
LOCH ARD FOREST
A886
A814
2556
BEINN BHEULA
560
DRUM OF CLASHMORE
1898
BEINN BHREAC
Gartmore
Minard

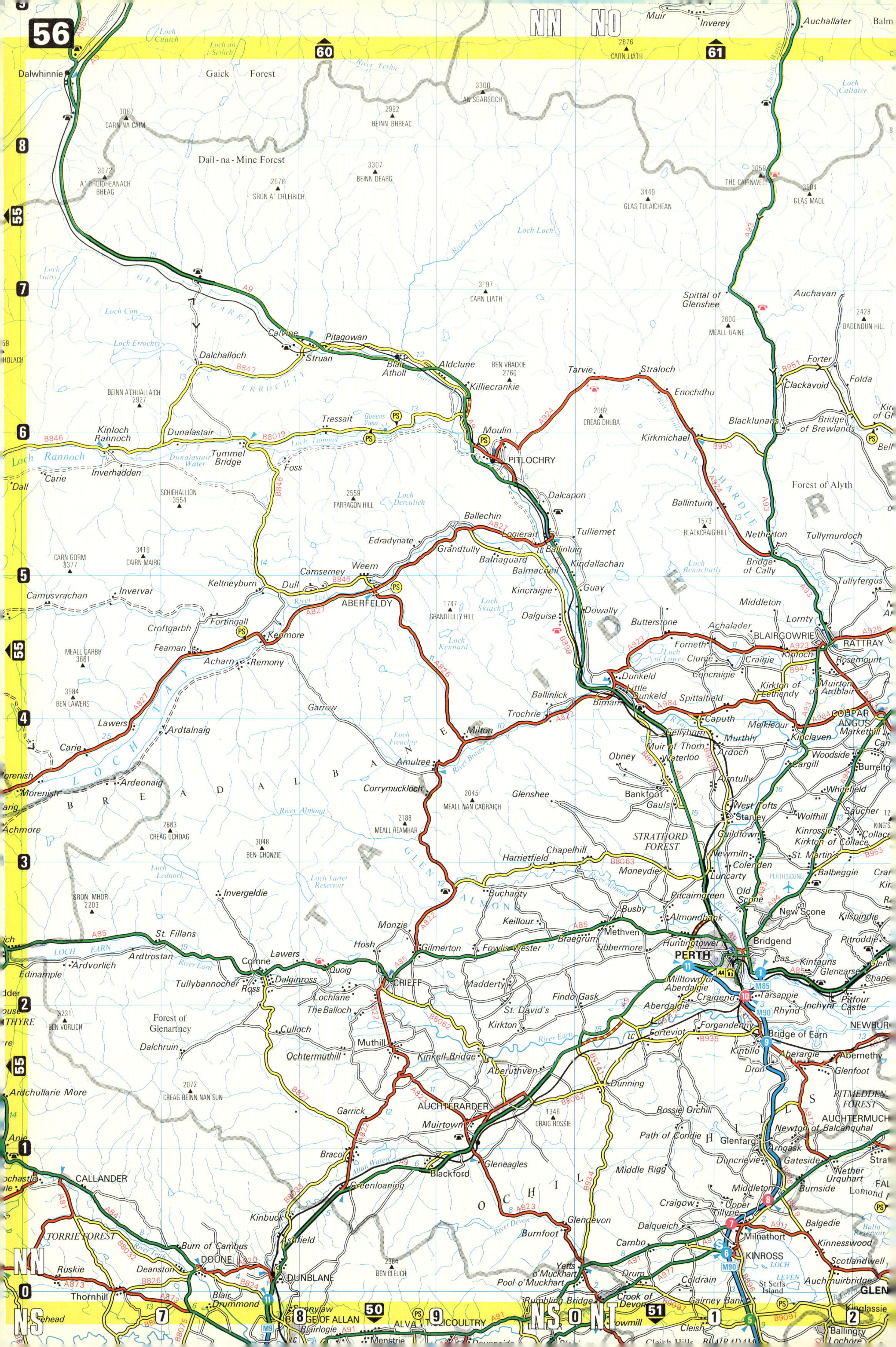
NN
NO
60
61
55
Dalwhinnie
Gaick Forest
Loch Cuaich
Loch an t-Seilich
River Feshie
3300 AN SGARSOCH
2676 CARN LIATH
Muir
Inverey
Auchallater
Balm
Loch Callater
3087 CARN NA CAIM
2992 BEINN BHREAC
Dail-na-Mine Forest
3072 A' BHUIDHEANACH BHEAG
2678 SRON A' CHLEIRICH
3307 BEINN DEARG
3059 THE CAIRNWELL
3504 GLAS MAOL
3449 GLAS TULAICHEAN
Loch Loch
River Tilt
Loch Garry
Loch Con
Loch Errochty
GLEN GARRY
GLEN ERROCHTY
3197 CARN LIATH
Spittal of Glenshee
Auchavan
2600 MEALL UAINE
2428 BADENDUN HILL
Calvine
Pitagowan
Struan
Dalchalloch
Blair Atholl
Aldclune
BEN VRACKIE 2760
Killiecrankie
Tarvie
Straloch
Enochdhu
Forter
Clackavoid
Folda
BEINN A' CHUALLAICH 2927
Tressait
Queens View
2092 CREAG DHUBA
Moulin
PITLOCHRY
Kirkmichael
Blacklunans
Bridge of Brewlands
Kinloch Rannoch
Dunalastair
Loch Tummel
Dunalastair Water
Tummel Bridge
Loch Rannoch
Carie
Inverhadden
Foss
Dall
SCHIEHALLION 3554
2559 FARRAGON HILL
Loch Derculich
Dalcapon
STRATHARDLE
Forest of Alyth
Ballintuim
1573 BLACKCRAIG HILL
Netherton
Tullymurdoch
Ballechin
Logierait
Ballinluig
Tulliemet
Edradynate
Grandtully
Balnaguard
Balmacneil
Kindallachan
CARN GORM 3377
3419 CARN MAIRG
Camserney
Weem
Loch Benachally
Bridge of Cally
Tullyfergus
Camusvrachan
Invervar
Keltneyburn
Dull
ABERFELDY
Kincraigie
Guay
Dowally
Loch Skiach
1747 GRANDTULLY HILL
Middleton
Croftgarbh
Fortingall
Kenmore
River Tay
Dalguise
Butterstone
Achalader
Lornty
BLAIRGOWRIE
RATTRAY
MEALL GARBH 3661
Fearnan
Acharn
Remony
Loch Kennard
Forneth
Loch of Lowes
Clunie
Craigie
Kinloch
Rosemount
3984 BEN LAWERS
Concraigie
Dunkeld
Little Dunkeld
Spittalfield
Kirkton of Lethendy
Muirton of Ardblair
Garrow
Ballinlick
Trochrie
Birnam
Lawers
Ardtalnaig
Milton
Loch Freuchie
Caputh
Meikleour
COUPAR ANGUS
Carie
LOCH TAY
Murthly
Kinclaven
Gellyburn
Muir of Thorn
Waterloo
Ardoch
Obney
Woodside
Burrelton
Amulree
River Braan
Morenish
Ardeonaig
BREADALBANE
Corrymuckloch
Glenshee
Airntully
Cargill
Whitefield
2045 MEALL NAN CADRAICH
Bankfoot
Gauls
West Tofts
Stanley
Wolfhill
Saucher
2883 CREAG UCHDAG
2188 MEALL REAMHAR
River Almond
Achmore
STRATHORD FOREST
Guildtown
Kinrossie
Kirkton of Collace
St. Martins
3048 BEN CHONZIE
GLEN ALMOND
Harrietfield
Chapelhill
Moneydie
Newmiln
Colenden
Luncarty
Balbeggie
Loch Lednock
Loch Turret Reservoir
Buchanty
Pitcairngreen
Old Scone
SRON MHOR 2203
Invergeldie
Keillour
Busby
Almondbank
New Scone
Kilspindie
Monzie
Methven
Braegrum
Huntingtower
Tibbermore
Bridgend
Pitroddie
St. Fillans
LOCH EARN
Ardtrostan
Ardvorlich
Lawers
Comrie
Quoig
Hosh
Gilmerton
Fowlis Wester
PERTH
Kinfauns
Glencarse
Edinample
Tullybannocher
Ross
Dalginross
CRIEFF
Madderty
Milltown of Aberdalgie
Craigend
Tarsappie
Rhynd
Inchyra
Pitfour Castle
Lochlane
The Balloch
Findo Gask
St. David's
Aberdalgie
3231 BEN VORLICH
Forest of Glenartney
Culloch
Kirkton
River Earn
Forteviot
Forgandenny
Bridge of Earn
NEWBURGH
Dalchruin
Muthill
Ochtermuthill
Kinkell Bridge
Aberuthven
Kintillo
Aberargie
Abernethy
Dron
Glenfoot
Ardchullarie More
2072 CREAG BEINN NAN EUN
Dunning
PITMEDDEN FOREST
Garrick
AUCHTERARDER
1346 CRAIG ROSSIE
Rossie Ochill
AUCHTERMUCHTY
Muirtown
Path of Condie
Glenfarg
Newton of Balcanquhal
Braco
Arngask
Gateside
Strathmiglo
Allan Water
Gleneagles
Duncrievie
Nether Urquhart
Blackford
OCHIL HILLS
Middle Rigg
Middleton
Burnside
Falkland
CALLANDER
Greenloaning
Craigow
Upper Tillyrie
Lomond
TORRIE FOREST
Kinbuck
River Devon
Glendevon
Dalqueich
Milnathort
Balgedie
Burnfoot
Ashfield
Carnbo
KINROSS
Kinnesswood
Burn of Cambus
DOUNE
2384 BEN CLEUCH
Drum
Loch Leven
Scotlandwell
Ruskie
Deanston
River Teith
Yetts o'Muckhart
Pool o'Muckhart
Coldrain
St Serfs Island
Auchmuirbridge
Glenrothes
Thornhill
Blair Drummond
DUNBLANE
Rumbling Bridge
Crook of Devon
Gairney Bank
Kinglassie
NS
NT
50
51
BRIDGE OF ALLAN
ALVA
TILLICOULTRY
Blairlogie
Menstrie
Powmill
Cleish
Ballingry
Lochore

57
61
62
51
52
53
3
4
5
6
7
8
NO
NT
MOUNT KEEN
HILL OF CAT
HILL OF SAUGHS
MOUNT BATTOCK
LEACHIE HILL
CAIRN O' MOUNT
CRUYS
BEN TIRRAN
DRIESH
HILL OF WARREN
FINBRACKS
HILL OF COUTERNACH
HILL OF FINAVON
ARK HILL
Mergie
Rickarton
Kirktown of Fetteresso
STO
Bridge of Dye
Spittal of Glenmuick
Glaslaw
Mains of Dillavaird
Drumlithie
Fiddes
Barras
Glenbervie
Crawt
Auchronie
Tarfside
Cairncross
Auchenblae
Mondynes
Pitforthie
Catterline
Clatterin' Brig
Glensaugh
East Cairnbeg
Brownmuir
Roadside of Kinneff
Fordoun
Parkneuk
Kinneff
Braedownie
Clova
Fasque
Thaneston
Arbuthnott
Allardice
INVERBERVIE
Auchmull
Fettercairn
Dalbog
Meikle Strath
Mains of Thorton
Tulloch
Bervie Bay
Wheen
LAURENCEKIRK
Gourdon
Rottal
Gannochy
Sauchieburn
Edzell
Luthermuir
Benholm
Bridgend
Balfield
Dunlappie
Johnshaven
Runtaleave
Tillyarblet
Pitcarity
Inchbare
Marykirk
Pert
Craigo
Lochside
Milton Ness
St. Cyrus
Glenmoy
Kirkton of Menmuir
Tigerton
Newtonmill
Keithock
Logie Pert
Logie
Morphie
Redheugh
Auchnacree
Belliehill
Mains of Balhall
Easter Lednathie
Glenquiech
Ogil
Trinity
Muirton of Ballochy
Hillside
Little Brechin
West Muir
Horiehaugh
Newmill of Inshewan
Fern
Careston
Dykehead
Kirkhill
Dun
Attithol
Balintore
Pearsie
Cortachy
Memus
Tannadice
BRECHIN
MONTROSE
Netherton
Barnhead
Scurdie Ness
Dykends
Balloch
Murthill
Finavon
Middle Drums
Maryton
Inverquharity
Shielhill
Bonnyton
Ferryden
Kirkton of Kingoldrum
Kinnordy
Northmuir
Oathlaw
Aberlemno
Farnell
Kirkton of Craig
Carcary
Fishtown of Usan
Loch of Lintrathen
Bridgend of Lintrathen
Pitkennedy
KIRRIEMUIR
Westerton
Westmuir
Dubton
Boddin
Lunanhead
Turin
Bolshan
Braehead
Kirkton of Airlie
Mains of Ballindarg
Mosside
Glasterlaw
Lunan
Reswallie
Kinnell
LUNAN BAY
FORFAR
Balgavies
Craigton
Leys of Cossans
Drumgley
Guthrie
Burnside
Inverkeilor
Boysack
Redcastle
Kingsmuir
Pitmuies
Dunnichen
Friockheim
Chapelton
Ruthven
Douglastown
Letham
Lownie Moor
Cauldcots
South Mains
Balhary
Glamis
Craichie
Leysmill
Kirkton
Eassie and Nevay
Thornton
Drunkendub
Meigle
Charleston
Tulloes
Colliston
Leitfie
Foffarty
Mosston
Marywell
Balkeerie
Milton
Whigstreet
Redford
Kirkinch
Gateside
Greystone
Auchmithie
St. Vigeans
Kirkbuddo
Wester Denoon
Carmyllie
Newbigging
Nether Handwick
Denhead of Arbirlot
The Deil's Heid
Gallowfauld
Hayhillock
ARBROATH
Newtyle
Arbirlot
Bonnington
Wormiehills
Smiddy
Keillor
Kirkton of Auchterhouse
Kirkton of Tealing
Balgray
Monikie
Kirkton of Monikie
Salmond's Muir
Bonnyton
North Kingennie
Craigton
Muirdrum
Leys
Auchterhouse
Newbigging
Leoch
East March
Bucklerheads
Lundie
Pitcur
Newbigging
Dronley
Kirkton of Strathmartine
Kellas
Panbride
Muirhead
Birkhill
Drumsturdy
Barry
Littleton
Feus
Burnside of Duntrune
CARNOUSTIE
Fowlis
Liff
AA 24 hour
Downfield
Douglas and Angus
Mains of Ardestie
Knapp
Benvie
Denhead of Gray
Lochee
MONIFIETH
Invergowrie
BUDDON NESS
Ballindean
DUNDEE
Broughty Ferry
Longforgan
Kingoodie
Toll
Inchture
Scotscraig
TAYPORT
DUNDEE (RIVERSIDE PARK)
NEWPORT-ON-TAY
Wormit
Grange
Woodhaven
TENTSMUIR FOREST
Kirkton
Balmerino
Bottomcraig
FIRTH OF TAY
Errol
Gauldry
Carrick
Hazelton Walls
Creich
Lucklawhill
Leuchars
Kilmany
Brunton
Balmullo
ST ANDREWS BAY
Rathillet
Logie
Guardbridge
Luthrie
Glenduckie
Moonzie
Kincaple
Lindores
Dunbog
Dairsie or Osnaburgh
AA
ST. ANDREWS
Strathkinness
Fernie
Kemback
Blebocraigs
Letham
Monimail
CUPAR
Boarhills
Denhead
Prior Muir
Cupar Muir
Collessie
Pitscottie
Bridgend
Kingsbarns
Bow of Fife
Springfield
Ceres
Baldinnie
Cameron Reservoir
Stravithie
Kinlock
Prior
Dunino
LADYBANK
Craigrothie
Dunshelt
Pitlessie
Radernie
Peat Inn
Kingsmuir
Balcomie
FIFE NESS
Kingskettle
Balmalcolm
New Gilston
Lathones
CRAIL
Kettlebridge
Largoward
Lochty Private Railway
Backmuir of New Gilston
Bonnybank
Freuchie
Montrave
Carnbee
Arncroach
Langdyke
Wester Newburn
KILRENNY
Muirhead
Star
Kirkton of Largo
Colinsburgh
Lundin Links
Kennoway
Abercrombie
ANSTRUTHER
Cadham
Lower Largo
Drumeldrie
PITTENWEEM
MARKINCH
Balcurvie
LEVEN
Kilconquhar
ST. MONANS
Innerleven
LARGO BAY
Milton of Balgonie
Windygates
ELIE
Coaltown of Balgonie
METHIL
EARLSFERRY
Sauchar Point
Isle of May
Thornton
BUCKHAVEN
Coaltown of
East
A92
A94
A935
A933
A934
A90
A926
A928
A929
A932
A923
A927
A930
A972
A85
A91
A913
A914
A915
A916
A917
A921
A911
B974
B966
B9120
B967
B955
B951
B954
B9134
B957
B9113
B965
B9128
B978
B9127
B961
B945
B946
B939
B940
B9131
B9171
B942
B941
B937
B936
B927
B9130

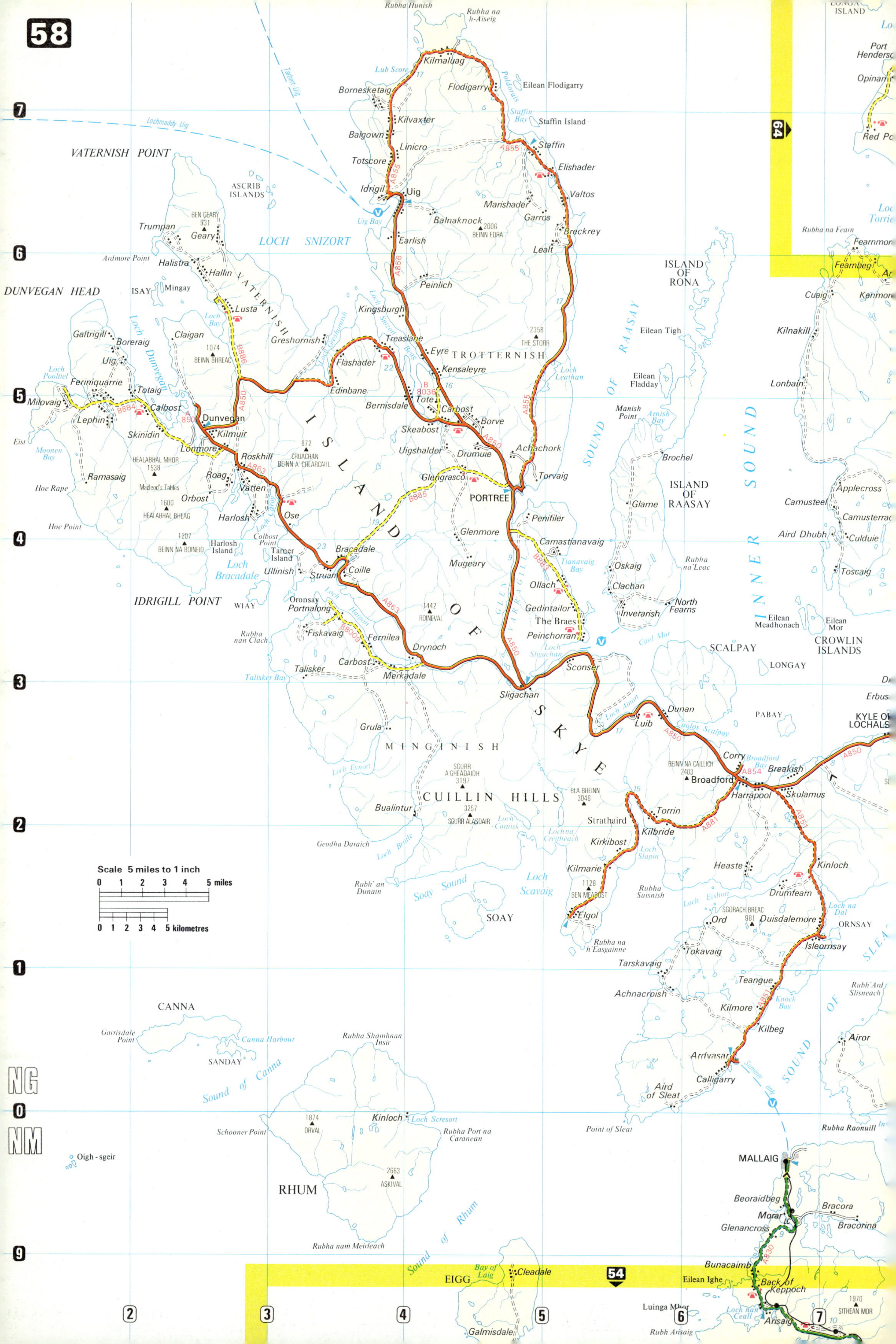
Rubha Hunish
Rubha na h-Aiseig
Kilmaluag
Lub Score
Borneskétaig
Flodigarry
Eilean Flodigarry
Staffin Bay
Staffin Island
Kilvaxter
Balgown
Linicro
Staffin
Totscore
Elishader
Idrigil
Uig
Uig Bay
Valtos
Marishader
Balnaknock
2006 BEINN EDRA
Garros
Brecktrey
Earlish
Lealt
Peinlich
VATERNISH POINT
ASCRIB ISLANDS
BEN GEARY 931
Trumpan
Geary
LOCH SNIZORT
Ardmore Point
Halistra
Hallin
VATERNISH
DUNVEGAN HEAD
ISAY
Mingay
Lusta
Loch Bay
Kingsburgh
Galtrigill
Boreraig
Claigan
Greshornish
Treaslane
1074 BEINN BHREAC
Eyre
TROTTERNISH
2358 THE STORR
Uig
Loch Pooltiel
Feriniquarrie
Flashader
Kensaleyre
Totaig
Edinbane
Milovaig
Calbost
Dunvegan
Bernisdale
Tote
Carbost
Borve
Lephin
Kilmuir
Skeabost
Skinidin
Eist
Moonen Bay
Lonmore
Uigshader
Drumuie
Achachork
Roskhill
872 CRUACHAN BEINN A' CHEARCAILL
HEALABHAL MHOR 1538
Ramasaig
Roag
Glengrasco
Torvaig
Hoe Rape
Macleod's Tables
Vatten
PORTREE
Orbost
1600 HEALABHAL BHEAG
Harlosh
Ose
Penifiler
Hoe Point
Glenmore
1207 BEINN NA BOINEID
Harlosh Island
Colbost Point
Camastianavaig
Tarner Island
Bracadale
Tianavaig Bay
Loch Bracadale
Ullinish
Struan
Coille
Mugeary
Ollach
IDRIGILL POINT
WIAY
Oronsay
Portnalong
1442 ROINEVAL
Gedintailor
The Braes
Fiskavaig
Fernilea
Peinchorran
Rubha nan Clach
Drynoch
Loch Sligachan
Carbost
Talisker
Merkadale
Talisker Bay
Sligachan
Sconser
ISLAND OF SKYE
ISLAND OF RONA
Eilean Tigh
SOUND OF RAASAY
Eilean Fladday
Manish Point
Arnish Bay
Brochel
ISLAND OF RAASAY
Glame
Oskaig
Clachan
Rubha na'Leac
North Fearns
Inverarish
Eilean Meadhonach
Eilean Mor
CROWLIN ISLANDS
SCALPAY
LONGAY
INNER SOUND
Caol Mor
Dunan
Luib
PABAY
Loch Ainort
Caolas Scalpay
KYLE OF LOCHALSH
Grula
MINGINISH
Corry
Broadford Bay
BEINN NA CAILLICH 2403
Broadford
Breakish
Loch Eynort
SGURR A'GHEADAIDH 3197
CUILLIN HILLS
BLA BHEINN 3046
Harrapool
Skulamus
Bualintur
3257 SGURR ALASDAIR
Loch Coruisk
Strathaird
Torrin
Kilbride
Geodha Daraich
Loch Brittle
Loch na Creitheach
Kirkibost
Loch Slapin
Heaste
Kinloch
Kilmarie
Rubh' an Dunain
Soay Sound
Loch Scavaig
1128 BEN MEABOST
Rubha Suisnish
Loch Eishort
Drumfearn
SOAY
SGORACH BREAC 981
Ord
Duisdalemore
Loch na Dal
ORNSAY
Elgol
Rubha na h'Easgainne
Tokavaig
Isleornsay
Tarskavaig
Teangue
Achnacroish
Kilmore
Knock Bay
Kilbeg
Ardvasar
Calligarry
Aird of Sleat
Point of Sleat
CANNA
Garrisdale Point
Canna Harbour
SANDAY
Sound of Canna
Rubha Shamhnan Insir
Kinloch
Loch Scresort
1874 ORVAL
Schooner Point
Rubha Port na Caranean
Oigh-sgeir
2663 ASKIVAL
RHUM
Rubha nam Meirleach
Sound of Rhum
Bay of Laig
Cleadale
EIGG
Galmisdale
Luinga Mhor
Rubh Arisaig
Eilean Ighe
MALLAIG
Beoraidbeg
Morar
Bracora
Glenancross
Bracorina
Bunacaimb
Back of Keppoch
Loch nan Ceall
Arisaig
1970 SITHEAN MOR
Port Henderson
Opinan
Red Point
Loch Torridon
Rubha na Fearn
Fearnmore
Fearnbeg
Cuaig
Kenmore
Kilnakill
Lonbain
Applecross
Camusteel
Camusterrach
Aird Dhubh
Culduie
Toscaig
Erbusaig
Rubh'Ard Slisneach
Airor
Rubha Raonuill
SOUND OF SLEAT
Tarbert Uig
Lochmaddy Uig
A850
A855
A856
A863
A87
B884
B886
B885
B8036
B883
B8009
A881
A851
A830
A854
64
54
7 6 5 4 3 2 1 0 9
2 3 4 5 6 7
NG
NM
Scale 5 miles to 1 inch
0 1 2 3 4 5 miles
0 1 2 3 4 5 kilometres

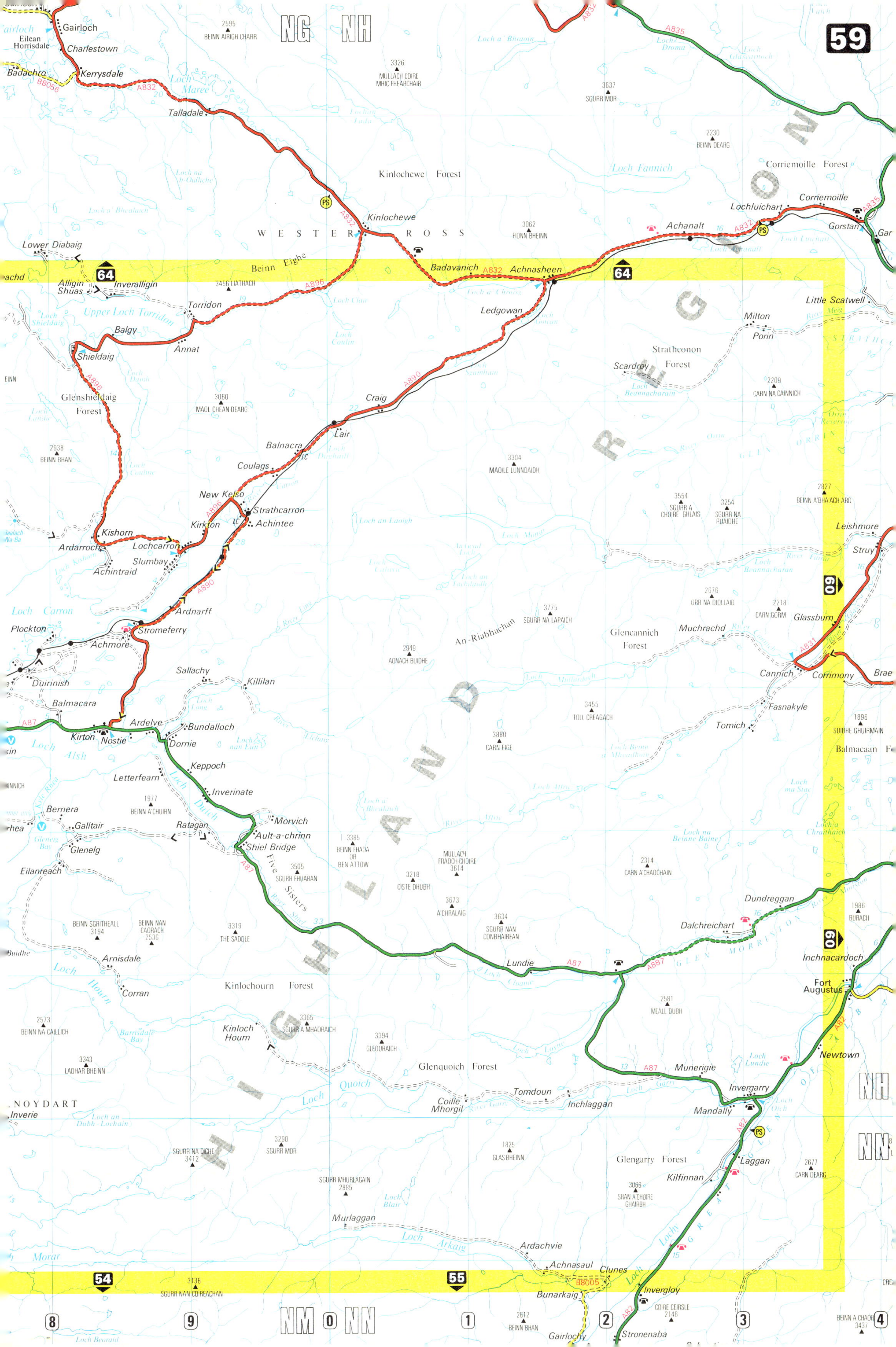
NG NH
Gairloch
Charlestown
Kerrysdale
Badachro
Talladale
Loch Maree
Kinlochewe Forest
Kinlochewe
WESTER ROSS
Lower Diabaig
Beinn Eighe
Alligin Shuas
Inveralligin
Torridon
Upper Loch Torridon
Balgy
Annat
Shieldaig
Glenshieldaig Forest
Badavanich
Achnasheen
Achanalt
Lochluichart
Corriemoille
Corriemoille Forest
Gorstan
Loch Fannich
Ledgowan
Craig
Lair
Balnacra
Coulags
New Kelso
Strathcarron
Achintee
Kirkton
Kishorn
Ardarroch
Lochcarron
Slumbay
Achintraid
Loch Carron
Plockton
Stromeferry
Achmore
Ardnarff
Duirinish
Balmacara
Sallachy
Killilan
Kirkton
Nostie
Ardelve
Bundalloch
Dornie
Keppoch
Letterfearn
Invernate
Bernera
Galltair
Glenelg
Ratagan
Morvich
Ault-a-chrinn
Shiel Bridge
Five Sisters
Eilanreach
Arnisdale
Corran
Loch Hourn
Kinlochourn Forest
Kinloch Hourn
Strathconon Forest
Scardroy
Milton
Porin
Little Scatwell
Leishmore
Struy
Glassburn
Glencannich Forest
Muchrachd
Cannich
Corrimony
Brae
Fasnakyle
Tomich
An-Riabhachan
Lundie
Dalchreichart
Dundreggan
Glen Moriston
Inchnacardoch
Fort Augustus
Newtown
Munerigie
Invergarry
Mandally
Laggan
Kilfinnan
Glenquoich Forest
Tomdoun
Coille Mhorgil
Inchlaggan
Glengarry Forest
Loch Quoich
Loch Arkaig
Murlaggan
Ardachvie
Achnasaul
Clunes
Bunarkaig
Invergloy
Stronenaba
Gairlochy
Knoydart
Inverie
Loch Morar
HIGHLAND REGION
A832 A835 A896 A890 A87 A887 A82 A831 B8056 B8005
3326 MULLACH COIRE MHIC FHEARCHAIR
3637 SGURR MOR
3456 LIATHACH
3060 MAOL CHEAN DEARG
3304 MAOILE LUNNDAIDH
3554 SGURR A CHOIRE GHLAIS
3254 SGURR NA RUAIDHE
3775 SGURR NA LAPAICH
3455 TOLL CREAGACH
3880 CARN EIGE
3385 BEINN FHADA OR BEN ATTOW
3505 SGURR FHUARAN
3614 MULLACH FRAOCH CHOIRE
3673 A'CHRALAIG
3634 SGURR NAN CONBHAIREAN
3365 SGURR A MHAORAICH
3394 GLEOURAICH
NM NN
8 9 0 1 2 3 4
64 60 54 55

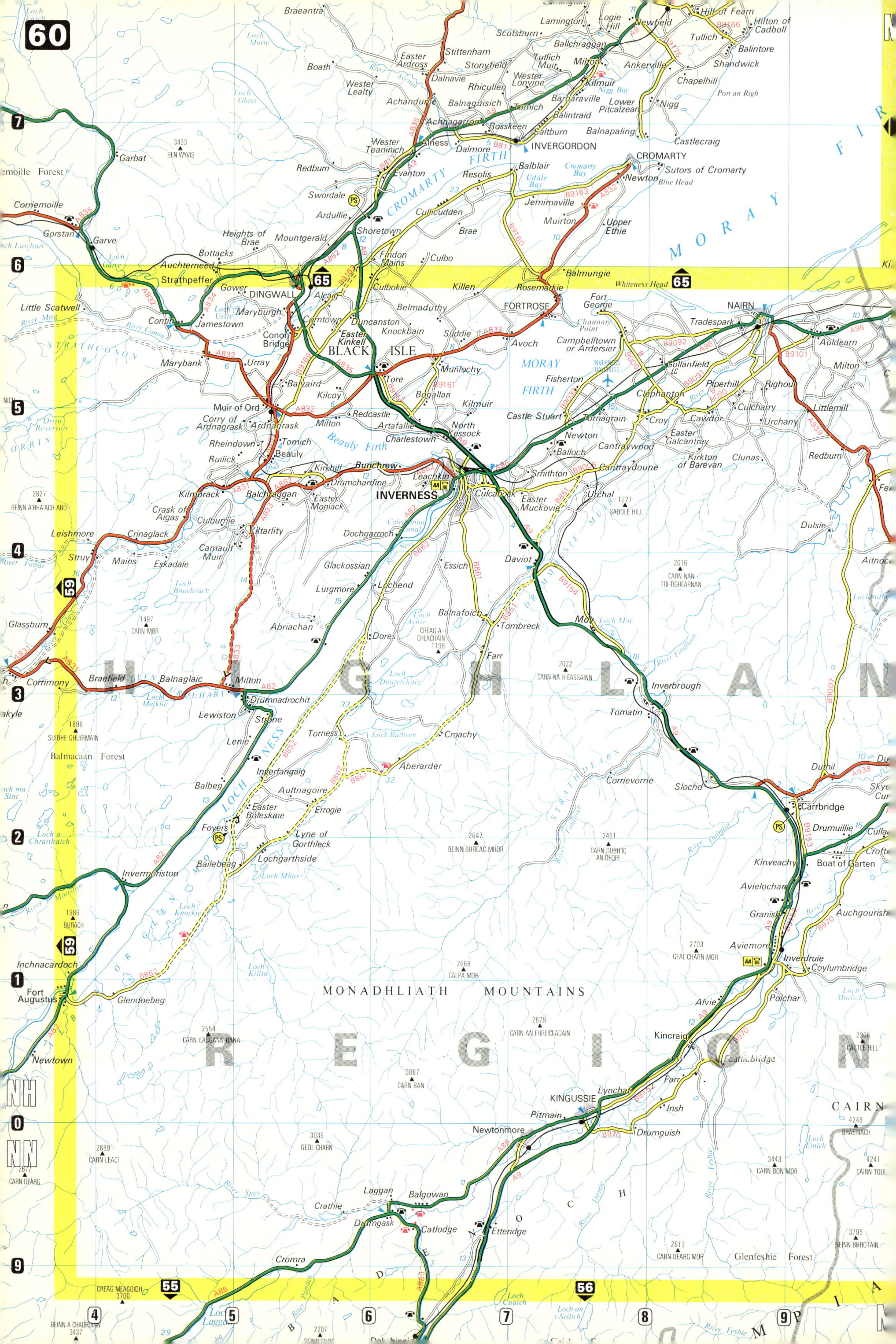

HIGHLAND REGION
MONADHLIATH MOUNTAINS
MORAY FIRTH
CROMARTY FIRTH
BLACK ISLE
Beauly Firth
LOCH NESS
STRATHCONON
STRATH DEARN
INVERNESS
DINGWALL
INVERGORDON
CROMARTY
FORTROSE
NAIRN
KINGUSSIE
Braeantra
Lamington
Logie Hill
Newfield
Hill of Fearn
Hilton of Cadboll
Scotsburn
Tullich
Balintore
Shandwick
Stittenham
Ballchraggan
Easter Ardross
Boath
Stonyfield
Tullich Muir
Milton
Ankerville
Dalnavie
Wester Lonvine
Kilmuir
Chapelhill
Wester Lealty
Rhicullen
Nigg Bay
Port an Righ
Achandunie
Balnaguisich
Barbaraville
Tomich
Lower Pitcalzean
Nigg
Achnagarron
Rosskeen
Balintraid
Saltburn
Balnapaling
Castlecraig
Alness
Wester Teaninich
Dalmore
Garbat
BEN WYVIS 3433
Corriemoille
Gorstan
Garve
Redburn
Evanton
Resolis
Balblair
Cromarty Bay
Udale Bay
Sutors of Cromarty
Newton
Blue Head
Swordale
Jemimaville
Ardullie
Cullicudden
Muirton
Upper Ethie
Shoretown
Brae
Heights of Brae
Mountgerald
Bottacks
Findon Mains
Culbo
Auchterneed
Strathpeffer
Balmungie
Rosemarkie
Whiteness Head
Gower
Alcaig
Culbokie
Killen
Fort George
Little Scatwell
Contin
Jamestown
Maryburgh
Conon Bridge
Corntown
Duncanston
Belmaduthy
Chanonry Point
Tradespark
Easter Kinkell
Knockbain
Suddie
Avoch
Campbelltown or Ardersier
Auldearn
Marybank
Urray
Munlochy
Gollanfield
Milton
Balvaird
Tore
Fisherton
INVERNESS (DALCROSS)
Piperhill
Righoul
Kilcoy
Bogallan
Clephanton
Culcharry
Littlemill
Muir of Ord
Redcastle
Kilmuir
Castle Stuart
Tornagrain
Croy
Cawdor
Urchany
Corry of Ardnagrask
Ardnagrask
Milton
Artafallie
North Kessock
Easter Galcantray
Rheindown
Tomich
Charlestown
Newton
Cantraywood
Beauly
Balloch
Kirkton of Barevan
Clunas
Redburn
Ruilick
Kirkhill
Bunchrew
Leachkin
Smithton
Cantraydoune
Kilmorack
Balchraggan
Drumchardine
Culcabock
Urchal
Easter Moniack
Easter Muckovie
SADDLE HILL 1227
BEINN A'BHA'ACH ARD 2827
Crask of Aigas
Culburnie
Kiltarlity
Dochgarroch
Caledonian Canal
Dulsie
Leishmore
Crinaglack
Camault Muir
Struy
Mains
Eskadale
Glackossian
Essich
Daviot
CARN NAN TRI-TIGHEARNAN 2016
Aitnoch
Lurgmore
Lochend
Loch Bruicheach
Glassburn
CARN MOR 1497
Abriachan
Balnafoich
Tombreck
Moy
Loch Moy
Dores
Loch Ashie
CREAG A CHLACHAIN 1196
Farr
River Findhorn
CARN NA H-EASGAINN 2022
Corrimony
Braefield
Balnaglaic
Milton
Loch Duntelchaig
Inverbrough
Drumnadrochit
Loch Meikle
Lewiston
Strone
Tomatin
SUIDHE GHUIRMAIN 1896
Torness
Loch Ruthven
Croachy
Lenie
Balmacaan Forest
Aberarder
Duthil
Inverfarigaig
Corrievorrie
Slochd
Balbeg
Aultnagoire
Carrbridge
Easter Boleskine
Errogie
Foyers
Lyne of Gorthleck
Drumuillie
BEINN BHREAC MHOR 2647
CARN DUBH 'IC AN DEOIR 2461
Kinveachy
Boat of Garten
Bailebeag
Lochgarthside
Loch Mhor
Invermoriston
Avielochan
BURACH 1986
Loch Knockie
Granish
Auchgourish
River Moriston
GEAL CHARN MOR 2703
Aviemore
Inverdruie
Coylumbridge
CALPA MOR 2668
Inchnacardoch
Loch Killin
Fort Augustus
Glendoebeg
Loch Morlich
Polchar
Alvie
CARN AN FHREICEADAIN 2879
CARN EASGANN BANA 2554
CASTLE HILL 2366
Kincraig
Feshiebridge
Newtown
CARN BAN 3087
Lynchat
Farr
Insh
CAIRN
BRAERIACH 4248
Pitmain
Newtonmore
Drumguish
Loch Einich
GEOL CHARN 3036
CARN LEAC 2889
CARN DEARG
CARN BON MOR 3443
CAIRN TOUL 4241
Laggan
Balgowan
Crathie
River Spey
Drumgask
Catlodge
Etteridge
BEINN BHROTAIN 3795
CARN DEARG MOR 2813
Cromra
Glenfeshie Forest
CREAG MEAGAIDH 3700
Loch Cuaich
Loch an t-Seilich
River Feshie
BEINN A CHAORAINN 3437
NH
NN
55
56
59
65

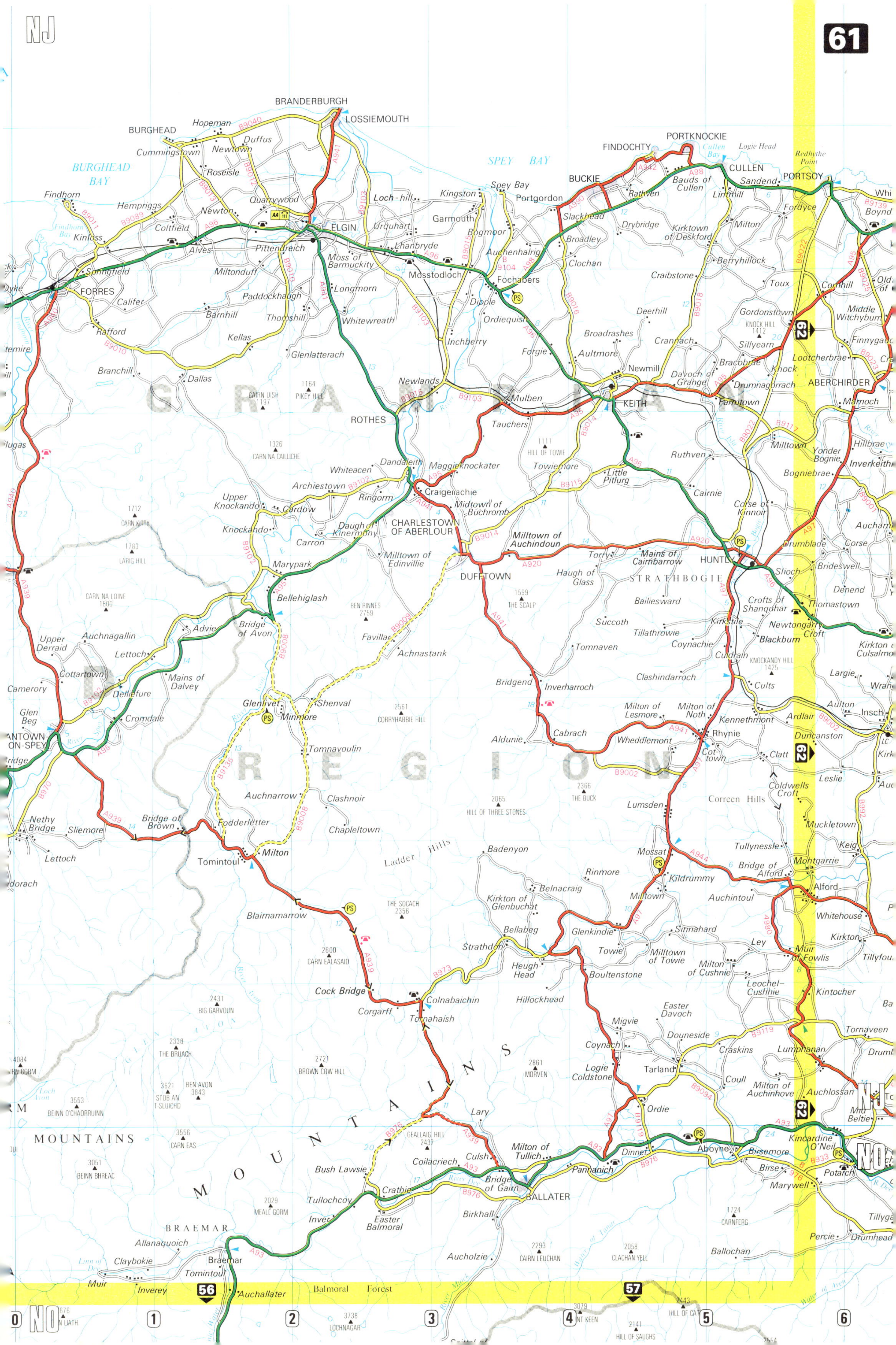
NJ
BRANDERBURGH
LOSSIEMOUTH
BURGHEAD
Hopeman
Duffus
Cummingstown
Newton
BURGHEAD BAY
Roseisle
Findhorn
Hempriggs
Quarrywood
Newton
Coltfield
Kinloss
ELGIN
Alves
Pittendreich
Springfield
Miltonduff
FORRES
Califer
Paddockhaugh
Barnhill
Thornshill
Rafford
Kellas
Branchill
Dallas
Glenlatterach
Longmorn
Whitewreath
Moss of Barmuckity
Lhanbryde
Urquhart
Loch-hill
Kingston
Garmouth
Spey Bay
Portgordon
SPEY BAY
Bogmoor
Auchenhalrig
Mosstodloch
Fochabers
Dipple
Ordiequish
Inchberry
Forgie
Newlands
ROTHES
Mulben
Tauchers
GRAMPIAN
CAIRN UISH 1197
PIKEY HILL 1164
CARN NA CAILLICHE 1326
Dandaleith
Whiteacen
Archiestown
Maggieknockater
Craigellachie
Ringorm
Upper Knockando
Cardow
Knockando
Daugh of Kinermony
CHARLESTOWN OF ABERLOUR
Carron
Midtown of Buchromb
Marypark
Milltown of Edinvillie
Bellehiglash
DUFFTOWN
Milltown of Auchindoun
CARN KITTY 1712
LARIG HILL 1783
CARN NA LOINE 1800
BEN RINNES 2759
THE SCALP 1599
Bridge of Avon
Advie
Upper Derraid
Auchnagallin
Lettoch
Cottartown
Mains of Dalvey
Camerory
Dellefure
Glen Beg
Cromdale
Favillar
Achnastank
Glenlivet
Minmore
Shenval
Tomnavoulin
CORRYHABBIE HILL 2561
Auchnarrow
Clashnoir
Chapeltown
Fodderletter
Bridge of Brown
Tomintoul
Milton
Nethy Bridge
Sliemore
Lettoch
Blairnamarrow
Ladder Hills
CARN EALASAID 2600
THE SOCACH 2356
Cock Bridge
Corgarff
Colnabaichin
Tornahaish
BIG GARVOUN 2431
THE BRUACH 2338
BROWN COW HILL 2721
STOB AN T-SLUICHD 3621
BEN AVON 3843
BEINN A'CHAORAINN 3553
CARN EAS 3556
BEINN BHREAC 3051
MOUNTAINS
CAIRNGORM
MOUNTAINS
BRAEMAR
MEALL GORM 2029
Allanaquoich
Claybokie
Braemar
Tomintoul
Muir
Inverey
Auchallater
Balmoral Forest
LOCHNAGAR 3738
Bush Lawsie
Tullochcoy
Inver
Crathie
Easter Balmoral
Coilacriech
Culsh
Bridge of Gairn
BALLATER
Birkhall
Aucholzie
CAIRN LEUCHAN 2293
CLACHAN YELL 2058
GEALLAIG HILL 2437
Lary
Milton of Tullich
Pannanich
Dinnet
Aboyne
Birsemore
Birse
Marywell
Kincardine O'Neil
Potarch
CAIRNFERG 1724
Ballochan
Percie
Drumhead
Ordie
Tarland
Logie Coldstone
Coynach
Migvie
Douneside
Craskins
Coull
Milton of Auchinhove
Lumphanan
Auchlossan
Easter Davoch
Hillockhead
Heugh-head
Strathdon
Bellabeg
Towie
Glenkindie
Boultenstone
Milltown of Towie
Milton of Cushnie
Leochel-Cushnie
Kintocher
Sinnahard
Ley
Muir of Fowlis
Kirkton of Glenbuchat
Belnacraig
Rinmore
Badenyon
Kildrummy
Milltown
Mossat
Auchintoul
Bridge of Alford
Montgarrie
Alford
Whitehouse
Tullynessle
Muckletown
Lumsden
Correen Hills
HILL OF THREE STONES 2065
THE BUCK 2366
Cabrach
Aldunie
Wheddlemont
Rhynie
Cot-town
Clatt
Kennethmont
Milton of Lesmore
Milton of Noth
Bridgend
Inverharroch
Clashindarroch
Tomnaven
Tillathrowie
Coynachie
Culdrain
KNOCKANDY HILL 1425
Cults
Succoth
Bailiesward
STRATHBOGIE
Haugh of Glass
Torry
Mains of Cairnbarrow
HUNTLY
Kirkstile
Crofts of Shanquhar
Newtongarry Croft
Blackburn
Thomastown
Drumblade
Corse
Slioch
Brideswell
Denend
Corse of Kinnoir
Cairnie
Ruthven
Little Pitlurg
Towiemore
HILL OF TOWIE 1111
KEITH
Newmill
Aultmore
Broadrashes
Crannach
Davoch of Grange
Bracobrae
Knock
Drumnagorrach
Farmtown
Milltown
Yonder Bognie
Bogniebrae
Deerhill
Craibstone
Berryhillock
Kirktown of Deskford
Clochan
Broadley
Drybridge
Slackhead
BUCKIE
Rathven
FINDOCHTY
PORTKNOCKIE
Cullen Bay
Logie Head
Bauds of Cullen
CULLEN
Sandend
Lintmill
Milton
Fordyce
PORTSOY
Redhythe Point
Boyndie
Toux
Cornhill
Gordonstown
KNOCK HILL 1412
Sillyearn
Lootcherbrae
ABERCHIRDER
Marnoch
Hillbrae
Inverkeithny
Auchaber
Largie
Ardlair
Duncanston
Aulton
Insch
Leslie
Coldwells Croft
Keig
Kirkton of Culsalmond
Middle Witchyburn
Finnygaud
Tillyfourie
Tornaveen
Mid Beltie
Tillygarmond
NO
0
1
2
3
4
5
6
56
57
62

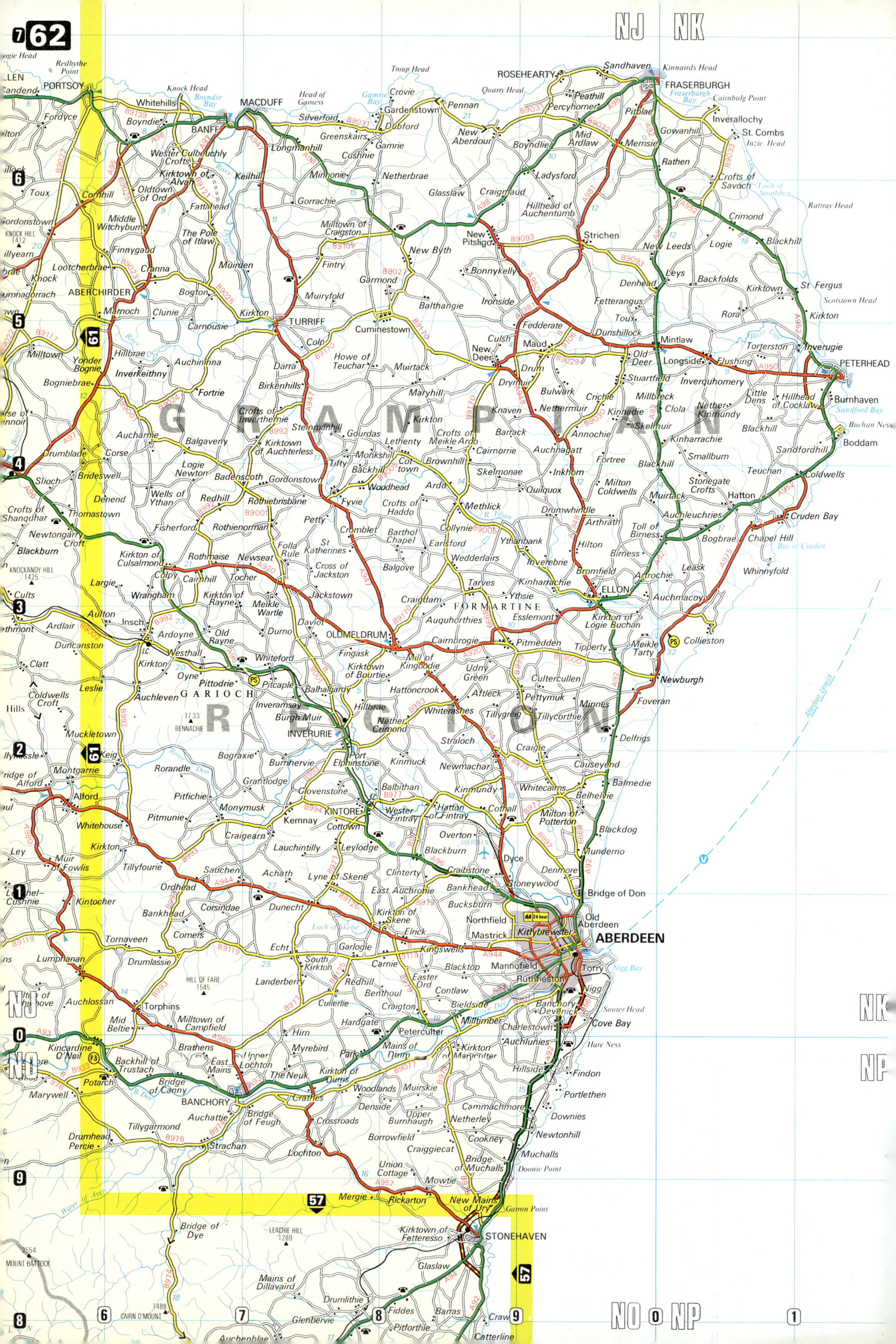
NJ NK
PORTSOY
Redhythe Point
Knock Head
Boyndie Bay
Whitehills
MACDUFF
BANFF
Head of Garness
Gamrie Bay
Troup Head
Crovie
Gardenstown
Pennan
ROSEHEARTY
Quarry Head
Sandhaven
Kinnairds Head
FRASERBURGH
Fraserburgh Bay
Cairnbulg Point
Inverallochy
St. Combs
Inzie Head
Fordyce
Boyndie
Silverford
Dubford
New Aberdour
Boyndlie
Peathill
Percyhorner
Pitblae
Mid Ardlaw
Memsie
Gowanhill
Rathen
Wester Culbeuchly
Crofts
Kirktown of Alvah
Keilhill
Longmanhill
Greenskairs
Cushnie
Gamrie
Minnonie
Netherbrae
Glasslaw
Craigmaud
Ladysford
Crofts of Savoch
Loch of Strathbeg
Rattray Head
Toux
Cornhill
Oldtown of Ord
Fattahead
Gorrachie
Hillhead of Auchentumb
Crimond
Gordonstown
KNOCK HILL 1412
Middle Witchyburn
The Pole of Itlaw
Milltown of Craigston
New Pitsligo
Strichen
Blackhill
Logie
New Leeds
Finnygaud
Fintry
New Byth
Bonnykelly
Denhead
Leys
Backfolds
Kirktown
St Fergus
Scotstown Head
Lootcherbrae
Knock
Cranna
Muirden
Garmond
Ironside
Fetterangus
ABERCHIRDER
Bogton
Muiryfold
Balthangie
Toux
Rora
Kirkton
Marnoch
Clunie
Kirkton
TURRIFF
Cuminestown
Fedderate
Dunshillock
Mintlaw
Inverugie
Carnousie
Colp
Culsh
New Deer
Maud
Old Deer
Longside
Flushing
Torterston
PETERHEAD
Milltown
Yonder Bognie
Hillbrae
Auchininna
Darra
Howe of Teuchar
Muirtack
Drum
Drymuir
Stuartfield
Inverquhomery
Bogniebrae
Inverkeithny
Birkenhills
Bulwark
Crichie
Millbreck
Little Dens
Hillhead of Cocklaw
Burnhaven
Sandford Bay
Buchan Ness
Fortrie
Maryhill
Nethermuir
Kinnadie
Clola
Nether Kinmundy
Boddam
GRAMPIAN
Crofts of Inverthernie
Kirkton
Knaven
Skelmuir
Blackhill
Aucharnie
Steinmanhill
Gourdas
Crofts of Meikle Ardo
Barrack
Annochie
Kinharrachie
Sandfordhill
Balgaveny
Kirktown of Auchterless
Lethenty
Cairnorrie
Auchnagatt
Smallburn
Drumblade
Corse
Logie Newton
Monkshill
Cot-town
Brownhill
Fortree
Blackhill
Slioch
Brideswell
Badenscoth
Gordonstown
Tifty
Backhill
Skelmonae
Inkhorn
Stonegate Crofts
Teuchan
Coldwells
Wells of Ythan
Woodhead
Ardo
Quilquox
Milton of Coldwells
Muirtack
Hatton
Denend
Redhill
Rothiebrisbane
Fyvie
Crofts of Haddo
Methlick
Drumwhindle
Auchleuchries
Cruden Bay
Crofts of Shanquhar
Thomastown
B9001
Petty
Arthrath
Toll of Birness
Newtongarry Croft
Fisherford
Rothienorman
Cromblet
Barthol Chapel
Collynie
Ythanbank
Hilton
Bogbrae
Chapel Hill
Bay of Cruden
Blackburn
Kirkton of Culsalmond
Rothmaise
Newseat
Folla Rule
St Katherines
Earlsford
Birness
KNOCKANDY HILL 1425
Colpy
Cairnhill
Tocher
Cross of Jackston
Balgove
Wedderlairs
Inverebrie
Leask
Whinnyfold
Largie
Bromfield
Artrochie
Cults
Wrangham
Kirkton of Rayne
Meikle Wartle
Jackstown
Tarves
Kinharrachie
ELLON
Auchmacoy
Aulton
Craigdam
Ythsie
FORMARTINE
Ardlair
Insch
Ardoyne
Old Rayne
Durno
Daviot
Auquhorthies
Esslemont
Kirkton of Logie Buchan
Collieston
Duncanston
OLDMELDRUM
Cairnbrogie
Pitmedden
Tipperty
Meikle Tarty
Westhall
Fingask
Mill of Kingoodie
Clatt
Kirkton
Whiteford
Kirktown of Bourtie
Udny Green
Culterculien
Newburgh
Oyne
Pittodrie
Pitcaple
Balhalgardy
Hattoncrook
Leslie
Coldwells Croft
Auchleven
GARIOCH
Inveramsay
Artleck
Pettymuk
Minnes
Foveran
Hills
Hillbrae
Whiterashes
Tillygreig
Tillycorthie
1733 BENNACHIE
REGION
Burgh Muir
Nether Crimond
INVERURIE
Straloch
Delfrigs
Muckletown
Keig
Bograxie
Port Elphinstone
Kinmuck
Newmachar
Craigie
Causeyend
Montgarrie
Rorandle
Burnhervie
Balmedie
Alford
Grantlodge
Balbithan
Kinmundy
Whitecairns
Pitfichie
Clovenstone
Belhelvie
Monymusk
KINTORE
Wester Fintray
Hatton of Fintray
Cothall
Milton of Potterton
Pitmunie
Kemnay
Whitehouse
Cottown
Blackdog
Craigearn
Overton
Ley
Muir of Fowlis
Kirkton
Lauchintilly
Leylodge
Blackburn
Dyce
Munderno
Tillyfourie
Sauchen
Achath
Lyne of Skene
Clinterty
Denmore
Ordhead
Kintocher
Craibstone
Stoneywood
Bridge of Don
Corsindae
Dunecht
East Auchronie
Bankhead
Bankhead
Kirkton of Skene
Bucksburn
Old Aberdeen
Northfield
Tornaveen
Comers
Loch of Skene
Elrick
Mastrick
Kittybrewster
ABERDEEN
Echt
Garlogie
Kingswells
Lumphanan
Drumlassie
South Kirkton
Carnie
Blacktop
Mannofield
Torry
Nigg Bay
HILL OF FARE 1545
Landerberry
Redhill
Easter Ord
Ruthrieston
Benthoul
Contlaw
Nigg
Auchlossan
Torphins
Cullerlie
Craigton
Bieldside
Banchory Devenick
Souter Head
Mid Beltie
Milltown of Campfield
Hirn
Hardgate
Peterculter
Milltimber
Charlestown
Cove Bay
Kincardine O'Neil
Brathens
Myrebird
Park
Mains of Drum
Kirkton of Maryculter
Auchlunies
Hare Ness
Backhill of Trustach
East Mains
Upper Lochton
Hillside
Findon
Potarch
Bridge of Canny
The Neuk
Kirkton of Durris
Marywell
Crathes
Woodlands
Muirskie
Portlethen
BANCHORY
Auchattie
Bridge of Feugh
Denside
Cammachmore
Downies
Crossroads
Upper Burnhaugh
Netherley
Tillygarmond
Newtonhill
Drumhead
Percie
Strachan
Borrowfield
Cookney
Lochton
Craiggiecat
Muchalls
Bridge of Muchalls
Doonie Point
Union Cottage
Mowtie
Water of Aven
Mergie
Rickarton
New Mains of Ury
Garron Point
Bridge of Dye
LEACHIE HILL 1289
Kirktown of Fetteresso
STONEHAVEN
2554 MOUNT BATTOCK
Glaslaw
Mains of Dillavaird
Drumlithie
1488 CAIRN O'MOUNT
Fiddes
Barras
Crawton
Glenbervie
Pitforthie
Auchenblae
Catterline
NO NP
NK
NP
NJ
NO
61
61
57
57
A98
A947
A950
A952
A90
A92
A96
A93
A944
A920
A980
A957
A97
B9001
B9170
B976

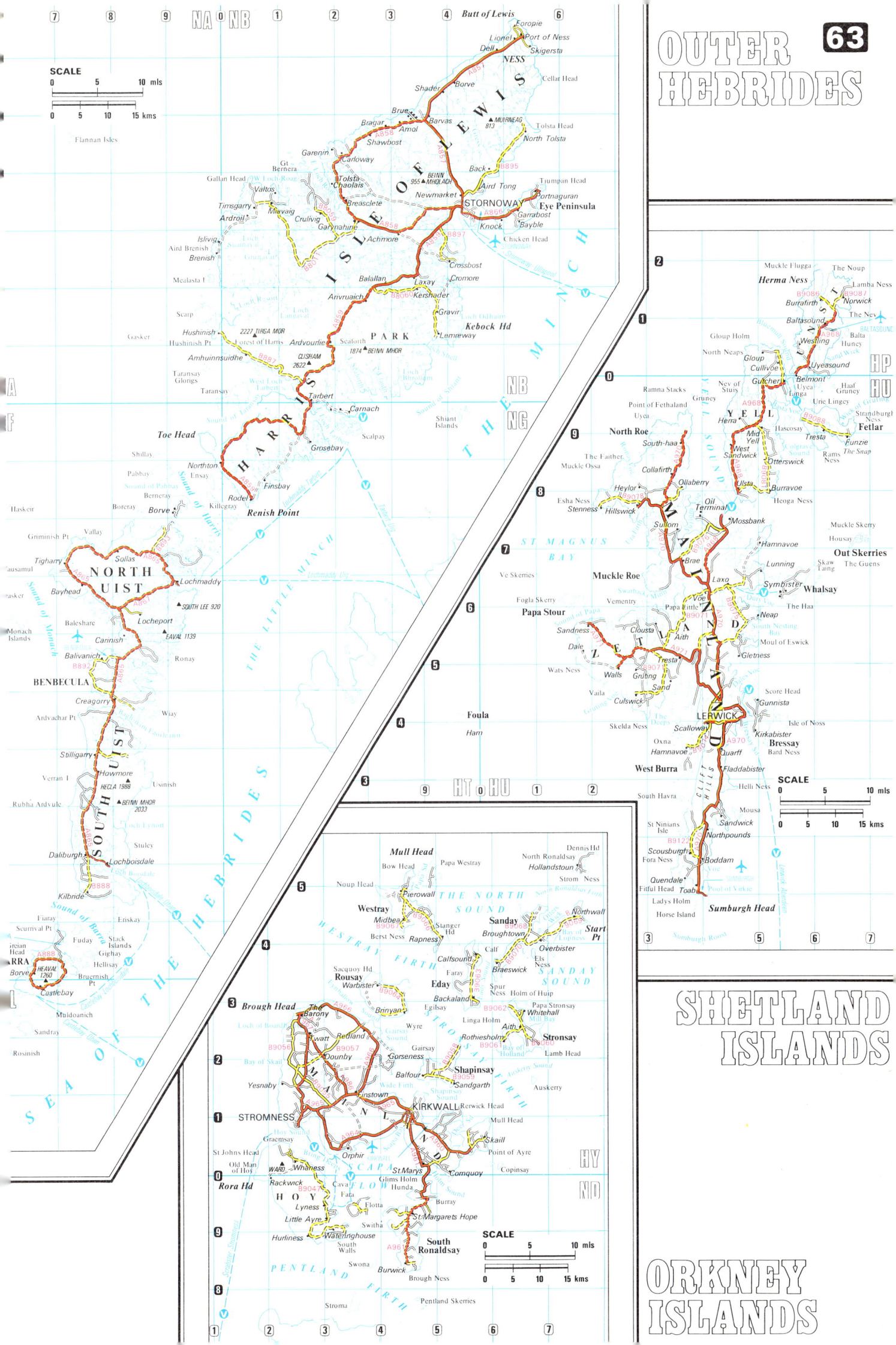

Outer Hebrides / Shetland Islands / Orkney Islands

63

64

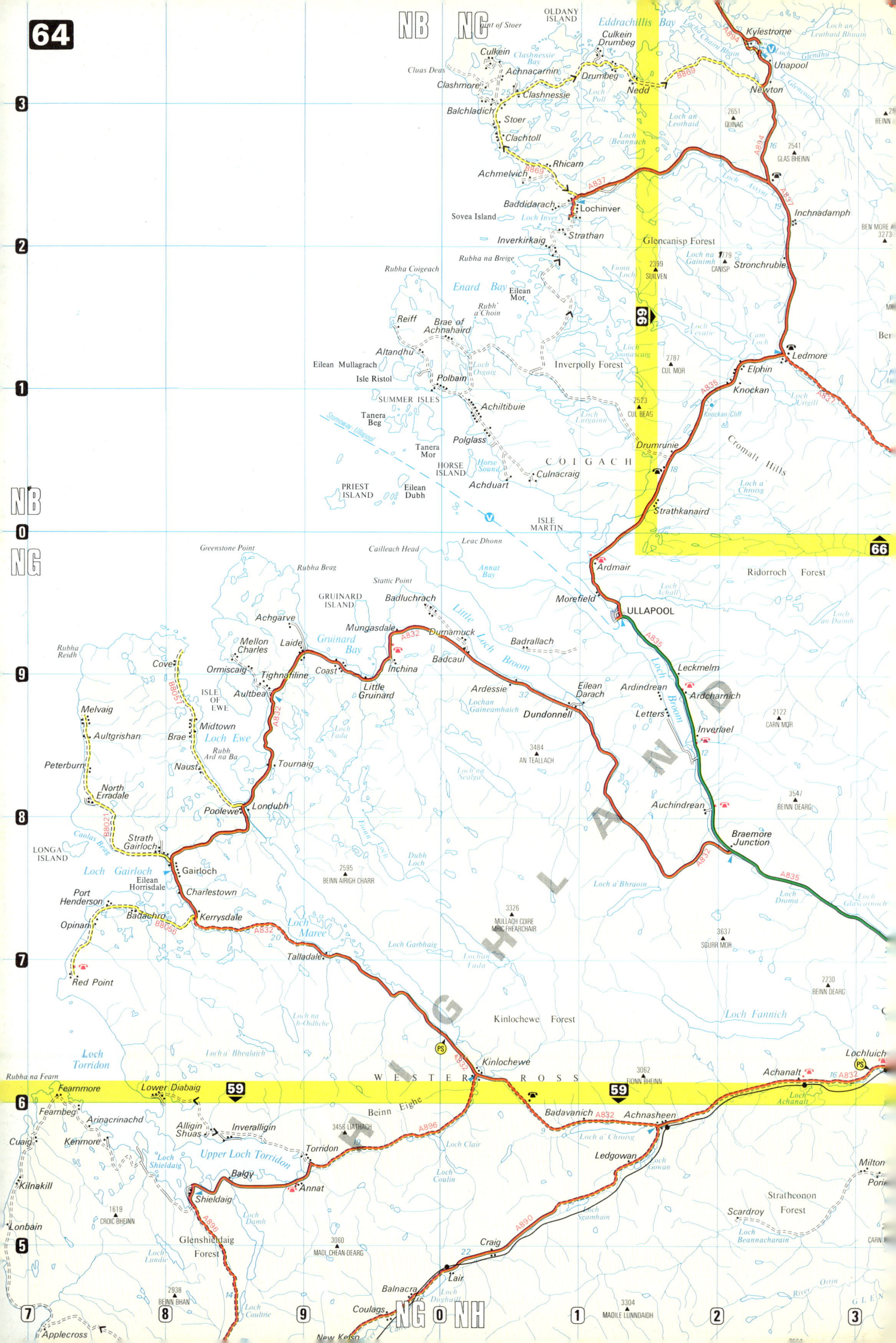

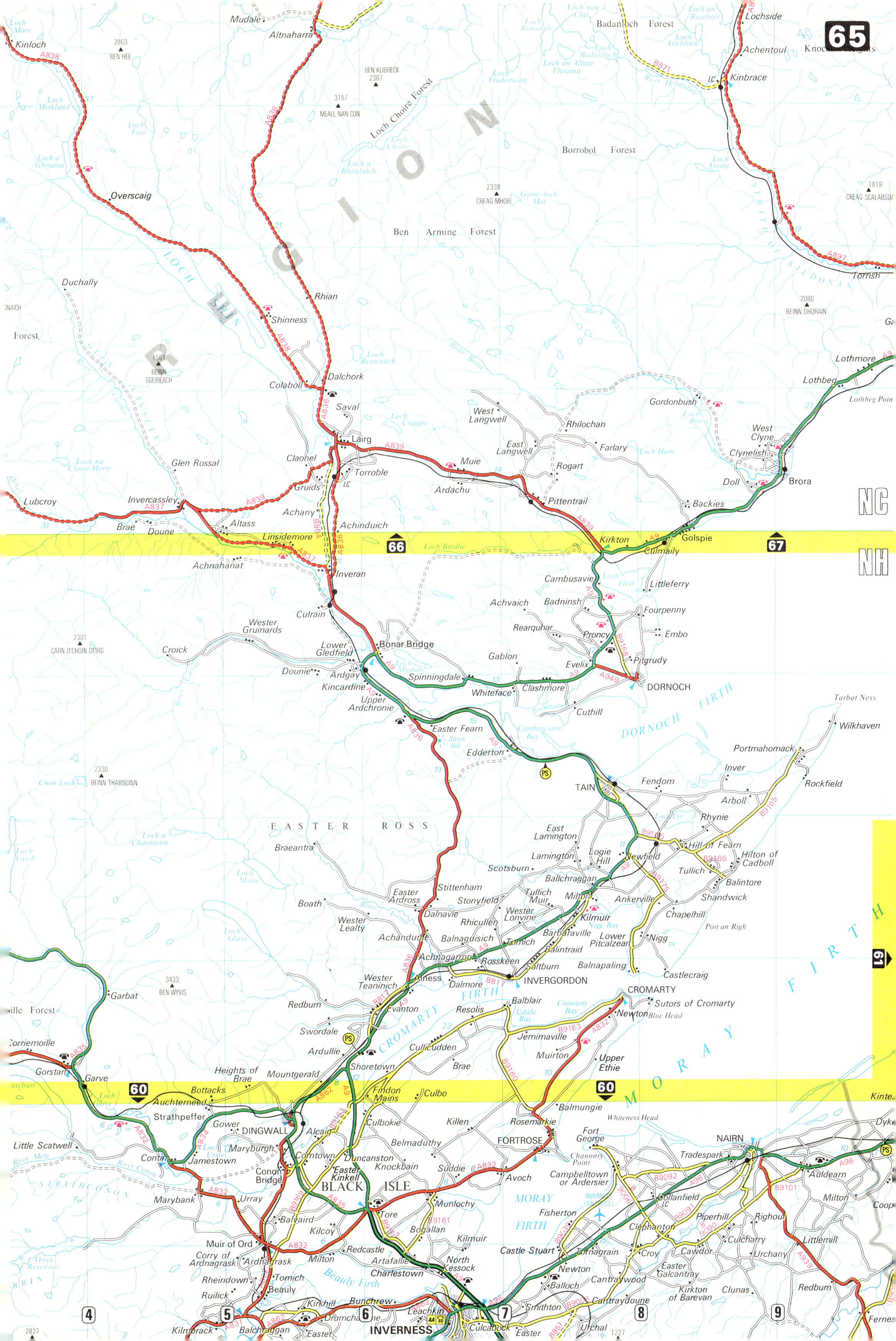
Mudale
Altnaharra
Kinloch
2863
BEN HEE
A838
BEN KLIBRECK
2367
3157
MEALL NAN CON
Loch Choire Forest
Loch More
Loch Merkland
Loch Fiag
Loch a' Ghriama
Loch Choire
Loch a' Bhealaich
REGION
Overscaig
LOCH SHIN
Badanloch Forest
Loch Rimsdale
Loch Badanloch
Loch an Alltan Fhearna
Loch Truderscaig
Lochside
Achentoul
Knockfin Heights
Kinbrace
B871
River Helmsdale
Borrobol Forest
2338
CREAG MHOR
Gorm-loch Mor
Ben Armine Forest
1819
CREAG SCALABSDALE
A897
Torrish
STRATH OF KILDONAN
2060
BEINN DHORAIN
Duchally
Rhian
Shinness
A838
A836
Forest
1561
BEINN SGEIREACH
GLEN CASSLEY
River Cassley
Loch Beannach
Black Water
River Brora
Lothmore
Lothbeg
Lothbeg Point
Colaboll
Dalchork
Saval
Lairg
A839
Gordonbush
Loch Brora
West Langwell
Rhilochan
East Langwell
Farlary
Loch Horn
West Clyne
Clynelish
Brora
Doll
Glen Rossal
Loch na Claise Moire
Claonel
Gruids
Torroble
Muie
Rogart
Ardachu
Pittentrail
Backies
Lubcroy
Invercassley
A837
Brae
Doune
Altass
Achany
Achinduich
B864
Linsidemore
Kirkton
Golspie
Culmaily
66
67
Loch Buidhe
NC
NH
Achnahanat
Inveran
Cambusavie
Loch Fleet
Littleferry
Culrain
Achvaich
Badninsh
Fourpenny
Wester Gruinards
Rearquhar
Proncy
Embo
2301
CARN CHUINNEAG
CARN D'CHOIN DEIRG
Croick
Lower Gledfield
Bonar Bridge
Gablon
Evelix
B9168
Pitgrudy
Dounie
Ardgay
Loch Migdale
Spinningdale
Clashmore
A949
DORNOCH
Kincardine
Whiteface
Cuthill
Upper Ardchronie
DORNOCH FIRTH
Tarbat Ness
Wilkhaven
Easter Fearn
Struie Hill
Edderton
Cambuscurrie Bay
PS
Portmahomack
Inver
Rockfield
2330
BEINN THARSUINN
Crom Loch
TAIN
Fendom
Arboll
Rhynie
EASTER ROSS
Loch a' Chaorainn
Loch Vaich
Braeantra
East Lamington
Lamington
Logie Hill
Newfield
B9165
Hill of Fearn
B9166
Hilton of Cadboll
Tullich
Loch Morie
Scotsburn
Ballchraggan
Balintore
Stittenham
Easter Ardross
Tullich Muir
Milton
Shandwick
Boath
Stonyfield
Ankerville
Dalnavie
Rhicullen
Wester Lonvine
Kilmuir
Chapelhill
Wester Lealty
Nigg Bay
Port an Righ
Loch Glass
Achandunie
Balnaguisich
Tomich
Barbaraville
Lower Pitcalzean
Nigg
Balintraid
Achnagarron
Rosskeen
Saltburn
Balnapaling
Castlecraig
Garbat
3433
BEN WYVIS
Wester Teaninich
Alness
Dalmore
B817
INVERGORDON
CROMARTY
Sutors of Cromarty
Redburn
Evanton
Resolis
Balblair
Udale Bay
Cromarty Bay
Newton
Blue Head
Swordale
CROMARTY FIRTH
Jemimaville
B9163
A832
MORAY FIRTH
Corriemoille
Forest
Gorstan
Ardullie
Cullicudden
Muirton
Upper Ethie
Garve
Heights of Brae
Mountgerald
Shoretown
Brae
B9160
Loch Garve
60
Bottacks
Auchterneed
Findon Mains
Culbo
Balmungie
Kinte
Strathpeffer
Gower
DINGWALL
Alcaig
Culbokie
Killen
Rosemarkie
Whiteness Head
Fort George
Dyke
Little Scatwell
Loch Ussie
Maryburgh
Belmaduthy
FORTROSE
Chanonry Point
NAIRN
Tradespark
A96
River Meig
Contin
Jamestown
River Conon
Conon Bridge
Conon
Duncanston
Easter Kinkell
Knockbain
Suddie
Avoch
Campbelltown or Ardersier
B9092
Auldearn
Milton
B9101
STRATHCONON
Marybank
Urray
BLACK ISLE
Munlochy
MORAY
Gollanfield
B9006
Balvaird
Tore
B9161
Fisherton
INVERNESS (DALCROSS)
Piperhill
Righoul
Coop
Kilcoy
Bogallan
FIRTH
B9039
Clephanton
B9090
B9091
River Nairn
Muir of Ord
Kilmuir
Culcharry
Littlemill
Corry of Ardnagrask
Ardnagrask
Milton
Redcastle
North Kessock
Castle Stuart
Tornagrain
Croy
Cawdor
Urchany
A939
Orrin Reservoir
Artafallie
Newton
Easter Galcantray
Rheindown
Tomich
Charlestown
Beauly Firth
Cantraywood
Kirkton of Barevan
Clunas
Redburn
Ruilick
Beauly
Balloch
Bunchrew
Kirkhill
B9006
Cantraydoune
Smithton
Leachkin
Drumchardine
4
5
6
7
8
9
2827
Kilmorack
A831
Balchraggan
A862
Easter
INVERNESS
Culcabock
Easter
B851
Urchal
1227
Ferness
61

66

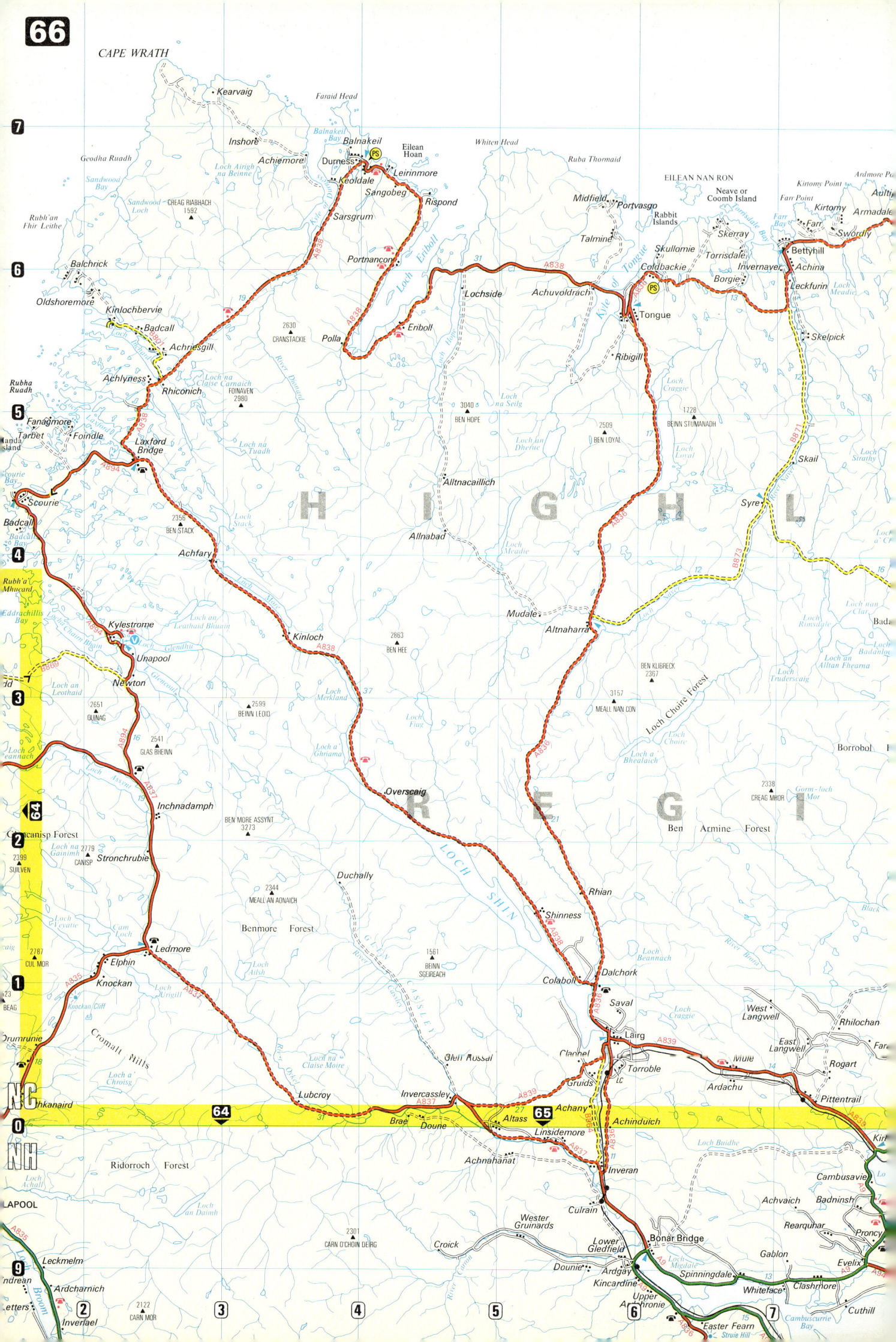

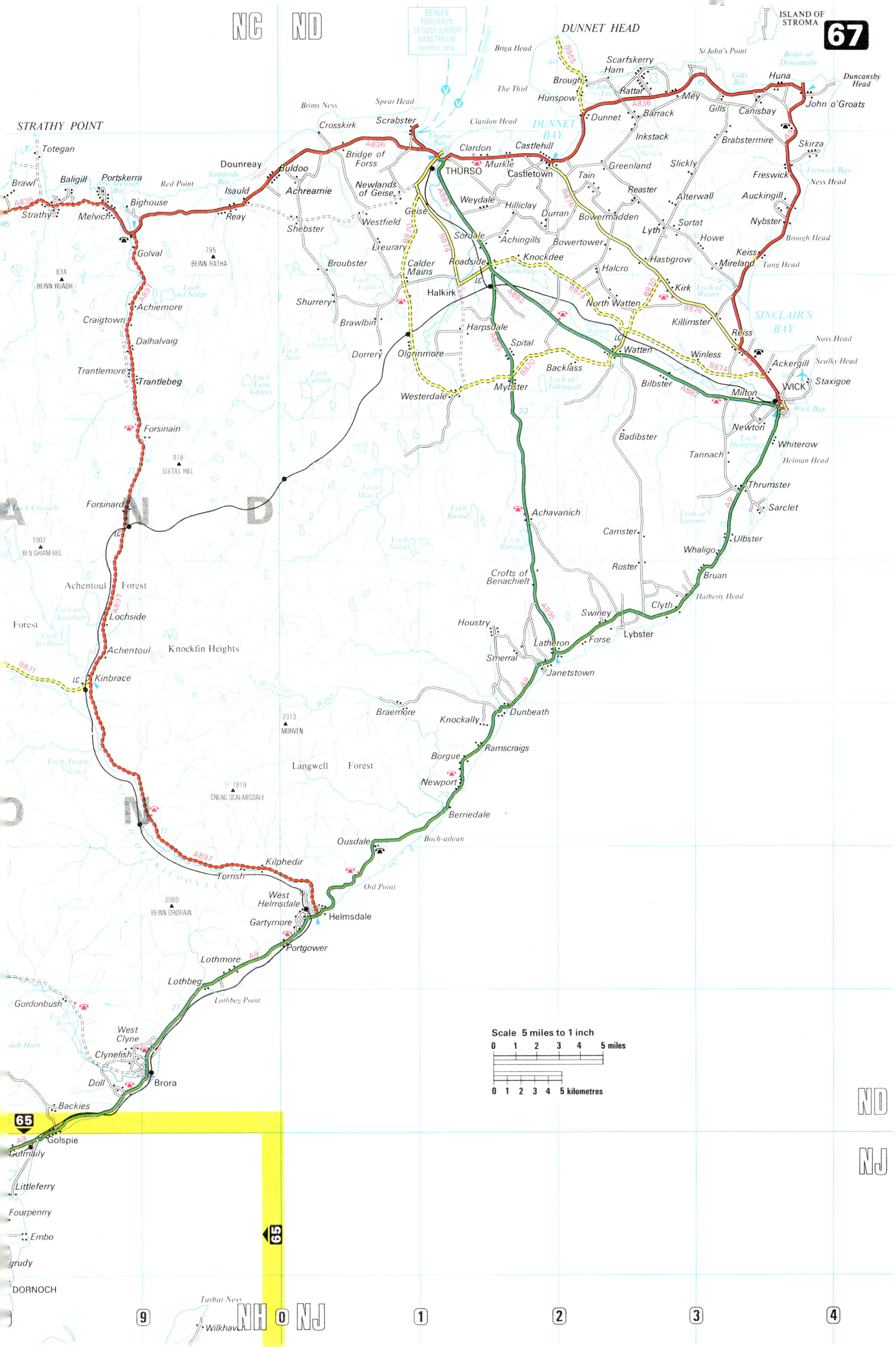
NC
ND
BERGEN
TORSHAVN
SEYDISFJORDUR
HANSTHOLM
summer only
Scrabster Stromness
DUNNET HEAD
ISLAND OF STROMA
Briga Head
St John's Point
Boars of Duncansby
Duncansby Head
Scarfskerry
Ham
Brough
Hunspow
Rattar
Mey
Gills
Gills Bay
Huna
John o'Groats
Canisbay
The Thirl
Dunnet
Barrack
A836
B855
Brims Ness
Spear Head
Clardon Head
DUNNET BAY
Inkstack
Brabstermire
Skirza
STRATHY POINT
Crosskirk
Scrabster
Thurso Bay
Clardon
Castlehill
Totegan
Bridge of Forss
Murkle
Castletown
Greenland
Slickly
Freswick
Freswick Bay
Ness Head
Dounreay
Sandside Bay
Buldoo
THURSO
Loch Heilen
Tain
Brawl
Baligill
Portskerra
Red Point
Isauld
Achreamie
Newlands of Geise
Reaster
Alterwall
Auckingill
Strathy
Melvich
Bighouse
Reay
Weydale
Hilliclay
Durran
Bowermadden
Lyth
Sortat
Nybster
Shebster
Geise
Westfield
Brough Head
Sordale
Achingills
Bowertower
Howe
Golval
795
BEINN RATHA
Leurary
B870
B874
Knockdee
Hastigrow
Keiss
Mireland
Tang Head
Broubster
Calder Mains
Roadside
Loch Scarmclate
Halcro
834
BEINN RUADH
Loch na Seilge
Loch Calder
Halkirk
A882
B874
North Watten
Kirk
Loch of Wester
Achiemore
Shurrery
B876
SINCLAIR'S BAY
Craigtown
Brawlbin
Harpsdale
Killimster
Reiss
Dalhalvaig
Loch Shurrery
Olgrinmore
Spital
Loch Watten
Watten
Noss Head
Loch Seye
Dorrery
Winless
Ackergill
Sealky Head
Trantlemore
Loch Calium
Backlass
Trantlebeg
Loch Tuim Ghlais
Westerdale
Mybster
Loch of Toftingall
Bilbster
Milton
WICK
Staxigoe
Wick Bay
Forsinain
A895
Newton
Badibster
Loch Hempriggs
Whiterow
918
SLETILL HILL
Tannach
Helman Head
Thrumster
Loch More
Sarclet
Loch Crocach
Forsinard
Loch Ruard
Achavanich
Loch of Yarrows
1902
BEN GRIAM BEG
Loch Sand
Camster
Ulbster
Loch Rangag
Whaligo
Roster
Achentoul
Forest
Crofts of Benachielt
Bruan
Halberry Head
A897
Loch an Ruathair
Clyth
Forest
Lochside
Swiney
Houstry
A895
Loch Arichlinie
Forse
Lybster
Achentoul
Knockfin Heights
Latheron
Smerral
B871
Janetstown
Kinbrace
Berriedale Water
Braemore
Dunbeath
Knockally
2313
MORVEN
Ramscraigs
Borgue
Loch Ascaig
Langwell
Forest
Newport
1819
CREAG SCALABSDALE
Berriedale
Boch-ailean
Ousdale
A897
Kilphedir
Torrish
Ord Point
West Helmsdale
2060
BEINN DHORAIN
Helmsdale
Gartymore
Portgower
Lothmore
Lothbeg
Lothbeg Point
Gordonbush
Loch Brora
West Clyne
Clynelish
Doll
Brora
Backies
65
Golspie
Culmaily
Littleferry
Fourpenny
Embo
DORNOCH
Tarbat Ness
Wilkhaven
Scale 5 miles to 1 inch
0 1 2 3 4 5 miles
0 1 2 3 4 5 kilometres
ND
NJ
NH
0
9
1
2
3
4

MILEAGE CHART

The distances between towns on the mileage chart are given to the nearest mile, and are measured along the normal AA recommended routes. It should be noted that AA recommended routes do not necessarily follow the shortest distances between places but are based on the quickest travelling time, making maximum use of motorways or dual-carriageway roads.

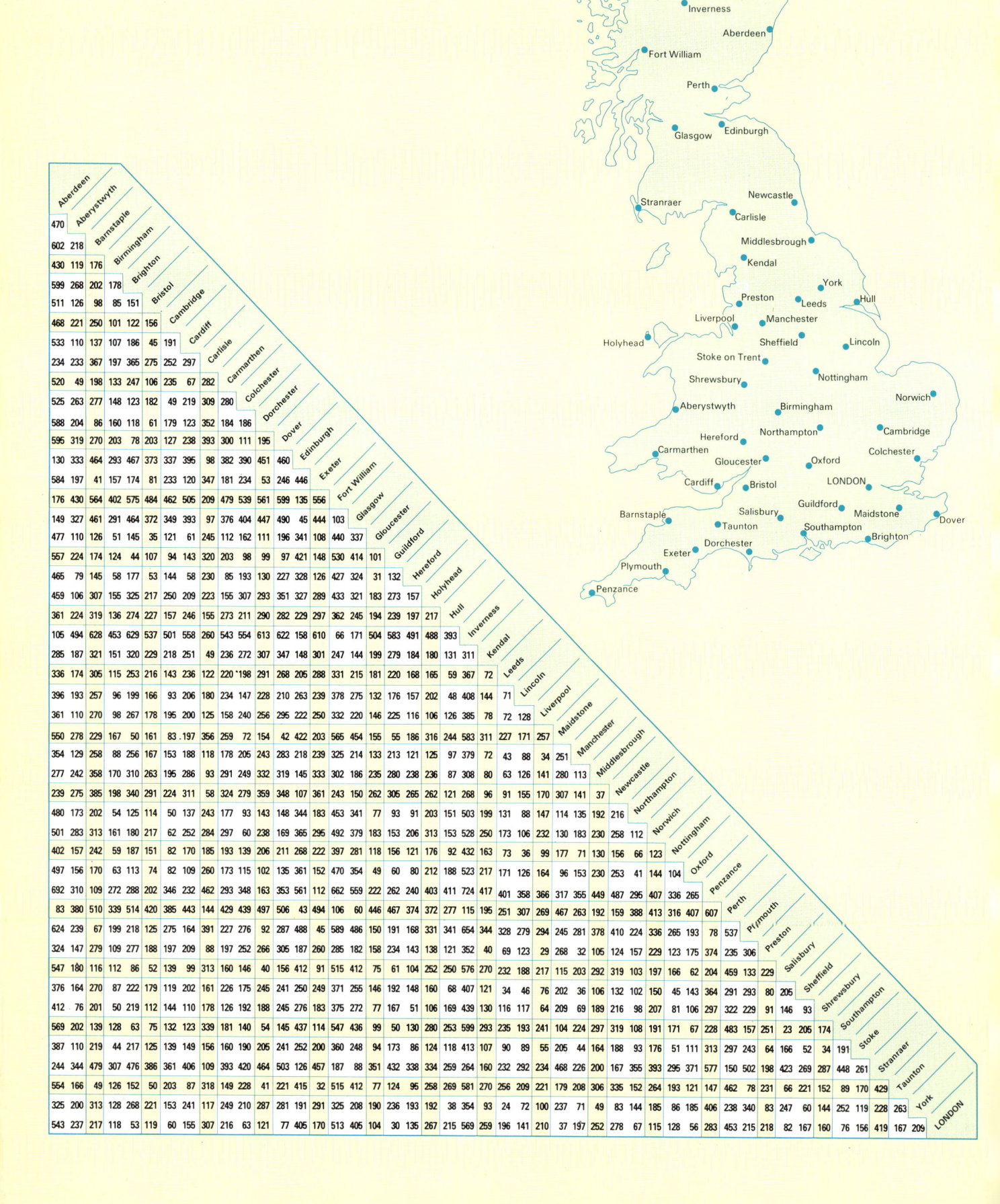

INDEX To Place Names

Ab Kettleby–Ashburton

Ab Kettleby 34 SK7223
Abbas Combe 8 ST7022
Abberley 24 SO7567
Abberton (Essex) 21 TM0019
Abberton (Here. and Worc.) 25 SO9953
Abberwick 53 NU1213
Abbess Roding 20 TL5711
Abbey 5 ST1410
Abbey Dore 24 SO3830
Abbey Hulton 33 SJ9148
Abbey St. Bathans 53 NT7662
Abbey Town 45 NY1750
Abbey Wood 12 TQ4779
Abbeycwmhir 23 SO0571
Abbeystead 36 SD5654
Abbot's Salford 25 SP0650
Abbots Bickington 4 SS3813
Abbots Bromley 33 SK0824
Abbots Langley 19 TL0902
Abbots Leigh 16 ST5473
Abbots Morton 25 SP0255
Abbots Ripton 27 TL2377
Abbotsbury 7 SY5785
Abbotsford 52 NT5034
Abbotsham 6 SS4226
Abbotskerswell 5 SX8569
Abbotsley 27 TL2256
Abbotswood 9 SU3722
Abbotts Ann 10 SU3243
Abdon 24 SO5786
Aber (Dyfed) 22 SN4748
Aber (Gwyn.) 30 SH6572
Aber-banc 22 SN3541
Aber-nant (Mid Glam.) 16 SO0103
Aberaeron 22 SN4562
Aberaman 16 SO0101
Aberangell 22 SH8409
Aberargie 56 NO1615
Aberarth 22 SN4763
Aberbeeg 16 SO2102
Abercanaid 16 SO0503
Abercarn 16 ST2195
Abercegir 22 SH8001
Aberchirder 62 NJ6252
Abercraf 15 SN8212
Abercrombie 57 NO5102
Abercych 16 SN2441
Abercynon 16 ST0894
Aberdalgie 56 NO0720
Aberdare 15 SO0002
Aberdaron 30 SH1726
Aberdeen 62 NJ9305
Aberdour 51 NT1885
Aberdulais 15 SS7799
Aberdyfi 22 SN6196
Aberedw 23 SO0747
Abereiddy 14 SM7931
Abererch 30 SH3936
Aberfan 16 SO0700
Aberfeldy 56 NN8549
Aberffraw 30 SH3568
Aberffrwd 22 SN6878
Aberford 38 SE4336
Aberfoyle 55 NN5200
Abergavenny 16 SO2914
Abergele 31 SH9477
Abergorlech 15 SN5833
Abergwesyn 22 SN8552
Abergwili 15 SN4421
Abergwynant 30 SH6717
Abergwynfi 15 SS8996
Abergynolwyn 22 SH6706
Aberhosan 22 SN8197
Aberkenfig 15 SS8983
Aberlady 52 NT4679
Aberlemno 57 NO5255
Aberllefenni 22 SH7609
Abermeurig 22 SN5655
Abermule 23 SO1694
Abernaint 31 SJ1221
Abernant (Dyfed) 14 SN3423
Abernethy 56 NO1816
Abernyte 57 NO2531
Aberporth 14 SN2651
Abersoch 30 SH3128
Abersychan 16 SO2704
Abertillery 16 SO2104
Abertridwr (Mid Glam.) 16 ST1289
Abertridwr (Powys) 31 SJ0319
Abertysswg 16 SO1305
Aberuthven 56 NN9715
Aberyscir 16 SN9929
Aberystwyth 22 SN5881
Abingdon 18 SU4997
Abinger Common 11 TQ1145
Abington 51 NS9323
Abington Pigotts 20 TL3044
Ablington 17 SP1007
Abney 33 SK1979
Aboyne 61 NO5298
Abram 36 SD6001
Abriachan 60 NH5535
Abridge 20 TQ4696
Abthorpe 26 SP6446
Abune-the-Hill 63 HY2928
Aby 35 TF4178
Acaster Malbis 38 SE5845
Acaster Selby 38 SE5741
Accrington 37 SD7528
Acha 48 NM1854
Achachork 58 NG4746
Achahamara 49 NE7887
Achahoish 49 NR7877
Achallader 55 NN3345
Achanalt 64 NH2561
Achandunie 65 NH6471
Achaphubuil 55 NN0875
Acharacle 54 NM6767
Acharn (Tays.) 56 NN7543
Achath 62 NJ7311
Achavanich 67 ND1742
Achduart 64 NC0403
Achentoul 67 NC8733
Achfary 66 NC2939
Achgarve 64 NG8893
Achiemore (Highld.) 67 NC8958
Achiltibuie 64 NC0208
Achina 66 NC7060
Achinduich 65 NH5899
Achintee (Highld.) 59 NG9441
Achintraid 59 NG8438
Achleck 54 NM4145
Achlyness 66 NC2452
Achmelvich 64 NC0524
Achmore (Central) 56 NN5832
Achmore (Highld.) 59 NG8533
Achmore (Isle of Lewis) 63 NB3029
Achnacarnin 64 NC0431
Achnacroish 54 NM8541
Achnagarron 65 NH6870
Achnaha 54 NM4668
Achnahanat 65 NH5098
Achnasaul 59 NN1589
Achnasheen 59 NH1658
Achnastank 61 NJ2733
Achosnich 54 NM4467
Achreamie 67 ND0166
Achriabhach 55 NN1468
Achriesgill 66 NC2554
Achurch 27 TL0282
Achuvoldrach 66 NC5659
Achvaich 65 ND7194
Ackergill 67 ND3553
Acklam (Cleve.) 42 NZ4817
Acklam (N Yorks.) 38 SE7861
Ackleton 24 SO7798
Acklington 47 NU2201
Ackton 38 SE4121
Ackworth Moor Top 38 SE4316
Acle 29 TG3910
Acock's Green 25 SP1383
Acol 13 TR3067
Acomb 47 NY9366
Aconbury 24 SO5133
Acre 37 SD7824
Acrefair 31 SJ2743
Acrise Place 13 TQ0843
Acton (Ches.) 37 SJ6253
Acton (Gtr London) 19 TQ2080
Acton (Salop) 23 SO3184
Acton (Suff.) 21 TL8945
Acton Beauchamp 24 SO6750
Acton Bridge 32 SJ5975
Acton Burnell 24 SJ5301
Acton Green 24 SO6395
Acton Pigott 24 SJ5402
Acton Round 24 SO6395
Acton Scott 24 SO4589
Acton Trussell 33 SJ9317
Acton Turville 17 ST8080
Adbaston 32 SJ7627
Adber 8 ST5920
Adderbury 18 SP4635
Adderley 32 SJ6639
Adderstone 53 NU1330
Addiewell 51 NS9962
Addingham 37 SE0749
Addington (Bucks.) 18 SP7428
Addington (Kent) 12 TQ6559
Addlestone 11 TQ0464
Addlethorpe 35 TF5469
Adeney 32 SJ6918
Adfa 23 SJ0501
Adforton 24 SO4071
Adisham 13 TR2253
Adlestrop 18 SP2427
Adlingfleet 39 SE8421
Adlington (Ches.) 33 SJ9180
Adlington (Lancs.) 36 SD6013
Admaston (Salop) 24 SJ6313
Admaston (Staffs.) 33 SK0423
Admington 26 SP1945
Adstock 18 SP7329
Adstone 26 SP5951
Advie 61 NJ1234
Adwell 18 SU6999
Adwick le Street 38 SE5308
Adwick upon Dearne 38 SE4601
Adziel 62 NJ9453
Ae Village 45 NX9889
Affleck 62 NJ8623
Affpuddle 8 SY8093
Agglethorpe 41 SE0886
Aignish 63 NB4832
Aike 39 TA0445
Aiketgate 46 NY4846
Aikton 46 NY2753
Ailey 23 SO3348
Ailsworth 27 TL1199
Ainderby Quernhow 42 SE3480
Ainderby Steeple 42 SE3392
Aingers Green 21 TM1120
Ainsdale 36 SD3111
Ainstable 46 NY5346
Ainsworth 37 SD7610
Aintree 36 SJ3798
Aird (Dumf. and Galwy.) 44 NX0960
Aird (Isle of Lewis) 63 NB5635
Aird Dell 63 NB4762
Aird Uig 63 NB0437
Aird of Sleat 58 NG5900
Aird, The (Island of Skye) 58 NG3952
Aird, The (Island of Skye) 58 NG4375
Airdrie 50 NS7665
Airdriehill 50 NS7867
Airmyn 38 SE7224
Airntully 56 NO0935
Airor 58 NG7105
Airth 50 NS8987
Airton 37 SD9059
Aisby (Lincs.) 34 SK8792
Aisby (Lincs.) 34 TF0138
Aiskew 42 SE2788
Aislaby (Cleve) 42 NZ4012
Aislaby (N Yorks.) 43 NZ8508
Aislaby (N Yorks.) 43 SE7785
Aisthorpe 34 SK9479
Aith (Fetlar) 63 HU6390
Aith (Orkney) 63 HY2417
Aith (Shetl.) 63 HU3455
Akeld 53 NT9529
Akeley 18 SP7037
Akenham 21 TM1448
Albaston 4 SX4270
Alberbury 24 SJ3514
Albourne 11 TQ2616
Albrighton (Salop) 32 SJ4918
Albrighton (Salop) 25 SJ8103
Alburgh 29 TM2786
Albury (Herts.) 20 TL4324
Albury (Surrey) 11 TQ0547
Alby Hill 29 TG1934
Alcaig 60 NH5657
Alcaston 24 SO4587
Alciston 12 TQ5005
Alconbury 27 TL1875
Alconbury Weston 27 TL1777
Aldborough (N Yorks.) 38 SE4065
Aldborough (Norf.) 29 TG1834
Aldbourne 10 SU2675
Aldbrough (Humbs.) 39 TA2338
Aldbrough (N Yorks.) 42 NZ2011
Aldbury 19 SP9612
Aldclune 56 NN9064
Aldeburgh 21 TM4656
Aldeby 29 TM4593
Aldenham 19 TQ1198
Alderbury (Salop) 32 SJ3614
Alderbury (Wilts.) 8 SU1827
Alderford 29 TG1218
Alderholt 8 SU1212
Alderley 17 ST7690
Alderley Edge 33 SJ8478
Aldermaston 10 SO6000
Aldermaston Soke 10 SU6263
Aldermaston Wharf 10 SU6067
Alderminster 26 SP2248
Aldershot 11 SU8650
Alderton (Glos.) 25 SP0033
Alderton (Northants.) 26 SP7346
Alderton (Salop) 32 SJ4923
Alderton (Suff.) 21 TM3441
Alderton (Wilts.) 17 ST8382
Alderwasley 33 SK3153
Aldfield 37 SE2669
Aldford 32 SJ4159
Aldham 21 TL9125
Aldingbourne 11 SU9205
Aldingham 40 SD2871
Aldington (Here. and Worc.) 25 SP0644
Aldington (Kent) 13 TR0736
Aldochlay 50 NS3591
Aldreth 27 TL4473
Aldridge 25 SK0500
Aldringham 29 TM4460
Aldsworth 17 SP1509
Aldwark (Derby.) 33 SK2257
Aldwark (N. Yorks.) 38 SE4663
Aldwick 11 SZ9199
Aldwincle 27 TL0081
Aldworth 10 SU5579
Alexandria 50 NS3979
Alfardisworthy 4 SS2911
Alfington 7 SY1197
Alfold 11 TQ0333
Alford (Grampn.) 61 NJ5715
Alford (Lincs.) 35 TF4575
Alford (Somer.) 8 ST6032
Alfreton 33 SK4155
Alfrick 24 SO7453
Alfriston 12 TQ5103
Alhampton 8 ST6234
Alkborough 39 SE8721
Alkerton 26 SP3743
Alkham 13 TR2441
Alkington 32 SJ5239
Alkmonton 33 SK1838
All Cannings 17 SU0661
All Saints South Elmham 29 TM3482
All Stretton 24 SO4395
Allaleigh 5 SX8053
Allanaquoich 61 NO1191
Allanton (Borders) 53 NT8654
Allanton (Strath.) 50 NS8457
Allendale 47 NY8455
Allenheads 47 NY8645
Allensmore 24 SO4635
Aller 7 ST4029
Aller Dean 53 NT9847
Allerby 40 NY0839
Allerford 6 SS9047
Allerston 43 SE8782
Allerthorpe 38 SE7847
Allerton 32 SJ3986
Allerton Bywater 38 SE4127
Allestree 33 SK3439
Allexton 26 SK8100
Allgreave 33 SJ9767
Allhallows 12 TQ8377
Alligin Shuas 59 NG8358
Allimore Green 33 SJ8519
Allington (Lincs.) 34 SK8540
Allington (Wilts.) 17 SU0663
Allington (Wilts.) 10 SU2039
Allithwaite 40 SD3876
Alloa 50 NS8893
Allonby 45 NY0842
Alloway 49 NS3318
Alltwalis 15 SN4431
Alltwen 15 SN7303
Allweston 8 ST6614
Almeley 23 SO3351
Almer 8 SY9098
Almington 32 SJ7034
Almondbank 56 NO0626
Almondbury 37 SE1614
Almondsbury 17 ST6083
Alne 38 SE4965
Alness 65 NH6669
Alnham 53 NT9910
Alnmouth 53 NU2410
Alnwick 53 NU1912
Alphamstone 21 TL8735
Alpheton 21 TL8850
Alphington 5 SX9190
Alport 33 SK2164
Alpraham 32 SJ5859
Alresford 21 TM0621
Alrewas 33 SK1715
Alsager 32 SJ7955
Alsagers bank 32 SJ8048
Alsop en le Dale 33 SK1655
Alston 46 NY7146
Alstone 25 SO9832
Alstonfield 33 SK1355
Alswear 6 SS7222
Altandhu 64 NB9812
Altanduin 67 NC8025
Altarnun 4 SX2281
Altassmore 66 NC5000
Alterwall 67 ND2865
Altgaltraig 49 NS0473
Altham 37 SD7632
Althorne 21 TQ9098
Althorpe 39 SE8309
Altnaharra 66 NC5635
Altofts 38 SE3723
Alton (Derby.) 33 SK3664
Alton (Hants.) 10 SU7139
Alton (Staffs.) 33 SK0742
Alton Pancras 8 ST6902
Alton Priors 17 SU1062
Altrincham 32 SJ7687
Alva 50 NS8897
Alvanley 32 SJ4973
Alvaston 33 SK3933
Alvechurch 25 SP0272
Alvecote 26 SK2404
Alvediston 8 ST9723
Alveley 24 SO7584
Alverdiscott 6 SS5225
Alverstoke 9 SZ5998
Alverstone 9 SZ5785
Alverton 34 SK7942
Alves 61 NJ1362
Alvescot 18 SP2704
Alveston (Avon) 17 ST6388
Alveston (Warw.) 26 SP2256
Alvie 60 NH8609
Alvingham 35 TF3691
Alvington 17 SO6000
Alwalton 27 TL1395
Alwen Resr. 31 SH9454
Alwinton 47 NT9206
Alyth 57 NO2448
Amber Hill 35 TF2346
Ambergate 33 SK3451
Amberley (Glos.) 17 SO8401
Amberley (W. Susx.) 11 TQ0313
Amble 47 NU2604
Amblecote 25 SO8885
Ambleside 40 NY3704
Ambleston 14 SN0026
Ambrosden 18 SP6019
Amcotts 39 SE8514
Amersham 19 SU9597
Amesbury 8 SU1541
Amington 26 SK2304
Amisfield Town 45 NY0082
Amlwch 30 SH4392
Ammanford 15 SN6212
Amotherby 43 SE7473
Ampfield 9 SU3923
Ampleforth 42 SE5878
Ampney Crucis 17 SP0602
Ampney St. Mary 17 SP0802
Ampney St. Peter 17 SP0701
Amport 10 SU2944
Ampthill 19 TL0337
Ampton 28 TL8671
Amroth 14 SN1607
Amulree 56 NN8936
Anaheilt 54 NM8162
Ancaster 34 SK9843
Anchor 23 SO1785
Ancroft 53 NT9945
Ancrum 52 NT6224
Ancton 11 SU9800
Anderby 35 TF5275
Anderson 8 SY8797
Anderton 32 SJ6475
Andover 10 SU3645
Andover Down 10 SU3946
Andoversford 17 SP0219
Andreas 43 SC4199
Angersleigh 7 ST1918
Angle 14 SM8603
Angmering 11 TQ0704
Angram 38 SE5148
Ankerville 65 NH8174
Anlaby 39 TA0328
Anmer 28 TF7429
Anna Valley 10 SU3444
Annan 45 NY1966
Annaside 40 SD0986
Annat (Highld.) 59 NG8954
Annat (Strath.) 55 NN0322
Annathill 50 NS7270
Annbank 50 NS4022
Annesley Woodhouse 34 SK4953
Annet 2 SV8608
Annfield Plain 47 NZ1551
Annochie 62 NJ9342
Annscroft 24 SJ4407
Ansley 26 SP2991
Anslow 33 SK2125
Anslow Gate 33 SK2024
Anstey (Herts.) 20 TL4032
Anstey (Leic.) 26 SK5408
Anston 34 SK5184
Anstruther 57 NO5603
Ansty (W Susx.) 11 TQ2923
Ansty (Warw.) 26 SP3983
Ansty (Wilts.) 8 ST9526
Anthill Common 9 SU6412
Anthorn 45 NY1958
Antingham 29 TG2533
Antony 4 SX3954
Antrobus 32 SJ6479
Anwick 35 TF1150
Anwoth 45 NX5856
Aonach Eagach (Mt.) 55 NN1557
Apethorpe 27 TL0295
Apley 35 TF1075
Apperknowle 33 SK3878
Apperley 17 SO8628
Appleby (Cumbr.) 41 NY6820
Appleby (Humbs.) 39 SE9414
Appleby Magna 26 SK3110
Appleby Parva 26 SK3109
Appleby Street 20 TL3304
Applecross 58 NG7144
Appledore (Devon) 6 SS4630
Appledore (Devon) 7 ST0614
Appledore (Kent) 13 TQ9529
Appleford 18 SU5293
Appleshaw 10 SU3048
Appleton (Ches.) 32 SJ6484
Appleton (Oxon.) 18 SP4401
Appleton Roebuck 38 SE5542
Appleton Wiske 42 NZ3904
Appleton-le-Moors 43 SE7387
Appleton-le-Street 43 SE7373
Appletreehall 52 NT5117
Appletreewick 37 SE0560
Appley 7 ST0721
Appley Bridge 36 SD5209
Apse Heath 9 SZ5682
Apsley End 19 TL1232
Apuldram 10 SU8403
Arbeadie 62 NO6996
Arbirlot 57 NO6040
Arboll 65 NH8881
Arborfield 10 SU7567
Arborfield Cross 10 SU7666
Arborfield Garrison 10 SU7665
Arbroath 57 NO6340
Arbuthnott 57 NO8074
Archiestown 61 NJ2344
Arclid Green 32 SJ7962
Ardachu 66 NC6703
Ardachvie 59 NN1490
Ardanaiseig 55 NN0824
Ardarroch 59 NG8339
Ardbeg 48 NR4146
Ardcharnich 64 NH1789
Ardchiavaig 54 NM3818
Ardchyle 55 NN5229
Arddleen 31 SJ2516
Ardeley 20 TL3127
Ardelve 59 NG8727
Arden 50 NS3684
Ardens Grafton 25 SP1154
Ardentinny 49 NS1887
Ardeonaig 56 NN6635
Ardersier or Campbeltown 60 NH7854
Ardery 54 NM7562
Ardessie 64 NH0589
Ardfern 54 NM8004
Ardgartan 55 NN2702
Ardgay 65 NH5990
Ardindrean 64 NH1588
Ardingly 12 TQ3229
Ardington 18 SU4388
Ardivachar 63 NF7445
Ardlamont Point 49 NR9963
Ardleigh 21 TM0529
Ardler 57 NO2641
Ardley 18 SP5427
Ardlui 55 NN3115
Ardmair 64 NH1198
Ardmay 55 NN2802
Ardminish 48 NR6448
Ardmolich 54 NM7171
Ardmore (Strath.) 50 NS3178
Ardnadam 49 NS1580
Ardnagrask 60 NH5149
Ardnarff 59 NG8935
Ardnastang 54 NM8061
Ardo 62 NJ8538
Ardoch 56 NO0937
Ardorlich 56 NN6322
Ardoyne 62 NJ6527
Ardpatrick 48 NR7560
Ardpeaton 49 NS2185
Ardrishaig 49 NR8585
Ardroil 63 NB0432
Ardross 65 NH6173
Ardrossan 49 NS2342
Ardshealach 54 NM6967
Ardsley 38 SE3805
Ardsley East 37 SE3024
Ardslignish 54 NM5661
Ardtalnaig 56 NN7039
Ardullie 65 NH5963
Ardvasar 58 NG6303
Ardvey 63 NG1292
Ardwell 46 NX1045
Areley Kings 24 SO8070
Argoed Mill 23 SN9962
Aridhglas 54 NM3123
Arinacrinachd 58 NG7458
Arinagour 48 NM2257
Arion 63 HY2514
Arivruach 63 NB2417
Arkendale 38 SE3860
Arkengarthdale 41 NZ0001
Arkesden 20 TL4834
Arkholme 36 SD5871
Arkley 19 TQ2296
Arksey 38 SE5706
Arkwright Town 33 SK4270
Arlecdon 40 NY0419
Arlesey 19 TL1935
Arleston 24 SJ6410
Arley (Ches.) 32 SJ6780
Arley (Warw.) 26 SP2890
Arlingham 17 SO7010
Arlington (Devon) 6 SS6140
Arlington (Glos.) 17 SP1006
Arlington (E Susx) 12 TQ5407
Armadale (Highld.) 66 NC7864
Armadale (Lothian) 51 NS9368
Armadale Castle 58 NG6404
Armathwaite 46 NY5046
Arminghall 29 TG2504
Armitage 33 SK0816
Armscote 26 SP2444
Armthorpe 38 SE6105
Arnabost 48 NM2159
Arncliffe 37 SD9371
Arncliffe Cote 37 SD9470
Arncott 18 SP6117
Arncroach 57 NO5105
Arne 8 SY9788
Arnesby 26 SP6192
Arngask 56 NO1310
Arnicle 48 NR7138
Arnisdale 59 NG8410
Arnish 58 NG5948
Arniston Engine 51 NT3462
Arnol 63 NB3148
Arnprior 50 NS6194
Arnside 40 SD4578
Aros Mains 54 NM5645
Arpafeelie 60 NH6150
Arrad Foot 40 SD3080
Arram 39 TA0344
Arrathorne 42 SE2093
Arreton 9 SZ5386
Arrington 20 TL3250
Arrochar 55 NN2904
Arrow 25 SP0856
Artafallie 60 NH6249
Arthington 37 SE2644
Arthingworth 26 SP7581
Arthog 30 SH6414
Arthrath 62 NJ9636
Arthurstone 57 NO2642
Artrochie 62 NK0032
Arundel 11 TQ0107
Aryhoulan 55 NN0168
Asby 40 NY0620
Ascog 49 NS1063
Ascot 11 SU9168
Ascott-under-Wychwood 18 SP2918
Asenby 42 SE3975
Asfordby 34 SK7018
Asfordby Hill 34 SK7219
Asgarby (Lincs.) 35 TF1145
Asgarby (Lincs.) 35 TF3366
Ash (Kent) 12 TQ5964
Ash (Kent) 13 TR2958
Ash (Somer.) 7 ST4720
Ash (Surrey) 11 SU8950
Ash Bullayne 5 SS7704
Ash Magna 32 SJ5739
Ash Mill 6 SS7823
Ash Priors 7 ST1429
Ash Thomas 5 ST0010
Ashampstead 10 SU5676
Ashbocking 21 TM1654
Ashbourne 33 SK1846
Ashbrittle 5 ST0521
Ashburton 5 SX7569

Ashbury

Barton-le-Willows

Ashbury (Devon.)	4	SX 5097
Ashbury (Oxon.)	18	SU 2685
Ashby	39	SE 9008
Ashby Folville	26	SK 7012
Ashby Magna	26	SP 5690
Ashby Parva	26	SP 5288
Ashby St. Ledgers	26	SP 5768
Ashby St. Mary	29	TG 3202
Ashby by Partney	35	TF 4266
Ashby cum Fenby	39	TA 2500
Ashby de la Launde	35	TF 0455
Ashby-de-la-Zouch	33	SK 3516
Ashchurch	25	SO 9233
Ashcombe	5	SX 9179
Ashcott	7	ST 4336
Ashdon	20	TL 5842
Asheldham	21	TL 9701
Ashen	20	TL 7442
Ashendon	18	SP 7014
Ashfield (Central)	56	NN 7803
Ashfield (Suff.)	29	TM 2062
Ashfield Green	29	TM 2673
Ashford (Derby.)	33	SK 1969
Ashford (Devon.)	6	SS 5335
Ashford (Kent)	13	TR 0142
Ashford (Surrey)	11	TQ 0671
Ashford Bowdler	24	SO 5170
Ashford Carbonel	24	SO 5270
Ashford Hill	10	SU 5562
Ashgill	50	NS 7849
Ashiesteel Hill	52	NT 4134
Ashill (Devon)	7	ST 0811
Ashill (Norf.)	28	TF 8804
Ashill (Somer.)	7	ST 3217
Ashingdon	21	TQ 8693
Ashington (Northum.)	47	NZ 2687
Ashington (W Susx)	11	TQ 1315
Ashkirk	52	NT 4722
Ashleworth	17	SO 8125
Ashley (Cambs.)	28	TL 6961
Ashley (Devon.)	5	SS 6411
Ashley (Glos.)	17	ST 9394
Ashley (Hants.)	9	SU 3831
Ashley (Northants.)	26	SP 7991
Ashley (Staffs.)	32	SJ 7536
Ashley Green	19	SP 9705
Ashley Heath	8	SU 1105
Ashmansworth	10	SU 4156
Ashmansworthy	4	SS 3317
Ashmore	8	ST 9117
Ashorne	26	SP 3057
Ashover	33	SK 3463
Ashow	26	SP 3170
Ashperton	24	SO 6441
Ashprington	5	SX 8157
Ashreigney	5	SS 6213
Ashtead	11	TQ 1858
Ashton (Ches.)	32	SJ 5069
Ashton (Corn.)	2	SW 6028
Ashton (Devon.)	5	SX 8584
Ashton (Here. and Worc.)	24	SO 5164
Ashton (Northants.)	26	SP 7649
Ashton (Northants.)	27	TL 0588
Ashton Common	17	ST 8958
Ashton Keynes	17	SU 0494
Ashton under Hill	25	SO 9938
Ashton upon Mersey	32	SJ 7792
Ashton-in-Makerfield	36	SJ 5799
Ashton-under-Lyne	37	SJ 9399
Ashurst (Hants.)	9	SU 3310
Ashurst (Kent)	12	TQ 5038
Ashurst (W Susx)	11	TQ 1716
Ashurstwood	12	TQ 4236
Ashwater	4	SX 3895
Ashwell (Herts.)	19	TL 2639
Ashwell (Leic.)	27	SK 8613
Ashwellthorpe	29	TM 1397
Ashwick	8	ST 6447
Ashwicken	28	TF 7018
Askam in Furness	40	SD 2177
Askern	38	SE 5613
Askerswell	7	SY 5292
Askett	18	SP 8105
Askham (Cumbr.)	40	NY 5123
Askham (Notts.)	34	SK 7374
Askham Bryan	38	SE 5548
Askham Richard	38	SE 5347
Askrigg	41	SD 9491
Askwith	37	SE 1648
Aslackby	35	TF 0830
Aslacton	29	TM 1591
Aslockton	34	SK 7440
Asloun	62	NJ 5414
Aspatria	45	NY 1442
Aspenden	20	TL 3528
Aspley Guise	19	SP 9436
Aspley Heath	19	SP 9334
Aspull	36	SD 6108
Asselby	38	SE 7127
Assington	21	TL 9338
Astbury	33	SJ 8461
Astcote	26	SP 6753
Asterley	24	SJ 3707
Asterton	24	SO 3991
Asthall	18	SP 2811
Asthall Leigh	18	SP 3012
Astley (Here. and Worc.)	24	SO 7867
Astley (Salop)	32	SJ 5218
Astley (Warw.)	26	SP 3189
Astley Abbots	24	SO 7096
Astley Cross	24	SO 8069
Astley Green	36	SJ 7099
Aston (Berks.)	18	SU 7884
Aston (Ches.)	32	SJ 5578
Aston (Ches.)	32	SJ 6046
Aston (Derby.)	33	SK 1883
Aston (Here. and Worc.)	24	SO 4571
Aston (Herts.)	19	TL 2722
Aston (Oxon.)	18	SP 3302
Aston (S Yorks.)	34	SK 4685
Aston (Salop)	32	SJ 5228
Aston (Salop)	24	SJ 6109
Aston (Staffs.)	32	SJ 7540
Aston (Staffs.)	33	SJ 9131
Aston (W Mids)	25	SP 0789
Aston Abbotts	19	SP 8420
Aston Blank (Cold Aston)	17	SP 1219
Aston Botterell	24	SO 6284
Aston Cantlow	25	SP 1359
Aston Clinton	19	SP 8812
Aston Crews	17	SO 6723
Aston End	19	TL 2724
Aston Eyre	24	SO 6594
Aston Fields	25	SO 9669
Aston Flamville	26	SP 4692
Aston Ingham	17	SO 6823
Aston Magna	25	SP 1935
Aston Rogers	23	SJ 3406
Aston Rowant	18	SU 7299
Aston Sandford	18	SP 7507
Aston Somerville	25	SP 0438
Aston Subedge	25	SP 1341
Aston Tirrold	18	SU 5586
Aston Upthorpe	18	SU 5586
Aston juxta Mondrum	32	SJ 6556
Aston le Walls	26	SP 4950
Aston on Clun	24	SO 3981
Aston-on-Trent	33	SK 4129
Astwick	19	TL 2138
Astwood	27	SP 9547
Astwood Bank	25	SP 0362
Aswarby (Lincs.)	35	TF 0639
Aswardby (Lincs.)	35	TF 3770
Atcham	24	SJ 5408
Athelington	29	TM 2170
Athelney	7	ST 3428
Athelstaneford	52	NT 5377
Atherington	6	SS 5923
Atherstone	26	SP 3097
Atherstone on Stour	26	SP 2050
Atherton	36	SD 6703
Atlow	33	SK 2248
Attenborough	34	SK 5134
Attleborough (Norf.)	29	TM 0495
Attleborough (Warw.)	26	SP 3790
Attlebridge	29	TG 1216
Atwick	39	TA 1850
Atworth	17	ST 8565
Aubourn	34	SK 9262
Auchagallon	49	NR 8934
Auchallater	61	NO 1688
Aucharnie	62	NJ 6341
Auchattie	62	NO 6994
Auchenblae	57	NO 7278
Auchenbowie	50	NS 7988
Auchenbreck	49	NS 0281
Auchencairn	45	NX 7951
Auchencarroch	50	NS 4182
Auchencrow	53	NT 8560
Auchendinny	51	NT 2561
Auchengray	51	NS 9953
Auchengruith	45	NS 8209
Auchenhalrig	61	NJ 3661
Auchenheath	50	NS 8043
Auchentiber	50	NS 3647
Auchgourish	60	NH 9315
Auchindrain	55	NN 0303
Auchindrean	64	NH 1980
Auchininna	62	NJ 6446
Auchinleck (Dumf and Galwy.)	44	NX 4570
Auchinleck (Strath.)	50	NS 5422
Auchinloch	50	NS 6670
Auchintool	61	NJ 5316
Auchintore	55	NN 0972
Auchleuchries	62	NK 0136
Auchleven	62	NJ 6224
Auchlochan	50	NS 8037
Auchlossan	61	NO 5703
Auchlyne	55	NN 5129
Auchmillan	50	NS 5129
Auchmithie	57	NO 6744
Auchmuirbridge	56	NO 2101
Auchnacree	57	NO 4663
Auchnagatt	62	NJ 9341
Auchronie	57	NO 4480
Auchterarder	56	NN 9312
Auchterderran	51	NT 2195
Auchterhouse	57	NO 3337
Auchtermuchty	56	NO 2311
Auchterneed	60	NH 4959
Auchtertool	51	NT 2190
Auchtoo	55	NN 5620
Auckingill	67	ND 3764
Auckley	38	SE 6501
Audenshaw	33	SJ 9196
Audlem	32	SJ 6543
Audley	32	SJ 7950
Auds	62	NJ 6564
Aughton (Humbs.)	38	SE 7038
Aughton (Lancs.)	36	SD 3804
Aughton (Lancs.)	36	SD 5467
Aughton (S Yorks.)	34	SK 4586
Aughton Park	36	SD 4106
Auldearn	60	NH 9155
Aulden	24	SO 4654
Auldhame	52	NT 5984
Auldhouse	50	NS 6250
Ault-a-chrinn	59	NG 9420
Aultbea	64	NG 8789
Aultgrishan	64	NG 7485
Aultiphurst	67	NC 8065
Aultmore (Grampn.)	61	NJ 4053
Aultnagoire	60	NH 5423
Aulton	62	NJ 6028
Aundorach	60	NH 9716
Aunsby	35	TF 0438
Auquhorthies	62	NJ 8329
Aust	17	ST 5789
Austerfield	34	SK 6594
Austonley	37	SE 1207
Austrey	26	SK 2906
Austwick	37	SD 7668
Authorpe	35	TF 3980
Authorpe Row	35	TF 5373
Avebury	17	SU 0969
Aveley	20	TW 5680
Avening	17	ST 8797
Averham	34	SK 7654
Aveton Gifford	5	SX 6947
Avielochan	60	NH 9016
Aviemore	60	NH 8912
Avington	10	SU 3767
Avoch	60	NH 6955
Avon	8	SZ 1498
Avon Castle	8	SU 1303
Avon Dassett	26	SP 4150
Avonbridge	50	NS 9072
Avonmouth	16	ST 5177
Avonwick	5	SX 7158
Awbridge	9	SU 3323
Awkley	17	ST 5885
Awliscombe	7	ST 1301
Awre	17	SO 7008
Awsworth	34	SK 4843
Axbridge	16	ST 4254
Axford (Hants.)	10	SU 6043
Axford (Wilts.)	10	SU 2369
Axminster	7	SY 2998
Axmouth	7	SY 2591
Aylburton	17	SO 6101
Ayle	46	NY 7149
Aylesbeare	7	SY 0391
Aylesbury	18	SP 8213
Aylesby	39	TA 2007
Aylesford	12	TQ 7359
Aylesham	13	TR 2352
Aylestone	26	SK 5701
Aylmerton	29	TG 1839
Aylsham	29	TG 1926
Aylton	24	SO 6537
Aymestrey	24	SO 4265
Aynho	18	SP 5133
Ayot St. Lawrence	19	TL 1916
Ayot St. Peter	19	TL 2115
Ayr	49	NS 3321
Aysgarth	41	SE 0088
Ayside	40	SD 3983
Ayston	27	SK 8601
Aythorpe Roding	20	TL 5815
Ayton (Berwick.)	53	NT 9260
Ayton (N Yorks.)	43	SE 9884
Aywick (Yell)	63	HU 5386
Azerley	42	SE 2574
Babbinswood	32	SJ 3329
Babcary	7	ST 5628
Babel	15	SN 8235
Babell	31	SJ 1574
Babraham	20	TL 5150
Babworth	34	SK 6880
Back	63	NB 4840
Back of Keppoch	58	NM 6587
Backaland	63	HY 5630
Backbarrow	40	SD 3584
Backford	32	SJ 3971
Backhill of Clackriach	62	NJ 9347
Backies	67	NC 8302
Backmuir of New Gilston	57	NO 4308
Backwell	16	ST 4868
Backworth	47	NZ 2972
Bacon End	20	TL 6018
Baconsthorpe	29	TG 1237
Bacton (Here. and Worc.)	24	SO 3732
Bacton (Norf.)	29	TG 3434
Bacton (Suff.)	29	TM 0466
Bacup	37	SD 8622
Badachro	64	NG 7873
Badbury	17	SU 1980
Badby	26	SP 5559
Badcall (Highld.)	66	NC 1541
Badcall (Highld.)	66	NC 2355
Badcaul	64	NH 0191
Baddeley Green	33	SJ 9250
Baddesley Ensor	26	SP 2798
Baddidarach	64	NC 0923
Badenscoth	62	NJ 7038
Badenyon	61	NJ 3419
Badger	24	SO 7699
Badgers Mount	12	TQ 5061
Badgeworth (Glos.)	17	SO 9019
Badgworth (Somer.)	16	ST 3952
Badingham	29	TM 3067
Badlesmere	13	TR 0154
Badluarach	64	NG 9994
Badminton	17	ST 8082
Badrallach	64	NH 0691
Badsey	25	SP 0743
Badsworth	38	SE 4614
Badwell Ash	29	TL 9969
Bagby	42	SE 4680
Bagendon	17	SP 0006
Bagillt	31	SJ 2175
Baginton	26	SP 3474
Baglan	15	SS 7493
Bagley	32	SJ 4027
Bagnall	33	SJ 9250
Bagshot (Surrey)	11	SU 9163
Bagshot (Wilts.)	10	SU 3165
Bagthorpe (Norf.)	28	TF 7932
Bagthorpe (Notts.)	34	SK 4751
Bagworth	26	SK 4408
Bagwy Llydiart	16	SO 4427
Bail Uachdraich	63	NF 8160
Baildon	37	SE 1539
Baile Boidheach	48	NR 7473
Baile Mor	54	NM 2824
Bailebeag	60	NH 5018
Baillieston	50	NS 6764
Bainbridge	41	SD 9390
Bainton (Cambs.)	27	TF 0906
Bairnkine	52	NT 6515
Baker Street	20	TQ 6381
Baker's End	20	TL 3917
Bakewell	33	SK 2168
Bala	31	SH 9236
Balallan	63	NB 2720
Balbeg	60	NH 4924
Balbeggie	56	NO 1629
Balbithan	62	NJ 7917
Balblair	65	NH 7066
Balchladich	64	NC 0330
Balchraggan	60	NH 5343
Balchrick	66	NC 1960
Balcombe	12	TQ 3130
Balcurvie	57	NO 3400
Baldersby	42	SE 3578
Balderstone	36	SD 6332
Balderton	34	SK 8151
Baldhu	2	SW 7743
Baldinnie	57	NO 4311
Baldock	19	TL 2434
Baldrine	43	SC 4281
Baldwin	43	SC 3581
Baldwin's Gate	32	SJ 7939
Baldwinholme	46	NY 3351
Bale	29	TG 0136
Balemartine	48	NL 9841
Balephuil	48	NL 9640
Balerno	51	NT 1666
Balfield	57	NO 5468
Balfour	63	HY 4716
Balfron	50	NS 5488
Balgaveny	62	NJ 6640
Balgavies	57	NO 5351
Balgedie	56	NO 1603
Balgonar	51	NT 0395
Balgove	62	NJ 8133
Balgowan	60	NN 6394
Balgown	58	NG 3868
Balgray	57	NO 4138
Balgrochan	50	NS 6278
Balhalgardy	62	NJ 7623
Balhary	57	NO 2646
Baliasta	63	HP 6009
Baligill	67	NC 8566
Balintore (Highld.)	65	NH 8675
Balintore (Tays.)	57	NO 2859
Balintraid	65	NH 7370
Balivanich	63	NF 7755
Balkeerie	57	NO 3244
Balkholme	38	SE 7828
Balkissock	44	NX 1381
Ball	31	SJ 3026
Ball Hill	10	SU 4263
Ballabeg	43	SC 2470
Ballacannell	43	SC 4382
Ballacarnane Beg	43	SC 3088
Ballajora	43	SC 4790
Ballamodha	43	SC 2773
Ballantree	46	NX 0882
Ballantrushal	63	NB 3853
Ballasalla (I. of M.)	43	SC 2870
Ballasalla (I. of M.)	43	SC 3497
Ballater	61	NO 3695
Ballaugh	43	SC 3493
Ballchraggan	65	NH 7775
Ballechin	56	NN 9353
Ballencrieff	52	NT 4878
Ballevullin	48	NL 9546
Balliekine	49	NR 8739
Balliemore (Strath.)	54	NM 8228
Ballig	43	SC 2882
Ballinaby	48	NR 2267
Ballindean	57	NO 2529
Ballinger Common	19	SP 9103
Ballingham	24	SO 5731
Ballingry	51	NT 1797
Ballinluig	56	NN 9852
Ballintuim	56	NO 1054
Balloch (Highld)	60	NH 7346
Balloch (Strath.)	50	NS 3981
Balloch (Tays.)	56	NN 8419
Balloch (Tays.)	57	NO 3557
Ballochan	61	NO 5290
Ballochroy	48	NR 7252
Balls Cross	11	SU 9826
Ballsalla (I. of M.)	43	SC 3497
Ballygown	54	NM 4343
Ballygrant	48	NR 3966
Ballymichael	49	NR 9231
Balmacara	59	NG 8028
Balmaclellan	45	NX 6578
Balmacneil	56	NN 9850
Balmae	45	NX 6845
Balmaha	50	NS 4290
Balmalcolm	57	NO 3108
Balmartin	63	NF 7273
Balmedie	62	NJ 9617
Balmerino	57	NO 3542
Balmerlawn	9	SU 3003
Balmore	50	NS 6073
Balmullo	57	NO 4220
Balmungie	60	NH 7359
Balnabodach	63	NF 7101
Balnacra	59	NG 9746
Balnaglaic	0	NH 4531
Balnaguard	56	NN 9451
Balnaguisich	65	NH 6771
Balnahard	54	NM 4534
Balnahard	54	NR 4199
Balnakeil	66	NC 3968
Balnaknock	58	NG 4162
Balnamoon	57	NO 5463
Balnapaling	65	NH 7969
Balquhidder	55	NN 5320
Balranald	63	NF 7169
Balsall Common	26	SP 2377
Balscote	26	SP 3841
Balsham	20	TL 5850
Baltasound (Unst)	63	HP 6208
Balterley	32	SJ 7550
Balthangie	62	NJ 8351
Baltonsborough	7	ST 5434
Balvaird	60	NH 5452
Balvarban	56	NO 0762
Balvicar	54	NM 7616
Balvraid	60	NH 8231
Bamburgh	53	NU 1834
Bamford	33	SK 2083
Bampton (Cumbr.)	40	NY 5118
Bampton (Devon.)	7	SS 9522
Bampton (Oxon.)	18	SP 3103
Banavie	55	NN 1177
Banbury	18	SP 4540
Banc Cwmhelen	15	SN 6811
Banc-y-ffordd	22	SN 4037
Banchory	62	NO 6995
Banchory-Devenick	62	NJ 9101
Bancyfelin	14	SN 3218
Banff	62	NJ 6863
Bangor	30	SH 5872
Bangor-is-y-coed	32	SJ 3945
Banham	29	TM 0688
Bank	9	SU 2807
Bank Newton	37	SD 9152
Bank Street	24	SO 6362
Bankend (Dumf. and Galwy.)	45	NY 0268
Bankend (Strath.)	50	NS 8033
Bankfoot	56	NO 0635
Bankglen	50	NS 5912
Bankhead (Grampn.)	62	NJ 6608
Bankhead (Grampn.)	62	NJ 8910
Banknock	50	NS 7779
Banks (Cumbr.)	46	NY 5664
Banks (Lancs.)	36	SD 3820
Bankshill	45	NY 1981
Banningham	29	TG 2129
Bannister Green	20	TL 6920
Bannockburn	50	NS 8190
Banstead	11	TQ 2559
Bantham	5	SX 6643
Banton	50	NS 7479
Banwell	16	ST 3959
Bapchild	13	TQ 9363
Baramore	54	NM 6474
Barassie	49	NS 3232
Barbaraville	65	NH 7471
Barber Booth	33	SK 1184
Barbon	41	SD 6282
Barbrook	6	SS 7147
Barby	26	SP 5470
Barcheston	18	SP 2639
Barcombe	12	TQ 4214
Barcombe Cross	12	TQ 4216
Barden	42	SE 1493
Bardfield Saling	20	TL 6826
Bardister	63	HU 3577
Bardney	35	TF 1169
Bardon Mill	46	NY 7764
Bardowie	50	NS 5873
Bardrainney	49	NS 3372
Bardsea	40	SD 3074
Bardsey	38	SE 3643
Bardsley	37	SD 9201
Bardwell	29	TL 9473
Barewood	24	SO 3856
Barford (Norf.)	29	TG 1007
Barford (Warw.)	29	SP 2660
Barford St. Martin	8	SU 0531
Barford St. Michael	26	SP 4332
Barfreston	13	TR 2650
Bargoed	16	SO 1500
Bargrennan	44	NX 3476
Barham (Cambs.)	27	TL 1375
Barham (Kent)	13	TR 2050
Barham (Suff.)	21	TM 1451
Barholm	27	TF 0811
Barkby	26	SK 6309
Barkestone-le-Vale	34	SK 7734
Barkham	10	SU 7866
Barking (Gtr London)	20	TQ 4785
Barking (Suff.)	21	TM 0653
Barkingside	20	TQ 4489
Barkisland	37	SE 0419
Barkston (Lincs.)	34	SK 9241
Barkston (N Yorks.)	38	SE 4936
Barkway	20	TL 3835
Barkwith	35	TF 1681
Barlaston	33	SJ 8938
Barlavington	11	SU 9716
Barlborough	34	SK 4777
Barlby	38	SE 6334
Barlestone	26	SK 4205
Barley (Herts.)	20	TL 4038
Barley (Lancs.)	37	SD 8240
Barleythorpe	27	SK 8409
Barling	21	TQ 9289
Barlow (Derby.)	33	SK 3474
Barlow (N Yorks.)	38	SE 6428
Barlow (Tyne and Wear)	47	NZ 1560
Barmby Moor	38	SE 7748
Barmby on the Marsh	38	SE 6828
Barmer	28	TF 8133
Barmouth	30	SH 6115
Barmpton	42	NZ 3118
Barmston	39	TA 1659
Barnack	27	TF 0705
Barnacle	26	SP 3884
Barnard Castle	41	NZ 0516
Barnard Gate	18	SP 4010
Barnardiston	20	TL 7148
Barnburgh	38	SE 4803
Barnby	29	TM 4789
Barnby Dun	38	SE 6109
Barnby Moor	34	SK 6684
Barnby in the Willows	34	SK 8552
Barnes	11	TQ 2276
Barnet	19	TQ 2494
Barnetby le Wold	39	TA 0509
Barney	29	TF 9932
Barnham (Suff.)	28	TL 8779
Barnham (W Susx)	11	SU 9604
Barnham Broom	29	TG 0807
Barnhead	57	NO 6657
Barnhill	61	NJ 1457
Barnhills	44	NW 9871
Barningham (Durham)	41	NZ 0810
Barningham (Suff.)	29	TL 9676
Barnoldby le Beck	39	TA 2303
Barnoldswick	37	SD 8746
Barns Green	11	TQ 1227
Barnsley (Glos.)	17	SP 0705
Barnsley (S Yorks.)	38	SE 3406
Barnstaple	6	SS 5533
Barnston (Essex)	20	TL 6519
Barnston (Mers.)	31	SJ 2783
Barnt Green	25	SP 0073
Barnton	32	SJ 6374
Barnwell	27	TL 0485
Barnwood	17	SO 8518
Barr	44	NX 2794
Barrachan	44	NX 3649
Barrack (Grampn)	62	NJ 8942
Barraglom	63	NB 1634
Barrapoll	48	NL 9542
Barras	57	NO 8580
Barrasford	47	NY 9273
Barregarrow	43	SC 3288
Barrhead	50	NS 5058
Barrhill (Strath.)	44	NX 2382
Barrington (Cambs.)	20	TL 3949
Barrington (Somer.)	7	ST 3918
Barripper	2	SW 6338
Barrmill	50	NS 3651
Barrock	67	ND 2571
Barrow (Lancs.)	36	SD 7338
Barrow (Leic.)	34	SK 8815
Barrow (Salop)	24	SJ 6500
Barrow (Somer.)	8	ST 7231
Barrow (Suff.)	28	TL 7663
Barrow Gurney	16	ST 5267
Barrow Street	8	ST 8330
Barrow upon Humber	39	TA 0721
Barrow upon Soar	34	SK 5717
Barrow upon Trent	33	SK 3528
Barrow-in-Furness	36	SD 1969
Barroway Drove	28	TF 5703
Barrowby	34	SK 8736
Barrowden	27	SK 9400
Barrowford	37	SD 8538
Barry (S Glam.)	16	ST 1168
Barry (Tays)	57	NO 5334
Barry Island	16	ST 1166
Barsby	26	SK 6911
Barsham	29	TM 3989
Barston	26	SP 2078
Bartestree	24	SO 5641
Barthol Chapel	62	NJ 8134
Barthomley	32	SJ 7652
Bartley	9	SU 3012
Bartlow	20	TL 5845
Barton (Cambs.)	20	TL 4055
Barton (Ches.)	32	SJ 4454
Barton (Devon.)	5	SX 9067
Barton (Glos.)	17	SP 0925
Barton (Lancs.)	36	SD 5136
Barton (N Yorks.)	42	NZ 2208
Barton (Warw.)	25	SP 1051
Barton Bendish	28	TF 7105
Barton Common	29	TG 3522
Barton Hartshorn	18	SP 6431
Barton Mills	28	TL 7273
Barton Moss	32	SJ 7397
Barton Seagrave	27	SP 8877
Barton St. David	7	ST 5431
Barton Stacey	10	SU 4340
Barton Turf	29	TG 3421
Barton in Fabis	34	SK 5232
Barton in the Beans	26	SK 3906
Barton in the Clay	19	TL 0831
Barton on Sea	9	SZ 2493
Barton-Upon-Humber	39	TA 0222
Barton-le-Street	43	SE 7274
Barton-le-Willows	38	SE 7163

Barton-on-the-Heath
Blandford Forum

Barton-on-the-Heath 18 SP 2532
Barton-under-Needlewood 33 SK 1818
Barvas 63 NB 3649
Barway 28 TL 5475
Barwell 26 SP 4496
Barwick 7 ST 5513
Barwick in Elmet 38 SE 3937
Baschurch 32 SJ 4222
Bascote 26 SP 4063
Basford Green 33 SJ 9951
Bashall Eaves 36 SD 6943
Bashley 9 SZ 2496
Basildon (Berks.) 10 SU 6078
Basildon (Essex) 20 TQ 7189
Basing 10 SU 6652
Basingstoke 10 SU 6351
Baslow 33 SK 2572
Bason Bridge 7 ST 3445
Bassenthwaite 40 NY 2332
Bassett 9 SU 4116
Bassingbourn 20 TL 3344
Bassingfield 34 SK 6137
Bassingham 34 SK 9059
Bassingthorpe 34 SK 9628
Basta 63 HU 5295
Baston 35 TF 1114
Bastwick 29 TG 4217
Batcombe (Dorset) 8 ST 6104
Batcombe (Somer.) 8 ST 6838
Bate Heath 32 SJ 6879
Bath 17 ST 7464
Bathampton 17 ST 7765
Bathealton 7 ST 0724
Batheaston 17 ST 7767
Bathford 17 ST 7866
Bathgate 51 NS 9768
Bathley 34 SK 7759
Bathpool 4 SX 2874
Batley 37 SE 2424
Batsford 25 SP 1834
Battersea 11 TQ 2876
Battisford 21 TM 0554
Battisford Tye 21 TM 0254
Battle (E Susx.) 12 TQ 7416
Battle (Powys) 15 SO 0031
Battlefield 32 SJ 5117
Battlesbridge 20 TQ 7794
Battlesden 19 SP 9628
Battleton 6 SS 9127
Battramsley 9 SZ 3099
Baughurst 10 SU 5859
Baulking 18 SU 3190
Baumber 35 TF 2174
Baunton 17 SP 0204
Baverstock 8 SU 0231
Bawburgh 29 TG 1508
Bawdeswell 29 TG 0420
Bawdrip 7 ST 3339
Bawdsey 21 TM 3440
Bawtry 34 SK 6592
Baxenden 37 SD 7726
Baxterley 26 SP 2796
Bayble 63 NB 5231
Baycliff 40 SD 2872
Baydon 10 SU 2877
Bayford 20 TL 3108
Bayhead 63 NF 7468
Bayles 46 NY 7044
Baylham 21 TM 1051
Bayston Hill 24 SJ 4809
Bayton 24 SO 6973
Beachampton 18 SP 7737
Beachley 16 ST 5591
Beacon 7 ST 1705
Beacon End 21 TL 9524
Beacon Hill (Dorset) 8 SY 9794
Beacon's Bottom 18 SU 7895
Beaconsfield 19 SU 9490
Beacontree 20 TQ 4886
Beacravik 63 NG 1190
Beadlam 42 SE 6584
Beadnell 53 NU 2329
Beaford 4 SS 5514
Beal (N Yorks.) 38 SE 5325
Beal (Northum.) 53 NU 0642
Bealings 21 TM 2348
Beaminster 7 ST 4801
Beamish 47 NZ 2253
Beamsley 37 SE 0752
Bean 12 TQ 5972
Beanacre 17 ST 9066
Beanley 53 NU 0818
Beaquoy 63 HY 3022
Beare Green 11 TQ 1842
Bearley 25 SP 1760
Bearpark 47 NZ 2343
Bearsbridge 46 NY 7857
Bearsden 50 NS 5471
Bearsted 12 TQ 8055
Bearwood 8 SZ 0496
Beattock 45 NT 0702
Beauchamp Roding 20 TL 5809
Beauchief 33 SK 3381
Beaufort 16 SO 1611
Beaulieu 9 SU 3801
Beauly 60 NH 5246
Beaumaris 30 SH 6076
Beaumont (Cumbr.) 46 NY 3459
Beaumont (Essex) 21 TM 1725
Beausale 26 SP 2470
Beaworthy 4 SX 4699
Beazley End 20 TL 7428
Bebington 32 SJ 3384
Bebside 47 NZ 2881
Beccles 29 TM 4290
Becconsall 36 SD 4422
Beck Foot (Cumbr.) 41 SD 6196
Beck Hole 43 NZ 8102
Beck Row 28 TL 6977
Beck Side 40 SD 2382
Beckbury 24 SJ 7601
Beckenham 12 TQ 3769
Beckermet 40 NY 0206
Beckfoot (Cumbr.) 45 NY 0949
Beckfoot (Cumbr.) 40 NY 1600
Beckford 25 SO 9735
Beckhampton 17 SU 0868
Beckingham (Lincs.) 34 SK 8753
Beckingham (Notts.) 34 SK 7790
Beckington 17 ST 7951
Beckley (E Susx.) 13 TQ 8423
Beckley (Oxon) 18 SP 5611
Beckton 20 TQ 4381
Beckwithshaw 37 SE 2653
Bedale 42 SE 2688
Bedburn 41 NZ 1031
Beddau 16 ST 0585
Beddgelert 30 SH 5848
Beddingham 12 TQ 4408
Beddington 12 TQ 3165
Bedfield 29 TM 2266
Bedford 27 TL 0449
Bedhampton 9 SU 6906
Bedingfield 29 TM 1768
Bedlington 47 NZ 2581
Bedlinog 16 SO 0901
Bedmond 19 TL 0903
Bednall 33 SJ 9517
Bedrule 52 NT 6017
Bedstone 24 SO 3675
Bedwas 16 ST 1689
Bedworth 26 SP 3587
Beeby 26 SK 6608
Beech (Hants.) 10 SU 6938
Beech (Staffs.) 33 SJ 8538
Beech Hill 10 SU 6964
Beechamwell 28 TF 7405
Beechingstoke 17 SU 0859
Beedon 10 SU 4877
Beeford 39 TA 1254
Beeley 33 SK 2667
Beelsby 39 TA 2001
Beenham 10 SU 5868
Beer 7 SY 2289
Beer Hackett 8 ST 5911
Beercrocombe 7 ST 3220
Beesby 35 TF 4680
Beeson 5 SX 8140
Beeston (Beds.) 27 TL 1648
Beeston (Ches.) 32 SJ 5358
Beeston (Norf.) 28 TF 9015
Beeston (Notts.) 34 SK 5336
Beeston (W Yorks.) 38 SE 2930
Beeston Regis 29 TG 1742
Beeswing 45 NX 8969
Beetham 40 SD 4979
Beetley 29 TF 9718
Begbroke 18 SP 4613
Begelly 14 SN 1107
Beguildy 23 SO 1979
Beighton (Norf.) 29 TG 3808
Beighton (S Yorks.) 34 SK 4483
Beith 49 NS 3454
Bekesbourne 13 TR 1955
Belaugh 29 TG 2818
Belbroughton 25 SO 9177
Belchamp Otten 20 TL 8041
Belchamp St. Paul 20 TL 7942
Belchamp Walter 20 TL 8240
Belchford 35 TF 2975
Belford 53 NU 1033
Belhelvie 62 NJ 9417
Bell Busk 37 SD 9056
Bellabeg 61 NJ 3513
Bellanoch 49 NR 7992
Bellaty 57 NO 2459
Belleau 35 TF 4078
Bellehiglash 61 NJ 1837
Bellerby 41 SE 1192
Belliehill 57 NO 5663
Bellingdon 19 SP 9405
Bellingham 47 NY 8383
Belloch 48 NR 6737
Bellochantuy 48 NR 6632
Bells Yew Green 12 TQ 6136
Bellsbank 44 NS 4804
Bellshill (Northum.) 53 NU 1230
Bellshill (Strath.) 50 NS 7360
Bellspool 51 NT 1635
Bellsquarry 51 NT 0465
Belmaduthy 60 NH 6556
Belmesthorpe 27 TF 0410
Belmont (Lancs.) 36 SD 6715
Belmont (Unst) 63 HP 5600
Belnacraig 61 NJ 3716
Belowda 2 SW 9661
Belper 33 SK 3447
Belsay 47 NZ 1078
Belses 52 NT 5725
Belsford 5 SX 7659
Belstead 21 TM 1341
Belston 50 NS 3820
Belstone 5 SX 6193
Belthorn 36 SD 7124
Beltoft 39 SE 8006
Belton (Humbs.) 38 SE 7806
Belton (Leic.) 34 SK 4420
Belton (Leic.) 26 SK 8101
Belton (Lincs.) 34 SK 9239
Belton (Norf.) 29 TG 4802
Belvedere 12 TQ 4978
Belvoir 34 SK 8133
Bembridge 9 SZ 6488
Bemersyde 52 NT 5933
Bempton 39 TA 1972
Benacre 29 TM 5184
Benenden 12 TQ 8033
Bengate 29 TG 3027
Benholm 57 NO 8069
Beningbrough 38 SE 5257
Benington (Herts.) 20 TL 3023
Benington (Lincs.) 35 TF 3946
Benllech 30 SH 5182
Benmore (Central) 55 NN 4125
Bennacott 4 SX 2991
Bennan (Island of Arran) 49 NR 9821
Bennecarrigan 49 NR 9423
Benniworth 35 TF 2081
Benover 12 TQ 7048
Benson 18 SU 6191
Benthall (Northum.) 53 NU 2328
Benthall (Salop) 24 SJ 6602
Bentham 17 SO 9116
Bentley (Hants.) 10 SU 7844
Bentley (Here. and Worc.) 25 SO 9966
Bentley (Humbs.) 39 TA 0135
Bentley (S Yorks.) 38 SE 5605
Bentley (Warw.) 26 SP 2895
Bentley Heath 25 SP 1676
Benton 6 SS 6536
Bentpath 46 NY 3190
Bentworth 10 SU 6640
Benvie 57 NO 3231
Benwick 27 TL 3490
Beoley 25 SP 0669
Beoraidbeg 58 NM 6793
Bepton 11 SU 8518
Berden 20 TL 4629
Bere Alston 4 SX 4466
Bere Ferrers 4 SX 4563
Bere Regis 8 SY 8494
Berea 14 SM 7929
Berepper 2 SW 6522
Bergh Apton 29 TG 3000
Berinsfield 18 SU 5696
Berkeley 17 ST 6899
Berkhamsted 19 SP 9907
Berkley 8 ST 8049
Berkswell 26 SP 2479
Bermondsey 12 TQ 3579
Bernisdale 58 NG 4050
Berrick Salome 18 SU 6293
Berriedale Water 67 ND 0630
Berriew 23 SJ 1801
Berrington (Northum.) 53 NU 0043
Berrington (Salop) 24 SJ 5206
Berrow 7 ST 2952
Berrow Green 24 SO 7458
Berry Hill 17 SO 5712
Berry Pomeroy 5 SX 8261
Berryhillock 61 NJ 5060
Berrynarbor 6 SS 5546
Bersham 32 SJ 3048
Berstane 63 HY 4610
Bersted 11 SU 9300
Berwick 12 TQ 5105
Berwick Hill 47 NZ 1775
Berwick St. James 8 SU 0739
Berwick St. John 8 ST 9421
Berwick St. Leonard 8 ST 9233
Berwick-upon-Tweed 53 NT 9953
Besford 25 SO 9144
Bessacarr 38 SE 6101
Bessels Leigh 18 SP 4501
Bessingham 29 TG 1636
Besthorpe (Norf.) 29 TM 0695
Besthorpe (Notts.) 34 SK 8264
Beswick 39 TA 0148
Betchworth 11 TQ 2149
Bethel 30 SH 5265
Bethersden 13 TQ 9240
Bethesda (Dyfed) 14 SN 0918
Bethesda (Gwyn.) 30 SH 6266
Bethlehem 15 SN 6825
Bethnal Green 20 TQ 3583
Betley 32 SJ 7548
Betsham 12 TQ 6071
Betteshanger 13 TR 3152
Bettiscombe 7 SY 3999
Bettisfield 32 SJ 4535
Betton (Salop) 32 SJ 6836
Betton (Salop.) 23 SJ 3102
Bettws (Gwent) 16 ST 2991
Bettws (Mid Glam.) 15 SS 9086
Bettws Bledrws 22 SN 5952
Bettws Cedewain 23 SO 1296
Bettws Evan 22 SN 3047
Bettws Gwerfil Goch 31 SJ 0346
Bettws Malpas 16 ST 3090
Bettws-Newydd 16 SO 3606
Bettyhill 66 NC 7061
Betws 15 SN 6311
Betws Garmon 30 SH 5357
Betws-y-coed 31 SH 7956
Betws-yn-Rhos 31 SH 9073
Beulah (Dyfed) 14 SN 2846
Beulah (Powys) 22 SN 9251
Bevendean 12 TQ 3406
Bevercotes 34 SK 6972
Beverley 39 TA 0339
Beverston 17 ST 8693
Bevington 17 ST 6596
Bewaldeth 40 NY 2134
Bewcastle 46 NY 5674
Bewdley 24 SO 7875
Bewerley 37 SE 1564
Bewholme 39 TA 1650
Bexhill 12 TQ 7407
Bexley 12 TQ 4553
Bexwell 28 TF 6303
Beyton 29 TL 9363
Bibury 17 SP 1106
Bicester 18 SP 5822
Bickenhall 7 ST 2818
Bickenhill 25 SP 1882
Bicker 35 TF 2237
Bickerstaffe 36 SD 4404
Bickerton (Ches.) 32 SJ 5052
Bickerton (N Yorks.) 38 SE 4450
Bickington (Devon.) 6 SS 5332
Bickington (Devon.) 5 SX 7972
Bickleigh (Devon.) 5 SS 9407
Bickleigh (Devon.) 4 SX 5262
Bickleton 6 SS 5031
Bickley 12 TQ 4268
Bickley Moss 32 SJ 5448
Bicknacre 20 TL 7802
Bicknoller 7 ST 1039
Bicknor 13 TQ 8658
Bickton 8 SU 1412
Bicton (Salop) 32 SJ 4415
Bicton (Salop) 23 SO 2882
Bidborough 12 TQ 5643
Biddenden 13 TQ 8538
Biddenham 27 TL 0250
Biddestone 17 ST 8673
Biddisham 16 ST 3853
Biddlesden 18 SP 6340
Biddlestone 53 NT 9508
Biddulph 33 SJ 8857
Biddulph Moor 33 SJ 9057
Bideford 6 SS 4526
Bidford-on-Avon 25 SP 1052
Bidston 31 SJ 3089
Bielby 38 SE 7843
Bieldside 62 NJ 8702
Bierley 9 SZ 5077
Bierton 19 SP 8415
Big Sand 64 NG 7579
Bigbury 5 SX 6646
Bigbury-on-Sea 5 SX 6544
Bigby 39 TA 0507
Biggar (Cumbr.) 36 SD 1966
Biggar (Strath.) 51 NT 0437
Biggin (Derby.) 33 SK 1559
Biggin (Derby.) 33 SK 2548
Biggin (N. Yorks.) 38 SE 5434
Biggin Hill 12 TQ 4159
Biggleswade 27 TL 1944
Bighouse 67 NC 8964
Bighton 9 SU 6134
Bignor 11 SU 9814
Bilberry 3 SX 0159
Bilborough 34 SK 5241
Bilbrook 25 SJ 8703
Bilbrough 38 SE 5246
Bilbster 67 ND 2852
Bildeston 21 TL 9949
Billericay 20 TQ 6794
Billesdon 26 SK 7103
Billesley 25 SP 1456
Billingborough 35 TF 1134
Billinge 36 SD 5300
Billingford (Norf.) 29 TG 0120
Billingford (Norf.) 29 TM 1678
Billingham 42 NZ 4624
Billinghay 35 TF 1554
Billingley 38 SE 4304
Billingshurst 11 TQ 0825
Billingsley 24 SO 7085
Billington (Beds.) 19 SP 9422
Billington (Lancs.) 36 SD 7235
Billockby 29 TG 4213
Billy Row 42 NZ 1637
Bilsborrow 36 SD 5140
Bilsby 35 TF 4776
Bilsington 13 TR 0434
Bilsthorpe 34 SK 6560
Bilston (Lothian) 51 NT 2664
Bilston (W Mids) 25 SO 9496
Bilstone 33 SK 3606
Bilting 13 TR 0549
Bilton (Humbs.) 39 TA 1532
Bilton (N Yorks.) 38 SE 4750
Bilton (Northum.) 53 NU 2210
Bilton (Warw.) 26 SP 4873
Binbrook 35 TF 2093
Bincombe 8 SY 6884
Binegar 8 ST 6149
Binfield 11 SU 8471
Binfield Heath 10 SU 7478
Bingfield 47 NY 9772
Bingham 34 SK 7039
Bingham's Melcombe 8 ST 7701
Bingley 37 SE 1039
Binham 29 TF 9839
Binley (Hants.) 10 SU 4153
Binley (W Mids) 26 SP 3778
Binniehill 50 NS 8572
Binstead (Hants.) 10 SU 7741
Binstead (I. of W.) 9 SZ 5792
Binton 25 SP 1454
Bintree 29 TG 0123
Binweston 23 SJ 3004
Birch (Essex) 21 TL 9419
Birch (Gtr. Mches.) 37 SD 8507
Birch Green 21 TL 9418
Birch Vale 33 SK 0286
Bircham Newton 28 TF 7633
Bircham Tofts 28 TF 7732
Birchanger 20 TL 5122
Bircher 24 SO 4765
Birchgrove (S Glam.) 16 ST 1679
Birchgrove (W Glam.) 15 SS 7098
Birchington 13 TR 3069
Birchover 33 SK 2462
Bircotes 34 SK 6391
Bird End 25 SP 0193
Birdbrook 20 TL 7041
Birdham 10 SU 8200
Birdingbury 26 SP 4368
Birdlip 17 SO 9214
Birdsgreen 24 SO 7685
Birdston 50 NS 6575
Birdwell 38 SE 3401
Birdwood 17 SO 7318
Birgham 53 NT 7939
Birkdale 36 SD 3214
Birkenhead 32 SJ 3188
Birkenhills 62 NJ 7445
Birkenshaw (Strath.) 50 NS 6962
Birkenshaw (W Yorks.) 37 SE 2028
Birkhall 61 NO 3493
Birkhill Feus 57 NO 3433
Birkin 38 SE 5226
Birley 24 SO 4553
Birling (Kent) 12 TQ 6860
Birling (Northum.) 47 NU 2406
Birlingham 25 SO 9343
Birmingham 25 SP 0787
Birnam 56 NO 0341
Birness 62 NJ 9933
Birse 61 NO 5596
Birsemore 61 NO 5297
Birstall 26 SK 5809
Birstall Smithies 37 SE 2226
Birstwith 37 SE 2459
Birtley (Here. and Worc.) 24 SO 3669
Birtley (Northum.) 47 NY 8778
Birtley (Tyne and Wear) 47 NZ 2755
Birts Street 24 SO 7836
Bisbrooke 27 SP 8899
Bishampton 25 SO 9851
Bishop Auckland 42 NZ 2029
Bishop Burton 39 SE 9839
Bishop Caundle 8 ST 6912
Bishop Middleham 42 NZ 3231
Bishop Monkton 38 SE 3266
Bishop Norton 34 SK 9892
Bishop Sutton 17 ST 5859
Bishop Thornton 37 SE 2663
Bishop Wilton 38 SE 7955
Bishop's Castle 23 SO 3288
Bishop's Caundle 8 ST 6912
Bishop's Cleeve 17 SO 9527
Bishop's Frome 24 SO 6648
Bishop's Itchington 26 SP 3857
Bishop's Nympton 6 SS 7523
Bishop's Offley 32 SJ 7729
Bishop's Stortford 20 TL 4821
Bishop's Sutton 9 SU 6031
Bishop's Tachbrook 26 SP 3161
Bishop's Tawton 6 SS 5630
Bishop's Waltham 9 SU 5517
Bishop's Wood (Staffs.) 25 SJ 8309
Bishopbriggs 50 NS 6070
Bishops Cannings 17 SU 0364
Bishops Lydeard 7 ST 1629
Bishopsbourne 13 TR 1852
Bishopsteignton 5 SX 9173
Bishopstoke 9 SU 4619
Bishopston 15 SS 5889
Bishopstone (Bucks.) 18 SP 8010
Bishopstone (E Susx.) 12 TQ 4701
Bishopstone (Here. and Worc.) 24 SO 4143
Bishopstone (Wilts.) 8 SU 0625
Bishopstone (Wilts.) 18 SU 2483
Bishopswood (Somer.) 7 ST 2512
Bishopsworth 17 ST 5768
Bishopthorpe 38 SE 5947
Bishopton (Durham) 42 NZ 3621
Bishopton (Strath.) 50 NS 4371
Bishton 16 ST 3887
Bisley (Glos.) 17 SO 9005
Bisley (Surrey) 11 SU 9559
Bispham 36 SD 3139
Bissoe 2 SW 7741
Bisterne Close 9 SU 2202
Bitchfield 34 SK 9828
Bittadon 6 SS 5441
Bittaford 5 SX 6557
Bittering 29 TF 9317
Bitterley 24 SO 5577
Bitterne 9 SU 4513
Bitteswell 26 SP 5385
Bitton 17 ST 6769
Bix 18 SU 7285
Bixter 63 HU 3352
Blaby 26 SP 5697
Black Bourton 18 SP 2804
Black Callerton 47 NZ 1769
Black Clauchrie 44 NX 2984
Black Crofts 54 NM 9234
Black Dog (Devon) 7 SS 8009
Black Down (Devon) 5 ST 0907
Black Down (Devon) 4 SX 5081
Black Down (Dorset) 7 SY 6087
Black Marsh 21 SO 3399
Black Mount (Strath) 55 NN 2842
Black Notley 20 TL 7620
Black Torrington 4 SS 4605
Blackacre 45 NY 0490
Blackadder 53 NT 8452
Blackawton 5 SX 8050
Blackborough 7 ST 0909
Blackborough End 28 TF 6614
Blackboys 12 TQ 5220
Blackbrook 32 SJ 7639
Blackburn (Grampn.) 63 NJ 5434
Blackburn (Grampn.) 62 NJ 8212
Blackburn (Lancs.) 36 SD 6827
Blackburn (Lothian) 51 NS 9865
Blackden Heath 32 SJ 7871
Blackdog (Grampn.) 62 NJ 9514
Blackfield 9 SU 4402
Blackford (Cumbr.) 46 NY 3962
Blackford (Somer.) 8 ST 6526
Blackford (Somer.) 7 ST 4147
Blackford (Tays.) 56 NN 8908
Blackfordby 33 SK 3318
Blackgang 9 SZ 4876
Blackhall Colliery 42 NZ 4539
Blackhall Rocks 42 NZ 4739
Blackham 12 TQ 4839
Blackhaugh 52 NT 4238
Blackheath (Essex) 21 TM 0021
Blackheath (Surrey) 11 TQ 0346
Blackhill (Gramp.) 63 NK 0039
Blackhill (Grampn.) 63 NK 0757
Blackhill (Grampn.) 62 NK 0843
Blackland 17 SU 0168
Blackley 37 SD 8503
Blacklunans 56 NO 1560
Blackmill 15 SS 9386
Blackmoor 10 SU 7833
Blackmoor Gate 6 SS 6443
Blackmore 20 TL 6001
Blackmore End 20 TL 7430
Blackness 51 NT 0579
Blacknest 10 SU 7941
Blacko 37 SD 8541
Blackpill 15 SS 6290
Blackpool 36 SD 3035
Blackpool Gate 46 NY 5377
Blackridge 50 NS 8967
Blackrock (Gwent) 16 SO 2112
Blackrock (Islay) 48 NR 3063
Blackrod 36 SD 6110
Blackshaw 45 NY 0465
Blacksmith's Corner 21 TM 0131
Blackstone 11 TQ 2416
Blackthorn 18 SP 6219
Blackthorpe 28 TL 9063
Blacktoft 39 SE 8424
Blacktop 62 NJ 8604
Blackwater (Corn.) 2 SW 7346
Blackwater (Hants.) 11 SU 8559
Blackwater (I. of W.) 9 SZ 5086
Blackwater (Suff.) 29 TM 5077
Blackwaterfoot 49 NR 8928
Blackwell (Derby.) 33 SK 1272
Blackwell (Durham) 42 NZ 2712
Blackwell (Here. and Worc.) 25 SO 9972
Blackwood (Gwent) 16 ST 1797
Blackwood (Strath.) 50 NS 7943
Blackwood Hill 33 SJ 9255
Blacon 32 SJ 3767
Bladnoch 44 NX 4254
Bladon 18 SP 4414
Blaen Dyryn 15 SN 9336
Blaenannerch 14 SN 2449
Blaenau Ffestiniog 30 SH 7045
Blaenavon 16 SO 2509
Blaenawey 16 SO 2919
Blaenffos 12 SN 1837
Blaengarw 15 SS 9092
Blaengwrach 15 SN 8605
Blaengwynfi 15 SS 8996
Blaenpennal 22 SN 6365
Blaenplwyf 22 SN 5775
Blaenporth 14 SN 2648
Blaenrhondda 15 SS 9299
Blaenwaun 14 SN 2327
Blagdon (Avon) 17 ST 5059
Blagdon Hill (Somerset) 7 ST 2118
Blaich 55 NN 0476
Blaina 16 SO 2008
Blair Atholl 56 NN 8765
Blair Castle (Tays) (ant.) 56 NN 8666
Blair Drummond 56 NS 7398
Blairadam Forest 51 NT 1693
Blairdenon Hill 56 NN 8601
Blairdrummond Moss 56 NS 7297
Blairfindy Castle (ant.) 61 NJ 1928
Blairgowrie 56 NO 1745
Blairhall 51 NT 0089
Blairingone 51 NS 9896
Blairlogie 50 NS 8396
Blairmore 49 NS 1982
Blairnamarrow 62 NJ 2117
Blairskaith 50 NS 5975
Blaisdon 17 SO 7016
Blakebrook 24 SO 8077
Blakedown 25 SO 8778
Blakelaw 53 NT 7730
Blakemere 24 SO 3641
Blakeney (Glos.) 17 SO 6707
Blakeney (Norf.) 29 TG 0243
Blakenhall (Ches.) 32 SJ 7247
Blakenhall (W Mids) 25 SO 9297
Blakeshall 25 SO 8381
Blakesley 26 SP 6250
Blanchland 47 NY 9650
Bland Hill 37 SE 2053
Blandford Forum 8 ST 8806

Blandford St. Mary

Brightwalton

Blandford St. Mary 8 ST8805
Blanefield 50 NS5579
Blankney 35 TF0660
Blara Chaorvinn 57 NN1068
Blarghour 55 NM9913
Blarmachfoldach 55 NN0969
Blarnaleyoch 64 NH1490
Blashford 8 SU1406
Blaston 26 SP8095
Blatherwycke 27 SP9795
Blawith 40 SD2888
Blaxhall 21 TM3657
Blaxton 38 SE6600
Blaydon 47 NZ1863
Bleadon 16 ST3456
Blean 13 TR1260
Bleasby 34 SK7049
Blebocraigs 57 NO4214
Bleddfa 23 SO2068
Bledington 18 SP2422
Bledlow 18 SP7802
Bledlow Ridge 18 SU7898
Blegbie 52 NT4861
Blencarn 41 NY6331
Blencogo 45 NY1947
Blencow 40 NY4532
Blendworth 10 SU7113
Blennerhasset 45 NY1741
Bletchingdon 18 SP5017
Bletchingley 12 TQ3250
Bletchley (Bucks.) 19 SP8733
Bletchley (Salop) 32 SJ6233
Bletherston 14 SN0721
Bletsoe 27 TL0258
Blewbury 18 SU5385
Blickling 29 TG1728
Blidworth 34 SK5855
Blindburn 53 NT8310
Blindcrake 40 NY1434
Blindley Heath 12 TQ3645
Blisland 3 SX0973
Bliss Gate 24 SO7472
Blissford 8 SU1713
Blisworth 26 SP7253
Blo Norton 29 TM0179
Blockley 25 SP1634
Blofield 29 TG3309
Blore 33 SK1349
Bloxham 18 SP4235
Bloxwich 25 SJ9902
Bloxworth 8 SY8894
Blubberhouses 37 SE1655
Blue Anchor 7 ST0343
Blue Bell Hill 12 TQ7462
Blunderston 29 TM5197
Blunham 27 TL1551
Blunsdon St. Andrew 17 SU1389
Bluntisham 27 TL3674
Blyborough 34 SK9394
Blyford 29 TM4276
Blymhill 25 SJ8112
Blyth (Northum.) 47 NZ3181
Blyth (Notts.) 34 SK6287
Blyth Bridge 51 NT1345
Blythburgh 29 TM4575
Blythe Bridge 33 SJ9541
Blyton 34 SK8594
Bo'Ness 51 NS9981
Boarhills 57 NO5614
Boarhunt 9 SU6008
Boarshead 12 TQ5332
Boarstall 18 SP6214
Boasley Cross 4 SX5093
Boat of Garten 60 NH9419
Boath 65 NH5773
Bobbing 13 TQ8865
Bobbington 24 SO8090
Bobbingworth 20 TL5305
Bocaddon 4 SX1758
Bocking 20 TL7623
Bocking Churchstreet 20 TL7525
Boconnoc 4 SX1460
Boddam (Grampn.) 62 NK1342
Boddam (Shetld.) 63 HU3915
Boddington 17 SO8925
Bodedern 30 SH3380
Bodelwyddan 31 SJ0075
Bodenham (Here. and Worc.) 24 SO5251
Bodenham (Wilts.) 8 SU1626
Bodewryd 30 SH3990
Bodfari 31 SJ0970
Bodffordd 30 SH4276
Bodfuan 30 SH3237
Bodham Street 29 TG1240
Bodiam 12 TQ7826
Bodicote 18 SP4537
Bodieve 3 SW9973
Bodior 30 SH2876
Bodle Street Green 12 TQ6514
Bodmin 3 SX0767
Bodney 28 TL8398
Bodorgan 30 SH3867
Bog, The 24 SO3597
Bogbrae 62 NK0335
Bogend 50 NS3932
Boghall 51 NS9968
Bogmoor 61 NJ3562
Bogniebrae 62 NJ5945
Bognor Regis 11 SZ9399
Bograxie 62 NJ7119
Bogside 50 NS8353
Bogton 62 NJ6751
Bogue 45 NX6481
Bohortha 2 SW8632
Bohuntine 55 NN2882
Boisdale 63 NF7414
Bojewyan 2 SW3934
Bolam 42 NZ1922
Bold Heath 32 SJ5389
Boldon 47 NZ3661
Boldon Colliery 47 NZ3462
Boldre 9 SZ3198
Boldron 41 NZ0314
Bole 34 SK7987
Bolehill 33 SK2955
Boleside 52 NT4933
Bolham Water 7 ST1612
Bolingey 2 SW7653
Bollington (Ches.) 32 SJ7286
Bollington (Ches.) 33 SJ9377
Bolney 11 TQ2622
Bolnhurst 27 TL0859
Bolshan 57 NO6252
Bolsover 34 SK4770
Bolsterstone 33 SK2696
Bolstone 24 SO5532
Boltby 42 SE4886
Bolton (Cumbr.) 41 NY6323
Bolton (Gtr Mches.) 36 SD7108
Bolton (Humbs.) 38 SE7752
Bolton (Lothian) 52 NT5070
Bolton (Northum.) 53 NU1013
Bolton Abbey 37 SE0754
Bolton Percy 38 SE5341
Bolton Upon Dearne 38 SE4502
Bolton by Bowland 37 SD7849
Bolton le Sands 36 SD4867
Bolton-on-Swale 42 SE2599
Boltonfellend 46 NY4768
Boltongate 46 NY2340
Bolventor 4 SX1876
Bomere Heath 32 SJ4719
Bonar-Bridge 65 NH6191
Bonawe 55 NN0133
Bonawe Quarries 55 NN0133
Bonby 39 TA0015
Boncath 14 SN2038
Bonchester Bridge 52 NT5811
Bondleigh 5 SS6504
Bonehill 25 SK1902
Bonhill 50 NS3979
Boningale 25 SJ8102
Bonjedward 52 NT6523
Bonkle 50 NS8356
Bonnington (Kent) 13 TR0536
Bonnington (Lothian) 51 NT1269
Bonnington Smiddy 57 NO5739
Bonnybank 57 NO3503
Bonnybridge 50 NS8280
Bonnykelly 62 NJ8553
Bonnyrigg 51 NT3065
Bonnyton (Tays.) 57 NO3338
Bonnyton (Tays.) 57 NO6655
Bonsall 33 SK2758
Bont 16 SO3819
Bont Newydd (Gwyn.) 31 SH7720
Bont-dolgadfan 22 SH8800
Bontddu 30 SH6618
Bontgoch Elerch 22 SN6886
Bontnewydd (Gwyn.) 30 SH4859
Bontuchel 31 SJ0857
Bonvilston 16 ST0674
Booker 19 SU8491
Booley 32 SJ5725
Boosbeck 42 NZ6516
Boot 40 NY1700
Boothby Graffoe 34 SK9859
Boothby Pagnell 34 SK9730
Boothstown 36 SD7200
Bootle (Cumbr.) 40 SD1088
Bootle (Mers.) 32 SJ3394
Bootle Station 40 SD0989
Boquhan 50 NS5387
Boraston 24 SO6170
Borden 13 TQ8863
Bordley 37 SD9465
Bordon Camp 9 SU7937
Boreham (Essex) 20 TL7509
Boreham (Wilts.) 8 ST8944
Boreham Street 12 TQ6611
Borehamwood 19 TQ1996
Boreland (Dumf. and Galwy.) 45 NY1790
Boreraig 58 NG1853
Borgie 66 NC6759
Borgue (Dumf. and Galwy.) 45 NX6248
Borgue (Highld.) 67 ND1325
Borley 20 TL8442
Bornesketaig 58 NG3771
Borness 45 NX6145
Borough Green 12 TQ6057
Boroughbridge 38 SE3966
Borras Head 32 SJ3653
Borrobol Lodge 67 NC8626
Borrowash 33 SK4134
Borrowby 42 SE4289
Borrowdale (Cumbr.) 40 NY2514
Borth 22 SN6089
Borthwickbrae 52 NT4113
Borthwickshiels 52 NT4315
Borve (Barra) 63 NF6501
Borve (Berneray) 63 NF9181
Borve (Island of Skye) 58 NG4448
Borvemore 63 NG0294
Borwick 36 SD5273
Bosavern 2 SW3730
Bosbury 24 SO6943
Boscastle 3 SX0990
Boscombe (Dorset) 8 SZ1191
Boscombe (Wilts.) 10 SU2038
Boscoppa 3 SX0353
Bosham 10 SU8004
Bosherton 14 SR9694
Boskednan 2 SW4434
Bosley 33 SJ9165
Bossall 38 SE7160
Bossiney 3 SX0688
Bossingham 13 TR1549
Bostock Green 32 SJ6769
Boston 35 TF3244
Boston Spa 38 SE4245
Botallack 2 SW3632
Botcheston 26 SK4804
Botesdale 29 TM0475
Bothal 47 NZ2386
Bothamsall 34 SK6773
Bothel 40 NY1838
Bothenhampton 7 SY4791
Bothwell 50 NS7058
Botley (Bucks.) 19 SP9802
Botley (Hants.) 9 SU5112
Botley (Oxon.) 18 SP4806
Botolphs 11 TQ1909
Bottacks 65 NH4860
Bottesford (Humbs.) 39 SE9107
Bottesford (Leic.) 34 SK8038
Bottisham 28 TL5460
Bottomcraig 57 NO3724
Bottoms 37 SD9321
Botusfleming 4 SX4061
Botwnnog 30 SH2631
Boughrood 23 SO1239
Boughspring 16 ST5597
Boughton (Norf.) 28 TF7002
Boughton (Northants.) 26 SP7565
Boughton (Notts.) 34 SK6768
Boughton Aluph 13 TR0348
Boughton Green 12 TQ7651
Boughton Lees 13 TR0247
Boughton Malherbe 13 TQ8849
Boughton Street 13 TR0559
Boulby 43 NZ7519
Bouldon 24 SO5485
Boulmer 53 NU2614
Boulston 14 SM9812
Boultham 34 SK9568
Bourn 20 TL3256
Bourne 35 TF0920
Bourne End (Beds.) 27 SP9644
Bourne End (Bucks.) 19 SU8987
Bourne End (Herts.) 19 TL0206
Bournebridge 20 TQ5194
Bournemouth 8 SZ0991
Bournes Green 17 SO9104
Bournheath 25 SO9474
Bournmoor 47 NZ3051
Bournville 25 SP0480
Bourton (Avon) 16 ST3864
Bourton (Dorset) 8 ST7630
Bourton (Oxon.) 18 SU2387
Bourton (Salop) 24 SO5996
Bourton on Dunsmore 26 SP4370
Bourton-on-the-Hill 25 SP1732
Bourton-on-the-Water 17 SP1620
Bousd 48 NM2563
Boveney 11 SU9377
Boverton 16 SS9868
Bovey Tracey 5 SX8178
Bovingdon 19 TL0103
Bovington Camp 8 SY8389
Bow (Devon.) 5 SS7201
Bow (Flotta) (Ork) 63 ND3693
Bow Brickhill 19 SP9034
Bow Street 22 SN6284
Bow of Fife 57 NO3112
Bowbank 41 NY9423
Bowburn 42 NZ3038
Bowcombe 9 SZ4786
Bowd 7 SY1190
Bowden (Borders) 52 NT5530
Bowden (Devon.) 5 SX8448
Bowden Hill 17 ST9367
Bowdon 32 SJ7586
Bower 46 ND2463
Bowerchalke 8 SU0122
Bowermadden 67 ND2364
Bowers Gifford 20 TQ7588
Bowershall 51 NT0991
Bowertower 67 ND2362
Bowes 41 NY9913
Bowhill 52 NT4227
Bowland Bridge 40 SD4189
Bowley 24 SO5352
Bowlhead Green 11 SU9138
Bowling 50 NS4473
Bowling Bank 32 SJ3948
Bowling Green 25 SO8151
Bowmanstead 40 SD3096
Bowmore 48 NR3159
Bowness-on-Solway 46 NY2262
Bowness-on-Windermere 40 SD4097
Bowsden 53 NT9941
Bowthorpe 29 TG1709
Box (Glos.) 17 SO8600
Box (Wilts.) 17 ST8268
Boxbush 17 SO7412
Boxford (Berks.) 10 SU4271
Boxford (Suff.) 21 TL9640
Boxgrove 11 SU9007
Boxley 12 TQ7759
Boxted (Essex) 21 TM0033
Boxted (Suff) 20 TL8251
Boxworth 27 TL3464
Boyden Gate 13 TR2264
Boylestone 33 SK1835
Boyndie 62 NJ6463
Boyndie Bay 62 NJ6765
Boyndlie 62 NJ9162
Boynton 39 TA1368
Boysack 57 NO6249
Boyton (Corn.) 4 SX3192
Boyton (Suff.) 21 TM3747
Boyton (Wilts.) 8 ST9539
Bozeat 27 SP9059
Braaid 43 SC3176
Brabling Green 29 TM2964
Brabourne Lees 13 TR0840
Brabstermire 67 ND3169
Bracadale 58 NG3538
Braceborough 27 TF0713
Bracebridge Heath 34 SK9767
Braceby 34 TF0135
Bracewell 37 SD8648
Brackenfield 33 SK3759
Brackenthwaite 40 NY1522
Brackletter 55 NN1882
Brackley (Northants.) 18 SP5837
Brackley (Strath.) 49 NR7941
Bracknell 11 SU8769
Braco 56 NN8309
Bracobrae 61 NJ5053
Bracon Ash 29 TM1899
Bracora 58 NM7192
Bracorina 58 NM7292
Bradbourne 33 SK2052
Bradbury 42 NZ3128
Bradda 43 SC1970
Bradden 26 SP6448
Braddock 4 SX1662
Bradenham 18 SU8297
Bradenstoke 17 SU0079
Bradfield (Berks.) 10 SU6072
Bradfield (Essex) 21 TM1430
Bradfield (Norf.) 29 TG2633
Bradfield (S Yorks.) 33 SK2692
Bradfield Combust 21 TL8957
Bradfield Green 32 SJ6859
Bradfield St. Clare 21 TL9057
Bradfield St. George 21 TL9059
Bradford (Devon.) 4 SS4207
Bradford (Northum.) 53 NU1532
Bradford (W Yorks.) 37 SE1633
Bradford Abbas 8 ST5814
Bradford Leigh 17 ST8362
Bradford Peverell 8 SY6592
Bradford on Avon 17 ST8260
Bradford-on-Tone 7 ST1722
Brading 9 SZ6087
Bradley (Derby.) 33 SK2145
Bradley (Hants.) 10 SU6341
Bradley (Here. and Worc.) 25 SO9860
Bradley (Humbs.) 39 TA2406
Bradley (N Yorks.) 41 SE0380
Bradley (Staffs.) 33 SJ8717
Bradley Green 25 SO9861
Bradley in the Moors 33 SK0541
Bradmore 34 SK5831
Bradninch 5 SS9903
Bradnop 33 SK0155
Bradpole 7 SY4794
Bradshaw 36 SD7312
Bradstone 4 SX3880
Bradwell (Bucks.) 19 SP8339
Bradwell (Derby.) 33 SK1781
Bradwell (Essex) 20 TL8023
Bradwell (Norf.) 29 TG5003
Bradwell Green 32 SJ7563
Bradwell Grove 18 SP2308
Bradwell Waterside 21 TL9907
Bradwell-on-Sea 21 TM0006
Bradworthy 4 SS3213
Brae (Highld.) 65 NC4302
Brae (Highld.) 64 NG8185
Brae (Highld.) 65 NH6662
Brae (Shetld.) 63 HU3567
Brae of Achnahaird 64 NB9913
Braeantra 61 NH5678
Braedownie 57 NO2875
Braefield 60 NH4130
Braegrum 56 NO0024
Braehead (Dumf. and Galwy.) 44 NX4252
Braehead (Orkney.) 63 HY5101
Braehead (Strath.) 50 NS8134
Braehead (Strath.) 51 NS9550
Braehead (Tays.) 57 NO6852
Braehead (Wigtown.) 63 NX4252
Braehoulland 63 HU2479
Braemar 61 NO1592
Braemore 67 ND0630
Braes, The 55 NG5334
Braeside 49 NS2375
Braeswick 63 HY6037
Brafferton (Durham) 42 NZ2921
Brafferton (N Yorks.) 38 SE4370
Brafield-on-the-Green 26 SP8158
Bragar 63 NB2847
Bragbury End 19 TL2621
Braides 35 SD4453
Braidwood 50 NS8448
Braigo 48 NR2369
Brailes 26 SP3139
Brailsford 33 SK2541
Braintree 20 TL7622
Braiseworth 29 TM1371
Braishfield 9 SU3725
Braithwaite 40 NY2323
Braithwell 34 SK5394
Bramber 11 TQ1810
Bramborough 32 SJ3582
Bramcote 34 SK5037
Bramdean 9 SU6127
Bramerton 29 TG2904
Bramfield (Herts.) 19 TL2915
Bramfield (Suff.) 29 TM4073
Bramford 21 TM1246
Bramhall 33 SJ8984
Bramham 38 SE4242
Bramhope 37 SE2443
Bramley (Hants.) 10 SU6358
Bramley (S Yorks.) 34 SK4892
Bramley (Surrey) 11 TQ0044
Brampford Speke 5 SX9298
Brampton (Cambs.) 27 TL2170
Brampton (Cumbr.) 46 NY5361
Brampton (Cumbr.) 41 NY6723
Brampton (Lincs.) 34 SK8479
Brampton (Norf.) 29 TG2224
Brampton (S Yorks.) 38 SE4101
Brampton (Suff.) 29 TM4381
Brampton Abbotts 17 SO6026
Brampton Ash 26 SP7887
Brampton Bryan 24 SO3672
Bramshall 33 SK0633
Bramshaw 9 SU2615
Bramshill 10 SU7461
Bramshott 10 SU8432
Bran End 20 TL6525
Branault 54 NM5369
Brancaster 28 TF7743
Brancepeth 42 NZ2238
Branchill 61 NJ0852
Branderburgh 61 NJ2371
Brandesburton 39 TA1147
Brandeston 29 TM2460
Brandiston 29 TG1321
Brandon (Durham) 42 NZ2439
Brandon (Lincs.) 34 SK9048
Brandon (Northum.) 53 NU0417
Brandon (Suff.) 28 TL7886
Brandon (Warw.) 26 SP4076
Brandon Bank 28 TL6289
Brandon Creek 28 TL6091
Brandon Parva 29 TG0708
Brands Hatch 12 TQ5764
Brandsby 38 SE5872
Brane 2 SW4028
Branksome Park 8 SZ0490
Branscombe 7 SY1988
Bransdale 42 SE6296
Bransford 24 SO7952
Bransgore 8 SZ1897
Branston (Leic.) 34 SK8029
Branston (Lincs.) 34 TF0167
Branston (Staffs.) 33 SK2221
Branstone 9 SZ5583
Brant Broughton 34 SK9154
Brantham 21 TM1034
Branthwaite (Cumbr) 40 NY0525
Brantingham 39 SE9429
Branton 53 NU0416
Branxholm Park 52 NT4612
Branxholme 52 NT4611
Branxton 53 NT8937
Brassington 33 SK2354
Brasted 12 TQ4733
Brasted Chart 12 TQ4653
Bratoft 35 TF4765
Brattleby 34 SK9480
Bratton 17 ST9152
Bratton Clovelly 4 SX4691
Bratton Fleming 6 SS6437
Bratton Seymour 8 ST6729
Braughing 20 TL3925
Braunston (Leic.) 27 SK8306
Braunston (Northants.) 26 SP5366
Braunstone 26 SK5502
Braunton 6 SS4836
Brawby 43 SE7378
Brawl 67 NC8066
Brawlbin 67 ND0757
Bray 11 SU9079
Bray Shop 4 SX3374
Braybrooke 26 SP7684
Brayford 6 SS6834
Brayton 38 SE6030
Brazacott 4 SX2691
Breachwood Green 19 TL1522
Breaclete 63 NB1537
Breadsall 33 SK3639
Breadstone 17 SO7000
Breage 2 SW6128
Breakish 58 NG6723
Bream 17 SO6005
Breamore 8 SU1517
Brean 16 ST2955
Brearton 38 SE3260
Breasclete 63 NB2135
Breaston 34 SK4533
Brechfa 15 SN5230
Brechin 57 NO5960
Breckles 29 TL9594
Breckrey 58 NG5061
Brecon 16 SO0428
Bredbury 33 SJ9292
Brede 12 TQ8218
Bredenbury 24 SO6058
Bredfield 21 TM2653
Bredgar 13 TQ8860
Bredhurst 12 TQ7962
Bredon 25 SO9236
Bredon's Norton 25 SO9339
Bredwardine 23 SO3344
Breedon on the Hill 33 SK4022
Breibister 63 HU2149
Breich 51 NS9560
Breighton 38 SE7033
Breinton 24 SO4739
Breivig 63 NL6998
Bremhill 17 ST9873
Bremia (ant.) 22 SN6456
Brenchley 12 TQ6741
Brendon 6 SS7648
Brenish 63 NA9926
Brent 19 TQ2084
Brent Eleigh 21 TL9447
Brent Knoll 7 ST3350
Brent Pelham 20 TL4330
Brentford 11 TQ1778
Brentwood 20 TQ5993
Brenzett 13 TR0027
Brereton 33 SK0516
Brereton Green 32 SJ7764
Brereton Heath 32 SJ8064
Bressingham 29 TM0780
Bretabister 63 HU4857
Bretby 33 SK2923
Bretford 26 SP4277
Bretforton 25 SP0943
Bretherton 36 SD4720
Brettenham (Norf) 29 TL9383
Brettenham (Suff.) 21 TL9653
Bretton 32 SJ3563
Brewham 8 ST7136
Brewood 25 SJ8808
Briantspuddle 8 SY8193
Bricket Wood 19 TL1301
Bricklehampton 25 SO9842
Bride 43 NX4501
Bridekirk 40 NY1133
Bridell 14 SN1742
Bridestowe 4 SX5189
Brideswell 61 NJ5739
Bridford 5 SX8186
Bridge 13 TR1854
Bridge End (Lincs.) 35 TF1436
Bridge Green 20 TL4636
Bridge Sollers 24 SO4142
Bridge Street 21 TL8749
Bridge Trafford 32 SJ4471
Bridge of Alford 61 NJ5617
Bridge of Allan 50 NS7897
Bridge of Avon 61 NJ1835
Bridge of Balgie 55 NN5746
Bridge of Brown 61 NJ1220
Bridge of Cally 56 NO1351
Bridge of Canny 62 NO6597
Bridge of Craigisla 57 NO2553
Bridge of Dee 45 NX7360
Bridge of Don 62 NJ9409
Bridge of Dun 57 NO6658
Bridge of Dye 57 NO6585
Bridge of Earn 56 NO1318
Bridge of Feugh 62 NO7094
Bridge of Gairn 61 NO3597
Bridge of Gaur 55 NN5056
Bridge of Muchalls 62 NO8991
Bridge of Orchy 55 NN2939
Bridge of Tilt 56 NN8765
Bridge of Weir 50 NS3865
Bridgefoot 40 NY0529
Bridgemary 9 SU5702
Bridgend (Borders) 52 NT5235
Bridgend (Cumbr.) 40 NY3914
Bridgend (Dumf. and Galwy.) 51 NT0708
Bridgend (Fife.) 57 NO3911
Bridgend (Grampn.) 61 NJ3731
Bridgend (Grampn.) 61 NJ5135
Bridgend (Islay) 48 NR3362
Bridgend (Lothian) 51 NT0475
Bridgend (Mid Glam.) 15 SS9079
Bridgend (Strath.) 49 NR8592
Bridgend (Strath.) 50 NS6970
Bridgend (Tays.) 56 NO1224
Bridgend (Tays.) 57 NO5368
Bridgend of Lintrathen 57 NO2854
Bridgerule 4 SS2803
Bridges 24 SO3996
Bridgetown 6 SS9233
Bridgeyate 17 ST6873
Bridgham 29 TL9686
Bridgnorth 24 SO7193
Bridgtown 25 SJ9808
Bridgwater 7 ST3037
Bridlington 39 TA1766
Bridport 7 SY4692
Bridstow 17 SO5824
Brierfield 37 SD8436
Brierley (Glos.) 17 SP6215
Brierley (Here. and Worc.) 24 SO4956
Brierley (S Yorks.) 38 SE4011
Brierley Hill 25 SO9187
Brig o'Turk 55 NN5306
Brigg 39 TA0007
Brigham (Cumbr.) 40 NY0830
Brigham (Humbs.) 39 TA0753
Brighouse 37 SE1423
Brighstone 9 SZ4282
Brightgate 33 SK2659
Brighthampton 18 SP3803
Brightling 12 TQ6821
Brightlingsea 21 TM0816
Brighton (Corn.) 2 SW9054
Brighton (E Susx) 12 TQ3105
Brightons 50 NS9277
Brightwalton 10 SU4278

Brightwell

Carhampton

Brightwell (Oxon.) 18 SU 5790
Brightwell (Suff.) 21 TM 2543
Brightwell Baldwin 18 SU 6594
Brignall 41 NZ 0712
Brigsley 39 TA 2501
Brigsteer 40 SD 4889
Brigstock 27 SP 9485
Brill 18 SP 6513
Brilley 23 SO 2549
Brimfield 24 SO 5267
Brimington 33 SK 4073
Brimpsfield 17 SO 9312
Brimpton 10 SU 5564
Brims 63 ND 2888
Brind 38 SE 7430
Brindle 36 SD 5924
Brindley Ford 33 SJ 8754
Brindley Heath 25 SJ 9914
Brineton 24 SJ 8013
Bringewood Chase 24 SO 4573
Bringhurst 27 SP 8492
Brington 27 TL 0875
Briningham 29 TG 0334
Brinkhill 35 TF 3773
Brinkley 20 TL 6254
Brinklow 26 SP 4379
Brinkworth 17 SU 0184
Brinscall 36 SD 6321
Brinsley 34 SK 4548
Brinsop 24 SO 4344
Brinsworth 33 SK 4190
Brinton 29 TG 0335
Brinyan 63 HY 4327
Brisley 29 TF 9421
Brislington 17 ST 6170
Bristol 17 ST 5872
Briston 29 TG 0632
Britannia 37 SD 8821
Britford British Legion Village 12 TQ 7257
Briton Ferry 15 SS 7394
Britwell Salome 18 SU 6792
Brixham 5 SX 9255
Brixton 4 SX 5452
Brixton Deverill 8 ST 8638
Brixworth 26 SP 7470
Brize Norton 18 SP 2907
Broad Blunsdon 17 SU 1490
Broad Campden 25 SP 1537
Broad Chalke 8 SU 0325
Broad Green 24 SO 7656
Broad Haven 14 SM 8613
Broad Hill (Cambs.) 28 TL 5976
Broad Hinton 17 SU 1076
Broad Laying 10 SU 4362
Broad Marston 25 SP 1346
Broad Oak (Cumbr.) 40 SD 1194
Broad Oak (E Susx) 12 TQ 8320
Broad Oak (Here. and Worc.) 16 SO 4721
Broad Street 12 TQ 8356
Broad Town 17 SU 0977
Broadbottom 33 SJ 9993
Broadbridge 10 SU 8105
Broadbridge Heath 11 TQ 1431
Broadclyst 5 SX 9897
Broadford 58 NG 6423
Broadhampston 5 SX 8066
Broadhaugh 52 NT 4509
Broadheath (Gtr Mches.) 32 SJ 7689
Broadheath (Here. and Worc.) 24 SO 6665
Broadheath (Here. and Worc.) 25 SO 8156
Broadhembury 7 ST 1004
Broadhempston 5 SX 8066
Broadley (Grampn.) 61 NJ 4161
Broadley (Gtr Mches.) 37 SD 8716
Broadley Common 20 TL 4207
Broadmayne 8 SY 7286
Broadmeadows 52 NT 4130
Broadmere 10 SU 6247
Broadoak (Dorset) 7 SY 4496
Broadoak (E Susx) 12 TQ 6022
Broadoak (Kent) 13 TR 1661
Broadrashes 61 NJ 4354
Broadstairs 13 TR 3967
Broadstone (Dorset) 8 SZ 0095
Broadstone (Salop) 24 SO 5389
Broadwas 24 SO 7555
Broadwater 11 TQ 1504
Broadway (Here. and Worc.) 25 SP 0937
Broadway (Somer.) 7 ST 3215
Broadway Hill 25 SP 1136
Broadwell (Glos.) 18 SP 2027
Broadwell (Oxon.) 18 SP 2503
Broadwell (Warw.) 26 SP 4565
Broadwell Lane End 17 SO 5811
Broadwey 8 SY 6683
Broadwindsor 7 ST 4302
Broadwood-Kelly 5 SS 6105
Broadwoodwidger 4 SX 4089
Brobury 23 SO 3444
Brochel 55 NG 5848
Brockbridge 9 SU 6018
Brockdam 53 NU 1624
Brockdish 29 TM 2179
Brockenhurst 9 SU 2902
Brocketsbrae 50 NS 8236
Brockford Street 29 TM 1166
Brockhall 26 SP 6362
Brockham 11 TQ 2049
Brockhampton (Glou.) 15 SP 0423
Brockhampton (Here and worc.) 24 SO 5932
Brockholes 37 SE 1411
Brynna 16 SS 9883
Brynrefail 30 SH 4786
Brynsadler 16 ST 0380
Brynsiencyn 30 SH 4867
Brynteg 30 SH 4982
Bualintur 58 NG 4020
Bubbenhall 26 SP 3672
Bubwith 28 SE 7136
Buccleuch 51 NT 3214
Buchanty 56 NN 9328
Buchlyvie 50 NS 5793
Buck's Cross 6 SS 3422
Buck's Mills 6 SS 3523
Buckabank 46 NY 3749
Buckden (Cambs.) 27 TL 1967
Buckden (N Yorks.) 41 SD 9477
Buckenham 29 TG 3505
Buckerell 7 ST 1200
Buckfast 5 SX 7367
Buckfastleigh 5 SX 7466
Buckhaven 57 NT 3598
Buckholm 52 NT 4838
Buckhorn Weston 8 ST 7524
Buckhurst Hill 20 TQ 4193
Buckie 61 NJ 4265
Buckies 67 ND 1063
Buckingham 18 SP 6933
Buckland (Bucks.) 19 SP 8812
Buckland (Devon.) 5 SX 6743
Buckland (Glos.) 25 SP 0836
Buckland (Herts.) 20 TL 3533
Buckland (Kent) 13 TR 2942
Buckland (Oxon.) 18 SU 3497
Buckland (Surrey) 11 TQ 2250
Buckland Brewer 6 SS 4120
Buckland Common 19 SP 9306
Buckland Dinham 8 ST 7550
Buckland Filleigh 6 SS 4609
Buckland Monachorum 4 SX 4868
Buckland Newton 8 ST 6905
Buckland St. Mary 7 ST 2713
Buckland in the Moor 5 SX 7273
Buckland-Tout-Saints 5 SX 7546
Bucklebury 10 SU 5570
Bucklerheads 57 NO 4636
Bucklers Hard 9 SZ 4099
Bucklesham 21 TM 2442
Buckley 31 SJ 2764
Buckminster 34 SK 8722
Bucknall (Lincs.) 35 TF 1668
Bucknall (Staffs.) 33 SJ 9147
Bucknell (Oxon.) 18 SP 5525
Bucknell (Salop) 24 SO 3574
Bucks Green 11 TQ 0732
Bucks Hill 19 TL 0500
Bucks Horn Oak 10 SU 8142
Bucksburn 62 NJ 8909
Buckton (Here. and Worc.) 24 SO 3873
Buckton (Northum.) 53 NU 0838
Buckworth 27 TL 1476
Budbrooke 26 SP 2565
Budby 34 SK 6169
Bude 4 SS 2006
Budlake 5 SS 9700
Budle 53 NU 1534
Budleigh Salterton 5 SY 0682
Budock Water 2 SW 7832
Buerton 32 SJ 6843
Bugbrooke 26 SP 6757
Bugle 3 SX 0158
Bugthorpe 38 SE 7757
Builth Road 15 SO 0253
Builth Wells 23 SO 0351
Bulby 35 TF 0526
Buldoo 67 NC 9967
Bulford 8 SU 1643
Bulkeley 32 SJ 5254
Bulkington (Warw.) 26 SP 3986
Bulkington (Wilts.) 17 ST 9458
Bulkworthy 4 SS 3914
Bulley 17 SO 7519
Bullwood 49 NS 1674
Bulmer (Essex) 20 TL 8440
Bulmer (N Yorks.) 38 SE 6967
Bulmer Tye 20 TL 8438
Bulphan 20 TQ 6385
Bulverhythe 12 TQ 7809
Bulwell 34 SK 5345
Bulwick 27 SP 9694
Bumble's Green 20 TL 4005
Bunacaimb 58 NM 6588
Bunarkaig 59 NN 1887
Bunaveneadar 63 NB 1304
Bunbury 32 SJ 5658
Bunchrew 60 NH 6145
Buncton 11 TQ 1413
Bundalloch 59 NG 8927
Buness (Unst) 63 HP 6309
Bunessan 54 NM 3821
Bungay 29 TM 3389
Bunnahabhainn 48 NR 4173
Bunny 34 SK 5829
Buntingford 20 TL 3629
Bunwell 29 TM 1293
Bunwell Street 29 TM 1194
Burbage (Derby.) 33 SK 0472
Burbage (Leic.) 26 SP 4492
Burbage (Wilts.) 10 SU 2261
Burcombe (Wilts.) 8 SU 0630
Burcot 18 SU 5595
Burdale 39 SE 8762
Bures 21 TL 9034
Burford 18 SP 2512
Burgar 63 HY 3427
Burgess Hill 12 TQ 3118
Burgh (Suff.) 21 TM 2251
Burgh Heath 11 TQ 2458
Burgh Le Marsh 35 TF 5065
Burgh Muir 62 NJ 7622
Burgh St. Margaret 29 TG 4413
Burgh St. Peter 29 TM 4693
Burgh by Sands 46 NY 3259
Burgh next Aylsham 29 TG 2125
Burgh on Bain 35 TF 2186
Burghclere 10 SU 4660
Burghead 61 NJ 1168
Burghfield 10 SU 6668
Burghfield Common 10 SU 6466
Burghfield Hill 10 SU 6567
Burghill 24 SO 4744
Burghwallis 38 SE 5312
Burham 12 TQ 7262
Buriton 10 SU 7319
Burland 32 SJ 6153
Burlawn 3 SW 9970
Burleigh 11 SU 9069
Burlescombe 7 ST 0716
Burleston 8 SY 7794
Burley (Hants.) 8 SU 2103
Burley (Leic.) 27 SK 8810
Burley Gate 24 SO 5947
Burley Street 8 SU 2004
Burley in Wharfdale 37 SE 1646
Burleydam 32 SJ 6042
Burlingjobb 23 SO 2558
Burlton 32 SJ 4526
Burmarsh 13 TR 1032
Burmington 18 SP 2637
Burn 38 SE 5928
Burnage 33 SJ 8692
Burnaston 33 SK 2832
Burnby 39 SE 8346
Burneside 40 SD 5095
Burneston 42 SE 3084
Burnett 17 ST 6665
Burnfoot (Borders) 52 NT 4113
Burnfoot (Borders) 52 NT 5116
Burnfoot (Tays.) 56 NN 9804
Burnham (Berks. — Bucks.) 19 SU 9382
Burnham (Humbs.) 39 TA 0517
Burnham Beeches 19 SU 9585
Burnham Deepdale 28 TF 8044
Burnham Green 19 TL 2616
Burnham Market 28 TF 8342
Burnham Norton 28 TF 8243
Burnham Overy 28 TF 8442
Burnham Thorpe 28 TF 8541
Burnham-on-Crouch 21 TQ 9496
Burnham-on-Sea 7 ST 3049
Burnhaven 62 NK 1244
Burnhead 45 NX 8595
Burnhervie 62 NJ 7319
Burnhill Green 24 SJ 7800
Burnhope 47 NZ 1948
Burnhouse 50 NS 3850
Burniston 43 TA 0193
Burnley 37 SD 8332
Burnmouth 53 NT 9560
Burnopfield 47 NZ 1756
Burnsall 37 SE 0363
Burnside (Fife.) 56 NO 1607
Burnside (Lothian) 51 NT 0971
Burnside (Shetld.) 63 HU 2778
Burnside (Strath) 50 NS 5922
Burnside (Tays.) 57 NO 5050
Burnside of Duntrune 57 NO 4434
Burnt Fen 28 TL 6085
Burnt Yates 37 SE 2461
Burntisland 51 NT 2385
Burntwood 25 SK 0609
Burpham (Surrey) 11 TQ 0151
Burpham (W. Susx.) 11 TQ 0408
Burra Firth (Unst.) 63 HP 6113
Burradon (Northum.) 47 NT 9806
Burradon (Tyne and Wear) 47 NZ 2772
Burravoe (Shetld.) 63 HU 3666
Burravoe (Yell.) 63 HU 5280
Burrelton 56 NO 1936
Burridge 9 SU 5110
Burrill 42 SE 2387
Burringham 39 SE 8309
Burrington (Avon) 16 ST 4759
Burrington (Devon.) 5 SS 6316
Burrington (Here. and Worc.) 24 SO 4472
Burrough Green 20 TL 6355
Burrough on the Hill 21 SK 7510
Burrow Bridge 7 ST 3530
Burrowhill 11 SU 9763
Burry Port 15 SN 4400
Burscough 36 SD 4310
Burscough Bridge 36 SD 4411
Bursea 39 SE 8033
Burshill 39 TA 0948
Bursledon 9 SU 4809
Burslem 33 SJ 8749
Burstall 21 TM 0944
Burstock 7 ST 4202
Burston (Norf.) 29 TM 1383
Burston (Staffs.) 33 SJ 9330
Burstow 12 TQ 3141
Burstwick 39 TA 2228
Burtersett 41 SD 8989
Burton (Ches.) 32 SJ 3174
Burton (Ches.) 32 SJ 5063
Burton (Cumbr.) 40 SD 5276
Burton (Dorset) 8 SZ 1794
Burton (Dyfed) 14 SM 9805
Burton (Lincs.) 34 SK 9574
Burton (Northum.) 53 NU 1732
Burton (Somer.) 7 ST 1944
Burton (Wilts.) 17 ST 8179
Burton Agnes 39 TA 1063
Burton Bradstock 7 SY 4889
Burton Coggles 34 SK 9725
Burton Constable 39 TA 1836
Burton Fleming 39 TA 0872
Burton Green (Clwyd) 32 SJ 3458
Burton Green (Warw.) 26 SP 2675
Burton Hastings 26 SP 4189
Burton Joyce 34 SK 6443
Burton Latimer 27 SP 9074
Burton Lazars 34 SK 7716
Burton Leonard 38 SE 3263
Burton Overy 26 SP 6798
Burton Pedwardine 35 TF 1142
Burton Pidsea 39 TA 2431
Burton Salmon 38 SE 4827
Burton in Lonsdale 36 SD 6572
Burton on the Wolds 34 SK 5281
Burton upon Stather 39 SE 8617
Burton upon Trent 33 SK 2423
Burtonwood 32 SJ 5692
Burwardsley 32 SJ 5156
Burwarton 24 SO 6185
Burwash 12 TQ 6724
Burwash Common 12 TQ 6423
Burwell (Cambs.) 28 TL 5866
Burwell (Lincs.) 35 TF 3579
Burwick (Shetld.) 63 HU 3940
Burwick (South Ronaldsay) 63 ND 4384
Bury (Cambs.) 27 TL 2883
Bury (Gtr. Mches.) 37 SD 8010
Bury (Somer.) 6 SS 9427
Bury (W. Susx.) 11 TQ 0113
Bury Green 20 TL 4521
Bury St. Edmunds 28 TL 8564
Burythorpe 38 SE 7964
Busbridge 11 SU 9842
Busby (Strath.) 50 NS 5856
Busby (Tays.) 56 NO 0327
Buscot 18 SU 2297
Bush Green 29 TM 2187
Bushbury 25 SJ 9202
Bushey 19 TQ 1395
Bushey Heath 19 TQ 1594
Bushley 25 SO 8734
Bushton 17 SU 0677
Busta 63 HU 3466
Butcher's Pasture 20 TL 6024
Butcombe 16 ST 5161
Butleigh 7 ST 5233
Butleigh Wootton 7 ST 5034
Butlers Marston 26 SP 3150
Butley 21 TM 3651
Butsfield 47 NZ 1044
Butt Green 32 SJ 6651
Buttercrambe 38 SE 7358
Butterknowle 41 NZ 1025
Butterleigh 5 SS 9708
Buttermere (Cumbr.) 40 NY 1717
Buttermere (Wilts.) 10 SU 3361
Buttershaw 37 SE 1329
Butterstone 56 NO 0646
Butterton 33 SK 0756
Butterwick (Humbs.) 39 SE 8305
Butterwick (Lincs.) 35 TF 3045
Butterwick (N. Yorks.) 43 SE 7377
Butterwick (N. Yorks.) 39 SE 9971
Buttington 23 SJ 2408
Buttock's Booth 26 SP 7864
Buttonoak 24 SO 7578
Buxhall 21 TM 0057
Buxted 12 TQ 4923
Buxton (Derby.) 33 SK 0673
Buxton (Norf.) 29 TG 2222
Buxton Heath 29 TG 1821
Bwlch 16 SO 1422
Bwlch-y-cibau 31 SJ 1717
Bwlch-y-ffridd 23 SO 0695
Bwlch-y-groes (Dyfed) 14 SN 2436
Bwlch-y-sarnau 23 SO 0274
Bwlchgwyn 31 SJ 2653
Bwlchllan 22 SN 5758
Bwlchtocyn 30 SH 3126
Byers Green 42 NZ 2234
Byfield 26 SP 5153
Byfleet 11 TQ 0461
Byford 24 SO 3943
Bygrave 19 TL 2636
Byker 47 NZ 2763
Bylchau 31 SH 9762
Byley 32 SJ 7269
Bythorn 27 TL 0575
Byton 24 SO 3664
Byworth 11 SU 9921
Cabourne 39 TA 1301
Cabrach (Grampn.) 61 NJ 3826
Cadbury 5 SS 9105
Cadbury Barton 5 SS 6917
Cadder 50 NS 6172
Caddington 19 TL 0619
Caddonfoot 52 NT 4534
Cade Street 12 TQ 6021
Cadeby (Leic.) 21 SK 4202
Cadeby (S Yorks.) 38 SE 5100
Cadeleigh 5 SS 9107
Cadgwith 2 SW 7214
Cadham 57 NO 2701
Cadishead 32 SJ 7091
Cadle 15 SS 6297
Cadley 10 SU 2066
Cadmore End 18 SU 7892
Cadnam 9 SU 2913
Cadney 39 TA 0103
Cadole 31 SJ 2062
Caeathro 30 SH 5061
Caehopkin 15 SN 8212
Caeo 22 SN 6739
Caerau (Mid Glam.) 15 SS 8594
Caerau (S Glam.) 16 ST 1375
Caerdeon 30 SH 6418
Caergeiliog 30 SH 3178
Caergwrle 31 SJ 3057
Caerleon 16 ST 3390
Caernarfon 30 SH 4862
Caerphilly 16 ST 1587
Caersws 23 SO 0392
Caerwent 16 ST 4790
Caerwys 31 SJ 1272
Caethle 22 SN 6099
Cairnbaan 49 NR 8390
Cairnbrogie 62 NJ 8527
Cairncross 53 NT 8963
Cairndow 55 NN 1810
Cairness 62 NK 0360
Cairneyhill 51 NT 0486
Cairngaan 44 NX 1232
Cairngarroch (Dumf. and Galwy.) 44 NX 0649
Cairnhill (Grampn.) 62 NJ 6732
Cairnie 61 NJ 4945
Cairnorrie 62 NJ 8640
Cairnryan 44 NX 0668
Caister-on-Sea 29 TG 5212
Caistor 39 TA 1101
Caistor St. Edmund 29 TG 2303
Caistron 47 NT 9901
Caitha 52 NT 4640
Calbost 63 NB 4117
Calbourne 9 SZ 4286
Calcot 10 SU 6672
Caldbeck 40 NY 3239
Caldbergh 41 SE 0984
Caldecote (Cambs.) 27 TL 1488
Caldecote (Cambs.) 20 TL 3456
Caldecote (Herts.) 19 TL 2338
Caldecott (Leic.) 27 SP 8693
Caldecott (Northants.) 27 SP 9968
Calder Bridge 40 NY 0405
Calder Mains 67 ND 0959
Calder Vale 36 SD 5345
Calderbank 50 NS 7662
Calderbrook 37 SD 9418
Caldercruix 50 NS 8167
Caldermill 50 NS 6641
Caldhame 57 NO 4748
Caldicot 16 ST 4888
Caldwell 42 NZ 1613
Caldy 31 SJ 2285
Caledrhydiau 22 SN 4753
Calgary 54 NM 3751
Califer 61 NJ 0857
California (Central) 50 NS 9076
California (Norf.) 29 TG 5114
Calke 33 SK 3722
Callaly 53 NU 0509
Callander 56 NN 6208
Callanish 63 NB 2133
Callestick 2 SW 7750
Calligarry 58 NG 6203
Callington 4 SX 3669
Callow 24 SO 4934
Callow End 25 SO 8349
Callow Hill (Here. and Worc.) 24 SO 7473
Callow Hill (Wilts) 17 SU 0385
Callows Grave 24 SO 5966
Calmore 9 SU 3314
Calmsden 17 SP 0408
Calne 17 ST 9971
Calow 33 SK 4071
Calshot 9 SU 4701
Calstock 4 SX 4368
Calthorpe 29 TG 1831
Calthwaite 46 NY 4640
Calton (N Yorks.) 37 SD 9059
Calton (Staffs.) 33 SK 1050
Calvely 32 SJ 5958
Calver 33 SK 2374
Calver Hill 24 SO 3748
Calverhall 32 SJ 6037
Calverleigh 5 SS 9214
Calverley 37 SE 2036
Calvert 18 SP 6824
Calverton (Bucks) 18 SP 7938
Calverton (Notts.) 34 SK 6149
Calvine 56 NN 8066
Calzeat 51 NT 1136
Cam 17 ST 7599
Camas-luinie 59 NG 9128
Camastianavaig 58 NG 5039
Camasunary 58 NG 5119
Camault Muir 65 NH 5040
Camber 12 TQ 9619
Camberley 11 SU 8760
Camberwell 12 TQ 3376
Camblesforth 38 SE 6425
Cambo 47 NZ 0285
Cambois 47 NZ 3083
Camborne 2 SW 6440
Cambridge (Cambs.) 20 TL 4658
Cambus 50 NS 8593
Cambusbarron 50 NS 7792
Cambuskenneth 50 NS 8094
Cambuslang 50 NS 6459
Camden 19 TQ 2784
Camelford 3 SX 1083
Camelon 50 NS 8680
Camelsdale 11 SU 8932
Camerory 61 NJ 0231
Camerton (Avon) 17 ST 6857
Camerton (Cumbr.) 40 NY 0330
Camghouran 55 NN 5556
Cammachmore 62 NO 9295
Cammeringham 34 SK 9482
Camp, The 17 SO 9308
Campbelltown or Ardersier 60 NH 7854
Campbelton 49 NS 1950
Campbeltown 48 NR 7120
Campmuir 56 NO 2137
Campsall 38 SE 5313
Campsea Ashe 21 TM 3356
Campton 19 TL 1238
Camrose 14 SM 9220
Camserney 56 NN 8149
Camusteel 58 NG 7042
Camusterrach 58 NG 7141
Camusvrachan 56 NN 6248
Canada 9 SU 2817
Canal Foot 40 SD 3177
Candlesby 35 TF 4567
Cane End 10 SU 6779
Canewdon 21 TQ 8994
Canford Bottom 8 SU 0300
Canford Cliffs 8 SZ 0689
Canisbay 67 ND 3472
Cann Common 8 ST 8920
Cannich 59 NH 3331
Cannington 7 ST 2539
Cannock 25 SJ 9710
Cannock Wood 25 SK 0412
Canon Bridge 24 SO 4341
Canon Frome 24 SO 6543
Canon Pyon 24 SO 4549
Canonbie 46 NY 3976
Canons Ashby 26 SP 5750
Canonstown 2 SW 5335
Canterbury 13 TR 1557
Cantley (Norf.) 29 TG 3704
Cantley (S Yorks) 38 SE 6202
Cantlop 24 SJ 5205
Canton 16 ST 1577
Cantraydoune 60 NH 7946
Cantraywood 60 NH 7748
Cantsfield 41 SD 6172
Canwick 34 SK 9869
Canworthy Water 4 SX 2291
Caol 55 NN 1076
Caoles 48 NM 0848
Capel 11 TQ 1740
Capel Bangor 22 SN 6580
Capel Betws Lleucu 22 SN 6058
Capel Carmel 30 SH 1628
Capel Coch 30 SH 4582
Capel Curig 30 SH 7258
Capel Cynon 22 SN 3849
Capel Dewi 22 SN 4542
Capel Garmon 31 SH 8155
Capel Gwyn (Dyfed) 15 SN 4622
Capel Gwyn (Gwyn) 30 SH 3575
Capel Gwynfe 15 SN 7222
Capel Hendre 15 SN 5911
Capel Isaac 15 SN 5982
Capel Iwan 14 SN 2836
Capel Llanilterne 16 ST 0979
Capel St. Mary 21 TM 0838
Capelle Ferne 13 TR 2439
Capel-y-ffin 23 SO 2531
Capenhurst 32 SJ 3673
Capernwray 36 SD 5372
Capheaton 47 NZ 0380
Cappercleuch 51 NT 2423
Capstone 12 TQ 7865
Capton 5 SX 8353
Caputh 56 NO 0940
Car Colston 34 SK 7142
Carbis Bay 2 SW 5339
Carbost (Island of Skye) 58 NG 3731
Carbost (Island of Skye) 58 NG 4248
Carbrooke 29 TF 9402
Carburton 34 SK 6173
Carcary 57 NO 6455
Carclew 2 SW 7838
Carcroft 38 SE 5409
Cardenden 51 NT 2195
Cardeston 24 SJ 3912
Cardiff 16 ST 1877
Cardigan 14 SN 1846
Cardington (Beds.) 27 TL 0847
Cardington (Salop) 24 SO 5095
Cardinham 3 SX 1268
Cardney House 56 NO 0545
Cardow 61 NJ 1942
Cardrona 51 NT 3038
Cardross (Strath.) 50 NS 3477
Cardurnock 45 NY 1758
Careby 34 TF 0216
Careston 57 NO 5260
Carew 14 SN 0403
Carew Cheriton 14 SN 0402
Carew Newton 14 SN 0404
Carey 24 SO 5631
Carfrae 52 NT 5769
Cargen 45 NX 9672
Cargenbridge 45 NX 9474
Cargill 56 NO 1536
Cargo 46 NY 3659
Cargreen 4 SX 4262
Carham 53 NT 7938
Carhampton 7 ST 0042

Carharrack Clachan

Carharrack	2	SW 7241
Carie (Tays.)	56	NN 6157
Carie (Tays.)	56	NN 6437
Carinish	63	NF 8159
Carisbrooke	9	SZ 4888
Cark	40	SD 3676
Carlby	35	TF 0414
Carlcotes	37	SE 1703
Carleton (Cumbr.)	46	NY 4253
Carleton (Lancs.)	36	SD 3339
Carleton (N Yorks.)	37	SD 9749
Carleton Forehoe	29	TG 0805
Carleton Rode	29	TM 1192
Carlingcott	17	ST 6958
Carlisle	46	NY 3955
Carlops	51	NT 1656
Carloway	63	NB 2042
Carlton (Beds.)	27	SP 9555
Carlton (Cambs.)	20	TL 6453
Carlton (Cleve.)	42	NZ 3921
Carlton (Leic.)	26	SK 3905
Carlton (N Yorks.)	42	NZ 5004
Carlton (N Yorks.)	41	SE 0684
Carlton (N Yorks.)	42	SE 6086
Carlton (N Yorks.)	38	SE 6423
Carlton (Notts.)	34	SK 6141
Carlton (S Yorks.)	38	SE 3610
Carlton (Suff.)	29	TM 3864
Carlton (W Yorks.)	38	SE 3327
Carlton Colville	29	TM 5190
Carlton Curlieu	26	SP 6997
Carlton Husthwaite	42	SE 4976
Carlton Miniott	42	SE 3980
Carlton Scroop	34	SK 9445
Carlton in Lindrick	34	SK 5984
Carlton-le-Moorland	34	SK 9058
Carlton-on-Trent	34	SK 7963
Carluke	50	NS 8450
Carmacoup	50	NS 7927
Carmathen	15	SN 4120
Carmel (Clwyd)	31	SJ 1676
Carmel (Dyfed)	15	SN 5816
Carmel (Gwyn.)	30	SH 3882
Carmel (Gwyn.)	30	SH 4954
Carmunnock	50	NS 5957
Carmyle	50	NS 6461
Carmyllie	57	NO 5542
Carna	54	NM 6259
Carnaby	39	TA 1465
Carnach (Harris)	63	NG 2297
Carnach (Highld.)	59	NH 0228
Carnan (South Uist)	63	NF 8143
Carnbee	57	NO 5306
Carnbo	56	NO 0503
Carne	2	SW 9138
Carnell	50	NS 4632
Carnforth	36	SD 4970
Carnhell Green	2	SW 6137
Carnie	62	NJ 8105
Carno	23	SN 9696
Carnock	51	NT 0489
Carnon Downs	2	SW 7940
Carnousie	62	NJ 6650
Carnoustie	57	NO 5634
Carnwath	51	NS 9746
Carnyorth	2	SW 3733
Carperby	41	SE 0089
Carr Shield	46	NY 8047
Carr Vale	34	SK 4669
Carradale	49	NR 8138
Carragrich	63	NG 2098
Carrbridge	60	NH 9022
Carreglefn	30	SH 3889
Carrick (Fife.)	57	NO 4422
Carrick (Strath)	49	NR 9187
Carrieden	51	NT 0181
Carrine	48	NR 6709
Carrington (Gtr Mches.)	32	SJ 7492
Carrington (Lincs.)	35	TF 3155
Carrington (Lothian)	51	NT 3160
Carrog	31	SJ 1043
Carron (Central)	50	NS 8882
Carron (Grampn.)	61	NJ 2241
Carron Bridge (Central)	0	NS 7484
Carronbridge (Dumf. & Galwy.)	45	NX 8697
Carronshore	50	NS 8983
Carrutherstown	45	NY 1071
Carrville	47	NZ 3043
Carsaig	54	NM 5421
Carseriggen	44	NX 3167
Carsethorn	45	NX 9959
Carshalton	11	TQ 2764
Carsington	33	SK 2553
Carskiey	48	NR 6508
Carsluith	44	NX 4854
Carsphairn	45	NX 5693
Carstairs	51	NS 9345
Carstairs Junction	51	NS 9545
Carswell Marsh	18	SU 3198
Carter's Clay	9	SU 3024
Carterton	18	SP 2706
Carthew	3	SX 0055
Carthorpe	42	SE 3083
Cartington	47	NU 0304
Cartland	50	NS 8646
Cartmel	40	SD 3778
Cartmel Fell	40	SD 4188
Carway	15	SN 4606
Cashmoor	8	ST 9813
Cassington	18	SP 4510
Casswell's Bridge	35	TF 1627
Castell Howell	15	SN 4448
Castell-y-bwch	16	ST 2792
Casterton	41	SD 6279
Castle Acre	28	TF 8115
Castle Ashby	27	SP 8659
Castle Bank	[illegible]	[illegible]
Castle Bolton	41	SE 0391
Castle Bromwich	25	SP 1489
Castle Bytham	34	SK 9818
Castle Caereinion	23	SJ 1605
Castle Camps	20	TL 6343
Castle Carrock	46	NY 5455
Castle Cary (Somer.)	8	ST 6332
Castle Combe	17	ST 8477
Castle Donington	34	SK 4427
Castle Douglas	45	NX 7662
Castle Eaton	17	SU 1495
Castle Eden	42	NZ 4338
Castle Frome	24	SO 6645
Castle Green	40	SD 5292
Castle Gresley	33	SK 2718
Castle Heaton	53	NT 9041
Castle Hedingham	20	TL 7835
Castle Hill (Suff.)	21	TM 1646
Castle Kennedy	44	NX 1059
Castle Morris	14	SM 9031
Castle O'er	46	NY 2492
Castle Pulverbatch	24	SJ 4202
Castle Rising	28	TF 6624
Castle Stuart	60	NH 7449
Castle Toward	49	NS 1168
Castlebay	63	NL 6698
Castlebythe	14	SN 0229
Castlecary (Strath.)	50	NS 7878
Castlecraig (Borders)	51	NT 1344
Castleford	38	SE 4225
Castlehill (Strath.)	50	NS 8452
Castlemartin	14	SR 9198
Castlemorton	24	SO 7937
Castleside	47	NZ 0748
Castlethorpe	26	SP 7944
Castleton (Borders)	46	NY 5190
Castleton (Derby.)	33	SK 1582
Castleton (Gwent)	16	ST 2583
Castleton (N Yorks.)	42	NZ 6808
Castletown (Highld.)	67	ND 1967
Castletown (I. of M.)	43	SC 2667
Castletown (Tyne and Wear)	47	NZ 3558
Caston	29	TL 9598
Castor	27	TL 1298
Cat's Ash	16	ST 3790
Catacol	49	NR 9149
Catbrain	16	ST 5580
Catcliffe	33	SK 4288
Catcott	7	ST 3939
Caterham	12	TQ 3455
Catesby	26	SP 5159
Catfield	29	TG 3821
Catfirth (Shetld.)	63	HU 4354
Catford	12	TQ 3872
Catforth	36	SD 4735
Cathcart	50	NS 5960
Cathedine	16	SO 1425
Catherington	9	SU 6914
Catherton	24	SO 6578
Catlodge	60	NN 6392
Catlowdy	46	NY 4676
Catmore	18	SU 4579
Caton	36	SD 5364
Cator Court	5	SX 6877
Catrine	50	NS 5225
Catsfield	12	TQ 7213
Catshill	25	SO 9674
Cattal	38	SE 4454
Cattawade	21	TM 1033
Catterall	36	SD 4942
Catterick	42	SE 2397
Catterick Bridge	42	SE 2299
Catterick Camp	42	SE 1897
Catterlen	40	NY 4833
Catterline	57	NO 8678
Catterton	38	SE 5045
Catthorpe	26	SP 5578
Cattistock	8	SY 5999
Catton (N Yorks)	42	SE 3778
Catton (Norf.)	29	TG 2312
Catton (Northum.)	46	NY 8257
Catwick	39	TA 1245
Catworth	27	TL 0873
Caulcott	18	SP 5024
Cauldcotts	57	NO 6547
Cauldhame	50	NS 6494
Cauldon	33	SK 0749
Cauldside	46	NY 4480
Cauldwell	33	SK 2517
Caulkerbush	45	NX 9358
Caunsall	25	SO 8481
Caunton	34	SK 7460
Causewayhead	50	NS 8195
Causey Park	47	NZ 1794
Causeyend	62	NJ 9419
Cautley	41	SD 6994
Cavendish	20	TL 8046
Cavenham	28	TL 7669
Caver's Hill	51	NT 3921
Caversfield	18	SP 5824
Caversham	10	SU 7274
Caversta	63	NB 3619
Caverswall	33	SJ 9442
Cawdor	60	NH 8450
Cawood	38	SE 5737
Cawsand	4	SX 4350
Cawston	29	TG 1324
Cawthorne	37	SE 2807
Cawton	42	SE 6476
Caxton	20	TL 3058
Caxton End	20	TL 3157
Caynham	24	SO 5473
Caythorpe (Lincs.)	34	SK 9348
Caythorpe (Notts.)	34	SK 6845
Cayton	43	TA 0583
Cefn Coch Powys)	31	SJ 1026
Cefn Cribwr	15	SS 8582
Cefn Cross	15	SS 8682
Cefn-Einion	23	SO 2886
Cefn-brith	31	SH 9350
Cefn-coed-y-cymmer	16	SO 0307
Cefn-ddwysarn	31	SH 9638
Cefn-mawr (Clywd)	31	SJ 2842
Cefn-y-bedd	32	SJ 3156
Cefn-y-coed	23	SO 2093
Cefn-y-pant	14	SN 1925
Ceidio	30	SH 4085
Ceint	30	SH 4874
Cellan	22	SN 6149
Cellarhead (Staffs.)	33	SJ 9547
Cemaes	30	SH 3793
Cemmaes	22	SH 8306
Cemmaes Road	22	SH 8204
Cenarth	14	SN 2641
Cennin	30	SH 4645
Ceres	57	NO 4011
Cerne Abbas	[illegible]	[illegible]
Cerney Wick	17	SU 0796
Cerrigceinwen	30	SH 4273
Cerrigydrudion	31	SH 9548
Cessford	53	NT 7323
Chaceley	25	SO 8530
Chacewater	2	SW 7444
Chackmore	18	SP 6835
Chacombe	26	SP 4943
Chad Valley	25	SP 0385
Chadderton	37	SD 9005
Chaddesden	33	SK 3737
Chaddesley Corbett	25	SO 8973
Chaddleworth	10	SU 4177
Chadlington	18	SP 3221
Chadshunt	26	SP 3453
Chadwell St. Mary	12	TQ 6478
Chadwick End	26	SP 2073
Chaffcombe	7	ST 3510
Chagford	5	SX 7087
Chailey	12	TQ 3919
Chainhurst	12	TQ 7347
Chalbury Common	8	SU 0206
Chaldon	12	TQ 3155
Chaldon Herring or East Chaldon	8	SY 7983
Chale	9	SZ 4877
Chale Green	9	SZ 4879
Chalfont St. Giles	19	SU 9993
Chalfont St. Peter	19	SU 9990
Chalford	17	SO 8902
Chalgrove	18	SU 6396
Chalk	12	TQ 6772
Challacombe	6	SS 6941
Challoch	44	NX 3867
Challock Lees	13	TR 0050
Chalton (Beds.)	19	TL 0326
Chalton (Hants.)	9	SU 7316
Chalvington	12	TQ 5109
Chandler's Cross	19	TQ 0698
Chandler's Ford	9	SU 4320
Channerwick	63	HU 4023
Chantry (Somer.)	8	ST 7146
Chantry (Suff.)	21	TM 1443
Chapel	51	NT 2593
Chapel Allerton (Somer.)	7	ST 4050
Chapel Allerton (W Yorks.)	38	SE 2936
Chapel Amble	3	SW 9975
Chapel Brampton	26	SP 7266
Chapel Chorlton	32	SJ 8037
Chapel Haddlesey	38	SE 5826
Chapel Hill (Grampn.)	62	NK 0635
Chapel Hill (Gwent)	16	SO 5200
Chapel Hill (Lincs.)	35	TF 2054
Chapel Hill (Tays.)	56	NO 2021
Chapel Lawn	23	SO 3176
Chapel Le Dale	41	SD 7377
Chapel Row	10	SU 5669
Chapel St. Leonards	35	TF 5572
Chapel Stile	40	NY 3205
Chapel of Garioch	62	NJ 7124
Chapel-en-le-Frith	33	SK 0580
Chapelend Way	20	TL 7039
Chapelgate	35	TF 4124
Chapelhall	50	NS 7826
Chapelhill (Highld.)	65	NH 8273
Chapelhill (Tays.)	56	NO 0030
Chapelknowe	46	NY 3173
Chapelton (Devon.)	6	SS 5826
Chapelton (Strath.)	50	NS 6848
Chapelton (Tays.)	57	NO 6247
Chapeltown (Grampn.)	61	NJ 2421
Chapeltown (Lancs.)	36	SD 7315
Chapeltown (S Yorks.)	33	SK 3596
Chapmanslade	8	ST 8427
Chappel	21	TL 8928
Chard	7	ST 3208
Chardstock	7	ST 3004
Charfield	17	ST 7292
Charing	13	TQ 9549
Charing Heath	13	TQ 9148
Charingworth	18	SP 1939
Charlbury	18	SP 3519
Charlcombe	17	ST 7467
Charlcote	26	SP 2656
Charles	6	SS 6832
Charles Tye	21	TM 0252
Charleston	57	NO 3845
Charlestown (Corn.)	3	SX 0351
Charlestown (Dorset)	6	SY 6597
Charlestown (Fife.)	51	NT 0683
Charlestown (Grampn.)	62	NJ 9300
Charlestown (Highld.)	64	NG 8174
Charlestown (Highld.)	60	NH 6448
Charlestown of Aberlour	61	NJ 2642
Charlesworth	33	SK 0092
Charlinch	7	ST 2337
Charlton (Gtr London)	12	TQ 4278
Charlton (Here. and Worc.)	25	SP 0045
Charlton (Northants.)	18	SP 5236
Charlton (W Susx.)	11	SU 8812
Charlton (Wilts.)	8	ST 9021
Charlton (Wilts.)	17	ST 9698
Charlton (Wilts.)	17	SU 1155
Charlton (Wilts.)	8	SU 1723
Charlton Abbots	17	SP 0324
Charlton Adam	7	ST 5328
Charlton Horethorne	8	ST 6623
Charlton Kings	17	SO 9620
Charlton Mackrell	7	ST 5228
Charlton Marshall	8	ST 8903
Charlton Musgrove	8	ST 7229
Charlton-on-Otmoor	18	SP 5615
Charlwood	11	TQ 2441
Charminster	8	SY 6792
Charmouth	7	SY 3693
Charndon	18	SP 6724
Charney Bassett	18	SU 3894
Charnock Richard	36	SD 5415
Charsfield	21	TM 2556
Chart Sutton	12	TQ 8049
Charter Alley	10	SU 5957
Charterhouse	16	ST 4955
Chartershall	50	NS 7990
Charterville Allotments	18	SP 3110
Chartham	18	TR 1054
Chartham Hatch	13	TR 1056
Chartridge	19	SP 9303
Charwelton	26	SP 5455
Chase Terrace	25	SK 0409
Chasetown	25	SK 0408
Chastleton	18	SP 2429
Chatburn	37	SD 7644
Chatcull	32	SJ 7934
Chatham	12	TQ 7567
Chathill	53	NU 1826
Chattenden	12	TQ 7672
Chatteris	27	TL 3986
Chattisham	21	TM 0942
Chatton	53	NU 0528
Chawleigh	5	SS 7112
Chawston	27	TL 1556
Chawton	10	SU 7037
Cheadle (Gtd Mches.)	33	SJ 8788
Cheadle (Staffs.)	33	SK 0043
Cheadle Hulme	33	SJ 8686
Cheam	11	TQ 2463
Chearsley	18	SP 7110
Chebsey	33	SJ 8528
Checkendon	18	SU 6682
Checkley (Ches.)	32	SJ 7245
Checkley (Staffs.)	33	SK 0237
Chedburgh	20	TL 7957
Cheddar	16	ST 4553
Cheddington	19	SP 9217
Cheddleton	33	SJ 9651
Cheddon Fitzpaine	7	ST 2327
Chedgrave	29	TM 3699
Chedington	7	ST 4805
Chediston	29	TM 3577
Chedworth	17	SP 0511
Chedzoy	7	ST 3337
Cheetham Hill	57	SD 8401
Cheldon	5	SS 7313
Chelford	32	SJ 8174
Chellaston	33	SK 3830
Chellington	27	SP 9656
Chelmarsh	24	SO 7187
Chelmondiston	21	TM 2037
Chelmorton	33	SK 1169
Chelmsford	20	TL 7006
Chelsfield	12	TQ 4864
Chelsworth	21	TL 9748
Cheltenham	17	SO 9422
Chelveston	27	SP 9969
Chelvey	16	ST 4668
Chelwood	17	ST 6361
Chelwood Gate	12	TQ 4130
Cheney Longville	24	SO 4184
Chenies	19	TQ 0198
Chepstow	16	ST 5393
Cherhill	17	SU 0370
Cherington (Warw.)	18	SP 2936
Cherington (Glos.)	17	ST 9098
Cheriton (Devon.)	6	SS 7346
Cheriton (Devon.)	7	ST 1001
Cheriton (Hants.)	9	SU 5828
Cheriton (Somer.)	8	ST 6825
Cheriton (W Glam.)	15	SS 4593
Cheriton Bishop	5	SX 7793
Cheriton Fitzpaine	5	SS 8606
Cherrington	32	SJ 6619
Cherry Burton	39	SE 9842
Cherry Cobb Sands	39	TA 2121
Cherry Hinton	20	TL 4857
Cherry Willingham	34	TF 0173
Chertsey	11	TQ 0466
Cheselbourne	8	SY 7699
Chesham	19	SP 9601
Chesham Bois	19	SU 9698
Cheshunt	20	TL 3502
Cheslyn Hay	25	SJ 9707
Chessington	11	TQ 1863
Chester	32	SJ 4066
Chester-le-Street	47	NZ 2751
Chesterblade	8	ST 6641
Chesterfield (Derby.)	33	SK 3871
Chesterfield (Staffs.)	25	SK 1005
Chesteron (Cambs.)	27	TL 4560
Chesters (Borders)	52	NT 6210
Chesterton (Cambs.)	27	TL 1295
Chesterton (Cambs.)	27	TL 4560
Chesterton (Oxon.)	18	SP 5621
Chesterton (Staffs.)	32	SJ 8249
Chesterton Green	26	SP 3558
Chestfield	13	TR 1365
Cheswardine	32	SJ 7129
Cheswick	53	NU 0346
Chetnole	8	ST 6008
Chettiscombe	5	SS 9614
Chettisham	28	TL 5483
Chettle	8	ST 9513
Chetton	24	SO 6690
Chetwode	18	SP 6429
Chetwynd Aston	32	SJ 7517
Cheveley	28	TL 6760
Chevening	12	TQ 4857
Chevington	20	TL 7859
Chevington Drift	47	NZ 2699
Chevithorne	5	SS 9715
Chew Magna	17	ST 5763
Chew Stoke	16	ST 5561
Chewton Mendip	17	ST 5952
Chicheley	27	SP 9046
Chichester	11	SU 8605
Chickerell	8	SY 6480
Chicklade	8	ST 9134
Chidden	9	SU 6517
Chiddingfold	11	SU 9635
Chiddingly	12	TQ 5414
Chiddingstone	12	TQ 5045
Chiddingstone Causeway	12	TQ 5147
Chideock	7	SY 4292
Chidham	10	SU 7803
Chieveley	10	SU 4773
Chignall Smealy	20	TL 6611
Chignall St. James	20	TL 6709
Chigwell	20	TQ 4493
Chigwell Row	20	TQ 4693
Chilbolton	10	SU 3939
Chilcomb (Hants.)	9	SU 5028
Chilcombe (Dorset)	7	SY 5291
Chilcompton	17	ST 6452
Chilcote	26	SK 2811
Child Okeford	8	ST 8312
Child's Ercall	32	SJ 6625
Childer Thornton	32	SJ 3677
Childrey	18	SU 3687
Childswickham	25	SP 0738
Childwall	32	SJ 4089
Chilfrome	8	SY 5898
Chilgrove	10	SU 8314
Chilham	13	TR 0753
Chillaton	4	SX 4381
Chillenden	13	TR 2753
Chillerton	9	SZ 4883
Chillesford	21	TM 3852
Chillingham	53	NU 0625
Chillington (Devon.)	5	SX 7942
Chillington (Somer.)	7	ST 3811
Chilmark	8	ST 9632
Chilson	18	SP 3119
Chilsworthy (Corn.)	4	SX 4172
Chilsworthy (Devon.)	4	SS 3206
Chilthorne Domer	7	ST 5219
Chilton (Bucks.)	18	SP 6811
Chilton (Durham)	42	NZ 3031
Chilton (Oxon.)	18	SU 4885
Chilton Buildings	42	NZ 2929
Chilton Cantelo	7	ST 5621
Chilton Foliat	10	SU 3170
Chilton Polden	7	ST 3739
Chilton Street	20	TL 7547
Chilton Trinity	7	ST 2939
Chilworth	9	SU 4018
Chimney	18	SP 3500
Chineham	10	SU 6554
Chingford	20	TQ 3893
Chinley	33	SK 0382
Chinnor	18	SP 7500
Chipnall	32	SJ 7231
Chippenham (Cambs.)	28	TL 6669
Chippenham (Wilts.)	17	ST 9173
Chipperfield	19	TL 0401
Chipping (Herts.)	20	TL 3532
Chipping (Lancs.)	36	SD 6243
Chipping Campden	25	SP 1539
Chipping Hill	20	TL 8215
Chipping Norton	18	SP 3127
Chipping Ongar	20	TL 5502
Chipping Sodbury	17	ST 7282
Chipping Warden	26	SP 4948
Chipstable	7	ST 0427
Chipstead (Kent)	12	TQ 5056
Chipstead (Surrey)	11	TQ 2756
Chirbury	23	SO 2598
Chirk	31	SJ 2937
Chirmorie	44	NX 2076
Chirnside	53	NT 8756
Chirnsidebridge	53	NT 8556
Chirton	17	SU 0757
Chisbury	10	SU 2766
Chiselborough	7	ST 4614
Chiseldon	17	SU 1879
Chislehampton	18	SU 5999
Chislehurst	12	TQ 4470
Chislet	13	TR 2264
Chiswellgreen	19	TL 1303
Chiswick	11	TQ 2077
Chisworth	33	SJ 9991
Chithurst	10	SU 8423
Chittering	28	TL 4970
Chitterne	8	ST 9843
Chittlehamholt	6	SS 6420
Chittlehampton	6	SS 6325
Chittoe	17	ST 9666
Chivelstone	5	SX 7838
Chobham	11	SU 9761
Cholderton	10	SU 2242
Cholesbury	19	SP 9307
Chollerton	47	NY 9372
Cholsey	18	SU 5886
Cholstrey	24	SO 4659
Choppington	47	NZ 2583
Chopwell	47	NZ 1158
Chorley (Ches.)	32	SJ 5650
Chorley (Lancs.)	36	SD 5817
Chorley (Salop)	24	SO 6983
Chorley (Staffs.)	25	SK 0711
Chorleywood	19	TQ 0396
Chorlton	32	SJ 7250
Chorlton Lane	32	SJ 4547
Chorlton-cum-Hardy	37	SJ 8093
Chowley	32	SJ 4756
Chrishall	20	TL 4439
Christchurch (Cambs.)	28	TL 4996
Christchurch (Dorset)	8	SZ 1593
Christchurch (Glos.)	17	SO 5713
Christian Malford	17	ST 9678
Christleton	32	SJ 4365
Christmas Common	18	SU 7193
Christon	16	ST 3956
Christon Bank	53	NU 2122
Christow	5	SX 8385
Chudleigh	5	SX 8679
Chudleigh Knighton	5	SX 8477
Chulmleigh	5	SS 6814
Chunal	33	SK 0391
Church	36	SD 7428
Church Brampton	26	SP 7165
Church Broughton	33	SK 2033
Church Crookham	10	SU 8152
Church Eaton	33	SJ 8417
Church End (Beds.)	19	SP 9921
Church End (Beds.)	19	TL 1937
Church End (Cambs.)	27	TF 3909
Church End (Cambs.)	20	TL 4857
Church End (Essex)	20	TL 5841
Church End (Hants.)	10	SU 6756
Church End (Warw.)	26	SP 2892
Church End (Wilts.)	17	SU 0278
Church Fenton	38	SE 5136
Church Gresley	33	SK 2918
Church Hanborough	18	SP 4212
Church Knowle	8	SY 9481
Church Langton	26	SP 7293
Church Lawford	26	SP 4476
Church Lawton	32	SJ 8255
Church Leigh	33	SK 0235
Church Lench	25	SP 0251
Church Minshull	32	SJ 6660
Church Norton	11	SZ 8695
Church Preen	24	SO 5398
Church Pulverbatch	24	SJ 4303
Church Stoke	23	SO 2694
Church Stowe (Northants.)	26	SP 6357
Church Street	12	TQ 7174
Church Stretton	24	SO 4593
Church Warsop	34	SK 5668
Churcham	17	SO 7618
Churchdown	17	SO 8819
Churchend (Essex)	20	TL 6323
Churchend (Essex)	21	TR 0092
Churchill (Avon)	16	ST 4359
Churchill (Here. and Worc.)	25	SO 8779
Churchill (Oxon.)	18	SP 2824
Churchingford	7	ST 2112
Churchover	26	SP 5080
Churchstanton	7	ST 1914
Churchstow (Devon.)	5	SX 7145
Churchtown (I. of M.)	43	SC 4294
Churchtown (Lancs.)	36	SD 4842
Churchtown (Mers.)	36	SD 3618
Churt	10	SU 8538
Churton	32	SJ 4156
Churwell	37	SE 2729
Chwilog	30	SH 4338
Chyandour	2	SW 4731
Cilcain	31	SJ 1765
Cilcennin	22	SN 5160
Cilfor	30	SH 6237
Cilfrew	15	SN 7600
Cilfynydd	16	ST 0892
Cilgerran	14	SN 1943
Cilgwyn	15	SN 7430
Ciliau-Aeron	22	SN 5058
Cilmalieu	54	NM 8955
Cilmery	23	SO 0051
Cilrhedyn	14	SN 2734
Ciltalgarth	31	SH 8840
Cilycwm	22	SN 7540
Cinderford	17	SO 6513
Cioch Mhor	65	NH 5063
Cirean Geardail	64	NC 0034
Cirencester	17	SP 0201
City Dulas	30	SH 4687
Clachaig	49	NS 1181
Clachan (Benbecula)	63	NF 7746
Clachan (Lismore Island)	54	NM 8543
Clachan (North Uist)	63	NF 8163
Clachan (Raasay)	58	NG 5436
Clachan (Strath.)	54	NM 7819
Clachan (Strath.)	48	NR 7656

Clachan Mor Cowden

Clachan Mor 48 NL9847
Clachan of Campsie 50 NS6179
Clachan of Glendaruel 49 NR9984
Clachan-Seil 54 NM7718
Clachbreck 48 NR7675
Clachtoll 64 NC0427
Clackavoid 56 NO1463
Clackmannan 50 NS9191
Clacton-on-Sea 21 TM1715
Cladach Kirkibost 63 NF7865
Cladich 55 NN0921
Claggan 54 NM7049
Claigan 58 NG2354
Claines 25 SO8559
Clandown 17 ST6955
Clanfield (Hants.) 9 SU6916
Clanfield (Oxon.) 18 SP2801
Clannaborough Barton 5 SS7402
Clanville 10 SU3148
Clanyard 44 NX1037
Claonaig 49 NR8656
Claonel 66 NC5604
Clapgate 8 SU0102
Clapham (Beds.) 27 TL0252
Clapham (Gtd London) 11 TQ2875
Clapham (N Yorks.) 36 SD7469
Clapham (W Susx) 11 TQ0906
Clappers 53 NT9455
Clappersgate 40 NY3603
Clapton (Glos.) 17 SP1617
Clapton (Somer.) 7 ST4106
Clapton-in-Gordano 16 ST4774
Clapworthy 6 SS6724
Clarbeston 14 SN0421
Clarbeston Road 14 SN0121
Clarborough 34 SK7383
Clardon 67 ND1468
Clare 20 TL7645
Clarebrand 45 NX7666
Claremont Park 11 TQ1363
Clarencefield 45 NY0968
Clarkston 50 NS5757
Clashmore 65 NH7489
Clashnessie 64 NC0530
Clathy 56 NN9919
Clatt 61 NJ5426
Clatter 23 SN9994
Clattering Brig 57 NO6678
Clatworthy 7 ST0530
Claughton (Lancs.) 36 SD5242
Claughton (Lancs.) 36 SD5666
Claverdon 25 SP1964
Claverham 16 ST4566
Clavering 20 TL4832
Claverley 24 SO7993
Claverton 17 ST7864
Clawdd-newydd 31 SJ0852
Clawton 4 SX3599
Claxby (Lincs.) 35 TF1194
Claxby (Lincs.) 35 TF4571
Claxton (N Yorks.) 38 SE6960
Claxton (Norf.) 29 TG3303
Clay Common 29 TM4781
Clay Coton 26 SP5977
Clay Cross 33 SK3963
Claybokie 61 NO0889
Claybrooke Magna 26 SP4988
Claydon (Oxon.) 26 SP4550
Claydon (Suff.) 21 TM1350
Claygate 11 TQ1563
Claygate Cross 12 TQ6155
Clayhanger (Devon.) 7 ST0223
Clayhanger (W Mids.) 25 SK0404
Clayhidon 7 ST1615
Clayock 67 ND1659
Claypole 34 SK8449
Clays of Allan 65 NH8376
Clayton (S Yorks.) 38 SE4507
Clayton (Staffs.) 33 SJ8443
Clayton (W Susx.) 12 TQ3014
Clayton (W Yorks.) 37 SE1131
Clayton West 37 SE2511
Clayton-le-Moors 36 SD7431
Clayton-le-Woods 36 SD5722
Clayworth 34 SK7288
Cleadale 58 NM4789
Cleadon 47 NZ3862
Clearwell 17 SO5708
Cleasby 42 NZ2713
Cleat 63 ND4585
Cleatlam 41 NZ1118
Cleator 40 NY0113
Cleator Moor 40 NY0214
Cleckheaton 37 SE1825
Clee St. Margaret 24 SO5684
Cleedownton 24 SO5880
Cleehill 24 SO5975
Cleethorpes 39 TA3008
Cleeton St. Mary 24 SO6178
Cleeve 16 ST4566
Cleeve Hill 17 SO9827
Cleeve Prior 25 SP0849
Clehonger 24 SO4637
Cleigh 54 NM8725
Cleish 56 NT0998
Cleland 50 NS7958
Clench Common 17 SU1765
Clenchwarton 28 TF5820
Clent 25 SO9179
Cleobury Mortimer 24 SO6775
Cleobury North 24 SO6187
Cleongart 48 NR6734
Clephanton 60 NH8450
Clerklands 52 NT5024
Cleughbrae 45 NY0774
Clevancy 17 SU0475
Clevedon 16 ST4071
Cleveleys 36 SD3142
Cleverton 17 ST9785
Clewer 7 ST4350
Cley next the Sea 29 TG0444
Cliasamol 63 NB0706
Cliburn 41 NY5824
Cliddesden 10 SU6349
Cliff End 13 TQ8813
Cliffe (Kent) 12 TQ7376
Cliffe (N Yorks.) 38 SE6631
Cliffe Woods 12 TQ7373
Clifford (Here. and Worc.) 23 SO2445
Clifford (W Yorks.) 38 SE4244
Clifford Chambers 25 SP1952
Clifford's Mesne 17 SO7023
Cliffsend 13 TR3464
Clifton (Avon) 17 ST5673
Clifton (Beds.) 27 TL1739
Clifton (Central) 55 NN3230
Clifton (Cumbr.) 40 NY0429
Clifton (Cumbr.) 40 NY5326
Clifton (Derby.) 33 SK1644
Clifton (Here. and Worc.) 25 SO8446
Clifton (Lancs.) 36 SD4630
Clifton (Northum.) 47 NZ2082
Clifton (Notts.) 34 SK5434
Clifton (Oxon.) 18 SP4831
Clifton Campville 26 SK2510
Clifton Hampden 18 SU5495
Clifton Reynes 27 SP9051
Clifton upon Dunsmore 26 SP5276
Clifton upon Teme 24 SO7161
Climping 11 TQ0002
Clint 37 SE2559
Clint Green 29 TG0210
Clinterty 62 NJ8311
Clintmains 52 NT6132
Clippesby 29 TG4214
Clipsham 34 SK9616
Clipston (Northants.) 26 SP7181
Clipston (Notts.) 34 SK6333
Clipstone 34 SK6064
Clitheroe 36 SD7441
Clive 32 SJ5124
Clivocast 63 HP6000
Clocaenog 31 SJ0854
Clochan 61 NJ4060
Clock Face 32 SJ5291
Clodock 16 SO3227
Clola 62 NK0043
Clophill 19 TL0838
Clopton 27 TL0680
Clopton Green 20 TL7654
Close Clark 43 SC2775
Closeburn 45 NX8992
Clothall 19 TL2732
Clothan 63 HU4581
Clotton 32 SJ5263
Clough Foot 37 SD9123
Cloughton 43 TA0094
Cloughton Newlands 43 TA0096
Clousta 63 HU3157
Clova (Grampn.) 61 NJ4522
Clova (Tays.) 57 NO3273
Clovelly 6 SS3124
Clovenfords 52 NT4436
Clovenstone 62 NJ7717
Clovulin 55 NN0063
Clowne 34 SK4975
Clows Top 24 SO7171
Cluer 63 NG1490
Clun 23 SO3081
Clunas 60 NH8846
Clunbury 24 SO3780
Clunes 59 NN2088
Clungunford 24 SO3978
Clunie (Grampn.) 62 NJ6350
Clunie (Tays.) 56 NO1043
Clunton 23 SO3381
Cluny 51 NT2495
Clutton (Avon) 17 ST6159
Clutton (Ches.) 32 SJ4654
Clwt-y-bont 30 SH5763
Clydach (Gwent) 16 SO2213
Clydach (W Glam.) 15 SN6801
Clydach Vale 16 SS9793
Clydebank 50 NS5069
Clydey 14 SN2535
Clyffe Pypard 17 SU0776
Clynder 49 NS2484
Clynderwen 14 SN1219
Clynelish 67 NC8905
Clynnog-fawr 30 SH4149
Clyro 23 SO2143
Clyst Honiton 5 SX9893
Clyst Hydon 7 ST0301
Clyst St. George 5 SX9888
Clyst St. Lawrence 7 ST0200
Clyst St. Mary 5 SX9890
Clyth 67 ND2837
Cnwch Coch 22 SN6775
Coad's Green 4 SX2976
Coal Aston 33 SK3679
Coalbrookdale 24 SJ6604
Coalburn 50 NS8034
Coalcleugh 46 NY8045
Coaley 17 SO7701
Coalpit Heath 17 ST6780
Coalport 24 SJ6902
Coalsnaughton 50 NS9195
Coaltown of Balgonie 57 NT2999
Coaltown of Wemyss 51 NT3295
Coalville 26 SK4214
Coast 64 NG9290
Coatbridge 50 NS7265
Coatdyke 50 NS7464
Coate (Wilts.) 17 SU0361
Coate (Wilts.) 17 SU1782
Coates (Cambs.) 17 TL3097
Coates (Glos.) 17 SO9700
Coatham 42 NZ5925
Coatham Mundeville 42 NZ2919
Coatsgate 45 NT0605
Cobbaton 6 SS6127
Coberley 17 SO9615
Cobham (Kent) 12 TQ6768
Cobham (Surrey) 11 TQ1060
Cobnash 24 SO4560
Cock Bridge 61 NJ2509
Cock Clarks 20 TL8102
Cockayne 42 SE6298
Cockayne Hatley 27 TL2549
Cockburnspath 53 NT7770
Cockenzie and Port Seton 52 NT4075
Cockerham 36 SD4651
Cockerington 35 TF3789
Cockermouth 40 NY1230
Cockernhoe Green 19 TL1223
Cockfield (Durham) 49 NZ1224
Cockfield (Suff.) 21 TL9054
Cockfosters 19 TQ2896
Cocking 11 SU8717
Cockington 5 SX8964
Cocklake 7 ST4349
Cockley Cley 28 TF7904
Cockpole Green 18 SU7981
Cockshutt 32 SJ4329
Cockthorpe 29 TF9842
Cockwood 5 SX9780
Coddenham 21 TM1354
Coddington (Ches.) 32 SJ4455
Coddington (Here. and Worc.) 24 SO7142
Coddington (Notts.) 34 SK8354
Codford St. Mary 8 ST9739
Codford St. Peter 8 ST9640
Codicote 19 TL2118
Codnor 33 SK4149
Codrington 17 ST7278
Codsall 25 SJ8603
Codsall Wood 25 SJ8405
Coed-y-paen 16 ST3398
Coedana 30 SH4381
Coedely 16 ST0285
Coedkernew 16 ST2783
Coedpoeth 31 SJ2850
Coelbren 15 SN8411
Coffinswell 5 SX8868
Cofton Hackett 25 SP0075
Cogan 16 ST1772
Cogenhoe 27 SP8360
Coggeshall 20 TL8522
Coillaig 55 NN0120
Coille Coire Chrannaig 55 NN4888
Coille Mhorgil 59 NH1001
Coilloire 58 NG3538
Coity 15 SS9281
Coker 7 ST5312
Colaboll 66 NC5610
Colan 2 SW8661
Colaton Raleigh 7 SY0787
Colbost 58 NG2148
Colby (Cumbr.) 41 NY6620
Colby (I. of M.) 43 SC2370
Colby (Norf.) 29 TG2131
Colchester 21 TM0025
Cold Ash 10 SU5169
Cold Ashby 26 SP6576
Cold Ashton 17 ST7472
Cold Brayfield 27 SP9252
Cold Hanworth 35 TF0393
Cold Hesledon 47 NZ4147
Cold Higham 26 SP6653
Cold Kirby 42 SE5384
Cold Newton 26 SK7106
Cold Norton 20 TL8500
Cold Overton 26 SK8110
Coldbackie 66 NC6160
Coldblow 12 TQ5173
Coldean 12 TQ3408
Coldeast 5 SX8274
Colden Common 9 SU4822
Coldfair Green 29 TM4361
Coldharbour 11 TQ1443
Coldingham 53 NT9065
Coldrain 56 NO0700
Coldred 13 TR2747
Coldridge 5 SS6907
Coldstream 53 NT8539
Coldwaltham 11 TQ0216
Coldwells 62 NK1039
Coldwells Croft 61 NJ4723
Cole 8 ST6633
Colebatch 23 SO3187
Colebrook 7 ST0006
Colebrooke 5 SX7799
Coleby (Humbs.) 39 SE8919
Coleby (Lincs.) 34 SK9760
Coleford (Devon.) 5 SS7701
Coleford (Glos.) 17 SO5710
Coleford (Somer.) 8 ST6848
Colehill 8 SU0300
Coleman's Hatch 12 TQ4533
Colemere 32 SJ4232
Colenden 56 NO1029
Coleorton 33 SK3917
Colerne 17 ST8171
Colesbourne 17 SO9913
Colesden 27 TL1255
Coleshill (Bucks.) 19 SU9495
Coleshill (Oxon.) 18 SU2393
Coleshill (Warw.) 25 SP1989
Colgate 11 TQ2332
Colgrain 49 NS3280
Colinsburgh 57 NO4703
Colinton 51 NT2169
Colintraive 49 NS0374
Colkirk 28 TF9126
Coll (Isle of Lewis) 63 NB4739
Collace 56 NO2032
Collafirth (Shetld.) 63 HU3482
Collafirth (Shetld.) 63 HU4368
Collaton St. Mary 5 SX8660
Collessie 57 NO2813
Collier Row 20 TQ4991
Collier Street 12 TQ7145
Collier's End 20 TL3720
Colliery Row 47 NZ3449
Collieston 62 NK0328
Collin 45 NY0276
Collingbourne Ducis 10 SU2453
Collingbourne Kinston 10 SU2355
Collingham (Notts.) 34 SK8261
Collingham (W. Yorks.) 38 SE3845
Collington 24 SO6460
Collingtree 26 SP7555
Colliston 57 NO6045
Collynie 62 NJ8436
Collyweston 27 SK9903
Colmonell 44 NX1586
Colmworth 27 TL1058
Coln Rogers 17 SP0809
Coln St. Aldwyns 17 SP1405
Coln St. Dennis 17 SP0810
Colnabaichin 61 NJ2908
Colnbrook 11 TQ0277
Colne (Cambs.) 27 TL3776
Colne (Lancs.) 37 SD8839
Colne Engaine 20 TL8530
Colne Valley 20 TL8529
Colney 29 TG1808
Colney Heath 19 TL2005
Colney Street 19 TL1502
Colp 62 NJ7448
Colpy 62 NJ6432
Colsterdale 42 SE1280
Colsterworth 34 SK9224
Colston Bassett 34 SK7033
Coltfield 61 NJ1163
Coltishall 29 TG2619
Colton (Cumbr.) 40 SD3186
Colton (N. Yorks.) 38 SE5444
Colton (Norf.) 29 TG1009
Colton (Staffs.) 33 SK0520
Colvister 63 HU5196
Colwall Green 24 SO7541
Colwall Stone 24 SO7542
Colwell 47 NY9575
Colwich 33 SK0121
Colwinston 15 SS9475
Colworth 11 SU9102
Colwyn Bay 31 SH8478
Colyford 7 SY2492
Colyton 7 SY2493
Combe (Berks.) 10 SU3760
Combe (Here. and Worc.) 23 SO3463
Combe (Oxon.) 18 SP4115
Combe Florey 7 ST1531
Combe Hay 17 ST7359
Combe Hill 46 NT3900
Combe Martin 6 SS5846
Combe Moor 24 SO3663
Combe Raleigh 7 ST1502
Combe St. Nicholas 7 ST3011
Combeinteignhead 5 SX9071
Comberbach 32 SJ6477
Comberton 20 TL3856
Combrook 26 SP3051
Combs (Derby.) 33 SK0478
Combs (Suff.) 21 TM0456
Combs Ford 21 TM0457
Combwich 7 ST2542
Comers 62 NJ6707
Commins Coch 22 SH8403
Common Edge 36 SD3232
Common Moor 4 SX2369
Common Side 33 SK3375
Common, The 9 SU2432
Commondale 42 NZ6610
Compstall 33 SJ9690
Compton (Berks.) 18 SU5279
Compton (Devon.) 5 SX8664
Compton (Hants.) 9 SU4625
Compton (Surrey) 11 SU9547
Compton (W. Susx.) 10 SU7714
Compton (Wilts.) 17 SU1352
Compton Abbas 8 ST8718
Compton Abdale 17 SP0516
Compton Bassett 17 SU0372
Compton Beauchamp 18 SU2887
Compton Bishop 16 ST3955
Compton Chamberlayne 8 SU0229
Compton Dando 17 ST6464
Compton Dundon 7 ST4933
Compton Martin 16 ST5456
Compton Pauncefoot 8 ST6425
Compton Valence 8 SY5993
Comrie 56 NN7722
Conchra 49 NS0288
Concraigie 56 NO1044
Conderton 25 SO9637
Condicote 17 SP1528
Condorrat 50 NS7373
Condover 24 SJ4906
Coney Weston 29 TL9578
Coneyhurst Common 11 TQ1024
Coneysthorpe 38 SE7171
Congerstone 26 SK3605
Congham 28 TF7123
Congleton 33 SJ8562
Congresbury 16 ST4363
Coningsby 35 TF2258
Conington (Cambs.) 27 TL1785
Conington (Cambs.) 27 TL3266
Conisbrough 38 SK5098
Conisby 48 NR2661
Conisholme 35 TF3995
Coniston (Cumbr.) 40 SD3097
Coniston (Humbs.) 39 TA1535
Coniston Cold 37 SD9054
Conistone 37 SD9867
Connah's Quay 31 SJ2869
Connel 54 NM9134
Connel Park 50 NS6012
Connor Downs 2 SW5939
Conon Bridge 60 NH5455
Cononley 37 SD9846
Consall 33 SJ9748
Consett 47 NZ1150
Constable Burton 42 SE1690
Constantine 2 SW7229
Contin 60 NH4555
Contlaw 62 NJ8402
Conway 31 SH7777
Conyer 13 TQ9664
Cookbury 4 SS4005
Cookham 19 SU8985
Cookham Dean 19 SU8785
Cookham Rise 19 SU8884
Cookhill 25 SP0558
Cookley (Here. and Worc.) 25 SO8480
Cookley (Suff.) 29 TM3475
Cookley Green 18 SU6990
Cookney 62 NO8793
Cooksbridge 12 NO4013
Cooksmill GreeN 20 TL6306
Coolham 11 TQ1222
Cooling 12 TQ7575
Coombe (Corn.) 4 SS2011
Coombe (Corn.) 2 SW9551
Coombe Bissett 8 SU1026
Coombe Hill 17 SO8827
Coombe Keynes 8 SY8484
Coombes 11 TQ1908
Coopersale Common 20 TL4702
Copdock 21 TM1141
Copford Green 21 TL9222
Copister 63 HU4878
Cople 27 TL1048
Copley 41 NZ0825
Copley Dale 33 SK1679
Copmanthorpe 38 SE5646
Coppathorne 4 SS2000
Coppenhall 33 SJ9019
Coppingford 27 TL1680
Copplestone 5 SS7702
Coppull 36 SD5613
Copsale 11 TQ1724
Copster Green 36 SD6734
Copt Heath 25 SP1778
Copt Hewick 38 SE3371
Copt Oak 26 SK4812
Copthorne 12 TQ3139
Copythorne 9 SU3014
Corbridge 47 NY9964
Corby 27 SP8988
Corby Glen 34 SK9925
Coreley 24 SO6173
Corfe 7 ST2319
Corfe Castle 8 SY9681
Corfe Mullen 8 SY9798
Corfton 24 SO4985
Corgarff 61 NJ2708
Corhampton 9 SU6120
Corley 26 SP3085
Corley Ash 26 SP2886
Corley Moor 26 SP2884
Corn Holm (Copinsay) 63 HY5901
Cornelly 15 SS8281
Corney 40 SD1191
Cornforth 42 NZ3034
Cornhill 62 NJ5858
Cornhill-on-Tweed 53 NT8639
Cornholme (W Yorks.) 37 SD9025
Cornish Hall End 20 TL6836
Cornquoy 63 ND5299
Cornriggs 47 NY8441
Cornsay 47 NZ1443
Corntown 60 NH5657
Cornwell 18 SP2727
Cornwood 4 SX6059
Cornworthy 5 SX8255
Corpach 55 NN0976
Corpusty 29 TG1129
Corran (Highld.) 59 NG8509
Corran (Highld.) 55 NN0263
Corrany 43 SC4589
Corrie 49 NS0243
Corrie Common 46 NY2085
Corriemoillie 65 NH3663
Corrimony 60 NH3830
Corringham (Essex) 20 TQ7183
Corringham (Lincs.) 34 SK8691
Corris Uchaf 22 SH7408
Corry 58 NG6424
Corry of Ardnagrask 60 NH5048
Corscombe 7 ST5105
Corse 62 NJ6040
Corse of Kinnoir 61 NJ5443
Corsham 17 ST8669
Corsindae 62 NJ6808
Corsley 8 ST8246
Corsley Heath 8 ST8245
Corsock 45 NX7576
Corston (Avon) 17 ST6965
Corston (Wilts.) 17 ST9284
Corstorphine 51 NT1972
Cortachy 57 NO3959
Corton (Suff.) 29 TM5497
Corton (Wilts.) 8 ST9340
Corton Denham 8 ST6322
Corvanan Lodge 55 NN0668
Corwen 31 SJ0743
Coryton (Devon.) 4 SX4583
Coryton (Essex) 20 TQ7482
Cosby 26 SP5495
Coseley 25 SO9494
Cosgrove 26 SP7942
Cosham 9 SU6605
Cosheston 14 SN0003
Cossall 34 SK4842
Cosses 44 NX1182
Cossington (Leics.) 26 SK6013
Cossington (Somer.) 7 ST3540
Costa 63 HY3328
Costessey 29 TG1712
Costock 34 SK5726
Coston 34 SK8422
Cot-town (Grampn.) 62 NJ8140
Cot-town (Grampn.) 61 NJ5026
Cotebrook 32 SJ5765
Cotehill 46 NY4750
Cotes (Cumbr.) 40 SD4886
Cotes (Leic.) 34 SK5520
Cotes (Staffs.) 33 SJ8434
Cotesbach 26 SP5382
Cotgrave 34 SK6435
Cothall 62 NJ8716
Cotham 34 SK7984
Cothelstone 7 ST1831
Cotherstone 41 NZ0119
Cothill 18 SU4699
Cotleigh 7 ST2002
Coton (Cambs.) 20 TL4158
Coton (Northants.) 26 SP6771
Coton (Staffs.) 33 SJ9832
Coton Clanford 33 SJ8723
Coton in the Elms 33 SK2415
Cott 5 SX7861
Cottam (Lancs.) 36 SD4932
Cottam (Notts.) 34 SK8179
Cottartown 61 NJ0331
Cottenham 27 TL4567
Cotterdale 41 SD8393
Cottered 20 TL3129
Cotterstock 27 TL0490
Cottesbrooke 26 SP7073
Cottesmore 27 SK9013
Cottingham (Humbs.) 39 TA0532
Cottingham (Northants.) 18 SP8490
Cottisford 26 SP5831
Cotton 29 TM0667
Cotton End 27 TL0845
Cottown (Grampn.) 62 NJ7715
Cotwalton 33 SJ9234
Coughton 25 SP0760
Coulags 59 NG9645
Coull 61 NJ5102
Coulport 49 NS2087
Coulsdon 12 TQ3059
Coulter 51 NT0233
Coulton 42 SE6374
Cound 24 SJ5504
Coundon 42 NZ2329
Coundon Grange 42 NZ2327
Countersett 41 SD9287
Countesthorpe 26 SP5895
Countess Wear 5 SX9489
Countisbury 6 SS7449
Coupar Angus 56 NO2139
Coupland 53 NT9331
Cour 49 NR8248
Court Henry 15 SN5522
Courteachan 58 NM6897
Courteenhall 26 SP7653
Courtsend 21 TR0293
Courtway 7 ST2033
Cousland 51 NT3768
Cousley Wood 12 TQ6533
Cove (Devon.) 5 SS9519
Cove (Hants.) 10 SU8555
Cove (Highld.) 64 NG8190
Cove (Strath.) 49 NS2281
Cove Bay (Grampn.) 62 NJ9500
Cove Point 48 NR7107
Covehithe 29 TM5281
Coven 25 SJ9006
Coveney 28 TL4882
Covenham St. Bartholomew 35 TF3395
Covenham St. Mary 35 TF3394
Coventry 26 SP3379
Coverack 2 SW7818
Coverham 41 SE1086
Covington 27 TL0570
Cowan Bridge 41 SD6476
Cowbeech 12 TQ6114
Cowbit 35 TF2618
Cowbridge 16 SS9974
Cowden 12 TQ4640

Cowdenbeath Denend

Cowdenbeath 51 NT1619
Cowdenburn 51 NT2052
Cowes 9 SZ4995
Cowesby 42 SE4689
Cowfold 11 TQ2122
Cowick 38 SE6521
Cowie 50 NS8389
Cowley (Devon.) 5 SX9095
Cowley (Glos.) 17 SO9614
Cowley (Gtr London) 19 TQ0582
Cowley (Oxon.) 18 SP5404
Cowling (N Yorks.) 37 SD9743
Cowling (N Yorks.) 42 SD9743
Cowlinge 20 TL7154
Cowpen Bewley 43 NZ4824
Cowplain 9 SU7011
Cowshill 47 NY8540
Cowstrandburn 51 NT0390
Cox Common 29 TM4082
Coxbank 32 SJ6541
Coxbench 33 SK3743
Coxheath 12 TQ7451
Coxhoe 42 NZ3235
Coxley 7 ST5343
Coxwold 42 SE5377
Coychurch 15 SS9379
Coylton 50 NS4119
Coylumbridge 60 NH9110
Coynach 61 NJ4405
Crabbs Cross 25 SP0464
Crabtree 11 TQ2225
Crabtree Green 32 SJ3344
Crackenthorpe 41 NY6622
Crackington Haven 4 SX1496
Crackleybank 24 SJ7611
Crackpot 41 SD9796
Cracoe 37 SD9760
Cradley 24 SO7347
Crafthole 4 SX3654
Cragabus 48 NR3345
Cragg 37 SE0023
Craggan (Grampn.) 61 NJ0226
Craggan (Strath.) 55 NS2699
Craghead 47 NZ2150
Craibstone (Grampn.) 62 NJ8611
Craichie 57 NO5047
Craig (Dumf. and Galwy.) 45 NX6875
Craig (Highld.) 59 NH0349
Craig Castle 61 NJ4724
Craig Penllyn 16 SS9777
Craig-y-nos 15 SN8315
Craigcefnparc 15 SN6703
Craigdallie 57 NO2428
Craigdam 62 NJ8430
Craigdarroch 45 NS6306
Craigearn 62 NJ7214
Craigellachie (Grampn.) 61 NJ2844
Craigend 56 NO1120
Craigendoran 49 NS3181
Craiggiecat 62 NO8592
Craighat 50 NS4984
Craighoar Hill 45 NT0002
Craighouse 48 NR5267
Craigie (Grampn.) 62 NJ9119
Craigie (Strath.) 50 NS4232
Craigie (Tays.) 56 NO1143
Craiglockhart 51 NT2270
Craigmillar 51 NT2871
Craignant 31 SJ2535
Craigneuk (Strath.) 50 NS7656
Craigneuk (Strath.) 50 NS7764
Craignure 54 NM7236
Craigo 57 NO6864
Craigow 56 NO0806
Craigrothie 57 NO3710
Craigruie 55 NN5020
Craigton (Grampn.) 62 NJ8301
Craigton (Tays.) 57 NO3250
Craigton (Tays.) 57 NO5138
Craigtown 67 NC8856
Craik 51 NT3408
Crail 57 NO6107
Crailing 52 NT6824
Crailinghall 52 NT6921
Crakehall 42 SE2490
Crambe 38 SE7364
Cramlington 47 NZ2776
Cramond 51 NT1876
Cramond Bridge 51 NT1775
Cranage 32 SJ7568
Cranberry 32 SJ8236
Cranborne 8 SU0513
Cranbourne 11 SU9272
Cranbrook 12 TQ7735
Cranbrook Common 12 TQ7983
Cranfield 27 SP9542
Cranford 11 TQ1077
Cranford St. Andrew 27 SP9277
Cranford St. John 27 SP9276
Cranham (Essex) 20 TQ5787
Cranham (Glos.) 17 SO8912
Crank 36 SJ5099
Cranleigh 11 TQ0638
Cranmore (I. of W.) 9 SZ3990
Cranmore (Somer.) 8 ST6843
Cranna 62 NJ6352
Crannach 61 NJ4954
Cranoe 26 SP7695
Cransford 29 TM3164
Cranshaws 52 NT6961
Cranstal 43 NX4602
Crantock 2 SW7860
Cranwell 35 TF0349
Cranwich 28 TL7795
Cranworth 29 TF9804
Crapstone 4 SX5067
Crarae 55 NR9897
Craster 53 NU2519
Cratfield 29 TM3175
Crathes 62 NO7596
Crathie (Grampn.) 61 NO2695
Crathie (Highld.) 60 NN5893
Crathorne 42 NZ4407
Craven Arms 24 SO4382
Crawcrook 47 NZ1363
Crawford 51 NS9520
Crawfordjohn 50 NS8823
Crawick 50 NS7710
Crawley (Hants.) 9 SU4234
Crawley (Oxon.) 18 SP3312
Crawley (W Susx.) 11 TQ2636
Crawley Down 12 TQ3237
Crawleyside 47 NY9940
Crawshawbooth 37 SD8125
Crawton 57 NO8779
Cray (N Yorks.) 41 SD9479
Cray (Powys) 15 SN8924
Cray's Pond 18 SU6380
Crayford 12 TQ5157
Crayke 38 SE5670
Crays Hill 20 TQ7192
Creacombe 5 SS8119
Creagan 55 NM9744
Creagorry 63 NF7948
Creaton 26 SP7071
Credenhill 24 SO4543
Crediton 5 SS8300
Creech St. Michael 7 ST2725
Creed 2 SW9347
Creedy Park 5 SS8302
Creekmouth 20 TQ4581
Creeting St. Mary 21 TM0956
Creeton 34 TF0120
Creetown 44 NX4758
Creggans 55 NN0802
Cregneish 43 SC1967
Cregrina 23 SO1252
Creich (Fife.) 57 NO3221
Creich (Island of Mull) 54 NM3124
Creigiau 16 ST0881
Cressage 24 SJ5904
Cresselly 14 SN0606
Cressing 20 TL7920
Cresswell (Dyfed) 14 SN0506
Cresswell (Northum.) 47 NZ2993
Cresswell (Staffs.) 33 SJ9739
Creswell 34 SK5274
Cretingham 29 TM2260
Crew Green 32 SJ3215
Crewe (Ches.) 32 SJ4253
Crewe (Ches.) 32 SJ7055
Crewkerne 7 ST4409
Crianlarich 55 NN3825
Cribyn 22 SN5251
Criccieth 30 SH4938
Crich 33 SK3554
Crichie 62 NJ9544
Crichton 51 NT3862
Crick (Gwent) 16 ST4890
Crick (Northants.) 26 SP5872
Crickadarn 23 SO0942
Cricket St. Thomas 7 ST3708
Crickheath 31 SJ2923
Crickhowell 16 SO2118
Cricklade 17 SU0993
Cridling Stubbs 38 SE5221
Crieff 56 NN8621
Criggion 31 SJ2915
Crigglestone 38 SE3116
Crimond 62 NK0556
Crimplesham 28 TF6503
Crinaglack 60 NH4240
Crinan 49 NR7894
Cringleford 29 TG1905
Crinow 14 SN1214
Cripp's Corner 12 TQ7821
Cripplesease 2 SW5036
Croachy 60 NH6527
Crockenhill 12 TQ5067
Crockernwell 5 SX7592
Crockerton 8 ST8642
Crocketford or Ninemile Bar 45 NX8272
Crockey Hill 38 SE6246
Crockham Hill 12 TQ4450
Crockleford Heath 21 TM0426
Croes-y-mwyalch 16 ST3092
Croeserw 15 SS8695
Croesgoch 14 SM8330
Croesor 30 SH6344
Croesyceiliog (Dyfed) 15 SN4016
Croesyceiliog (Gwent) 16 ST3196
Croft (Ches.) 32 SJ6393
Croft (Leic.) 26 SP5195
Croft (Lincs.) 35 TF5162
Croft (N Yorks.) 42 NZ2909
Croftamie 50 NS4786
Crofton 38 SE3717
Crofts of Blackburn 61 NJ5433
Crofts of Shanquhar 61 NJ5536
Crofty 15 SS5295
Croggan 54 NM7027
Croglin 46 NY5747
Croick 65 NH4591
Croir 63 NB1539
Cromarty 65 NH7766
Cromdale 61 NJ0728
Cromer (Herts.) 19 TL2928
Cromer (Norf.) 29 TG2142
Cromford 33 SK2956
Cromhall 17 ST6990
Cromhall Common 17 ST6989
Cromore 63 NB4021
Cromra 60 NN5489
Cromwell 34 SK7961
Cronberry 50 NS6022
Crondall 10 SU7948
Cronk, The 43 SC3495
Cronk-y-Voddy 43 SC3086
Cronton 32 SJ4988
Crook (Cumbr.) 40 SD4694
Crook (Durham) 42 NZ1635
Crook of Devon 56 NO0301
Crookham (Berks.) 10 SU5364
Crookham (Northum.) 53 NT9138
Crookham Village 10 SU7952
Crookhouse 53 NT7627
Crooklands 40 SD5383
Cropredy 26 SP4646
Cropston 26 SK5511
Cropthorne 25 SO9944
Cropton 43 SE7589
Cropwell Bishop 34 SK6835
Cropwell Butler 34 SK6837
Crosbie 49 NS2150
Crosby (Cumbr.) 40 NY0738
Crosby (Humbs.) 39 SE8711
Crosby (I. of M.) 43 SC3279
Crosby (Mers.) 36 SJ3099
Crosby Garrett 41 NY7309
Crosby Ravensworth 41 NY6214
Croscombe 8 ST5844
Cross (Somerset) 16 ST4154
Cross (W Isles) 63 NB5061
Cross Ash 16 SO4019
Cross Green (Devon.) 4 SX3888
Cross Green (Suff.) 21 TL9952
Cross Hands 15 SN5612
Cross Houses (Salop) 24 SJ5307
Cross Inn (Dyfed) 22 SN3957
Cross Inn (Dyfed) 22 SN5464
Cross Inn (Mid Glam.) 16 ST0583
Cross Lanes (Clwyd) 32 SJ3746
Cross Street 29 TM1876
Cross in Hand 12 TQ5621
Cross of Jackston 62 NJ7432
Crossaig 49 NR8351
Crossapoll 48 NL9943
Crossbost 63 NB3924
Crosscanonby 40 NY0739
Crossdale Street 29 TG2239
Crossdougal 63 NF7520
Crossens 36 SD3719
Crossford (Fife.) 51 NT0686
Crossford (Strath.) 50 NS8246
Crossgates (Fife.) 51 NT1488
Crossgates (Powys) 23 SO0865
Crossgill 36 SD5562
Crosshill (Fife.) 51 NT1796
Crosshill (Strath.) 44 NS3206
Crosshouse (Strath.) 50 NS3938
Crossings 46 NY5177
Crosskeys (Gwent) 16 ST2292
Crosskirk 67 ND0370
Crosslanes (N Yorks.) 38 SE5264
Crosslanes (Salop.) 32 SJ3218
Crosslee 51 NT3018
Crossmichael 45 NX7267
Crossmoor 36 SD4438
Crossroads 62 NO7594
Crossroads 62 NO7594
Crossway 16 SO4419
Crossway Green 25 SO8368
Crosswell 14 SN1236
Crosthwaite 40 SD4491
Croston 36 SD4818
Crostwick 29 TG2515
Crostwight 29 TG3329
Crouch Hill 8 ST7010
Croughton 18 SP5433
Crovie 62 NJ8065
Crow Hill 17 SO6326
Crow Rock 14 SR8894
Crowan 2 SW6434
Crowborough 12 TQ5130
Crowcombe 7 ST1336
Crowfield (Northants.) 26 SP6141
Crowfield (Suff.) 21 TM1557
Crowhurst (E Susx) 12 TQ7512
Crowhurst (Surrey) 12 TQ3947
Crowland 27 TF2310
Crowlas 2 SW5133
Crowle (Here. and Worc.) 25 SO9256
Crowle (Humbs.) 38 SE7713
Crowlista 63 NB0433
Crowmarsh Gifford 18 SU6189
Crownhill 4 SX4857
Crownthorpe 29 TG0803
Crowthorne 10 SU8464
Crowton 32 SJ5774
Croxall 25 SK1913
Croxdale 42 NZ2636
Croxden 33 SK0639
Croxley Green 19 TQ0795
Croxton (Cambs.) 27 TL2459
Croxton (Humbs.) 39 TA0912
Croxton (Norf.) 28 TL8786
Croxton (Staffs.) 32 SJ7832
Croxton Kerrial 34 SK8329
Croy (Highld.) 60 NH7949
Croy (Strath.) 50 NS7275
Croyde 6 SS4439
Croydon (Cambs.) 20 TL3149
Croydon (Gtr London) 12 TQ3365
Cruban Beag 60 NN6692
Cruckmeole 24 SJ4309
Cruckton 24 SJ4210
Cruden Bay 62 NK0936
Crudgington 32 SJ6317
Crudwell 17 ST9592
Crug 23 SO1872
Crugmeer 2 SW9076
Crulivig 63 NB1733
Crumlin 16 ST2198
Crundale (Dyfed.) 14 SM9718
Crundale (Kent) 13 TR0749
Crunwear 14 SN1810
Cruwys Morchard 5 SS8712
Crux Easton 10 SU4256
Crwbin 15 SN4713
Crymmych 14 SN1833
Crynant 15 SN7095
Crystal Palace 12 TQ3470
Cuaig 58 NG7057
Cubbington 26 SP3368
Cubert 2 SW7857
Cublington 19 SP8422
Cuckfield 12 TQ3024
Cucklington 8 ST7527
Cuckney 34 SK5671
Cuddesdon 18 SP5902
Cuddington (Bucks.) 18 SP7311
Cuddington (Ches.) 32 SJ5971
Cuddington Heath 32 SJ4646
Cuddy Hill 36 SD4937
Cudham 12 TQ4459
Cudliptown 4 SX5278
Cudworth (S Yorks.) 38 SE3842
Cudworth (Somer.) 7 ST3810
Cuffley 20 TL3002
Cuiashader 63 NB5458
Cuier 63 NF6703
Culbo 65 NH6360
Culbokie 60 NH6059
Culburnie 60 NH4941
Culcabock 60 NH6844
Culcharry 60 NH8650
Culcheth 32 SJ6594
Culdrain 61 NJ5133
Culduie 58 NG7140
Culford 28 TL8370
Culgaith 41 NY6129
Culham 18 SU5095
Culkein 64 NC0333
Culkerton 17 ST9296
Cullachie 60 NH9720
Cullen 61 NJ5166
Cullercoats 47 NZ3571
Cullerlie 62 NJ7603
Cullicudden 65 NH6564
Cullingworth 37 SE0636
Cullipool 54 NM7313
Cullisse 65 NH8274
Cullivoe 63 HP5402
Culloch 56 NN7818
Cullompton 7 ST0207
Culmaily 65 NH8099
Culmington 24 SO4982
Culmstock 7 ST1013
Culnacraig 64 NC0603
Culrain 65 NH5794
Culross 51 NS9885
Culroy 49 NS3114
Culsh (Grampn.) 62 NJ8848
Culswick 63 HU2745
Cultercullen 62 NJ9124
Cults (Grampn.) 61 NJ5331
Cults (Grampn.) 62 NJ8903
Culverstone Green 12 TQ6363
Culverthorpe 34 TF0240
Culworth 26 SP5447
Cumb 63 HU5292
Cumbernauld 50 NS7676
Cumberworth 35 TF5073
Cuminestown 62 NJ8050
Cummersdale 46 NY3952
Cummertrees 45 NY1366
Cummingstown 61 NJ1368
Cumnock 50 NS5619
Cumnor 18 SP4604
Cumrew 46 NY5550
Cumwhinton 46 NY4552
Cumwhitton 46 NY5052
Cundall (N Yorks.) 38 SE4272
Cunninghamhead 50 NS3741
Cunningsburgh 63 HU4330
Cunnister 63 HU5296
Cupar 57 NO3714
Cupar Muir 57 NO3613
Curbar 33 SK2574
Curbridge (Hants.) 9 SU5211
Curbridge (Oxon.) 18 SP3208
Curdridge 9 SU5313
Curdworth 25 SP1892
Curland 7 ST2716
Currie 51 NT1867
Curry Mallet 7 ST3221
Curry Rivel 7 ST3824
Curtisden Green 12 TQ7440
Cury 2 SW6721
Cushnie 62 NJ7962
Cushuish 7 ST1930
Cusop 23 SO2341
Cuthill (Highld.) 65 NH7587
Cutiau 30 SH6317
Cutnall Green 25 SO8768
Cutsdean 25 SP0830
Cutthorpe 33 SK3473
Cutts 63 HU4038
Cuxham 18 SU6695
Cuxton 12 TQ7166
Cuxwold 39 TA1701
Cwm (Clwyd) 31 SJ0677
Cwm (Gwent) 16 SO1805
Cwm (W Glam.) 15 SS6895
Cwm Ceulan 22 SN6890
Cwm Irfon 22 SN8549
Cwm-Cewydd 22 SH8713
Cwm-Llinau 22 SH8407
Cwm-y-glo 30 SH5562
Cwmaman 16 SS9999
Cwmavon 15 SS7892
Cwmbach (Dyfed) 14 SN2525
Cwmbach (Mid Glam.) 15 SO0201
Cwmbelan 23 SN9481
Cwmbran 16 ST2894
Cwmcarn 16 ST2293
Cwmcarvan 16 SO4707
Cwmcoy 14 SN2941
Cwmdare 16 SN9803
Cwmdu (Dyfed) 15 SN6330
Cwmdu (Powys) 16 SO1823
Cwmduad 15 SN3731
Cwmfelin Boeth 14 SN1919
Cwmfelin Mynach 14 SN2324
Cwmffrwd 15 SN4217
Cwmgwrach 15 SN8605
Cwmisfael 15 SN4915
Cwmllynfell 15 SN7413
Cwmparc 15 SS9496
Cwmpengraig 14 SN3436
Cwmsychpant 22 SN4746
Cwmtillery 16 SO2106
Cwmtudu 22 SN3557
Cwmyoy 16 SO2923
Cwmystwyth 22 SN7873
Cwrt-newydd 22 SN4847
Cwrt-y-gollen 16 SO2317
Cyffylliog 31 SJ0557
Cymmer (Mid Glam.) 15 ST0290
Cymmer (W Glam.) 15 SS8696
Cynghordy 22 SN8139
Cynwyd 31 SJ0541
Cynwyl Elfed 15 SN3727

Dacre (Cumbr.) 40 NY4526
Dacre (N Yorks.) 37 SE1960
Dacre Banks 37 SE1961
Daddry Shield 41 NY8937
Dadford 18 SP6638
Dadlington 26 SP4098
Dafen 15 SN5201
Daffy Green 29 TF9609
Dagenham 20 TQ5084
Daglingworth 17 SO9905
Dagnall 19 SP9916
Daill 48 NR3662
Dailly 44 NS2701
Dairsie or Osnaburgh 57 NO4117
Dalavich 55 NM9612
Dalbeattie 45 NX8361
Dalbeg 63 NB2345
Dalblair 50 NS6419
Dalbog 57 NO5871
Dalby 43 SC2178
Dalcapon 56 NN9755
Dalchalloch 56 NN7264
Dalchenna 55 NN0706
Dalchreichart 59 NH2912
Dalcross 60 NH7748
Dalderby 35 TF2465
Dale (Derby.) 33 SK4338
Dale (Dyfed) 14 SM8005
Dale (Shetld.) 63 HU1852
Dale Head 40 NY4316
Dalelia 54 NM7369
Dalgarven 49 NS2945
Dalginross 56 NN7721
Dalguise 56 NN9947
Dalhalvaig 67 NC8954
Dalham 28 TL7261
Daliburgh 63 NF7421
Dalkeith 51 NT3367
Dall 56 NN5956
Dallas 61 NJ1252
Dalle Crucis Abbey (cnt.) 32 SJ2044
Dalleagles 50 NS5710
Dallinghoo 21 TM2654
Dallington 12 TQ6519
Dalmally 55 NN1527
Dalmary 50 NS5195
Dalmellington 46 NS4705
Dalmeny 51 NT1477
Dalmigavie 60 NH7419
Dalmore (Highld.) 65 NH6668
Dalnabreck 54 NM7069
Dalnavie 65 NH6483
Dalness 55 NN1751
Dalnessie 66 NC6315
Dalqueich 56 NO0704
Dalquharran Castle 44 NS2702
Dalreavoch 6 NC7508
Dalry 49 NS2949
Dalrymple 49 NS3514
Dalserf 50 NS7950
Dalston 46 NY3750
Dalswinton 45 NX9385
Dalton (Dumf. and Galwy.) 45 NY1173
Dalton (Lancs.) 36 SD4907
Dalton (N Yorks.) 41 NZ1108
Dalton (N Yorks.) 42 SE4376
Dalton (N Yorks.) 34 SK4593
Dalton (Northum.) 47 NY9158
Dalton (Northum.) 47 NZ1172
Dalton Piercy 42 NZ4631
Dalton in Furness 40 SD2374
Dalton-le-Dale 47 NZ4047
Dalton-on-Tees 42 NZ2908
Dalveich 56 NN6124
Dalwhinnie 56 NN6384
Dalwood 7 ST2400
Damerham 8 SU1015
Damgate 29 TG3909
Damnaglaur 44 NX1235
Danbury 20 TL7805
Danby 43 NZ7009
Danby Wiske 42 SE3398
Dandaleith 61 NJ2845
Danderhall 51 NT3069
Dane End 20 TL3321
Dane Hills 26 SK5605
Danebridge 33 SJ9665
Danehill 12 TQ4027
Danskine 52 NT5667
Daren-felen 16 SO2212
Darenth 12 TQ5671
Daresbury 32 SJ5782
Darfield 38 SE4104
Dargate 13 TR0861
Darite 4 SX2569
Darlaston 25 SO9796
Darlingscott 26 SP2324
Darlington 42 NZ2914
Darliston 32 SJ5833
Darlochan 48 NR6723
Darlton 34 SK7773
Darowen 22 SH8302
Darras Hall 47 NZ1571
Darrington 38 SE4919
Darsham 29 TM4170
Dartford 12 TQ5474
Dartington 5 SX7862
Dartmeet 5 SX6773
Dartmouth 5 SX8751
Darton 38 SE3110
Darvel 50 NS5637
Darwen 36 SD6922
Datchet 11 SU9876
Datchworth 19 TL2619
Dauntsey 17 ST9882
Davenham 32 SJ6570
Daventry 26 SP5762
Davidstow 4 SX1587
Davington 46 NT2302
Daviot (Grampn.) 62 NJ7528
Daviot (Highld.) 60 NH7139
Davoch of Grange 61 NJ4951
Dawley 24 SJ6807
Dawlish 5 SX9676
Dawlish Warren 5 SX9778
Dawn 31 SH8672
Dawsmere 35 TF4430
Daylesford 18 SP2425
Deadwater 46 NY6096
Deal 13 TR3752
Dean (Cumbr.) 40 NY0725
Dean (Devon) 5 SX7364
Dean (Hants.) 9 SU5619
Dean (Somer.) 8 ST6743
Dean Prior 5 SX7363
Dean Row 33 SJ8781
Deanburnhaugh 51 NT3911
Deane 10 SU5450
Deanland 8 ST9918
Deanscale 40 NY0926
Deanshanger 26 SP7639
Deanston 56 NN7101
Dearham 40 NY0736
Debach 21 TM2454
Debden 20 TL5533
Debden Cross 20 TL5832
Debenham 29 TM1763
Dechmont 51 NT0370
Deddington 18 SP4631
Dedham 21 TM0533
Deene 27 SP9492
Deenethorpe 27 SP9592
Deepcar 38 SK2897
Deepcut 11 SU9057
Deepdale (Cumbr.) 41 SD7284
Deeping Gate 27 TF1509
Deeping St. James 27 TF1609
Deeping St. Nicholas 35 TF2115
Deerhurst 17 SO8729
Defford 25 SO9143
Defynnog 15 SN9227
Deganwy 31 SH7779
Deighton (N Yorks.) 42 NZ3801
Deighton (N Yorks.) 38 SE6244
Deiniolen 30 SH5863
Delabole 3 SX0683
Delamere 32 SJ5668
Dell 63 NB4861
Delliefure 61 NJ0731
Delph 37 SD9807
Dembleby 35 TF0437
Den, The 50 NS3251
Denaby 38 SK4899
Denbigh 31 SJ0566
Denbury 5 SX8268
Denby 33 SK3946
Denby Dale 37 SE2208
Denchworth 18 SU3891
Denend 62 NJ6038

Denford
East Hendred

Denford 27 SP 9976
Dengie 21 TL 9801
Denham (Bucks.) 19 TQ 0386
Denham (Suff.) 28 TL 7561
Denham (Suff.) 29 TM 1974
Denham Green 19 TQ 0388
Denhead (Fife.) 57 NO 4613
Denhead (Grampn.) 62 NJ 9952
Denhead of Gray 57 NO 3431
Denholm 52 NT 5718
Denholme 37 SE 0633
Denmead 9 SU 6511
Dennington 29 TM 2866
Denny 50 NS 8182
Denny Lodge 9 SU 3305
Dennyloanhead 50 NS 8180
Denshaw 37 SD 9710
Denside 62 NO 8095
Densole 13 TR 2141
Denston 20 TL 7652
Denstone 33 SK 0940
Dent 41 SD 7087
Denton (Cambs.) 27 TL 1487
Denton (Durham) 42 NZ 2118
Denton (E Susx.) 12 TQ 4502
Denton (Gtr. Mches.) 33 SJ 9295
Denton (Kent) 13 TR 2146
Denton (Lincs.) 34 SK 8632
Denton (N Yorks.) 37 SE 1448
Denton (Norf.) 29 TM 2887
Denton (Northants.) 27 SP 8357
Denton (Oxon.) 18 SP 5902
Denver 28 TF 6101
Denwick (Northum.) 53 NU 2014
Deopham 29 TG 0400
Deopham Green 29 TM 0499
Depden Green 20 TL 7756
Deptford (Gtr London) 12 TQ 3676
Deptford (Wilts.) 8 SU 0038
Derby 33 SK 3435
Derbyhaven 43 SC 2867
Deri 16 SO 1202
Derringstone 13 TR 2049
Derrington 33 SJ 8822
Derry Hill 17 ST 9670
Derrythorpe 39 SE 8208
Dersingham 28 TF 6830
Dervaig 54 NM 4351
Derwen 31 SJ 0650
Desborough 26 SP 8083
Desford 26 SK 4703
Detchant 53 NU 0836
Detling 12 TQ 7958
Deuddwr 31 SJ 2317
Devauden 16 ST 4899
Devil's Bridge 22 SN 7477
Devizes 17 SU 0061
Devonport 4 SX 4554
Devonside 50 NS 9296
Devoran 2 SW 7939
Dewlish 8 SY 7798
Dewsall Court 24 SO 4833
Dewsbury 37 SE 2422
Dhoon 43 SC 4586
Dhoor 43 SC 4396
Dhowin 43 NX 4101
Diabaig 64 NG 8060
Dial Post 11 TQ 1519
Dibden 9 SU 3908
Dibden Purlieu 9 SU 4106
Dickleburgh 29 TM 1682
Didbrook 25 SP 0531
Didcot 18 SU 5290
Diddington 27 TL 1965
Diddlebury 24 SO 5085
Didley 24 SO 4432
Didmarton 17 ST 8287
Didsbury 33 SJ 8490
Didworthy 5 SX 6862
Digby 35 TF 0754
Diggle 37 SE 0008
Dihewyd 22 SN 4855
Dilham 29 TG 3325
Dilhorne 33 SJ 9743
Dilston 47 NY 9763
Dilton Marsh 8 ST 8449
Dilwyn 24 SO 4154
Dinas (Dyfed) 14 SN 0139
Dinas (Dyfed) 14 SN 2730
Dinas (Gwyn.) 30 SH 2736
Dinas Powis 16 ST 1571
Dinas-Mawddwy 31 SH 8514
Dinchope 24 SO 4583
Dinder 7 ST 5744
Dinedor 24 SO 5336
Dingley 26 SP 7687
Dingwall 60 NH 5458
Dinnet 61 NO 4698
Dinnington (S Yorks.) 34 SK 5386
Dinnington (Somer.) 7 ST 4012
Dinnington (Tyne and Wear) 47 NZ 2073
Dinorwic 30 SH 5961
Dinton 8 SU 0131
Dinwoodie Mains 45 NY 1090
Dinworthy 4 SS 3015
Dippen 49 NR 7937
Dippin 49 NS 0422
Dipple (Grampn.) 61 NJ 3258
Dipple (Strath.) 44 NS 2002
Diptford 5 SX 7256
Dipton 47 NZ 1554
Dirleton 52 NT 5183
Discoed 23 SO 2764
Diseworth 34 SK 4524
Dishes 63 HY 6523
Dishforth 42 SE 3873
Disley 33 SJ 9784
Diss 29 TM 1179
Disserth 23 SO 0458
Distington 40 NY 0023
Ditcheat 8 ST 6236
Ditchingham 29 TM 3391
Ditchling 12 TQ 3215
Dittisham 5 SX 8655
Ditton (Ches.) 32 SJ 4986
Ditton (Kent) 12 TQ 7158
Ditton Green 20 TL 6658
Ditton Priors 24 SO 6089
Dixton (Glos.) 25 SO 9830
Dixton (Gwent) 16 SO 5114
Dobwalls 4 SX 2165
Doccombe 5 SX 7786
Dochgarroch 60 NH 6140
Docking 28 TF 7637
Docklow 24 SO 5657
Dockray 40 NY 3921
Dodburn 52 NT 4707
Doddinghurst 20 TQ 5998
Doddington (Cambs.) 27 TL 4090
Doddington (Kent) 13 TQ 9357
Doddington (Lincs.) 34 SK 8970
Doddington (Northum.) 53 NU 0032
Doddington (Salop) 24 SO 6176
Doddiscombsleigh 5 SX 8586
Dodford (Here. and Worc.) 25 SO 9273
Dodford (Northants.) 26 SP 6160
Dodington (Avon) 17 ST 7579
Dodleston 32 SJ 3661
Dodworth 38 SE 3105
Doe Lea 34 SK 4566
Dog Village 5 SX 9896
Dogdyke 35 TF 2055
Dogmersfield 10 SU 7852
Dol-for (Powys) 22 SH 8006
Dolanog 23 SJ 0612
Dolau 23 SO 1367
Dolbenmaen 30 SH 5043
Dolfach 22 SN 9077
Dolfor (Powys) 23 SO 1087
Dolgarrog 31 SH 7766
Dolgellau 30 SH 7217
Doll 67 NC 8803
Dollar 51 NS 9697
Dolphinholme 36 SD 5153
Dolphinton 51 NT 1046
Dolton 4 SS 5712
Dolwen (Clwyd) 31 SH 8874
Dolwen (Powys) 23 SH 9707
Dolwyddelan 30 SH 7352
Dolyhir 23 SO 2458
Domgay 31 SJ 2819
Doncaster 38 SE 5803
Donhead St. Andrew 8 ST 9124
Donhead St. Mary 8 ST 9024
Donibristle 51 NT 1688
Donington 35 TF 2135
Donington on Bair 35 TF 2382
Donisthorpe 26 SK 3114
Donkey Town 11 SU 9460
Donnington (Berks.) 10 SU 4668
Donnington (Glos.) 17 SP 1928
Donnington (Here. and Worc.) 24 SO 7034
Donnington (Salop) 24 SJ 5807
Donnington (Salop) 24 SJ 7114
Donnington (W Susx.) 10 SU 8502
Donyatt 7 ST 3313
Doonfoot 49 NS 3218
Doonholm 49 NS 3317
Dorchester (Dorset) 8 SY 6990
Dorchester (Oxon.) 18 SU 5794
Dordon 26 SK 2600
Dore 33 SK 3081
Dores 60 NH 5934
Dorking 11 TQ 1649
Dormans Lane 12 TQ 4042
Dormanstown 42 NZ 5823
Dormington 24 SO 5840
Dorney 11 SU 9379
Dornie 59 NG 8826
Dornoch (Highld.) 65 NH 7989
Dornock (Dumf. and Galwy.) 46 NY 2366
Dorrery 67 ND 0754
Dorridge 25 SP 1774
Dorrington (Lincs.) 35 TF 0752
Dorrington (Salop) 24 SJ 4703
Dorsington 25 SP 1349
Dorstone 23 SO 3142
Dorton 18 SP 6714
Dosthill 26 SP 2199
Doublebois 4 SX 1964
Dougarie 49 NR 8837
Doughton 17 ST 8791
Douglas (I. of M.) 43 SC 3876
Douglas (Strath.) 50 NS 8330
Douglas Hill 30 SH 6065
Douglas and Angus 57 NO 4332
Douglastown 57 NO 4147
Doulting 8 ST 6443
Dounby 63 HY 2920
Doune (Tays.) 56 NN 7201
Douneside 61 NJ 4806
Dounie 65 NH 5590
Dounreay 67 NC 9966
Dousland 4 SX 5368
Dove Holes 33 SK 0778
Dovenby 40 NY 0933
Dover 13 TR 3141
Doverdale 25 SO 8566
Doveridge 33 SK 1134
Dowally 56 NO 0047
Dowdeswell 17 SO 9919
Dowland 4 SS 5610
Dowlish Wake 7 ST 3712
Down Ampney 17 SU 1097
Down Hatherley 17 SO 8622
Down St. Mary 5 SS 7404
Downderry 4 SX 3153
Downe 12 TQ 4361
Downend (Berks.) 10 SU 4775
Downend (I. of W.) 9 SZ 5387
Downfield 57 NO 3833
Downgate 4 SX 3772
Downham (Cambs.) 28 TL 5284
Downham (Essex) 20 TQ 7395
Downham (Lancs.) 37 SD 7844
Downham (Northum.) 53 NT 8633
Downham Market 38 TF 6003
Downhead 8 ST 6845
Downhill 2 SW 8669
Downholme 41 SE 1197
Downies 62 NO 9294
Downley 19 SU 8495
Downton (Hants.) 9 SZ 2693
Downton (Wilts.) 8 SU 1721
Downton on the Rock 24 SO 4273
Dowsby 35 TF 1129
Doxford 53 NU 1823
Doynton 17 ST 7173
Draffan 50 NS 7945
Drakeland Corner 4 SX 5758
Drakemyre 49 NS 2850
Drakes Broughton 25 SO 9248
Draughton (N. Yorks.) 37 SE 0352
Draughton (Northants.) 26 SP 7676
Drax 38 SE 6726
Draycote 26 SP 4469
Draycott (Derby) 34 SK 4433
Draycott (Glos.) 25 SP 1836
Draycott (Somer.) 7 ST 4750
Draycott in the Clay 33 SK 1528
Draycott in the Moors 33 SJ 9840
Drayton (Hants.) 9 SU 6605
Drayton (Here. and Worc.) 25 SO 9076
Drayton (Leic.) 27 SP 8392
Drayton (Norf.) 29 TG 1713
Drayton (Oxon.) 26 SP 4241
Drayton (Oxon.) 18 SU 4794
Drayton (Somer.) 7 ST 4042
Drayton Bassett 25 SK 1900
Drayton Parslow 19 SP 8428
Drayton St. Leonard 18 SU 5996
Drefach (Dyfed) 22 SN 3538
Drefach (Dyfed) 22 SN 5045
Drefach (Dyfed) 15 SN 5213
Dreghorn 49 NS 3538
Drem 52 NT 5079
Drewsteignton 5 SX 7391
Driby 35 TF 3874
Driffield 17 SU 0799
Drift 2 SW 4328
Drigg 40 SD 0698
Drighlington 37 SE 2229
Drimnin 54 NM 5553
Drimpton 7 ST 4104
Drinesheader 63 NG 1795
Drinkstone 29 TL 9561
Drinkstone Green 29 TL 9660
Drointon 33 SK 0226
Droitwich 25 SO 8962
Dron 56 NO 1415
Dronfield 33 SK 3578
Dronfield Woodhouse 33 SK 3278
Drongan 50 NS 4418
Dronley 57 NO 3435
Droxford 9 SU 6018
Droylsden 37 SJ 9098
Druid 31 SJ 0343
Druidale 43 SC 3688
Druidston 14 SM 8716
Druimarbin 55 NN 0861
Druimavuic 55 NN 0044
Drum (Grampn.) 62 NJ 8946
Drum (Tays.) 56 NO 0400
Drumbeg 64 NC 1232
Drumblade 61 NJ 5840
Drumbuie (Dumf. and Galwy.) 45 NX 5682
Drumbuie (Highld.) 59 NG 7730
Drumburgh 46 NY 2659
Drumchapel 50 NS 5270
Drumchardine 60 NH 5644
Drumclog 50 NS 6339
Drumeldrie 57 NO 4403
Drumelzier 51 NT 1333
Drumfearn 58 NG 6716
Drumgask 60 NN 6193
Drumgley 57 NO 4250
Drumguish 60 NN 7999
Drumhead 62 NO 6092
Drumlassie 62 NJ 6405
Drumlemble 48 NR 6619
Drumlithie 57 NO 7880
Drummore 44 NX 1336
Drumnadrochit 60 NH 5029
Drumnagorrach 61 NJ 5252
Drumrash 45 NX 6871
Drumrunie 66 NC 1706
Drums 62 NJ 9822
Drumsallie 55 NM 9578
Drumshang 49 NS 2515
Drumsturdy 57 NO 4935
Drumuie 58 NG 4546
Drumuillie 60 NH 9420
Drumvaich 56 NN 6803
Drumwhindle 62 NJ 9236
Drunkendub 57 NO 6646
Drury 31 SJ 2964
Dry Doddington 34 SK 8446
Dry Drayton 27 TL 3862
Drybeck 41 NY 6615
Drybridge (Grampn.) 61 NJ 4362
Drybridge (Strath.) 50 NS 3536
Drybrook 17 SO 6416
Dryhope 51 NT 2624
Drymen 50 NS 4788
Drymuir 62 NJ 9146
Drynoch 58 NG 4031
Dubford 62 NJ 7963
Dubton 57 NO 5652
Duck's Cross 27 TL 1156
Duckington 32 SJ 4851
Ducklington 18 SP 3507
Duddingston 51 NT 2972
Duddington 27 SK 9800
Duddleswell 12 TQ 4628
Duddo 53 NT 9342
Duddon 32 SJ 5164
Duddon Bridge 40 SD 1988
Dudleston Heath 32 SJ 3636
Dudley 25 SO 9390
Duffield 33 SK 3443
Duffryn 15 SS 8495
Dufftown 61 NJ 3240
Duffus 61 NJ 1668
Dufton 41 NY 6925
Duggleby 39 SE 8766
Duirinish 59 NG 7831
Duisdalemore 58 NG 6913
Duisky 55 NN 0176
Dukestown 16 SO 1410
Dukinfield 37 SJ 9497
Dulas (Gwyn.) 30 SH 4789
Dulcote 7 ST 5644
Dulford 7 ST 0606
Dull 56 NN 8049
Dullatur 50 NS 7476
Dullingham 20 TL 6357
Dulnain Bridge 61 NH 9924
Duloe (Beds.) 27 TL 1560
Duloe (Corn.) 4 SX 2358
Dulsie 60 NH 9341
Dulverton 6 SS 9127
Dulwich 12 TQ 3373
Dumbarton 50 NS 4075
Dumbleton 25 SP 0135
Dumfries 45 NX 9775
Dumgoyne 50 NS 5283
Dummer 10 SU 5845
Dun (Tays.) 57 NO 6659
Dunalastair 56 NN 7159
Dunan (Isle of Skye) 58 NG 5828
Dunan (Strath.) 49 NS 1571
Dunans 49 NS 0491
Dunball 7 ST 3140
Dunbar 52 NT 6878
Dunbeath 67 ND 1629
Dunbeg 54 NM 8734
Dunblane 56 NN 7801
Dunbog 57 NO 2817
Duncanston (Highld.) 60 NH 5956
Duncaston (Grampn.) 61 NJ 5826
Dunchurch 26 SP 4871
Duncote 26 SP 6750
Duncow 45 NX 9683
Duncrievie 56 NO 1309
Duncton 11 SU 9516
Dundee 57 NO 4030
Dundon 7 ST 4732
Dundonald 50 NS 3634
Dundonnell 64 NH 0886
Dundraw 46 NY 2149
Dundreggan 59 NH 3114
Dundrennan 45 NX 7447
Dundry 16 ST 5566
Dundurn 56 NN 7023
Dunecht 62 NJ 7509
Dunfermiline 51 NT 0987
Dunford Bridge 37 SE 1502
Dunham 34 SK 8174
Dunham Town 32 SJ 7488
Dunham-on-the-Hill 32 SJ 4772
Dunhampton 25 SO 8466
Dunholme 34 TF 0279
Dunino 57 NO 5311
Dunipace 50 NS 8083
Dunk's Green 12 TQ 6152
Dunkeld 56 NO 0242
Dunkeswell 7 ST 1407
Dunkirk 13 TR 0758
Dunlappie 57 NO 5967
Dunley 24 SO 7869
Dunlop 50 NS 4049
Dunmore (Central.) 50 NS 8989
Dunmore (Strath.) 49 NR 7961
Dunnet 67 ND 2171
Dunnichen 57 NO 5048
Dunning 56 NO 0114
Dunnington (Humbs.) 39 TA 1551
Dunnington (N. Yorks.) 38 SE 6652
Dunnington (Warw.) 25 SP 0653
Dunnockshaw 37 SD 8127
Dunollie 54 NM 8532
Dunoon 49 NS 1777
Dunragit 44 NX 1557
Duns 53 NT 7853
Duns Tew 18 SP 4528
Dunsby 35 TF 1026
Dunscore 45 NX 8684
Dunscroft 38 SE 6409
Dunsden Green 10 SU 7477
Dunsfold 11 TQ 0036
Dunsford 5 SX 8089
Dunshelt 57 NO 2410
Dunshillock 62 NJ 9848
Dunsley 43 NZ 8511
Dunsmore 19 SP 8605
Dunsop Bridge 36 SD 6549
Dunstable 19 TL 0221
Dunstall 33 SK 1920
Dunstall Green 28 TL 7460
Dunstan 53 NU 2419
Dunster 7 SS 9943
Dunston (Lincs.) 35 TF 0663
Dunston (Norf.) 29 TG 2302
Dunston (Staffs.) 33 SJ 9217
Dunston (Tyne and Wear) 47 NZ 2263
Dunsville 38 SE 6407
Dunswell 39 TA 0735
Dunsyre 51 NT 0748
Dunterton 4 SX 3779
Duntisbourne Abbots 17 SO 9707
Duntisbourne Leer 17 SO 9707
Duntisbourne Rouse 17 SO 9805
Duntish 8 ST 6906
Duntocher 50 NS 4972
Dunton (Beds.) 27 TL 2344
Dunton (Bucks.) 18 SP 8224
Dunton (Norf.) 28 TF 8730
Dunton Bassett 26 SP 5490
Dunton Green 12 TQ 5157
Dunton Wayletts 20 TQ 6590
Duntulum 58 NG 4174
Dunure 49 NS 2515
Dunvant 15 SS 5993
Dunvegan 58 NG 2548
Dunwich 29 TM 4770
Durdar 46 NY 4051
Durham 47 NZ 2742
Durisdeer 45 NS 8903
Durleigh 7 ST 2736
Durley (Hants.) 9 SU 5115
Durley (Wilts.) 10 SU 2364
Durley Street 9 SU 5217
Durnamuck 64 NH 0192
Durness 66 NC 4067
Durno 62 NJ 7128
Durran 67 ND 1863
Durrington (W Susx.) 11 TQ 1105
Durrington (Wilts.) 8 SU 1544
Dursley 17 ST 7597
Durston 7 ST 2828
Durweston 8 ST 8508
Dury 63 HU 4560
Duston 26 SP 7261
Duthil 60 NH 9324
Dutlas 23 SO 2077
Duton Hill 20 TL 6026
Dutton 32 SJ 5779
Duxford 20 TL 4846
Dwygyfylchi 30 SH 7377
Dwyran 30 SH 4466
Dyce 62 NJ 8812
Dyffryn 15 SS 8593
Dyffryn Ardudwy 30 SH 5822
Dyffryn Ceidrych 15 SN 7025
Dyffryn Cellwen 15 SN 8509
Dyke (Devon.) 6 SS 3123
Dyke (Grampn.) 60 NH 9858
Dyke (Lincs.) 35 TF 1022
Dykehead (Central) 50 NS 5997
Dykehead (Strath.) 50 NS 8759
Dykehead (Tays.) 57 NO 3860
Dykends 57 NO 2557
Dylife 22 SN 8594
Dymchurch 13 TR 1029
Dymock 24 SO 6931
Dynevor Castle 15 SN 6122
Dyrham 17 ST 7375
Dysart 51 NT 3093
Dyserth 31 SJ 0579

Eagland Hill 36 SD 4345
Eagle 34 SK 8767
Eaglescliffe 42 NZ 4215
Eaglesfield (Cumbr.) 40 NY 0928
Eaglesfield (Dumf and Galwy.) 46 NY 2374
Eaglesham 50 NS 5751
Eairy 43 SC 2977
Eakring 34 SK 6762
Ealand 38 SE 7811
Ealing 19 TQ 1781
Eamont Bridge 40 NY 5228
Earby 37 SD 9046
Earcroft 36 SD 6824
Eardington 24 SO 7290
Eardisland 24 SO 4158
Eardisley 23 SO 3149
Eardiston (Here. and Worcs.) 24 SO 6968
Eardiston (Salop 24 SJ 3725
Earith 27 TL 3875
Earl Shilton 26 SP 4697
Earl Soham 29 TM 2363
Earl Sterndale 33 SK 0967
Earl Stonham 21 TM 1158
Earl's Croome 25 SO 8642
Earl's Green 29 TM 0366
Earl's Hill 50 NS 7188
Earl's Seat (Central) (mt.) 50 NS 5783
Earle 53 NT 9826
Earlestown 32 SJ 5795
Earlham 29 TG 1908
Earlish 58 NG 3861
Earls Barton 27 SP 8563
Earls Colne 21 TL 8528
Earlsdon 21 SP 3177
Earlsferry 57 NO 4800
Earlsford 62 NJ 8334
Earlshall (cnt.) 57 NO 4621
Earlston (Borders) 52 NT 5738
Earlston (Strath.) 50 NS 4035
Earlstoun 45 NX 6183
Earlswood 25 SP 1174
Earlswood Common 16 ST 4595
Earnley 10 SZ 8096
Earsdon 47 NZ 3272
Earshaig 45 NT 0402
Earsham 29 TM 3289
Earswick 38 SE 6157
Eartham 11 SU 9309
Easby 42 NZ 5708
Easdale (Strath.) 54 NM 7317
Easebourne 11 SU 8922
Easenhall 26 SP 4679
Easington (Bucks.) 18 SP 6810
Easington (Cleve.) 43 NZ 7418
Easington (Durham) 47 NZ 4143
Easington (Humbs.) 39 TA 3919
Easington (Northum.) 53 NU 1234
Easington (Oxon.) 18 SU 6697
Easington Lane 47 NZ 3646
Easingwold 38 SE 5269
Easole Street 13 TR 2652
Eassie and Nevay 57 NO 3345
East Aberthaw 16 ST 0367
East Allington 5 SX 7648
East Anstey 6 SS 8626
East Ashling 10 SU 8207
East Barming 12 TQ 7254
East Barnet 19 TQ 2794
East Barsham 28 TF 9133
East Beckham 29 TG 1640
East Bedfont 11 TQ 1074
East Bergholt 21 TM 0734
East Bilney 29 TF 9519
East Blatchington 12 TQ 4800
East Boldre 9 SU 3700
East Boleskine 60 NH 5122
East Bradenham 29 TF 9208
East Brent 16 ST 3452
East Bridge 29 TM 4566
East Bridgford 34 SK 6943
East Buckland 6 SS 6731
East Budleigh 7 SY 0684
East Burra 63 HU 3833
East Burrafirth 63 HU 3658
East Burton 8 SY 8386
East Cairnbeg 57 NO 7076
East Calder 51 NT 0867
East Carleton (Norf.) 29 TG 1802
East Carlton (Northants.) 27 SP 8389
East Chaldon or Chaldon Herring 8 SY 7983
East Challow 18 SU 3988
East Chiltington 12 TQ 3715
East Chisenbury 17 SU 1352
East Clandon 11 TQ 0651
East Claydon 18 SP 7325
East Combe (Somer.) 7 ST 1631
East Cottingwith 38 SE 7042
East Coulston 17 ST 9454
East Cowes 9 SZ 5095
East Cowton 42 NZ 3103
East Cramlington 47 NZ 2876
East Creech 8 SY 9282
East Dean (Hants.) 9 SU 2726
East Dean (W Susx.) 11 SU 9013
East Dereham 29 TF 9913
East Down 6 SS 5941
East Drayton 34 SK 7775
East End (Avon) 16 ST 4770
East End (Dorset) 8 SY 9998
East End (Hants.) 10 SU 4161
East End (Hants.) 9 SZ 3697
East End (Herts.) 20 TL 4527
East End (Kent) 12 TQ 8335
East End (Oxon.) 18 SP 3914
East Farleigh 12 TQ 7353
East Farndon 26 SP 7185
East Ferry 38 SK 8199
East Garston 10 SU 3676
East Ginge 18 SU 4486
East Goscote 26 SK 6413
East Grafton 10 SU 2560
East Grimstead 9 SU 2227
East Grinstead 12 TQ 3938
East Guldeford 13 TQ 9321
East Haddon 26 SP 6668
East Hagbourne 18 SU 5388
East Halton 39 TA 1419
East Halton Skitter 39 TA 1423
East Ham (Gtr London) 20 T1 4283
East Hanney 18 SU 4192
East Hanningfield 20 TL 7601
East Hardwick 38 SE 4618
East Harling 29 TL 9986
East Harlsey 42 SE 4299
East Harptree 17 ST 5655
East Hartford 47 NZ 2679
East Harting 10 SU 7919
East Hatley 27 TL 2850
East Hauxwell 42 SE 1693
East Haven 57 NO 5836
East Heckington 35 TF 1944
East Hedleyhope 47 NZ 1540
East Hendred 18 SU 4588

East Heslerton
Farrington Gurney

East Heslerton 43 SE9276
East Hoathly 12 TQ5216
East Horrington 7 ST5846
East Horsley 11 TQ0952
East Huntspill 7 ST3444
East Hyde 19 TL1317
East Ilsley 18 SU4981
East Kennett 17 SU1167
East Keswick 38 SE3544
East Kilbride 50 NS6354
East Kirkby 35 TF3362
East Knighton 8 SY8185
Eaw Knoyle 8 ST8830
East Lambrook 7 ST4319
East Langdon 13 TR3346
East Langton 26 SP7292
East Langwell 66 NC7206
East Lavington 11 SU9416
East Layton 42 NZ1609
East Leake 34 SK5526
East Leigh (Devon.) 5 SS6905
East Lexham 28 TF8617
East Lilburn 53 NU0423
East Linton 52 NT5977
East Liss 10 SU7827
East Lochussie 60 NH5056
East Looe 4 SX2553
East Lound 38 SK7899
East Lulworth 8 SY8581
East Mains 62 NO6797
East Malling 12 TQ7057
East March 57 NO4436
East Marden 10 SU8014
East Markham 34 SK7472
East Marsh 14 SN2808
East Marton 37 SD9050
East Meon 9 SU6822
East Mersea 21 TM0414
East Molesey 11 TQ1568
East Morden 8 SY9194
East Morton 37 SE1042
East Norton 26 SK7800
East Oakley 10 SU5749
East Ogwell 5 SX8370
East Ord 53 NT9851
East Panson 4 SX3692
East Peckham 12 TQ6649
East Pennard 8 ST5937
East Plean 50 NS8387
East Poringland 29 TG2701
East Portlemouth 5 SX7438
East Prawle 5 SX7736
East Preston 11 TQ0702
East Putford 4 SS3616
East Quantoxhead 7 ST1343
East Rainton 47 NZ3347
East Ravendale 39 TF2399
East Raynham 28 TF8825
East Retford 34 SK7080
East Rudham 28 TF8228
East Runton 29 TG1942
East Saltoun 52 NT4767
East Shefford 10 SU3974
East Sleekburn 47 NZ2785
East Stoke (Dorset) 8 SY8787
East Stoke (Notts.) 34 SK7549
East Stour 8 ST8022
East Stourmouth 13 TR2662
East Stratton 10 SU5440
East Studdal 13 TR3149
East Taphouse 4 SX1863
East Thirston 47 NZ1999
East Tilbury 12 TQ6877
East Tisted 10 SU7032
East Torrington 35 TF1483
East Tuddenham 29 TG0811
East Tytherley 9 SU2929
East Tytherton 17 ST9674
East Village 5 SS8405
East Wall 24 SO5293
East Walton 28 TF7416
East Wellow 9 SU3020
East Wemyss 57 NT3396
East Whitburn 51 NS9665
East Wickham 12 TQ4576
East Williamston 14 SN0905
East Winch 28 TF6916
East Wittering 10 SZ7996
East Witton 42 SE1486
East Woodhay 10 SU4061
East Worldham 10 SU7538
East Wretham 28 TL9190
East Yell 63 HU5284
Eastbourne 12 TV6199
Eastbury (Berks.) 10 SU3477
Eastbury (Gtr London) 19 TQ0991
Eastchurch 13 TQ9871
Eastcombe (Glos.) 17 SO8804
Eastcote (Gtr London) 19 TQ1188
Eastcote (W Mids) 25 SP1979
Eastcott (Corn.) 4 SS2515
Eastcott (Wilts.) 17 SU0255
Eastcourt 17 ST9792
Eastdean (E Susx.) 12 TV5598
Eastend (Essex) 21 TQ9492
Easter Ardross 65 NH6373
Easter Balmoral 61 NO2693
Easter Compton 17 ST5782
Easter Galcantray 60 NH8147
Easter Kinkell 60 NH5756
Easter Lednathie 57 NO3363
Easter Moniack 60 NH5543
Easter Muckovie 60 NH7044
Easter Ord 62 NJ8304
Easter Skeld 63 HU3044
Easter Stanhope 51 NT1229
Eastergate [illegible] SU9405
Eastern Green 26 SP2780
Easterton 17 SU0154
Eastertown 16 ST3454
Eastfield (N Yorks.) 43 TA0484
Eastfield (Strath.) 50 NS7574
Eastfield (Strath.) 50 NS8964
Eastfield Hall 47 NU2206
Eastgate (Durham) 41 NY9538
Eastgate (Norf.) 29 TG1423
Eastham (Mers.) 32 SJ3580
Easthampstead 11 SU8667
Easthope 24 SO5695
Easthorpe 21 TL9121
Easthouses 51 NT3465
Eastington (Glos.) 17 SO7705
Eastington (Glos.) 17 SP1213
Eastleach Martin 18 SP1905
Eastleach Turville 17 SP1905
Eastleigh (Hants.) 9 SU4518
Eastling 13 TQ9656
Eastney 9 SZ6698
Eastnor 24 SO7337
Eastoft 39 SE8016
Easton (Cambs.) 27 TL1371
Easton (Cumbr.) 46 NY4372
Easton (Devon.) 5 SX7288
Easton (Dorset) 8 SY6871
Easton (Hants.) 9 SU5132
Easton (I. of W.) 9 SZ3485
Easton (Lincs.) 34 SK9226
Easton (Norf.) 29 TG1311
Easton (Somer.) 7 ST5147
Easton (Suff.) 21 TM2838
Easton Grey 17 ST8787
Easton Maudit 27 SP8858
Easton Royal 10 SU2060
Easton on the Hill 27 TF0004
Easton-in-Gordano 16 ST5175
Eastrea 27 TL2997
Eastriggs 46 NY2465
Eastrington 38 SE7929
Eastry 13 TR3155
Eastville 35 TF4057
Eastwell 34 SK7728
Eastwell Park 13 TR0147
Eastwick 20 TL4311
Eastwood (Essex) 21 TQ8588
Eastwood (Notts.) 34 SK4646
Eastwood (W Yorks.) 37 SD9625
Eathorpe 26 SP3969
Eaton (Ches.) 32 SJ5763
Eaton (Ches.) 33 SJ8765
Eaton (Leic.) 34 SK7929
Eaton (Norf.) 29 TG2006
Eaton (Notts.) 34 SK7077
Eaton (Oxon.) 18 SP4403
Eaton (Salop) 24 SO3789
Eaton (Salop) 24 SO4989
Eaton Bishop 24 SO4439
Eaton Bray 19 SP9720
Eaton Constantine 24 SJ5906
Eaton Hastings 18 SU2698
Eaton Socon 27 TL1658
Eaton upon Tern 32 SJ6523
Eaval (Mt) 63 NF8960
Ebberston 43 SE8983
Ebbesborne Wake 8 ST9824
Ebbw Vale (Gwent) 16 ST2094
Ebchester 47 NZ1055
Ebford 5 SX9887
Ebrington 25 SP1840
Ecchinswell 10 SU5060
Ecclaw 53 NT7568
Ecclefechan 45 NY1974
Eccles (Borders) 53 NT7641
Eccles (Gtr Mches) 37 SJ7798
Eccles (Kent) 12 TQ7260
Eccles Road 29 TM0190
Ecclesfield 33 SK3393
Ecclesgrieg 57 NO7365
Eccleshall 32 SJ8329
Ecclesmachan 51 NT0573
Eccleston (Ches.) 32 SJ4162
Eccleston (Lancs.) 36 SD5216
Eccleston (Mers.) 32 SJ4895
Eccup 38 SE2842
Echt 62 NJ7305
Eckford 52 NT7125
Eckington (Derby) 33 SK4379
Eckington (Here. and Worc.) 25 SO9241
Ecton 27 SP8263
Edale 33 SK1285
Eday Aerodrome 63 HY5634
Edburton 11 TQ2311
Edderton 65 NH7184
Eddleston 51 NT2447
Eden Park 12 TQ3868
Edenbridge 12 TQ4446
Edenfield 37 SD8019
Edenhall 41 NY5632
Edenham 35 TF0621
Edensor 33 SK2469
Edenthorpe 38 SE6206
Ederline 54 NM8702
Edern 30 SH2739
Edgbaston 25 SP0684
Edgcott 18 SP6722
Edge 24 SJ3908
Edge End 17 SO5913
Edge Hill 26 SP3747
Edgebolton 32 SJ5721
Edgefield 29 TG0934
Edgeworth 17 SO9406
Edgmond 32 SJ7119
Edgmond Marsh 32 SJ7120
Edgton 24 SO3885
Edgware 19 TQ2091
Edgworth 36 SD7416
Edinample 56 NN6022
Edinbane 58 NG3451
Edinburgh 51 NT2674
Edingale 26 SK2112
Edingley 34 SK6655
Edingthorpe 29 TG3132
Edington (Somer.) 7 ST3939
Edington (Wilts.) 17 ST9252
Edington Burtle 7 ST3943
Edith Weston 27 SK9205
Edithmead 7 ST3249
Edlesborough 19 SP9719
Edlingham 53 NU1108
Edlington 35 TF2371
Edmondbyers 47 NZ0150
Edmondsham 8 SU0611
Edmondsley 47 NZ2348
Edmondthorpe 34 SK8517
Edmonstone 33 [illegible]
Edmonton 20 TQ3493
Ednam 53 NT7337
Edradynate 56 NN8852
Edrom 53 NT8255
Edstaston 32 SJ5131
Edstone 25 SP1761
Edwalton 34 SK5935
Edwardstone 21 TL9442
Edwinsford 15 SN6334
Edwinstowe 34 SK6266
Edworth 27 TL2241
Edwyn Ralph 24 SO6457
Edzell 57 NO5968
Efail Isaf 16 ST0884
Efailnewydd 30 SH3536
Efenechtyd 31 SJ1155
Effingham 11 TQ1253
Effirth 63 HU3152
Efford 5 SS8901
Egerton (Gtr Mches.) 36 SD7014
Egerton (Kent) 13 TQ9047
Eggardon Hill 7 SY5494
Eggington 19 SP9525
Egginton 33 SK2628
Egglescliffe 42 NZ4213
Eggleston 41 NZ0023
Egham 11 TQ0171
Egleton 27 SK8707
Eglingham 53 NU1019
Egloshayle 3 SX0071
Egloskerry 4 SX2786
Eglwys-Brewis 16 ST0168
Eglwysbach 31 SH8070
Eglwyswrw 14 SN1438
Egmanton 34 SK7368
Egremont 40 NY0110
Egton 43 NZ8006
Egton Bridge 43 NZ8005
Eilanreach 59 NG8017
Eilean Darach 64 NH1087
Elan Village 23 SN9365
Elberton (Avon) 17 ST6088
Elburton (Devon.) 4 SX5353
Elcho 56 NO1620
Elcombe 17 SU1280
Eldernell 27 TL3298
Eldersfield 24 SO7931
Elderslie 50 NS4462
Eldroth 37 SD7665
Eldwick 37 SE1240
Elford (Northum.) 53 NU1830
Elford (Staffs.) 25 SK1810
Elgin 61 NJ2162
Elgol 58 NG5214
Elham 13 TR1744
Elie 57 NO4900
Elim 30 SH3584
Eling 9 SU3612
Elishader 58 NG5065
Elishaw 47 NY8694
Elkesley 34 SK6875
Elkstone 17 SO9612
Elland 37 SE1020
Ellary 48 NR7476
Ellastone 33 SK1143
Ellemford 53 NT7360
Ellen's Green 11 TQ1035
Ellenhall 33 SJ8426
Ellerbeck (N Yorks.) 42 SE4396
Ellerby (Humbs.) 39 TA1637
Ellerby (N Yorks.) 43 NZ7914
Ellerdine Heath 32 SJ6121
Ellerker 39 SE9229
Ellerton (Humbs.) 38 SE7039
Ellerton (Salop) 32 SJ7126
Ellesborough 19 SP8306
Ellesmere 32 SJ3934
Ellesmere Port 32 SJ4077
Ellingham (Norf.) 29 TM3592
Ellingham (Northum.) 53 NU1725
Ellingstring 42 SE1783
Ellington (Cambs.) 27 TL1671
Ellington (Northum.) 47 NZ2792
Ellisfield 10 SU6345
Ellistown 26 SK4311
Ellon 62 NJ9530
Ellough 29 TM4486
Elloughton 39 SE9428
Ellwood 17 SO5808
Elm 28 TF4607
Elm Park 20 TQ5385
Elmbridge 25 SO8967
Elmdon (Essex) 20 TL4639
Elmdon (W Mids) 25 SP1783
Elmdon Heath 25 SP1580
Elmesthorpe 26 SP4696
Elmhurst 25 SK1112
Elmley Castle 25 SO9841
Elmley Lovett 25 SO8669
Elmore 17 SO7715
Elmore Back 17 SO7716
Elmscott 4 SS2321
Elmsett 21 TM0546
Elmstead Market 21 TM0624
Elmsted Court 13 TR1145
Elmstone 13 TR2660
Elmstone Hardwicke 17 SO9226
Elmswell 29 TL9964
Elmton 34 SK5073
Elphin 66 NC2111
Elphinstone 51 NT3970
Elrick 62 NJ8206
Elrig 44 NX3247
Elsdon 47 NY9393
Elsecar 38 SE3800
Elsenham 20 TL5425
Elsfield 18 SP5409
Elsham 39 TA0312
Elsing 29 TG0516
Elslack 37 SD9349
Elsrickle 51 NT0643
Elstead (Surrey) 11 SU9043
Elsted (W Susx.) 10 SU8119
Elston 34 SK7548
Elstone 5 SS6716
Elstow 27 TL0547
Elstree 19 TQ1895
Elstronwick 39 TA2232
Elswick 36 SD4138
Elsworth 27 TL3163
Elterwater 40 NY3204
Eltham 12 TQ4274
Eltisley 27 TL2759
Elton (Cambs.) 27 TL0893
Elton (Ches.) 32 SJ4575
Elton (Clev.) 42 NZ4017
Elton (Derby) 33 SK2261
Elton (Glos.) 17 SO6914
Elton (Here. and Worc.) 24 SO4571
Elton (Notts.) 34 SK7638
Elvanfoot 51 NS9517
Elvaston 33 SK4132
Elveden 28 TL8279
Elvingston 52 NT4674
Elvington (Kent) 13 TR2750
Elvington (N Yorks.) 38 SE6947
Elwick (Cleve.) 42 NZ4532
Elwick (Northum.) 53 NU1136
Elworth 32 SJ7361
Elworthy 7 ST0835
Ely (Cambs.) 28 TL5380
Ely (S Glam.) 16 ST1476
Emberton 27 SP8849
Embleton (Cumbr.) 40 NY1630
Embleton (Northum.) 53 NU2322
Embo 65 NH8192
Emborough 8 ST6151
Embsay 37 SE0053
Emery Down 9 SU2808
Emley 37 SE2413
Emmer Green 10 SU7177
Emmington 18 SP7402
Emneth 28 TF4807
Emneth Hungate 28 TF5107
Empingham 27 SK9408
Empshott 10 SU7731
Emsworth 10 SU7405
Enaclete 63 NB1228
Enborne 10 SU4365
Enchmarsh 24 SO4996
End Moor 41 SD5584
Enderby 26 SP5399
Endon 33 SJ9253
Enfield 20 TQ3296
Enford 8 SU1351
Engine Common 17 ST6984
Englefield 10 SU6272
Englefield Green 11 SU9870
English Bicknor 17 SO5815
English Frankton 32 SJ4529
Englishcombe 17 ST7162
Enham-Alamein 10 SU3648
Enmore 7 ST2335
Ennerdale Bridge 40 NY0615
Enoch 45 NS8801
Enochdhu 5 NO0662
Ensbury 8 SZ0896
Ensdon 32 SJ4016
Ensis 6 SS5626
Enstone 18 SP3725
Enterkinfoot 45 NS8504
Enville 25 SO8286
Eorabus 54 NM3823
Eoropie 63 NB5156
Epperstone 34 SK6548
Epping 20 TL4602
Epping Green (Essex) 20 TL4305
Epping Green (Herts.) 19 TL2906
Epping Upland 20 TL4404
Eppleby 42 NZ1713
Epsom 11 TQ2160
Epwell 26 SP3540
Epworth 38 SE7803
Erbistock 32 SJ3541
Erbusaig 59 NG7629
Erdington 25 SP1291
Eredine 55 NM9609
Eriboll 66 NC4356
Ericstane 51 NT0710
Eridge Green 12 TQ5535
Erines 49 NR8575
Eriswell 28 TL7278
Erith 12 TQ5177
Erlestoke 17 ST9853
Ermington 5 SX6353
Erpingham 29 TG1831
Errogie 60 NH5622
Errol 57 NO2522
Ersary 63 NF7100
Ervie 44 NX0067
Erwarton 21 TM2234
Erwood 23 SO0943
Eryholme 42 NZ3208
Eryrys 31 SJ2057
Escalls 2 SW3627
Escrick 38 SE6243
Esgairgeiliog 22 SH7605
Esh 47 NZ1944
Esh Winning 47 NZ1942
Esher 11 TQ1464
Eshott 47 NZ2097
Eshton 37 SD9356
Eskadale 60 NH4539
Eskbank 51 NT3266
Eskdale Green 40 NY1400
Esprick 36 SD4035
Essendine 27 TF0412
Essendon 19 TL2708
Essich 60 NH6539
Essington 25 SJ9603
Esslemont 62 NJ9329
Eston 42 NZ5518
Etal 53 NT9339
Etchilhampton 17 SU0460
Etchingham 12 TQ7126
Etchinghill (Kent) 13 TR1639
Etchinghill (Staffs.) 33 SK0218
Eton 11 SU9678
Etteridge 60 NN6892
Ettington 26 SP2649
Etton (Humbs.) 39 SE9743
Etton (Cambs.) 27 TF1306
Ettrick 51 NT2714
Ettrickbridge End 51 NT3824
Etwall 33 SK2732
Euston 28 TL8978
Euxton 36 SD5518
Evanton 65 NH6066
Evedon 35 TF0947
Evelix 65 NH7690
Evenjobb 23 SO2662
Evenley 18 SP5834
Evenlode 18 SP2229
Evenwood 42 NZ1524
Everbay 63 HY6725
Evercreech 8 ST6438
Everdon 26 SP5957
Everingham 39 SE8042
Everleigh 10 SU1953
Everley 43 SE9789
Eversholt 19 SP9933
Evershot 7 ST5704
Eversley 10 SU7762
Eversley Cross 10 SU7961
Everton (Beds.) 27 TL2051
Everton (Hants) 9 SZ2993
Everton (Notts.) 34 SK6891
Evertown 46 NY3576
Evesbatch 24 SO6848
Evesham 25 SP0344
Evington 26 SK6203
Ewden Village 33 SK2797
Ewe Hill 51 NT0540
Ewell 11 TQ2262
Ewell Minnis 13 TR2643
Ewelme 18 SU6491
Ewen 17 SU0097
Ewenny 15 SS9077
Ewerby 35 TF1247
Ewesley 47 NZ0592
Ewhurst (E Susx) 12 TQ7924
Ewhurst (Surrey) 11 TQ0940
Ewloe 31 SJ3066
Eworthy 4 SX4494
Ewshot 10 SU8149
Ewyas Harold 16 SO3828
Exbourne 4 SS6002
Exbury 9 SU4200
Exebridge 6 SS9324
Exelby 42 SE2986
Exeter 5 SX9292
Exford 6 SS8538
Exhall 25 SP1055
Exminster 5 SX9487
Exmouth 7 SY0080
Exnaboe 63 HU3912
Exning 20 TL6265
Exton (Devon) 5 SX9886
Exton (Hants.) 9 SU6121
Exton (Leic.) 27 SK9211
Exton (Somer.) 6 SS9233
Eyam 33 SK2176
Eydon 26 SP5450
Eye (Cambs.) 27 TF2202
Eye (Here. and Worc.) 24 SO4963
Eye (Suffolk) 29 TM1473
Eyemouth 53 NT9464
Eyeworth 27 TL2545
Eyhorne Street 12 TQ8354
Eyke 21 TM3151
Eynesbury 27 TL1859
Eynsford 12 TQ5365
Eynsham 18 SP4309
Eype 7 SY4491
Eyre 58 NG4152
Eythorne 13 TR2849
Eyton (Here. and Worc.) 24 SO4761
Eyton (Salop) 24 SO3687
Eyton upon the Weald Moors 32 SJ6414

Faccombe 10 SY3857
Faceby 42 NZ4903
Faddiley 32 SJ5752
Fadmoor 42 SE6789
Faifley 50 NS5073
Failand 16 ST5272
Failford 50 NS4526
Failsworth 37 SD9002
Fair Oak (Hants.) 9 SY4918
Fairbourne 22 SH6113
Fairburn 38 SE4727
Fairfield 25 SO9475
Fairford 17 SP1501
Fairlie 49 NS2155
Fairlight 13 TQ8612
Fairmile 7 SY0997
Fairmilehead 51 NT2567
Fairoak (Staffs.) 32 SJ7632
Fairseat 12 TQ6261
Fairstead (Essex) 20 TL7616
Fairstead (Norf.) 29 TG2723
Fairwarp 12 TQ4626
Fairy Cross 6 SS4024
Fakenham 29 TF9229
Fala 52 NT4361
Fala Dam 52 NT4261
Falahill 51 NT3956
Faldingworth 35 TF0684
Falfield 17 ST6893
Falkenham 21 TM2939
Falkirk 50 NS8880
Falkland 57 NO2507
Falla 52 NT7013
Fallin 50 NS8391
Falmer 12 TQ3508
Falmouth 2 SW8032
Falstone 46 NY7287
Fan Hill 23 SN9388
Fan Llia 15 SN9318
Fanagmore 66 NC1750
Fangdale Beck 42 SE5694
Fangfoss 38 SE7653
Fanmore 54 NM4244
Fans 52 NT6140
Far Cotton 26 SP7458
Farcet 27 TL2094
Farden 24 SO5776
Fareham 9 SU5806
Farewell 25 SK0811
Faringdon 18 SU2895
Farington 36 SD5425
Farlam 46 NY5558
Farleigh 12 TQ3660
Farleigh Hungerford 17 ST7957
Farleigh Wallop 10 SU6246
Farlesthorpe 35 TF4774
Farleton 40 SD5380
Farley (Salop) 24 SJ3808
Farley (Staffs.) 33 SK0644
Farley (Wilts.) 9 SU2229
Farley Green 11 TQ0645
Farley Hill 10 SU7564
Farleys End 17 SO7615
Farlington 38 SE6167
Farlow 24 SO6380
Farmborough 17 ST6560
Farmcote 17 SP0629
Farmers 22 SN6444
Farmington 17 SP1315
Farmoor 18 SP4407
Farmtown 61 NJ5051
Farnborough (Berks.) 18 SU4381
Farnborough (Gtr London) 12 TQ4464
Farnborough (Hants.) 11 SU8753
Farnborough (Warw.) 26 SP4349
Farncombe 11 SU9755
Farndish 27 SP9263
Farndon (Ches.) 32 SJ4154
Farndon (Notts.) 34 SK7651
Farnell 57 NO6255
Farnham (Dorset) 8 ST9514
Farnham (Essex) 20 TL4724
Farnham (N Yorks.) 38 SE3460
Farnham (Suff.) 29 TM3660
Farnham (Surrey) 10 SU8446
Farnham Common 19 SU9584
Farnham Green 20 TL4625
Farnham Royal 19 SU9682
Farningham 12 TQ5566
Farnley 37 SE2147
Farnley Tyas 37 SE1612
Farnsfield 34 SK6456
Farnworth (Ches.) 32 SJ5187
Farnworth (Gtr Mches.) 36 SD7305
Farr (Highld.) 66 NC7163
Farr (Highld.) 60 NH6833
Farr (Highld.) 60 NH8203
Farringdon 7 SY0191
Farrington Gurney 17 ST6255

Farsley Gatebeck

Farsley 37 SE 2135
Farthinghoe 18 SP 5339
Farthingstone 26 SP 6155
Farway 7 SY 1895
Fasnacloich 55 NN 0247
Fasque 57 NO 6475
Fassfern 55 NN 0278
Fatfield 47 NZ 3053
Fattahead 62 NJ 6657
Faugh 46 NY 5154
Fauldhouse 50 NS 9260
Faulkbourne 20 TL 7917
Faulkland 17 ST 7354
Fauls 32 SJ 5933
Faversham 13 TR 0161
Favillar 61 NJ 2734
Fawfieldhead 33 SK 0763
Fawkham Green 12 TQ 5865
Fawler 18 SP 3717
Fawley (Berks.) 18 SU 3981
Fawley (Bucks.) 18 SU 7586
Fawley (Hants.) 9 SU 4503
Fawley Chapel 17 SO 5829
Faxfleet 39 SE 8624
Faygate 11 TQ 2134
Fazeley 26 SK 2001
Fearby 42 SE 1981
Fearnan 56 NN 7244
Fearnhead 32 SJ 6290
Fearnmore 64 NG 7260
Featherstone (Staffs.) 25 SJ 9305
Featherstone (W Yorks.) 38 SE 4222
Feckenham 25 SP 0061
Fedderate 62 NJ 8949
Feering 21 TL 8720
Feetham 41 SD 9898
Feizor 41 SD 7968
Felbridge 12 TQ 3739
Felbrigg 29 TG 2039
Felcourt 12 TQ 3841
Felden 19 TL 0404
Felindre (Dyfed) 15 SN 7027
Felindre (Powys) 23 SO 1681
Felindre (W Glam.) 15 SN 6302
Felinfach 23 SO 0933
Felinfoel 15 SN 5202
Felingwm Uchaf 15 SN 5024
Felixkirk 42 SE 4684
Felixstowe 21 TM 3034
Felkington 53 NT 9444
Felling 47 NZ 2762
Felmersham 27 SP 9957
Felmingham 29 TG 2529
Felpham 11 SZ 9599
Felsham 21 TL 9457
Felsted 20 TL 6720
Feltham 11 TQ 1072
Felthorpe 29 TG 1618
Felton (Avon) 16 ST 5165
Felton (Here. and Worc.) 24 SO 5748
Felton (Northum.) 47 NU 1800
Felton Butler 32 SJ 3917
Feltwell 28 TL 7190
Feltwell Anchor 28 TL 6789
Fen Ditton 28 TL 4860
Fen Drayton 27 TL 3468
Fen End 26 SP 2274
Fence 37 SD 8237
Fendike Corner 35 TF 4560
Feniscowles 36 SD 6425
Feniton 7 SY 1199
Fenny Bentley 33 SK 1750
Fenny Bridges 7 SY 1198
Fenny Compton 26 SP 4152
Fenny Drayton 26 SP 3597
Fenny Stratford 19 SP 8834
Fenrother 47 NZ 1792
Fenstanton 27 TL 3168
Fenton (Cambs.) 27 TL 3279
Fenton (Lincs.) 34 SK 8476
Fenton (Lincs.) 34 SK 8750
Fenton (Staffs.) 33 SJ 8944
Fenton Town 53 NT 9733
Fenwick (Northum.) 53 NU 0639
Fenwick (Northum.) 47 NZ 0572
Fenwick (S Yorks.) 38 SE 5916
Fenwick (Strath.) 50 NS 4643
Feock 2 SW 8238
Feolin Ferry 48 NR 4469
Feriniquarrie 58 NG 1750
Fern 57 NO 4861
Ferndale 16 SS 9997
Ferndown 8 SU 0700
Ferness 60 NH 9645
Fernham 18 SU 2991
Fernhill Heath 25 SO 8659
Fernhurst 11 SU 9028
Fernie 57 NO 3115
Fernilea 58 NG 3732
Fernilee 33 SK 0178
Ferrensby 38 SE 3660
Ferring 11 TQ 0902
Ferrybridge 38 SE 4824
Ferryden 57 NO 7156
Ferryhill 42 NZ 2832
Ferryside 15 SN 3610
Fersfield 29 TM 0682
Fersit 55 NN 3577
Feshiebridge 60 NH 8504
Fetcham 11 TQ 1555
Fetterangus 62 NJ 9850
Fettercairn 57 NO 6573
Fewston 37 SE 1954
Ffairfach 15 SN 6220
Ffestiniog 30 SH 7042
Fforest 15 SN 5804
Fforest-fach (W Glam.) 15 SS 6396
Ffostrasol 22 SN 3747
Ffrith 31 SJ 2855
Ffrwdgrech 15 SO 0227
Ffynnonddrain 15 SN 4021
Ffynnongroew 31 SJ 1382
Fiddes 57 NO 8181
Fiddington (Glos.) 25 SO 9231
Fiddington (Somer.) 7 ST 2140
Fiddlers Hamlet 20 TL 4701
Field 33 SK 0233
Field Broughton 40 SD 3881
Field Dalling 29 TG 0039
Field Head 26 SK 4909
Fifehead Magdalen 8 ST 7721
Fifehead Neville 8 ST 7610
Fifield (Berks.) 11 SU 9076
Fifield (Oxon.) 18 SP 2318
Figheldean 8 SU 1547
Fighting Cocks 42 NZ 3414
Filby 29 TG 4613
Filey 43 TA 1180
Filgrave 27 SP 8748
Filkins 18 SP 2304
Filleigh (Devon.) 6 SS 6628
Filleigh (Devon.) 5 SS 7410
Fillingham 34 SK 9485
Fillongley 26 SP 2787
Filton 17 ST 6079
Fimber 39 SE 8960
Finavon 57 NO 4957
Finavon Castle 57 NO 4956
Fincham 28 TF 6806
Finchampstead 10 SU 7963
Fincharn 54 NM 9003
Finchdean 10 SU 7312
Finchingfield 20 TL 6832
Finchley 19 TQ 2890
Findern 33 SK 3030
Findhorn 61 NJ 0464
Findhorn Bridge 60 NH 8027
Findo Gask 56 NO 0020
Findochty 61 NJ 4667
Findon (Grampn.) 62 NO 9397
Findon (W. Susx) 11 TQ 1208
Findon Mains 65 NH 6060
Finedon 27 SP 9272
Fingal Street 29 TM 2169
Fingask 62 NJ 7827
Fingest 18 SU 7791
Finghall 42 SE 1889
Fingringhoe 21 TM 0220
Finmere 18 SP 6333
Finnart 55 NN 5157
Finningham 29 TM 0669
Finningley 62 SK 6699
Finnygaud 62 NJ 6054
Finsbay 63 NG 0786
Finsbury 20 TQ 3282
Finstall 25 SO 9869
Finsthwaite 40 SD 3687
Finstock 18 SP 3516
Finstown 63 HY 3514
Fintry (Central) 50 NS 6186
Fintry (Grampn.) 62 NJ 7554
Fionnphort (Island of Mull) 54 NM 2923
Fir Tree 42 NZ 1334
Firbeck 34 SK 5688
Firgrove 37 SD 9113
Firsby 35 TF 4563
Firth 63 HU 4413
Fishbourne (I of W) 9 SZ 5592
Fishbourne (W Susx) 10 SU 8304
Fishburn 42 NZ 3632
Fishcross 50 NS 8995
Fisher's Pond 9 SU 4820
Fisherford 62 NJ 6635
Fisherstreet 11 SU 9531
Fisherton (Highld.) 60 NH 7451
Fisherton (Strath.) 49 NS 2717
Fishguard 14 SM 9637
Fishlake 38 SE 6513
Fishpool 37 SD 8009
Fishtoft 35 TF 3642
Fishtoft Drove 35 TF 3148
Fishtown of Usan 57 NO 7254
Fishwick 53 NT 9151
Fiskavaig 58 NG 3234
Fiskerton (Lincs.) 35 TF 0472
Fiskerton (Notts.) 34 SK 7351
Fittleton 8 SU 1449
Fittleworth 11 TQ 0119
Fitton End 27 TF 4312
Fitz 32 SJ 4417
Fitzhead 7 ST 1228
Fitzwilliam 38 SE 4115
Five Ashes 12 TQ 5525
Five Oak Green 12 TQ 6445
Five Oaks 11 TQ 0928
Five Penny Borve 63 NB 4055
Five Penny Ness 63 NB 5364
Five Roads 15 SN 4905
Fivehead 7 ST 3522
Flackwell Heath 19 SU 8890
Fladbury 25 SO 9946
Fladdabister 63 HU 4332
Flagg 33 SK 1368
Flamborough 39 TA 2270
Flamstead 19 TL 0814
Flansham 11 SU 9601
Flasby 37 SD 9456
Flash 33 SK 0267
Flashader 58 NG 3553
Flatt, The 46 NY 5678
Flaunden 19 TL 0100
Flawborough 34 SK 7842
Flawith 38 SE 4865
Flax Bourton 16 ST 5069
Flaxby 38 SE 3957
Flaxley 17 SO 6915
Flaxpool 7 ST 1435
Flaxton 38 SE 6762
Fleckney 26 SP 6493
Flecknoe 26 SP 5163
Fleet (Hants.) 10 SU 8054
Fleet (Lincs.) 35 TF 3823
Fleet Hargate 35 TF 3925
Fleetham 53 NU 1928
Fleetwood 36 SD 3247
Flemingston 16 ST 0170
Flemington 50 NS 6559
Flempton 28 TL 8169
Fletching 12 TQ 4323
Flexford 11 SU 9350
Flimby 40 NY 0233
Flimwell 12 TQ 7131
Flint 31 SJ 2472
Flint Mountain 31 SJ 2369
Flintham 34 SK 7446
Flinton 39 TA 2136
Flitcham 28 TF 7226
Flitton 19 TL 0536
Flitwick 19 TL 0335
Flixborough 39 SE 8715
Flixton (Gtr Mches.) 32 SJ 7494
Flixton (N Yorks.) 43 TA 0479
Flixton (Suff.) 29 TM 3186
Flockton 37 SE 2314
Flodda (Benbecula) 63 NF 8455
Flodden 53 NT 9235
Flodigarry 58 NG 4671
Flookburgh 40 SD 3675
Flordon 29 TM 1897
Flore 26 SP 6460
Flotterton 47 NT 9902
Flowton 21 TM 0847
Flushing (Corn.) 2 SW 8034
Flushing (Grampn.) 62 NK 0546
Flyford Flavell 25 SO 9754
Fobbing 20 TQ 7183
Fochabers 61 NJ 3458
Fochriw 16 SO 1005
Fockerby 39 SE 8419
Fodder Fen 28 TL 5287
Fodderletter 61 NJ 1421
Fodderty 60 NH 5159
Foel 23 SH 9911
Foffarty 57 NO 4145
Foggathorpe 38 SE 7537
Fogo 53 NT 7749
Foindle 66 NC 1948
Folda 56 NO 1964
Fole 33 SK 0437
Foleshill 26 SP 3582
Folke 8 ST 6513
Folkestone 13 TR 2336
Folkingham 35 TF 0433
Folkington 12 TQ 5604
Folksworth 27 TL 1490
Folkton 43 TA 0579
Folla Rule 62 NJ 7333
Follifoot 38 SE 3452
Folly Gate 4 SX 5797
Fonthill Bishop 8 ST 9332
Fonthill Gifford 8 ST 9231
Fontmell Magna 8 ST 8616
Fontwell 11 SU 9407
Foolow 33 SK 1976
Foots Cray 12 TQ 4770
Forcett 42 NZ 1712
Ford (Bucks.) 18 SP 7709
Ford (Glos.) 17 SP 0829
Ford (Mers.) 36 SJ 3598
Ford (Northum.) 53 NT 9437
Ford (Salop) 24 SJ 4113
Ford (Staffs.) 33 SK 0654
Ford (Strath.) 54 NM 8603
Ford (W Susx) 11 TQ 0003
Ford (Wilts.) 17 ST 8475
Ford End 20 TL 6716
Ford Street (Somer.) 7 ST 1518
Fordcombe 12 TQ 5240
Fordell 51 NT 1588
Forden 23 SJ 2201
Fordham (Cambs.) 28 TL 6370
Fordham (Essex) 21 TL 9228
Fordham (Norf.) 28 TL 6199
Fordingbridge 8 SU 1413
Fordon 43 TA 0475
Fordoun 57 NO 7475
Fordstreet (Essex) 21 TL 9227
Fordwells 18 SP 3013
Fordwich 13 TR 1859
Fordyce 61 NJ 5563
Foremark 33 SK 3326
Forest 41 NY 8629
Forest Gate 20 TQ 4085
Forest Green 11 TQ 1241
Forest Hall 41 NY 5401
Forest Head 46 NY 5857
Forest Hill 18 SP 5807
Forest Mill 51 NS 9594
Forest Moor 37 SE 2256
Forest Row 12 TQ 4235
Forest Town 34 SK 5662
Forestburn Gate 47 NZ 0696
Forestfield 50 NS 8566
Forestside 10 SU 7512
Forfar 57 NO 4550
Forgandenny 56 NO 0818
Forgie 61 NJ 3954
Formby 36 SD 2907
Forncett End 29 TM 1493
Forncett St. Mary 29 TM 1694
Forncett St. Peter 29 TM 1693
Forneth 56 NO 0945
Fornham All Saints 28 TL 8367
Fornham St. Martin 28 TL 8566
Forres 61 NJ 0358
Forsbrook 33 SJ 9641
Forse 67 ND 2234
Forsinard 67 NC 8842
Forstal, The 13 TQ 8946
Forston 8 SY 6695
Fort Augustus 60 NH 3709
Fort George 60 NH 7656
Fort William 55 NN 1074
Forter 56 NO 1864
Forteviot 56 NO 0517
Forth 51 NS 9453
Forthampton 25 SO 8532
Fortingall 56 NN 7447
Forton (Hants.) 9 SU 4243
Forton (Lancs.) 36 SD 4851
Forton (Salop) 32 SJ 4216
Forton (Somer.) 7 ST 3306
Forton (Staffs.) 32 SJ 7521
Fortrie 62 NJ 6645
Fortrose 60 NH 7256
Fortuneswell 8 SY 6873
Forty Hill 20 TQ 3398
Forward Green 21 TM 1059
Fosbury 10 SU 3157
Fosdyke 35 TF 3133
Foss 56 NN 7958
Foss-y-ffin 22 SN 4460
Fossebridge 17 SP 0811
Foster Street 20 TL 4909
Foston (Derby.) 33 SK 1831
Foston (Lincs.) 34 SK 8542
Foston (N Yorks.) 38 SE 6965
Foston on the Wolds 39 TA 1055
Fotherby 35 TF 3131
Fotheringhay 27 TL 0593
Foul Mile 12 TQ 6215
Foulden (Borders) 53 NT 9355
Foulden (Norf.) 28 TL 7699
Foulis Castle 65 NH 5964
Foulridge 37 SD 8942
Foulsham 29 TG 0324
Fountainhall 52 NT 4349
Four Ashes 29 TM 0070
Four Crosses (Powys) 32 SJ 0508
Four Crosses (Powys) 31 SJ 2718
Four Crosses (Staffs.) 25 SJ 9509
Four Elms 12 TQ 4648
Four Forks 7 ST 2336
Four Gotes 35 TF 4516
Four Lanes 2 SW 6838
Four Marks 9 SU 6634
Four Mile Bridge 30 SH 2778
Four Oaks (E Susx) 13 TQ 8624
Four Oaks (W Mids) 25 SP 1198
Four Oaks (W Mids) 26 SP 2480
Four Throws 12 TQ 7729
Fourcrosses (Gwyn.) 30 SH 3939
Fourlanes End 32 SJ 8059
Fourstones 47 NY 8967
Fovant 8 SU 0028
Foveran 62 NJ 9824
Fowey 3 SX 1251
Fowlis 57 NO 3133
Fowlis Wester 56 NN 9223
Fowlmere 20 TL 4245
Fownhope 24 SO 5734
Fox Lane 10 SU 8557
Foxdale 43 SC 2878
Foxearth 20 TL 8344
Foxfield 40 SD 2085
Foxham 17 ST 9777
Foxhole (Corn.) 2 SW 9654
Foxholes (N Yorks.) 43 TA 0173
Foxley (Norf.) 29 TG 0321
Foxley (Wilts.) 17 ST 8985
Foxt 33 SK 0348
Foxton (Cambs.) 20 TL 4148
Foxton (Leic.) 26 SP 7090
Foxup 41 SD 8676
Foxwist Green 32 SJ 6168
Foy 17 SO 5928
Foyers 60 NH 4921
Fraddon 2 SW 9158
Fradley 25 SK 1513
Fradswell 33 SJ 9831
Fraisthorpe 39 TA 1561
Framfield 12 TQ 4920
Framingham Earl 29 TG 2702
Framingham Pigot 29 TG 2703
Framlingham 29 TM 2863
Frampton (Dorset) 8 SY 6294
Frampton (Lincs.) 35 TF 3239
Frampton Cotterell 17 ST 6582
Frampton Mansell 17 SO 9202
Frampton West End 35 TF 3040
Frampton on Severn 17 SO 7407
Framsden 21 TM 1959
Framwellgate Moor 47 NZ 2644
Franche 25 SO 8178
Frankby 31 SJ 2486
Frankley 25 SO 9980
Frankton 26 SP 4270
Frant 12 TQ 5835
Fraserburgh 62 NJ 9966
Frating Green 21 TM 0923
Fratton 9 SU 6600
Freathy 4 SX 3952
Freckenham 28 TL 6672
Freckleton 36 SD 4228
Freeby 34 SK 8020
Freeland 18 SP 4112
Freester 63 HU 4553
Freethorpe 29 TG 4105
Freethorpe Common 29 TG 4004
Freiston 35 TF 3743
Fremington 6 SS 5132
Frenchay 17 ST 6377
Frenchbeer 5 SX 6785
Frensham 10 SU 8441
Fresgoe 67 NC 9566
Freshfield 36 SD 2807
Freshford 17 ST 7860
Freshwater 9 SZ 3487
Freshwater Bay 9 SZ 3485
Freshwater West 14 SR 8899
Fressingfield 29 TM 2677
Freston 21 TM 1739
Freswick 67 ND 3667
Frettenham 29 TG 2417
Freuchie 57 NO 2806
Friar's Gate 12 TQ 4933
Friday Bridge 28 TF 4605
Fridaythorpe 39 SE 8759
Friern Barnet 19 TQ 2892
Friesthorpe 35 TF 0683
Frieth 18 SU 7990
Frilford 18 SU 4497
Frilsham 10 SU 5373
Frimley 11 SU 8758
Frindsbury 12 TQ 7369
Fring 28 TF 7334
Fringford 18 SP 6028
Frinsted 13 TQ 8957
Frinton-on-Sea 21 TM 2319
Friockheim 57 NO 5949
Frisby on the Wreake 34 SK 6917
Friskney 35 TF 4555
Friston (E Susx) 12 TV 5498
Friston (Suff.) 29 TM 4160
Fritchley 33 SK 3553
Frith Bank 35 TF 3147
Frith Common 24 SO 6969
Fritham 9 SU 2413
Frithelstock 4 SS 4619
Frithville 35 TF 3250
Frittenden 12 TQ 8141
Fritton (Norf.) 29 TG 4700
Fritton (Norf.) 29 TM 2293
Fritwell 18 SP 5229
Frizington 40 NY 0316
Frocester 17 SO 7803
Frodesley 24 SJ 5101
Frodsham 32 SJ 5177
Froggatt 33 SK 2476
Froghall 33 SK 0247
Frogmore 10 SU 8360
Frolesworth 26 SP 5090
Frome 8 ST 7747
Frome St. Quintin 8 ST 5902
Fromes Hill 24 SO 6846
Fron (Gwyn.) 30 SH 3539
Fron (Powys) 23 SJ 2203
Fron (Powys) 23 SO 0865
Fron Cysyllte 31 SJ 2741
Fron-goch 31 SH 9039
Frosterley 41 NZ 0237
Froxfield 10 SU 2967
Froxfield Green 10 SU 7025
Fryerning 20 TL 6400
Fryton 42 SE 6875
Fulbeck 34 SK 9450
Fulbourn 20 TL 5256
Fulbrook 18 SP 2513
Fulford (N Yorks.) 38 SE 6149
Fulford (Somer.) 7 ST 2129
Fulford (Staffs.) 33 SJ 9438
Fulham 11 TQ 2576
Fulking 11 TQ 2411
Full Sutton 38 SE 7455
Fuller Street 20 TL 7415
Fuller's Moor 32 SJ 4953
Fullerton 10 SU 3739
Fulletby 35 TF 2973
Fullwood 50 NS 4450
Fulmer 19 SU 9985
Fulmodeston 29 TF 9931
Fulnetby 35 TF 0979
Fulstow 35 TF 3297
Fulwell 47 NZ 3959
Fulwood (Lancs.) 36 SD 5331
Fulwood (S Yorks.) 33 SK 3085
Funtington 10 SU 7908
Funzie 63 HU 6689
Furnace 55 NN 0200
Furneux Pelham 20 TL 4327
Furzehill 6 SS 7245
Fyfett 7 ST 2314
Fyfield (Essex) 20 TL 5707
Fyfield (Glos.) 18 SP 2003
Fyfield (Hants.) 10 SU 2946
Fyfield (Oxon.) 18 SU 4298
Fyfield (Wilts.) 17 SU 1468
Fylingthorpe 43 NZ 9405
Fyvie 62 NJ 7637

Gabroc Hill 50 NS 4551
Gaddesby 26 SK 6813
Gaer 16 SO 1721
Gaerwen 30 SH 4871
Gagingwell 18 SP 4025
Gailey 25 SJ 9110
Gainford 42 NZ 1716
Gainsborough 34 SK 8189
Gainsford End 20 TL 7235
Gairloch 64 NG 8076
Gairlochy 55 NN 1784
Gairney Bank 56 NT 1299
Gaitsgill 46 NY 3946
Galashiels 52 NT 4936
Galby 26 SK 6901
Galgate 36 SD 4855
Galhampton 8 ST 6329
Gall 56 NO 0734
Gallanach (Strath.) 48 NM 2261
Gallatown 51 NT 2994
Galley Common 26 SP 3192
Galleyend 20 TL 7103
Galleywood 20 TL 7002
Gallowfauld 57 NO 4342
Galltair 59 NG 8120
Galmisdale 54 NM 4784
Galmpton (Devon) 5 SX 6940
Galmpton (Devon) 5 SX 8856
Galphay 37 SE 2572
Galson 63 NB 4358
Galston 50 NS 5036
Galtrigill 58 NG 1854
Gamblesby 41 NY 6039
Gamlingay 27 TL 2452
Gamrie 62 NJ 7962
Gamston (Notts.) 34 SK 6037
Gamston (Notts.) 34 SK 7076
Ganarew 16 SO 5216
Ganavan 54 NM 8632
Ganllwyd 30 SH 7224
Gannochy 57 NO 5970
Ganstead 39 TA 1434
Ganthorpe 38 SE 6870
Ganton 43 SE 9877
Garbhallt (Strath.) 49 NS 0295
Garboldisham 29 TM 0081
Gardenstown 62 NJ 7964
Garderhouse 63 HU 3347
Gare Hill 8 ST 7840
Garelochhead 49 NS 2491
Garford 18 SU 4296
Garforth 38 SE 4033
Gargrave 37 SD 9354
Gargunnock 50 NS 7094
Garinin 63 NB 1944
Garlieston 44 NX 4746
Garlogie 62 NJ 7805
Garmond 62 NJ 8052
Garmouth 61 NJ 3364
Garn 30 SH 2734
Garn-Dolbenmaen 30 SH 4944
Garnant 15 SN 6813
Garnett Bridge 40 SD 5299
Garnkirk 50 NS 6768
Garrabost 63 NB 5133
Garraron 54 NM 8008
Garras 2 SW 7023
Garreg 30 SH 6141
Garreg Bank 23 SJ 2811
Garrick 56 NN 8412
Garrigill 46 NY 7441
Garros 58 NG 4963
Garrow 56 NN 8240
Garrynamonie 63 NF 7416
Garsdale 41 SD 7389
Garsdon 17 ST 9687
Garshall Green 33 SJ 9633
Garsington 18 SP 5802
Garstang 36 SD 4945
Garston 32 SJ 4083
Garswood 36 SJ 5599
Gartcosh 50 NS 6968
Garth (Clwyd) 31 SJ 2542
Garth (I. of M.) 43 SC 3177
Garth (Mid Glam.) 15 SS 8690
Garth (Powys) 23 SN 9549
Garth (Shetld.) 63 HU 2157
Garthbrengy 23 SO 0433
Gartheli 22 SN 5956
Garthmyl 23 SO 1999
Garthorpe (Humbs.) 39 SE 8419
Garthorpe (Leic.) 34 SK 8320
Gartmore 50 NS 5297
Gartness (Central) 50 NS 5086
Gartness (Strath.) 50 NS 7864
Gartocharn 50 NS 4286
Garton 39 TA 2635
Garton-on-the-Wolds 39 SE 9859
Gartymore 67 ND 0114
Garvald 52 NT 5870
Garvan 55 NM 9777
Garvard 48 NR 3691
Garve 65 NH 3961
Garvestone 29 TG 0207
Garvock 49 NS 2571
Garway 16 SO 4522
Garynahine 63 NB 2331
Gastard 17 ST 8868
Gasthorpe 29 TL 9780
Gatcombe 9 SZ 4885
Gate Burton 34 SK 8382
Gate Helmsley 38 SE 6955
Gatebeck 41 SD 5485

Gateforth Greta Bridge

Gateforth ... 38 ... SE 5528
Gatehead ... 50 ... NS 3936
Gatehouse ... 46 ... NY 7988
Gatehouse of Fleet ... 45 ... NX 5956
Gatelawbridge ... 45 ... NX 9096
Gateley ... 29 ... TF 9624
Gatenby ... 42 ... SE 3287
Gateshead ... 47 ... NZ 2562
Gatesheath ... 32 ... SJ 4760
Gateside (Fife.) ... 56 ... NO 1809
Gateside (Strath.) ... 50 ... NS 3653
Gateside (Tays.) ... 57 ... NO 4344
Gathurst ... 36 ... SD 5307
Gatley ... 32 ... SJ 8387
Gattonside ... 52 ... NT 5435
Gauldry ... 57 ... NO 3723
Gaunt's Common ... 8 ... SU 0205
Gautby ... 35 ... TF 1772
Gavinton ... 53 ... NT 7652
Gawber ... 38 ... SE 3207
Gawcott ... 18 ... SP 6831
Gawsworth ... 33 ... SJ 8869
Gawthrop ... 41 ... SD 6987
Gawthwaite ... 40 ... SD 2784
Gay Street ... 11 ... TQ 0820
Gaydon ... 26 ... SP 3654
Gayhurst ... 27 ... SP 8446
Gayles ... 42 ... NZ 1207
Gayton (Mers.) ... 31 ... SJ 2680
Gayton (Norf.) ... 28 ... TF 7219
Gayton (Northants.) ... 26 ... SP 7054
Gayton (Staffs.) ... 33 ... SJ 9728
Gayton Thorpe ... 28 ... TF 7418
Gayton le Marsh ... 35 ... TF 4284
Gaywood ... 28 ... TF 6320
Gazeley ... 28 ... TL 7264
Geary ... 58 ... NG 2661
Gedding ... 21 ... TL 9457
Geddington ... 27 ... SP 8983
Gedintailor ... 58 ... NG 5235
Gedney ... 35 ... TF 4024
Gedney Broadgate ... 35 ... TF 4022
Gedney Drove End ... 28 ... TF 4629
Gedney Dyke ... 35 ... TF 4126
Gedney Hill ... 27 ... TF 3311
Gee Cross ... 37 ... SJ 9593
Geilston ... 50 ... NS 3477
Geise ... 67 ... ND 1064
Geldeston ... 29 ... TM 3891
Gell ... 31 ... SH 8569
Gelli Gynan ... 31 ... SJ 1854
Gelligaer ... 16 ... ST 1397
Gellilydan ... 30 ... SH 6839
Gellioedd ... 31 ... SH 9344
Gelly ... 14 ... SN 0819
Gellyburn ... 56 ... NO 0939
Gellywen ... 14 ... SN 2723
Gelston ... 45 ... NX 7758
Genoch Mains ... 44 ... NX 1356
Gentleshaw ... 25 ... SK 0511
Geocrab ... 63 ... NG 1190
George Nympton ... 6 ... SS 7023
Georgeham ... 6 ... SS 4639
Georgetown ... 50 ... NS 4567
Georgia ... 2 ... SW 4836
Georth ... 63 ... HY 3626
Germansweek ... 4 ... SX 4394
Germoe ... 2 ... SW 5829
Gerrans ... 2 ... SW 8735
Gerrards Cross ... 19 ... TQ 0088
Geshader ... 63 ... NB 1131
Gestingthorpe ... 20 ... TL 8138
Geufordd ... 31 ... SJ 2114
Gibraltar ... 35 ... TF 5558
Gidea Park ... 20 ... TQ 5390
Gidleigh ... 5 ... SX 6788
Gifford ... 52 ... NT 5368
Giggleswick ... 37 ... SD 8163
Gilberdyke ... 39 ... SE 8329
Gilchriston ... 52 ... NT 4865
Gilcrux ... 40 ... NY 1138
Gildersome ... 37 ... SE 2429
Gildingwells ... 34 ... SK 5585
Gileston ... 16 ... ST 0167
Gilfach ... 16 ... ST 1598
Gilfach Goch ... 16 ... SS 9890
Gilfachrheda ... 22 ... SN 4058
Gillamoor ... 42 ... SE 6890
Gilling East ... 42 ... SE 6176
Gilling West ... 42 ... NZ 1805
Gillingham (Dorset) ... 8 ... ST 8026
Gillingham (Kent) ... 12 ... TQ 7768
Gillingham (Norf.) ... 29 ... TM 4191
Gillow Heath ... 33 ... SJ 8858
Gills ... 67 ... ND 3172
Gilmerton (Lothian) ... 51 ... NT 2968
Gilmerton (Tays.) ... 56 ... NN 8823
Gilmorton ... 26 ... SP 5787
Gilsland ... 46 ... NY 6366
Gilsland Spa ... 46 ... NY 6367
Gilston ... 52 ... NT 4456
Gilwern ... 16 ... SO 2414
Gimingham ... 29 ... TG 2836
Gipping ... 29 ... TM 0763
Gipsey Bridge ... 35 ... TF 2850
Girlsta ... 63 ... HU 4351
Girsby ... 42 ... NZ 3508
Girthon ... 45 ... NX 6053
Girton (Cambs.) ... 27 ... TL 4262
Girton (Notts.) ... 34 ... SK 8266
Girvan ... 44 ... NX 1897
Gisburn ... 37 ... SD 8248
Gisleham ... 29 ... TM 5188
Gislingham ... 29 ... TM 0771
Gissing ... 29 ... TM 1485
Gittisham ... 7 ... SY 1398
Glackossian ... 60 ... NH 5938
Gladestry ... 23 ... SO 2355
Gladsmuir ... 52 ... NT 4573
Glais ... 15 ... SN 7000
Glaisdale ... 43 ... NZ 7705
Glamis ... 57 ... NO 3846
Glan-Conwy ... 31 ... SH 8352
Glan-Mule ... 23 ... SO 1690
Glan-y-don ... 31 ... SJ 1679
Glan-yr-afon (Clwyd-Gwyn.) ... 31 ... SJ 0242
Glan-yr-afon (Gwyn.) ... 31 ... SH 9141
Glanaber Terrace ... 30 ... SH 7547
Glanaman ... 15 ... SN 6713
Glandford ... 29 ... TG 0441
Glandwr (Dyfed) ... 14 ... SN 1928
Glandwr (Gwent) ... 16 ... SO 2101
Glangrwyne ... 16 ... SO 2316
Glanrhyd ... 14 ... SN 1442
Glanton ... 53 ... NU 0714
Glanton Pike ... 53 ... NU 0514
Glanvilles Wootton ... 8 ... ST 6708
Glapthorn ... 27 ... TL 0290
Glapwell ... 34 ... SK 4766
Glasbury ... 23 ... SO 1739
Glascote ... 26 ... SK 2203
Glascwm ... 23 ... SO 1553
Glasdrum ... 55 ... NN 0046
Glasfryn ... 31 ... SH 9150
Glasgow ... 50 ... NS 5865
Glasinfryn ... 30 ... SH 5868
Glaspwll ... 22 ... SN 7397
Glasserton ... 44 ... NX 4238
Glassford ... 50 ... NS 7247
Glasshouse Hill ... 17 ... SO 7020
Glasshouses ... 37 ... SE 1764
Glasslaw ... 62 ... NJ 8659
Glasslie ... 56 ... NO 2305
Glasson (Cumbr.) ... 46 ... NY 2560
Glasson (Lancs.) ... 36 ... SD 4455
Glassonby ... 41 ... NY 5738
Glasterlaw ... 57 ... NO 6051
Glaston ... 27 ... SK 8900
Glastonbury ... 7 ... ST 4938
Glatton ... 27 ... TL 1586
Glazebury ... 32 ... SJ 6796
Glazeley ... 24 ... SO 7088
Gleadless Townend ... 33 ... SK 3883
Gleadsmoss ... 33 ... SJ 8469
Gleaston ... 36 ... SD 2570
Glemsford ... 20 ... TL 8247
Glen Auldyn ... 43 ... SC 4393
Glen Barry ... 62 ... NJ 5554
Glen Bernisdale ... 58 ... NG 4048
Glen Branter ... 55 ... NS 1097
Glen Breackerie ... 48 ... NR 6511
Glen Parva ... 26 ... SP 5798
Glen Village ... 50 ... NS 8878
Glen Vine ... 43 ... SC 3378
Glenalmond (Tays.) ... 56 ... NN 9627
Glenancross ... 58 ... NM 6691
Glenbarr ... 48 ... NR 6736
Glenbervie ... 57 ... NO 7680
Glenboig ... 50 ... NS 7268
Glenbreck ... 51 ... NT 0521
Glenbuck ... 50 ... NS 7429
Glenburn ... 50 ... NS 4761
Glencaple ... 45 ... NX 9968
Glencarse ... 56 ... NO 1922
Glencloy ... 49 ... NS 0036
Glencoe ... 55 ... NN 1058
Glencraig ... 51 ... NT 1795
Glendaruel ... 49 ... NR 9985
Glendevon ... 56 ... NN 9804
Glendoick ... 56 ... NO 2022
Glenduckie ... 57 ... NO 2818
Glenegedale ... 48 ... NR 3351
Glenelg ... 59 ... NG 8119
Glenfarg ... 56 ... NO 1310
Glenfield ... 26 ... SK 5306
Glenfinnan ... 54 ... NM 9080
Glenfoot ... 56 ... NO 1715
Glengarnock ... 49 ... NS 3252
Glengrasco ... 58 ... NG 4444
Glenkindie ... 61 ... NJ 4313
Glenlee ... 45 ... NX 6080
Glenlivet ... 61 ... NJ 2126
Glenluce ... 44 ... NX 1957
Glenmaye ... 43 ... SC 2380
Glenmore (Skye) ... 58 ... NG 4340
Glenmore (Strath.) ... 54 ... NM 8412
Glenridding ... 40 ... NY 3817
Glenrothes ... 57 ... NO 2600
Glensaugh ... 57 ... NO 6778
Glenshee ... 56 ... NN 9834
Glensluain ... 55 ... NS 0999
Glenstockdale ... 44 ... NX 0061
Glenstriven ... 49 ... NS 0878
Glentham ... 34 ... TF 0090
Glentress ... 51 ... NT 2839
Glentrool Village ... 44 ... NX 3578
Glentworth ... 34 ... SK 9488
Glespin ... 50 ... NS 8028
Gletness ... 63 ... HU 4651
Glewstone ... 16 ... SO 5522
Glinton ... 27 ... TF 1506
Glooston ... 26 ... SP 7596
Glossop ... 33 ... SK 0393
Gloster Hill ... 47 ... NU 2504
Gloucester ... 17 ... SO 8318
Gloup ... 63 ... HP 5004
Glusburn ... 37 ... SE 0344
Gluss ... 63 ... HU 3477
Glympton ... 18 ... SP 4221
Glyn ... 30 ... SH 7457
Glyn Ceiriog ... 31 ... SJ 2038
Glyn Dyfrdwy ... 31 ... SJ 1542
Glyn-Cywarch ... 30 ... SH 6034
Glyn-Neath ... 15 ... SN 8806
Glynarthen ... 22 ... SN 3148
Glyncorrwg ... 15 ... SS 8799
Glynde ... 12 ... TQ 4509
Glyndebourne ... 12 ... TQ 4510
Glyntaff ... 16 ... ST 0889
Glynteg ... 14 ... SN 3637
Glyntrefnant ... 22 ... SN 9192
Gnosall ... 32 ... SJ 8220
Gnosall Heath ... 33 ... SJ 8419
Goadby ... 26 ... SP 7598
Goadby Marwood ... 34 ... SK 7826
Goatacre ... 17 ... SU 0176
Goathill ... 8 ... ST 6717
Goathland ... 43 ... NZ 8301
Goathurst ... 7 ... ST 2534
Gobowen ... 32 ... SJ 3033
Godalming ... 11 ... SU 9743
Godmanchester ... 27 ... TL 2470
Godmanstone ... 8 ... SY 6697
Godmersham ... 13 ... TR 0650
Godney ... 7 ... ST 4842
Godolphin Cross ... 2 ... SW 6031
Godre'r-graig ... 15 ... SN 7507
Godshill (Hants.) ... 8 ... SU 1714
Godshill (I. of W.) ... 9 ... SZ 5281
Godstone ... 12 ... TQ 3551
Goetre ... 16 ... SO 3205
Goff's Oak ... 20 ... TL 3202
Gogar ... 51 ... NT 1672
Goginan ... 22 ... SN 6981
Golan ... 30 ... SH 5242
Golant ... 3 ... SX 1254
Golberdon ... 4 ... SX 3271
Golborne ... 36 ... SJ 6097
Golcar ... 37 ... SE 0915
Goldcliff ... 16 ... ST 3683
Golden Cross ... 12 ... TQ 5312
Golden Green ... 12 ... TQ 6348
Golden Grove ... 15 ... SN 5919
Golden Pot ... 10 ... SU 7143
Golden Valley ... 17 ... SO 9022
Goldenhill ... 33 ... SJ 8553
Golders Green ... 19 ... TQ 2488
Goldhanger ... 21 ... TL 9009
Golding ... 24 ... SJ 5403
Goldsborough (N Yorks.) ... 43 ... NZ 8314
Goldsborough (N Yorks.) ... 33 ... SE 3856
Goldsithney ... 2 ... SW 5430
Goldthorpe ... 38 ... SE 4604
Gollanfield ... 60 ... NH 8052
Golspie ... 65 ... NH 8399
Golval ... 67 ... NC 8962
Gomersal ... 37 ... SE 2026
Gomshall ... 11 ... TQ 0847
Gonalston ... 34 ... SK 6847
Gonfirth (Shetld.) ... 63 ... HU 3661
Good Easter ... 20 ... TL 6212
Gooderstone ... 28 ... TF 7602
Goodleigh ... 6 ... SS 5934
Goodmanham ... 39 ... SE 8842
Goodnestone (Kent) ... 13 ... TR 0461
Goodnestone (Kent) ... 13 ... TR 2554
Goodrich ... 17 ... SO 5719
Goodrington ... 5 ... SX 8958
Goodwick ... 14 ... SM 9438
Goodworth Clatford ... 10 ... SU 3642
Goodyers End ... 26 ... SP 3385
Goole ... 38 ... SE 7423
Goole Fields ... 38 ... SE 7519
Goonbell ... 2 ... SW 7249
Goonhavern ... 2 ... SW 7953
Gooseham ... 4 ... SS 2316
Goosetrey ... 32 ... SJ 7769
Goosey ... 18 ... SU 3591
Goosnargh ... 36 ... SD 5536
Gordon ... 52 ... NT 6443
Gordonbush ... 67 ... NC 8409
Gordonstoun ... 61 ... NJ 1368
Gordonstown (Grampn.) ... 61 ... NJ 5656
Gordonstown (Grampn.) ... 62 ... NJ 7138
Gorebridge ... 51 ... NT 3461
Gorefield ... 27 ... TF 4112
Goring ... 18 ... SU 6080
Goring-by-Sea ... 11 ... TQ 1102
Gorleston on Sea ... 29 ... TG 5203
Gorley ... 8 ... SU 1511
Gorrachie ... 62 ... NJ 7358
Gorran Haven ... 3 ... SX 0141
Gors ... 22 ... SN 6277
Gors-goch ... 23 ... SN 9393
Gorsedd ... 31 ... SJ 1476
Gorseinon ... 15 ... SS 5998
Gorslas ... 15 ... SN 5713
Gorsley ... 17 ... SO 6826
Gorsness ... 63 ... HY 4119
Gorstan ... 65 ... NH 3862
Gorsty Common ... 24 ... SO 4537
Gorton ... 33 ... SJ 8996
Gosbeck ... 21 ... TM 1555
Gosberton ... 35 ... TF 2331
Gosfield ... 20 ... TL 7829
Gosforth (Cumbr.) ... 40 ... NY 0603
Gosforth (Tyne and Wear) ... 47 ... NZ 2467
Gosmore ... 19 ... TL 1927
Gosport ... 9 ... SZ 6199
Gossabrough ... 63 ... HU 5383
Goswick ... 53 ... NU 0545
Gotham ... 34 ... SK 5330
Gotherington ... 17 ... SO 9629
Gott Bay ... 48 ... NM 0546
Goudhurst ... 12 ... TQ 7337
Goulceby ... 35 ... TF 2579
Gourdas ... 62 ... NJ 7741
Gourdon ... 57 ... NO 8270
Gourock ... 49 ... NS 2477
Govan ... 50 ... NS 5464
Gowanhill ... 62 ... NK 0363
Gowdall ... 38 ... SE 6122
Gowerton ... 15 ... SS 5896
Gowkhall ... 51 ... NT 0589
Goxhill (Humbs.) ... 39 ... TA 1021
Goxhill (Humbs.) ... 39 ... TA 1844
Graffham (W Susx.) ... 11 ... SU 9216
Grafham (Cambs.) ... 27 ... TL 1669
Grafton (Here. and Worc.) ... 24 ... SO 4937
Grafton (Here. and Worc.) ... 24 ... SO 5761
Grafton (N Yorks.) ... 38 ... SE 4163
Grafton (Oxon.) ... 18 ... SP 2600
Grafton Flyford ... 25 ... SO 9655
Grafton Regis ... 26 ... SP 7546
Grafton Underwood ... 27 ... SP 9280
Grafty Green ... 13 ... TQ 8748
Graianrhyd ... 31 ... SJ 2156
Graig (Clwyd) ... 31 ... SJ 0872
Graig (Gwyn.) ... 31 ... SH 8071
Graig-fechan ... 31 ... SJ 1454
Grain ... 13 ... TQ 8876
Grainsby ... 39 ... TF 2799
Grainthorpe ... 35 ... TF 3896
Graizelound ... 38 ... SK 7798
Grampound ... 2 ... SW 9348
Grampound Road ... 2 ... SW 9150
Gramsdale ... 63 ... NF 8255
Granborough ... 18 ... SP 7625
Granby ... 34 ... SK 7536
Grandborough ... 26 ... SP 4866
Grandtully ... 56 ... NN 9152
Grange (Cumbr.) ... 40 ... NY 2517
Grange (Mers.) ... 31 ... SJ 2286
Grange (N Yorks.) ... 42 ... SE 5796
Grange (Tays.) ... 57 ... NO 2725
Grange Crossroads ... 61 ... NJ 4754
Grange Hill ... 20 ... TQ 4492
Grange Moor ... 37 ... SE 2216
Grange Villa ... 47 ... NZ 2352
Grange of Lindores ... 57 ... NO 2516
Grange-over-Sands ... 40 ... SD 4077
Grangemouth ... 51 ... NS 9281
Grangepans ... 51 ... NT 0282
Grangetown ... 42 ... NZ 5420
Granish ... 60 ... NH 8914
Gransmoor ... 39 ... TA 1259
Granston ... 14 ... SM 8934
Grantchester ... 20 ... TL 4355
Grantham ... 34 ... SK 9135
Grantley ... 37 ... SE 2369
Grantlodge ... 62 ... NJ 7017
Granton (Dumf. and Galwy.) ... 51 ... NT 0709
Granton (Lothian) ... 51 ... NT 2277
Grantown-on-Spey ... 61 ... NJ 0327
Grantshouse ... 53 ... NT 8065
Grappenhall ... 32 ... SJ 6385
Grasby ... 39 ... TA 0804
Grasmere ... 40 ... NY 3307
Grasscroft ... 37 ... SD 9704
Grassendale ... 32 ... SJ 3985
Grassholme ... 41 ... NY 9221
Grassington ... 37 ... SE 0064
Grassmoor ... 33 ... SK 4067
Grassthorpe ... 34 ... SK 7967
Grateley ... 10 ... SU 2741
Gratwich ... 33 ... SK 0231
Graveley (Cambs.) ... 27 ... TL 2564
Graveley (Herts.) ... 19 ... TL 2328
Gravelly Hill ... 25 ... SP 1090
Gravels ... 23 ... SJ 3300
Graveney ... 13 ... TR 0562
Gravesend ... 12 ... TQ 6473
Gravir ... 63 ... NB 3715
Grayingham ... 34 ... SK 9395
Grayrigg ... 41 ... SD 5797
Grays ... 12 ... TQ 6177
Grayshott ... 11 ... SU 8735
Grayswood ... 11 ... SU 9234
Grazeley ... 10 ... SU 6966
Greasbrough ... 33 ... SK 4195
Greasby ... 31 ... SJ 2587
Great Abington ... 20 ... TL 5348
Great Addington ... 27 ... SP 9575
Great Alne ... 25 ... SP 1159
Great Altcar ... 36 ... SD 3206
Great Amwell ... 20 ... TL 3712
Great Asby ... 41 ... NY 6813
Great Ashfield ... 29 ... TM 0068
Great Ayton ... 42 ... NZ 5510
Great Baddow ... 20 ... TL 7204
Great Badminton ... 17 ... ST 8082
Great Bardfield ... 20 ... TL 6730
Great Barford ... 27 ... TL 1352
Great Barr ... 25 ... SP 0495
Great Barrington ... 18 ... SP 2013
Great Barrow ... 32 ... SJ 4668
Great Barton ... 28 ... TL 8967
Great Barugh ... 43 ... SE 7478
Great Bavington ... 47 ... NY 9880
Great Bedwyn ... 10 ... SU 2764
Great Bentley ... 21 ... TM 1121
Great Billing ... 26 ... SP 8162
Great Bircham ... 28 ... TF 7632
Great Blakenham ... 21 ... TM 1150
Great Bolas ... 32 ... SJ 6421
Great Bookham ... 11 ... TQ 1454
Great Bosullow ... 2 ... SW 4133
Great Bourton ... 26 ... SP 4545
Great Bowden ... 26 ... SP 7488
Great Bradley ... 20 ... TL 6753
Great Braxted ... 21 ... TL 8614
Great Bricett ... 21 ... TM 0350
Great Brickhill ... 19 ... SP 9030
Great Bridgeford ... 33 ... SJ 8827
Great Brington ... 26 ... SP 6665
Great Bromley ... 21 ... TM 0826
Great Broughton ... 42 ... NZ 5406
Great Budworth ... 32 ... SJ 6677
Great Burdon ... 42 ... NZ 3116
Great Burstead ... 20 ... TQ 6892
Great Busby ... 42 ... NZ 5105
Great Canfield ... 20 ... TL 5917
Great Carlton ... 35 ... TF 4185
Great Casterton ... 27 ... TF 0009
Great Chart ... 13 ... TQ 9842
Great Chatwell ... 32 ... SJ 7914
Great Chesterford ... 20 ... TL 5042
Great Cheverell ... 17 ... ST 9858
Great Chishill ... 20 ... TL 4238
Great Clacton ... 21 ... TM 1716
Great Coates ... 39 ... TA 2310
Great Comberton ... 25 ... SO 9542
Great Corby ... 46 ... NY 4754
Great Cornard ... 21 ... TL 8840
Great Coxwell ... 18 ... SU 2693
Great Cransley ... 27 ... SP 8376
Great Cressingham ... 28 ... TF 8501
Great Crosby ... 36 ... SJ 3199
Great Cubley ... 33 ... SK 1637
Great Dalby ... 34 ... SK 7414
Great Doddington ... 27 ... SP 8864
Great Driffield ... 39 ... TA 0257
Great Dunham ... 28 ... TF 8714
Great Dunmow ... 20 ... TL 6221
Great Durnford ... 8 ... SU 1338
Great Easton (Essex) ... 20 ... TL 6125
Great Easton (Leic.) ... 27 ... SP 8493
Great Eccleston ... 36 ... SD 4240
Great Edstone ... 43 ... SE 7084
Great Ellingham ... 29 ... TM 0196
Great Elm ... 8 ... ST 7449
Great Eversden ... 20 ... TL 3653
Great Fen ... 28 ... TL 5978
Great Finborough ... 21 ... TM 0157
Great Fransham ... 28 ... TF 8913
Great Gaddesden ... 19 ... TL 0211
Great Gidding ... 27 ... TL 1183
Great Givendale ... 39 ... SE 8153
Great Glemham ... 29 ... TM 3361
Great Glen ... 26 ... SP 6597
Great Gonerby ... 34 ... SK 8938
Great Gransden ... 27 ... TL 2756
Great Green (Norf.) ... 29 ... TM 2789
Great Green (Suff.) ... 21 ... TL 9155
Great Habton ... 43 ... SE 7576
Great Hallingbury ... 20 ... TL 5119
Great Hanwood ... 24 ... SJ 4309
Great Harrowden ... 27 ... SP 8871
Great Harwood ... 36 ... SD 7332
Great Haseley ... 18 ... SP 6401
Great Hatfield ... 39 ... TA 1842
Great Heck ... 38 ... SE 5920
Great Henny ... 21 ... TL 8738
Great Hinton ... 17 ... ST 9058
Great Hockham ... 29 ... TL 9592
Great Holland ... 21 ... TM 2119
Great Horkesley ... 21 ... TL 9731
Great Hormead ... 20 ... TL 4030
Great Horwood ... 18 ... SP 7731
Great Houghton (Northants.) ... 26 ... SP 7958
Great Houghton (S Yorks.) ... 38 ... SE 4206
Great Hucklow ... 33 ... SK 1777
Great Kelk ... 39 ... TA 1058
Great Kingshill ... 19 ... SU 8798
Great Langton ... 42 ... SE 2996
Great Leighs ... 20 ... TL 7317
Great Limber ... 39 ... TA 1308
Great Linford ... 27 ... SP 8542
Great Livermere ... 28 ... TL 8871
Great Longstone ... 33 ... SK 1971
Great Lumley ... 47 ... NZ 2949
Great Lyth ... 24 ... SJ 4507
Great Malvern ... 24 ... SO 7845
Great Maplestead ... 20 ... TL 8034
Great Marton ... 36 ... SD 3335
Great Massingham ... 28 ... TF 7922
Great Milton ... 18 ... SP 6302
Great Missenden ... 19 ... SP 8901
Great Mitton ... 36 ... SD 7138
Great Mongeham ... 13 ... TR 3451
Great Moulton ... 29 ... TM 1690
Great Musgrave ... 41 ... NY 7613
Great Ness ... 32 ... SJ 3918
Great Oakley (Essex) ... 21 ... TM 1927
Great Oakley (Northants.) ... 27 ... SP 8686
Great Offley ... 19 ... TL 1427
Great Ormside ... 41 ... NY 7017
Great Orton ... 46 ... NY 3254
Great Oxendon ... 26 ... SP 7383
Great Palgrave ... 28 ... TF 8312
Great Parndon ... 20 ... TL 4308
Great Paxton ... 27 ... TL 2164
Great Plumstead ... 29 ... TG 2910
Great Ponton ... 34 ... SK 9230
Great Postland ... 27 ... TF 2612
Great Preston ... 38 ... SE 4029
Great Raveley ... 27 ... TL 2581
Great Rissington ... 17 ... SP 1917
Great Rollright ... 18 ... SP 3231
Great Ryburgh ... 29 ... TF 9527
Great Ryle ... 53 ... NU 0212
Great Saling ... 20 ... TL 7025
Great Salkeld ... 41 ... NY 5536
Great Sampford ... 20 ... TL 6435
Great Sankey ... 32 ... SJ 5688
Great Saxham ... 28 ... TL 7862
Great Shefford ... 10 ... SU 3875
Great Shelford ... 20 ... TL 4652
Great Smeaton ... 42 ... NZ 3404
Great Snoring ... 29 ... TF 9434
Great Somerford ... 17 ... ST 9682
Great Soudley ... 32 ... SJ 7228
Great Stainton ... 42 ... NZ 3322
Great Stambridge ... 21 ... TQ 8991
Great Staughton ... 27 ... TL 1264
Great Steeping ... 35 ... TF 4364
Great Stonar ... 13 ... TR 3359
Great Strickland ... 41 ... NY 5522
Great Stukeley ... 27 ... TL 2275
Great Sturton ... 35 ... TF 2176
Great Swinburne ... 47 ... NY 9375
Great Tew ... 18 ... SP 3929
Great Tey ... 21 ... TL 8925
Great Torrington ... 4 ... SS 4919
Great Tosson ... 47 ... NU 0300
Great Totham (Essex) ... 21 ... TL 8511
Great Totham (Essex) ... 21 ... TL 8613
Great Wakering ... 21 ... TQ 9487
Great Waldingfield ... 21 ... TL 9143
Great Walsingham ... 29 ... TF 9437
Great Waltham ... 20 ... TL 6913
Great Warley ... 20 ... TQ 5890
Great Washbourne ... 25 ... SO 9834
Great Welnetham ... 21 ... TL 8759
Great Wenham ... 21 ... TM 0738
Great Whittington ... 47 ... NZ 0070
Great Wigborough ... 21 ... TL 9615
Great Wilbraham ... 20 ... TL 5557
Great Wishford ... 8 ... SU 0835
Great Witcombe ... 17 ... SO 9014
Great Witley ... 24 ... SO 7566
Great Wolford ... 18 ... SP 2434
Great Wratting ... 20 ... TL 6848
Great Wyrley ... 25 ... SJ 9907
Great Wytheford ... 32 ... SJ 5719
Great Yarmouth ... 29 ... TG 5207
Great Yeldham ... 20 ... TL 7638
Greatford ... 27 ... TF 0811
Greatham (Cleve.) ... 42 ... NZ 4927
Greatham (Hants.) ... 10 ... SU 7730
Greatham (W Susx) ... 11 ... TQ 0415
Greatstone-on-Sea ... 13 ... TR 0822
Greatworth ... 26 ... SP 5542
Green Hammerton ... 38 ... SE 4656
Green Hill (Northumb.) ... 47 ... NY 8647
Green Hill (Wilts.) ... 17 ... SU 0686
Green Ore ... 7 ... ST 5749
Green Street ... 19 ... TQ 1998
Green Street Green ... 12 ... TQ 4563
Green, The (Cumbr.) ... 40 ... SD 1784
Green, The (Wilts.) ... 8 ... ST 8731
Greenbank ... 36 ... SD 5254
Greenburn ... 51 ... NS 9360
Greendikes ... 53 ... NU 0628
Greenfield (Beds.) ... 19 ... TL 0534
Greenfield (Clwyd) ... 31 ... SJ 1977
Greenfield (Gtr Mches.) ... 37 ... SD 9904
Greenfield (Highld.) ... 59 ... NH 2000
Greenfield (Oxon.) ... 18 ... SU 7191
Greenford ... 19 ... TQ 1382
Greengairs ... 50 ... NS 7870
Greenham ... 10 ... SU 4865
Greenhaugh ... 46 ... NY 7987
Greenhead (Northum.) ... 46 ... NY 6665
Greenhill (Central) ... 50 ... NS 8278
Greenhill (Gtr London) ... 19 ... TQ 1688
Greenhill (S Yorks.) ... 33 ... SK 3481
Greenhithe ... 12 ... TQ 5974
Greenholm ... 50 ... NS 5637
Greenholme ... 41 ... NY 5905
Greenhow Hill ... 37 ... SE 1164
Greenigo ... 63 ... HY 4107
Greenland ... 67 ... ND 2367
Greenlaw ... 52 ... NT 7145
Greenloaning ... 56 ... NN 8307
Greenmount ... 37 ... SD 7714
Greenock ... 49 ... NS 2776
Greenodd ... 40 ... SD 3182
Greens Norton ... 26 ... SP 6649
Greenside ... 47 ... NZ 1362
Greenskairs ... 62 ... NJ 7863
Greenstead Green ... 20 ... TL 8227
Greensted ... 20 ... TL 5302
Greenwich ... 12 ... TQ 4077
Greet ... 25 ... SP 0230
Greete ... 24 ... SO 5770
Greetham (Leic.) ... 34 ... SK 9214
Greetham (Lincs.) ... 35 ... TF 3070
Greetland ... 37 ... SE 0821
Greinton ... 7 ... ST 4136
Grendon (Northants.) ... 27 ... SP 8760
Grendon (Warw.) ... 26 ... SK 2800
Grendon Common ... 26 ... SP 2799
Grendon Green ... 24 ... SO 5957
Grendon Underwood ... 18 ... SP 6720
Grenitote ... 63 ... NF 8274
Grenoside ... 33 ... SK 3394
Gresford ... 32 ... SJ 3454
Gresham ... 29 ... TG 1738
Greshornish ... 58 ... NG 3454
Gress ... 63 ... NB 4842
Gressenhall ... 29 ... TF 9615
Gressenhall Green ... 29 ... TF 9616
Gressingham ... 36 ... SD 5769
Greta Bridge ... 41 ... NZ 0813

Gretna Hazlemere

Gretna 46 NY3167
Gretna Green 46 NY3268
Gretton (Glos.) 25 SP0030
Gretton (Northants.) 27 SP8894
Gretton (Salop) 24 SO5195
Grewelthorpe 42 SE2276
Greygarth 37 SE1872
Greysouthen 40 NY0729
Greystoke 40 NY4330
Greystone 57 NO5343
Greywell 10 SU7151
Gribun 54 NM4533
Griff 26 SP3588
Griffithstown 16 ST2999
Grigghall 40 SD4691
Grimeford Village 36 SD6112
Grimethorpe 38 SE4109
Griminish 63 NF7851
Grimista 63 HU4643
Grimley 25 SO8360
Grimness (S. Ronaldsay) 63 ND4793
Grimoldby 35 TF3988
Grimsargh 36 SD5834
Grimsby 39 TA2810
Grimscote 26 SP6553
Grimscott 4 SS2606
Grimshader 63 NB4026
Grimsthorpe 35 TF0423
Grimston (Leic.) 34 SK6821
Grimston (Norf.) 28 TF7221
Grimstone 8 SY6393
Grindale 39 TA1371
Grindle 24 SJ7403
Grindleford 33 SK2477
Grindleton 37 SD7545
Grindlow 38 SK1877
Grindon (Northum.) 53 NT9144
Grindon (Staffs.) 33 SK0854
Gringley on the Hill 34 SK7390
Grinsdale 46 NY3758
Grinshill 32 SJ5223
Grinton 41 SE0498
Gristhorpe 43 TA0882
Griston 29 TL9499
Gritley 63 HY5605
Grittenham 17 SU0382
Grittleton 17 ST8579
Grizebeck 40 SD2384
Grizedale 40 SD3394
Grobister 63 HY6524
Groby 26 SK5207
Groes (Clwyd) 31 SJ0064
Groes (W Glam.) 15 SS7986
Groes-faen 16 ST0780
Groesffordd Marli 31 SJ0073
Groeslon 30 SH4755
Grogport 49 NR8044
Gronant 31 SJ0883
Groombridge 12 TQ5337
Grosebay 63 NG1592
Grosmont (Gwent) 16 SO4024
Grosmont (N Yorks.) 43 NZ8205
Groton 21 TL9641
Grove (Dorset) 8 SY6972
Grove (Kent) 13 TR2362
Grove (Notts.) 34 SK7379
Grove (Oxon.) 18 SU4090
Grove Park 12 TQ4172
Grovely Wood 8 SU0534
Grovesend 15 SN5900
Gruids 66 NC5604
Gruinart 48 NR2866
Grula 58 NG3826
Gruline 54 NM5440
Grunasound 63 HU3733
Grundisburgh 21 TM2251
Gruting 63 HU2748
Grutness 63 HU4009
Grwyne Fechan 16 SO2324
Gualachulain 55 NN1145
Guardbridge 57 NO4519
Guarlford 25 SO8145
Guay 56 NO0049
Guestling Green 13 TQ8513
Guestwick 29 TG0627
Gugh 2 SV8908
Guide Post 47 NZ2585
Guilden Morden 27 TL2744
Guilden Sutton 32 SJ4468
Guildford 11 TQ0049
Guildtown 56 NO1331
Guilsborough 26 SP6773
Guilsfield 23 SJ2111
Guisborough 42 NZ6115
Guisley 37 SE1941
Guist 29 TF9925
Guiting Power 17 SP0924
Gulberwick 63 HU4437
Gulf of Corryvreckan 54 NM6901
Gullane 52 NT4882
Gulval 2 SW4831
Gumfreston 14 SN1101
Gumley 26 SP6890
Gunby (Humbs.) 38 SE7135
Gunby (Lincs.) 34 SK9021
Gundleton 9 SU6133
Gunn 6 SS6333
Gunnerside 41 SD9598
Gunnerton 47 NY9074
Gunness 39 SE8411
Gunnislake 4 SX4371
Gunnista 63 HU5043
Gunthorpe (Norf.) 29 TG0135
Gunthorpe (Notts.) 34 SK6744
Gurnard 9 SZ4795
Gurney Slade 8 ST6249
Gurnos 15 SN7709
Gussage All Saints 8 SU0010
Gussage St. Michael 8 ST9811
Guston 13 TR3244
Gutcher 63 HU5498
Guthrie 57 NO5650
Guy's Head 28 TF4825
Guy's Marsh 8 ST8420
Guyhirn 27 TF3903
Guyzance 47 NU2103
Gwaenysgor 31 SJ0780
Gwalchmai 30 SH3975
Gwaun-Cae-Gurwen 15 SN7011
Gwbert-on-Sea 14 SN1650
Gweek 2 SW7026
Gwehelog 16 SO3804
Gwenddwr 23 SO0643
Gwennap 2 SW7340
Gwenter 2 SW7418
Gwernaffield 31 SJ2064
Gwernesney 16 SO4101
Gwernogle 15 SN5234
Gwernymynydd 31 SJ2162
Gwespyr 31 SJ1183
Gwinear 2 SW5937
Gwithian 2 SW5841
Gwrhyd 15 SN9339
Gwrych Castle 31 SH9277
Gwyddelwern 31 SJ0746
Gwyddgrug 15 SN4635
Gwytherin 31 SH8761
Gylchedd 31 SH8644
Gypsey Race 39 TA0970

Habberley (Here. and Worc.) 24 SO8077
Habberley (Salop) 24 SJ3903
Habost (Isle of Lewis) 63 NB3219
Habost (Isle of Lewis) 63 NB5362
Habrough 39 TA1514
Haccombe 5 SX8970
Hacconby 35 TF1025
Haceby 34 TF0236
Hacheston 21 TM3059
Hackenthorpe 33 SK4183
Hacketts 20 TL3208
Hackford 29 TG0502
Hackforth 42 SE2493
Hackland 63 HY3920
Hacklete 63 NB1534
Hackleton 26 SP8055
Hackness (N Yorks.) 43 SE9690
Hackness (South Walls) 63 ND3391
Hackney 20 TQ3585
Hackthorn 34 SK9882
Hackthorpe 41 NY5423
Hadden 53 NT7836
Haddenham (Bucks.) 18 SP7408
Haddenham (Cambs.) 27 TL4675
Haddington 52 NT5174
Haddiscoe 29 TM4497
Haddon 27 TL1392
Hademore 25 SK1708
Hadfield 33 SK0296
Hadham Cross 20 TL4218
Hadham Ford 20 TL4321
Hadleigh (Essex) 20 TQ8087
Hadleigh (Suff.) 21 TM0242
Hadley 24 SJ6712
Hadley End 33 SK1320
Hadlow 12 TQ6349
Hadlow Down 12 TQ5324
Hadnall 32 SJ5120
Hadstock 20 TL5645
Hadzor 25 SO9162
Haffenden Quarter 13 TQ8841
Hafod-Dinbych 31 SH8953
Hafodunos 31 SH8666
Haggbeck 46 NY4774
Hagley (Here. and Worc.) 24 SO5641
Hagley (Here. and Worc.) 25 SO9181
Hagworthingham 35 TF3469
Haigh 36 SD6108
Haighton Green 36 SD5634
Hail Weston 27 TL1662
Haile 40 NY0308
Hailes 25 SP0530
Hailey (Herts.) 20 TL3710
Hailey (Oxon.) 18 SP3512
Hailsham 12 TQ5909
Hainault 20 TQ4691
Hainford 29 TG2218
Hainton 35 TF1784
Haisthorpe 39 TA1264
Halam 34 SK6754
Halberton 7 ST0112
Halcro 67 ND2260
Hale (Ches.) 32 SJ4682
Hale (Gtr Mches.) 32 SJ7786
Hale (Hants.) 8 SU1919
Hale (Lincs.) 35 TF1443
Hale Bank 32 SJ4784
Hale Street 12 TQ6749
Halebarns 32 SJ7985
Hales (Norf.) 29 TM3897
Hales (Staffs.) 32 SJ7134
Hales Place 13 TR1459
Halesowen 25 SO9683
Halesworth 29 TM3877
Halewood 32 SJ4585
Halford (Salop) 24 SO4383
Halford (Warw.) 26 SP2545
Halfpenny Green 25 SO8292
Halfway (Dyfed) 15 SN6430
Halfway (Dyfed) 15 SN8232
Halfway House 23 SJ3411
Halfway Houses 13 TQ9373
Halifax 37 SE0825
Halistra 58 NG2459
Halket 50 NS4252
Halkirk 67 ND1359
Halkyn 31 SJ2071
Hall Dunnerdale 40 SD2195
Hall Green 25 SP1181
Hall's Green 19 TL2728
Halland 12 TQ5016
Hallaton 26 SP7896
Hallatrow 17 ST6356
Hallbankgate 46 NY5859
Hallen 16 ST5479
Hallin 58 NG2559
Halling 12 TQ7063
Hallington 47 NY9875
Halloughton 34 SK6851
Hallow 25 SO8258
Hallrule 52 NT5914
Halls 52 NT6572
Hallsands 5 SX8138
Halltoft End 35 TF3645
Hallworthy 4 SX1787
Hallyburton 52 NT6748
Hallyne 51 NT1940
Halmer End 32 SJ7949
Halmore 17 SO6902
Halmyre Mains 51 NT1749
Halnaker 11 SU9108
Halsall 36 SD3710
Halse (Northants.) 18 SP5640
Halse (Somer.) 7 ST1327
Halsetown 2 SW5038
Halsham 39 TA2627
Halsinger 6 SS5138
Halstead (Essex) 20 TL8130
Halstead (Kent) 12 TQ4961
Halstead (Leic.) 26 SK7505
Halstock 7 ST5308
Haltham 35 TF2463
Halton (Bucks.) 19 SP8710
Halton (Ches.) 32 SJ5381
Halton (Clwyd) 32 SJ3039
Halton (Lancs.) 36 SD5065
Halton East 37 SE0454
Halton Gill 41 SD8876
Halton Holegate 35 TF4165
Halton Lea Gate 46 NY6558
Halton West 37 SD8454
Haltwhistle 46 NY7064
Halvergate 29 TG4206
Halwell 5 SX7753
Halwill 4 SX4299
Halwill Junction 4 SS4400
Ham (Bressay) 63 HU4939
Ham (Foula) 63 HT9739
Ham (Glos.) 17 ST6898
Ham (Gtr London) 11 TQ1672
Ham (Highld.) 67 ND2373
Ham (Kent) 13 TR3354
Ham (Wilts.) 10 SU3262
Ham Green (Avon) 16 ST5575
Ham Green (Here. and Worc.) 25 SP0063
Ham Street (Somer.) 7 ST5534
Hamble 9 SU4806
Hambleden (Bucks.) 18 SU7886
Hambledon (Hants.) 9 SU6414
Hambledon (Surrey) 11 SU9638
Hambleton (Lancs.) 36 SD3742
Hambleton (N Yorks.) 38 SE5430
Hambridge 7 ST3921
Hambrook (Avon) 17 ST6378
Hambrook (W Susx.) 10 SU7806
Hameringham 35 TF3167
Hamerton 27 TL1379
Hamilton 50 NS7255
Hammersmith 11 TQ2279
Hammerwich 25 SK0707
Hammoon 8 ST8114
Hamnavoe (Shetld.) 63 HU4971
Hamnavoe (West Burra) 63 HU3635
Hamnavoe (Yell) 63 HU4980
Hampden 19 SP8603
Hampden Park 12 TQ6002
Hampden Row 19 SP8402
Hampnett 17 SP0915
Hampole 38 SE5010
Hampreston 8 SZ0598
Hampstead 19 TQ2485
Hampstead Norris 10 SU5276
Hampsthwaite 37 SE2558
Hampton (Gtr London) 11 TQ1369
Hampton (Salop) 24 SO7486
Hampton Bishop 24 SO5538
Hampton Heath 32 SJ4949
Hampton Lovett 25 SO8865
Hampton Lucy 26 SP2557
Hampton Poyle 18 SP5015
Hampton in Arden 26 SP2081
Hampton on the Hill 26 SP2564
Hamsey 12 TQ4112
Hamstall Ridware 33 SK1019
Hamstead (I. of W.) 9 SZ3991
Hamstead (W Mids) 25 SP0593
Hamstead Marshall 10 SU4165
Hamsterley (Durham) 41 NZ1131
Hamsterley (Durham) 47 NZ1156
Hamstreet (Kent) 13 TR0034
Hamtoun 63 HT9637
Hamworthy 8 SY9990
Hanbury (Here and Worc.) 25 SO9663
Hanbury (Staffs.) 33 SK1727
Hanchurch 33 SJ8441
Handbridge 32 SJ4164
Handcross 11 TQ2630
Handforth 33 SJ8883
Handley 32 SJ4567
Handsacre 33 SK0916
Handsworth (S Yorks.) 33 SK4086
Handsworth (W Mids) 25 SP0490
Hanford 33 SJ8642
Hanging Langford 8 SU0237
Hanham 17 ST6372
Hankelow 32 SJ6645
Hankerton 17 ST9690
Hankham 12 TQ6105
Hanky Childe 24 SO6565
Hanley 33 SJ8847
Hanley Castle 25 SO8342
Hanley Swan 25 SO8143
Hanley William 24 SO6765
Hanlith 37 SD9061
Hanmer 32 SJ4540
Hannington (Hants.) 10 SU5355
Hannington (Northants.) 26 SP8171
Hannington (Wilts.) 17 SU1793
Hannington Wick 17 SU1795
Hanslope 26 SP8046
Hanthorpe 35 TF0824
Hanwell 26 SP4343
Hanworth (Gtr London) 11 TQ1271
Hanworth (Norf.) 29 TG1935
Happendon 50 NS8533
Happisburgh 29 TG3731
Happisburgh Common 29 TG3729
Hapsford 32 SJ4774
Hapton (Lancs.) 37 SD7931
Hapton (Norf.) 29 TM1796
Harberton 5 SX7758
Harbertonford 5 SX7856
Harbledown 13 TR1358
Harborne 25 SP0384
Harborough Magna 26 SP4779
Harbottle 47 NT9304
Harbury 26 SP3759
Harby (Leic.) 34 SK7431
Harby (Notts.) 34 SK8770
Harcombe 7 SY1590
Harden 37 SE0838
Hardenhuish 17 ST9074
Hardgate 62 NJ7801
Hardham 11 TQ0317
Hardingham 29 TG0403
Hardings Wood 32 SJ8054
Hardingstone 26 SP7657
Hardington 17 ST7452
Hardington Mandeville 7 ST5111
Hardington Marsh 7 ST5009
Hardley 9 SU4205
Hardley Street 29 TG3801
Hardmead 27 SP9347
Hardrow 41 SD8691
Hardstoft 34 SK4463
Hardway (Hants.) 9 SU6101
Hardway (Somer.) 8 ST7134
Hardwick (Bucks.) 18 SP8019
Hardwick (Cambs.) 20 TL3758
Hardwick (Norf.) 29 TM2290
Hardwick (Northants.) 27 SP8569
Hardwick (Oxon.) 18 SP3706
Hardwick (Oxon.) 18 SP5729
Hardwicke (Glos.) 17 SO7912
Hardwicke (Glos.) 17 SO9127
Hare Hatch 10 SU8077
Hare Street 20 TL3929
Hareby 35 TF3365
Hareden 36 SD6350
Harefield 19 TQ0590
Harehope 53 NU0920
Harescombe 17 SO8410
Haresfield 17 SO8110
Harewood 38 SE3245
Harford 5 SX6359
Hargrave (Ches.) 32 SJ4862
Hargrave (Northants.) 27 TL0370
Hargrave Green 20 TL7759
Haringey 20 TQ3290
Harker 46 NY3960
Harkstead 21 TM1935
Harlaston 26 SK2111
Harlaxton 34 SK8832
Harle Skye 37 SD8634
Harlech 30 SH5831
Harlesden 19 TQ2383
Harleston (Norf.) 29 TM2483
Harleston (Suff.) 29 TM0160
Harlestone 26 SP7064
Harley 24 SJ5901
Harling Road 29 TL9788
Harlington 19 TL0330
Harlosh 58 NG2841
Harlow 20 TL4711
Harlow Hill 47 NZ0768
Harlthorpe 38 SE7337
Harlton 20 TL3852
Harman's Cross 8 SY9880
Harmby 42 SE1289
Harmer Green 19 TL2516
Harmer Hill 32 SJ4822
Harmston 34 SK9762
Harnhill 17 SP0600
Harold Hill 20 TQ5391
Harold Wood 20 TQ5590
Haroldston West 14 SM8615
Haroldswick 63 HP6412
Harome 42 SE6482
Harpenden 19 TL1314
Harpford 7 SY0890
Harpham 39 TA0961
Harpley (Here. and Worc.) 24 SO6861
Harpley (Norf.) 28 TF7826
Harpole 26 SP6961
Harpsdale 67 ND1256
Harpsden 18 SU7680
Harpswell 34 SK9389
Harpur Hill 33 SK0671
Harpurhey 37 SD8701
Harrapool 58 NG6523
Harrietfield 56 NN9829
Harrietsham 13 TQ8753
Harrington (Cumbr.) 40 NX9926
Harrington (Lincs.) 35 TF3671
Harrington (Northants.) 26 SP7780
Harringworth 27 SP9197
Harriseahead 33 SJ8656
Harrogate 38 SE3055
Harrold 27 SP9456
Harrow 19 TQ1388
Harrow on the Hill 19 TQ1586
Harrowbarrow 4 SX3969
Harrowden 27 TL0646
Harsgeir 63 NB1040
Harston (Cambs.) 20 TL4251
Harston (Leic.) 34 SK8331
Hart 42 NZ4735
Hartburn 47 NZ0886
Hartest 20 TL8352
Hartfield 12 TQ4735
Hartford (Cambs.) 27 TL2572
Hartford (Ches.) 32 SJ6372
Hartford End 20 TL6817
Hartfordbridge 10 SU7757
Harthill (Ches.) 32 SJ4955
Harthill (Lothian) 50 NS9064
Harthill (S Yorks.) 34 SK4980
Hartington 33 SK1360
Hartland 4 SS2624
Hartland Quay 4 SS2224
Hartlebury 25 SO8470
Hartlepool 42 NZ5032
Hartley (Cumbr.) 41 NY7808
Hartley (Kent) 12 TQ6166
Hartley (Kent) 12 TQ7634
Hartley (Northum.) 47 NZ3475
Hartley Wespall 10 SU6958
Hartley Wintney 10 SU7756
Hartlip 12 TQ8364
Harton (N Yorks.) 38 SE7061
Harton (Salop) 24 SO4888
Harton (Tyne and Wear) 47 NZ3864
Hartpury 17 SO7924
Hartshill 26 SP3293
Hartshorne 33 SK3221
Hartsop 40 NY4013
Hartwell 26 SP7850
Hartwood 50 NS8459
Harvel 12 TQ6563
Harvington 25 SP0548
Harvington Cross 25 SP0549
Harwell 18 SU4989
Harwich 21 TM2431
Harwood (Durham) 41 NY8133
Harwood (Gtr Mches.) 36 SD7411
Harwood Dale 43 SE9595
Harworth 34 SK6291
Hascombe 11 TQ0039
Haselbech 26 SP7177
Haselbury Plucknett 7 ST4711
Haseley 26 SP2368
Haselor 25 SP1257
Hasfield 17 SO8227
Hasguard 14 SM8509
Haskayne 36 SD3507
Hasketon 21 TM2550
Hasland 33 SK3969
Haslemere 11 SU9032
Haslingden 37 SD7823
Haslingden Grane 37 SD7523
Haslingfield 20 TL4052
Haslington 32 SJ7355
Hassall 32 SJ7667
Hassall Green 32 SJ7758
Hassell Street 13 TR0946
Hassendean 52 NT5420
Hassingham 29 TG3605
Hassocks 12 TQ3015
Hassop 33 SK2272
Hastigrow 67 ND2661
Hastingleigh 13 TR0945
Hastings 12 TQ8009
Hastingwood 20 TL4807
Hastoe 19 SP9209
Haswell 47 NZ3743
Hatch (Beds.) 27 TL1547
Hatch (Hants.) 10 SU6752
Hatch (Wilts.) 8 ST9228
Hatch Beauchamp 7 ST3020
Hatch End 19 TQ1391
Hatching Green 19 TL1313
Hatchmere 32 SJ5571
Hatcliffe 39 TA2100
Hatfield (Here. and Worc.) 24 SO5859
Hatfield (Herts.) 19 TL2309
Hatfield (S Yorks.) 38 SE6609
Hatfield Broad Oak 20 TL5516
Hatfield Heath 20 TL5215
Hatfield Peverel 20 TL7911
Hatfield Woodhouse 38 SE6708
Hatford 18 SU3394
Hatherden 10 SU3450
Hatherleigh 6 SS5404
Hathern 34 SK5022
Hatherop 17 SP1505
Hathersage 33 SK2381
Hatherton (Ches.) 32 SJ6847
Hatherton (Staffs.) 25 SJ9610
Hatley St. George 27 TL2851
Hattingley 10 SU6437
Hatton (Ches.) 32 SJ5982
Hatton (Derby.) 33 SK2130
Hatton (Grampn.) 62 NK0537
Hatton (Gtr London) 11 TQ1075
Hatton (Lincs.) 35 TF1776
Hatton (Salop) 24 SO4690
Hatton (Warw.) 26 SP2367
Hatton Heath 32 SJ4561
Hatton of Fintray 62 NJ8316
Hattoncrook 62 NJ8424
Haugh Head 53 NU0026
Haugh of Urr 45 NX8066
Haugham 35 TF3381
Haughley 29 TM0262
Haughley Green 29 TM0364
Haughton (Notts.) 34 SK6772
Haughton (Salop) 32 SJ3727
Haughton (Salop) 32 SJ5516
Haughton (Salop) 24 SO6795
Haughton (Staffs.) 33 SJ8620
Haughton Green 33 SJ9393
Haughton Moss 32 SJ5756
Haunton 26 SK2411
Hauxley 47 NU2703
Hauxton 20 TL4351
Havant 10 SU7106
Haven 24 SO4054
Havenstreet 9 SZ5690
Haverfordwest 14 SM9515
Haverhill 20 TL6745
Haverigg 40 SD1578
Havering 20 TQ5587
Havering's Grove 20 TQ6594
Havering-atte-Bower 20 TQ5193
Haversham 27 SP8343
Haverthwaite 40 SD3483
Hawarden 32 SJ3165
Hawes 41 SD8789
Hawford 25 SO8460
Hawick 52 NT5014
Hawkchurch 7 ST3400
Hawkedon 20 TL7952
Hawkeridge 17 ST8653
Hawkerland 7 SY0588
Hawkes End 26 SP2983
Hawkesbury 17 ST7687
Hawkesbury Upton 17 ST7786
Hawkhill 53 NU2212
Hawkhope 46 NY7188
Hawkhurst 12 TQ7630
Hawkinge 13 TR2139
Hawkley 10 SU7429
Hawkridge 6 SS8630
Hawkshead 40 SD3598
Hawksland 50 NS8439
Hawkstone 32 SJ5830
Hawkswick 37 SD9570
Hawksworth (Notts.) 34 SK7543
Hawksworth (W Yorks.) 37 SE1641
Hawkwell 21 TQ8691
Hawley (Hants.) 10 SU8558
Hawley (Kent) 12 TQ5571
Hawling 17 SP0623
Hawnby 42 SE5389
Haworth 37 SE0337
Hawsker 43 NZ9207
Hawstead 21 TL8559
Hawthorn Hill 11 SU8873
Hawton 34 SK7851
Haxby 38 SE6057
Haxey 38 SK7699
Hay-on-Wye 23 SO2342
Haydock 32 SJ5696
Haydon 8 ST6615
Haydon Bridge 47 NY8464
Haydon Wick 17 SU1388
Haye 4 SX3570
Hayes (Gtr London) 19 TQ0980
Hayes (Gtr London) 12 TQ4165
Hayfield 33 SK0386
Hayhillock 57 NO5242
Hayle 2 SW5537
Hayling Island 9 SU7201
Haynes 27 TL0841
Hayscastle 14 SM8926
Hayscastle Cross 14 SM9125
Hayton (Cumbr.) 45 NY1041
Hayton (Cumbr.) 46 NY5057
Hayton (Humbs.) 39 SE8145
Hayton (Notts.) 34 SK7284
Hayton's Bent 24 SO5280
Haytor Vale 5 SX7677
Haywards Heath 12 TQ3324
Haywood Oaks 34 SK6055
Hazel Grove 33 SJ9287
Hazelbank 50 NS8344
Hazelbury Bryan 8 ST7408
Hazeley 10 SU7459
Hazelrigg 53 NU0533
Hazelslade 25 SK0212
Hazelton Walls 57 NO3321
Hazelwood 33 SK3245
Hazlemere 19 SU8895

Hazlerigg Hornblotton Green

Hazlerigg 47 NZ2472
Hazleton 17 SP0718
Heacham 28 TF6737
Head of Muir 50 NS8080
Headbourne Worthy 9 SU4831
Headcorn 12 TQ8344
Headington 18 SP5407
Headlam 42 NZ1818
Headless Cross 25 SP0365
Headley (Hants.) 10 SU5162
Headley (Hants.) 10 SU8236
Headley (Surrey) 11 TQ2054
Headon 34 SK7476
Heads Nook 46 NY4955
Heage 33 SK3650
Healaugh (N Yorks.) 41 SE0198
Healaugh (N Yorks.) 38 SE4947
Heale 6 SS6446
Healey (Lancs.) 37 SD8817
Healey (N Yorks.) 42 SE1780
Healey (Northum.) 47 NZ0158
Healeyfield 47 NZ0648
Healing 39 TA2110
Heamoor 2 SW4631
Heanchardon 6 SS5035
Heanish 48 NM0343
Heanor 33 SK4346
Heanton Punchardon 6 SS5035
Heapham 34 SK8788
Hearthstane 51 NT1125
Heaste 58 NG6417
Heath 34 SK4467
Heath End (Hants.) 10 SU5762
Heath End (Hants.) 11 SU8550
Heath Hayes 25 SK0110
Heath Hill 24 SJ7614
Heath House 7 ST4146
Heath and Reach 19 SP9228
Heath, The 21 TL9043
Heathcote 33 SK1460
Heather 26 SK3910
Heathfield (Devon.) 5 SX8376
Heathfield (E Susx) 12 TQ5821
Heathfield (Somer.) 7 ST1526
Heathton 25 SO8192
Heatley 32 SJ6988
Heaton (Lancs.) 36 SD4460
Heaton (Staffs.) 33 SJ9462
Heaton (Tyne and Wear) 47 NZ2665
Heaton Moor 37 SJ8691
Heaverham 12 TQ5758
Heaviley 33 SJ9088
Hebburn 47 NZ3265
Hebden 37 SE0263
Hebden Bridge 37 SD9927
Hebden Green 32 SJ6365
Hebron 47 NZ1989
Heckfield 10 SU7260
Heckfield Green 29 TM1875
Heckington 35 TF1444
Heckmondwike 37 SE2123
Heddington 17 ST9966
Heddle 63 HY3512
Heddon-on-the-Wall 47 NZ1366
Hedenham 29 TM3193
Hedge End 9 SU4812
Hedgerley 19 SU9787
Hedging 7 ST3029
Hedley on the Hill 47 NZ0759
Hednesford 25 SK0012
Hedon 39 TA1828
Hedsor 19 SU9086
Hegdon Hill 24 SO5854
Heglibister 63 HU3952
Heighington (Durham) 42 NZ2522
Heighington (Lincs.) 34 TF0269
Heights of Brae 65 NH5161
Heights of Kinlochewe 64 NH0764
Heilam 66 NC4560
Heiton 52 NT7130
Heldon Hill 61 NJ1257
Hele (Devon.) 6 SS5347
Hele (Devon.) 5 SS9902
Helensburgh 49 NS2982
Helford 2 SW7526
Helhoughton 28 TF8626
Helions Bumpstead 20 TL6541
Helland 3 SX0770
Hellesdon 29 TG1810
Hellidon 26 SP5158
Hellifield 37 SD8556
Hellingly 12 TQ5812
Hellington 29 TG3103
Hellister 63 HU3949
Helmdon 26 SP5843
Helmingham 21 TM1857
Helmsdale 67 ND0215
Helmshore 37 SD7821
Helmsley 42 SE6183
Helperby 38 SE4369
Helperthorpe 39 SE9570
Helpringham 35 TF1340
Helpston 27 TF1205
Helsby 32 SJ4875
Helston 2 SW6527
Helstone 3 SX0881
Helton 40 NY5122
Helwith Bridge 41 SD8169
Hemblington 29 TG3411
Hemel Hempstead 19 TL0506
Hemingbrough 38 SE6730
Hemingby 35 TF2374
Hemingford Abbots 27 TL2870
Hemingford Grey 27 TL2970
Hemingstone 21 TM1453
Hemington (Northants.) 27 TL0985
Hemington (Somer.) 17 ST7253
Hemley 21 TM2842
Hempholme 39 TA0850
Hempnall 29 TM2494
Hempnall Green 29 TM2593
Hempriggs 61 NJ1064
Hempstead (Essex) 20 TL6338
Hempstead (Norf.) 29 TG4028
Hempsted (Glos) 17 SO8117
Hempsted (Norf.) 29 TG1037
Hempton (Norf.) 28 TF9129
Hempton (Oxon.) 18 SP4431
Hemsby 29 TG4917
Hemswell 34 SK9290
Hemsworth 38 SE4213
Hemyock 7 ST1313
Henbury (Avon) 16 ST5478
Henbury (Ches.) 33 SJ8873
Hendersyde Park 53 NT7435
Hendon (Gtr London) 19 TQ2389
Hendon (Tyne and Wear) 47 NZ4055
Hendy 15 SN5804
Heneglwys 30 SH4276
Henfield 11 TQ2116
Hengoed (Mid Glam.) 16 ST1495
Hengoed (Powys) 23 SO2253
Hengoed (Salop) 31 SJ2833
Hengrave 28 TL8268
Henham 20 TL5428
Heniarth 23 SJ1108
Henley (Salop) 24 SO5476
Henley (Somer.) 7 ST4232
Henley (Suff.) 21 TM1551
Henley (W Susx) 11 SU8926
Henley Park 11 SU9352
Henley on Thames 18 SU7682
Henley-in-Arden 25 SP1465
Henllan (Clwyd) 31 SJ0268
Henllan (Dyfed) 22 SN3540
Henllan Amgoed 14 SN1820
Henllys 16 ST2693
Henlow 19 TL1738
Hennock 5 SX8380
Henry's Moat (Castell Hendre) 14 SN0428
Henryd 31 SH7674
Hensall 38 SE5923
Henshaw 46 NY7664
Henstead 29 TM4986
Henstridge 8 ST7219
Henstridge Marsh 8 ST7420
Henton (Oxon.) 18 SP7602
Henton (Somer.) 7 ST4845
Henwick 25 SO8354
Henwood 4 SX2673
Heogan 63 HU4743
Heol Senni 15 SN9223
Heol-y-Cyw 15 SS9484
Hepburn 53 NU0724
Hepple 47 NT9800
Hepscott 47 NZ2284
Heptonstall 37 SD9827
Hepworth (Suff.) 29 TL9874
Hepworth (W Yorks.) 37 SE1606
Herbrandston 14 SM8708
Hereford 24 SO5040
Hergest 23 SO2655
Heriot 51 NT3952
Hermitage (Berks.) 10 SU5072
Hermitage (Borders) 46 NY5095
Hermitage (Dorset.) 8 ST6306
Hermitage (Hants.) 10 SU7505
Hermitage, The 11 TQ2253
Hermon (Dyfed) 14 SN2032
Hermon (Dyfed) 14 SN3630
Hermon (Gwyn.) 30 SH3868
Herne 13 TR1866
Herne Bay 13 TR1768
Herner 6 SS5926
Hernhill 13 TR0660
Herodsfoot 4 SX2160
Herongate 20 TQ6391
Heronsgate 19 TQ0294
Herriard 10 SU6645
Herringfleet 29 TM4797
Herringswell 28 TL7170
Herrington 47 NZ3553
Hersden 13 TR1961
Hersham 11 TQ1164
Herstmonceux 12 TQ6312
Hertford 20 TL3212
Hertford Heath 20 TL3510
Hertingfordbury 20 TL3112
Hesket Newmarket 40 NY3438
Hesketh Bank 36 SD4323
Hesketh Lane 36 SD6141
Heskin Green 36 SK5315
Hesleden 42 NZ4438
Hesleyside 46 NY8183
Heslington 38 SE6250
Hessay 38 SE5253
Hessenford 4 SX3057
Hessett 29 TL9361
Hessle 39 TA0326
Hest Bank 36 SD4566
Heston 11 TQ1277
Heswall 31 SJ2682
Hethe 18 SP5929
Hethersett 29 TG1505
Hethersgill 46 NY4767
Hethpool 53 NT8928
Hett 42 NZ2836
Hetton 37 SD9658
Hetton-le-Hole 47 NZ3548
Heugh 47 NZ0873
Heugh-Head 61 NJ3711
Heveningham 29 TM3372
Hever 12 TQ4744
Heversham 40 SD4983
Hevingham 29 TG2022
Hewelsfield 17 SO5602
Hewish (Avon) 16 ST4064
Hewish (Somer.) 7 ST4108
Hexham 47 NY9364
Hextable 12 TQ5170
Hexton 19 TL1030
Hexworthy 5 SX6572
Heybridge (Essex) 21 TL8508
Heybridge (Essex) 20 TQ6498
Heybridge Basin 21 TL8707
Heybrook Bay 4 SX4948
Heydon (Cambs.) 20 TL4340
Heydon (Norf.) 29 TG1127
Heydour 34 TF0039
Heyford 26 SP6558
Heylipoll 48 NL9643
Heylor 63 HU2881
Heysham 36 SD4161
Heyshott 11 SU8918
Heytesbury 8 ST9242
Heythrop 18 SP3527
Heywood (Gtr Mches.) 37 SD8510
Heywood (Wilts.) 17 ST8753
Hibaldstow 39 SE9702
Hickleton 38 SE4805
Hickling (Norf.) 29 TG4124
Hickling (Notts.) 34 SK6929
Hickling Green 29 TG4023
Hickling Heath 29 TG4022
Hidcote Boyce 25 SP1742
High Ackworth 38 SE4317
High Banton 50 NS7480
High Beach 20 TQ4097
High Bentham 36 SD6669
High Bickington 6 SS5920
High Birkwith 41 SD8076
High Blantyre 50 NS6756
High Bonnybridge 50 NS8378
High Buston 53 NU2308
High Callerton 47 NZ1670
High Catton 38 SE7153
High Cogges 18 SP3709
High Coniscliffe 42 NZ2215
High Cross (Hants.) 10 SU7126
High Cross (Herts.) 20 TL3618
High Cross Bank 33 SK3018
High Easter 20 TL6214
High Ellington 42 SE1983
High Ercall 32 SJ5917
High Etherley 42 NZ1628
High Garrett 20 TL7726
High Grange 42 NZ1731
High Grantley 42 SE2369
High Green (Here. and Worc.) 25 SO8745
High Green (Norf.) 29 TG1305
High Green (S Yorks.) 38 SK3397
High Halden 13 TQ9037
High Halstow 12 TQ7875
High Ham 7 ST4231
High Hatton 32 SJ6024
High Hesket 46 NY4744
High Hoyland 37 SE2710
High Hunsley 39 SE9535
High Hurstwood 12 TQ4926
High Lane 24 SO6760
High Laver 20 TL5208
High Legh 30 SJ6984
High Littleton 17 ST6458
High Lorton 40 NY1625
High Melton 38 SE5001
High Newton 40 SD4082
High Newton-by-the-Sea 53 NU2325
High Offley 32 SJ7826
High Ongar 20 TL5603
High Onn 32 SJ8216
High Roding 20 TL6017
High Salvington 11 TQ1206
High Shaw 41 SD8791
High Spen 47 NZ1359
High Street (Corn.) 2 SW9753
High Street (Suff.) 21 TM4355
High Street Green 21 TM0055
High Toynton 35 TF2869
High Trewhitt 47 NU0105
High Wray 40 SD3799
High Wych 20 TL4614
High Wycombe 19 SU8593
Higham (Derby.) 33 SK3959
Higham (Kent) 12 TQ7171
Higham (Lancs.) 37 SD8036
Higham (Suff.) 28 TL7465
Higham (Suff.) 21 TM0335
Higham Dykes 47 NZ1375
Higham Ferrers 27 SP9669
Higham Gobion 19 TL1033
Higham Wood 12 TQ6048
Higham on the Hill 26 SP3895
Highampton 4 SS4804
Highbridge 7 ST3147
Highbrook 12 TQ3630
Highburton 37 SE1813
Highbury 8 ST6849
Highclere 10 SU4360
Highcliffe 8 SZ2193
Higher Ansty 8 ST7603
Higher Ballam 36 SD3630
Higher Penwortham 36 SD5128
Higher Tale 7 ST0601
Higher Walreddon 4 SX4771
Higher Walton (Ches.) 32 SJ5985
Higher Walton (Lancs.) 36 SD5727
Higher Wych 32 SJ4943
Highfield (Strath.) 49 NS3050
Highfield (Tyne and Wear) 47 NZ1459
Highfields 20 TL3559
Highleadon 17 SO7623
Highleigh 10 SZ8498
Highley 24 SO7483
Highmoor Cross 18 SU7084
Highmoor Hill 16 ST4689
Highnam 17 SO7919
Highsted 13 TQ9161
Hightae 45 NY0979
Hightown (Ches.) 33 SJ8762
Hightown (Mers.) 36 SD2903
Highway 17 SU0474
Highweek 5 SX8472
Highworth 18 SU2092
Hilborough (Norf.) 28 TF8200
Hildenborough 12 TQ5648
Hildersham 20 TL5448
Hilderstone 33 SJ9434
Hilderthorpe 39 TA1765
Hilgay 28 TL6298
Hill 17 ST6495
Hill Brow 10 SU7926
Hill Dyke 35 TF3447
Hill End (Durham) 41 NZ0135
Hill End (Fife.) 51 NT0495
Hill Head (Hants.) 9 SU5402
Hill Ridware 33 SK0718
Hill Row 27 TL4475
Hill Top (Hants.) 9 SU4002
Hill Top (W Yorks.) 38 SE3315
Hill of Beath 51 NT1690
Hill of Fearn 65 NH8377
Hill of Maud Crofts 61 NJ4661
Hill, The 40 SD1783
Hillam 38 SE5028
Hillbeck 41 NY7915
Hillberry 43 SC3879
Hillborough (Kent) 13 TR2168
Hillbrae (Grampn.) 62 NJ6047
Hillbrae (Grampn.) 62 NJ7923
Hillend (Fife.) 51 NT1483
Hillesden 18 SP6828
Hillesley 17 ST7689
Hillfarrance 7 ST1624
Hillhead (Devon.) 5 SX9053
Hillhead (Strath.) 50 NS4219
Hillhead of Auchentumb 62 NJ9258
Hillhead of Cocklaw 62 NK0844
Hilliard's Cross 25 SK1412
Hilliclay 67 ND1764
Hillingdon 19 TQ0882
Hillington 28 TF7225
Hillmorton 26 SP5374
Hillockhead 61 NJ3809
Hillside (Grampn.) 62 NO9298
Hillside (Shetld.) 63 HU4063
Hillside (Tays.) 57 NO7061
Hillswick 63 HU2877
Hillwell 63 HU3714
Hilmarton 17 SU0175
Hilperton 17 ST8759
Hilsea 9 SU6503
Hilton (Cambs.) 27 TL2966
Hilton (Cleve.) 42 NZ4611
Hilton (Cumbr.) 41 NY7320
Hilton (Derby.) 33 SK2430
Hilton (Dorset) 8 ST7802
Hilton (Durham) 42 NZ1621
Hilton (Grampn.) 62 NJ9434
Hilton (Salop) 24 SO7795
Hilton of Cadboll 65 NH8776
Himbleton 25 SO9458
Himley 25 SO8891
Hincaster 40 SD5148
Hinckley 26 SP4294
Hinderclay 29 TM0276
Hinderwell 43 NZ7916
Hindford 32 SJ3333
Hindhead 11 SU8736
Hindley 36 SD6104
Hindley Green 36 SD6403
Hindlip 25 SO8758
Hindolveston 29 TG0329
Hindon 8 ST9032
Hindringham 29 TF9836
Hingham 29 TG0202
Hinstock 32 SJ6926
Hintlesham 21 TM0843
Hinton (Avon) 17 ST7376
Hinton (Hants.) 8 SZ2095
Hinton (Northants.) 26 SP5352
Hinton (Salop) 24 SJ4008
Hinton Ampner 9 SU5927
Hinton Blewett 17 ST5956
Hinton Charterhouse 17 ST7758
Hinton Marsh 9 SU5827
Hinton Martell 8 SU0106
Hinton Parva 18 SU2283
Hinton St. George 7 ST4212
Hinton St. Mary 8 ST7816
Hinton Waldrist 18 SU3799
Hinton on the Green 25 SP0204
Hinton-in-the-Hedges 18 SP5537
Hints (Salop) 24 SO6175
Hints (Staffs.) 25 SK1503
Hinwick 27 SP9361
Hinxhill 13 TR0442
Hinxton 20 TL4945
Hinxworth 19 TL2340
Hipperholme 37 SE1225
Hirn 63 NJ7300
Hirnant 31 SJ0423
Hirst 47 NZ2787
Hirst Courtney 38 SE6124
Hirwaun 15 SN9505
Hiscott 6 SS5426
Histon 27 TL4363
Hitcham 21 TL9851
Hitchin 19 TL1829
Hither Green 12 TQ3874
Hittisleigh 5 SX7395
Hixon 33 SK0026
Hoaden 13 TR2759
Hoaldalbert 16 SO3923
Hoar Cross 33 SK1223
Hoarwithy 16 SO5429
Hoath 13 TR2064
Hobarris 23 SO3078
Hobbister 63 HY3807
Hobkirk 52 NT5810
Hobson 47 NZ1755
Hoby 34 SK6617
Hockering 29 TG0713
Hockerton 34 SK7156
Hockley 20 TQ8293
Hockley Heath 25 SP1572
Hockliffe 19 SP9726
Hockwold cum Wilton 28 TL7288
Hockworthy 7 ST0319
Hoddesdon 20 TL3709
Hoddlesdon 36 SD7122
Hodgeston 14 SS0399
Hodnet 32 SJ6128
Hodthorpe 34 SK5476
Hoe 29 TF9916
Hoe Gate 9 SU6213
Hoggeston 18 SP8025
Hoghton 36 SD6125
Hognaston 33 SK2350
Hogsthorpe 35 TF5372
Holbeach 35 TF3625
Holbeach Bank 35 TF3627
Holbeach Drove 27 TF3212
Holbeach Hurn 35 TF3927
Holbeach St. Johns 35 TF3418
Holbeach St. Marks 35 TF3731
Holbeach St. Matthew 35 TF4132
Holbeck 34 SK5473
Holberrow Green 25 SP0259
Holbeton 5 SX6150
Holborn 20 TQ3181
Holbrook (Derby) 33 SK3645
Holbrook (Suff.) 21 TM1636
Holburn 53 NU0436
Holbury 9 SU4303
Holcombe (Devon.) 5 SX9574
Holcombe (Somer.) 8 ST6649
Holcombe Rogus 7 ST0519
Holcot 26 SP7969
Holden 37 SD7749
Holdenby 26 SP6967
Holdgate 24 SO5589
Holdingham 35 TF0547
Holestane 45 NX8799
Holford 7 ST1541
Holker 40 SD3577
Holkham 28 TF8944
Hollacombe 4 SS3702
Holland (Papa Westray) 63 HY4851
Holland (Stronsay) 63 HY6622
Holland Fen 35 TF2445
Holland-on-Sea 21 TM2016
Hollandstoun 63 HY7553
Hollesley 21 TM3544
Hollingbourne 13 TQ8455
Hollington (Derby) 33 SK2239
Hollington (E Susx.) 12 TQ7911
Hollington (Staffs.) 33 SK0538
Hollingworth 33 SK0096
Hollins 37 SD8108
Hollins Green 32 SJ6990
Hollinsclough 33 SK0666
Hollinswood 24 SJ6909
Hollinwood 32 SJ5236
Hollocombe 5 SS6311
Holloway 33 SK3256
Hollowell 26 SP6972
Holly End 28 TF4906
Hollybush (Gwent) 16 SO1603
Hollybush (Here. and Worc.) 24 SO7636
Hollybush (Strath.) 50 NS3914
Hollym 39 TA3425
Holm (Isle of Lewis) 63 NB4531
Holmbury St. Mary 11 TQ1144
Holme (Cambs.) 27 TL1987
Holme (Cumbr.) 40 SD5278
Holme (Notts.) 34 SK8059
Holme (W Yorks.) 37 SE1005
Holme Chapel 37 SD8728
Holme Hale 28 TF8807
Holme Lacy 24 SO5535
Holme Marsh 23 SO3354
Holme next the Sea 28 TF7043
Holme on the Wolds 39 SE9646
Holme upon Spalding Moor 39 SE8138
Holmer 24 SO5042
Holmer Green 19 SU9097
Holmes Chapel 32 SJ7667
Holmesfield 33 SK3277
Holmeswood 36 SD4316
Holmewood 33 SK4365
Holmfirth 37 SE1408
Holmhead 50 NS5620
Holmpton 39 TA3623
Holmrook 40 SD0799
Holmsgarth 63 HU4642
Holne 5 SX7069
Holnest 8 ST6509
Holsworthy 4 SS3403
Holsworthy Beacon 4 SS3508
Holt (Clwyd) 32 SJ4053
Holt (Dorset) 8 SU0203
Holt (Here. and Worc.) 25 SO8262
Holt (Norf.) 29 TG0738
Holt (Wilts.) 17 ST8661
Holt End 25 SP0769
Holt Heath 25 SO8163
Holtby 38 SE6754
Holton (Oxon.) 18 SP6006
Holton (Somer.) 8 ST6826
Holton (Suff.) 29 TM4077
Holton Heath 8 SY9491
Holton St. Mary 21 TM0537
Holton cum Beckering 35 TF1181
Holton le Clay 39 TA2802
Holton le Moor 39 TF0797
Holwell (Herts.) 19 TL1633
Holwell (Leic.) 34 SK7323
Holwell (Oxon) 18 SP2309
Holwick 41 NY9026
Holworth 8 SY7683
Holy Cross 25 SO9279
Holybourne 10 SU7341
Holyhead 30 SH2482
Holymoorside 33 SK3369
Holyport 11 SU8977
Holystone 47 NT9502
Holytown 50 NS7760
Holywell (Cambs.) 27 TL3370
Holywell (Clwyd) 31 SJ1875
Holywell (Corn.) 2 SW7658
Holywell (Dorset) 8 ST5904
Holywell Green 37 SE0918
Holywell Lake 7 ST1020
Holywell Row 28 TL7077
Holywood 45 NX9480
Hom Green 17 SO5822
Homer 24 SJ6101
Homersfield 29 TM2885
Homington 8 SU1226
Honey Hill 13 TR1161
Honeyborough 14 SM9506
Honeybourne 25 SP1144
Honeychurch 5 SS6202
Honiley 26 SP2472
Honing 29 TG3227
Honingham 29 TG1011
Honington (Lincs.) 34 SK9443
Honington (Suff.) 28 TL9174
Honington (Warw.) 26 SP2642
Honiton 7 ST1600
Honley 37 SE1311
Hoo (Kent) 12 TQ7872
Hoo Green 21 TM2559
Hooe (Devon.) 4 SX5052
Hooe (E Susx) 12 TQ6809
Hook (Dyfed) 14 SM9811
Hook (Hants.) 10 SU7254
Hook (Humbs.) 38 SE7525
Hook (Surrey) 11 TQ1764
Hook (Wilts.) 17 SU0784
Hook Norton 18 SP3533
Hooke (Dorset) 7 ST5300
Hookgate 32 SJ7435
Hookway 5 SX8598
Hookwood 11 TQ2643
Hoole 32 SJ4367
Hooton 32 SJ3679
Hooton Levitt 34 SK5291
Hooton Pagnell 38 SE4808
Hooton Roberts 38 SK4897
Hope (Clwyd) 32 SJ3058
Hope (Derby.) 33 SK1783
Hope (Devon.) 5 SX6740
Hope (Powys) 23 SJ2507
Hope (Salop) 23 SJ3401
Hope Bagot 24 SO5874
Hope Bowdler 24 SO4792
Hope Mansell 17 SO6219
Hope under Dinmore 24 SO5052
Hopeman 61 NJ1469
Hopesay 24 SO3883
Hopton (Norf.) 29 TG5200
Hopton (Salop) 32 SJ5926
Hopton (Staffs.) 33 SJ9426
Hopton (Suff.) 29 TL9979
Hopton Cangeford 24 SO5480
Hopton Castle 24 SO3678
Hopton Wafers 24 SO6476
Hopwas 25 SK1705
Hopwood 25 SP0375
Horam 12 TQ5717
Horbling 35 TF1135
Horbury 38 SE2918
Horden 47 NZ4441
Horderley 24 SO4086
Hordle 9 SZ2795
Hordley 32 SJ3730
Horeb 22 SN3942
Horham 29 TM2172
Horkesley Heath 21 TL9829
Horkstow 39 SE9818
Horley (Oxon.) 26 SP4143
Horley (Surrey) 11 TQ2843
Horn Hill 19 TQ0292
Hornblotton Green 8 ST5833

Hornby
Kestle Mill

Hornby (Lancs.) 36 SD 5868
Hornby (N Yorks.) 42 NZ 3605
Horncastle 35 TF 2669
Hornchurch 20 TQ 5487
Horncliffe 53 NT 9249
Horndean 9 SU 7013
Horndon on the Hill 20 TQ 6683
Horne 12 TQ 3344
Horning 29 TG 3417
Horninghold 26 SP 8097
Horninglow 33 SK 2324
Horningsea 28 TL 4962
Horningsham 8 ST 8241
Horningtoft 29 TF 9323
Hornsby 46 NY 5150
Hornsea 39 TA 2047
Hornsey 20 TQ 3089
Hornton 26 SP 3945
Horrabridge 4 SX 5169
Horringer 28 TL 8261
Horsebridge (E Susx) 12 TQ 5911
Horsebridge (Hants.) 9 SU 3430
Horsebridge (Staffs.) 33 SJ 9553
Horsebrook 25 SJ 8810
Horsehay 24 SJ 6707
Horseheath 20 TL 6147
Horsehouse 41 SE 0481
Horsell 11 SU 9959
Horseman's Green 32 SJ 4441
Horseway 27 TL 4287
Horsey 29 TG 4523
Horsford 29 TF 1915
Horsforth 37 SE 2337
Horsham (Here. and Worc.) 24 SO 7357
Horsham (W Susx) 11 TQ 1730
Horsham St. Faith 29 TG 2114
Horsington (Lincs.) 35 TF 1868
Horsington (Somer.) 8 ST 7023
Horsley (Derby.) 33 SK 3744
Horsley (Glos.) 17 ST 8398
Horsley (Northum.) 47 NY 8496
Horsley (Northum.) 47 NZ 0966
Horsley Cross 21 TM 1227
Horsley Woodhouse 33 SK 3945
Horsleycross Street 21 TM 1228
Horsleyhill 52 NT 5319
Horsmonden 12 TQ 7040
Horspath 18 SP 5704
Horstead 29 TG 2619
Horsted Keynes 12 TQ 3828
Horton (Avon) 17 ST 7684
Horton (Berks.) 11 TQ 0175
Horton (Bucks.) 19 SP 9219
Horton (Dorset) 8 SU 0307
Horton (Lancs.) 37 SD 8550
Horton (Northants.) 26 SP 8254
Horton (Northum.) 53 NU 0230
Horton (Staffs.) 33 SJ 9457
Horton (W Glam.) 15 SS 4785
Horton (Wilts.) 17 SU 0463
Horton Green 32 SJ 4549
Horton Heath 9 SU 4916
Horton Kirby 12 TQ 5668
Horton in Ribblesdale 37 SD 8172
Horwich 36 SD 6311
Horwood 6 SS 5027
Hose 34 SK 7329
Hosh 56 NN 8523
Hoswick 63 HU 4124
Hotham 39 SE 8934
Hothfield 13 TQ 9644
Hoton 34 SK 5722
Houbie 63 HU 6390
Hough 32 SJ 7151
Hough Green 32 SJ 4885
Hough-on-the-Hill 34 SK 9246
Hougham 34 SK 8844
Hougharry 63 NF 7071
Houghton (Cambs.) 27 TL 2871
Houghton (Cumbr.) 46 NY 4159
Houghton (Dyfed) 14 SM 9807
Houghton (Hants.) 9 SU 3331
Houghton (W Susx) 11 TQ 0111
Houghton Conquest 27 TL 0441
Houghton Regis 19 TL 0224
Houghton St. Giles 29 TF 9235
Houghton le Spring 47 NZ 3450
Houghton on the Hill 26 SK 6703
Houlsyke 43 NZ 7308
Hound Green 10 SU 7259
Houndslow 52 NT 6347
Houndwood 53 NT 8464
Hounslow 11 TQ 1276
Housetter 63 HU 3784
Houston 50 NS 4067
Houstry 67 ND 1534
Hove 11 TQ 2805
Hoveringham 34 SK 6946
Hoveton 29 TG 3018
Hovingham 42 SE 6675
How 46 NY 5056
How Caple 24 SO 6030
Howden 38 SE 7428
Howden-le-Wear 42 NZ 1633
Howe (Cumbr.) 40 SD 4588
Howe (Highld.) 67 ND 3062
Howe (Norf.) 29 TM 2799
Howe Green 20 TL 7403
Howe Street (Essex) 20 TL 6914
Howe Street (Essex) 20 TL 6934
Howe of Teuchar 62 NJ 7947
Howe, The 43 SC 1967
Howell 35 TF 1346
Howey 23 SO 0558
Howgate 51 NT 2457
Howick 53 NU 2517
Howlaws 53 NT 7242
Howle 32 SJ 6823
Howlett End 20 TL 5834
Howmore 63 NF 7636
Hownam 53 NT 7719
Hownam Law 53 NT 7921
Hownam Mains 53 NT 7820
Howsham (Humbs.) 39 TA 0404
Howsham (N Yorks.) 38 SE 7362
Howton 16 SO 4129
Howwood 50 NS 3960
Hoxne 29 TM 1877
Hoylake 31 SJ 2189
Hoyland Nether 38 SE 3600
Hoyland Swaine 37 SE 2604
Hubbert's Bridge 35 TF 2643
Huby 38 SE 5665
Hucclecote 17 SO 8717
Hucking 12 TQ 8358
Hucknall 34 SK 5349
Huddersfield 37 SE 1416
Huddington 25 SO 9457
Hudswell 42 NZ 1400
Huggate 39 SE 8855
Hugh Town 2 SV 9010
Hughenden Valley 19 SU 8695
Hughley 24 SO 5697
Hugmore 32 SJ 3752
Huish (Devon.) 4 SS 5311
Huish (Wilts.) 17 SU 1463
Huish Champflower 7 ST 0429
Huish Episcopi 7 ST 4226
Hulcott 19 SP 8516
Hulland 33 SK 2447
Hullavington 17 ST 8982
Hullbridge 20 TQ 8194
Hulme End 33 SK 1059
Hulme Walfield 33 SJ 8465
Hulne Park 53 NU 1514
Hulver Street 29 TM 4686
Humber Court 24 SO 5356
Humberston 39 TA 3105
Humberstone 26 SK 6206
Humbie 52 NT 4562
Humbleton (Humbs.) 39 TA 2234
Humbleton (Northum.) 53 NT 9728
Hume 52 NT 7041
Humshaugh 47 NY 9171
Huna 67 ND 3573
Huncoat 37 SD 7730
Huncote 26 SP 5197
Hundalee 52 NT 6418
Hunderthwaite 41 NY 9821
Hundleby 35 TF 3966
Hundleton 14 SM 9600
Hundon 20 TL 7348
Hundred Acres 9 SU 5911
Hundred End 36 SD 4122
Hundred, The 24 SO 5264
Hungarton 26 SK 6807
Hungerford (Berks.) 10 SU 3368
Hungerford (Hants.) 8 SU 1612
Hungerford Newtown 10 SU 3571
Hunmanby 43 TA 0977
Hunningham 26 SP 3768
Hunsdon 20 TL 4114
Hunsingore 38 SE 4253
Hunsonby 41 NY 5835
Hunspow 67 ND 2172
Hunstanton 28 TF 6741
Hunstanworth 47 NY 9449
Hunston (Suff.) 29 TI 9768
Hunston (W Susx) 11 SU 8601
Hunstrete 17 ST 6462
Hunt End 25 SP 0364
Hunt's Cross 32 SJ 4385
Hunter's Quay 49 NS 1879
Huntingdon 27 TL 2371
Huntingfield 29 TM 3374
Huntington (Here. and Worc.) 23 SO 2553
Huntington (Lothian) 52 NT 4875
Huntington (N Yorks.) 38 SE 6156
Huntington (Staffs) 25 SJ 9713
Huntingtower 56 NO 0725
Huntley 17 SO 7219
Huntly 61 NJ 5339
Hunton (Kent) 12 TQ 7149
Hunton (N Yorks.) 42 SE 1892
Huntsham 7 ST 0020
Huntspill 7 ST 3045
Huntworth 7 ST 3134
Hunwick 42 NZ 1832
Hunworth 29 TG 0635
Hurdsfield 33 SJ 9274
Hurley (Berks.) 19 SU 8283
Hurley (Warw.) 26 SP 2495
Hurlford 50 NS 4536
Hurliness 63 ND 2888
Hurn 8 SZ 1296
Hursley 9 SU 4225
Hurst (Berks.) 10 SU 7972
Hurst (Gtr Mches.) 37 SD 9400
Hurst (N Yorks.) 42 NZ 0402
Hurst Green (E Susx) 12 TQ 7327
Hurst Green (Lancs.) 36 SD 6838
Hurst Green (Surrey) 12 TQ 3951
Hurstbourne Priors 10 SU 4346
Hurstbourne Tarrant 10 SU 3853
Hurstpierpoint 11 TQ 2816
Hurtwood Common 11 TQ 0743
Hurworth 42 NZ 3010
Hury 41 NY 9619
Husbands Bosworth 26 SP 6484
Husborne Crawley 19 SP 9535
Husinish 63 NA 9812
Husthwaite 42 SE 5175
Huthwaite 34 SK 4659
Huttoft 35 TF 5176
Hutton (Avon) 16 ST 3458
Hutton (Borders) 53 NT 9053
Hutton (Cumbr.) 40 NY 4326
Hutton (Essex) 20 TQ 6394
Hutton (Lancs.) 36 SD 4926
Hutton (N Yorks.) 38 SE 7667
Hutton Bonville 42 NZ 3300
Hutton Buscel 43 SE 9784
Hutton Conyers 42 SE 3273
Hutton Cranswick 39 TA 0252
Hutton End 40 NY 4538
Hutton Henry 42 NZ 4236
Hutton Magna 42 NZ 1212
Hutton Roof (Cumbr.) 40 NY 3734
Hutton Roof (Cumbr.) 41 SD 5777
Hutton Rudby 42 NZ 4606
Hutton Sessay 42 SE 4776
Hutton Wandesley 38 SE 5050
Hutton-le-Hole 43 SE 7090
Huxley 32 SJ 5061
Huxter (Shetld.) 63 HU 5662
Huyton 32 SJ 4490
Hycemoor 40 SD 0989
Hyde (Glos.) 17 SO 8801
Hyde (Gtr. Mches.) 33 SJ 9294
Hyde Heath 19 SP 9300
Hydestile 11 SU 9740
Hynish 48 NL 9839
Hyssington 23 SO 3194
Hythe (Hants.) 9 SU 4207
Hythe (Kent) 13 TR 1635
Hythe End 11 TQ 0172
Hythie 62 NK 0051

Ibberton 8 ST 7807
Ible 33 SK 2457
Ibsley 8 SU 1509
Ibstock 26 SK 4010
Ibstone 18 UU 7593
Ibthorpe 10 SU 3753
Ibworth 10 SU 5654
Ickburgh 28 TL 8195
Ickenham 19 TQ 0786
Ickford 18 SP 6407
Ickham 13 TR 2258
Ickleford 19 TL 1831
Icklesham 13 TQ 8816
Ickleton 20 TL 4943
Icklingham 28 TL 7772
Ickwell Green 27 TL 1545
Icomb 18 SP 2122
Idbury 18 SP 2320
Iddesleigh 4 SS 5608
Ide 5 SX 8990
Ide Hill 12 TQ 4851
Ideford 5 SX 8977
Iden 13 TQ 9123
Iden Green 12 TQ 8031
Idlicote 26 SP 2844
Idmiston 8 SU 1937
Idridgehay 33 SK 2849
Idrigil 58 NG 3863
Idstone 18 SU 2584
Idvies 57 NO 5347
Ifield (W Susx) 11 TQ 2537
Ifield or Singlewell (Kent) 12 TQ 6471
Ifold 11 TQ 0231
Iford 12 TQ 4007
Ifton Heath 32 SJ 3236
Ightfield 32 SJ 5938
Ightman 12 TQ 5956
Iken 21 TM 4155
Ilam 33 SK 1351
Ilchester 7 ST 5222
Ilderton 53 NU 0121
Ilford 20 TQ 4586
Ilfracombe 6 SS 5147
Ilkeston 34 SK 4642
Ilketshall St. Andrew 29 TM 3887
Ilketshall St. Margaret 29 TM 3485
Ilkley 37 SE 1147
Illey 25 SO 9881
Illingworth 37 SE 0728
Illogan 2 SW 6643
Illston on the Hill 26 SP 7099
Ilmer 18 SP 7605
Ilmington 26 SP 2143
Ilminster 7 ST 3614
Ilsington 5 SX 7876
Ilston 15 SS 5590
Ilton (N. Yorks.) 42 SE 1878
Ilton (Somer.) 7 ST 3517
Imachar 49 NR 8640
Imber 8 ST 9648
Immingham 39 TA 1714
Impington 27 TL 4463
Ince 32 SJ 4476
Ince Blundell 36 SD 3203
Ince-in-Makersfield 36 SD 5903
Inchbare 57 NO 6065
Inchberry 61 NJ 3155
Inchinnan 50 NS 4768
Inchlaggan 59 NH 1801
Inchnacardoch 60 NH 3710
Inchnadamph 66 NC 2522
Inchture 57 NO 2728
Inchyra 56 NO 1820
Indian Queens 2 SW 9158
Ingatestone 20 TQ 6499
Ingbirchworth 37 SE 2205
Ingestre 33 SJ 9724
Ingham (Lincs.) 34 SK 9483
Ingham (Norf.) 29 TG 3825
Ingham (Suff.) 28 TL 8570
Ingleby Arncliffe 42 NZ 4400
Ingleby Greenhow 42 NZ 5806
Inglesbatch 17 ST 7061
Inglesham 18 SU 2098
Ingleton (Durham) 42 NZ 1720
Ingleton (N Yorks.) 41 SD 6972
Inglewhite 36 SD 5439
Ingoe 47 NZ 0374
Ingoldisthorpe 28 TF 6832
Ingoldmells 35 TF 5668
Ingoldsby 34 TF 0030
Ingram 53 NU 0116
Ingrave 20 TQ 6292
Ings 40 SD 4498
Ingst 17 ST 5887
Ingworth 29 TG 1929
Inkberrow 25 SP 0157
Inkhorn 62 NJ 9239
Inkpen 10 SU 3564
Inkstack 67 ND 2570
Innellan 49 NS 1469
Innerleithen 51 NT 3336
Innerleven 57 NO 3700
Innermessan 44 NX 0863
Innerwick (Lothian) 52 NT 7273
Innerwick (Tays.) 56 NN 5947
Insch 62 NJ 6327
Insh 60 NH 8101
Inskip 36 SD 4537
Instow 6 SS 4730
Inver (Grampn.) 61 NO 2393
Inver (Highld.) 65 NH 8682
Inver (Tays.) 56 NO 0142
Inver Mallie 55 NN 1388
Inverailort 54 NM 7681
Inveralligin 59 NG 8457
Inverallochy 62 NK 0464
Inveramsay 62 NJ 7424
Inveran 65 NH 5797
Inveraray 55 NN 0908
Inverarish 58 NG 5535
Inverarity 57 NO 4444
Inverarnan 55 NN 3118
Inverasdale 64 NG 8286
Inverbervie 57 NO 8372
Invercreran 55 NN 0147
Inverdruie 60 NJ 9010
Inverebrie 62 NJ 9233
Inveresk 51 NT 3471
Inverey 61 NO 0889
Inverfarigaig 60 NH 5224
Invergarry 59 NH 3101
Invergeldie 56 NN 7427
Invergloy House 59 NN 2288
Invergordon 65 NH 7168
Invergowrie 57 NO 3430
Inverguseran 58 NG 7407
Inverhadden 56 NN 6757
Inverharroch 61 NJ 3831
Inverie 59 NG 7600
Inverinan 55 NM 9917
Inverinate 59 NG 9122
Inverkeilor 57 NO 6649
Inverkeithing 51 NT 1383
Inverkeithny 62 NJ 6246
Inverkip 49 NS 2071
Inverkirkaig 64 NC 0819
Inverlael 64 NH 1885
Inverlochlarig 55 NH 4318
Invermoriston 60 NH 4117
Invernaver 66 NC 7060
Inverness 60 NH 6645
Invernoaden 55 NS 1197
Inverquharity 57 NO 4057
Inverquhomery 62 NK 0246
Inverroy 55 NN 2581
Inverugie 62 NK 0947
Inveruglas 55 NN 3109
Inverurie 62 NJ 7721
Invervar 56 NN 6648
Inwardleigh 4 SX 5599
Inworth 21 TL 8717
Iping 10 SU 8522
Ipplepen 5 SX 8366
Ipsden 18 SU 6385
Ipstones 33 SK 0249
Ipswich 21 TM 1744
Irby 31 SJ 2584
Irby in the Marsh 35 TF 4763
Irby upon Humber 39 TA 1904
Irchester 27 SP 9265
Ireby (Cumbr.) 40 NY 2338
Ireby (Lancs.) 41 SD 6575
Ireland (Shetld.) 63 HU 3722
Ireleth 40 SD 2277
Ireshopeburn 41 NY 8638
Irlam 32 SJ 7194
Irnham 34 TF 0226
Iron Acton 17 ST 6783
Iron Cross 25 SP 0552
Iron-Bridge 24 SJ 6703
Ironside 62 NJ 8852
Ironville 34 SK 4351
Irstead 29 TG 3620
Irthington 46 NY 4961
Irthlingborough 27 SP 9470
Irton 43 TA 0084
Irvine 49 NS 3239
Isauld 67 NC 9765
Isbister (Shetld.) 63 HU 3791
Isbister (Whalsay) 63 HU 5763
Isfield 12 TQ 4417
Isham 27 SP 8873
Islawr-dref 22 SH 6815
Isle Abbotts 7 ST 3520
Isle Brewers 7 ST 3621
Isle of Whithorn 44 NX 4736
Isleham 28 TL 6474
Isleornsay 58 NG 6912
Islesburgh 63 HU 3369
Isleworth 11 TQ 1675
Isley Walton 33 SK 4225
Islington 20 TQ 3085
Islip (Northants.) 27 SP 9879
Islip (Oxon.) 18 SP 5214
Islivig 63 NA 9927
Istead Rise 12 TQ 6369
Itchen Abbas 9 SU 5332
Itchen Stoke 9 SU 5532
Itchingfield 11 TQ 1328
Itchington 17 ST 6586
Itteringham 29 TG 1430
Itton (Devon.) 5 SX 6898
Itton (Gwent) 16 ST 4896
Ivegill 46 NY 4143
Ivelet 41 SD 9398
Iver 19 TQ 0381
Iver Heath 19 TQ 0283
Iveston 47 NZ 1350
Ivinghoe 19 SP 9416
Ivinghoe Aston 19 SP 9518
Ivington 24 SO 4756
Ivington Green 24 SO 4656
Ivy Hatch 12 TQ 5854
Ivybridge 5 SX 6356
Ivychurch 13 TR 0227
Iwade 13 TQ 9067
Iwerne Courney or Shroton 8 ST 8512
Iwerne Minster 8 ST 8614
Ixworth 29 TL 9370
Ixworth Thorpe 28 TL 9172

Jack Hill 37 SE 1951
Jackstown 62 NJ 7531
Jackton 50 NS 5953
Jacobstow (Corn.) 4 SX 1995
Jacobstowe (Devon) 4 SS 5801
Jameston 14 SS 0599
Jamestown (Dumf. and Galwy.) 46 NY 2996
Jamestown (Highld.) 60 NH 4756
Jamestown (Strath.) 50 NS 3981
Janetstown 67 ND 1932
Jarrow 47 NZ 3265
Jawcraig 50 NS 8475
Jaywick 21 TM 1513
Jedburgh 52 NT 6520
Jeffreyston 14 SN 0906
Jemimaville 65 NH 7165
Jevington 12 TQ 5601
Johnby 40 NY 4333
Johnshaven 57 NO 7966
Johnston (Dyfed) 14 SM 9310
Johnstone (Strath.) 50 NS 4263
Johnstonebridge 45 NY 1091
Jordans 19 SU 9791
Jordanston 14 SN 9132
Jump 38 SE 3701
Juniper Green 51 NT 2068
Jurby East 43 SC 3899
Jurby West 43 SC 3598

Kaber 41 NY 7911
Kaimes (Lothian) 51 NT 2767
Kames (Strath.) 54 NM 8211
Kames (Strath.) 49 NR 9771
Kames (Strath.) 50 NS 6926
Kea 2 SW 8042
Keadby 39 SE 8311
Keal 35 TF 3763
Keal Cotes 35 TF 3661
Kearsley 37 SD 7504
Kearstwick 41 SD 6079
Kearton 41 SD 9999
Keasden 36 SD 7266
Keddington (Lincs.) 35 TF 3388
Kedington (Suff.) 20 TL 7046
Kedleston 33 SK 2941
Keelby 39 TA 1610
Keele 32 SJ 8045
Keeley Green 27 TL 0046
Keeston 14 SM 9019
Keevil 17 ST 9157
Kegworth 34 SK 4826
Kehelland 2 SW 6241
Keig 62 NJ 6119
Keighley 37 SE 0641
Keilarsbrae 50 NS 8993
Keilhill 62 NJ 7259
Keillor 57 NO 2640
Keillour 56 NN 9725
Keilmore 48 NR 6880
Keils 48 NR 5268
Keinton Mandeville 7 ST 5430
Keir Mill 7 NX 8593
Keisby 35 TF 0328
Keiss 67 ND 3461
Keith 61 NJ 4350
Keithock 57 NO 6063
Kelbrook 37 SD 9044
Kelby 34 TF 0041
Keld (Cumbr.) 41 NY 5514
Keld (N Yorks.) 41 NY 8901
Keldholme 43 SE 7086
Kelfield 38 SE 5938
Kelham 34 SK 7755
Kellan 54 NM 5342
Kellas (Grampn.) 61 NJ 1654
Kellas (Tays.) 57 NO 4535
Kellaton 5 SX 8039
Kelleth 41 NY 6605
Kelling 29 TG 0942
Kellington 38 SE 5524
Kelloe 42 NZ 3435
Kelly 4 SX 3981
Kelly Bray 4 SX 3571
Kelmarsh 26 SP 7379
Kelmscot 18 SU 2499
Kelsale 29 TM 3865
Kelsall 32 SJ 5268
Kelshall 20 TL 3236
Kelso 53 NT 7333
Kelstern 35 TF 2590
Kelston 17 ST 6966
Keltneyburn (Tays.) 56 NN 7749
Kelty 51 NT 1494
Kelvedon 21 TL 8618
Kelvedon Hatch 20 TQ 5698
Kelynack 2 SW 3729
Kemback 57 NO 4115
Kemberton 24 SJ 7204
Kemble 17 ST 9897
Kemerton 25 SO 9437
Kemeys Commander 16 SO 3405
Kemnay 62 NJ 7315
Kemp Town 12 TQ 3303
Kempley 17 SO 6729
Kempsey 25 SO 8549
Kempsford 17 SU 1596
Kempston 27 TL 0347
Kempston Hardwick 27 TL 0244
Kempton 24 SO 3582
Kemsing 12 TQ 5558
Kenardington 13 TQ 9732
Kenchester 24 SO 4343
Kencot 18 SP 2504
Kendal 40 SD 5192
Kenderchurch 16 SO 4028
Kenfig 15 SS 8081
Kenfig Hill 15 SS 8483
Kenilworth 26 SP 2872
Kenley (Gtr London) 12 TQ 3259
Kenley (Salop) 24 SJ 5600
Kenmore (Highld.) 58 NG 7557
Kenmore (Tays.) 56 NN 7745
Kenn (Avon) 16 ST 4168
Kenn (Devon.) 5 SX 9285
Kennacley 63 NG 1794
Kennerleigh 5 SS 8107
Kennet 50 NS 9291
Kennethmont 61 NJ 5328
Kennett 28 TL 6968
Kennford 5 SX 9186
Kenninghall 29 TM 0386
Kennington (Kent) 13 TR 0245
Kennington (Oxon) 18 SP 5202
Kennoway 57 NO 3402
Kennyhill 28 TL 6680
Kennythorpe 38 SE 7865
Kenovay 48 NL 9946
Kensaleyre 58 NG 4251
Kensington and Chelsea 11 TQ 2778
Kensworth 19 TL 0318
Kensworth Common 19 TL 0317
Kent's Green 17 SO 7423
Kent's Oak 9 SU 3224
Kentallen 55 NN 0057
Kentchurch 16 SO 4125
Kentford 28 TL 7066
Kentisbeare 7 ST 0608
Kentisbury 6 SS 6144
Kentmere 40 NY 4504
Kenton (Devon.) 5 SX 9583
Kenton (Suff.) 29 TM 1965
Kentra 54 NM 6568
Kents Bank 40 SD 3975
Kenwick 32 SJ 4230
Kenwyn 2 SW 8145
Kenyon 32 SJ 6295
Keoldale 66 NC 3866
Keose 63 NB 3521
Keppanach 55 NN 0262
Keppoch 59 NG 9621
Kepwick 42 SE 4690
Keresley 26 SP 3182
Kerne Bridge 17 SO 5819
Kerridge 33 SJ 9376
Kerris 2 SW 4427
Kerry 23 SO 1490
Kerry's Gate 24 SO 3933
Kerrycroy 49 NS 1061
Kersall 34 SK 7162
Kersey 21 TM 0044
Kershader 63 NB 3419
Kershopefoot 46 NY 4782
Kersoe 25 SO 9939
Kerswell 7 ST 0806
Kerswell Green 25 SO 8646
Kesgrave 21 TM 2245
Kessingland 29 TM 5286
Kestle Mill 2 SW 8459

Keston Laneast

Keston 12 TQ4164
Keswick (Cumbr.) 40 NY2723
Keswick (Norf.) 29 TG2004
Keswick (Norf.) 29 TG3533
Kettering 27 SP8778
Ketteringham 29 TG1503
Kettins 56 NO2338
Kettlebaston 21 TL9650
Kettlebridge 57 NO3007
Kettlebrook 26 SK2103
Kettleburgh 29 TM2660
Kettleness 43 NZ8315
Kettleshulme 33 SJ9879
Kettlesing Bottom 37 SE2257
Kettlestone 29 TF9631
Kettlethorpe 34 SK8475
Kettlewell 37 SD9772
Ketton 27 SK9704
Kew 11 TQ1877
Kewstoke 16 ST3363
Kexbrough 38 SE3009
Kexby (Lincs.) 34 SK8785
Kexby (N Yorks.) 38 SE7050
Key Green 33 SJ8963
Keyham 26 SK6606
Keyhaven 9 SZ3091
Keymer 12 TQ3115
Keyingham 39 TA2425
Keynsham 17 ST6568
Keysoe 27 TL0763
Keysoe Row 27 TL0861
Keyston 27 TL0475
Keyworth 34 SK6130
Kibblesworth 47 NZ2456
Kibworth Beauchamp 26 SP6893
Kibworth Harcourt 26 SP6894
Kidbrooke 12 TQ4076
Kiddemore Green 25 SJ8509
Kidderminster 25 SO8376
Kiddington 18 SP4122
Kidlington 18 SP4913
Kidmore End 10 SU6979
Kidsgrove 32 SJ8354
Kidstones 41 SD9581
Kidwelly 15 SN4106
Kielder 46 NY6293
Kiells 48 NR4168
Kilbarchan 50 NS4063
Kilbeg 58 NG6506
Kilberry 48 NR7164
Kilbirnie 49 NS3154
Kilbride (S. Uist) 63 NF7514
Kilbride (Skye) 58 NG5820
Kilbride (Strath.) 54 NM8525
Kilburn (Derby.) 33 SK3845
Kilburn (N Yorks.) 42 SE5179
Kilby 26 SP6295
Kilcadzow 50 NS8848
Kilchattan (Bute) 49 NS1054
Kilchattan (Colonsay) 48 NR3795
Kilchenzie 48 NR6725
Kilcheran 54 NM8238
Kilchiaran 48 NR2060
Kilchoan 54 NM4963
Kilchoman 48 NR2163
Kilchrenan 55 NN0322
Kilconquhar 57 NO4802
Kilcot 17 SO6925
Kilcoy 60 NH5751
Kilcreggan 49 NS2380
Kildale 42 NZ6009
Kildalloig 48 NR7518
Kildavanan 49 NS0266
Kildonan (Highld.) 67 NC9121
Kildonan (Island of Arran) 49 NS0321
Kildonnan 54 NM4985
Kildrummy 61 NJ4617
Kildwick 37 SE0145
Kilfinan 49 NR9378
Kilfinnan 59 NN2795
Kilgetty 14 SN1207
Kilgwrrwg Common 16 ST4797
Kilham (Humbs.) 39 TA0564
Kilham (Northumb.) 53 NT8832
Kilkenneth 48 NL9444
Kilkerran 44 NS3003
Kilkhampton 4 SS2511
Killamarsh 34 SK4680
Killay 15 SS6092
Killchianaig 48 NR6486
Killean 48 NR6944
Killearn 50 NS5286
Killen 60 NH6758
Killerby 42 NZ1919
Killichonan 55 NN5458
Killichronan 54 NM5441
Killiechanate 55 NN2481
Killiecrankie 56 NN9162
Killilan 59 NG9430
Killimster 67 ND3156
Killin 55 NN5732
Killinghall 38 SE2858
Killingholm 39 TA1416
Killington 41 SD6188
Killochyett 52 NT4545
Killocraw 48 NB6630
Killundine 54 NM5849
Kilmacolm 50 NS3569
Kilmahumaig 49 NR7893
Kilmaluag 58 NG4374
Kilmany 57 NO3821
Kilmarie 58 NG5417
Kilmarnock 50 NS4237
Kilmaron Castle 57 NO3516
Kilmartin 54 NR8398
Kilmaurs 50 NS4141
Kilmelford 54 NM8413
Kilmeny 48 NR3865
Kilmersdon 17 ST6952
Kilmeston 9 SU5825
Kilmichael Glassary 49 NR8593
Kilmichael of Inverlussa 49 NR7785
Kilmington (Devon.) 7 SY2798
Kilmington (Wilts.) 8 ST7736
Kilmorack 60 NH4944
Kilmore (Island of Skye) 58 NG6507
Kilmore (Strath.) 54 NM8824
Kilmory (Highld.) 54 NM5270
Kilmory (Island of Arran) 49 NR9621
Kilmory (Rhum) 58 NG3603
Kilmory (Strath.) 48 NR7075
Kilmory Castle 49 NR8686
Kilmuir (Highld.) 60 NH6749
Kilmuir (Highld.) 65 NH7573
Kilmuir (Island of Skye) 58 NG2547
Kilmun 49 NS1781
Kiln Pit Hill 47 NZ0454
Kilnave 48 NR2871
Kilndown 12 TQ7035
Kilnhurst 38 SK4697
Kilninian 54 NM3945
Kilninver 54 NM8221
Kilnsea 39 TA4015
Kilnsey 37 SD9767
Kilnwick 39 SE9949
Kiloran 48 NR3996
Kilpatrick 49 NR9027
Kilpeck 24 SO4430
Kilpheder 63 NF7419
Kilphedir 67 NC9818
Kilpin 38 SE7726
Kilrenny 57 NO5705
Kilsby 26 SP5671
Kilspindie 56 NO2225
Kilsyth 50 NS7178
Kiltarlity 60 NH5041
Kilton 7 ST1644
Kilvaxter 58 NG3869
Kilve 7 ST1443
Kilvington 34 SK7942
Kilwinning 49 NS3043
Kimberley (Norf.) 29 TG0704
Kimberley (Notts.) 34 SK4944
Kimble 18 SP8206
Kimble Wick 18 SP8007
Kimblesworth 47 NZ2547
Kimbolton (Cambs.) 27 TL0967
Kimbolton (Here. and Worc.) 24 SO5261
Kimcote 26 SP5888
Kimmeridge 8 SY9179
Kimmerston 53 NT9535
Kimpton (Hants.) 10 SU2746
Kimpton (Herts.) 19 TL1718
Kinbrace 67 NC8631
Kinbuck 56 NN7905
Kincaple 57 NO4518
Kincardine (Fife.) 51 NS9387
Kincardine (Highld.) 65 NH6089
Kincardine O'Neil 62 NO5999
Kinclaven 56 NO1538
Kincorth 62 NJ9302
Kincraig 60 NH8305
Kincraigie 56 NN9849
Kindallachan 56 NN9950
Kineton (Glos.) 17 SP0926
Kineton (Warw.) 26 SP3351
Kinfauns 56 NO1622
King Sterndale 33 SK0972
King's Bromley 33 SK1216
King's Cliffe 27 TL0097
King's Coughton 25 SP0858
King's Delph 27 TL2595
King's Heath 25 SP0781
King's Lynn 28 TF6220
King's Norton (Leic.) 26 SK6800
King's Norton (W Mids) 25 SP0579
King's Nympton 5 SS6819
King's Pyon 24 SO4350
King's Somborne 9 SU3631
King's Stag 8 ST7210
King's Stanley 17 SO8103
King's Sutton 18 SP4936
King's Walden 19 TL1623
Kingarth 49 NS0956
Kingcoed 16 SO4205
Kingham 18 SP2523
Kingholm Quay 45 NX9773
Kinghorn 51 NT2686
Kinglassie 56 NT2298
Kingoodie 57 NO3329
Kings Caple 17 SO5628
Kings Langley 19 TL0702
Kings Meaburn 41 NY6221
Kings Muir (Borders) 51 NT2539
Kings Ripton 27 TL2576
Kings Worthy 9 SU4932
Kingsand 4 SX4350
Kingsbarns 57 NO5912
Kingsbridge (Devon.) 5 SX7344
Kingsbridge (Somer.) 7 SS9837
Kingsburgh 58 NG3955
Kingsbury (Gtr London) 19 TQ1989
Kingsbury (Warw.) 26 SP2196
Kingsbury Episcopi 7 ST4320
Kingsclere 10 SU5258
Kingscote 17 ST8196
Kingscott 4 SS5318
Kingscross 49 NS0428
Kingsdon 7 ST5126
Kingsdown 13 TR3748
Kingseat 51 NT1290
Kingsey 18 SP7406
Kingsfold 11 TQ1636
Kingsford 25 SO8281
Kingshall Street 28 TL9161
Kingshouse 55 NN5620
Kingskerswell 5 SX8767
Kingskettle 57 NO3008
Kingsland 24 SO4461
Kingsley (Ches) 32 SJ5474
Kingsley (Hants.) 10 SU7838
Kingsley (Staffs.) 33 SK0047
Kingsley Green 11 SU8930
Kingsmuir (Fife) 57 NO5409
Kingsmuir (Tays.) 57 NO4849
Kingsnorth 13 TR0039
Kingstanding 25 SP0794
Kingsteignton 5 SX8773
Kingsthorne 24 SO4932
Kingsthorpe 26 SP7563
Kingston (Cambs.) 20 TL3455
Kingston (Devon.) 5 SX6347
Kingston (Dorset) 8 ST7509
Kingston (Dorset) 8 SY9579
Kingston (Grampn.) 61 NJ3365
Kingston (Hants.) 8 SU1401
Kingston (I. of W.) 9 SZ4781
Kingston (Kent) 13 TR1951
Kingston (Lothian) 52 NT5482
Kingston Bagpuize 18 SU4098
Kingston Blount 18 SU7399
Kingston Deverill 8 ST8436
Kingston Lisle 18 SU3287
Kingston Russell 8 SY5891
Kingston Setmour 16 ST3966
Kingston St. Mary 7 ST2229
Kingston by Sea 11 TQ2205
Kingston near Lewes 12 TQ3908
Kingston on Soar 34 SK5027
Kingston upon Hull 39 TA0929
Kingston upon Thames 11 TQ1869
Kingstone (Here. and Worc.) 24 SO4235
Kingstone (Somer.) 7 ST3713
Kingstone (Staffs.) 33 SK0629
Kingstown 46 NY3959
Kingswear 5 SX8851
Kingswells 62 NJ8606
Kingswinford 25 SO8888
Kingswood (Avon) 17 ST6473
Kingswood (Bucks) 18 SP6819
Kingswood (Glos.) 17 ST7491
Kingswood (Kent) 13 TQ8351
Kingswood (Powys) 23 SJ2402
Kingswood (Surrey) 11 TQ2455
Kingswood (Warw.) 25 SP1871
Kingswood Common 23 SO2854
Kington (Here. and Worc.) 23 SO2956
Kington (Here. and Worc.) 25 SO9955
Kington Langley 17 ST9276
Kington Magna 8 ST7622
Kington St. Michael 17 ST9077
Kingussie 60 NH7500
Kingweston 7 ST5230
Kinharrachie (Grampn.) 62 NJ9231
Kinkell Bridge 56 NN9316
Kinknockie 62 NK0041
Kinlet 24 SO7280
Kinloch (Fife.) 57 NO2812
Kinloch (Highld.) 66 NC3434
Kinloch (Tays.) 56 NO1444
Kinloch (Tays.) 57 NO2644
Kinloch Hourn 59 NG9407
Kinloch Rannoch 56 NN6658
Kinlochard 55 NN4502
Kinlochbervie 66 NC2156
Kinlocheil 55 NM9779
Kinlochewe 64 NH0261
Kinlochleven 55 NN1861
Kinlochmore 55 NN1962
Kinloss 61 NJ0661
Kinmel Bay 31 SH9881
Kinmuck 62 NJ8119
Kinmundy 62 NJ8817
Kinnadie 62 NJ9643
Kinnaird 57 NO2428
Kinneff 57 NO8574
Kinnelhead 45 NT0201
Kinnell 57 NO6050
Kinnerley 32 SJ3321
Kinnersley (Here. and Worc.) 23 SO3449
Kinnersley (Here. and Worc.) 25 SO8743
Kinnerton (Ches.) 32 SJ3361
Kinnerton (Powys) 23 SO2463
Kinnesswood 56 NO1702
Kinninvie 41 NZ0521
Kinnordy 57 NO3654
Kinoulton 34 SK6730
Kinross 56 NO1102
Kinrossie 56 NO1832
Kinsham 24 SO3664
Kinsley 38 SE4114
Kinson 8 SZ0696
Kintbury 10 SU3866
Kintessack 61 NJ0060
Kintillo 56 NO1317
Kintocher 61 NJ5709
Kintore 62 NJ7916
Kintra 48 NR3248
Kinuachdrach Harbour 54 NR7098
Kinveachy 60 NH9118
Kinver 25 SO8433
Kippax 38 SE4130
Kippen 50 NS6594
Kippford or Scaur 45 NX8355
Kirbister (Orkney) 63 HY3607
Kirbuster 63 HY2825
Kirby Bedon 29 TG2705
Kirby Cane 29 TM3794
Kirby Cross 21 TM2120
Kirby Grindalythe 39 SE9067
Kirby Hill (N Yorks.) 42 NZ1306
Kirby Hill (N Yorks.) 38 SE3868
Kirby Knowle 42 SE4687
Kirby Mills 43 SE7185
Kirby Misperton 43 SE7779
Kirby Muxloe 26 SK5104
Kirby Row 29 TM3792
Kirby Sigston 42 SE4194
Kirby Underdale 39 SE8158
Kirby Wiske 42 SE3784
Kirby le Soken 21 TM2222
Kirdford 11 TQ0226
Kirivick 63 NB2041
Kirk 67 ND2859
Kirk Bramwith 38 SE6111
Kirk Connel (Dumf. and Galwy.) 50 NS7312
Kirk Deighton 38 SE3950
Kirk Ella 39 TA0129
Kirk Hallam 34 SK4540
Kirk Hammerton 38 SE4655
Kirk Ireton 33 SK2650
Kirk Langley 33 SK2838
Kirk Merrington 42 NZ2631
Kirk Michael (I. of M.) 43 SC3190
Kirk Sandall 38 SE6007
Kirk Smeaton 38 SE5116
Kirk Yetholm 53 NT8227
Kirk of Shotts 50 NS8462
Kirkabister 63 HU4938
Kirkandrews upon Eden 46 NY3558
Kirkbampton 46 NY3056
Kirkbean 45 NX9859
Kirkbride 46 NY2356
Kirkbuddo 57 NO5043
Kirkburn (Humbs.) 39 SE9855
Kirkburton 37 SE1912
Kirkby (Lincs.) 35 TF0692
Kirkby (Mers.) 36 SJ4098
Kirkby (N Yorks.) 42 NZ5306
Kirkby Bellars 34 SK7117
Kirkby Fleetham 42 SE2984
Kirkby Green 35 TF0857
Kirkby Lonsdale 41 SD6178
Kirkby Malham 37 SD8960
Kirkby Mallory 26 SK4500
Kirkby Malzeard 42 SE2374
Kirkby Overblow 38 SE3249
Kirkby Stephen 41 NY7708
Kirkby Thore 41 NY6325
Kirkby Underwood 35 TF0727
Kirkby in Ashfield 34 SK4956
Kirkby la Thorpe 35 TF0946
Kirkby on Bain 35 TF2362
Kirkbymoorside 43 SE6986
Kirkcaldy 51 NT2791
Kirkcambeck 46 NY5368
Kirkcarswell 45 NX7549
Kirkcolm 44 NX0268
Kirkcowan 44 NX3260
Kirkcudbright 45 NX6851
Kirkfieldbank 50 NS8643
Kirkgunzeon 45 NX8666
Kirkham (Lancs.) 36 SD4231
Kirkham (N Yorks.) 38 SE7365
Kirkhamgate 38 SE2922
Kirkharle 47 NZ0182
Kirkheaton (Northum.) 47 NZ0177
Kirkheaton (W Yorks.) 37 SE1817
Kirkhill (Highld.) 60 NH5545
Kirkhill (Tays.) 57 NO6860
Kirkhope (Borders) 51 NT3823
Kirkhouse 51 NT3233
Kirkibost (Island of Skye) 58 NG5417
Kirkibost (Lewis) 63 NB1835
Kirkinch 57 NO3144
Kirkinner 44 NX4251
Kirkintilloch 50 NS6573
Kirkland (Cumbr.) 40 NY0718
Kirkland (Cumbr.) 41 NY6432
Kirkland (Dumf. and Galwy.) 50 NS7214
Kirkland (Dumf. and Galwy.) 45 NX8090
Kirkleatham 42 NZ5921
Kirklevington 42 NZ4309
Kirkley 29 TM5491
Kirkleyditch 33 SJ8778
Kirklington (N Yorks.) 42 SE3181
Kirklington (Notts.) 34 SK6757
Kirklinton 46 NY4366
Kirkliston 51 NT1274
Kirkmaiden 44 NX1236
Kirkmichael (Strath.) 49 NS3408
Kirkmichael (Tays.) 56 NO0860
Kirkmond le Mire 39 TF1892
Kirkmuirhill 50 NS7943
Kirknewton (Lothian) 51 NT1166
Kirknewton (Northum.) 53 NT9130
Kirkoswald (Cumbr.) 46 NY5541
Kirkoswald (Strath.) 49 NS2407
Kirkpatrick Durham 45 NX7870
Kirkpatrick-Fleming 46 NY2770
Kirksanton 40 SD1380
Kirkstall 37 SE2635
Kirkstead 35 TF1762
Kirkstile (Dumf. and Galwy.) 46 NY3690
Kirkstile (Grampn.) 61 NJ5235
Kirkton (Borders) 52 NT5413
Kirkton (Dumf. and Galwy.) 45 NX9781
Kirkton (Fife.) 57 NO3625
Kirkton (Grampn.) 62 NJ6112
Kirkton (Grampn.) 62 NJ6425
Kirkton (Grampn.) 62 NJ6950
Kirkton (Grampn.) 62 NJ8243
Kirkton (Grampn.) 62 NK1050
Kirkton (Highld.) 59 NG9141
Kirkton (Highld.) 65 NH7998
Kirkton (Strath.) 51 NS9422
Kirkton (Tays.) 56 NN9618
Kirkton (Tays.) 57 NO4246
Kirkton Manor 51 NT2137
Kirkton of Airlie 57 NO3151
Kirkton of Auchterhouse 57 NO3338
Kirkton of Barevan 60 NH8347
Kirkton of Collace 56 NO1931
Kirkton of Craig 57 NO7055
Kirkton of Durris 62 NO7796
Kirkton of Glenbuchat 61 NJ3715
Kirkton of Glenisla 56 NO2160
Kirkton of Kingoldrum 57 NO3354
Kirkton of Largo 57 NO4203
Kirkton of Lethendy 56 NO1241
Kirkton of Logie Buchan 62 NJ9829
Kirkton of Maryculter 62 NO8599
Kirkton of Menmuir 57 NO5364
Kirkton of Monikie 57 NO5138
Kirkton of Rayne 62 NJ6930
Kirkton of Skene 62 NJ8007
Kirkton of Strathmartine 57 NO3735
Kirkton of Tealing 57 NO4037
Kirktown 62 NK0952
Kirktown of Alvah 62 NJ6760
Kirktown of Auchterless 62 NJ7141
Kirktown of Bourtie 62 NJ8024
Kirktown of Deskford 61 NJ5061
Kirktown of Fetteresso 57 NO8585
Kirkwall 63 HY4410
Kirkwhelpington 47 NY9984
Kirmington 39 TA1011
Kirn 49 NS1878
Kirriemuir 57 NO3854
Kirstead Green 29 TM2997
Kirtlebridge 46 NY2372
Kirtling 20 TL6857
Kirtling Green 20 TL6855
Kirtlington 18 SP4919
Kirtomy 66 NC7463
Kirton (Lincs.) 35 TF3038
Kirton (Notts.) 34 SK6869
Kirton (Suff.) 21 TM2739
Kirton End 35 TF2840
Kirton Holme 35 TF2642
Kirton in Lindsey 39 SK9398
Kishorn 59 NG8340
Kislingbury 26 SP6959
Kites Hardwick 26 SP4668
Kittybrewster 62 NJ9208
Kitwood 9 SU6633
Kiveton Park 34 SK4982
Knaith 34 SK8284
Knap Corner 8 ST8023
Knaphill 11 SU9658
Knapp (Somer.) 7 ST3025
Knapp (Tays) 57 NO2831
Knapton (N Yorks.) 38 SE5652
Knapton (N Yorks.) 43 SE8775
Knapton (Norf.) 29 TG3034
Knapwell 27 TL3362
Knaresborough 38 SE3557
Knarsdale 46 NY6753
Knaven 62 NJ8943
Knayton 42 SE4387
Knebworth 19 TL2520
Kneesall 34 SK7064
Kneesworth 20 TL3444
Kneeton 34 SK7146
Knelston 15 SS4689
Knightacott 6 SS6439
Knightcote 26 SP3954
Knighton (Devon.) 5 SX5249
Knighton (Leic.) 26 SK6001
Knighton (Powys) 23 SO2872
Knighton (Staffs.) 32 SJ7240
Knighton (Staffs.) 32 SJ7427
Knightwick 24 SO7355
Knill 23 SO2960
Knipton 34 SK8231
Knitsley 47 NZ1148
Kniveton 33 SK2050
Knock (Cumbr.) 41 NY6826
Knock (Grampn.) 61 NJ5452
Knock (Island of Mull) 54 NM5438
Knock (Isle of Lewis) 63 NB4931
Knockally 67 ND1428
Knockan 66 NC2110
Knockando 61 NJ1941
Knockbain 60 NH6255
Knockbrex 45 NX5849
Knockdee 67 ND1761
Knockdolian 44 NX1285
Knockenkelly 49 NS0426
Knockentiber 50 NS3939
Knockholt 12 TQ4658
Knockholt Pound 12 TQ4859
Knockie Lodge 60 NH4413
Knockin 32 SJ3322
Knocknaha 48 NR6817
Knockrome 48 NR5571
Knocksharry 43 SC2785
Knodishall 29 TM4261
Knolls Green 32 SJ8079
Knolton 32 SJ3738
Knook 8 ST9341
Knossington 26 SK8008
Knott End-on-Sea 36 SD3548
Knotting 27 TL0063
Knottingley 38 SE5023
Knotty Green 19 SU9392
Knowbury 24 SO5774
Knowe 44 NX3171
Knowehead 45 NX6090
Knowesgate 47 NY9885
Knoweside 49 NS2512
Knowetownhead 52 NT5418
Knowl Hill 10 SU8279
Knowle (Avon) 17 ST6170
Knowle (Devon.) 6 SS4938
Knowle (Devon.) 5 SS7801
Knowle (W Mids) 25 SP1876
Knowle Green 36 SD6337
Knowlton 13 TR2853
Knowsley 32 SJ4395
Knowstone 6 SS8223
Knucklas 23 SO2574
Knutsford 32 SJ7578
Knypersley 33 SJ8856
Kyle of Lochalsh 59 NG7627
Kyleakin 58 NG7526
Kylerhea 59 NG7820
Kylesmorar 59 NM8093
Kylestrome 66 NC2234
Kyloe 53 NU0540
Kynnersley 32 SJ6716
Kyre Park 24 SO6263

Labost 63 NB2748
Laceby 39 TA2106
Lacey Green 18 SP8200
Lach Dennis 32 SJ7071
Lackalee 63 NG1292
Lackford 28 TL7970
Lacock 17 ST9168
Ladbroke 26 SP4158
Laddingford 12 TQ6948
Lade Bank 35 TF3954
Ladock 2 SW8950
Ladybank (Fife.) 57 NO3009
Ladybank (Strath.) 44 NS2102
Ladykirk 53 NT8847
Ladysford 62 NJ9060
Lagavulin 48 NR4045
Lagg (Island of Arran) 49 NR9521
Lagg (Jura) 48 NR5978
Laggan (Highld.) 59 NN2997
Laggan (Highld.) 60 NN6194
Lagganulva 54 NM4541
Laid 66 NC4159
Laide 64 NG8992
Laindon 20 TQ6889
Lair 59 NH0148
Lairg 66 NC5806
Lake 8 SU1239
Lake Side 40 SD3787
Lakenham 29 TG2307
Lakenheath 28 TL7182
Lakesend 28 TL5196
Laleham 11 TQ0568
Laleston 15 SS8779
Lamarsh 21 TL8935
Lamas 29 TG2423
Lamberhurst 12 TQ6735
Lamberton 53 NT9657
Lambeth 12 TQ3074
Lambfell Moar 43 SC2984
Lambley (Northum.) 46 NY6758
Lambley (Notts.) 34 SK6245
Lambourn 10 SU3278
Lambourne End 20 TQ4894
Lambs Green 11 TQ2136
Lambston 14 SM9016
Lamerton 4 SX4476
Lamesley 47 NZ2557
Lamington (Highld.) 65 NH7577
Lamington (Strath.) 51 NS9730
Lamlash 49 NS0231
Lamonby 40 NY4135
Lamorna 2 SW4524
Lamorran 2 SW8741
Lampeter 22 SN5748
Lampeter-Velfrey 14 SN1514
Lamphey 14 SN0100
Lamplugh 40 NY0820
Lamport 26 SP7574
Lamyatt 8 ST6535
Lana 4 SX3496
Lanark 50 NS8843
Lancaster 36 SD4761
Lanchester 47 NZ1647
Landbeach 28 TL4765
Landcross 4 SS4524
Landerberry 62 NJ7404
Landewednack 2 SW7012
Landford 9 SU2519
Landimore 15 SS4693
Landkey 6 SS5931
Landore 15 SS6595
Landrake 4 SX3760
Landscove 5 SX7766
Landshipping 14 SN0211
Landulph 4 SX4261
Landwade 28 TL6268
Landywood 25 SJ9806
Lane End 18 SU8091
Lane Green 25 SJ8802
Laneast 4 SX2283

Laneham Llanbedr-y-cennin

Laneham 34 SK8076
Laneshawbridge 37 SD9240
Langar 34 SK7234
Langbank 50 NS3873
Langbar 37 SE0951
Langcliffe 37 SD8264
Langdale End 43 SE9391
Langdon Hills 20 TQ6786
Langdyke 57 NO3304
Langenhoe 21 TM0018
Langford (Beds.) 27 TL1841
Langford (Devon.) 7 ST0203
Langford (Essex) 20 TL8408
Langford (Notts.) 34 SK8258
Langford (Oxon.) 18 SP2402
Langford Budville 7 ST1122
Langford End 27 TL1654
Langham (Essex) 21 TM0233
Langham (Leic.) 27 SK8411
Langham (Norf.) 29 TG0041
Langham (Suff.) 29 TL9769
Langho 36 SD7034
Langholm 46 NY3684
Langley (Berks.) 11 TQ0078
Langley (Ches.) 33 SJ9471
Langley (Essex) 20 TL4435
Langley (Hants.) 9 SU4400
Langley (Herts.) 19 TL2122
Langley (Kent) 12 TQ8051
Langley (W Susx) 10 SU8029
Langley (Warw.) 25 SP1962
Langley Burrell 17 ST9275
Langley Hill 17 SP0028
Langley Marsh 7 ST0729
Langley Park 47 NZ2144
Langley Street 29 TG3601
Langney 12 TQ6302
Langold 34 SK5887
Langore 4 SX3086
Langport 7 ST4226
Langrick 35 TF2648
Langridge 17 ST7369
Langrigg 45 NY1645
Langrish 10 SU7023
Langsett 37 SE2100
Langshaw 52 NT5139
Langstone 9 SU7104
Langthorne 42 SE2491
Langthorpe 38 SE3867
Langthwaite 41 NZ0002
Langtoft (Humbs.) 39 TA0166
Langtoft (Lincs.) 27 TF1212
Langton (Durham) 42 NZ1719
Langton (Lincs.) 35 TF2368
Langton (Lincs.) 35 TF3970
Langton (N Yorks.) 38 SE7967
Langton Green 12 TQ5439
Langton Herring 8 SY6182
Langton Matravers 8 SY9978
Langton by Wragby 35 TF1476
Langtree 4 SS4415
Langwathby 41 NY5733
Langworth 35 TF0676
Lanivet 3 SX0364
Lanlivery 3 SX0759
Lanner 2 SW7139
Lanreath 4 SX1756
Lansallos 4 SX1751
Lanteglos Highway 4 SX1453
Lanton (Borders) 52 NT6221
Lanton (Northum.) 53 NT9231
Lapford 5 SS7308
Laphroaig 48 NR3845
Lapley 25 SJ8713
Lapworth 25 SP1671
Larachbeg 54 NM6948
Larbert 50 NS8582
Largie 62 NJ6131
Largiemore 49 NR9486
Largoward 57 NO4607
Largs 49 NS2058
Largybeg 49 NS0423
Largymore 49 NS0424
Larkfield 49 NS2376
Larkhall 50 NS7651
Larkhill 8 SU1243
Larling 29 TL9889
Larriston 46 NY5494
Lartington 41 NZ0117
Lasham 10 SU6742
Lassodie 51 NT1292
Lasswade 51 NT3066
Lastingham 43 SE7290
Latchingdon 21 TL8800
Latchley 4 SX4173
Lately Common 36 SJ6797
Lathbury 27 SP8745
Latheron 67 ND1933
Lathones 57 NO4708
Latimer 19 TQ0099
Latteridge 17 ST6684
Lattiford 8 ST6926
Latton 17 SU0995
Lauder 52 NT5347
Laugharne 14 SN3011
Laughterton 34 SK8375
Laughton (E Susx) 12 TQ4913
Laughton (Leic.) 26 SP6589
Laughton (Lincs.) 34 SK8497
Laughton-en-le-Morthen 34 SK5188
Launcells 4 SS2405
Launceston 4 SX3384
Launton 18 SP6022
Laurencekirk 57 NO7171
Laurieston 45 NX6864
Lavant 11 SU8608
Lavendon 27 SP9153
Lavenham 21 TL9149
Laverhay 45 NY1498
Laverstock 8 SU1530
Laverstoke 10 SU4948
Laverton (Glos.) 25 SP0735
Laverton (N Yorks) 42 SE2273
Laverton (Somer.) 17 ST7753
Law 50 NS8252
Lawers (Tays.) 56 NN6739
Lawford 21 TM0830
Lawhitton 4 SX3582
Lawkland 37 SD7766
Lawley 24 SJ6608
Lawnhead 32 SJ8224
Lawrenny 14 SN0107
Lawshall 21 TL8654
Lawton 24 SO4459
Laxay 63 NB3321
Laxdale 63 NB4234
Laxey 43 SC4384
Laxfield 29 TM2972
Laxford Bridge 66 NC2347
Laxo 63 HU4463
Laxobigging 63 HU4172
Laxton (Humbs.) 38 SE7825
Laxton (Northants.) 27 SP9496
Laxton (Notts.) 34 SK7266
Laycock 37 SE0340
Layer Breton 21 TL9417
Layer-de-la-Haye 21 TL9620
Layham 21 TM0340
Layland's Green 10 SU3866
Laysters Pole 24 SO5563
Laytham 38 SE7439
Lazenby 42 NZ5719
Lazonby 41 NY5439
Lea (Derby.) 33 SK3357
Lea (Here. and Worc.) 17 SO6521
Lea (Lincs.) 34 SK8286
Lea (Salop) 24 SJ4108
Lea (Salop) 24 SO3589
Lea (Wilts.) 17 ST9586
Lea Marston 26 SP2093
Lea Town 36 SD4930
Leayeat 41 SD7587
Leachkin 60 NH6344
Leadburn 51 NT2355
Leaden Roding 20 TL5913
Leadenham 34 SK9452
Leadgate (Cumbr.) 46 NY7043
Leadgate (Durham) 47 NZ1251
Leadhills 50 NS8814
Leafield 18 SP3115
Leake Common Side 35 TF3952
Leake Hurn's End 35 TF4248
Lealholm 43 NZ7607
Lealt (Island of Skye) 58 NG5060
Leamington Hastings 26 SP4467
Leargybreck 48 NR5371
Learmouth 53 NT8537
Leasgill 40 SD4984
Leasingham 35 TF0548
Leask 62 NK0232
Leatherhead 11 TQ1656
Leathley 37 SE2346
Leaton 32 SJ4618
Leaveland 13 TQ9854
Leavening 38 SE7863
Leaves Green 12 TQ4162
Lebberston 43 TA0882
Lechlade 18 SU2199
Leckford 10 SU3737
Leckfurin 66 NC7059
Leckgruinart 48 NR2769
Leckhampstead (Berks.) 10 SU4375
Leckhampstead (Bucks.) 18 SP7237
Leckhampton 17 SO9419
Leckmelm 64 NH1690
Leckwith 16 ST1574
Leconfield 39 TA0143
Ledaig 54 NM9037
Ledburn 19 SP9022
Ledbury 24 SO7037
Ledgemoor 24 SO4150
Ledicot 24 SO4162
Ledmore Junction 66 NC2412
Ledsham (Ches.) 32 SJ3574
Ledsham (W Yorks.) 38 SE4529
Ledston 38 SE4328
Ledwell 18 SP4128
Lee (Devon.) 6 SS4846
Lee (Hants.) 9 SU3617
Lee (Island of Mull) 54 NM4022
Lee (Lancs.) 36 SD5655
Lee (Salop) 32 SJ4032
Lee Brockhurst 32 SJ5426
Lee Clump 19 SP9004
Lee Green 32 SJ6561
Lee Moor 4 SX5862
Lee, The 19 SP9904
Lee-on-the-Solent 9 SU5600
Leebotwood 24 SO4798
Leece 36 SD2469
Leeds (Kent) 12 TQ8253
Leeds (W Yorks.) 38 SE3034
Leedstown 2 SW6034
Leek 33 SJ9856
Leek Wootton 26 SP2868
Leeming 42 SE2989
Leeming bar 42 SE2889
Lees (Derby.) 33 SK2637
Lees (Gtr Mches) 37 SD9504
Leeswood 31 SJ2759
Legbourne 35 TF3684
Legerwood 52 NT5843
Legsby 35 TF1385
Leicester 26 SK5904
Leicester Forest East 26 SK5203
Leigh (Dorset) 8 St6108
Leigh (Glos.) 17 SO8725
Leigh (Gtr Mches) 36 SJ6699
Leigh (Here. and Worc.) 24 SO7853
Leigh (Kent) 12 TQ5546
Leigh (Salop) 23 SJ3303
Leigh (Surrey) 11 TQ2246
Leigh (Wilts.) 17 SU0692
Leigh Beck 20 TQ8182
Leigh Common 8 ST7329
Leigh Delamere 17 ST8879
Leigh Green 13 TQ8933
Leigh Sinton 24 SO7750
Leigh Woods 16 ST5572
Leigh upon Mendip 8 ST6847
Leigh-on-Sea 20 TQ8385
Leighterton 17 ST8290
Leighton (Poweys) 23 SJ2405
Leighton (Salop) 24 SJ6105
Leighton (Somer.) 8 ST7043
Leighton Bromswold 27 TL1175
Leighton Buzzard 19 SP9225
Leinthall Earls 24 SO4467
Leinthall Starkes 24 SO4369
Leintwardine 24 SO4074
Leire 26 SP5290
Leirinmore 66 NC4267
Leishmore 60 NH3940
Leiston 29 TM4462
Leitfie 57 NO2545
Leith 51 NT2676
Leitholm 53 NT7944
Lelant 2 SW5437
Lelley 39 TA2032
Lem Hill 24 SO7274
Lempitlaw 53 NT7832
Lemreway 63 NB3711
Lendalfoot 44 NX1390
Lenham 13 TQ8952
Lenham Heath 13 TQ9249
Lenie 60 NH5127
Lennel 53 NT8540
Lennoxtown 50 NS6277
Lenton 34 TF0230
Lenwade 29 TG0918
Lenzie 50 NS6571
Leoch 57 NO3638
Leochel-Cushnie 61 NJ5210
Leominster 24 SO4959
Leonard Stanley 17 SO8003
Lepe 9 SZ4498
Leperstone Resr 50 NS3571
Lephin 58 NG1749
Lephinmore 49 NR9892
Leppington 38 SE7661
Lepton 37 SE2015
Lerryn 4 SX1356
Lerwick (Shetld.) 63 HU4741
Lesbury 53 NU2311
Leslie (Fife.) 57 NO2401
Leslie (Grampn.) 62 NJ5924
Lesmahagow 50 NS8139
Lesnewth 4 SX1390
Lessingham 29 TG3928
Lessonhall 46 NY2250
Leswalt 44 NX0263
Letchmore Heath 19 TQ1597
Letchworth 19 TL2132
Letcombe Bassett 18 SU3785
Letcombe Regis 18 SU3786
Letham (Fife.) 57 NO3014
Letham (Tays.) 57 NO5248
Letham Grange 57 NO6245
Lethenty 62 NJ8041
Letheringham 21 TM2757
Letheringsett 29 TG0638
Lettaford 5 SX7084
Letterewe 64 NG9571
Letterfearn 59 NG8823
Lettermore 54 NM4948
Letters 64 NH1687
Letterston 14 SM9429
Lettoch 61 NJ0932
Letton (Here. and Worc.) 23 SO3346
Letton (Here. and Worc.) 24 SO3770
Letty Green 19 TL2810
Letwell 34 SK5587
Leuchars 57 NO4521
Leurbost 63 NB3725
Levedale 33 SJ8916
Leven (Fife.) 57 NO3700
Leven (Humbs.) 39 TA1045
Levens 40 SD4886
Levenshulme 33 SJ8794
Levenwick 63 HU4021
Leverburgh 63 NG0186
Leverington 27 TF4410
Leverton 35 TF3947
Levington 21 TM2339
Levisham 43 SE8390
Lew 18 SP3206
Lewannick 4 SX2780
Lewdown 4 SX4486
Lewes 12 TQ4110
Leweston 14 SM9422
Lewisham 12 TQ3674
Lewiston 60 NH5029
Lewknor 18 SU7197
Leworthy 6 SS6638
Lewtrenchard 4 SX4586
Ley (Corn.) 4 SX1766
Ley (Grampn.) 61 NJ5312
Leybourne 12 TQ6858
Leyburn 41 SE1190
Leycett 32 SJ7846
Leyland 36 SD5421
Leylodge 62 NJ7713
Leys (Grampn.) 62 NK0052
Leys (Tays.) 57 NO2537
Leys of Cossans 57 NO3749
Leysdown-on-Sea 13 TR0370
Leysmill 57 NO6047
Leyton 20 TQ3886
Lezant 4 SX3378
Lhanbryde 61 NJ2761
Lhen, The 43 NX3801
Libberton 51 NS9943
Liberton 51 NT2769
Lichfield 25 SK1209
Lickey 25 SO0075
Lickey End 25 So9772
Lickfold 11 SU9225
Liddel 63 ND4683
Liddington 18 SU2081
Lidgate 20 TL7258
Lidlington 19 SP9939
Lidstone 18 SP3524
Liff 57 NO3332
Lifton 4 SX3885
Lighthazles 37 SE0220
Lighthorne 26 SP3355
Lightwater 11 SU9262
Lightwood 33 SJ9041
Lightwood Green 32 SJ3840
Lilbourne 26 SP5677
Lilleshall 32 SJ7315
Lilley 19 TL1226
Lilliesleaf 52 NT5325
Lillingstone Dayrell 18 SP7039
Lillingstone Lovell 26 SP7140
Lillington 8 ST6212
Lilstock 7 ST1644
Limbrick 36 SD6016
Limefield 37 SD8012
Limekilnburn 50 NS7050
Limekilns 51 NT0783
Limerigg 50 NS8570
Limington 7 ST5422
Limpenhoe 29 TG3903
Limpley Stoke 17 ST7760
Limpsfield 12 TQ4152
Linby 34 SK5350
Linchmere 11 SU8630
Lincoln 34 SK9771
Lincomb 25 SO8268
Lincombe 5 SX7458
Lindal in Furness 40 SD2575
Lindale 40 SD4180
Lindean 52 NT4931
Lindfield 12 TQ3425
Lindford 10 SU8136
Lindores 57 NO2616
Lindridge 24 SO6769
Lindsell 20 TL6427
Lindsey 21 TL9744
Linford (Essex) 12 TQ6779
Linford (Hants.) 8 SU1707
Lingague 43 SC2172
Lingdale 42 NZ6716
Lingen 24 SO3667
Lingfield 12 TQ3943
Lingwood 29 TG3609
Liniclett 63 NF7949
Linicro 58 NG3967
Linkenholt 10 SU3657
Linkinhorne 4 SX3173
Linksness (Hoy) 63 HY2403
Linktown 51 NT2790
Linley 24 SO3593
Linley Green 24 SO6953
Linlithgow 51 NS9977
Linlithgow Bridge 51 NS9877
Linshader (Isle of Lewis) 63 NB2031
Linsidemore 65 NH5498
Linslade 19 SP9125
Linstead Parva 29 TM3377
Linstock 46 NY4258
Linthwaite 37 SE0913
Lintlaw 53 NT8258
Lintmill 61 NJ5165
Linton (Borders) 53 NT7726
Linton (Cambs.) 20 TL5646
Linton (Derby.) 33 SK2716
Linton (Here. and Worc.) 17 SO6625
Linton (Kent) 12 TQ7550
Linton (N Yorks.) 37 SD9962
Linton-on-Ouse 38 SE4960
Linwood (Hants.) 8 SU1809
Linwood (Lincs.) 35 TF1186
Linwood (Strath.) 50 NS4464
Lionel 63 NB5263
Liphook 10 SU8431
Liscombe 6 SS8732
Liskeard 4 SX2564
Liss 10 SU7727
Liss Forest 10 SU7929
Lissett 39 TA1458
Lissington 35 TF1083
Lisvane 16 ST1983
Liswerry 16 ST3487
Litcham 28 TF8817
Litchborough 26 SP6354
Litchfield 10 SU4553
Litherland 36 SJ3397
Litlington (Cambs.) 20 TL3142
Litlington (E Susx) 12 TQ5201
Little Abington 20 TL5349
Little Addington 27 SP9573
Little Alne 25 SP1361
Little Amwell 20 TL3511
Little Aston 25 SK0900
Little Atherfield 9 SZ4680
Little Ayre 63 ND3091
Little Ayton 42 NZ5710
Little Baddow 20 TL7807
Little Badminton 17 ST8084
Little Ballinluig 56 NN9152
Little Bardfield 20 TL6530
Little Barford 27 TL1857
Little Barningham 29 TG1333
Little Barrington 18 SP2012
Little Barugh 43 SE7579
Little Bedwyn 10 SU2966
Little Bentley 21 TM1125
Little Berkhamsted 19 TL2907
Little Billing 26 SP8061
Little Birch 24 SO5031
Little Blakenham 21 TM1048
Little Bowden 26 SP7487
Little Bradley 20 TL6852
Little Brampton 24 SO3681
Little Brechin 57 NO5862
Little Brickhill 19 SP9032
Little Brington 26 SP6663
Little Bromley 21 TM0928
Little Budworth 32 SJ5965
Little Burstead 20 TQ6691
Little Bytham 34 TF0118
Little Carlton 35 TF3985
Little Casterton 27 TF0109
Little Cawthorpe 35 TF3583
Little Chalfont 19 SU9997
Little Chart 13 TQ9245
Little Chesterford 20 TL5141
Little Cheverell 17 ST9853
Little Chishill 20 TL4237
Little Clacton 21 TM1618
Little Comberton 25 SO9643
Little Common 12 TQ7107
Little Compton 18 SP2530
Little Cowarne 24 SO6051
Little Coxwell 18 SU2893
Little Cressingham 28 TF8600
Little Dalby 34 SK7714
Little Dens 62 NK0744
Little Dewchurch 24 SO5231
Little Dunham 28 TF8613
Little Dunkeld 56 NO0242
Little Dunmow 20 TL6521
Little Easton 20 TL6023
Little Eaton 33 SK3641
Little Ellingham 29 TM0099
Little End 20 TL5400
Little Eversden 20 TL3752
Little Fakenham 28 TL9076
Little Faringdon 18 SP2201
Little Fenton 38 SE5135
Little Fransham 28 TF9011
Little Gaddesden 19 SP9913
Little Garway 16 SO4424
Little Gidding 27 TL1382
Little Glemham 21 TM3458
Little Gransden 27 TL2755
Little Gruinard 64 NG9484
Little Hadham 20 TL4422
Little Hallingbury 20 TL5017
Little Harrowden 27 SP8771
Little Haseley 18 SP6400
Little Hautbois 29 TG2521
Little Haven 14 SM8513
Little Hay 25 SK1202
Little Haywood 33 SK0021
Little Hereford 24 SO5568
Little Hill 23 SO1267
Little Horkesley 21 TL9531
Little Horsted 12 TQ4718
Little Horwood 18 SP7930
Little Houghton (Northants.) 26 SP8059
Little Hucklow 33 SK1678
Little Hulton 36 SD7103
Little Kingshill 19 SU8999
Little Langford 8 SU0436
Little Laver 20 TL5409
Little Leigh 32 SJ6175
Little Leighs 20 TL7116
Little Lever 37 SD7507
Little London (E Susx) 12 TQ5420
Little London (Hants.) 10 SU3749
Little London (Hants.) 10 SU6259
Little London (Lincs.) 35 TF2321
Little Longstone 33 SK1871
Little Malvern 24 SO7741
Little Maplestead 20 TL8233
Little Marcle 24 SO6736
Little Marlow 19 SU8788
Little Massingham 28 TF7924
Little Melton 29 TG1506
Little Mill (Gwent) 16 SO3102
Little Milton 18 SP6100
Little Missenden 19 SU9298
Little Ness (Salop) 32 SJ4019
Little Newcastle 14 SM9829
Little Newsham 41 NZ1217
Little Oakley (Essex) 21 TM2229
Little Oakley (Northants.) 27 SP8985
Little Orton 46 NY3555
Little Paxton 27 TL1862
Little Petherick 2 SW9172
Little Plumstead 29 TG3112
Little Raveley 27 TL2579
Little Ribston 38 SE3853
Little Rissington 17 SP1819
Little Ryburgh 29 TF9628
Little Ryle 53 NU0211
Little Salkeld 41 NY5636
Little Sampford 20 TL6533
Little Saxham 28 TL7963
Little Scatwell 59 NH3756
Little Shelford 20 TL4551
Little Smeaton 38 SE5219
Little Snoring 29 TF9532
Little Somerford 17 ST9684
Little Stainton 42 NZ3420
Little Stanney 32 SJ4173
Little Staughton 27 TL1062
Little Steeping 35 TF4362
Little Stonham 29 TM1160
Little Stretton (Leic.) 26 SK6600
Little Stretton (Salop) 24 SO4491
Little Strickland 41 NY5619
Little Stukeley 27 TL2075
Little Tew 18 SP3828
Little Thetford 28 TL5376
Little Thurrock 12 TQ6477
Little Torrington 4 SS4816
Little Totham 21 TL8812
Little Town (Cumbr.) 40 NY2319
Little Wakering 21 TQ9388
Little Walden 20 TL5441
Little Waldingfield 21 TL9245
Little Walsingham 29 TF9336
Little Waltham 20 TL7012
Little Warley 20 TQ6090
Little Weighton 39 SE9833
Little Welnetham 21 TL8859
Little Wenlock 24 SJ6406
Little Whittingham Green 29 TM2877
Little Wilbraham 20 TL5458
Little Witley 24 SO7863
Little Wittenham 18 SU5693
Little Wolford 18 SP2635
Little Wyrley 25 SK0105
Little Yeldham 20 TL7739
Littleborough (Gtr Mches) 37 SD9316
Littleborough (Notts.) 34 SK8282
Littlebourne 13 TR2057
Littlebredy 8 SY5888
Littlebury 20 TL5139
Littlebury Green 20 TL4938
Littledean 17 SO6713
Littleferry 65 NH8095
Littleham (Devon.) 6 SS4323
Littleham (Devon.) 7 SY0281
Littlehampton 11 TQ0202
Littlehempston 5 SX8162
Littlehoughton (Northum.) 53 NU2316
Littlemill (Highld.) 61 NH9150
Littlemill (Strath.) 50 NS4515
Littlemore 18 SP5302
Littleover 33 SK3234
Littleport 28 TL5686
Littlestone-on-Sea 13 TR0824
Littlethorpe 38 SE3269
Littleton (Ches.) 32 SJ4366
Littleton (Hants) 10 SU4532
Littleton (Somer.) 7 ST4830
Littleton (Surrey) 11 TQ0768
Littleton (Tays.) 57 NO2633
Littleton Drew 17 ST8280
Littleton Pannell 17 ST9954
Littleton-on-Severn 17 ST5990
Littletown (Durham) 47 NZ3343
Littlewick Green 10 SU8379
Littleworth (Here. and Worc.) 25 SO8850
Littleworth (Oxon.) 18 SU3197
Littleworth (Staffs.) 25 SK0111
Litton (Derby) 33 SK1674
Litton (N Yorks.) 41 SD9074
Litton (Somer.) 17 ST5954
Litton Cheney 7 SY5490
Liverpool 32 SJ3591
Liversedge 37 SE2024
Liverton 43 NZ7115
Livingston 51 NT0568
Livingston Village 51 NT0366
Lixwm 31 SJ1617
Lizard 2 SW6912
Llanaber 30 SH6018
Llanaehaearn 30 SH3844
Llanafan 22 SN6872
Llanafan-fechan 23 SN9650
Llanallgo 30 SH5085
Llanarmon 30 SH4239
Llanarmon Dyffryn Ceirog 31 SJ1532
Llanarmon-yn-Ial 31 SJ1856
Llanarth (Dyfed) 22 SN4257
Llanarth (Gwent.) 16 SO3711
Llanarthney 15 SN5320
Llanasa 31 SJ1081
Llanbabo 30 SH3786
Llanbadarn Fawr 22 SN6080
Llanbadarn Fynydd 23 SO0977
Llanbadarn-y-garreg 23 SO1148
Llanbadrig 30 SH3794
Llanbeder 16 ST3890
Llanbedr (Gwyn.) 30 SH5826
Llanbedr (Powys) 23 SO1346
Llanbedr (Powys) 16 SO2320
Llanbedr-Dyffryn-Clwyd 31 SJ1459
Llanbedr-y-cennin 30 SH7659

Llanbedrgoch Ludford

Llanbedrgoch 30 SH5180
Llanbedrog 30 SH3231
Llanberis 30 SH5760
Llanbister 23 SO1073
Llanblethian 16 SS9873
Llanbodwel 31 SJ2423
Llanboidy 14 SN2123
Llanbradach 16 ST1490
Llanbrynmair 22 SH9002
Llancarfan 16 ST0570
Llancayo 16 SO3603
Llancynfelyn 22 SN6492
Llandaff 16 ST1578
Llandanwg 30 SH5728
Llandawke 14 SN2811
Llanddaniel Fab 30 SH4970
Llanddarog 15 SN5016
Llanddeiniol 22 SN5672
Llanddeiniolen 30 SH5465
Llandderfel 31 SH9837
Llanddeusant (Dyfed) 15 SN7724
Llanddeusant (Gwyn.) 30 SH3485
Llanddew 23 SO0530
Llanddewi 15 SS4689
Llanddewi Brefi 22 SN6655
Llanddewi Rhydderch 16 SO3412
Llanddewi Velfrey 14 SN1417
Llanddewi Ystradenni 23 SO1068
Llanddewi'r Cwm 23 SO0348
Llanddoget 31 SH8063
Llanddona 30 SH5779
Llanddowror 14 SN2514
Llanddulas 31 SH9078
Llanddyfnan 30 SH5078
Llandebie 15 SN6215
Llandefaelog 15 SN4111
Llandefaelog Fach 23 SO0322
Llandefaelog-te'r-graig 23 SO1230
Llandefalle 23 SO1135
Llandegai 30 SH5970
Llandegfan 30 SH5674
Llandegla 31 SJ1952
Llandegley 23 SO1363
Llandegveth 16 ST3395
Llandeilo 15 SN6322
Llandeilo Graban 23 SO0944
Llandeilo'r Fan 15 SN8943
Llandeloy 14 SM8526
Llandenny 16 SO4104
Llandevenny 16 ST4186
Llandinabo 16 SO5128
Llandinam 23 SO0288
Llandissilio 14 SN1221
Llandogo 16 SO5204
Llandough (S Glam.) 16 SS9972
Llandough (S Glam.) 16 ST1673
Llandovery 15 SN7634
Llandow 15 SS9473
Llandre (Dyfed) 22 SN6286
Llandre (Dyfed) 22 SN6642
Llandrillo 31 SJ0337
Llandrillo-yn-Rhos 31 SH8380
Llandrindod Wells 23 SO0561
Llandrinio 31 SJ2917
Llandudno 31 SH7782
Llandudno Junction 31 SH7977
Llandwrog 30 SH4556
Llandyfan 15 SN6417
Llandyfodwg 15 SS9587
Llandyfriog 22 SN3241
Llandyfrydog 30 SH4485
Llandygwydd 14 SN2443
Llandyrnog 31 SJ1064
Llandyssil 23 SO1995
Llandysul 22 SN4140
Llanedeyrn 16 ST2182
Llanefydd 21 SH9770
Llanegryn 22 SH5905
Llanegwad 15 SN5121
Llaneilian 30 SH4692
Llanelian-yn-Rhos 31 SH8376
Llanelidan 31 SJ1050
Llanelieu 23 SO1834
Llanellen 16 SO3010
Llanelli (Dyfed) 15 SN5000
Llanelltyd 30 SH7119
Llanelly (Gwent) 16 SO2314
Llanelwedd 23 SO0451
Llanenddwyn 30 SH5823
Llanengan 30 SH2927
Llanerchymedd 30 SH4138
Llanerfyl 23 SJ0309
Llanfachraeth 30 SH3182
Llanfachreth 30 SH7522
Llanfaelog 30 SH3373
Llanfaes 30 SH6077
Llanfaethlu 30 SH3186
Llanfaglan 30 SH4760
Llanfair 30 SH5729
Llanfair Caereinion 23 SJ1006
Llanfair Clydogau 22 SN6251
Llanfair Dyffryn Clwyd 31 SJ1355
Llanfair P. G. 30 SH5371
Llanfair Talhaiarn 31 SH9269
Llanfair Waterdine 23 SO2476
Llanfair-Nant-Gwyn 14 SN1637
Llanfair-yn-Neubwll 30 SH3077
Llanfairfechan 30 SH6874
Llanfairynghornwy 30 SH3290
Llanfallteg 14 SN1520
Llanfallteg West 14 SN1519
Llanfaredd 23 SO0651
Llanfechain 31 SJ1820
Llanfechell 30 SH3691
Llanfendigaid 22 SH5605
Llanferres 31 SJ1860
Llanfflewyn 30 SH3689
Llanfihangel 31 SJ0817
Llanfihangel Crucomey 16 SO3220
Llanfihangel Glyn Myfyr 31 SH9849
Llanfihangel Nant Bran 15 SN9434
Llanfihangel Rhydithon 23 SO1466
Llanfihangel Rogiet 16 ST4487
Llanfihangel ar-Arth 22 SN4539
Llanfihangel-Tal-y-llyn 16 SO1128
Llanfihangel-nant-Melan 23 SO1758
Llanfihangel-uwch-Gwili 15 SN4822
Llanfihangel-y-Creuddyn 22 SN6676
Llanfihangel-y-pennant (Gwyn.) 30 SH5245
Llanfihangel-y-pennant (Gwyn.) 22 SH6708
Llanfihangel-y-traethau 30 SH5935
Llanfilo 23 SO1133
Llanfoist 16 SO2813
Llanfor 31 SH9336
Llanfrechfa 16 ST3193
Llanfrothen 30 SH6241
Llanfrynach 16 SO0726
Llanfwrog (Clwyd) 31 SJ1157
Llanfwrog (Gwyn.) 30 SH3083
Llanfyllin 31 SJ1419
Llanfynydd (Clwyd) 31 SJ2756
Llanfynydd (Dyfed) 15 SN5527
Llanfyrnach 14 SN2231
Llangadfan 23 SJ0010
Llangadog 15 SN7028
Llangadwaladr (Clwyd) 31 SJ1730
Llangadwaladr (Gwyn.) 30 SH3869
Llangaffo 30 SH4468
Llangain 15 SN3815
Llangammarch Wells 23 SN9347
Llangan 15 SS9577
Llangarron 16 SO5221
Llangasty-Talyllyn 16 SO1426
Llangathen 15 SN5822
Llangattock 16 SO2117
Llangattock Lingoed 16 SO3620
Llangattock-Vibon-Avel 16 SO4515
Llangedwyn 31 SJ1824
Llangefni 30 SH4575
Llangeinor 15 SS9187
Llangeinwen 30 SH4365
Llangeitho 22 SN6159
Llangeler 22 SN3739
Llangelynin 22 SH5707
Llangendeirne 15 SN4514
Llangennech 15 SN5601
Llangennith 15 SS4291
Llangenny 16 SO2418
Llangernyw 31 SH8767
Llangian 30 SH2928
Llangiwg 15 SN7205
Llanglydwen 14 SN1826
Llangoed 30 SH6079
Llangoedmor 14 SN2045
Llangollen 31 SJ2141
Llangolman 14 SN1127
Llangorse 16 SO1327
Llangorwen 22 SN6084
Llangovan 16 SO4505
Llangower 31 SH9032
Llangranog 22 SN3154
Llangristiolus 30 SH4373
Llangrove 16 SO5219
Llangua 16 SO3926
Llangunllo 23 SO2171
Llangunnor 15 SN4219
Llangurig 22 SN9080
Llangwm (Clwyd) 31 SH9644
Llangwm (Dyfed) 14 SM9909
Llangwm (Gwent) 16 ST4299
Llangwm-isaf 16 SO4200
Llangwnadl 30 SH2033
Llangwyfan 31 SJ1266
Llangwyllog 30 SH4379
Llangwyryfon 22 SN5970
Llangybi (Dyfed) 22 SN6053
Llangybi (Gwent) 16 ST3796
Llangybi (Gwyn.) 30 SH4240
Llangyfelach 15 SS6499
Llangynhafal 31 SJ1263
Llangynidr 16 SO1519
Llangynin 14 SN2519
Llangynog (Dyfed) 14 SN3316
Llangynog (Powys) 31 SJ0526
Llanhamlach 16 SO0926
Llanharan 16 ST0083
Llanharry 16 ST0080
Llanhennock 16 ST3592
Llanhilleth 16 SO2101
Llanidloes 23 SN9584
Llaniestyn 30 SH2633
Llanigon 23 SO2139
Llanilar 22 SN6275
Llanilid 16 SS9781
Llanishen (Gwent) 16 SO4703
Llanishen (S Glam.) 16 ST1781
Llanllechid 30 SH6268
Llanlleonfel 23 SN9350
Llanllowell 16 ST3998
Llanllugan 23 SJ0402
Llanllwch 15 SN3818
Llanllwchaiarn 23 SO1192
Llanllyfni 30 SH4651
Llanmadoc 15 SS4493
Llanmaes 16 SS9869
Llanmartin 16 ST3989
Llanmerewig 23 SO1593
Llanmihangel 16 SS9771
Llanmorlais 15 SS5294
Llannon 15 SN5408
Llannor 30 SH3537
Llanon 22 SN5167
Llanpumsaint 15 SN4129
Llanreithan 14 SM8628
Llanrhaeadr 31 SJ0763
Llanrhaeadr-ym-Mochnant 31 SJ1226
Llanrhidian 15 SS3992
Llanrhos 31 SH7880
Llanrhyddlad 30 SH3389
Llanrhystud 22 SN5369
Llanrian 14 SM8131
Llanrothal 16 SO4618
Llanrug 30 SH5363
Llanrwst 31 SH7961
Llansadurnen 14 SN2810
Llansadwrn (Dyfed) 15 SN6931
Llansadwrn (Gwyn.) 30 SH5575
Llansaint 15 SN3808
Llansamlet 15 SS6997
Llansannan 31 SH9365
Llansannor 16 SS9977
Llansantffraed 16 SO1223
Llansantffraed-Cwmdeuddwr 23 SN9667
Llansantffraed-in-Elvel 23 SO0954
Llansantffraid 22 SN5167
Llansantffraid Glan Conway 31 SH8075
Llansantffraid-ym-Mechain 31 SJ2220
Llansawel 15 SN6136
Llansilin 31 SJ2028
Llansoy 16 SO4402
Llanspyddid 16 SO0328
Llanstadwell 14 SM9505
Llanstephan (Dyfed) 15 SN3511
Llanstephan (Powys) 23 SO1142
Llantarnam 16 ST3093
Llanthony 16 SO2827
Llantilio Pertholey 16 SO3116
Llantilio-Crossenny 16 SO3914
Llantrisant (Gwent) 16 ST3996
Llantrisant (Mid Glam.) 16 ST0483
Llantrithyd 16 ST0472
Llantwit Fardre 16 ST0785
Llantwit Major 16 SS9768
Llantysilio 31 SJ1943
Llanuwchllyn 31 SH8730
Llanvaches 16 ST4391
Llanvair-Discoed 16 ST4492
Llanvapley 16 SO3614
Llanvetherine 16 SO3617
Llanveynoe 23 SO3031
Llanvihangel Gobion 16 SO3409
Llanvihangel-Ystern-Llewern 16 SO4313
Llanwarne 16 SO5028
Llanwddyn 31 SJ0219
Llanwenog 22 SN4945
Llanwern 16 ST3688
Llanwinio 14 SN2626
Llanwnda (Dyfed) 14 SM9339
Llanwnda (Gwyn.) 30 SH4758
Llanwnen 22 SN5347
Llanwnog 23 SO0293
Llanwrda 15 SN7131
Llanwrin 22 SH7803
Llanwrthwl 23 SN9763
Llanwrtyd 22 SN8647
Llanwrtyd Wells 22 SN8746
Llanwyddelan 23 SJ0801
Llanyblodwel 32 SJ2322
Llanybri 14 SN3312
Llanybyther 22 SN5244
Llanycefn 14 SN0923
Llanychaer Bridge 14 SM9835
Llanycrwys 22 SN6445
Llanymawddwy 31 SH9019
Llanymynech 31 SJ2620
Llanynghenedl 30 SH3181
Llanynys 31 SJ1062
Llanyre 23 SO0462
Llanystumdwy 30 SH4738
Llanywern 23 SO1028
Llawhaden 14 SN0717
Llawnt 31 SJ2430
Llawryglyn 22 SN9291
Llay 32 SJ3255
Llechcynfarwy 30 SH3881
Llechfaen 16 SO0828
Llechryd (Dyfed) 14 SN2243
Llechryd (Mid Glam.) 16 SO1009
Llechrydau 31 SJ2234
Lledrod (Clwyd) 31 SJ2229
Lledrod (Dyfed) 22 SN6470
Llidiadnenog 15 SN5437
Llidiardau 30 SH1929
Llithfaen 30 SH3543
Llong 31 SJ2562
Llowes 23 SO1941
Llwydcoed 16 SN9905
Llwyn 23 SO2880
Llwyncelyn 22 SN4459
Llwyndafydd 22 SN3755
Llwynderw 23 SJ2004
Llwyndyrys 30 SH3741
Llwyngwril 22 SH5909
Llwynhendy 15 SS5599
Llwynmawr 31 SJ2236
Llwynypia 16 SS9993
Llynclys 31 SJ2924
Llynfaes 30 SH4178
Llys-y-fran 14 SN0424
Llysfaen 31 SH8977
Llyswen 23 SO1337
Llysworney 15 SS9674
Llywel 15 SN8630
Loan 51 NS9575
Loanend 53 NT9450
Loanhead 51 NT2765
Loans 49 NS3431
Loch Lubnaig 55 NN5713
Loch Sionascaig 64 NC1213
Loch Skealtar 63 NF8968
Loch Skeen 51 NT1716
Loch Skerrow 45 nx6068
Loch Skiach 56 NN9547
Loch Skipport (South Uist) 63 NF8238
Loch Tollaidh 64 NG8478
Lochailort (Highld.) 54 NM7682
Lochaline (Highld.) 54 NM6744
Lochans 44 NX0656
Locharbriggs 45 NX9980
Lochawe (Strath.) 55 NN1227
Lochboisdale (S. Uist) 63 NF7820
Lochbuie (Strath.) 54 NM6125
Lochcarron (Highld.) 59 NG9039
Lochdonhead 54 NM7333
Lochearnhead 56 NN5823
Lochee 57 NO3631
Lochend (Highld.) 67 ND2668
Lochend (Highld.) 60 NH5937
Locheport (N. Uist) 63 NF8563
Lochfoot 45 NX8973
Lochgair 49 NR9290
Lochgarthside 60 NH5219
Lochgelly 51 NT1893
Lochgilphead 49 NR8687
Lochgoilhead 55 NN1901
Lochhill 61 NJ2964
Lochinver 64 NC0922
Lochlane 56 NN8320
Lochluichart 64 NH3262
Lochmaben 45 NY0882
Lochnaw 44 NW9962
Lochore 51 NT1796
Lochranza (Island of Arran) 49 NR9350
Lochside (Grampn.) 57 NO7464
Lochside (Highland.) 67 NC8735
Lochton 62 NO7592
Lochwinnoch 49 NS3558
Lochwood (Dumf. and Galwy.) 45 NY0896
Lochwood (Strath.) 50 NS6966
Lockengate 3 SX0361
Lockerbie 45 NY1381
Lockeridge 17 SU1467
Lockerley 9 SU2925
Locking 16 ST3659
Lockington (Humbs.) 39 SE9947
Lockington (Leic.) 34 SK4628
Lockleywood 32 SJ6828
Lockmaddy 63 NF9168
Locks Heath 9 SU5207
Lockton 43 SE8489
Loddington (Leic.) 26 SK7802
Loddington (Northants.) 26 SP8178
Loddiswell 5 SX7148
Loddon 29 TM3698
Lode 28 TL5362
Loders 7 SY4994
Lodsworth 11 SU9223
Lofthouse (N Yorks.) 41 SE1073
Lofthouse (W Yorks.) 38 SE3325
Loftus 43 NZ7118
Logan 50 NS5820
Logan Mains 44 NX0942
Loggerheads 32 SJ7336
Loggie 64 NH1491
Logie (Fife) 57 NO4020
Logie (Grampn.) 62 NK0356
Logie (Tays.) 57 NO6963
Logie Coldstone 61 NJ4304
Logie Hill 65 NH7776
Logie Newton 62 NJ6638
Logie Pert 57 NO6664
Logierait 56 NN9752
Login 14 SN1623
Lolworth 27 TL3664
Lonbain 58 NG6853
Londesborough 39 SE8645
London 12 TQ3079
London Colney 19 TL1603
Londonderry 42 SE3087
Londonthorpe 34 SK9537
Londubh 64 NG8680
Long Ashton 16 ST5470
Long Bennington 34 SK8344
Long Bredy 7 SY5690
Long Buckby 26 SP6267
Long Clawson 34 SK7227
Long Common 9 SU5014
Long Compton (Staffs.) 33 SJ8522
Long Compton (Warw.) 18 SP2832
Long Crendon 18 SP6908
Long Crichel 8 ST9710
Long Ditton 11 TQ1666
Long Drax 38 SE6528
Long Duckmanton 34 SK4371
Long Eaton 34 SK4933
Long Hanborough 18 SP4114
Long Hermiston 51 NT1770
Long Itchington 26 SP4165
Long Lawford 26 SP4775
Long Load 7 ST4623
Long Marston (Herts.) 19 SP8915
Long Marston (N Yorks.) 38 SE4951
Long Marston (Warw.) 25 SP1548
Long Marton 41 NY6624
Long Melford 21 TL8646
Long Newnton (Glos.) 17 ST9092
Long Preston 37 SD8357
Long Riston 39 TA1242
Long Stratton 29 TL1992
Long Street 26 SP7946
Long Sutton (Hants.) 10 SU7347
Long Sutton (Lincs.) 35 TF4322
Long Sutton (Somer.) 7 ST4625
Long Whatton 34 SK4723
Long Wittenham 18 SU5493
Longbenton 47 NZ2668
Longborough 17 SP1729
Longbridge (W Mids) 25 SP0178
Longbridge (Warw.) 24 SP2662
Longbridge Deverill 8 ST8640
Longburton 8 ST6412
Longcliffe 33 SK2255
Longcot 18 SU2790
Longcroft 50 NS7979
Longden 24 SJ4306
Longdon (Here. and Worc.) 25 SO8336
Longdon (Staffs.) 33 SK0714
Longdon upon Tern 32 SJ6215
Longdown 5 SX8691
Longdowns 2 SW7434
Longfield 12 TQ6068
Longford (Derby.) 33 SK2137
Longford (Glos.) 17 SO8320
Longford (Gtr London) 11 TQ0576
Longford (Salop) 32 SJ6433
Longford (Salop) 32 SJ7218
Longford (W Mids.) 26 SP3583
Longforgan 57 NO3129
Longformacus 52 NT6957
Longframlington 47 NU1201
Longham (Dorset) 8 SZ0697
Longham (Norf.) 29 TF9415
Longhirst 47 NZ2289
Longhope 17 SO6819
Longhorsley 47 NZ1494
Longhoughton 53 NU2414
Longley Green 24 SO7350
Longmanhill 62 NJ7462
Longmoor Camp 10 SU7930
Longmorn 61 NJ2358
Longnewton (Bord) 52 NT5827
Longnewton (Gleve.) 42 NZ3816
Longney 17 SO7612
Longniddry 52 NT4476
Longnor (Salop) 24 SJ4800
Longnor (Staffs.) 33 SK0864
Longparish 10 SU4344
Longridge (Lancs.) 36 SD6037
Longridge (Lothian) 51 NS9462
Longriggend 50 NS8270
Longsdon 33 SJ9554
Longside 62 NK0347
Longsleddale 40 NY4902
Longslow 32 SJ6535
Longstanton 27 TL3966
Longstock 9 SU3536
Longstowe 20 TL3054
Longthorpe 27 TL1698
Longton (Lancs.) 36 SD4725
Longton (Staffs.) 33 SJ9043
Longtown (Cumbr.) 46 NY3768
Longtown (Here. and Worc.) 16 SO3228
Longville in the Dale 24 SO5393
Longwick 18 SP7805
Longwitton 47 NZ0700
Longwood 24 SJ6007
Longworth 18 SU3899
Longyester 52 NT5465
Lonmore 58 NG2646
Loose 12 TQ7552
Loosley Row 18 SP8100
Lootcherbrae 62 NJ6054
Lopcombe Corner 9 SU2435
Lopen 7 ST4214
Loppington 32 SJ4629
Lorbottle 47 NU0306
Lornty 56 NO1746
Loscoe 33 SK4247
Lossiemouth 61 NJ2370
Lossit 48 NR1856
Lostock Gralam 32 SJ6874
Lostwithiel 3 SX1059
Lothbeg 67 NC9410
Lothersdale 37 SD9545
Lothmore 67 NC9611
Loudwater 19 SU8990
Loughborough 34 SK5319
Loughor 15 SS5898
Loughton (Bucks.) 19 SP8337
Loughton (Essex) 20 TQ4296
Loughton (Salop) 24 SO6183
Lound (Lincs.) 35 TF0618
Lound (Notts.) 34 SK6986
Lound (Suff.) 29 TM5099
Lount 33 SK3819
Louth 35 TF3287
Love Clough 37 SD8126
Lover 8 SU2120
Loversall 38 SK5798
Loves Green 20 TL6404
Loveston 14 SN0808
Lovington 8 ST5931
Low Bradfield 33 SK2691
Low Bradley 37 SE0048
Low Braithwaite 46 NY4242
Low Brunton 47 NY9269
Low Burnham 38 SE7702
Low Catton 38 SE7053
Low Coniscliffe 42 NZ2514
Low Crosby 46 NY4459
Low Dinsdale 42 NZ3411
Low Eggborough 38 SE5522
Low Gate 47 NY9064
Low Ham 7 ST4329
Low Hartsop 40 NY4013
Low Hesket 46 NY4646
Low Hesleyhurst 47 NZ0997
Low Mill 42 SE6795
Low Moor 36 SD7241
Low Redford 41 NZ0731
Low Row (Cumbr.) 46 NY5863
Low Row (N Yorks.) 41 SD9897
Low Santon 39 SE9312
Low Street 29 TG3424
Low Thurlton 29 TM4299
Low Torry 51 NT0086
Low Waters 50 NS7353
Low Worsall 42 NZ3909
Lowca 40 NX9821
Lowdham 34 SK6646
Lower Aisholt 7 ST2035
Lower Assendon 18 SU7484
Lower Beeding 11 TQ2227
Lower Benefield 27 SP9888
Lower Bentham 36 SD6469
Lower Boddington 26 SP4752
Lower Bullingham 24 SO5038
Lower Cam 17 SO7401
Lower Chapel 23 SO0235
Lower Chute 10 SU3153
Lower Cwmtwrch 15 SN7710
Lower Darwen 36 SD6824
Lower Down 23 SO3384
Lower Dunsforth 38 SE4464
Lower Farringdon 10 SU7035
Lower Frankton 32 SJ3732
Lower Froyle 10 SU7544
Lower Gledfield 65 NH5990
Lower Halstow 13 TQ8567
Lower Hardres 13 TR1453
Lower Heyford 18 SP4824
Lower Higham 12 TQ7172
Lower Hordley 32 SJ3929
Lower Killeyan 48 NR2743
Lower Langford 16 ST4660
Lower Largo 67 NO4102
Lower Lemington 18 SP2134
Lower Lye 24 SO4067
Lower Maes-coed 23 SO3431
Lower Mayland 21 TL9101
Lower Moor 25 SO9847
Lower Nazeing 20 TL3906
Lower Penarth 16 ST1869
Lower Penn 25 SO8696
Lower Pennington 9 SZ3193
Lower Peover 32 SJ7474
Lower Pitcalzean 65 NH8070
Lower Quinton 25 SP1847
Lower Quinton 25 SP1847
Lower Shader 63 NB3854
Lower Shelton 27 SP9942
Lower Shiplake 10 SU7779
Lower Shuckburgh 26 SP4862
Lower Slaughter 17 SP1622
Lower Stanton St. Quintin 17 ST9180
Lower Sundon 19 TL0526
Lower Swanwick 9 SU4909
Lower Swell 17 SP1725
Lower Tysoe 26 SP3445
Lower Upham 9 SU5219
Lower Vexford 7 ST1135
Lower Weare 16 ST4053
Lower Wield 10 SU6340
Lower Winchendon 18 SP7312
Lower Woodend 18 SU8088
Lower Woodford 8 SU1235
Lowesby 26 SK7207
Lowestoft 29 TM5493
Lowestoft End 29 TM5394
Loweswater 40 NY1421
Lowgill (Cumbr.) 41 SD6297
Lowgill (Lancs.) 36 SD6564
Lowick (Cumbr.) 40 SD2985
Lowick (Northants.) 27 SP9781
Lowick (Northum.) 53 NU0139
Lownie Moor 57 NO4848
Lowsonford 25 SP1867
Lowthorpe 39 TA0860
Lowton 36 SJ6197
Lowton Common 36 SJ6397
Loxbeare 5 SS9116
Loxhill 11 TQ0037
Loxhore 6 SS6138
Loxley 26 SP2553
Loxton 16 ST3755
Loxwood 11 TQ0431
Lubenham 26 SP7087
Luccombe 6 SS9144
Luccombe Village 9 SZ5880
Lucker 53 NU1530
Luckett 4 SX3873
Luckington 17 ST8383
Lucklawhill 57 NO4222
Luckwell Bridge 6 SS9038
Lucton 24 SO4364
Ludag 63 NF7714
Ludborough 35 TF2995
Ludchurch 14 SN1411
Luddenden 37 SE0425
Luddesdown 12 TQ6766
Luddington 39 SE8216
Ludford (Lincs.) 35 TF1989
Ludford (Salop) 24 SO5173

Ludgershall Middleton in Teesdale

Ludgershall (Bucks.) 18 SP 6617
Ludgershall (Wilts.) 10 SU 2650
Ludgvan 2 SW 5033
Ludham 29 TG 3818
Ludlow 24 SO 5175
Ludwell 8 ST 9122
Ludworth 47 NZ 3641
Luffincott 4 SX 3394
Luffness 52 NT 4780
Lugar 50 NS 5821
Luggiebank 50 NS 7672
Lugton 50 NS 4152
Lugwardine 24 SO 5441
Luib 58 NG 5628
Lulham 24 SO 4041
Lullingstone Castle 12 TQ 5364
Lullington (Derby.) 26 SK 2513
Lullington (Somer.) 17 ST 7851
Lulsgate Bottom 16 ST 5065
Lulsley 24 SO 7455
Lumb 37 SE 0221
Lumby 38 SE 4830
Lumloch 50 NS 6369
Lumphanan 61 NJ 5804
Lumphinnans 51 NT 1692
Lumsdaine 53 NT 8769
Lumsden 61 NJ 4722
Lunan 57 NO 6851
Lunanhead 57 NO 4752
Luncarty 56 NO 0929
Lund (Humbs.) 39 SE 9648
Lund (N Yorks.) 38 SE 6532
Lundie (Tays.) 57 NO 2836
Lundin Links 57 NO 4002
Lunna 63 HU 4969
Lunning 63 HU 5066
Lunsford's Cross 12 TQ 7210
Lunt 36 SD 3401
Luntley 24 SO 3955
Luppitt 7 ST 1606
Lupton 41 SD 5581
Lurgashall 11 SU 9326
Lurgmore 60 NH 5937
Lusby 35 TF 3367
Luskentyre 63 NG 0699
Luss 50 NS 3592
Lusta 58 NG 2756
Lustleigh 5 SX 7881
Luston 24 SO 4863
Luthermuir 57 NO 6568
Luthrie 57 NO 3219
Luton (Beds.) 19 TL 0821
Luton (Devon) 5 SX 9076
Luton (Kent) 12 TQ 7766
Lutterworth 26 SP 5484
Lutton (Devon.) 4 SX 5959
Lutton (Lincs.) 35 TF 4325
Lutton (Northants.) 27 TL 1187
Luxborough 7 SS 9738
Luxulyan 3 SX 0458
Lybster 67 ND 2435
Lydbury North 23 SO 3486
Lydcott 6 SS 6936
Lydd 13 TR 0421
Lydd-on-Sea 13 TR 0819
Lydden 13 TR 2645
Lyddington 27 SP 8797
Lydeard St. Lawrence 7 ST 1232
Lydford (Devon.) 4 SX 5084
Lydford (Somer.) 7 ST 5731
Lydgate 37 SD 9225
Lydham 23 SO 3391
Lydiard Millicent 17 SU 0986
Lydiate 36 SD 3604
Lydlinch 8 ST 7413
Lydney 17 SO 6203
Lydstep 14 SS 0898
Lye 25 SO 9284
Lye Green 19 SP 9703
Lyford 18 SU 3994
Lymbridge Green 13 TR 1243
Lyme Regis 7 SY 3492
Lyminge 13 TR 1641
Lymington 9 SZ 3295
Lyminster 11 TQ 0204
Lymm 32 SJ 6786
Lymore 9 SZ 2992
Lympne 13 TR 1235
Lympsham 16 ST 3454
Lympstone 5 SX 9984
Lynchat 60 NH 7801
Lyndhurst 9 SU 2907
Lyndon 27 SK 9004
Lyne 11 TQ 0166
Lyne of Gorthleck 60 NH 5420
Lyne of Skene 62 NJ 7610
Lyneal 32 SJ 4433
Lyneham (Oxon.) 18 SP 2720
Lyneham (Wilts.) 17 SU 0179
Lynemouth 47 NZ 2991
Lyness 63 ND 3094
Lyng (Norf.) 29 TG 0617
Lyng (Somer.) 7 ST 3328
Lynmouth 6 SS 7249
Lynsted 13 TQ 9461
Lynton 6 SS 7149
Lyon's Gate 8 ST 6605
Lyonshall 23 SO 3356
Lytchett Matravers 8 SY 9495
Lytchett Minster 8 SY 9593
Lyth 67 ND 2763
Lytham 36 SD 3727
Lytham St. Anne's 36 SD 3427
Lythe 43 NZ 8413
Lythes 63 ND 4589

Maaruig 63 NB 1906
Mabe Burnthouse 2 SW 7634
Mabie 45 NX 9570
Mablethorpe 35 TF 5085
Macclesfield 33 SJ 9173
Macduff 62 NJ 7064
Machany 56 NN 9015
Macharioch 48 NR 7309
Machen 16 ST 2189
Machrihanish 48 NR 6220
Machynlleth 22 SH 7401
Mackworth 33 SK 3137
Macmerry 52 NT 4372
Madderty 56 NN 9522
Maddiston 51 NS 9476
Madehurst 11 SU 9810
Madeley (Salop) 24 SJ 6904
Madeley (Staffs.) 32 SJ 7744
Madingley 27 TL 3960
Madley 24 SO 4138
Madresfield 24 SO 8047
Madron 2 SW 4532
Maenclochog 14 SN 0827
Maendy 16 ST 0176
Maentwrog 30 SH 6640
Maer 32 SJ 7938
Maerdy (Clwyd) 31 SJ 0144
Maerdy (Mid Glam.) 16 SS 9798
Maes-glas 16 ST 2985
Maes-y-cwmmer 16 ST 1794
Maesbrook 32 SJ 3121
Maesbury Marsh 32 SJ 3125
Maesgwynne 14 SN 2024
Maeshafn 31 SJ 2061
Maesllyn 22 SN 3644
Maesmynis 23 SO 0148
Maesteg 15 SS 8591
Maesybont 15 SN 5616
Magdalen Laver 20 TL 5108
Maggieknockater 61 NJ 3145
Magham Down 12 TQ 6111
Maghull 36 SD 3702
Magor 16 ST 4287
Maiden Bradley 8 ST 8038
Maiden Law 47 NZ 1749
Maiden Newton 8 SY 5997
Maidencombe 5 SX 9268
Maidenhead 19 SU 8881
Maidens 49 NS 2107
Maidenwell 0 SX 1470
Maidford 26 SP 6052
Maids' Moreton 18 SP 7035
Maidstone 12 TQ 7656
Maidwell 26 SP 7477
Mail 63 HU 4328
Mains 60 NH 4239
Mains of Ardestie 57 NO 5034
Mains of Balhall 57 NO 5163
Mains of Ballindarg 57 NO 4051
Mains of Dalvey 61 NJ 1132
Mains of Drum 62 NO 8099
Mains of Melgund 57 NO 5456
Mains of Thornton 57 NO 6871
Mains of Throsk 57 NS 8690
Mainstone 23 SO 2687
Maisemore 17 SO 8121
Malborough 5 SX 7039
Malden 11 TQ 2166
Maldon 20 TL 8506
Malham 37 SD 9062
Mallaig 58 NM 6796
Malleny Mills 51 NT 1665
Mallwyd 22 SH 8612
Malmesbury 17 ST 9387
Malpas (Ches.) 32 SJ 4847
Malpas (Cornwall) 2 SW 8442
Maltby (Cleve.) 42 NZ 4613
Maltby (S Yorks.) 34 SK 5392
Maltby le Marsh 35 TF 4681
Malting Green 21 TL 9720
Maltman's Hill 13 TQ 9043
Malton 38 SE 7871
Malvern Link 24 SO 7848
Malvern Wells 24 SO 7742
Mamble 24 SO 6871
Manaccan 2 SW 7625
Manafon 23 SJ 1102
Manaton 5 SX 7481
Manby 35 TF 3986
Mancetter 26 SP 3196
Manchester 37 SJ 8397
Mancot 32 SJ 3267
Mandally 59 NH 2900
Manea 28 TL 4789
Manfield 42 NZ 2213
Mangersta 63 NB 0131
Mangotsfield 17 ST 6676
Manish (Harris) 63 NG 1089
Manish (Isle of Lewis) 63 NA 9513
Mankinholes 37 SD 9523
Manley 32 SJ 5071
Manmoel 16 SO 1703
Mannel 48 NL 9840
Manning's Heath 11 TQ 2028
Manningford Bohune 17 SU 1357
Manningford Bruce 17 SU 1359
Mannington 8 SU 0605
Manningtree 21 TM 1031
Mannofield 62 NJ 9104
Manorbier 14 SS 0698
Manorhill 52 NT 6632
Manorowen 14 SM 9336
Mansell Gamage 24 SO 3944
Mansell Lacy 24 SO 4245
Mansergh 41 SD 6082
Mansfield (Notts.) 34 SK 5361
Mansfield (Strath.) 50 NS 6214
Mansfield Woodhouse 34 SK 5363
Mansriggs 40 SD 2880
Manston 8 ST 8115
Manthorpe 35 TF 0616
Manton (Humbs.) 39 SE 9302
Manton (Leic.) 27 SK 8704
Manton (Wilts.) 17 SU 1768
Manuden 20 TL 4926
Maple Cross 19 TQ 0392
Maplebeck 34 SK 7160
Mapledurham 10 SU 6776
Mapledurwell 10 SU 6851
Maplehurst 11 TQ 1924
Mapleton 33 SK 1648
Mapperley 33 SK 4343
Mapperton 7 SY 5099
Mappleborough Green 25 SP 0866
Mappleton 39 TA 2244
Mappowder 8 ST 7105
Marazion 2 SW 5130
Marbury 32 SJ 5545
March 27 TL 4197
Marcham 18 SU 4596
Marchamley 32 SJ 5929
Marchbankwood 45 NY 0899
Marchington 33 SK 1330
Marchington Woodlands 33 SK 1128
Marchwiel 32 SJ 3547
Marchwood 9 SU 3809
Marcross 15 SS 9269
Marden (Here. and Worc.) 24 SO 5247
Marden (Kent) 12 TQ 7444
Marden (Wilts.) 17 SU 0857
Mardy 16 SO 3016
Mare Green 7 ST 3326
Marefield 26 SK 7408
Mareham le Fen 35 TF 2761
Mareham on the Hill 35 TF 2867
Maresfield 12 TQ 4624
Marfleet 39 TA 1329
Margam 15 SS 7887
Margaret Marsh 8 ST 8218
Margaret Roding 20 TL 5912
Margaretting 20 TL 6601
Margate 13 TR 3670
Margnaheglish 49 NS 0331
Marham 28 TF 7110
Marhamchurch 4 SS 2203
Marholm 27 TF 1402
Marian-glas 30 SH 5084
Mariansleigh 6 SS 7422
Marishader 58 NG 4963
Maristow 4 SX 4764
Mariveg 63 NB 4119
Mark 7 ST 3747
Mark Causeway 7 ST 3547
Mark Cross 12 TQ 5831
Markbeech 12 TQ 4842
Markby 35 TF 4878
Market Bosworth 26 SK 4003
Market Deeping 27 TF 1310
Market Drayton 32 SJ 6734
Market Harborough 26 SP 7387
Market Lavington 17 SU 0154
Market Overton 34 SK 8816
Market Rasen 35 TF 1089
Market Stainton 35 TF 2279
Market Street 29 TG 2921
Market Weighton 39 SE 8741
Market Weston 29 TL 9877
Markethill 56 NO 2239
Markfield 26 SK 4810
Markham 16 SO 1600
Markinch 57 NO 2901
Markington 38 SE 2864
Marks Tey 21 TL 9123
Marksbury 17 ST 6662
Markwell 4 SX 3658
Markyate 19 TL 0616
Marlborough 17 SU 1869
Marlcliff 25 SP 0950
Marldon 5 SX 8663
Marlesford 21 TM 3258
Marley Green 32 SJ 5745
Marlingford 29 TG 1208
Marloes 14 SM 7908
Marlow 19 SU 8587
Marlpit Hill 12 TQ 4447
Marnhull 8 ST 7718
Marnoch 62 NJ 5950
Marple 33 SJ 9588
Marr 38 SE 5105
Marrick 41 SE 0798
Marrister 63 HU 5464
Marros 14 SN 2008
Marsden 37 SE 0411
Marsett 41 SD 9086
Marsh 5 ST 2410
Marsh Baldon 18 SU 5699
Marsh Gibbon 18 SP 6423
Marsh Green (Devon.) 7 SY 0493
Marsh Green (Kent) 12 TQ 4344
Marsh Green (Salop) 24 SJ 6014
Marsh, The 23 SO 3197
Marshall's Heath 19 TL 1515
Marsham 29 TG 1924
Marshaw 36 SD 5853
Marshborough 13 TR 2958
Marshbrook 24 SO 4389
Marshchapel 39 TF 3598
Marshfield (Avon) 17 ST 7773
Marshfield (Gwent) 16 ST 2582
Marshgate 4 SX 1592
Marshside 36 SD 3419
Marshwood 7 SY 3899
Marske 41 NZ 1000
Marske-by-the-Sea 42 NZ 6322
Marston (Ches.) 32 SJ 6474
Marston (Here. and Worc.) 24 SO 3657
Marston (Lincs.) 34 SK 8943
Marston (Oxon.) 18 SP 5208
Marston (Staffs.) 25 SJ 8314
Marston (Staffs.) 33 SJ 9227
Marston (Warw.) 26 SP 2095
Marston (Wilts.) 17 ST 9656
Marston Green 25 SP 1685
Marston Magna 8 ST 5922
Marston Meysey 17 SU 1297
Marston Montgomery 33 SK 1338
Marston Moretaine 27 SP 9941
Marston St. Lawrence 26 SP 5342
Marston Stannett 24 SO 5655
Marston Trussell 26 SP 6986
Marston on Dove 33 SK 2329
Marstow 16 SO 5519
Marsworth 19 SP 9214
Marten 10 SU 2860
Marthall 32 SJ 8076
Martham 29 TG 4518
Martin (Hants.) 8 SU 0719
Martin (Lincs.) 35 TF 1259
Martin Drove End 8 SU 0420
Martin Hussingtree 25 SO 8860
Martinhoe 6 SS 6648
Martinscroft 32 SJ 6589
Martinstown 8 SY 6488
Martlesham 21 TM 2547
Martletwy 14 SN 0310
Martley 24 SO 7559
Martock 7 ST 4619
Marton (Ches.) 33 SJ 8468
Marton (Cleve.) 42 NZ 5115
Marton (Lincs.) 34 SK 8381
Marton (N Yorks.) 38 SE 4162
Marton (N Yorks.) 43 SE 7383
Marton (Salop) 23 SJ 2802
Marton (Warw.) 21 SP 4069
Marwood 6 SS 5437
Mary Tavy 4 SX 5079
Marybank 60 NH 4753
Maryburgh 60 NH 5456
Marygold 53 NT 8160
Maryhill 62 NJ 8245
Marykirk 57 NO 6865
Marylebone 36 SD 5807
Marypark 61 NJ 1938
Maryport (Cumbr.) 40 NY 0336
Maryport (Dumf. & Galwy) 44 NX 1434
Marystow 4 SX 4382
Maryton 57 NO 6856
Marywell (Grampn.) 61 NO 5896
Marywell (Tays.) 57 NO 6544
Masham 42 SE 2280
Mashbury 20 TL 6511
Mason 47 NZ 2073
Mastrick 62 NJ 9007
Matching 20 TL 5212
Matching Green 20 TL 5311
Matching Tye 20 TL 5111
Matfen 47 NZ 0371
Matfield 12 TQ 6541
Mathern 16 ST 5291
Mathon 24 SO 7345
Mathry 14 SM 8832
Matlaske 29 TG 1534
Matlock 33 SK 3060
Matlock Bath 33 SK 2958
Matson 17 SO 8316
Matterdale End 40 NY 3923
Mattersey 34 SK 6889
Mattingley 10 SU 7357
Mattishall 29 TG 0510
Mattishall Burgh 29 TG 0511
Mauchline 50 NS 4927
Maud 62 NJ 9247
Maugersbury 17 SP 1925
Maughold 43 SC 4991
Maulden 19 TL 0538
Maulds Meaburn 41 NY 6216
Maunby 42 SE 3486
Maund Bryan 24 SO 5550
Mautby 29 TG 4712
Mavesyn Ridware 33 SK 0817
Mavis Enderby 35 TF 3666
Maw Green 25 SP 0197
Mawbray 45 NY 0846
Mawdesley 36 SD 4914
Mawgan 2 SW 7024
Mawla 2 SW 6945
Mawnan 2 SW 7827
Mawnan Smith 2 SW 7728
Maxey 27 TF 1208
Maxstoke 26 SP 2386
Maxton 52 NT 6129
Maxwellheugh 53 NT 7333
Maxwellston 44 NS 2600
Maybole 49 NS 3009
Mayfield (E Susx) 12 TQ 5827
Mayfield (Staffs.) 33 SK 1545
Mayford 11 SU 9956
Maypole 16 SO 4716
Maypole Green 29 TM 4195
Maywick 63 HU 3824
Meadle 18 SP 8005
Meadowtown 23 SJ 3101
Meal Bank 41 SD 5495
Mealsgate 46 NY 2141
Mearbeck 37 SD 8160
Meare 7 ST 4541
Mears Ashby 27 SP 8366
Measham 26 SK 3312
Meathop 40 SD 4380
Meaux 39 TA 0939
Meavy 4 SX 5467
Medbourne 26 SP 7993
Meddon 4 SS 2717
Medmenham 18 SU 8084
Medstead 10 SU 6537
Meer End 26 SP 2474
Meerbrook 33 SJ 9860
Meesden 20 TL 4432
Meeth 4 SS 5408
Meidrim 14 SN 2820
Meifod 23 SJ 1513
Meigle 57 NO 2844
Meikle Earnock 50 NS 7253
Meikle Strath 57 NO 6471
Meikle Tarty 62 NJ 9928
Meikle Wartle 62 NJ 7230
Meikleour 56 NO 1539
Meinciau 15 SN 4610
Meir 33 SJ 9342
Melbost 63 NB 4632
Melbourn (Cambs.) 20 TL 3844
Melbourne (Derby.) 33 SK 3825
Melbourne (Humbs.) 38 SE 7543
Melbury Bubb 8 ST 5906
Melbury Osmond 7 ST 5707
Melbury Sampford 7 ST 5705
Melchbourne 27 TL 0265
Melcombe Bingham 8 ST 7602
Meldon (Devon) 4 SX 5592
Meldon (Northum.) 47 NZ 1284
Meldreth 20 TL 3746
Melfort 54 NM 8314
Meliden 31 SJ 0580
Melin Court 15 SN 8201
Melin-y-coed 31 SH 8160
Melin-y-ddol 23 SJ 0807
Melin-y-grug 23 SJ 0507
Melin-y-wig 31 SJ 0448
Melkinthorpe 41 NY 5525
Melkridge 46 NY 7363
Melksham 17 ST 9063
Melldalloch 49 NR 9375
Melling (Lancs.) 36 SD 5970
Melling (Mers.) 36 SD 3800
Mellis 29 TM 0974
Mellon Charles 64 NG 8491
Mellon Udrigle 64 NG 8895
Mellor (Gtr Mches.) 33 SJ 9888
Mellor (Lancs.) 36 SD 6530
Mellor Brook 36 SD 6331
Mells 8 ST 7249
Melmerby (Cumbr.) 41 NY 6137
Melmerby (N Yorks.) 41 SE 0785
Melmerby (N Yorks.) 42 SE 3376
Melplash 7 SY 4797
Melrose 52 NT 5433
Melsetter 63 ND 2689
Melsonby 42 NZ 1908
Meltham 37 SE 0910
Melton 21 TM 2850
Melton Constable 29 TG 0433
Melton Mowbray 34 SK 7518
Melton Ross 39 TA 0610
Meltonby 38 SE 7952
Melvaig 64 NG 7486
Melverley 32 SJ 3316
Melvich 67 NC 8864
Membury 7 ST 2703
Memsie 62 NJ 9762
Memus 57 NO 4258
Menabilly 3 SX 0951
Menai Bridge 30 SH 5572
Mendham 29 TM 2783
Mendlesham 29 TM 1065
Mendlesham Green 29 TM 0963
Menheniot 4 SX 2862
Mennock 50 NS 8008
Menston 37 SE 1743
Menstrie 50 NS 8596
Mentmore 19 SP 9019
Meole Brace 24 SJ 4811
Meonstoke 9 SU 6119
Meopham 12 TQ 6466
Meopham Station 12 TQ 6467
Mepal 27 TL 4481
Meppershall 19 TL 1336
Merbach 23 SO 3045
Mere (Ches.) 32 SJ 7281
Mere (Wilts.) 8 ST 8132
Mere Brow 36 SD 4118
Mere Green 25 SP 1298
Mereclough 37 SD 8730
Merevale 26 SP 2897
Mereworth 12 TQ 6553
Mergie 62 NO 7988
Meriden 26 SP 2482
Merkadale 58 NG 3831
Merkland 44 NX 2491
Merlin's Bridge 14 SM 9414
Merrington 32 SJ 4621
Merriott 7 ST 4412
Merrivale 4 SX 5475
Merrymeet 4 SX 2766
Mersham 13 TR 0539
Merstham 11 TQ 2953
Merston 11 SU 8903
Merstone 9 SZ 5285
Merther 2 SW 8644
Merthyr 14 SN 3520
Merthyr Cynog 23 SN 9837
Merthyr Dyfan 15 ST 1169
Merthyr Mawr 15 SS 8877
Merthyr Tydfil 16 SO 0406
Merthyr Vale 16 ST 0899
Merton (Devon.) 4 SS 5212
Merton (Gtr London) 11 TQ 2569
Merton (Norf.) 28 TL 9098
Merton (Oxon.) 18 SP 5717
Mervinslaw 52 NT 6713
Meshaw 5 SS 7519
Messing 21 TL 8918
Messingham 39 SE 8904
Metfield 29 TM 2980
Metheringham 35 TF 0661
Methil 57 NT 3699
Methley 38 SE 3826
Methlick 62 NJ 8537
Methven 56 NO 0225
Methwold 28 TL 7394
Methwold Hythe 28 TL 7195
Mettingham 29 TM 3689
Mevagissey 3 SX 0144
Mexborough 38 SK 4799
Mey 67 ND 2872
Meysey Hampton 17 SU 1199
Miavaig 63 NB 0834
Michaelchurch 16 SO 5125
Michaelchurch Escley 23 SO 3134
Michaelchurch-on-Arrow 23 SO 2450
Michaelston-le-Pit 16 ST 1573
Michaelston-y-Fedw 16 ST 2484
Michaelstow 3 SX 0778
Micheldever 10 SU 5138
Michelmersh 9 SU 3426
Mickfield 29 TM 1361
Mickle Trafford 32 SJ 4469
Mickleby 43 NZ 8013
Micklefield 38 SE 4433
Mickleham 11 TQ 1753
Mickleover 33 SK 3034
Mickleton (Durham) 41 NY 9623
Mickleton (Glos.) 25 SP 1543
Mickley 42 SE 2576
Mickley Square 47 NZ 0761
Mid Ardlaw 62 NJ 9464
Mid Beltie 62 NJ 6200
Mid Cairncross 57 NO 4979
Mid Sannox 49 NS 0145
Mid Thundergay 49 NR 8846
Mid Yell 63 HU 4991
Midbea 63 HY 4444
Middle Assendon 18 SU 7385
Middle Aston 18 SP 4726
Middle Barton 18 SP 4326
Middle Claydon 18 SP 7125
Middle Drums 57 NO 5957
Middle Littleton 25 SP 0747
Middle Maes-coed 23 SO 3334
Middle Mill 14 SM 8025
Middle Rasen 35 TF 0889
Middle Tysoe 26 SP 3344
Middle Wallop 10 SU 2937
Middle Winterslow 9 SU 2432
Middle Witchyburn 62 NJ 6356
Middle Woodford 8 SU 1136
Middlebie 46 NY 2176
Middleham 42 SE 1287
Middlehope 24 SO 4988
Middlemarsh 8 ST 6707
Middlesbrough 42 NZ 4920
Middlesmoor 41 SE 0974
Middlestone Moor 42 NZ 2532
Middlestown 37 SE 2617
Middleton (Cumbr.) 41 SD 6286
Middleton (Derby.) 33 SK 1963
Middleton (Derby.) 33 SK 2755
Middleton (Essex) 20 TL 8639
Middleton (Grampn.) 62 NJ 8419
Middleton (Gtr Mches.) 37 SD 8606
Middleton (Hants.) 10 SU 4243
Middleton (Here. and Worc.) 24 SO 5469
Middleton (Lancs.) 36 SD 4258
Middleton (Lothian) 51 NT 3657
Middleton (N Yorks.) 43 SE 7885
Middleton (N Yorks.—W Yorks.) 37 SE 1249
Middleton (Norf.) 28 TF 6616
Middleton (Northants.) 27 SP 8489
Middleton (Northum.) 53 NU 0024
Middleton (Northum.) 53 NU 1035
Middleton (Northum.) 47 NZ 0585
Middleton (Salop) 32 SJ 3128
Middleton (Salop) 23 SO 2999
Middleton (Salop) 24 SO 5377
Middleton (Suff.) 29 TM 4267
Middleton (Tays.) 56 NO 1206
Middleton (Tiree) 48 NL 9443
Middleton (W Yorks.) 38 SE 3027
Middleton (Warw.) 25 SP 1798
Middleton Cheney 26 SP 4941
Middleton Green 33 SJ 9935
Middleton Hall 53 NT 9825
Middleton Priors 24 SO 6290
Middleton Scriven 24 SO 6787
Middleton St. George 42 NZ 3412
Middleton Stoney 18 SP 5323
Middleton Tyas 42 NZ 2205
Middleton in Teesdale 41 NY 9425

Middleton on the Hill
Nettleton

Middleton on the Hill 24 SO 5464
Middleton-on-Sea 11 SU 9800
Middleton-on-the-Wolds 39 SE 9449
Middletown 23 SJ 3012
Middlewich 32 SJ 7066
Middlewood Green 29 TM 0961
Middleyard 50 NS 5132
Middlezoy 7 ST 3733
Middridge 42 NZ 2526
Midfield 66 NC 5864
Midge Hall 36 SD 5123
Midgeholme 46 NY 6458
Midgham 10 SU 5567
Midgley 37 SE 0226
Midhopestones 37 SK 2399
Midhurst 11 SU 8821
Midlem 52 NT 5227
Midsomer Norton 17 ST 6654
Midtown (Highld.) 64 NG 8285
Midville 35 TF 3857
Migvie 61 NJ 4306
Milborne Port 8 ST 6718
Milborne St. Andrew 8 SY 7997
Milborne Wick 8 ST 6620
Milbourne 47 NZ 1175
Milburn (Cumbr.) 41 NY 6529
Milbury Heath 17 ST 6690
Milcombe 18 SP 4134
Milden 21 TL 9546
Mildenhall (Suff.) 28 TL 7074
Mildenhall (Wilts.) 10 SU 2069
Mile Elm 17 ST 9968
Mile End 21 TL 9827
Milebrook 23 SO 3172
Milebush 12 TQ 7546
Mileham 28 TF 9119
Milesmark 51 NT 0688
Milfield 53 NT 9333
Milford (Derby.) 33 SK 3445
Milford (Staffs.) 33 SJ 9721
Milford (Surrey) 11 SU 9442
Milford Haven (Dyfed) 14 SM 9006
Milford on Sea 9 SZ 2891
Milkwall 17 SO 5809
Mill Bank 37 SE 0321
Mill End (Bucks.) 18 SU 7885
Mill End (Herts.) 20 TL 3332
Mill Green (Essex) 20 TL 6400
Mill Hill 19 TQ 2292
Mill Lane 10 SU 7850
Mill Street 29 TG 0118
Mill of Kingoodie 62 NJ 8425
Milland 10 SU 8228
Milland Marsh 10 SU 8326
Millbounds 63 HY 5635
Millbreck 62 NK 0045
Millbridge 10 SU 8542
Millbrook (Beds.) 19 TL 0138
Millbrook (Corn.) 4 SX 4252
Millbrook (Hants.) 9 SU 4012
Millburn (Strath.) 50 NS 4429
Millcorner 12 TQ 8223
Milldens 57 NO 5450
Miller's Dale 33 SK 1373
Millerhill 51 NT 3269
Millgreen (Salop) 32 SJ 6727
Millheugh 50 NS 7551
Millholme 41 SD 5690
Millhouse 49 NR 9570
Millikenpark 50 NS 4162
Millington 39 SE 8351
Millmeece 32 SJ 8333
Millom 40 SD 1780
Millport 49 NS 1655
Millthrop 41 SD 6691
Milltimber 62 NJ 8501
Milltown of Auchriachan 61 NJ 1718
Milltown of Corsindae 62 NJ 6809
Milltown of Murtle 62 NJ 8702
Milltown (Derby.) 33 SK 3561
Milltown (Dumf. and Galwy.) 46 NY 3375
Milltown (Grampn.) 61 NJ 4616
Milltown (Grampn.) 61 NJ 5447
Milltown of Aberdalgie 56 NO 0720
Milltown of Auchindown 61 NJ 3540
Milltown of Campfield 62 NJ 6400
Milltown of Craigston 62 NJ 7655
Milltown of Edinvillie 61 NJ 2369
Milltown of Towie 61 NJ 4612
Milnathort 56 NO 1204
Milngavie 50 NS 5574
Milnrow 37 SD 9212
Milnthorpe 40 SD 4981
Milovaig 58 NG 1550
Milson 24 SO 6372
Milstead 13 TQ 9058
Milston 8 SU 1645
Milton (Cambs.) 28 TL 4762
Milton (Central) 55 NN 5001
Milton (Central) 50 NS 4490
Milton (Cumbr.) 46 NY 5560
Milton (Dumf. and Galwy.) 44 NX 2154
Milton (Dumf. and Galwy.) 45 NX 8470
Milton (Grampn.) 61 NJ 5163
Milton (Highld.) 67 ND 3451
Milton (Highld.) 59 NH 3055
Milton (Highld.) 60 NH 4930
Milton (Highld.) 65 NH 7674
Milton (Highld.) 60 NH 9553
Milton (Highld.) 60 NH 5749
Milton (Oxon.) 18 SP 4535
Milton (Oxon.) 18 SU 4892
Milton (Staffs.) 33 SJ 9050
Milton (Strath.) 50 NS 4274
Milton (Tays.) 56 NN 9138
Milton (Tays.) 57 NO 3843
Milton Abbas 8 ST 8001
Milton Abbot 4 SX 4079
Milton Bridge 51 NT 2363
Milton Bryan 19 SP 9730
Milton Clevedon 8 ST 6637
Milton Coldwells 62 NJ 9538
Milton Combe 4 SX 4866
Milton Damerel 4 SS 3810
Milton Ernest 27 TL 0156
Milton Green 32 SJ 4558
Milton Hill 18 SU 4790
Milton Keynes 27 SP 8738
Milton Lilbourne 17 SU 1860
Milton Malsor 26 SP 7355
Milton Morenish 56 NN 6135
Milton Regis 13 TQ 9064
Milton of Auchinhove 61 NJ 5503
Milton of Balgonie 57 NO 3100
Milton of Braicklaich 60 NH 7851
Milton of Campsie 50 NS 6576
Milton of Cushnie 61 NJ 5111
Milton of Lesmore 61 NJ 4628
Milton of North 61 NJ 5028
Milton of Potterton 62 NJ 9415
Milton of Tullich 61 NO 3897
Milton on Stour 8 ST 7928
Milton-under-Wychwood 18 SP 2618
Miltonduff 61 NJ 1760
Milverton 7 ST 1225
Milwich 33 SJ 9632
Milwr 31 SJ 1974
Minard 49 NR 9796
Minchinhampton 17 SO 8600
Mindrum 53 NT 8432
Minehead 7 SS 9746
Minera 31 SJ 2651
Minety 17 SU 0290
Minffordd 30 SH 5938
Mingary 63 NF 7426
Miningsby 35 TF 3264
Minions 4 SX 2671
Minishant 49 NS 3314
Minley Manor 10 SU 8157
Minnes 62 NJ 9423
Minnigaff 44 NX 4166
Minskip 38 SE 3864
Minstead 9 SU 2811
Minster (Kent) 13 TQ 9573
Minster (Kent) 13 TR 3164
Minster Lovell 18 SP 3111
Minsteracres 47 NZ 0255
Minsterley 24 SJ 3705
Minsterworth 17 SO 7717
Minterne Magna 8 ST 6504
Minting 35 TF 1873
Mintlaw 62 NK 0048
Minto 52 NT 5620
Minton 24 SO 4290
Minwear 14 SN 0413
Minworth 25 SP 1592
Mirbister 63 HY 3019
Mireland 67 ND 3160
Mirfield 37 SE 2019
Miserden 17 SO 9308
Miskin 16 ST 0481
Misson 34 SK 6895
Misterton (Leic.) 26 SP 5584
Misterton (Notts.) 34 SK 7694
Misterton (Somer.) 7 ST 4508
Mistley 21 TM 1231
Mitcham 11 TQ 2868
Mitchel Troy 16 SO 4910
Mitcheldean 17 SO 6618
Mitchell 2 SW 8554
Mitford 47 NZ 1786
Mithian 2 SW 7450
Mitton 33 SJ 8815
Mixbury 18 SP 6033
Mixon 33 SK 0457
Mobberley 32 SJ 7880
Moccas 24 SO 3542
Mochdre (Clwyd) 31 SH 8278
Mochdre (Powys) 23 SO 0788
Mochrum 44 NX 3446
Mockerkin 40 NY 0923
Modbury 5 SX 6551
Moddershall 33 SJ 9236
Moel Tryfan 30 SH 5155
Moelfre (Clwyd) 31 SJ 1828
Moelfre (Gwyn.) 30 SH 5186
Moffat 45 NT 0805
Mogerhanger 27 TL 1349
Moira 33 SK 3216
Molash 13 TR 0251
Mold 31 SJ 2363
Molehill Green 20 TL 5624
Molescroft 39 TA 0140
Molesworth 27 TL 0775
Molland 6 SS 8028
Mollington (Ches.) 32 SJ 3870
Mollington (Northants.) 26 SP 4347
Mollinsburn 50 NS 7171
Monachty 22 SN 5062
Monboddo 57 NO 7478
Mondynes 57 NO 7879
Monewden 21 TM 2358
Moneydie 56 NO 0629
Moniaive 45 NX 7791
Monifieth 57 NO 5033
Monikie 57 NO 4938
Monimail 57 NO 2914
Monington 14 SN 1344
Monk Fryston 38 SE 5029
Monk Sherborne 10 SU 6056
Monk Soham 29 TM 2165
Monken Hadley 19 TQ 2497
Monkhopton 24 SO 6293
Monkland 24 SO 4557
Monkleigh 4 SS 4520
Monknash 15 SS 9270
Monkokehampton 4 SS 5805
Monks Eleigh 21 TL 9647
Monks Kirby 26 SP 4683
Monks' Heath 33 SJ 8873
Monkshill 62 NJ 7941
Monksilver 7 ST 0737
Monkswood 16 SO 3403
Monkton (Devon.) 7 ST 1803
Monkton (Kent) 13 TR 2865
Monkton (Strath.) 49 NS 3527
Monkton (Tyne and Wear) 47 NZ 3463
Monkton Combe 17 ST 7761
Monkton Deverill 8 ST 8537
Monkton Farleigh 17 ST 8065
Monkton Heathfield 7 ST 2526
Monkton Up Wimborne 8 SU 0113
Monkwood 9 SU 6730
Monmouth 16 SO 5113
Monnington on Wye 24 SO 3743
Monreith 44 NX 3641
Monreith Mains 44 NX 3643
Montacute 7 ST 4916
Montford 32 SJ 4114
Montgarrie 61 NJ 5717
Montgomery 23 SO 2296
Montgreenan 49 NS 3343
Montrave 57 NO 3706
Montrose 57 NO 7157
Monxton 10 SU 3144
Monyash 33 SK 1566
Monymusk 62 NJ 6815
Monzie 56 NN 8725
Moonzie 57 NO 3317
Moor Crichel 8 ST 9908
Moor Monkton 38 SE 5056
Moor Nook 36 SD 6537
Moor, The 12 TQ 7529
Moorby 35 TF 2964
Moorcot 24 SO 3555
Moordown 8 SZ 0994
Moore 32 SJ 5584
Moorends 38 SE 6915
Moorhall 33 SK 3175
Moorhampton 24 SO 3846
Moorhouse (Cumbr.) 46 NY 3356
Moorhouse (Notts.) 34 SK 7566
Moorland or Northmoor Green 7 ST 3332
Moorlinch 7 ST 3936
Moorsholm 43 NZ 6814
Moorside 37 SD 9507
Moortown (Hants.) 9 SZ 4283
Moortown (Lincs.) 39 TF 0699
Morar 58 NM 6792
Morborne 27 TL 1391
Morchard Bishop 5 SS 7607
Morcombelake 7 SY 4093
Morcott 27 SK 9200
Morda 31 SJ 2827
Morden (Dorset) 8 SY 9195
Morden (Gtr London) 11 TQ 2567
Mordiford 24 SO 5637
Mordon 42 NZ 3326
More 23 SO 3491
Morebath 5 SS 9525
Morebattle 53 NT 7724
Morecambe 36 SD 4364
Morefield 64 NH 1195
Moreleigh 5 SX 7652
Morenish 56 NN 6035
Moresby 40 NX 9821
Morestead 9 SU 5125
Moreton (Dorset) 8 SY 8089
Moreton (Essex) 20 TL 5307
Moreton (Mers.) 31 SJ 2689
Moreton (Oxon.) 18 SP 6904
Moreton Corbet 32 SJ 5523
Moreton Jeffries 24 SO 6048
Moreton Morrell 26 SP 3155
Moreton Pinkney 26 SP 5749
Moreton Say 32 SJ 6234
Moreton Valence 17 SO 7809
Moreton on Lugg 24 SO 5045
Moreton-in-Marsh 18 SP 2032
Moretonhampstead 5 SX 7586
Morfa Bychan 30 SH 5437
Morfa Glas 15 SN 8606
Morfa Nefyn 30 SH 2840
Morgan's Vale 8 SU 1921
Morland 41 NY 6022
Morley (Derby.) 33 SK 3941
Morley (Durham) 42 NZ 1227
Morley (W Yorks.) 37 SE 2627
Morley Green 32 SJ 8282
Morley St. Botolph 29 TM 0799
Morningside 51 NT 2471
Morningthorpe 29 TM 2192
Morpeth 47 NZ 2085
Morphie 57 NO 7164
Morrey 33 SK 1218
Morriston 15 SS 6698
Morston 29 TG 0043
Mortehoe 6 SS 4545
Mortimer 10 SU 6564
Mortimer West End 10 SU 6363
Mortimer's Cross 24 SO 4263
Mortlake 11 TQ 2075
Morton (Avon) 17 ST 6491
Morton (Derby.) 33 SK 4060
Morton (Lincs.) 34 SK 8091
Morton (Lincs.) 35 TF 0924
Morton (Norf.) 29 TG 1217
Morton (Salop) 31 SJ 2824
Morton Bagot 25 SP 1164
Morton-on-Swale 42 SE 3292
Morvah 2 SW 4035
Morval 4 SX 2556
Morvich 59 NG 9621
Morville 24 SO 6694
Morwenstow 4 SS 2015
Morwick Hall 47 NU 2303
Mosborough 33 SK 4281
Moscow 50 NS 4840
Mosedale 40 NY 3532
Moseley (Here. and Worc.) 25 SO 8159
Moseley (W Mids) 25 SP 0883
Moss (Clwyd) 31 SJ 3052
Moss (Highld.) 54 NM 6868
Moss (S Yorks.) 38 SE 5914
Moss (Tiree) 48 NL 9644
Moss Bank (Cumbr.) 36 SJ 5198
Moss Nook 32 SJ 8385
Moss Side 36 SD 3830
Moss of Barmuckity 61 NJ 2461
Mossat 61 NJ 4719
Mossbank (Shetld.) 63 HU 4475
Mossburnford 52 NT 6616
Mossdale 45 NX 6571
Mossend 50 NS 7460
Mosside 57 NO 4252
Mossley 37 SD 9702
Mosston 57 NO 5444
Mosterton 7 ST 4505
Mostyn 31 SJ 1680
Motcombe 8 ST 8425
Motherwell 50 NS 7557
Mottingham 12 TQ 4272
Mottisfont 9 SU 3226
Mottistone 9 SZ 4083
Mottram in Logendale 33 SJ 9995
Mouldsworth 32 SJ 5171
Moulin 56 NN 9459
Moulsecoomb 12 TQ 3307
Moulsford 18 SU 5984
Moulsoe 27 SP 9041
Moulton (Ches.) 32 SJ 6569
Moulton (Lincs.) 35 TF 3023
Moulton (N Yorks.) 42 NZ 2303
Moulton (Northants.) 26 SP 7866
Moulton (Suff.) 28 TL 6964
Moulton Chapel 35 TF 2918
Moulton Seas End 35 TF 3227
Mount (Corn.) 2 SW 7856
Mount (Corn.) 4 SX 1467
Mount Bures 21 TL 9032
Mount Hawke 2 SW 7147
Mount Pleasant 29 TM 5077
Mountain Ash 16 ST 0498
Mountain Cross 51 NT 1446
Mountain Water 14 SM 9224
Mountbenger 51 NT 3125
Mountfield 12 TQ 7320
Mountgerald 65 NH 5661
Mountjoy 2 SW 8760
Mountnessing 20 TQ 6297
Mounton 16 ST 5193
Mountsorrel 34 SK 5814
Mountstuart (Strath.) 49 NS 1059
Mousehole 2 SW 4626
Mouswald 45 NY 0672
Mow Cop 33 SJ 8557
Mowhaugh 53 NT 8120
Mowsley 26 SP 6489
Mowtie 62 NO 8388
Moy 55 NN 4282
Moy Hall 60 NH 7635
Moy House 61 NJ 0159
Moylgrove 14 SN 1244
Muasdale 48 NR 6840
Much Birch 24 SO 5030
Much Cowarne 24 SO 6147
Much Dewchurch 24 SO 4831
Much Hadham 20 TL 4319
Much Hoole 36 SD 4723
Much Marcle 24 SO 6533
Much Wenlock 24 SO 6199
Muchalls 62 NO 9091
Muchelney 7 ST 4224
Muchlarnick 4 SX 2156
Muckfoot 44 NX 2185
Mucking 20 TQ 6881
Mucklestone 32 SJ 7237
Muckleton 32 SJ 5821
Muckletown 61 NJ 5621
Muckton 35 TF 3781
Muddiford 6 SS 5638
Mudeford 8 SZ 1892
Mudford 7 ST 5719
Mudgley 7 ST 4445
Mugdock 50 NS 5576
Mugeary 58 NG 4438
Mugginton 33 SK 2843
Muggleswick 47 NZ 0450
Muie 66 NC 6704
Muir 61 NO 0689
Muir of Fowlis 61 NJ 5612
Muir of Ord 60 NH 5250
Muirdrum 57 NO 5637
Muirhead (Fife.) 57 NO 2805
Muirhead (Strath.) 50 NS 3530
Muirhead (Strath.) 50 NS 6869
Muirhead (Tays.) 57 NO 3434
Muirhouses 51 NT 0180
Muirkirk 50 NS 6927
Muirshearlich 55 NN 1380
Muirskie 62 NO 8295
Muirtack (Grampn.) 62 NJ 8146
Muirtack (Grampn.) 62 NJ 9937
Muirton 65 NH 7463
Muirton of Ardblair 56 NO 1743
Muirton of Ballochy 57 NO 6462
Muirtown 56 NN 9211
Muiryfold 62 NJ 7651
Muker 41 SD 9198
Mulbarton 29 TG 1901
Mulben 61 NJ 3450
Mulgrave Castle 43 NZ 8412
Mulindry 48 NR 3659
Mullion 2 SW 6719
Mumbles, The 15 SS 6287
Mumby 35 TF 5174
Muncaster Castle 40 SD 1096
Munderfield Row 24 SO 6451
Munderfield Stocks 24 SO 6550
Mundesley 29 TG 3136
Mundford 28 TL 8093
Mundham (Norf.) 29 TM 3298
Mundham (W Susx) 11 SU 8701
Mundon Hill 21 TL 8702
Mundorno 62 NJ 9413
Munerigie 59 NH 2602
Mungrisdale 40 NY 3630
Munlochy 60 NH 6453
Munsley 24 SO 6640
Munslow 24 SO 5187
Munslow Aston 24 SO 5086
Murcott 18 SP 5815
Murkle 67 ND 1668
Murlaggan (Highld.) 55 NN 3181
Murrow 27 TF 3707
Mursley 18 SP 8128
Murthill 57 NO 4657
Murthly 56 NO 0938
Murton (Cumbr.) 41 NY 7221
Murton (Durham) 47 NZ 3947
Murton (N Yorks.) 38 SE 6452
Murton (Northum.) 53 NT 9748
Musbury 7 SY 2794
Muscoates 42 SE 6880
Musselburgh 51 NT 3472
Muston (Leic.) 34 SK 8237
Muston (N Yorks.) 43 TA 0979
Mustow Green 25 SO 8774
Mutford 29 TM 4888
Muthill 56 NN 8616
Mutterton 7 ST 0304
Mybster 67 ND 1652
Myddfai 15 SN 7730
Myddle 32 SJ 4623
Mydroilyn 22 SN 4555
Mylor Bridge 2 SW 8036
Mynachlog-ddu 14 SN 1430
Myndtown 24 SO 3889
Mynytho 30 SH 3031
Myrebird 62 NO 7498
Mytchett 11 SU 8855
Mytholm 37 SD 9827
Mytholmroyd 37 SE 0125
Myton-on-Swale 38 SE 4366
Naburn 38 SE 5945
Nackington 13 TR 1554
Nacton 21 TM 2240
Nafferton 39 TA 0559
Nailsea 16 ST 4670
Nailstone 26 SK 4107
Nailsworth 17 ST 8499
Nairn 60 NH 8756
Nancegollan 2 SW 6632
Nanhoron 30 SH 2831
Nannau 30 SH 7420
Nannerch 31 SJ 1669
Nanpantan 34 SK 5017
Nanpean 2 SW 9556
Nant-ddu 16 SO 0015
Nant-glas 23 SN 9965
Nant-y-derry 16 SO 3306
Nant-y-moel 15 SS 9393
Nanternis 22 SN 3756
Nantgaredig 15 SN 4921
Nantgarw 16 ST 1285
Nantglyn 31 SJ 0061
Nantlle 30 SH 5053
Nantmawr 31 SJ 2424
Nantmel 23 SO 0366
Nantmor 30 SH 6046
Nantwich 32 SJ 6552
Nantyffyllon 15 SS 8492
Nantyglo 16 SO 1911
Naphill 19 SU 8496
Nappa 37 SD 8553
Napton on the Hill 26 SP 4661
Narberth 14 SN 1114
Narborough (Leic.) 26 SP 5497
Narborough (Norf.) 28 TF 7413
Nasareth 30 SH 4749
Naseby 26 SP 6878
Nash (Bucks.) 18 SP 7734
Nash (Gwent) 16 ST 3483
Nash (Here. and Worc.) 23 SO 3062
Nash (Salop) 24 SO 6071
Nash Lee 19 SP 8408
Nassington 27 TL 0696
Nasty 20 TL 3624
Nateby (Cumbr.) 41 NY 7706
Nateby (Lancs.) 36 SD 4644
Natland 40 SD 5289
Naughton 21 TM 0249
Naunton (Glos.) 17 SP 1123
Naunton (Here. and Worc.) 25 SO 8739
Naunton Beauchamp 25 SO 9652
Naust 64 NG 8283
Navenby 34 SK 9857
Navestock 20 TQ 5397
Navestock Side 20 TQ 5697
Nawton 42 SE 6584
Nayland 21 TL 9734
Nazeing 20 TL 4106
Neacroft 8 SZ 1897
Neal's Green 26 SP 3384
Neap 63 HU 5060
Near Cotton 33 SK 0646
Neasham 42 NZ 3210
Neath 15 SS 7597
Neatishead 29 TG 3421
Nebo (Dyfed) 22 SN 5465
Nebo (Gwyn.) 30 SH 4750
Nebo (Gwyn.) 31 SH 8356
Necton 28 TF 8709
Nedd 64 NC 1332
Nedging Tye 21 TM 0149
Needham 29 TM 2281
Needham Market 21 TM 0855
Needingworth 27 TL 3472
Neen Savage 24 SO 6777
Neen Sollars 24 SO 6572
Neenton 24 SO 6487
Nefyn 30 SH 3040
Neilston 50 NS 4657
Nelson (Lancs.) 37 SD 8737
Nelson (Mid Glam.) 16 ST 1195
Nelson Village 47 NZ 2577
Nemphlar 50 NS 8544
Nempnett Thrubwell 16 ST 5360
Nenthead 46 NY 7743
Nenthorn 52 NT 6837
Nercwys 31 SJ 2260
Nereabolls 48 NR 2255
Nerston 50 NS 6457
Nesbit 53 NT 9833
Ness (Ches.) 32 SJ 3075
Ness (N Yorks.) 43 SE 6878
Nesscliffe 32 SJ 3819
Neston (Ches.) 31 SJ 2877
Neston (Wilts.) 17 ST 8667
Nether Alderley 33 SJ 8476
Nether Blainslie 52 NT 5443
Nether Broughton 34 SK 6925
Nether Burrow 41 SD 6174
Nether Cerne 8 SY 6698
Nether Compton 8 ST 5907
Nether Crimond 62 NJ 8222
Nether Dallachy 61 NJ 3663
Nether Exe 5 SS 9300
Nether Handwick 57 NO 3641
Nether Haugh 33 SK 4196
Nether Howecleuch 51 NT 0312
Nether Kellet 36 SD 5067
Nether Kinmundy 62 NK 0444
Nether Kirkton 50 NS 4757
Nether Langwith 34 SK 5371
Nether Padley 33 SK 2478
Nether Poppleton 38 SE 5654
Nether Silton 42 SE 4592
Nether Stowey 7 ST 1939
Nether Wallop 9 SU 3036
Nether Whitacre 26 SP 2393
Nether Worton 18 SP 4230
Netheravon 8 SU 1448
Netherbrae 62 NJ 7959
Netherburn 50 NS 7947
Netherbury 7 SY 4799
Netherby 46 NY 3971
Netherend 17 SO 5900
Netherfield 12 TQ 7018
Netherhampton 8 SU 1029
Netherlaw 45 NX 7445
Netherley 62 NO 8593
Nethermill 45 NY 0487
Nethermuir 62 NJ 9143
Netherplace 50 NS 5155
Netherseal 26 SK 2813
Netherstreet 17 ST 9764
Netherthird 50 NS 5818
Netherthong 37 SE 1309
Netherton (Central) 50 NS 5579
Netherton (Devon.) 3 SX 8571
Netherton (Here. and Worc.) 25 SO 9941
Netherton (Mers.) 36 SD 3500
Netherton (Northum.) 53 NT 9907
Netherton (Tays.) 56 NO 1452
Netherton (Tays.) 57 NO 5457
Netherton (W Yorks.) 38 SE 2716
Nethertown (Cumbr.) 40 NX 9807
Nethertown (Highld.) 67 ND 3578
Netherwitton 47 NZ 1090
Nethy Bridge 61 NJ 0020
Netley 9 SU 4508
Netley Marsh 9 SU 3312
Nettlebed 18 SU 7086
Nettlebridge 8 ST 6448
Nettlecombe 7 SY 5195
Nettleden 19 TL 0210
Nettleham 34 TF 0075
Nettlestead 12 TQ 6852
Nettlestead Green 12 TQ 6850
Nettlestone 9 SZ 6290
Nettleton (Lincs.) 39 TA 1000

Nettleton

Oakwoodhill

Nettleton (Wilts.) 17 ST 8178
Neuk, The 62 NO 7397
Nevendon 20 TQ 7390
Nevern 14 SN 0840
New Abbey 45 NX 9665
New Aberdour 62 NJ 8863
New Addington 12 TQ 3863
New Alresford 9 SU 5832
New Alyth 57 NO 2447
New Annesley 34 SK 5153
New Bewick 53 NU 0620
New Bolingbroke 35 TF 3058
New Brighton 31 SJ 3093
New Brinsley 34 SK 4550
New Buckenham 29 TM 0890
New Byth 62 NJ 8254
New Clipstone 34 SK 5863
New Costessey 29 TG 1710
New Cross 22 SN 6376
New Cumnock 50 NS 6113
New Deer 62 NJ 8846
New Duston 26 SP 7162
New Earswick 38 SE 6155
New Edlington 38 SK 5399
New Ellerby 39 TA 1639
New Eltham 12 TQ 4573
New End 25 SP 0560
New Farnley 37 SE 2431
New Ferry 32 SJ 3385
New Fryston 38 SE 4526
New Galloway 45 NX 6377
New Gilston 57 NO 4207
New Hartley 47 NZ 3076
New Hedges 14 SN 1302
New Hey 37 SD 9311
New Holland 39 TA 0724
New Houghton (Derby.) 34 SK 4965
New Houghton (Norf.) 28 TF 7827
New Houses 41 SD 8073
New Hutton 41 SD 5691
New Hythe 12 TQ 7159
New Inn (Gwent) 16 SO 4800
New Inn (Gwent) 16 ST 3099
New Inn (N Yorks.) 37 SD 8072
New Invention 23 SO 2976
New Kelso 59 NG 9442
New Lanark 50 NS 8742
New Lane 36 SD 4212
New Leake 35 TF 4057
New Leeds 62 NJ 9954
New Longton 36 SD 5125
New Luce 44 NX 1764
New Mains of Ury 62 NO 8787
New Marske 42 NZ 6221
New Marton 32 SJ 3334
New Mill (Corn.) 2 SW 4534
New Mill (Herts.) 19 SP 9212
New Mill (W Yorks.) 37 SE 1608
New Mills (Corn.) 2 SW 8952
New Mills (Derby.) 33 SK 0085
New Mills (Gwent) 16 SO 5107
New Mills (Powys) 23 SJ 0901
New Milton 9 SZ 2495
New Moat 14 SN 0625
New Park 9 SU 2904
New Pitsligo 62 NJ 8855
New Polzeath 2 SW 9379
New Prestwick 49 NS 3424
New Quay (Dyfed) 22 SN 3859
New Rackheath 29 TG 2812
New Radnor 23 SO 2161
New Rent 40 NY 4536
New Romney 13 TR 0624
New Rossington 38 SK 6198
New Sauchie 50 NS 8993
New Scone 56 NO 1325
New Silksworth 47 NZ 3853
New Stevenston 50 NS 7659
New Tolsta 63 NB 5349
New Town (Lothian) 52 NT 4470
New Tredegar 16 SO 1403
New Tupton 33 SK 3966
New Ulva 48 NR 7080
New Walsoken 28 TF 4709
New Waltham 39 TA 2804
New Wimpole 20 TL 3450
New Winton 52 NT 4271
New Yatt 18 SP 3713
New York (Lincs.) 35 TF 2455
New York (Tyne and Wear) 47 NZ 3270
Newark (Cambs.) 27 TF 2100
Newark (Ork.) 63 HY 7242
Newark-on-Trent 34 SK 7953
Newarthill 50 NS 7859
Newbald 39 SE 9136
Newbiggin (Cumbr.) 46 NY 5649
Newbiggin (Cumbr.) 41 NY 6228
Newbiggin (Cumbr.) 36 SD 2669
Newbiggin (Durham) 41 NY 9127
Newbiggin (N Yorks.) 41 SD 9591
Newbiggin (N. Yorks.) 41 SD 9985
Newbiggin Common 41 NY 9131
Newbiggin-by-the-Sea 47 NZ 3187
Newbiggin-on-Lune 41 NY 7005
Newbigging (Strath.) 51 NT 0145
Newbigging (Tays.) 57 NO 2841
Newbigging (Tays.) 57 NO 4237
Newbigging (Tays.) 57 NO 4936
Newbold (Derby) 33 SK 3773
Newbold (Leic.) 33 SK 4018
Newbold Pacey 26 SP 2957
Newbold Verdon 26 SK 4403
Newbold on Avon 26 SP 4877
Newbold on Stour 26 SP 2446
Newborough (Cambs.) 27 TF 2006
Newborough (Gwyn.) 30 SH 4265
Newborough (Staffs.) 33 SK 1325
Newbottle 18 SP 5236
Newbourn 21 TM 2743
Newbridge (Clwyd) 51 SJ 2841
Newbridge (Corn.) 2 SW 4231
Newbridge (Gwent) 16 ST 2197
Newbridge (Hants.) 9 SU 2915
Newbridge (I. of W.) 9 SZ 4187
Newbridge (Lothian) 51 NT 1272
Newbridge on Wye 23 SO 0158
Newbridge-on-Usk 16 ST 3894
Newbrough 47 NY 8767
Newburgh (Fife) 56 NO 2318
Newburgh (Grampn.) 62 NJ 9925
Newburgh (Lancs.) 36 SD 4810
Newburn 47 NZ 1765
Newbury 10 SU 4666
Newby (Cumbr.) 41 NY 5921
Newby (N Yorks.) 42 NZ 5012
Newby (N Yorks.) 36 SD 7269
Newby Bridge 40 SD 3686
Newby East 46 NY 4758
Newby West 46 NY 3653
Newby Wiske 42 SE 3687
Newcastle (Gwent) 16 SO 4417
Newcastle (Salop) 23 SO 2482
Newcastle Emlyn 22 SN 3040
Newcastle upon Tyne 47 NZ 2464
Newcastle-under-Lyme 33 SJ 8445
Newcastleton 46 NY 4887
Newchapel (Dyfed) 14 SN 2239
Newchapel (Staffs.) 33 SJ 8654
Newchapel (Surrey) 12 TQ 3642
Newchurch (Dyfed) 15 SN 3724
Newchurch (Gwent) 16 ST 4597
Newchurch (I. of W.) 9 SZ 5585
Newchurch (Kent) 13 TR 0531
Newchurch (Powys) 23 SO 2150
Newchurch in Pendle 37 SD 8239
Newcott 7 ST 2309
Newdigate 11 TQ 2042
Newell Green 11 SU 8771
Newenden 12 TQ 8327
Newent 17 SO 7226
Newfield (Durham) 42 NZ 2033
Newfield (Highld.) 65 NH 7877
Newgale 14 SM 8422
Newgate 29 TG 0443
Newgate Street 20 TL 3005
Newgord 63 HP 5706
Newgrounds 17 SO 7204
Newhall (Ches.) 32 SJ 6045
Newhall (Derby.) 33 SK 2821
Newham (Gtr London) 20 TQ 4082
Newham (Northum.) 53 NU 1728
Newham Hall 53 NU 1729
Newhaven 12 TQ 4401
Newholm 43 NZ 8610
Newhouse 50 NS 7961
Newick 12 TQ 4121
Newington (Kent) 13 TQ 8665
Newington (Kent) 13 TR 1737
Newington (Oxon.) 18 SU 6196
Newland (Glos.) 16 SO 5509
Newland (Here. and Worc.) 24 SO 7948
Newland (N Yorks.) 38 SE 6824
Newlandrig 51 NT 3662
Newlands (Grampn.) 61 NJ 3051
Newlands (Northum.) 47 NZ 0955
Newlands of Geise 67 ND 0865
Newlyn 2 SW 4628
Newlyn East 2 SW 8256
Newmachar 62 NJ 8819
Newmains 50 NS 8256
Newmarket (Isle of Lewis) 63 NB 4235
Newmarket (Suff.) 28 TL 6463
Newmill (Borders) 52 NT 4510
Newmill (Grampn.) 61 NJ 4352
Newmill of Inshewan 57 NO 4260
Newmills (Lothian) 51 NT 1667
Newmiln 56 NO 1230
Newmilns 50 NS 5337
Newnham (Glos.) 17 SO 6911
Newnham (Hants) 10 SU 7054
Newnham (Herts.) 19 TL 2437
Newnham (Kent) 13 TQ 9557
Newnham (Northants.) 26 SP 5859
Newnham Bridge 24 SO 6469
Newport (Devon) 6 SS 5631
Newport (Dyfed) 14 SN 0639
Newport (Essex) 20 TL 5234
Newport (Glos.) 17 ST 7097
Newport (Gwent) 16 ST 3187
Newport (Highld.) 67 ND 1224
Newport (Humbs) 39 SE 8530
Newport (I. of W.) 9 SZ 4989
Newport (Norf.) 29 TG 5017
Newport (Salop) 32 SJ 7419
Newport Pagnell 27 SP 8743
Newport-on-Tay 57 NO 4228
Newpound Common 11 TQ 0627
Newquay (Corn.) 2 SW 8161
Newseat (Grampn.) 62 NJ 7033
Newseat (Grampn.) 62 NK 0749
Newsham (N Yorks.) 41 NZ 1010
Newsham (Northum.) 47 NZ 3079
Newsholme (Humbs.) 38 SE 7229
Newsholme (Lancs.) 37 SD 8451
Newstead (Borders) 52 NT 5634
Newstead (Northum.) 53 NU 1526
Newstead (Notts.) 34 SK 5252
Newthorpe 38 SE 4632
Newtimber Place 11 TQ 2613
Newton (Borders) 52 NT 6020
Newton (Cambs.) 35 TF 4314
Newton (Cambs.) 20 TL 4349
Newton (Ches.) 32 SJ 5059
Newton (Ches.) 32 SJ 5274
Newton (Cumbr.) 36 SD 2371
Newton (Dumf. and Galwy.) 45 NY 1194
Newton (Grampn.) 61 NJ 1663
Newton (Here. and Worc.) 23 SO 3433
Newton (Here. and Worc.) 24 SO 5054
Newton (Highld.) 66 NC 2331
Newton (Highld.) 67 ND 3449
Newton (Highld.) 60 NH 7448
Newton (Highld.) 65 NH 7866
Newton (Lancs.) 41 SD 5974
Newton (Lancs.) 36 SD 6950
Newton (Lincs.) 35 TF 0436
Newton (Lothian) 51 NT 0877
Newton (Mid Glam.) 15 SS 8377
Newton (N. Uist.) 63 NF 8877
Newton (Norf.) 28 TF 8315
Newton (Northants.) 27 SP 8883
Newton (Northum.) 47 NZ 0364
Newton (Notts.) 34 SK 6841
Newton (Staffs.) 33 SK 0325
Newton (Strath.) 55 NS 0498
Newton (Strath.) 50 NS 6560
Newton (Strath.) 51 NS 9331
Newton (Suff.) 21 TL 9140
Newton (W Glam.) 15 SS 6088
Newton (W Yorks.) 38 SE 4427
Newton (Warw.) 26 SP 5378
Newton (Wilts) 9 SU 2322
Newton Abbot 5 SX 8671
Newton Arlosh 45 NY 1955
Newton Aycliffe 42 NZ 2824
Newton Bewley 42 NZ 4626
Newton Blossomville 27 SP 9251
Newton Bromswold 27 SP 9966
Newton Burgoland 26 SK 3609
Newton Ferrers 4 SX 5447
Newton Flotman 29 TM 2198
Newton Harcourt 26 SP 6397
Newton Kyme 38 SE 4644
Newton Longville 19 SP 8431
Newton Mearns 50 NS 5456
Newton Mountain 14 SM 9807
Newton Poppleford 7 SY 0889
Newton Purcell 18 SP 6230
Newton Regis 26 SK 2707
Newton Reigny 40 NY 4731
Newton Solney 33 SK 2825
Newton St. Cyres 5 SX 8797
Newton St. Faith 29 TG 2117
Newton St. Loe 17 ST 7064
Newton St. Petrock 4 SS 4112
Newton Stacey 10 SU 4040
Newton Stewart 44 NX 4165
Newton Toney 10 SU 2140
Newton Tracey 6 SS 5226
Newton Valence 10 SU 7232
Newton by Toft 35 TF 0487
Newton of Balcanquhal 56 NO 1510
Newton on Trent 34 SK 8374
Newton under Roseberry 42 NZ 5613
Newton upon Derwent 38 SE 7149
Newton-le-Willows (Mers.) 32 SJ 5894
Newton-le-Willows (N Yorks.) 42 SE 2189
Newton-on-Ouse 38 SE 5059
Newton-on-Rawcliffe 43 SE 8090
Newton-on-the-Moor 47 NU 1605
Newtongarry Croft 61 NJ 5735
Newtongrange 51 NT 3364
Newtonhill 62 NO 9193
Newtonmill 57 NO 6064
Newtonmore 60 NN 7199
Newtown (Ches.) 32 SJ 6247
Newtown (Ches.) 33 SJ 9784
Newtown (Corn.) 2 SW 7323
Newtown (Cumbr.) 46 NY 5062
Newtown (Dorset) 8 SZ 0393
Newtown (Hants.) 9 SU 2710
Newtown (Hants.) 9 SU 3023
Newtown (Hants.) 10 SU 4763
Newtown (Hants.) 9 SU 6013
Newtown (Here. and Worc.) 24 SO 6145
Newtown (Highld.) 59 NH 3504
Newtown (I. of M.) 43 SC 3273
Newtown (I. of W.) 9 SZ 4290
Newtown (Northum.) 53 NT 9731
Newtown (Northum.) 47 NU 0300
Newtown (Northum.) 53 NU 0425
Newtown (Powys) 23 SO 1091
Newtown (Salop) 32 SJ 4831
Newtown (Staffs.) 33 SJ 9060
Newtown (Wilts.) 8 ST 9128
Newtown Linford 26 SK 5110
Newtown St. Boswells 52 NT 5731
Newtyle 57 NO 2941
Neyland 14 SM 9605
Nibley 17 ST 6882
Nicholashayne 7 ST 1015
Nicholaston 15 SS 5188
Nidd 42 SE 3060
Nigg (Grampn.) 62 NJ 9402
Nigg (Highld.) 65 NH 8071
Nightcott 6 SS 8925
Nine Ashes 20 TL 5902
Ninebanks 46 NY 7853
Ninfield 12 TQ 7012
Ningwood 9 SZ 3989
Nisbet 52 NT 6725
Niton 9 SZ 5076
Nitshill 50 NS 5160
No Man's Heath (Ches.) 32 SJ 5148
No Man's Heath (Warw.) 26 SK 2709
Noak Hill 20 TQ 5493
Nobottle 26 SP 6763
Nocton 35 TF 0564
Noke 18 SP 5413
Nolton 14 SM 8718
Nomansland (Devon) 5 SS 8313
Nomansland (Wilts.) 9 SU 2517
Noneley 32 SJ 4727
Nonington 13 TR 2552
Nook 46 NY 4679
Noran Water 57 NO 4860
Norbury (Ches.) 32 SJ 5547
Norbury (Derby.) 33 SK 1242
Norbury (Salop) 24 SO 3693
Norbury (Staffs.) 32 SJ 7823
Nordelph 28 TF 5501
Norden (Dorset) 8 SY 9483
Norden (Gtr Mches) 37 SD 8514
Nordley 24 SO 6998
Norham 53 NT 9047
Norley 32 SJ 5672
Norleywood 9 SZ 3597
Norman Cross 27 TL 1691
Norman's Green 7 ST 0503
Normanby (Humbs.) 39 SE 8716
Normanby (Lincs.) 34 SK 9988
Normanby (N Yorks.) 43 SE 7381
Normanby le Wold 35 TF 1294
Normandy 11 SU 9251
Normanton (Derby.) 33 SK 3433
Normanton (Lincs.) 34 SK 9446
Normanton (Notts.) 34 SK 7054
Normanton (W Yorks.) 38 SE 3822
Normanton le Heath 26 SK 3712
Normanton on Soar 34 SK 5123
Normanton on Trent 34 SK 7868
Normanton on the Wolds 34 SK 6232
Normoss 36 SD 3437
Norrington Common 17 ST 8864
Norris Hill 33 SK 3216
North Ashton 36 SD 5401
North Aston 18 SP 4728
North Baddesley 9 SU 3920
North Ballchulish 55 NN 0560
North Barrow 8 ST 6029
North Barsham 28 TP 9135
North Benfleet 20 TQ 7590
North Berwick 52 NT 5485
North Boarhunt 9 SU 6010
North Bovey 5 SX 7483
North Bradley 17 ST 8554
North Brentor 4 SX 4781
North Buckland 6 SS 4740
North Burlingham 29 TG 3610
North Cadbury 8 ST 6327
North Cairn 44 NW 9770
North Carlton 34 SK 9477
North Cave 39 SE 8832
North Cerney 17 SP 0208
North Charford 8 SU 1919
North Charlton 53 NU 1622
North Cliffe 39 SE 8737
North Clifton 34 SK 8272
North Cotes 39 TA 3400
North Cove 29 TM 4689
North Cowton 42 NZ 2803
North Crawley 27 SP 9244
North Cray 12 TQ 4972
North Creake 28 TF 8538
North Curry 7 ST 3125
North Dalton 39 SE 9352
North Dawn 63 HY 4803
North Deighton 38 SE 3851
North Duffield 38 SE 6837
North Elkington 35 TF 2890
North Elmham 29 TF 9820
North End (Avon) 16 ST 4167
North End (Berks.) 10 SU 4063
North End (Hants.) 9 SU 6502
North End (W Susx) 11 TQ 1209
North Erradale 64 NG 7481
North Fearns 58 NG 5835
North Ferriby 39 SE 9826
North Frodingham 39 TA 1053
North Green 29 TM 2288
North Grimston 39 SE 8467
North Haven (Grampn.) 62 NK 1138
North Hayling 10 SU 7203
North Heasley 6 SS 7333
North Heath 11 TQ 0621
North Hill 4 SX 2776
North Hinksey 18 SP 4806
North Holmwood 11 TQ 1646
North Huish 5 SX 7156
North Hykeham 34 SK 9465
North Kelsey 39 TA 0401
North Kessock 60 NH 6548
North Kilvington 42 SE 4285
North Kilworth 26 SP 6183
North Kingennie 57 NO 4736
North Kyme 35 TF 1452
North Lancing 11 TQ 1805
North Lee (Bucks.) 19 SP 8309
North Leigh (Oxon.) 18 SP 3813
North Leverton with Habblesthorpe 34 SK 7882
North Littleton 25 SP 0847
North Lopham 29 TM 0383
North Luffenham 27 SK 9303
North Marden 10 SU 8015
North Marston 18 SP 7722
North Middleton 51 NT 3559
North Molton 6 SS 7329
North Moreton 18 SU 5689
North Muskham 34 SK 7958
North Newbald 39 SE 9136
North Newington 18 SP 4139
North Newnton 17 SU 1257
North Newton 7 ST 2931
North Nibley 17 ST 7396
North Oakley 10 SU 5354
North Ockendon 20 TQ 5984
North Ormsby 35 TF 2893
North Otterington 42 SE 3589
North Owersby 35 TF 0594
North Perrott 7 ST 4709
North Petherton 7 ST 2832
North Petherwin 4 SX 2889
North Pickenham 28 TF 8606
North Piddle 25 SO 9654
North Poorton 7 SY 5197
North Queensferry 51 NT 1380
North Rigton 38 SE 2749
North Rode 33 SJ 8866
North Runcton 28 TF 6416
North Scale 36 SD 1769
North Scarle 34 SK 8466
North Seaton 47 NZ 2986
North Shian 54 NM 9143
North Shields 47 NZ 3468
North Shoebury 21 TQ 9286
North Shore 36 SD 3037
North Side 27 TL 2799
North Somercotes 35 TF 4296
North Stainley 42 SE 2876
North Stainmore 41 NY 8215
North Stifford 20 TQ 6080
North Stoke (Avon) 17 ST 7068
North Stoke (Oxon.) 18 SU 6186
North Stoke (W Susx) 11 TQ 0211
North Street (Berks.) 10 SU 6372
North Street (Hants.) 9 SU 6433
North Sunderland 53 NU 2131
North Tamerton 4 SX 3197
North Tawton 5 SS 6601
North Thoresby 39 TF 2998
North Tidworth 10 SU 2248
North Tolsta 63 NB 5347
North Tuddenham 29 TG 0413
North Walsham 29 TG 2730
North Waltham 10 SU 5546
North Warnborough 10 SU 7351
North Water Bridge 57 NO 6566
North Watten 67 ND 2458
North Weald Basset 20 TL 4904
North Whilborough 5 SX 8766
North Wick (Avon) 17 ST 5865
North Widcombe 17 ST 5758
North Willingham 35 TF 1688
North Wingfield 33 SK 4064
North Witham 34 SK 9221
North Wootton (Dorset) 8 ST 6614
North Wootton (Norf.) 28 TF 6424
North Wootton (Somer.) 7 ST 5641
North Wraxall 17 ST 8174
North Wroughton 17 SU 1581
Northallerton 42 SE 3793
Northam (Devon.) 6 SS 4429
Northam (Hants.) 9 SU 4312
Northampton 26 SP 7561
Northaw 19 TL 2802
Northborough 27 TF 1508
Northbourne 13 TR 3352
Northchapel 11 SU 9529
Northchurch 19 SP 9708
Northcott 4 SX 3392
Northend (Avon) 17 ST 7867
Northend (Bucks.) 18 SU 7392
Northend (Warw.) 26 SP 3852
Northfield (Borders) 53 NT 9167
Northfield (Grampn.) 62 NJ 9008
Northfield (W Mids.) 25 SP 0179
Northfleet 12 TQ 6274
Northiam 12 TQ 8324
Northill 27 TL 1446
Northington 10 SU 5637
Northlands 35 TF 3453
Northleach 17 SP 1114
Northleigh (Devon.) 7 SY 1995
Northlew 4 SX 5099
Northmoor 18 SP 4202
Northmoor Green or Moorland 7 ST 3332
Northmuir 57 NO 3855
Northolt 19 TQ 1285
Northop 31 SJ 2468
Northop Hall 31 SJ 2767
Northorpe (Lincs.) 34 SK 8996
Northorpe (Lincs.) 35 TF 0917
Northover 7 ST 5223
Northowram 37 SE 1127
Northrepps 29 TG 2439
Northton 63 NF 9889
Northway 25 SO 9234
Northwich 32 SJ 6573
Northwick (Avon) 16 ST 5586
Northwold 28 TL 7596
Northwood (Gtr London) 19 TQ 1090
Northwood (I. of W.) 9 SZ 4992
Northwood (Salop) 32 SJ 4633
Northwood Green 17 SO 7216
Norton (Ches.) 32 SJ 5581
Norton (Cleve.) 42 NZ 4421
Norton (Glos.) 17 SO 8624
Norton (Here. and Worc.) 25 SO 8750
Norton (Here. and Worc.) 25 SP 0447
Norton (Herts.) 19 TL 2234
Norton (I. of W.) 9 SZ 3489
Norton (N Yorks.) 38 SE 7971
Norton (Northants.) 26 SP 6063
Norton (Notts.) 34 SK 5772
Norton (Powys) 23 SO 3067
Norton (S Yorks.) 38 SE 5415
Norton (S Yorks.) 33 SK 3581
Norton (Salop) 24 SJ 5609
Norton (Salop) 24 SJ 7200
Norton (Salop) 24 SO 4581
Norton (Suff.) 29 TL 9565
Norton (W Susx) 11 SU 9306
Norton (Wilts.) 17 ST 8884
Norton Bavant 8 ST 9043
Norton Canes 25 SK 0108
Norton Canon 24 SO 3847
Norton Disney 34 SK 8859
Norton Ferris 8 ST 7936
Norton Fitzwarren 7 ST 1925
Norton Green 9 SZ 3388
Norton Hawkfield 17 ST 5964
Norton Heath 20 TL 6004
Norton Lindsey 26 SP 2263
Norton Maireward 17 ST 6064
Norton St. Philip 17 ST 7755
Norton Subcourse 29 TM 4098
Norton in Hales 32 SJ 7038
Norton in the Moors 33 SJ 8951
Norton sub Hamdon 7 ST 4615
Norton-Juxta-Twycross 26 SK 3207
Norton-le-Clay 38 SE 4071
Norwell 34 SK 7661
Norwell Woodhouse 34 SK 7462
Norwich 29 TG 2308
Norwick (Unst) 63 HP 6414
Norwood Green 11 TQ 1378
Norwood Hill 11 TQ 2443
Noseley 26 SP 7398
Noss Mayo 4 SX 5447
Nosterfield 42 SE 2780
Nostie 59 NG 8527
Notgrove 17 SP 1020
Nottage 15 SS 8278
Nottingham 34 SK 5741
Notton (W Yorks.) 38 SE 3413
Notton (Wilts.) 17 ST 9169
Nounsbrough 63 HU 2957
Nounsley 20 TL 7910
Noutard's Green 24 SO 7966
Nox 24 SJ 4010
Nuffield 18 SU 6687
Nun Monkton 38 SE 5057
Nunburnholme 39 SE 8548
Nuneaton 26 SP 3592
Nuneham Courtenay 18 SU 5599
Nunney 8 ST 7345
Nunnington 42 SE 6679
Nunnykirk 47 NZ 0892
Nunthorpe 42 NZ 5313
Nunton (Benbecula) 63 NF 7653
Nunton (Wilts.) 8 SU 1525
Nunwick 47 NY 8774
Nursling 9 SU 3615
Nursted 10 SU 7621
Nutbourne 11 TQ 0718
Nutfield 12 TQ 3150
Nuthall 34 SK 5144
Nuthampstead 20 TL 4134
Nuthurst 11 TQ 1926
Nutley 12 TQ 4427
Nutwell 38 SE 6303
Nybster 67 ND 3663
Nyetimber 11 SZ 8998
Nyewood 10 SU 8021
Nymet Rowland 5 SS 7108
Nymet Tracey 5 SS 7200
Nympsfield 17 SO 8000
Nynehead 7 ST 1422
Nyton 11 SU 9305

Oad Street 13 TQ 8762
Oadby 26 SK 6200
Oakamoor 33 SK 0544
Oakbank 51 NT 0866
Oakdale 16 ST 1898
Oake 7 ST 1525
Oaken 25 SJ 8502
Oakenclough 36 SD 5447
Oakengates 24 SJ 7010
Oakenshaw (Durham) 42 NZ 2036
Oakenshaw (W Yorks.) 37 SE 1727
Oakford (Devon.) 6 SS 9021
Oakford (Dyfed) 22 SN 4557
Oakgrove 33 SJ 9169
Oakham 27 SK 8509
Oakhanger 10 SU 7635
Oakhill 8 ST 6347
Oakington 27 TL 4164
Oaklands 31 SH 8158
Oakle Street 17 SO 7517
Oakley (Beds.) 27 TL 0153
Oakley (Bucks.) 18 SP 6412
Oakley (Fife.) 51 NT 0289
Oakley (Hants.) 10 SU 5650
Oakley (Suff.) 29 TM 1678
Oakley Green 11 SU 9376
Oakleypark 23 SN 9886
Oakridge 17 SO 9103
Oaks 24 SJ 4204
Oaksey 17 ST 9893
Oakthorpe 26 SK 3213
Oakwoodhill 11 TQ 1337

Oakworth

Petton

Oakworth ... 37 ... SE0238
Oare (Kent) ... 13 ... TR0062
Oare (Somer.) ... 6 ... SS8047
Oare (Wilts.) ... 17 ... SU1563
Oasby ... 34 ... TF0039
Oathlaw ... 57 ... NO4756
Oban ... 54 ... NM8630
Obney ... 56 ... NO0336
Oborne ... 8 ... ST6518
Occlestone Green ... 32 ... SJ6962
Occold ... 23 ... TM1570
Ochertyre ... 56 ... NN8323
Ochiltree ... 50 ... NS5121
Ochtermuthill ... 56 ... NN8216
Ockbrook ... 33 ... SK4235
Ockham ... 11 ... TQ0756
Ockle ... 54 ... NM5570
Ockley ... 11 ... TQ1640
Ocle Pychard ... 24 ... SO5946
Odcombe ... 7 ... ST5015
Oddingley ... 25 ... SO9159
Oddington (Glos.) ... 18 ... SP2225
Oddington (Oxon.) ... 18 ... SP5514
Odell ... 27 ... SP9658
Odiham ... 10 ... SU7350
Odstock ... 8 ... SU1426
Odstone ... 26 ... SK3907
Offchurch ... 26 ... SP3565
Offenham ... 25 ... SP0546
Offham (E Susx) ... 12 ... TQ4012
Offham (Kent) ... 12 ... TQ6557
Offord Cluny ... 27 ... TL2267
Offord Darcy ... 27 ... TL2266
Offton ... 21 ... TM0649
Offwell ... 7 ... SY1999
Ogbourne Maizey ... 17 ... SU1871
Ogbourne St. Andrew ... 17 ... SU1872
Ogbourne St. George ... 17 ... SU2074
Ogil ... 57 ... NO4561
Ogle ... 47 ... NZ1378
Ogmore ... 15 ... SS8877
Ogmore Vale ... 15 ... SS9490
Ogmore-by-Sea ... 15 ... SS8674
Okeford Fitzpaine ... 8 ... ST8010
Okehampton ... 4 ... SX5895
Okehampton Camp ... 4 ... SX5893
Okraquoy ... 63 ... HU4331
Old ... 26 ... SP7873
Old Aberdeen ... 62 ... NJ9408
Old Alresford ... 9 ... SU5834
Old Bewick ... 53 ... NU0621
Old Bolingbroke ... 35 ... TF3564
Old Brampton ... 33 ... SK3371
Old Bridge of Urr ... 45 ... NX7767
Old Buckenham ... 29 ... TM0691
Old Burghclere ... 10 ... SU4657
Old Byland ... 42 ... SE5486
Old Cleeve ... 7 ... ST0342
Old Colwyn ... 31 ... SH8678
Old Dailly ... 44 ... NX2299
Old Dalby ... 34 ... SK6723
Old Deer ... 62 ... NJ9747
Old Felixstowe ... 21 ... TM3135
Old Fletton ... 27 ... TL1997
Old Hall (Highld.) ... 67 ... ND2056
Old Hall, The (Humbs.) ... 39 ... TA2717
Old Heath ... 21 ... TM0122
Old Hutton ... 41 ... SD5688
Old Kea ... 2 ... SW8441
Old Kilpatrick ... 50 ... NS4673
Old Knebworth ... 19 ... TL2320
Old Leake ... 35 ... TF4050
Old Malton ... 43 ... SE7972
Old Milverton ... 26 ... SP2967
Old Monkland ... 50 ... NS7163
Old Newton ... 29 ... TM0662
Old Philpstoun ... 51 ... NT0577
Old Radnor ... 23 ... SO2559
Old Rayne ... 62 ... NJ6728
Old Romney ... 13 ... TR0325
Old Scone ... 56 ... NO1226
Old Sodbury ... 17 ... ST7581
Old Somerby ... 34 ... SK9633
Old Town (Northum.) ... 47 ... NY8891
Old Warden ... 27 ... TL1343
Old Weston ... 27 ... TL0977
Old Windsor ... 11 ... SU9874
Old Wives Lees ... 13 ... TR0755
Oldberrow ... 25 ... SP1165
Oldborough ... 5 ... SS7706
Oldbury (Salop) ... 24 ... SO7092
Oldbury (W Mids.) ... 25 ... SO9889
Oldbury (Warw.) ... 26 ... SP3194
Oldbury on the Hill ... 17 ... ST8089
Oldbury-on-Severn ... 17 ... ST6092
Oldcastle ... 16 ... SO3224
Oldcotes ... 34 ... SK5888
Oldfield ... 25 ... SO8464
Oldford ... 8 ... ST7849
Oldham ... 37 ... SD9305
Oldhamstocks ... 53 ... NT7470
Oldhurst ... 27 ... TL3077
Oldland ... 17 ... ST6771
Oldmeldrum ... 62 ... NJ8027
Oldpark ... 24 ... SJ6909
Oldshore ... 66 ... NC2059
Oldstead ... 42 ... SE5280
Oldtown of Ord ... 62 ... NJ6259
Oldways End ... 6 ... SS8624
Oldwhat ... 62 ... NJ8551
Olgrinmore ... 67 ... ND0955
Oliver ... 51 ... NT0924
Oliver's Battery ... 9 ... SU4527
Ollaberry ... 63 ... HU3680
Ollach ... 58 ... NG5137
Ollerton (Ches.) ... 32 ... SJ7776
Ollerton (Notts.) ... 34 ... SK6567
Ollerton (Salop) ... 32 ... SJ6425
Olney ... 27 ... SP8851
Olton ... 25 ... SP1282
Olveston ... 17 ... ST6087
Ombersley ... 25 ... SO8463
Ompton ... 34 ... SK6865
Onchan ... 43 ... SC4078
Onecote ... 33 ... SK0555
Ongar Hill ... 28 ... TF5724
Ongar Street ... 24 ... SO3967
Onibury ... 24 ... SO4579
Onich ... 55 ... NN0261
Onllwyn ... 15 ... SN8310
Onneley ... 32 ... SJ7542
Onslow Village ... 11 ... SU9849
Opinan (Highld.) ... 64 ... NG7472
Opinan (Highld.) ... 64 ... NG8796
Orby ... 35 ... TF4967
Orchard ... 8 ... ST8216
Orchard Portman ... 7 ... ST2421
Orcheston ... 8 ... SU0545
Orcop ... 16 ... SO4726
Ord ... 58 ... NG6113
Ordhead ... 62 ... NJ6610
Ordiequish ... 61 ... NJ3357
Ore ... 12 ... TQ8311
Oreham Common ... 11 ... TQ2214
Oreton ... 24 ... SO6580
Orford (Ches.) ... 32 ... SJ6090
Orford (Suff.) ... 21 ... TM4250
Orgreave ... 33 ... SK1415
Orlestone ... 13 ... TR0034
Orleton (Here. and Worc.) ... 24 ... SO4967
Orleton (Here. and Worc.) ... 24 ... SO6967
Orlingbury ... 27 ... SP8572
Ormesby ... 42 ... NZ5317
Ormesby St. Margaret ... 29 ... TG4915
Ormesby St. Michael ... 29 ... TG4814
Ormiscaig ... 64 ... NG8590
Ormiston ... 52 ... NT4169
Ormsaigmore ... 54 ... NM4763
Ormskirk ... 36 ... SD4107
Orosay (Isle of Lewis) ... 63 ... NB3612
Orphir ... 63 ... HY3404
Orpington ... 12 ... TQ4665
Orrell ... 36 ... SD5203
Orrin Rest ... 60 ... NH3850
Orrisdale Head ... 43 ... SC3192
Orroland ... 45 ... NX7746
Orsay ... 48 ... NR1651
Orsett ... 20 ... TQ6481
Orslow ... 32 ... SJ8015
Orston ... 34 ... SK7741
Orton (Cumbr.) ... 41 ... NY6208
Orton (Northants.) ... 26 ... SP8079
Orton Longueville ... 27 ... TL1696
Orton Waterville ... 27 ... TL1596
Orton-on-the-Hill ... 26 ... SK3004
Orval ... 58 ... NM3399
Orwell ... 20 ... TL3650
Osbaldeston ... 36 ... SD6431
Osbaston ... 26 ... SK4204
Osborne ... 9 ... SZ5194
Osborne Bay ... 9 ... SZ5395
Osbournby ... 35 ... TF0638
Oscroft ... 32 ... SJ5066
Osdale ... 58 ... NG3241
Ose ... 58 ... NG3442
Osea Island ... 21 ... TL9106
Osgathorpe ... 33 ... SK4219
Osgodby (Lincs.) ... 35 ... TF0792
Osgodby (N Yorks.) ... 38 ... SE6433
Osgodby (N Yorks.) ... 43 ... TA0585
Oskaig ... 58 ... NG5438
Oskamull ... 54 ... NM4540
Osmaston ... 33 ... SK1944
Osmington ... 8 ... SY7282
Osmington Mills ... 8 ... SY7381
Osmotherley ... 42 ... SE4597
Osnaburgh or Dairsie ... 57 ... NO4117
Ospringe ... 13 ... TQ9960
Ossett ... 37 ... SE2720
Ossington ... 34 ... SK7564
Ostend ... 21 ... TQ9397
Oswaldkirk ... 42 ... SE6279
Oswaldtwistle ... 36 ... SD7327
Oswestry ... 31 ... SJ2829
Otford ... 12 ... TQ5359
Otham ... 12 ... TQ7954
Othery ... 7 ... ST3831
Otley (Suff.) ... 21 ... TM2055
Otley (W Yorks.) ... 37 ... SE2045
Otter Ferry ... 49 ... NR9384
Otterbourne ... 9 ... SU4522
Otterburn (N Yorks.) ... 37 ... SD8857
Otterburn (Northum.) ... 47 ... NY8893
Otterburn Camp ... 47 ... NY8995
Otterham ... 4 ... SX1690
Ottershaw ... 11 ... TQ0264
Otterswick (Yell) ... 63 ... HU5185
Otterton ... 7 ... SY0785
Ottery St. Mary ... 7 ... SY0995
Ottringham ... 39 ... TA2624
Oughtershaw ... 41 ... SD8781
Oughtibridge ... 33 ... SK3093
Oulston ... 42 ... SE5474
Oulton (Cumbr.) ... 46 ... NY2551
Oulton (Norf.) ... 29 ... TG1328
Oulton (Staffs.) ... 33 ... SJ9035
Oulton (Suff.) ... 29 ... TM5194
Oulton (W Yorks.) ... 38 ... SE3627
Oulton Broad ... 29 ... TM5292
Oulton Street ... 29 ... TG1527
Oundle ... 27 ... TL0488
Ousby ... 41 ... NY6134
Ousdale ... 67 ... ND0620
Ousden ... 20 ... TL7359
Ouseburn ... 38 ... SE4461
Ousefleet ... 39 ... SE8223
Ouston ... 47 ... NZ2554
Out Newton ... 39 ... TA3822
Out Rawcliffe ... 36 ... SD4041
Outertown ... 63 ... HY2310
Outgate ... 40 ... SD3599
Outhgill ... 41 ... NY7801
Outlane ... 37 ... SE0817
Outwell ... 28 ... TF5104
Outwood (Surrey) ... 12 ... TQ3246
Outwood (W Yorks.) ... 37 ... SE3223
Oval, The ... 17 ... ST7363
Ovenden ... 37 ... SE0727
Over (Avon) ... 17 ... ST5882
Over (Cambs.) ... 27 ... TL3770
Over Haddon ... 33 ... SK2066
Over Kellet ... 36 ... SD5169
Over Kiddington ... 18 ... SP4122
Over Norton ... 18 ... SP3128
Over Silton ... 42 ... SE4593
Over Wallop ... 10 ... SU2838
Over Whitacre ... 26 ... SP2591
Overbury ... 25 ... SO9537
Overseal ... 33 ... SK2915
Overstone ... 26 ... SP8066
Overstrand ... 29 ... TG2440
Overton (Clwyd) ... 32 ... SJ3741
Overton (Dumf. and Galwy.) ... 45 ... NX9864
Overton (Grampn.) ... 62 ... NJ8714
Overton (Hants.) ... 10 ... SU5149
Overton (Lancs.) ... 36 ... SD4357
Overton (Salop) ... 24 ... SO4972
Overton Green ... 32 ... SJ7960
Overtown ... 50 ... NS8052
Overy Staithe ... 28 ... TF8444
Oving (Bucks.) ... 18 ... SP7821
Oving (W Susx) ... 11 ... SU9005
Ovingdean ... 12 ... TA3503
Ovingham ... 47 ... NZ0863
Ovington (Durham) ... 42 ... NZ1314
Ovington (Essex) ... 20 ... TL7742
Ovington (Hants.) ... 9 ... SU5631
Ovington (Norf.) ... 29 ... TF9202
Ovington (Northum.) ... 47 ... NZ0663
Ower ... 9 ... SU3216
Owermoigne ... 8 ... SY7685
Owlswick ... 18 ... SP7906
Owmby ... 34 ... SK9987
Owslebury ... 9 ... SU5123
Owston ... 26 ... SK7708
Owston Ferry ... 39 ... SE8000
Owstwick ... 39 ... TA2732
Owthorpe ... 34 ... SK6733
Oxborough ... 28 ... TF7401
Oxen Park ... 40 ... SD3187
Oxenholme ... 40 ... SD5390
Oxenhope ... 37 ... SE0334
Oxenton ... 25 ... SO9531
Oxenwood ... 10 ... SU3059
Oxford ... 18 ... SP5305
Oxhill ... 26 ... SP3145
Oxley ... 25 ... SJ9002
Oxley's Green ... 12 ... TQ6921
Oxnam ... 52 ... NT7018
Oxshott ... 11 ... TQ1460
Oxspring ... 37 ... SE2601
Oxted ... 12 ... TQ3852
Oxton (Borders) ... 52 ... NT4953
Oxton (Notts.) ... 34 ... SK6351
Oxwich ... 15 ... SS4986
Oxwick ... 28 ... TF9125
Oykel Bridge ... 66 ... NC3800
Oyne ... 62 ... NJ6725

Packington ... 33 ... SK3614
Padanaram ... 57 ... NO4251
Padbury ... 18 ... SP7130
Paddington ... 12 ... TQ2482
Paddlesworth ... 13 ... TR1939
Paddock Wood ... 12 ... TQ6645
Paddockhaugh ... 61 ... NJ2058
Paddolgreen ... 32 ... SJ5032
Padeswood ... 31 ... SJ2761
Padiham ... 37 ... SD7933
Padstow ... 2 ... SW9175
Pagham ... 11 ... SZ8897
Paglesham ... 21 ... TQ9292
Paible (W Isles) ... 63 ... NF7367
Paible (W Isles) ... 63 ... NG0299
Paignton ... 5 ... SX8960
Pailton ... 26 ... SP4781
Painscastle ... 23 ... SO1646
Painswick ... 17 ... SO8609
Paisley ... 50 ... NS4864
Pakefield ... 29 ... TM5390
Pakenham ... 29 ... TL9267
Pale ... 31 ... SH9836
Palestine ... 10 ... SU2640
Paley Street ... 11 ... SU8776
Palgowan ... 44 ... NX3783
Palgrave ... 29 ... TM1178
Palmerstown ... 16 ... ST1369
Palnackie ... 45 ... NX8257
Palnure ... 44 ... NX4563
Palterton ... 33 ... SK4768
Pamber End ... 10 ... SU6158
Pamber Green ... 10 ... SU6059
Pamber Heath ... 10 ... SU6262
Pamphill ... 8 ... ST9900
Pampisford ... 20 ... TL4948
Panbride ... 57 ... NO5635
Pancrasweek ... 4 ... SS2905
Pandy (Clwyd) ... 31 ... SJ1935
Pandy (Gwent) ... 16 ... SO3322
Pandy (Powys) ... 22 ... SH9004
Pandy Tudur ... 31 ... SH8564
Panfield ... 20 ... TL7325
Pangbourne ... 10 ... SU6376
Pannal ... 38 ... SE3051
Pant ... 31 ... SJ2722
Pant Mawr ... 22 ... SN8482
Pant-glas (Gwyn.) ... 30 ... SH4747
Pant-pastynog ... 31 ... SJ0461
Pant-y-dwr ... 23 ... SN9875
Pant-y-ffridd ... 23 ... SJ1502
Pantglas (Powys) ... 22 ... SN7898
Pantgwyn ... 14 ... SN2446
Panton ... 35 ... TF1778
Pantperthog ... 22 ... SH7504
Pantyffynnon ... 15 ... SN6210
Panxworth ... 29 ... TG3413
Papcastle ... 40 ... NY1131
Papple ... 52 ... NT5972
Papplewick ... 34 ... SK5451
Papworth Everard ... 27 ... TL2862
Papworth St. Agnes ... 27 ... TL2664
Par ... 3 ... SX0653
Parbold ... 36 ... SD4911
Parbrook ... 7 ... ST5736
Parc ... 30 ... SH4486
Parcllyn ... 14 ... SN2451
Pardshaw ... 40 ... NY0924
Parham ... 29 ... TM3060
Park (Grampn.) ... 62 ... NO7798
Park (Strath.) ... 54 ... NM9340
Park Corner ... 18 ... SU6988
Park End (Northum.) ... 47 ... NY8775
Park Gate (Hants.) ... 9 ... SU5108
Parkend (Glos.) ... 17 ... SO6108
Parkeston ... 21 ... TM2332
Parkgate (Ches.) ... 31 ... SJ2778
Parkgate (Ches.) ... 32 ... SJ7874
Parkgate (Dumf. and Galwy.) ... 45 ... NY0288
Parkgate (Surrey) ... 11 ... TQ2043
Parkham ... 6 ... SS3821
Parkham Ash ... 6 ... SS3620
Parkhouse ... 16 ... SO5002
Parkhurst ... 9 ... SZ4991
Parkneuk ... 57 ... NO7976
Parkstone ... 8 ... SZ0491
Parley Common ... 8 ... SZ0999
Parley Cross ... 8 ... SZ0898
Parracombe ... 6 ... SS6744
Parrog ... 14 ... SN0439
Parson Drove ... 27 ... TF3708
Partick ... 50 ... NS5567
Partington ... 32 ... SJ7191
Partney ... 35 ... TF4168
Parton (Cumbr.) ... 40 ... NX9720
Parton (Dumf. and Galwy.) ... 45 ... NX6970
Partridge Green ... 11 ... TQ1919
Parwich ... 33 ... SK1854
Passenham ... 18 ... SP7839
Paston ... 29 ... TG3235
Patcham ... 12 ... TQ3009
Patching ... 11 ... TQ0806
Patchole ... 6 ... SS6142
Patchway ... 17 ... ST6082
Pateley Bridge ... 37 ... SE1565
Path of Condie ... 56 ... NO0711
Pathhead (Fife.) ... 51 ... NT2892
Pathhead (Grampn.) ... 57 ... NO7363
Pathhead (Lothian) ... 51 ... NT3964
Pathhead (Strath.) ... 50 ... NS6114
Patmore Heath ... 20 ... TL4526
Patna ... 50 ... NS4110
Patney ... 17 ... SU0758
Patrick ... 43 ... SC2482
Patrick Brompton ... 42 ... SE2290
Patrington ... 39 ... TA3122
Patrixbourne ... 13 ... TR1855
Patterdale ... 40 ... NY3915
Pattingham ... 25 ... SO8299
Pattishall ... 26 ... SP6654
Paul ... 2 ... SW4627
Paulerspury ... 26 ... SP7145
Paull ... 39 ... TA1626
Paulton ... 17 ... ST6456
Pauperhaugh ... 47 ... NZ1099
Pavenham ... 27 ... SP9955
Pawlett ... 7 ... ST2942
Pawston ... 53 ... NT8532
Paxford ... 25 ... SP1837
Paxhill Park ... 12 ... TQ3626
Paxton ... 53 ... NT9352
Payhembury ... 7 ... ST0801
Paythorne ... 37 ... SD8251
Peacehaven ... 12 ... TQ4101
Peachley ... 24 ... SO8057
Peak Dale ... 33 ... SK0976
Peak Forest ... 33 ... SK1179
Peakirk ... 27 ... TF1606
Pearsie ... 57 ... NO3659
Peasedown St. John ... 17 ... ST7057
Peasemore ... 10 ... SU4576
Peasenhall ... 29 ... TM3569
Peaslake ... 11 ... TQ0844
Peasmarsh ... 13 ... TQ8822
Peaston Bank ... 52 ... NT4466
Peat Hill (Tays.) ... 57 ... NO5067
Peat Inn ... 57 ... NO4509
Peathill (Grampn.) ... 62 ... NJ9365
Peatling Magna ... 26 ... SP5992
Peatling Parva ... 26 ... SP5889
Peaton ... 24 ... SO5385
Pebmarsh ... 21 ... TL8533
Pebworth ... 25 ... SP1347
Pecket Well ... 37 ... SD9929
Peckforton ... 32 ... SJ5356
Peckleton ... 26 ... SK4701
Pedmore ... 25 ... SO9182
Pedwell ... 7 ... ST4236
Peebles ... 51 ... NT2540
Peel ... 43 ... SC2484
Pegswood ... 47 ... NZ2287
Pegwell Bay ... 13 ... TR3563
Peinchorran ... 58 ... NG5233
Peinlich ... 58 ... NG4158
Pelaw ... 47 ... NZ2962
Peldon ... 21 ... TL9816
Pelsall ... 25 ... SK0103
Pelton ... 47 ... NZ2553
Pelutho ... 45 ... NY1249
Pelynt ... 4 ... SX2055
Pembrey ... 15 ... SN4201
Pembridge ... 24 ... SO3858
Pembroke ... 14 ... SM9901
Pembroke Dock ... 14 ... SM9603
Pembury ... 12 ... TQ6240
Pen Coed (Powys) ... 23 ... SH9808
Pen-Sarn (Gwyn.) ... 30 ... SH4344
Pen-Sarn (Gwyn.) ... 30 ... SH5728
Pen-bont Rhydybeddau ... 22 ... SN6783
Pen-ffordd ... 14 ... SN0722
Pen-isa'r-cwm ... 31 ... SJ0018
Pen-llyn (Gwyn.) ... 30 ... SH3482
Pen-twyn ... 16 ... SO5209
Pen-y-bont (Clwyd) ... 31 ... SJ2123
Pen-y-bryn ... 30 ... SH6919
Pen-y-bwlch ... 22 ... SN7763
Pen-y-cae (Powys) ... 15 ... SN8413
Pen-y-cae-mawr ... 16 ... ST4195
Pen-y-cefn ... 31 ... SJ1175
Pen-y-clawdd ... 16 ... SO4508
Pen-y-coedcae ... 16 ... ST0587
Pen-y-garn ... 15 ... SN5731
Penallt ... 16 ... SO5210
Penally ... 14 ... SS1199
Penant ... 22 ... SN5163
Penare ... 3 ... SW9940
Penarth ... 16 ... ST1871
Penbryn ... 14 ... SN2952
Pencader ... 15 ... SN4436
Pencaitland ... 52 ... NT4468
Pencarreg ... 22 ... SN5345
Pencelli ... 16 ... SO0925
Penclawdd ... 15 ... SS5495
Pencoed (Mid Glam.) ... 15 ... SS9581
Pencombe ... 24 ... SO5952
Pencoyd ... 16 ... SO5126
Pencraig (Here. and Worc.) ... 17 ... SO5722
Pencraig (Powys) ... 31 ... SJ0427
Pendeen ... 2 ... SW3834
Penderyn ... 15 ... SN9408
Pendine ... 14 ... SN2308
Pendlebury ... 37 ... SD7802
Pendleton ... 37 ... SD7539
Pendock ... 24 ... SO7832
Pendoggett ... 3 ... SX0279
Pendoylan ... 16 ... ST0567
Penegoes ... 22 ... SH7701
Pengam ... 16 ... ST1797
Penge ... 12 ... TQ3570
Penhalvean ... 2 ... SW7037
Penhow ... 16 ... ST4290
Penhurst ... 12 ... TQ6916
Peniarth ... 22 ... SH6105
Penicuik ... 51 ... NT2359
Penifiler ... 58 ... NG4841
Peninver ... 48 ... NR7524
Penisar Waun ... 30 ... SH5564
Penistone ... 37 ... SE2402
Penjerrick ... 2 ... SW7730
Penketh ... 32 ... SJ5687
Penkill ... 44 ... NX2398
Penkridge ... 33 ... SJ9214
Penley ... 32 ... SJ4039
Penllergaer ... 15 ... SS6199
Penllyn (S Glam.) ... 16 ... SS9776
Penmachno ... 31 ... SH7950
Penmaen ... 15 ... SS5288
Penmaenmawr ... 30 ... SH7176
Penmaenpool ... 30 ... SH6918
Penmark ... 16 ... ST0568
Penmon ... 30 ... SH6381
Penmorfa ... 30 ... SH5440
Penmynydd ... 30 ... SH5174
Penn ... 19 ... SU9193
Penn Street ... 19 ... SU9296
Pennal ... 22 ... SH0900
Pennan ... 62 ... NJ8465
Pennant ... 22 ... SN8897
Pennant-Melangell ... 31 ... SJ0226
Pennard ... 15 ... SS5688
Pennerley ... 24 ... SO3599
Pennington ... 40 ... SD2577
Penny Bridge ... 40 ... SD3082
Pennycross ... 54 ... NM5025
Pennygown ... 54 ... NM6042
Pennymoor ... 5 ... SS8611
Penparc ... 14 ... SN2148
Penparcau ... 22 ... SN5980
Penperlleni ... 16 ... SO3204
Penpillick ... 3 ... SX0756
Penpol ... 2 ... SW8139
Penpoll ... 4 ... SX1454
Penpont (Dumf. and Galwy.) ... 45 ... NX8494
Penpont (Powys) ... 16 ... SN9728
Penrherber ... 14 ... SN2839
Penrhiwceiber ... 16 ... ST0597
Penrhiwllan ... 22 ... SN3742
Penrhiwpal ... 22 ... SN3445
Penrhos (Gwent) ... 16 ... SO4111
Penrhos (Gwyn.) ... 30 ... SH2781
Penrhos (Gwyn.) ... 30 ... SH3433
Penrhos (Powys) ... 15 ... SN8011
Penrhyn Bay ... 31 ... SH8281
Penrhyn-side ... 31 ... SH8181
Penrhyncoch ... 22 ... SN6484
Penrhyndeudraeth ... 30 ... SH6139
Penrice ... 15 ... SS4988
Penrith ... 40 ... NY5130
Penrose ... 2 ... SW8770
Penruddock ... 40 ... NY4227
Penryn ... 2 ... SW7834
Pensarn (Clwyd) ... 31 ... SH9478
Pensax ... 24 ... SO7269
Pensby ... 31 ... SJ2683
Penselwood ... 8 ... ST7531
Pensford ... 17 ... ST6163
Penshaw ... 47 ... NZ3253
Penshurst ... 12 ... TQ5243
Pensilva ... 4 ... SX2969
Pentewan ... 3 ... SX0147
Pentir ... 30 ... SH5767
Pentire ... 2 ... SW7961
Pentney ... 28 ... TF7213
Penton Mewsey ... 10 ... SU3247
Pentraeth ... 30 ... SH5278
Pentre (Clwyd) ... 31 ... SJ0862
Pentre (Clwyd) ... 31 ... SJ2840
Pentre (Powys) ... 31 ... SO0686
Pentre (Powys) ... 23 ... SO2466
Pentre (Salop) ... 32 ... SJ3617
Pentre Berw ... 30 ... SH4772
Pentre Halkyn ... 31 ... SJ2072
Pentrety gwyn ... 15 ... SN8135
Pentre'r-felin ... 15 ... SN9130
Pentre-Dolau-Honddu ... 23 ... SN9943
Pentre-Gwenlais ... 15 ... SN6116
Pentre-bach (Powys) ... 15 ... SN9033
Pentre-celyn (Clwyd) ... 31 ... SJ1453
Pentre-cwrt ... 22 ... SN3938
Pentre-dwfr ... 32 ... SJ1946
Pentre-dwr ... 15 ... SS6996
Pentre-poeth ... 16 ... ST2686
Pentre-tafarn-y-fedw ... 31 ... SH8162
Pentrebach (Mid Glam.) ... 16 ... SO0604
Pentrebeirdd ... 23 ... SJ1913
Pentrefelin ... 30 ... SH5239
Pentrefoelas ... 31 ... SH8751
Pentregat ... 22 ... SN3551
Pentrich ... 33 ... SK3852
Pentridge ... 8 ... SU0317
Pentyrch ... 16 ... ST1082
Penuwch ... 22 ... SN5962
Penwithick ... 3 ... SX0256
Penybanc ... 15 ... SN6124
Penybont (Powys) ... 23 ... SO1164
Penybontfawr ... 31 ... SJ0824
Penycae (Clwyd) ... 31 ... SJ2745
Penyffordd ... 32 ... SJ3061
Penygarnedd ... 31 ... SJ1023
Penygraig ... 16 ... SS9991
Penygroes (Dyfed) ... 15 ... SN5813
Penygroes (Gwyn.) ... 30 ... SH4753
Penysarn ... 30 ... SH4690
Penywaun ... 16 ... SN9704
Penzance ... 2 ... SW4730
Peopleton ... 25 ... SO9350
Peover Heath ... 32 ... SJ7973
Peper Harow ... 11 ... SU9344
Peplow ... 32 ... SJ6324
Percie ... 62 ... NO5991
Percyhorner ... 62 ... NJ9565
Perivale ... 19 ... TQ1682
Perranarworthal ... 2 ... SW7738
Perranporth ... 2 ... SW7554
Perranuthnoe ... 2 ... SW5329
Perranzabuloe ... 2 ... SW7752
Perry ... 27 ... TL1466
Perry Barr ... 25 ... SP0791
Perry Green ... 20 ... TL4317
Pershore ... 25 ... SO9446
Pert ... 57 ... NO6565
Pertenhall ... 27 ... TL0865
Perth ... [illegible] ... NO1123
Perthy ... 32 ... SJ3633
Perton ... 25 ... SO8598
Peter Tavy ... 4 ... SX5177
Peter's Green ... 19 ... TL1419
Peterborough ... 27 ... TL1999
Peterchurch ... 23 ... SO3438
Peterculter ... 62 ... NJ8400
Peterhead ... 62 ... NK1346
Peterlee ... 47 ... NZ4440
Peters Marland ... 4 ... SS4713
Petersfield ... 10 ... SU7423
Peterston-super Ely ... 16 ... ST0876
Peterstone Wentlooge ... 16 ... ST2680
Peterstow ... 17 ... SO5624
Petham ... 13 ... TR1251
Petrockstow ... 4 ... SS5109
Pett ... 13 ... TQ8714
Pettaugh ... 21 ... TM1659
Pettinain ... 51 ... NS9542
Pettistree ... 21 ... TM2954
Petton (Devon.) ... 7 ... ST0024

Petton
Ratcliffe Culey

Petton (Salop) 32 SJ4326
Petty 62 NJ7636
Pettycur 51 NT2686
Pettymuk 62 NJ9024
Petworth 11 SU9721
Pevensey 12 TQ6405
Philham 4 SS2522
Philiphaugh 52 NT4427
Phillack 2 SW5539
Philleigh 2 SW8639
Philpstoun 51 NT0577
Phoenix Green 10 SU7655
Pica 40 NY0222
Piccotts End 19 TL0509
Pickering 43 SE7983
Picket Piece 10 SU3947
Picket Post 8 SU1905
Pickhill 42 SE3483
Picklescott 24 SO4399
Pickmere 32 SJ6876
Pickwell (Devon.) 6 SS4540
Pickwell (Leic.) 26 SK7811
Pickworth (Leic.) 34 SK9913
Pickworth (Lincs.) 35 TF0433
Picton (N Yorks.) 42 NZ4107
Picton Castle (ant.) 14 SN0113
Piddinghoe 12 TQ4303
Piddington (Northants.) 26 SP8054
Piddington (Oxon.) 18 SP6317
Piddlehinton 8 SY7197
Piddletrenthide 8 SY7099
Pidley 27 TL3377
Piercebridge 42 NZ2115
Pierowall 63 HY4348
Pigdon 47 NZ1588
Pikehall 33 SK1959
Pilgrims Hatch 20 TQ5895
Pilham 34 SK8693
Pill 16 ST5275
Pillaton 4 SX3664
Pillerton Hersey 26 SP2948
Pillerton Priors 26 SP2947
Pilleth 23 SO2568
Pilley 38 SE3300
Pilling 36 SD4048
Pilling Lane 36 SD3749
Pilning 16 ST5585
Pilsbury 33 SK1163
Pilsdon 7 SY4199
Pilsley (Derby.) 33 SK2471
Pilsley (Derby.) 33 SK4262
Pilton (Leic.) 27 SK9102
Pilton (Northants.) 27 TL0284
Pilton (Somer.) 8 ST5940
Pimperne 8 ST9009
Pinchbeck 35 TF2425
Pinchbeck West 35 TF2024
Pinfold 36 SD3811
Pinhoe 5 SX9694
Pinmore 44 NX2090
Pinner 19 TQ1289
Pinvin 25 SO9548
Pinwherry 44 NX1987
Pinxton 34 SK4555
Pipe Gate 32 SJ7442
Pipe and Lyde 24 SO5044
Piperhill 60 NH8650
Pipewell 27 SP8385
Pippacott 6 SS5237
Pirbright 11 SU9455
Pirnmill 49 NR8744
Pirton (Here. and Worc.) 25 SO8847
Pirton (Herts.) 19 TL1431
Pishill 18 SU7289
Pistyll 30 SH3242
Pitagowan 56 NN8266
Pitblae 62 NJ9865
Pitcairngreen 56 NO0627
Pitcaple 62 NJ7225
Pitcarity 57 NO3265
Pitch Green 18 SP7703
Pitch Place 11 SU9752
Pitchcombe 17 SO8408
Pitchcott 18 SP7720
Pitchford 24 SJ5303
Pitcombe 8 ST6732
Pitcox 52 NT6475
Pitcur 57 NO2536
Pitfichie 62 NJ6716
Pitforthie 57 NO8079
Pitfour Castle 56 NO1921
Pitgrudy 65 NH7990
Pitkennedy 57 NO5454
Pitkevy 57 NO2403
Pitlessie 57 NO3309
Pitlochry 56 NN9458
Pitmedden 62 NJ8927
Pitminster 7 ST2119
Pitmuies 57 NO5649
Pitmunie 62 NJ6615
Pitney 7 ST4428
Pitroddie 56 NO2224
Pitscottie 57 NO4113
Pitsea 20 TQ7488
Pitsford 26 SP7568
Pitstone 19 SP9415
Pitt Down 9 SU4128
Pittendreich 61 NJ1961
Pittentrail 66 NC7202
Pittenweem 57 NO5402
Pittington 47 NZ3245
Pitton 8 SU2131
Pixey Green 29 TM2475
Place Newton 39 SE8872
Plains 50 NS7966
Plaish 24 SO5296
Plaistow 11 TQ0030
Plaitford 9 SU2719
Plas Gogerddan 22 SN6283
Plas Gwynant 30 SH6250
Plas Isaf 31 SJ0442
Plas Llwyd 31 SH9979
Plas Llwyngwern 22 SH7504
Plas Llysyn 23 SN9597
Plas Nantyr 31 SJ1537
Plas-yn-Cefn 31 SJ0171
Plashetts 46 NY6690
Plastow Green 10 SU5361
Platt 12 TQ6257
Plawsworth 47 NZ2647
Plaxtol 12 TQ6053
Play Hatch 10 SU7376
Playden 13 TQ9121
Playford 21 TM2148
Playing Place 2 SW8141
Plealey 24 SJ4206
Plean 50 NS8386
Pleasington 36 SD6425
Pleasley 34 SK5064
Plenmeller 46 NY7162
Pleshey 20 TL6614
Plockton 59 NG8033
Ploughfield 24 SO3841
Plowden 24 SO3888
Ploxgreen 24 SJ3604
Pluckley 13 TQ9045
Plumbland 40 NY1438
Plumley 32 SJ7275
Plumpton (E Susx.) 12 TQ3613
Plumpton (Lancs.) 36 SD3732
Plumpton Green 12 TQ3616
Plumpton Head 40 NY5035
Plumpton Wall 40 NY4937
Plumstead 29 TG1335
Plumtree 34 SK6133
Plungar 34 SK7633
Pluscarden 61 NJ1455
Plush 8 ST7102
Plwmp 22 SN3652
Plymouth 4 SX4755
Plympton 4 SX5356
Plymstock 4 SX5152
Plymtree 7 ST0502
Pockley 42 SE6385
Pocklington 39 SE8048
Pode Hole 35 TF2122
Podimore 7 ST5424
Podington 27 SP9462
Podmore 32 SJ7835
Pointon 35 TF1131
Pokesdown 8 SZ1292
Polapit Tamar 4 SX3389
Polbae 44 NX2873
Polbain 64 NB9910
Polbathic 4 SX3456
Polbeth 51 NT0364
Polchar 60 NH8909
Polebrook 27 TL0687
Polegate 12 TQ5805
Polesworth 26 SK2602
Polglass 64 NC0307
Polgooth 3 SW9950
Poling 11 TQ0405
Polkerris 3 SX0952
Pollachar 63 NF7414
Pollington 38 SE6119
Polloch 54 NM7068
Pollokshaws 50 NS5560
Pollokshields 50 NS5663
Polmassick 2 SW9745
Polmont 50 NS9378
Polnessan 50 NS4111
Polperro 4 SX2051
Polruan 4 SX1250
Polsham 7 ST5142
Polstead 21 TL9938
Poltimore 5 SX9696
Polton 51 NT2964
Polwarth 53 NT7450
Polyphant 4 SX2682
Polzeath 2 SW9378
Ponders End 20 TQ3695
Pondersbridge 27 TL2691
Ponsanooth 2 SW7336
Ponsworthy 5 SX7073
Pont Cyfyng 30 SH7357
Pont Nedd Fechan 15 SN9007
Pont Pen-y-benglog 30 SH6460
Pont Rhyd-y-cyff 15 SS8788
Pont-Llogel 31 SJ0315
Pont-faen (Powys) 23 SN9934
Pont-rhyd-y-fen 15 SS7994
Pont-rug 30 SH5163
Pont-y-pant 30 SH7554
Pontamman 15 SN6312
Pontantwn 15 SN4412
Pontardawe 15 SN7204
Pontardulais 15 SN5903
Pontarsais 15 SN4428
Pontefract 38 SE4522
Ponteland 47 NZ1672
Ponterwyd 22 SN7481
Pontesbury 24 SJ3905
Pontfadog 31 SJ2338
Pontfaen (Dyfed) 14 SN0234
Ponthenry 15 SN4709
Ponthirwaun 14 SN2645
Pontllanfraith 16 ST1895
Pontlliw 15 SN6101
Pontlottyn 16 SO1206
Pontlyfni 30 SH4352
Pontnewydd 16 ST2896
Pontrhydfendigaid 22 SN7366
Pontrhydygroes 22 SN7472
Pontrilas 16 SO3927
Pontrobert 23 SJ1112
Ponts Green 12 TQ6717
Pontshaen 22 SN4346
Pontshill 17 SO6321
Pontsticill 16 SO0511
Pontyates 15 SN4708
Pontyberem 15 SN4911
Pontybodkin 31 SJ2759
Pontyclun 16 ST0381
Pontycymer 15 SS9091
Pontypool 16 SO2701
Pontypridd 16 ST0690
Pontywaun 16 ST2293
Pooksgreen 9 SU3710
Pool (W Yorks.) 37 SE2445
Pool Quay 23 SJ2512
Pool Street 20 TL7637
Pool of Muckhart 56 NO0001
Poole (Dorset) 8 SZ0190
Poole Green 32 SJ6355
Poole Keynes 17 ST9995
Poolewe 64 NG8580
Pooley Bridge 40 NY4724
Poolhill 17 SO7329
Popeswood 11 SU8469
Popham 10 SU5543
Poplar 20 TQ3781
Porchfield 9 SZ4491
Porin 59 NH3155
Porkellis 2 SW6933
Porlock 6 SS8846
Port Ann 49 NR9086
Port Appin 54 NM9045
Port Askaig 48 NR4369
Port Bannatyne 49 NS0867
Port Carlisle 46 NY2461
Port Charlotte 48 NR2558
Port Corbert 48 NR6528
Port Cornaa 43 SC4787
Port Dinorwic 30 SH5267
Port Doir'a'Chrorain 48 NR5875
Port Driseach 49 NR9973
Port Ellen 48 NR3645
Port Elphinstone 62 NJ7719
Port Erin 43 SC1969
Port Gaverne 3 SX0080
Port Glasgow 49 NS3274
Port Henderson 64 NG7573
Port Isaac 3 SW9980
Port Logan 46 NX0940
Port Mulgrave 43 NZ7917
Port Quin 2 SW9780
Port Ramsey 54 NM8845
Port St. Mary 43 SC2067
Port Sunlight 32 SJ3483
Port Talbot 15 SS7690
Port Vasgo 66 NC5865
Port Wemyss 48 NR1751
Port William 44 NX3343
Port e Vullen 43 SC4793
Port of Menteith 56 NN5801
Port of Ness 63 NB6363
Port-Eynon 15 SS4685
Portachoillan 48 NR7557
Portavadie 49 NR9369
Portbury 16 ST4975
Portchester 9 SU6105
Portencross 49 NS1748
Portesham 8 SY6085
Portfield Gate 14 SM9115
Portgain 14 SM8132
Portgate 4 SX4185
Portgordon 61 NJ3964
Portgower 67 ND0013
Porth 16 ST0291
Porth Mellin 2 SW6618
Porth Navas 2 SW7428
Porthallow 2 SW7923
Porthcawl 15 SS8176
Porthcurno 2 SW3822
Porthgain 14 SM8132
Porthkerry 16 ST0866
Porthleven 2 SW6225
Porthmadog 30 SH5638
Porthmeor 2 SW4337
Portholland 2 SW9541
Porthoustock 2 SW8021
Porthpean 3 SX0350
Porthtowan 2 SW6847
Porthyrhyd (Dyfed) 15 SN5115
Porthyrhyd (Dyfed) 15 SN7137
Portincaple 49 NS2392
Portington 38 SE7830
Portinnisherrich 55 NM9711
Portishead 16 ST4676
Portknockie 61 NJ4868
Portland Harbour 8 SY6876
Portlethen 62 NO9396
Portloe 2 SW9339
Portmahomack 65 NH9184
Portmeirion 30 SH5937
Portmore (Hants.) 9 SZ3397
Portnacroish 54 NM9247
Portnaguiran 63 NB5537
Portnahaven 48 NR1652
Portnalong 58 NG3434
Portnancon 66 NC4260
Portobello (Dumf and Galwy) 44 NW9666
Portobello (Lothian) 51 NT3073
Porton 8 SU1836
Portpatrick 44 NZ0054
Portreath 2 SW6545
Portree 58 NG4843
Portrye 49 NS1758
Portscatho 2 SW8735
Portsea 9 SU6300
Portskerra 67 NC8765
Portskewett 16 ST4988
Portslade 11 TQ2506
Portslade-by-Sea 11 TQ2604
Portsmouth 9 SU6501
Portsmouth City Airport 9 SU6603
Portsoy 62 NJ5865
Portswood 9 SU4314
Portuairk 54 NM4468
Portvoller 63 NB5636
Portway (Warw.) 25 SP0872
Portwrinkle 4 SX3563
Poslingford 20 TL7648
Possingworth Park 12 TQ5420
Postbridge 5 SX6579
Postcombe 18 SU7099
Postling 13 TR1439
Postwick 29 TG2907
Potarch 62 NO6097
Potsgrove 19 SP9529
Pott Row 28 TF7021
Pott Shrigley 33 SJ9479
Potten End 19 TL0108
Potter Heigham 29 TG4119
Potter Street 20 TL4608
Potter's Cross 25 SO8484
Potterhanworth 35 TF0566
Potterne 17 ST9958
Potterne Wick 17 ST9957
Potters Bar 19 TL2501
Pottersbury 26 SP7543
Potto 42 NZ4703
Potton 27 TL2249
Poulton Island 21 TQ9591
Poughill (Corn.) 4 SS2207
Poughill (Devon.) 5 SS8508
Poulshot 17 ST9659
Poulton 17 SP1001
Poulton-le-Fylde 36 SD3439
Pound Bank 24 SO7373
Pound Hill 11 TQ2937
Poundon 18 SP6425
Poundsgate 5 SX7072
Poundstock 4 SX2099
Powburn (Nothum.) 53 NU0616
Powderham 5 SX9784
Powerstock 7 SY5196
Powfoot 45 NY1465
Powick 25 SO8351
Powmill 51 NT0197
Poxwell 8 SY7484
Poyle 11 TQ0376
Poynings 11 TQ2612
Poyntington 8 ST6419
Poynton 33 SJ9283
Poynton Green 32 SJ5618
Poys Street 29 TM3570
Poystreet Green 21 TL9858
Praa Sands 2 SW5828
Pratt's Bottom 12 TQ4762
Praze-an-Beeble 2 SW6336
Predannack Wollas 2 SW6616
Prees 32 SJ5533
Prees Green 32 SJ5631
Prees Higher Heath 32 SJ5636
Preesall 36 SD3646
Preesgweene 31 SJ3135
Pren-gwyn 22 SN4244
Prendwick 53 NU0012
Prenteg 30 SH5841
Prenton 32 SJ3184
Prescot (Mers.) 32 SJ4692
Prescott (Salop) 32 SJ4221
Pressen 53 NT8335
Prestatyn 31 SJ0682
Prestbury (Ches.) 33 SJ8976
Prestbury (Glos.) 17 SO9724
Presteigne 23 SO3164
Presthope 24 SO5897
Prestleigh 8 ST6340
Preston (Borders) 53 NT7957
Preston (Devon.) 5 SX8574
Preston (Dorset) 8 SY7082
Preston (E Susx) 12 TQ3107
Preston (Glos.) 24 SO6734
Preston (Glos.) 17 SP0400
Preston (Herts.) 19 TL1724
Preston (Humbs.) 39 TA1830
Preston (Kent) 13 TR0060
Preston (Kent) 13 TR2561
Preston (Lancs.) 36 SD5329
Preston (Leic.) 27 SK8602
Preston (Lothian) 52 NT5977
Preston (Suff.) 21 TL9450
Preston (Wilts.) 17 SU0377
Preston Bagot 25 SP1766
Preston Bissett 18 SP6530
Preston Brockhurst 32 SJ5324
Preston Brook 32 SJ5680
Preston Candover 10 SU6041
Preston Capes 26 SP5754
Preston Gubbals 32 SJ4819
Preston Wynne 24 SO5546
Preston on Stour 26 SP2049
Preston on Wye 24 SO3842
Preston upon the Weald Moors 32 SJ6815
Preston-under-Scar 41 SE0791
Prestonpans 51 NT3874
Prestwich 37 SD8103
Prestwick (Northum.) 47 NZ1872
Prestwick (Strath.) 49 NS3525
Prestwood 19 SP8700
Price Town 15 SS9392
Prickwillow 28 TL5982
Priddy 7 ST5250
Priest Hutton 40 SD5273
Priestweston 23 SO2997
Primethorpe 26 SP5293
Primrose Green 29 TG0616
Primrose Hill (Cambs.) 27 TL3889
Primrose Hill (Herts.) 19 TL0803
Princes Risborough 18 SP8003
Princethorpe 26 SP3970
Princetown 4 SX5873
Prior Muir 57 NO5213
Priors Hardwick 26 SP4756
Priors Marston 26 SP4857
Priory The 9 SZ6390
Priory Wood 23 SO2545
Priston 17 ST6960
Prittlewell 21 TQ8787
Privett 9 SU6726
Probus 2 SW8947
Prudhoe 47 NZ0962
Puckeridge 20 TL3823
Puckington 7 ST3718
Pucklechurch 17 ST6976
Puddington (Ches.) 32 SJ3273
Puddington (Devon) 5 SS8310
Puddledock 29 TM0592
Puddletown 8 SY7594
Pudleston 24 SO5659
Pudsey 37 SE2232
Pulborough 11 TQ0418
Puleston 32 SJ7322
Pulford 32 SJ3758
Pulham 8 ST7008
Pulham Market 29 TM1986
Pulham St. Mary 29 TM2185
Pulloxhill 19 TL0634
Pumpherston 51 NT0669
Pumsaint 22 SN6540
Puncheston 14 SN0029
Puncknowle 7 SY5388
Punnett's Town 12 TQ6220
Purbrook 9 SU6707
Purfleet 12 TQ5578
Puriton 7 ST3241
Purleigh 20 TL8301
Purley (Berks.) 10 SU6676
Purley (Gtr Lon.) 12 TQ3161
Purlogue 23 SO2877
Purls Bridge 28 TL4787
Purse Caundle 8 ST6917
Purslow 24 SO3680
Purston Jaglin 38 SE4319
Purton (Glos.) 17 SO6605
Purton (Glos.) 17 SO6904
Purton (Wilts.) 17 SU0887
Purton Stoke 17 SU0890
Pury End 26 SP7045
Pusey 18 SU3596
Putley 24 SO6437
Putney 11 TQ2274
Puttenham (Herts.) 19 SP8814
Puttenham (Surrey) 11 SU9347
Puxton 16 ST4063
Pwll 15 SN4801
Pwll-y-glaw 15 SS7993
Pwllcrochan 14 SM9202
Pwlldefaid 30 SH1526
Pwllheli 30 SH3735
Pwllmeyric 16 ST5192
Pye Corner 16 ST3485
Pyecombe 11 TQ2912
Pyle (I. of W.) 9 SZ4879
Pyle (Mid Glam.) 15 SS8282
Pylle 8 ST6038
Pymore 28 TL4986
Pyrford 11 TQ0458
Pyrton 18 SU6895
Pytchley 27 SP8574
Pyworthy 4 SS3102

Quabbs 23 SO2080
Quadring 35 TF2233
Quainton 18 SP7419
Quanter Ness 63 HY4114
Quarff 63 HU4235
Quarley 10 SU2743
Quarndon 33 SK3340
Quarrier's Homes 50 NS3666
Quarrington 35 TF0544
Quarrington Hill 42 NZ3337
Quarry Bank (W Mids.) 25 SO9386
Quarry, The 17 ST7399
Quarrybank (Ches.) 32 SJ5465
Quarryhill 65 NH7281
Quarrywood 61 NJ1864
Quarter 50 NS7251
Quatford 24 SO7390
Quatt 24 SO7588
Quebec 47 NZ1743
Quedgeley 17 SO8114
Queen Adelaide 28 TL5681
Queen Camel 8 ST5924
Queen Charlton 17 ST6366
Queenborough 13 TQ9471
Queenborough in Sheppey 13 TQ9174
Queensbury 37 SE1030
Queensferry (Clwyd) 32 SJ3168
Queensferry (Lothian) 51 NT1278
Queenzieburn 50 NS6977
Quendale 63 HU3713
Quendon 20 TL5130
Queniborough 26 SK6412
Quenington 17 SP1404
Quernmore 36 SD5160
Quethiock 4 SX3164
Quidenham 29 TM0287
Quidhampton (Hants) 10 SU5150
Quidhampton (Wilts.) 8 SU1030
Quilquox 62 NJ9038
Quindry 63 ND4392
Quinton 26 SP7754
Quoditch 4 SX4097
Quoig 56 NN8222
Quorndon 34 SK5616
Quothquan 51 NS9939
Quoyloo 63 HY2420
Quoys 63 HP6112

Raby 32 SJ3179
Rachub 30 SH6268
Rackenford 5 SS8418
Rackham 11 TQ0514
Rackheath 29 TG2814
Racks 45 NY0374
Rackwick (Hoy) 63 ND1999
Rackwick (Westray) 63 HY4449
Radcliffe (Gtr Mches) 37 SD7806
Radcliffe (Northum.) 47 NU2602
Radcliffe on Trent 34 SK6439
Radclive 18 SP6734
Radcot 18 SU2899
Radernie 57 NO4609
Radford Semele 26 SP3464
Radlett 19 TL1600
Radley 18 SU5398
Radnage 18 SU7897
Radstock 17 ST6854
Radstone 26 SP5840
Radway 26 SP3648
Radway Green 32 SJ7754
Radwell 19 TL2335
Radwinter 20 TL6037
Radyr 16 ST1380
Raerinish 63 NB4024
Rafford 61 NJ0656
Ragdale 34 SK6619
Raglan 16 SO4107
Ragnall 34 SK8073
Rahane 49 NS2386
Rainford 36 SD4700
Rainham (Gtr London) 20 TQ5282
Rainham (Kent) 12 TQ8165
Rainhill 32 SJ4990
Rainhill Stoops 32 SJ5090
Rainigadale 63 NB2201
Rainow 33 SJ9575
Rainton 42 SE3775
Rainworth 34 SK5958
Raisbeck 41 NY6407
Rait 56 NO2226
Raithby (Lincs.) 35 TF3084
Raithby (Lincs.) 35 TF3767
Rake 10 SU8027
Ram Lane 13 TQ9646
Ramasaig 58 NG1644
Rame (Corn.) 2 SW7233
Rame (Corn.) 4 SX4249
Rampisham 7 ST5502
Rampside 36 SD2366
Rampton (Cambs.) 27 TL4268
Rampton (Notts.) 34 SK7978
Ramsbottom 37 SD7916
Ramsbury 10 SU2771
Ramscraigs 67 ND1427
Ramsdean 10 SU7021
Ramsdell 10 SU5957
Ramsden 18 SP3515
Ramsden Bellhouse 20 TQ7194
Ramsden Heath 20 TQ7195
Ramsey (Cambs.) 27 TL2885
Ramsey (Essex) 21 TM2130
Ramsey (I. of M.) 43 SC4594
Ramsey Forty Foot 27 TL3187
Ramsey Hollow 27 TL3186
Ramsey Mereside 27 TL2889
Ramsey St. Mary's 27 TL2588
Ramsgate 13 TR3865
Ramsgate Street 29 TG0933
Ramsgill 37 SE1170
Ramshorn 33 SK0845
Ranby 34 SK6480
Rand 35 TF1078
Randwick 17 SO8206
Ranfurly 50 NS3865
Rangemore 33 SK1822
Rangeworthy 17 ST6886
Rankinston 50 NS4514
Ranskill 34 SK6587
Ranton 33 SJ8524
Ranworth 29 TG3514
Rascarrel 45 NX7948
Raskelf 38 SE4971
Rassau 16 SO1411
Rastrick 37 SE1321
Ratagan 59 NG9220
Ratby 26 SK5105
Ratcliffe Culey 26 SP3299

Ratcliffe on the Wreake
Salmond's Muir

Ratcliffe on the Wreake 34 SK6314
Rathen 62 NK0060
Rathillet 57 NO3620
Rathmell 37 SD8059
Ratho 51 NT1370
Rathven 61 NJ4465
Ratley 26 SP3847
Ratlinghope 24 SO4096
Rattar 67 ND2672
Ratten Row 36 SD4241
Rattery 5 SX7361
Rattlesden 21 TL9758
Rattray 56 NO1745
Rauceby 34 TF0146
Raughton Head 46 NY3745
Raunds 27 SP9972
Ravenfield 34 SK4895
Ravenglass 40 SD0896
Raveningham 29 TM3996
Ravenscar 43 NZ9801
Ravensdale 43 SC3592
Ravensden 27 TL0754
Ravenshead 34 SK5654
Ravensmoor 32 SJ6250
Ravensthorpe (Northants.) 26 SP6670
Ravensthorpe (W Yorks.) 37 SE2220
Ravenstone (Bucks.) 27 SP8450
Ravenstonedale 41 NY7203
Ravenstruther 50 NS9245
Ravensworth 42 NZ1407
Raw 43 NZ9305
Rawcliffe (Humbs.) 38 SE6822
Rawcliffe (N Yorks.) 38 SE5855
Rawcliffe Bridge 38 SE6921
Rawmarsh 38 SK4396
Rawreth 20 TQ7793
Rawridge 7 ST2006
Rawtenstall 37 SD8122
Raydon 21 TM0438
Raylees 47 NY9291
Rayleigh 20 TQ8090
Rayne 20 TL7222
Reach 28 TL5666
Read 37 SD7634
Reading 10 SU7272
Reading Street 13 TQ9230
Reagill 41 NY6017
Rearquhar 65 NH7492
Rearsby 34 SK6514
Rease Heath 32 SJ6454
Reaster 67 ND2565
Reawick 63 HU3244
Reay 67 NC9664
Reculver 13 TR2269
Red Dial 46 NY2545
Red Rock 36 SD5809
Red Roses 14 SN2012
Red Row 47 NZ2599
Red Street 32 SJ8251
Red Wharf Bay (Gwyn.) 30 SH5281
Redberth 14 SN0804
Redbourn 19 TL1012
Redbourne 39 SK9699
Redbridge 20 TQ4389
Redbrook 16 SO5310
Redbrook Street 13 TQ9336
Redburn (Highld.) 65 NH5767
Redburn (Highld.) 60 NH9447
Redcar 42 NZ6024
Redcastle (Highld.) 60 NH5849
Redcastle (Tays.) 57 NO6850
Redcliffe Bay 16 ST4475
Redding 50 NS9178
Reddingmuirhead 50 NS9177
Reddish 33 SJ8993
Redditch 25 SP0468
Rede 20 TL8055
Redenhall 29 TM2684
Redesmouth 47 NY8681
Redford 57 NO5644
Redgrave 29 TM0478
Redheugh 57 NO4463
Redhill (Avon) 16 ST4962
Redhill (Grampn.) 62 NJ6837
Redhill (Grampn.) 62 NJ7704
Redhill (Surrey) 11 TQ2850
Redisham 29 TM4084
Redland (Avon) 17 ST5875
Redland (Orkney) 63 HY3724
Redlingfield 29 TM1871
Redlynch (Somer.) 8 ST6933
Redlynch (Wilts.) 8 SU2020
Redmarley D'Abitot 24 SO7531
Redmarshall 42 NZ3821
Redmile 34 SK7935
Redmire 41 SE0491
Redmoor 3 SX0761
Rednal 32 SJ3628
Redpath 52 NT5835
Redpoint (Highld.) 64 NG7368
Redruth 2 SW6941
Redwick (Avon) 16 ST5485
Redwick (Gwent) 16 ST4184
Redworth 42 NZ2423
Reed 20 TL3636
Reedham 29 TG4201
Reedness 38 SE7922
Reef 63 NB1134
Reepham (Lincs.) 35 TF0373
Reepham (Norf.) 29 TG1023
Reeth 41 SE0499
Regaby 43 SC4397
Reiff 64 NB9614
Reigate 11 TQ2550
Reighton 43 TA1275
Reiss 67 ND3354
Rejerrah 2 SW8055
Relubbus 2 SW5632
Relugas 61 NH9948
Remenham 18 SU7784
Remenham Hill 18 SU7883
Rempstone 34 SK5724
Rendcomb 17 SP0109
Rendham 29 TM3564
Renfrew 50 NS4967
Renhold 27 TL0953
Renishaw 34 SK4477
Rennington 53 NU2118
Renton 50 NS3878
Renwick 46 NY5943
Repps 29 TG4116
Repton 33 SK3026
Rescobie 57 NO5152
Resipole 54 NM7264
Resolis 65 NH6765
Resolven 15 SN8202
Reston 53 NT8861
Reswallie 57 NO5051
Retew 2 SW9256
Rettendon 20 TQ7698
Revesby 35 TF2961
Rewe 5 SX9499
Reydon 29 TM4977
Reymerston 29 TG0206
Reynalton 14 SN0909
Reynoldston 15 SS4890
Rhandirmwyn 22 SN7843
Rhayader 23 SN9668
Rhedyn 30 SH3032
Rheindown 60 NH5147
Rhemore 54 NM5750
Rhes-y-cae 31 SJ1870
Rhewl (Clwyd) 31 SJ1060
Rhewl (Clwyd) 31 SJ1744
Rhiconich 66 NC2552
Rhicullen 65 NH6971
Rhigos 15 SN9205
Rhilochan 66 NC7407
Rhiroy 64 NH1589
Rhiwbryfdir 30 SH6946
Rhiwderyn 16 ST2587
Rhiwlas (Clwyd) 31 SJ1931
Rhiwlas (Gwyn.) 30 SH5765
Rhiwlas (Gwyn.) 31 SH9237
Rhodes Minnis 13 TR1542
Rhodesia 34 SK5680
Rhondda 16 SS9696
Rhonehouse or Kelton Hill 45 NX7459
Rhoose 16 ST0666
Rhos (Dyfed) 15 SN3835
Rhos (W Glam.) 15 SN7303
Rhos-fawr 30 SH3838
Rhos-on-Sea 31 SH8480
Rhos-y-gwaliau 31 SH9434
Rhos-y-llan 30 SH2337
Rhoscolyn 30 SH2675
Rhoscrowther 14 SM9002
Rhosesmor 31 SJ2168
Rhosgadfan 30 SH5057
Rhosgoch (Gwyn.) 30 SH4189
Rhosgoch (Powys) 23 SO1847
Rhoslan 30 SH4841
Rhoslefain 22 SH5705
Rhosllanerchrugog 31 SJ2946
Rhosmeirch 30 SH4677
Rhosneigr 30 SH3172
Rhosnesni 32 SJ3451
Rhossili 15 SS4188
Rhosson 14 SM7225
Rhostryfan 30 SH4958
Rhostyllen 32 SJ3148
Rhosybol 30 SH4288
Rhu (Strath.) 49 NS2783
Rhualt 31 SJ0774
Rhuban 63 NF7811
Rhuddlan 31 SJ0277
Rhue 64 NH0997
Rhulen 23 SO1350
Rhunahaorine 48 NR7048
Rhyd (Gwyn.) 30 SH6341
Rhyd-Ddu 30 SH5652
Rhyd-lydan 31 SH8950
Rhyd-y-clafdy 30 SH3235
Rhyd-y-meirch 16 SO3107
Rhyd-yr-onnen 22 SH6102
Rhydargaeau 15 SN4326
Rhydcymerau 22 SN5738
Rhydd 25 SO8345
Rhydding 15 SS7498
Rhydlewis 22 SN3447
Rhydlios 30 SH1830
Rhydowen 22 SN4445
Rhydrosser 22 SN5667
Rhydtalog 31 SJ2354
Rhydycroesau 31 SJ2330
Rhydyfelin (Dyfed) 22 SN5979
Rhydyfelin (Mid Glam.) 16 ST0988
Rhydyfro 15 SN7105
Rhydymain 31 SH7922
Rhydymwyn 31 SJ2066
Rhyl 31 SJ0181
Rhymney 16 SO1107
Rhyn 32 SJ3136
Rhynd 56 NO1520
Rhynie (Grampn.) 61 NJ4927
Rhynie (Highld.) 65 NH8578
Ribbesford 24 SO7874
Ribblesdale 37 SD8059
Ribbleton 36 SD5630
Ribchester 36 SD6435
Ribigill 66 NC5854
Riby 39 TA1807
Riccall 38 SE6237
Riccarton 50 NS4235
Richards Castle 24 SO4969
Richmond 42 NZ1701
Richmond upon Thames 11 TQ1874
Rickarton 62 NO8188
Rickinghall Inferior 29 TM0475
Rickinghall Superior 29 TM0475
Rickling 20 TL4931
Rickmansworth 19 TQ0594
Riddell 52 NT5124
Riddings 46 NY4075
Riddlecombe 5 SS6013
Riddlesden 37 SE0742
Ridge (Dorset) 8 SY9386
Ridge (Herts.) 19 TL2100
Ridge (Wilts.) 8 ST9531
Ridge Hill (Here. and Worcs.) 24 SO5035
Ridge Lane 26 SP2994
Ridgehill (Avon) 16 ST5362
Ridgemont 19 SP9736
Ridgeway Cross 24 SO7147
Ridgewell 20 TL7340
Ridgewood 12 TQ4719
Riding Mill 47 NZ0161
Ridlington (Leic.) 27 SK8402
Ridlington (Norf.) 29 TG3430
Ridsdale 47 NY9084
Riechip 56 NO0647
Rievaulx 42 SE5785
Rigg 46 NY2966
Riggend 50 NS7670
Righoul 60 NH8851
Rigside 50 NS8734
Rileyhill 33 SK1115
Rilla Mill 4 SX2973
Rillington 43 SE8574
Rimington 37 SD8045
Rimpton 8 ST6021
Rimswell 39 TA3128
Rinaston 14 SM9825
Ring's End 27 TF3902
Ringford 45 NX6857
Ringland 29 TG1313
Ringmer 12 TQ4412
Ringmore 5 SX6545
Ringorm 61 NJ2644
Ringsfield 29 TM4088
Ringsfield Corner 29 TM4187
Ringshall (Bucks.) 19 SP9814
Ringshall (Suff.) 21 TM0452
Ringshall Stocks 21 TM0551
Ringstead (Norf.) 28 TF7040
Ringstead (Northants.) 27 SP9875
Ringwood 8 SU1405
Ringwould 13 TR3648
Rinnigill 63 ND3193
Rinsey 2 SW5927
Ripe 12 TQ5010
Ripley (Derby.) 33 SK3950
Ripley (Hants.) 8 SZ1698
Ripley (N Yorks.) 38 SE2860
Ripley (Surrey) 11 TQ0556
Riplingham 39 SE9631
Ripon 38 SE3171
Rippingale 35 TF0927
Ripple (Here. and Worc.) 25 SO8737
Ripple (Kent) 13 TR3550
Ripponden 37 SE0319
Rireavach 64 NH0396
Risabus 48 NR3143
Risbury 24 SO5455
Risby (Humbs.) 39 SE9214
Risby (Suff.) 28 TL7966
Risca 16 ST2391
Rise 39 TA1541
Risegate 35 TF2029
Riseley (Beds.) 27 TL0463
Riseley (Berks.) 10 SU7263
Rishangles 29 TM1568
Rishton 36 SD7229
Rishworth 37 SE0317
Risley 34 SK4635
Risplith 37 SE2467
Rispond 66 NC4565
Rivar 10 SU3161
Rivenhall End 20 TL8316
River Bank 28 TL5368
Riverhead 12 TQ5156
Rivington 36 SD6214
Roa Island 36 SD2364
Roade 26 SP7551
Roadmeetings 50 NS8649
Roadside 67 ND1560
Roadside of Kinneff 57 NO8476
Roadwater 7 ST0238
Roag 58 NG2744
Roath 16 ST1978
Roberton (Borders) 52 NT4314
Roberton (Strath.) 51 NS9428
Robertsbridge 12 TQ7323
Roberttown 37 SE1922
Robeston Cross 14 SM8809
Robeston Wathen 14 SN0815
Robin Hood's Bay 43 NZ9505
Roborough 4 SS5717
Roby 32 SJ4291
Roby Mill 36 SD5106
Rocester 33 SK1039
Roch 14 SM8821
Rochdale 37 SD8913
Roche 3 SW9860
Rochester (Kent) 12 TQ7467
Rochester (Northum.) 47 NY8397
Rochford (Essex) 21 TQ8790
Rochford (Here. and Worc.) 24 SO6268
Rock (Corn.) 2 SW9475
Rock (Here. and Worc.) 24 SO7371
Rock (Northum.) 53 NU2020
Rock Ferry 32 SJ3386
Rockbeare 7 SY0195
Rockbourne 8 SU1118
Rockcliffe (Cumbr.) 46 NY3561
Rockcliffe (Dumf. and Galwy.) 45 NX8553
Rockfield (Gwent) 16 SO4814
Rockfield (Highld.) 65 NH9282
Rockhampton 17 ST6593
Rockingham 27 SP8691
Rockland All Saints 29 TL9896
Rockland St. Mary 29 TG3104
Rockland St. Peter 29 TL9897
Rockley 17 SU1571
Rockwell End 18 SU7988
Rodbourne 17 ST9383
Rodd 23 SO3162
Roddam 53 NU0220
Rodden 8 SY6184
Rode 17 ST8053
Rode Heath (Ches.) 32 SJ8056
Rodeheath (Ches.) 33 SJ8766
Rodel 63 NG0483
Roden 32 SJ5716
Rodhuish 7 ST0139
Rodington 32 SJ5814
Rodley 17 SO7411
Rodmarton 17 ST9397
Rodmell 12 TQ4106
Rodmersham 13 TQ9261
Rodney Stoke 7 ST4849
Rodsley 33 SK2040
Roecliffe 38 SE3765
Roehampton 11 TQ2373
Roesound 63 HU3365
Roewen 30 SH7571
Roffey 11 TQ1931
Rogart 66 NC7303
Rogate 10 SU8023
Rogerstone 16 ST2688
Rogerton 50 NS6256
Rogiet 16 ST4587
Roker 47 NZ4059
Rollesby 29 TG4415
Rolleston (Leic.) 26 SK7300
Rolleston (Notts.) 34 SK7452
Rolleston (Staffs.) 33 SK2337
Rolston 39 TA2145
Rolvenden 13 TQ8431
Rolvenden Layne 13 TQ8530
Romaldkirk 41 NY9921
Romanby 42 SE3693
Romannobridge 51 NT1547
Romansleigh 6 SS7220
Romford 20 TQ5188
Romiley 33 SJ9390
Romsey 9 SU3521
Romsley (Here. and Worc.) 25 SO9679
Romsley (Salop) 24 SO7883
Ronague 43 SC2472
Rookhope 47 NY9342
Rookley 9 SZ5084
Rooks Bridge 16 ST3652
Roos 39 TA2830
Rootpark 51 NS9554
Ropley 9 SU6431
Ropley Dean 9 SU6331
Ropsley 34 SK9834
Rora 62 NK0650
Rorrington 23 SJ3000
Rose 2 SW7754
Rose Ash 6 SS7821
Roseacre 36 SD4336
Rosebank 50 NS8049
Rosebrough 53 NU1326
Rosedale Abbey 43 SE7296
Roseden 53 NU0321
Rosehearty 62 NJ9367
Rosehill 32 SJ6630
Roseisle 61 NJ1367
Rosemarket 14 SM9508
Rosemarkie 60 NH7357
Rosemary Lane 7 ST1514
Rosemount (Strath.) 50 NS3729
Rosemount (Tays) 56 NO2043
Rosewell 51 NT2862
Roseworthy 2 SW6139
Rosgill 40 NY5316
Roshven 54 NM7078
Roskhill 58 NG2745
Rosley 46 NY3245
Roslin 51 NT2663
Rosliston 33 SK2416
Rosneath 49 NS2583
Ross (Dumf. and Galwy.) 45 NX6444
Ross (Northum.) 53 NU1336
Ross (Tays.) 56 NN7621
Ross-on-Wye 17 SO6024
Rossett 32 SJ3657
Rossington 38 SK6298
Rosskeen 65 NH6869
Rossland 50 NS4370
Roster 67 ND2639
Rostherne 32 SJ7483
Rosthwaite 40 NY2514
Roston 33 SK1241
Rosyth 51 NT1183
Rothbury 47 NU0601
Rotherby 34 SK6716
Rotherfield 12 TQ5529
Rotherfield Greys 18 SU7282
Rotherfield Peppard 18 SU7081
Rotherham 34 SK4392
Rothersthorpe 26 SP7156
Rotherwick 10 SU7156
Rothes 61 NJ2749
Rothesay 49 NS0864
Rothiebrisbane 62 NJ7437
Rothiemurchus 60 NH9206
Rothienorman 62 NJ7235
Rothiesholm 63 HY6123
Rothley 26 SK5812
Rothmaise 62 NJ6832
Rothwell (Lincs.) 39 TF1599
Rothwell (Northants.) 26 SP8181
Rothwell (W Yorks.) 38 SE3428
Rotsea 39 TA0651
Rottal 57 NO3769
Rottingdean 12 TQ3702
Rottington 40 NX9613
Roud 9 SZ5280
Rough Close 33 SJ9239
Rough Common 13 TR1359
Rougham 28 TF8320
Rougham Green 28 TL9061
Roughburn 55 NN3781
Roughlee 37 SD8440
Roughley 25 SP1399
Roughsike 46 NY5275
Roughton (Lincs.) 35 TF2364
Roughton (Norf.) 29 TG2136
Roughton (Salop) 24 SO7594
Roundhay 38 SE3235
Roundstreet Common 11 TQ0528
Roundway 17 SU0163
Rounton 42 NZ4103
Rous Lench 25 SP0153
Rousdon 7 SY2990
Routenburn 49 NS1961
Routh 39 TA0842
Row (Corn.) 3 SX0976
Row (Cumbr.) 40 SD4589
Rowanburn 46 NY4177
Rowde 17 ST9762
Rowfoot 46 NY6860
Rowhedge 21 TM0221
Rowhook 11 TQ1234
Rowington 26 SP2069
Rowland 33 SK2072
Rowland's Castle 10 SU7310
Rowland's Gill 47 NZ1658
Rowledge 10 SU8243
Rowley (Devon) 6 SS7219
Rowley (Humbs.) 39 SE9732
Rowley (Salop) 23 SJ3006
Rowley Regis 25 SO9787
Rowlstone 16 SO3727
Rowly 11 TQ0441
Rowney Green 25 SP0471
Rownhams 9 SU3816
Rowsham 19 SP8518
Rowsley 33 SK2566
Rowston 35 TF0856
Rowton (Ches.) 32 SJ4464
Rowton (Salop) 32 SJ6119
Roxburgh 52 NT6930
Roxby (Humbs.) 29 SE9217
Roxby (N Yorks) 43 NZ7616
Roxton 27 TL1554
Roxwell 20 TL6408
Royal Lemington Spa 26 SP3166
Royal Tunbridge Wells 12 TQ5839
Roybridge 55 NN2781
Roydon (Essex) 20 TL4009
Roydon (Norf.) 28 TF7022
Roydon (Norf.) 29 TM0980
Royston (Herts.) 20 TL3541
Royston (S Yorks.) 38 SE3611
Royton 37 SD9207
Ruabon 32 SJ3043
Ruaig 58 NM0647
Ruan Lanihorne 2 SW8942
Ruan Minor 2 SW7115
Ruardean 17 SO6117
Ruardean Woodside 17 SO6216
Rubery 25 SO9777
Ruckcroft 46 NY5344
Ruckinge 13 TR0233
Ruckland 35 TF3378
Ruckley 24 SJ5300
Ruddington 34 SK5733
Rudge 17 ST8252
Rudgeway 17 ST6286
Rudgwick 11 TQ0934
Rudhall 17 SO6225
Rudry 16 ST1986
Rudston 39 TA0967
Rudyard 33 SJ9557
Rufford 36 SD4515
Rufforth 38 SE5251
Rugby 26 SP5075
Rugeley 33 SK0418
Ruilick 60 NH5046
Ruishton 7 ST2624
Ruislip 19 TQ0987
Ruislip Common 19 TQ0789
Rumbling Bridge 56 NT0199
Rumburgh 29 TM3581
Rumford 2 SW8970
Rumney 16 ST2179
Runcorn 32 SJ5182
Runcton 11 SU8802
Runcton Holme 28 TF6109
Runfold 11 SU8747
Runhall 29 TG0507
Runham 29 TG4610
Runnington 7 ST1121
Runswick 43 NZ8016
Runtaleave 57 NO2867
Runwell 20 TQ7494
Rush Green 20 TQ5187
Rushall (Here. and Worc.) 24 SO6434
Rushall (Norf.) 29 TM1982
Rushall (W Mids.) 25 SK0201
Rushall (Wilts.) 17 SU1255
Rushbrooke 28 TL8961
Rushbury 24 SO5191
Rushden (Herts.) 20 TL3031
Rushden (Northants.) 27 SP9566
Rushford 29 TL9281
Rushlake Green 12 TQ6218
Rushmere 29 TM4987
Rushmere St. Andrew 21 TM2046
Rushmoor 11 SU8740
Rushock 25 SO8871
Rusholme 33 SJ8494
Rushton (Ches.) 32 SJ5863
Rushton (Northants) 27 SP8483
Rushton (Salop) 24 SJ6008
Rushton Spencer 33 SJ9363
Rushwick 25 SO8353
Rushyford 42 NZ2828
Ruskie 56 NN6200
Ruskington 35 TF0850
Rusland 40 SD3488
Rusper 11 TQ2037
Ruspidge 17 SO6512
Russell's Water 18 SU7089
Rustington 11 TQ0502
Ruston Parva 39 TA0661
Ruswarp 43 NZ8809
Rutherford 52 NT6530
Rutherglen 50 NS6161
Ruthernbridge 3 SX0166
Ruthin 31 SJ1257
Ruthrieston 62 NJ9204
Ruthven (Grampn.) 61 NJ5046
Ruthven (Highld.) 60 NH8133
Ruthven (Tays.) 57 NO2848
Ruthvoes 2 SW9360
Ruthwell 45 NY1067
Ruyton-XI-Towns 32 SJ3922
Ryal 47 NZ0174
Ryal Fold 36 SD6621
Ryall 7 SY4094
Ryarsh 12 TQ6659
Rydal 40 NY3606
Ryde 9 SZ5992
Rye 13 TQ9220
Rye Foreign 13 TQ8822
Rye Harbour 13 TQ9419
Ryhall 27 TF0311
Ryhill 38 SE3814
Ryhope 47 NZ4152
Ryknild Street (Warw.) (ant.) 25 SP0762
Rylstone 37 SD9758
Ryme Intrinseca 7 ST5810
Ryther 38 SE5539
Ryton (Glos.) 24 SO7232
Ryton (N Yorks.) 43 SE7975
Ryton (Salop) 24 SJ7502
Ryton (Tyne and wear) 47 NZ1564
Ryton-on-Dunsmore 26 SP3874

Sabden 37 SD7737
Sacombe 20 TL3419
Sacriston 47 NZ2447
Sadberge 42 NZ3416
Saddell 49 NR7832
Saddington 26 SP6591
Saddle Bow 28 TF6015
Saffron Walden 20 TL5438
Saham Toney 28 TF9002
Saighton 32 SJ4462
Saint Hill 12 TQ2835
Saintbury 25 SP1139
Salcombe 5 SX7338
Salcombe Regis 7 SY1488
Salcott 21 TL9413
Sale 32 SJ7990
Sale Green 25 SO9358
Saleby 36 TF1670
Salehurst 12 TQ7424
Salem (Dyfed) 15 SN6226
Salem (Dyfed) 22 SN6684
Salem (Gwyn.) 30 SH5456
Salen (Highld.) 54 NM6864
Salen (Island of Mull) 54 NM5743
Sales Point 21 TM0209
Salesbury 36 SD6732
Salford (Beds.) 27 SP9339
Salford (Gtr Mches.) 32 SJ7796
Salford (Oxon.) 18 SP2828
Salford Priors 25 SP0751
Salfords 11 TQ2846
Salhouse 29 TG3114
Saline 51 NT0292
Salisbury 8 SU1429
Sall 29 TG1024
Sallachy (Highld.) 66 NC5408
Sallachy (Highld.) 59 NG9130
Salmonby 35 TF3273
Salmond's Muir 57 NO5837

Salperton

Sinnington

Salperton	17	SP0720
Salph End	27	TL0752
Salsburgh	50	NS8262
Salt	33	SJ0994
Saltash	4	SX4239
Saltburn	65	NH7269
Saltburn-by-the-Sea	42	NZ6621
Saltby	34	SK8426
Saltcoats	49	NS2441
Saltdean	12	TQ3802
Salter	36	SD6063
Salterforth	37	SD8845
Saltergate	42	SE8594
Salterswall	32	SJ6267
Saltfleet	35	TF4593
Saltfleetby All Saints	35	TF4590
Saltfleetby St. Clements	35	TF4591
Saltfleetby St. Peter	35	TF4389
Saltford	17	ST6867
Salthouse	29	TG0743
Saltmarshe	38	SE7824
Saltney	32	SJ3864
Salton	43	SE7180
Saltwick	47	NZ1780
Saltwood	13	TR1536
Salwarpe	25	SO8762
Salwayash	7	SY4596
Samala	63	NF7962
Sambourne	25	SP0561
Sambrook	32	SJ7124
Samlesbury	25	SD5829
Samlesbury Bottoms	36	SD6229
Sampford Arundel	7	ST1018
Sampford Brett	7	ST0940
Sampford Courtnay	5	SS6301
Sampford Peverell	7	ST0214
Sampford Spiney	4	SX5372
Samuelston	52	NT4870
Sanaigmore	48	NR2370
Sancreed	2	SW4029
Sancton	39	SE8939
Sand	63	HU3447
Sand Hutton (N Yorks.)	38	SE6958
Sand Side	40	SD2282
Sandaig	58	NG7102
Sandbach	32	SJ7560
Sandbank	49	NS1580
Sandbanks	8	SZ0487
Sandend	61	NJ5566
Sanderstead	12	TQ3461
Sandford (Avon)	16	ST4159
Sandford (Cumbr.)	41	NY7216
Sandford (Devon)	5	SS8202
Sandford (Dorset)	8	SY9289
Sandford (Strath.)	50	NS7143
Sandford Orcas	8	ST6220
Sandford St. Martin	18	SP4226
Sandford-on-Thames	18	SP5301
Sandfordhill	62	NK1141
Sandgarth	63	HY5215
Sandgate	13	TR2035
Sandgreen	45	NX5752
Sandhaven	62	NJ9667
Sandhead	44	NX0949
Sandhoe	47	NY9766
Sandholme (Humbs.)	39	SE8230
Sandholme (Lincs.)	35	TF3370
Sandhurst (Berks.)	10	SU8361
Sandhurst (Glos.)	17	SO8223
Sandhurst (Kent)	12	TQ8028
Sandhutton (N Yorks.)	42	SE3881
Sandiacre	34	SK4736
Sandilands	35	TF5280
Sandiway	32	SJ6070
Sandleheath	8	SU1214
Sandleigh	18	SP4501
Sandling	12	TQ7558
Sandness	63	HU1956
Sandon (Essex)	20	TL7404
Sandon (Herts)	20	TL3234
Sandon (Staffs.)	33	SJ9429
Sandown	9	SZ5984
Sandplace	4	SX2457
Sandridge (Herts.)	19	TL1710
Sandridge (Wilts.)	17	ST9465
Sandringham	28	TF6928
Sandsend	43	NZ8512
Sandsound	63	HU3548
Sandtoft	38	SE7408
Sandwich	13	TR3358
Sandwick (Cumbr.)	40	NY4219
Sandwick (Isle of Lewis)	63	NB4432
Sandwick (Shetld)	63	HU4323
Sandy	27	TL1649
Sandy Lane	17	ST9668
Sandycroft	32	SJ3366
Sandygate	43	SC3797
Sangobeg	66	NC4266
Sanna	54	NM4569
Sanquhar	50	NS7809
Santon Bridge	40	NY1001
Santon Downham	28	TL8187
Sapcote	26	SP4893
Sapey Common	24	SO7064
Sapiston	28	TL9175
Sapperton (Glos.)	17	SO9403
Sapperton (Lincs.)	34	TF0133
Saracen's Head	35	TF3427
Sarclet	67	ND3443
Sarisbury	9	SU5008
Sarn (Mid Glam.)	15	SS9083
Sarn (Powys)	23	SO2090
Sarn Meyllteyrn	30	SH2432
Sarn-bach	30	SH3026
Sarnau (Dyfed)	22	SN3151
Sarnau (Dyfed)	14	SN3318
Sarnau (Gwyn.)	31	SH9739
Sarnau (Powys)	31	SJ2315
Sarnesfield	24	SO3750
Saron (Dyfed)	15	SN3738
Saron (Dyfed)	15	SN6012
Sarratt	19	TQ0499
Sarre	13	TR2565
Sarsden	18	SP2822
Satley	47	NZ1143
Satterleigh	6	SS6622
Satterthwaite	40	SD3392
Sauchchrie	39	NS3014
Sauchen	62	NJ7010
Saucher	56	NO1933
Sauchieburn	57	NO6669
Saughall	32	SJ3669
Saughtree	46	NY5696
Saul	17	SO7409
Saundby	34	SK7888
Saundersfoot	14	SN1304
Saunderton	18	SP7901
Saunton	6	SS4537
Sausthorpe	35	TF3869
Savalmore	66	NC5908
Sawbridgeworth	20	TL4814
Sawdon	43	SE9485
Sawley (Derby)	33	SK4731
Sawley (Lancs.)	37	SD7746
Sawley (N Yorks.)	37	SE2467
Sawrey	40	SD3694
Sawston	20	TL4849
Sawtry	27	TL1683
Saxby (Leic.)	34	SK8220
Saxby (Lincs.)	34	TF0086
Saxby All Saints	39	SE9816
Saxelbye	34	SK6921
Saxilby	34	SK8875
Saxlingham	29	TG0239
Saxlingham Nethergate	29	TM2397
Saxmundham	29	TM3863
Saxon Street	20	TL6859
Saxondale	34	SK6839
Saxtead	29	TM2665
Saxtead Green	29	TM2564
Saxthorpe	29	TG1130
Saxton	38	SE4736
Sayers Common	11	TQ2618
Scackleton	42	SE6472
Scadabay	63	NG1792
Scaftworth	23	SK6691
Scagglethorpe	39	SE8372
Scalasaig	48	NR3894
Scalby	43	TA0090
Scaldwell	26	SP7672
Scale Houses	46	NY5845
Scaleby	46	NY4563
Scalebyhill	46	NY4363
Scales (Cumbr.)	40	NY3426
Scales (Cumbr.)	36	SD2772
Scalford	34	SK7624
Scaling	43	NZ7413
Scalloway	63	HU4039
Scalpay (Harris)	63	NG2395
Scalpay (Island of Skye)	58	NG6030
Scamblesby	35	TF2778
Scamodale	54	NM8473
Scampston	43	SE8575
Scampton	34	SK9479
Scapa	63	HY4309
Scar	23	Y6745
Scarborough	43	TA0388
Scarcliffe	34	SK4968
Scarcroft	38	SE3540
Scardroy	59	NH2151
Scarff	63	HU2479
Scarfskerry	67	ND2673
Scargill	41	NZ0510
Scarinish	48	NM0444
Scarisbrick	36	SD3713
Scarning	29	TF9512
Scarrington	34	SK7341
Scarth Hill	36	SD4206
Scartho	39	TA2606
Scatsta	63	HU3872
Scaur or Kippford	45	NX8355
Scawby	39	SE9605
Scawton	42	SE5483
Scayne's Hill	12	TQ3723
Scethrog	16	SO1025
Scholar Green	32	SJ8357
Scholes (W Yorks.)	37	SE1507
Scholes (W Yorks.)	38	SE3736
Scleddau	14	SM9434
Sco Ruston	29	TG2821
Scole	29	TM1579
Scolton	14	SM9922
Sconser	58	NG5232
Scoor	54	NM4119
Scopwick	35	TF0658
Scoraig	64	NH0096
Scorborough	39	TA0145
Scorrier	2	SW7244
Scorton (Lancs.)	36	SD5048
Scorton (N Yorks.)	42	NZ2400
Scotby	46	NY4454
Scotforth	36	SD4759
Scothern	35	TF0377
Scotland Gate	47	NZ2584
Scotlandwell	56	NO1801
Scotney Castle	12	TQ6835
Scots' Gap	47	NZ0486
Scotsburn	65	NH7275
Scotscraig	57	NO4428
Scotstown	54	NM8263
Scotter	39	SE8800
Scotterthorpe	39	SE8701
Scotton (Lincs.)	39	SK8899
Scotton (N Yorks.)	42	SE1895
Scotton (N Yorks.)	38	SE3259
Scottow	29	TG2623
Scoughall	52	NT6183
Scoulton	29	TF9800
Scourie	66	NC1544
Scousburgh	63	HU3717
Scrabster	67	ND0970
Scrainwood	53	NT9909
Scrane End	35	TF3841
Scraptoft	26	SK6405
Scratby	29	TG5115
Scrayingham	38	SE7360
Scredington	35	TF0940
Scremby	35	TF4467
Scremerston	53	NU0049
Screveton	34	SK7343
Scriven	38	SE3458
Scrooby	34	SK6590
Scropton	33	SK1930
Scrub Hill	35	TF2355
Scruton	42	SE2992
Sculthorpe	28	TF8931
Scunthorpe	39	SE8910
Sea Palling	29	TG4327
Seaborough	7	ST4205
Seacombe	32	SJ3190
Seacroft	35	TF5660
Seafield	51	NT0066
Seaford	12	TV4899
Seaforth	32	SJ3297
Seagrave	34	SK6117
Seaham	47	NZ4149
Seahouses	53	NU2132
Seal	12	TQ5556
Sealand	32	SJ3268
Seamer (N Yorks.)	42	NZ4910
Seamer (N Yorks.)	43	TA0183
Seamill	49	NS2047
Searby	39	TA0605
Seasalter	13	TR0864
Seathwaite (Cumbr.)	40	NY2312
Seathwaite (Cumbr.)	40	SD2296
Seaton (Corn.)	4	SX3054
Seaton (Cumbr.)	40	NY0130
Seaton (Devon.)	7	SY2490
Seaton (Durham)	47	NZ4049
Seaton (Humbs.)	39	TA1646
Seaton (Leic.)	27	SP9098
Seaton (Northum.)	47	NZ3276
Seaton Carew	42	NZ5229
Seaton Delaval	47	NZ3075
Seaton Ross	38	SE7741
Seaton Sluice	47	NZ3376
Seave Green	42	NZ5600
Seaview Seavington St. Mary	7	ST3914
Seavington St. Michael	7	ST4015
Sebergham	46	NY3541
Seckington	26	SK2607
Sedbergh	41	SD6592
Sedbusk	41	SD8891
Sedgeberrow	25	SP0238
Sedgebrook	34	SK8537
Sedgefield	42	NZ3528
Sedgeford	28	TF7136
Sedgehill	8	ST8627
Sedgley	25	SO9193
Sedgwick	40	SD5186
Sedlescombe	12	TQ7818
Seend	17	ST9460
Seend Cleeve	17	ST9260
Seer Green	19	SU9691
Seething	29	TM3197
Sefton	36	SD3500
Seghill	47	NZ2874
Seighford	33	SJ8725
Seilebost	63	NG0696
Seisdon	25	SO8394
Selattyn	31	SJ2633
Selborne	10	SU7433
Selby	38	SE6132
Selham	11	SU9320
Selkirk	52	NT4728
Sellack	17	SO5627
Sellafirth	63	HU5198
Sellindge	13	TR0938
Selling	13	TR0358
Sells Green	17	ST9462
Selly Oak	25	SP0482
Selmeston	12	TQ5007
Selsden	12	TQ3562
Selsey	11	SZ8593
Selsfield Common	12	TQ3434
Selston	34	SK4553
Selworthy	6	SS9146
Semblister	63	HU3350
Semer	21	TL9946
Semington	17	ST8960
Semley	8	ST8926
Send	11	TQ0155
Senghenydd	16	ST1191
Sennen	2	SW3525
Sennen Cove	2	SW3425
Sennybridge	15	SN9228
Sessay	42	SE4575
Setchey	28	TF6313
Setley	9	SU3000
Settascarth	63	HY3618
Setter	63	HU4683
Settle	37	SD8263
Settrington	39	SE8370
Seven Kings	20	TQ4586
Seven Sisters	15	SN8108
Sevenhampton (Glos.)	17	SP0321
Sevenhampton (Wilts.)	18	SU2090
Sevenoaks	12	TQ5355
Sevenoaks Weald	12	TQ5351
Severn Beach	16	ST5384
Severn Stoke	25	SO8544
Sevington	13	TR0340
Sewards End	20	TL5738
Sewerby	39	TA2068
Seworgan	2	SW7030
Sewstern	34	SK8821
Sezincote	25	SP1731
Shabbington	18	SP6606
Shackerstone	26	SK3706
Shackleford	11	SU9345
Shadforth	47	NZ3441
Shadingfield	29	TM4383
Shadoxhurst	13	TQ9737
Shaftesbury	8	ST8622
Shafton	38	SE3810
Shalbourne	10	SU3163
Shalcombe	9	SZ3985
Shalden	10	SU6941
Shaldon	5	SX9272
Shalfleet	9	SZ4189
Shalford (Essex)	20	TL7229
Shalford (Surrey)	11	TQ0047
Shalford Green	20	TL7127
Shallowford	6	SS7144
Shalstone	18	SP6436
Shamley Green	11	TQ0344
Shandon	49	NS2586
Shangton	26	SP7196
Shanklin	9	SZ5881
Shap	41	NY5615
Shapwick (Dorset)	8	SY9301
Shapwick (Somer.)	7	ST4137
Shardlow	34	SK4330
Shareshill	25	SJ9406
Sharlston	38	SE3818
Sharnbrook	27	SP9959
Sharnford	26	SP4891
Sharoe Green	36	SD5332
Sharow	38	SE3271
Sharpenhoe	27	TL0630
Sharperton	47	NT9503
Sharpness	17	SO6702
Sharpthorne	12	TQ3732
Sharrington	29	TG0337
Shatterford	24	SO7980
Shaugh Prior	4	SX5463
Shaughlaige-e-Caine	43	SC3187
Shavington	32	SJ6951
Shaw (Berks.)	10	SU4768
Shaw (Gtr Mches.)	37	SD9308
Shaw (Wilts.)	17	ST8865
Shaw Hill	45	NX5871
Shaw Mills	37	SE2562
Shawbost	63	NB2646
Shawbury	32	SJ5521
Shawell	26	SP5480
Shawford	9	SU4624
Shawforth	37	SD8920
Shawhead	45	NX8675
Shawwood	50	NS5325
Shear Cross	8	ST8642
Shearsby	26	SP6291
Shebbear	4	SS4309
Shebdon	32	SJ7525
Shebster	67	ND0164
Shedfield	9	SU5512
Sheen	33	SK1161
Sheepscombe	17	SO8910
Sheepstor	4	SX5567
Sheepwash	4	SS4806
Sheepy Magna	26	SK3201
Sheepy Parva	26	SK3301
Sheering	20	TL5013
Sheerness	13	T19274
Sheet	10	SU7524
Sheffield	33	SK3587
Sheffield Bottom	10	SU6469
Shefford	19	TL1439
Sheinton	24	SJ6104
Shelderton	24	SO4077
Sheldon (Derby.)	33	SK1768
Sheldon (Devon.)	7	ST1208
Sheldon (W Mids.)	25	SP1584
Sheldwich	13	TR0156
Shelf	37	SE1228
Shelfanger	29	TM1083
Shelfield	25	SK0302
Shelford	34	SK6642
Shelley	37	SE2011
Shellingford	18	SU3193
Shellow Bowells	20	TL6108
Shelsley Beauchamp	24	SO7362
Shelsley Walsh	24	SO7263
Shelton (Beds.)	27	TL0368
Shelton (Norf.)	29	TM2191
Shelton (Notts.)	34	SK7744
Shelton Green	29	TM2390
Shelve	23	SO3399
Shelwick	24	SO5243
Shenfield	20	TQ6094
Shenington	26	SP3642
Shenley	19	TL1900
Shenley Brook End	19	SP8335
Shenley Church End	19	SP8336
Shenleybury	19	TL1802
Shenmore	24	SO3938
Shenstone (Here. and Worc.)	25	SO8673
Shenstone (Staffs.)	25	SK1004
Shenton	26	SK3800
Shenval	61	NJ2129
Shepherd's Green	18	SU7183
Shepherdswell or Sibertswold	13	TR2548
Shepley	37	SE1909
Shepperdine	17	ST6195
Shepperton	11	TQ0867
Shepreth	20	TL3947
Shepshed	34	SK4719
Shepton Beauchamp	7	ST4016
Shepton Mallet	7	ST6143
Shepton Montague	8	ST6731
Shepway	12	TQ7753
Sheraton	42	NZ4334
Sherborne (Dorset)	8	ST6316
Sherborne (Glos.)	17	SP1714
Sherborne St. John	10	SU6155
Sherbourne	26	SP2661
Sherburn (Durham)	47	NZ3142
Sherburn (N Yorks.)	43	SE9577
Sherburn in Elmet	38	SE4933
Shere	11	TQ0747
Shereford	28	TF8829
Sherfield English	9	SU2922
Sherfield on Loddon	10	SU6757
Sherford	5	SX7744
Sheriff Hutton	38	SE6566
Sheriffhales	24	SJ7512
Sheringham	29	TG1543
Sherington	27	SP8846
Shernborne	28	TF7132
Sherrington	8	ST9638
Sherston	17	ST8585
Sherwood Green	6	SS5520
Sheshader	63	NB5534
Shettleston	50	NS6464
Shevington	36	SD5408
Shevington Moor	36	SD5410
Sheviock	4	SX3655
Shiel Bridge	59	NG9318
Shieldaig	59	NG8154
Shieldhill (Central)	50	NS8976
Shielfoot	54	NM6669
Shifnal	24	SJ7407
Shilbottle	53	NU1908
Shildon	42	NZ2226
Shillingford (Devon.)	7	SS9723
Shillingford (Oxon.)	18	SU5992
Shillingford St. George	5	SX9087
Shillingstone	8	ST8211
Shillington	19	TL1234
Shillmoor (Northum.)	53	NT8807
Shiltenish	63	NB2819
Shilton (Oxon.)	18	SP2608
Shilton (Warw.)	26	SP4084
Shimpling (Norf.)	29	TM1583
Shimpling (Suff.)	21	TL8551
Shimpling Street	20	TL8652
Shiney Row	47	NZ3252
Shinfield	10	SU7368
Shinness	66	NC5314
Shipbourne	12	TQ5952
Shipdham	29	TF9607
Shipham	16	ST4457
Shiphay	5	SX8965
Shiplake	10	SU7678
Shipley (Salop)	24	SO8095
Shipley (W Susx.)	11	TQ1422
Shipley (W Yorks.)	37	SE1337
Shipmeadow	29	TM3789
Shippon	18	SU4898
Shipston on Stour	26	SP2540
Shipton (Glos.)	17	SP0318
Shipton (N Yorks)	38	SE5558
Shipton (Salop)	24	SO5591
Shipton Bellinger	10	SU2345
Shipton Gorge	7	SY4991
Shipton Green	10	SU8000
Shipton Moyne	17	ST8889
Shipton-on-Cherwell	18	SP4716
Shipton-under-Wychwood	18	SP2717
Shiptonthorpe	39	SE8543
Shirburn	18	SU6995
Shirdley Hill	36	SD3612
Shire Oak	25	SK0504
Shirebrook	34	SK5267
Shirehampton	16	ST5276
Shiremoor	47	NZ3171
Shirenewton	16	ST4793
Shirl Heath	24	SO4359
Shirland	33	SK3958
Shirley (Derby.)	33	SK2141
Shirley (Hants.)	9	SU4114
Shirley (W Mids.)	25	SP1277
Shirrell Heath	9	SU5714
Shirwell	6	SS5937
Shiskine	49	NR9129
Shobdon	24	SO3961
Shobrooke	5	SS8600
Shocklach	32	SJ4348
Shoeburyness	21	TQ9384
Sholden	13	TR3552
Sholing	9	SU4511
Shop (Corn.)	4	SS2214
Shop (Corn.)	2	SW8773
Shoreditch	20	TQ3284
Shoreham	12	TQ5261
Shoreham-by-Sea	11	TQ2105
Shoresdean	53	NT9546
Shoreswood	53	NT9446
Shoretown	65	NH6161
Shorncote	17	SU0296
Shorne	12	TQ6970
Short Cross	23	SJ2605
Short Heath (Leic.)	33	SK3014
Short Heath (W Mids.)	25	SP0992
Shortgate	12	TQ4915
Shortlanesend	2	SW8047
Shortless	50	NS4335
Shorwell	9	SZ4582
Shoscombe	17	ST7156
Shotesham	29	TM2599
Shotgate	20	TQ7692
Shotley Bridge	47	NZ0752
Shotley Gate	21	TM2433
Shotley Street	21	TM2335
Shottenden	13	TR0454
Shottermill	11	SU8732
Shottery	25	SP1854
Shotteswell	26	SP4245
Shottisham	21	TM3144
Shottle	33	SK3149
Shotton (Clwyd)	32	SJ3069
Shotton (Durham)	42	NZ4139
Shotton (Northum.)	53	NT8430
Shotton Colliery	47	NZ3941
Shotts	50	NS8760
Shotwick	32	SJ3371
Shouldham	28	TF6708
Shouldham Thorpe	28	TF6607
Shoulton	24	SO8058
Shrawley	24	SO8064
Shrewley	26	SP2167
Shrewsbury	24	SJ4912
Shrewton	8	SU0643
Shripney	11	SU9302
Shrivenham	18	SU2489
Shropham	29	TL9893
Shroton or Urwerne Courtney	8	ST8512
Shrub End	21	TL9723
Shucknall	24	SO5842
Shudy Camps	20	TL6244
Shulishader	63	NB5334
Shurdington	17	SO9118
Shurlock Row	10	SU8374
Shurrey	67	ND0458
Shurton	7	ST2044
Shustoke	26	SP2290
Shut End	25	SO9089
Shute	7	SY2597
Shutford	18	SP3840
Shuthonger	25	SO8935
Shutlanger	26	SP7249
Shuttington	26	SK2505
Shuttlewood	36	SK4672
Sibbertoft	26	SP6782
Sibdon Carwood	24	SO4083
Sibertswold or Shepherdswell	13	TR2548
Sibford Ferris	18	SP3537
Sibford Gower	18	SP3537
Sible Hedingham	20	TL7734
Sibsey	35	TF3551
Sibson (Cambs.)	27	TL0997
Sibson (Leic.)	26	SK3500
Sibthorpe	34	SK7645
Sicklesmere	21	TL8760
Sicklinghall	38	SE3548
Sidbury (Devon.)	7	SY1491
Sidbury (Salop)	24	SO6885
Sidcup	12	TQ4672
Siddington (Ches.)	33	SJ8470
Siddington (Glos.)	17	SU0399
Sidestrand	29	TG2539
Sidford	7	SY1390
Sidinish	63	NF8763
Sidlesham	10	SZ8599
Sidley	12	TQ7409
Sidmouth	7	SY1287
Siefton	24	SO4883
Sigford	5	SX7773
Sigglesthorne	39	TA1545
Silchester	10	SU6462
Sileby	34	SK6015
Silecroft	40	SD1281
Silian	22	SN5751
Silk Willoughby	35	TF0542
Silkstone	38	SE2905
Silkstone Common	38	SE2904
Silloth	45	NY1153
Sillyearn	61	NJ5254
Silpho	43	SE9692
Silsden	37	SE0446
Silsoe	19	TL0835
Silver End (Beds.)	27	TL0942
Silver End (Essex)	20	TL8019
Silverburn	51	NT2060
Silverdale (Lancs.)	40	SD4674
Silverdale (Staffs.)	32	SJ8146
Silverford	62	NJ7764
Silverley's Green	29	TM2976
Silverstone	26	SP6644
Silverton	5	SS9502
Silwick (Shetld.)	63	HU2942
Simonburn	47	NY8773
Simonsbath	6	SS7739
Simonstone	37	SD7734
Simprim	53	NT8545
Simpson	27	SP8836
Sinclairston	50	NS4716
Sinderby	42	SE3481
Sinderhope	47	NY8452
Sindlesham	10	SU7769
Singleton (Lancs.)	36	SD3838
Singleton (W Susx)	11	SU8713
Singlewell or Ifield	12	TQ6471
Sinnington	43	SE7485

Sinton Green Stanford Bishop

Sinton Green 25 SO8160
Sipson 11 TQ0877
Sirhowy 16 SO1410
Sissinghurst 12 TQ7937
Siston 17 ST6875
Sithney 2 SW6329
Sittenham 65 NH6574
Sittingbourne 13 TQ9163
Six Ashes 24 SO6988
Six Mile Bottom 20 TL5756
Sixhills 35 TF1787
Sixpenny Handley 8 ST9917
Sizewell 29 TM4762
Skaill (Mainland) (Orkney) 63 HY5806
Skares 50 NS5217
Skarpigarth 63 HU2049
Skateraw 53 NT7375
Skaw (Whalsay) 63 HU5866
Skeabost 58 NG4148
Skeabrae 63 HY2720
Skeeby 42 NZ1902
Skeffington 26 SK7402
Skeffling 39 TA3619
Skegby 34 SK4961
Skegness 35 TF5663
Skelberry 63 HU3916
Skelbo 65 NH7895
Skeldyke 35 TF3337
Skellingthorpe 34 SK9272
Skellister 63 HU4654
Skelmanthorpe 37 SE2210
Skelmersdale 36 SD4605
Skelmonae 62 NJ8839
Skelmorlie 49 NS1967
Skelmuir 62 NJ9842
Skelpick 66 NC7355
Skelton (Cleve.) 42 NZ6518
Skelton (Cumbr.) 40 NY4335
Skelton (N Yorks.) 41 NZ0900
Skelton (N Yorks.) 38 SE3568
Skelton (N Yorks.) 38 SE5656
Skelwith Bridge 40 NY3503
Skendleby 35 TF4369
Skenfrith 16 SO4520
Skerne 39 TA0455
Skeroblingarry 48 NR7026
Skerray 66 NC6563
Sketty 15 SS6293
Skewen 15 SS7297
Skewsby 38 SE6270
Skeyton 29 TG2425
Skidbrooke 35 TF4393
Skidby 39 TA0133
Skigersta 63 NB5461
Skilgate 7 SS9827
Skillington 34 SK8925
Skinburness 45 NY1255
Skinidin 58 NG2247
Skinningrove 43 NZ7119
Skipness 49 NR8957
Skipsea 39 TA1655
Skipton 37 SD9851
Skipton-on-Swale 42 SE3679
Skipwith 38 SE6538
Skirling 51 NT0739
Skirmett 18 SU7789
Skirpenbeck 38 SE7457
Skirpenbeck 38 SE7457
Skirwith (Cumbr.) 41 NY6132
Skirwith (N Yorks.) 41 SD7073
Skirza 67 ND3868
Skulamus 58 NG6722
Skullomie 66 NC6161
Skye of Curr 61 NH9924
Slack 37 SD9828
Slackhall 33 SK0781
Slackhead 61 NJ4063
Slad 17 SO8707
Slade 6 SS5046
Slade Green 12 TQ5276
Slaggyford 46 NY6752
Slaidburn 36 SD7152
Slaithwaite 37 SE0714
Slaley 47 NY9757
Slamannan 50 NS8573
Slapton (Bucks.) 19 SP9320
Slapton (Devon.) 5 SX8244
Slapton (Northants.) 26 SP6346
Slattocks 37 SD8808
Slaugham 11 TQ2528
Slawston 26 SP7794
Sleaford (Hants.) 10 SU8037
Sleaford (Lincs.) 35 TF0645
Sleagill 41 NY5919
Sleapford 32 SJ6315
Sledge Green 25 SO8134
Sledmere 39 SE9364
Sleightholme 41 NY9510
Sleights 43 NZ8607
Slepe 8 SY9293
Slickly 67 ND2966
Sliddery 49 NR9322
Sliemore 61 NJ0320
Sligachan 58 NG4829
Slimbridge 17 SO7303
Slindon (Staffs.) 32 SJ8232
Slindon (W Susx) 11 SU9608
Slinfold 11 TQ1131
Slingsby 43 SE6974
Slioch (Grampn.) 61 NJ5638
Slip End 19 TL0818
Slipton 27 SP9479
Slockavullin 54 NR8297
Sloley 29 TG2924
Slothby 35 TF4970
Slough 11 SU9779
Slyne 36 SD4765
Smailholm 52 NT6436
Small Dole 11 TQ2112
Small Hythe 13 TQ8930
Smallbridge 37 SD9114
Smallburgh 29 TG3324
Smallburn (Grampn.) 62 NK0141
Smallburn (Strath.) 50 NS6827
Smalley 33 SK4044
Smallfield 12 TQ3243
Smallridge 7 ST3001
Smardale 41 NY7308
Smarden 13 TQ8842
Smearisary 54 NM6477
Smeatharpe 5 ST1910
Smeeth 13 TR0739
Smeeton Westerby 26 SP6792
Smerclate 63 NF7415
Smerral 67 ND1733
Smethwick 25 SP0288
Smisby 33 SK3419
Smithfield 46 NY4465
Smithincott 7 ST0611
Smithton 60 NH7145
Snailbeach 24 SJ3702
Snailwell 28 TL6467
Snainton 43 SE9182
Snaith 38 SE6422
Snape (N Yorks.) 42 SE2684
Snape (Suff.) 21 TM3959
Snape Street 21 TM3958
Snarestone 26 SK3409
Snarford 35 TF0482
Snargate 13 TQ9928
Snave 13 TR0130
Snead 23 SO3191
Sneaton 43 NZ8907
Sneaton Thorpe 43 NZ9006
Snelland 35 TF0780
Snelston 33 SK1543
Snettisham 28 TF6834
Snishival 63 NF7534
Snitter 47 NU0203
Snitterby 34 SK9894
Snitterfield 26 SP2159
Snitton 24 SO5575
Snodhill 23 SO3140
Snodland 12 TQ7061
Snowshill 25 SP0933
Soberton 9 SU6016
Soberton Heath 9 SU6014
Soldon Cross 4 SS3210
Soldridge 9 SU6534
Sole Street 13 TR0949
Solihull 25 SP1479
Sollas 63 NF8074
Sollers Dilwyn 24 SO4255
Sollers Hope 24 SO6033
Sollom 36 SD4518
Solva 14 SM8024
Somerby 26 SK7710
Somercotes 33 SK4253
Somerford Keynes 17 SU0195
Somerley 10 SZ8198
Somerleyton 29 TM4897
Somersal Herbert 33 SK1335
Somersby 35 TF3472
Somersham (Cambs.) 27 TL3677
Somersham (Suff.) 21 TM0848
Somerton (Norf.) 29 TG4719
Somerton (Oxon.) 18 SP4928
Somerton (Somer.) 7 ST4828
Sompting 11 TQ1605
Sonning 10 SU7575
Sonning Common 18 SU7080
Sopley 8 SZ1596
Sopworth 17 ST8286
Sorbie 44 NX4346
Sordale 67 ND1462
Sorisdale 48 NM2763
Sorn 50 NS5526
Sornhill 50 NS5134
Sortat 67 ND2863
Sotby 35 TF2078
Sots Hole 35 TF1164
Sotterly 29 TM4584
Soughton 31 SJ2466
Soulbury 19 SP8827
Soulby 41 NY7410
Souldern 18 SP5231
Souldrop 27 SP9861
Sound (Shetld.) 63 HU3850
Sound (Shetld.) 63 HU4640
Soundwell 17 ST6574
Sourhope 53 NT8420
Sourin 63 HY4331
Sourton 4 SX5390
Soutergate 40 SD2281
South Acre 28 TF8014
South Alloa 50 NS8791
South Ambersham 11 SU9120
South Ballachulish 55 NN0559
South Bank 42 NZ5220
South Barrow 8 ST6027
South Benfleet 20 TQ7785
South Brent 5 SX6960
South Burlingham 29 TG3708
South Cadbury 8 ST6325
South Cairn 44 NW9768
South Carlton 34 SK9476
South Cave 39 SE9231
South Cerney 17 SU0497
South Chard 7 ST3205
South Charlton 53 NU1620
South Cliffe 39 SE8736
South Clifton 34 SK8270
South Cove 29 TM5081
South Creake 28 TF8536
South Croxton 26 SK6810
South Dalton 39 SE9645
South Darenth 12 TQ5669
South Duffield 38 SE6733
South Elkington 35 TF2988
South Elmsall 38 SE4711
South End (Berks.) 10 SU5970
South End (Cumbr.) 36 SD2063
South Erradale 64 NG7471
South Fambridge 21 TQ8694
South Fawley 10 SU3979
South Ferriby 39 SE9820
South Green 20 TQ6893
South Hall 49 NS0672
South Hanningfield 20 TQ7497
South Harting 10 SU7819
South Hayling 10 SZ7299
South Heath 19 SP9102
South Heighton 12 TQ4503
South Hetton 47 NZ3745
South Hiendley 38 SE3812
South Hill 4 SX3272
South Hole 4 SS2219
South Holmwood 11 TQ1745
South Hornchurch 20 TQ5283
South Hylton 47 NZ3556
South Kelsey 39 TF0398
South Kilvington 42 SE4283
South Kilworth 26 SP6082
South Kirkby 38 SE4410
South Kirkton 62 NJ7405
South Kyme 35 TF1749
South Lancing 11 TQ1804
South Leigh (Oxon.) 18 SP3908
South Leverton 34 SK7881
South Littleton 25 SP0746
South Lochboisdale 63 NF7817
South Lopham 29 TM0481
South Luffenham 27 SK9402
South Malling 12 TQ4211
South Marston 17 SU1987
South Milford 38 SE4931
South Milton 5 SX7042
South Mimms 19 TL2200
South Molton 6 SS7125
South Moor 47 NZ1952
South Moreton 18 SU5688
South Muskham 34 SK7957
South Newington 18 SP4033
South Newton 8 SU0834
South Normanton 34 SK4456
South Norwood 12 TQ3468
South Nutfield 12 TQ3048
South Ockendon 20 TQ5982
South Ormsby 35 TF3675
South Otterington 43 SE3787
South Oxhey 19 TQ1193
South Perrott 7 ST4706
South Petherton 7 ST4316
South Petherwin 4 SX3182
South Pickenham 28 TF8504
South Pool 5 SX7740
South Radworthy 6 SS7432
South Raynham 28 TF8723
South Reston 35 TF4082
South Runcton 28 TF6308
South Scarle 34 SK8463
South Shian 54 NM9042
South Shields 47 NZ3667
South Shore 36 SD3033
South Skirlaugh 39 TA1439
South Somercotes 35 TF4193
South Stainley 38 SE3063
South Stoke (Avon) 17 ST7461
South Stoke (Oxon.) 18 SU6083
South Stoke (W Susx) 11 TQ0210
South Street 12 TQ3918
South Tawton 5 SX6594
South Thoresby 35 TF4077
South Tidworth 10 SU2347
South Town (Hants.) 9 SU6536
South Walsham 29 TG3613
South Warnborough 10 SU7247
South Weald 20 TQ5793
South Weston 18 SU7098
South Wheatley 4 SX2492
South Widcombe 17 ST5756
South Wigston 26 SP5898
South Willingham 35 TF1983
South Wingfield 33 SK3755
South Witham 34 SK9219
South Wonston 9 SU4635
South Woodham Ferrers 20 TQ8097
South Wootton 28 TF6422
South Wraxall 17 ST8364
South Zeal 5 SX6593
South-haa 63 HU3688
Southall 19 TQ1280
Southam (Glos.) 17 SO9725
Southam (Warw.) 26 SP4161
Southampton 9 SU4212
Southborough 12 TQ5842
Southbourne (Dorset) 8 SZ1491
Southbourne (W Susx) 10 SU7705
Southburgh 29 TG0004
Southchurch 21 TQ9186
Southcott 4 SX5495
Southease 12 TQ4205
Southend (Strath.) 48 NR6908
Southend-on-Sea 21 TQ8885
Southerndown 15 SS8874
Southerness 45 NX9754
Southery 28 TL6294
Southfleet 12 TQ6171
Southgate (Gtr London) 20 TQ3093
Southgate (Norf.) 28 TF6833
Southgate (Norf.) 29 TG1324
Southill 27 TL1442
Southleigh (Devon) 7 SY2093
Southminster 21 TQ9699
Southoe 27 TL1864
Southolt 29 TM1968
Southorpe 27 TF0803
Southowram 37 SE1123
Southport 36 SD3316
Southrepps 29 TG2536
Southrey 35 TF1366
Southrop 17 SP1903
Southrope 10 SU6744
Southsea 9 SZ6498
Southwaite 46 NY4445
Southwark 12 TQ3278
Southwater 11 TQ1526
Southway 7 ST5142
Southwell (Dorset) 8 SY6870
Southwell (Notts.) 34 SK7053
Southwick (Hants.) 9 SU6208
Southwick (Northants.) 27 TL0192
Southwick (Tyne and Wear) 47 NZ3758
Southwick (W Susx) 11 TQ2405
Southwick (Wilts.) 17 ST8354
Southwold 29 TM5076
Southwood (Norf.) 29 TG3905
Southwood (Somer.) 7 ST5533
Soutra Mains 52 NT4559
Sowerby (N Yorks.) 42 SE4381
Sowerby (W Yorks.) 37 SE0423
Sowerby Bridge 37 SE0523
Sowerby Row 46 NY3940
Sowton 5 SX9792
Spa Common 29 TG2930
Spalding 35 TF2422
Spaldington 38 SE7533
Spaldwick 27 TL1272
Spalford 34 SK8369
Sparham 29 TG0619
Spark Bridge 40 SD3084
Sparkford 8 ST6026
Sparkwell 4 SX5767
Sparrowpit 33 SK0980
Sparsholt (Hants.) 9 SU4331
Sparsholt (Oxon.) 18 SU3487
Spaunton 43 SE7289
Spaxton 7 ST2236
Spean Bridge 55 NN2281
Speen (Berks.) 10 SU4568
Speen (Bucks.) 19 SU8499
Speeton 43 TA1574
Speke 32 SJ4383
Speldhurst 12 TQ5541
Spellbrook 20 TL4817
Spelsbury 18 SP3421
Spencers Wood 10 SU7166
Spennithorne 42 SE1489
Spennymoor 42 NZ2533
Spetchley 45 SO8953
Spettisbury 8 ST9002
Spexhall 29 TM3780
Spey Bay 61 NJ3866
Spilsby 35 TF4066
Spindlestone 53 NU1533
Spinningdale 65 NH6789
Spirthill 17 ST9975
Spital 67 ND1654
Spithurst 12 TQ4217
Spittal (Dyfed) 14 SM9723
Spittal (Lothian) 52 NT4677
Spittal (Northum.) 53 NU0051
Spittal of Gelnmuick 57 NO3184
Spittal of Glenshee 56 NO1070
Spittalfield 56 NO1040
Spixworth 29 TG2415
Spofforth 38 SE3650
Spondon 33 SK3935
Spooner Row 29 TM0997
Sporle 28 TF8411
Spott 52 NT6775
Spratton 26 SP7170
Spreakley 10 SU8341
Spreyton 5 SX6996
Spridlington 34 TF0084
Springburn 50 NS5968
Springfield (Fife.) 57 NO3411
Springfield (Grampn.) 61 NJ0559
Springfield (W Mids.) 25 SP1082
Springholm 45 NX8070
Springside 50 NS3639
Springthorpe 34 SK8789
Sproatley 39 TA1934
Sproston Green 32 SJ7367
Sprotbrough 38 SE5302
Sproughton 21 TM1244
Sprouston 53 NT7535
Sprowston 29 TG2412
Sproxton (Leic.) 34 SK8524
Sproxton (N Yorks.) 42 SE6181
Spurstow 32 SJ5556
St. Abbs 53 NT9167
St. Agnes (Corn.) 2 SW7150
St. Albans 19 TL1507
St. Allen 2 SW8250
St. Andrews 57 NO5016
St. Andrews Major 16 ST1471
St. Ann's (Dumf. and Galwy.) 45 NY0793
St. Ann's Chapel 4 SX4170
St. Anne's (Lancs.) 36 SD3129
St. Anthony 2 SW7725
St. Arvans 16 St5196
St. Asaph (Lanelwy) 31 SJ0374
St. Athan 16 ST0168
St. Austell 3 SX0152
St. Bees 40 NX9611
St. Blazey 3 SX0654
St. Boswells 52 NT5930
St. Breock 2 SW9771
St. Breward 3 SX0977
St. Briavels 16 SO5504
St. Bride's Major 15 SS8974
St. Brides 14 SM8010
St. Brides Netherwent 16 ST4289
St. Brides Wentlooge 16 ST2982
St. Brides-super-Ely 16 ST1078
St. Budeaux 4 SX4558
St. Buryan 1 SW4025
St. Catherines 55 NN1207
St. Clears 14 SN2716
St. Cleer 4 SX2468
St. Clement 2 SW8443
St. Clether 4 SX2084
St. Colmac 49 NS0467
St. Columb Major 2 SW9163
St. Columb Minor 2 SW8362
St. Columb Road 2 SW9059
St. Combs 62 NK0563
St. Cross South Elmham 29 TM2984
St. Cyrus 57 NO7464
St. Davids (Dyfed) 14 SM7525
St. Davids (Fife) 51 NT1582
St. Davids (Tays.) 56 NN9420
St. Day 2 SW7242
St. Dennis 2 SW9558
St. Devereux 24 SO4431
St. Dogmaels 14 SN1646
St. Dogwells 14 SM9728
St. Dominick 4 SX3967
St. Donats 15 SS9368
St. Edith's Marsh 17 ST9764
St. Endellion 3 SW9978
St. Enoder 2 SW8956
St. Erme 2 SW8449
St. Erth 2 SW5435
St. Erth Praze 2 SW5735
St. Ervan 2 SW8870
St. Ewe 2 SW9745
St. Fagans 16 ST1177
St. Fergus 62 NK0951
St. Fillans 56 NN6942
St. Florence 14 SN8801
St. Gennys 4 SX1497
St. George (Clwyd) 31 SH9775
St. Georges (S Glam.) 16 ST0976
St. Germans 4 SX3557
St. Giles in the Wood 4 SS5318
St. Giles-on-the-Heath 4 SX3590
St. Harmon 23 SN9872
St. Helen Auckland 42 NZ1826
St. Helena 29 TG1816
St. Helens (I. of W.) 9 SZ6288
St. Helens (Mers.) 32 SJ5095
St. Hilary 2 SW5531
St. Hilary (S Glam.) 16 ST0173
St. Illtyd 16 SO2102
St. Ippollitts 19 TL1927
St. Ishmaels 14 SM8307
St. Issey 2 Sw9271
St. Ive (Cambs.) 4 SX3167
St. Ives (Cambs.) 27 TL3171
St. Ives (Corn.) 2 Sw5140
St. Ives (Dorset) 8 SU1203
St. James South Elmham 29 TM3281
St. John (Corn.) 4 SX4053
St. John's (I. of M.) 43 Sc2781
St. John's Chapel 41 NY8837
St. John's Fen End 28 TF5311
St. John's Highway 28 TF5314
St. John's Town of Dairy 45 NX6281
St. Johns (Durham) 41 NZ0734
St. Johns (Here. and Worc.) 25 SO8453
St. Jude's 43 SC3996
St. Just (Corn.) 2 SW8435
St. Just. (Corn.) 2 SW3631
St. Katherines 62 NJ7834
St. Keverne 2 SW7821
St. Kew 3 SW0276
St. Kew Highway 3 SW0375
St. Keyne 4 SX2460
St. Lawrence (Corn.) 3 SX0466
St. Lawrence (Essex) 21 TL9604
St. Lawrence (I. of W.) 9 SZ5476
St. Lenords (Bucks.) 19 SP9006
St. Leonards (Dorset) 8 SU1002
St. Leonards (E Susx.) 12 TQ8009
St. Levan 2 SW3772
St. Lythans 16 ST1073
St. Mabyn 3 SX0373
St. Margaret South Elmham 29 TM3183
St. Margarets 24 SO3534
St. Margarets Hope (S Ronaldsay) 51 ND4493
St. Margarets at Cliffe 13 TR3644
St. Marks 43 SC2976
St. Martin (Corn.) 4 SX2555
St. Martin's Green 2 SW7324
St. Martins (Is. of Sc.) 2 SV9215
St. Martins (Salop) 32 SJ3236
St. Martins (Tays.) 56 NO1530
St. Mary Bourne 10 SU4250
St. Mary Church 16 ST0071
St. Mary Cray 12 TQ4767
St. Mary Hill 15 SS9678
St. Mary in the Marsh 13 TR0628
St. Mary's (Orkney) 63 HY4701
St. Mary's Bay 13 TR0927
St. Mary's Grove 16 ST4769
St. Mary's Hoo 12 TQ8076
St. Mary's Isle 45 NX6749
St. Marylebone 19 TQ2881
St. Mawes 2 SW8433
St. Mawgan 2 SW8765
St. Mellion 4 SX3865
St. Mellons 16 ST2281
St. Merryn 2 SW8874
St. Mewan 3 SW9951
St. Michael Caerhays 2 SW9642
St. Michael Penkevil 2 SW8542
St. Michael South Elmham 29 TM3483
St. Michaels (Here. & Worc.) 24 SO5765
St. Michaels (Kent) 13 TQ8835
St. Michaels Mount 2 SW5130
St. Michaels on Wyre 36 SD4640
St. Minver 2 SW9677
St. Monans 57 NO5201
St. Neot (Corn) 4 SX1867
St. Neots (Cambs.) 27 TL1860
St. Nicholas (Dyfed) 14 SM9035
St. Nicholas (S Glam.) 16 ST0874
St. Nicholas at Wade 13 TR2666
St. Ninians 50 NS7991
St. Osyth 21 TM1215
St. Owens Cross 16 SO5324
St. Paul's Walden 19 TL1922
St. Pauls Cray 12 TQ4768
St. Peter's 13 TR3668
St. Petrox 14 SR9797
St. Pinnock 4 SX2063
St. Quivox 50 NS3723
St. Stephen (Corn.) 2 SW9453
St. Stephens (Corn.) 4 SX3285
St. Stephens (Corn.) 4 SX4158
St. Teath 3 SX0680
St. Twynnells 14 SE9597
St. Vigeans 57 NO6443
St. Wenn 2 SW9664
St. Weonards 16 SO4924
Stackhouse 37 SD8165
Stacksteads 37 SD8421
Staddiscombe 4 SX5151
Staddlethorpe 39 SE8428
Stadhampton 18 SU6098
Staffield 46 NY5442
Staffin 58 NG4967
Stafford 33 SJ9223
Stagsden 27 SP9849
Stainburn 37 SE2448
Stainby 34 SK9022
Staincross 38 SE3210
Staindrop 41 NZ1220
Staines 11 TQ0471
Stainfield (Lincs.) 35 TF0724
Stainfield (Lincs.) 35 TF1173
Stainforth (N Yorks.) 37 SD8267
Stainforth (S Yorks.) 38 SE6411
Staining 36 SD3435
Stainland 37 SE0719
Stainsacre 43 NZ9108
Stainton (Cleve.) 42 NZ4714
Stainton (Cumbr.) 40 NY4827
Stainton (Cumbr.) 40 SD5285
Stainton (Durham) 41 NZ0718
Stainton (N Yorks.) 41 SE1096
Stainton (S Yorks.) 34 SK5593
Stainton by Langworth 35 TF0577
Stainton le Vale 35 TF1794
Stainton with Adgarley 36 SD2472
Staintondale 43 SE9898
Stair (Cumbr.) 40 NY2321
Stair (Strath.) 50 NS4323
Staithes 43 NZ7818
Stake Pool 36 SD4148
Stakeford 47 NZ2785
Stalbridge 8 ST7317
Stalbridge Weston 8 ST7216
Stalham 29 TG3725
Stalham Green 29 TG3824
Stalisfield Green 13 TQ9652
Stalling Busk 41 SD9185
Stallingborough 39 TA2011
Stalmine 36 SD3745
Stalybridge 37 SJ9698
Stambourne 20 TL7238
Stamford 27 TF0207
Stamford Bridge 38 SE7155
Stamfordham 47 NZ0772
Stanborough 19 TL2210
Stanbridge (Beds.) 19 SP9623
Stanbridge (Dorset) 8 SU0003
Stand 50 NS7668
Standburn 51 NS9274
Standeford 25 SJ9107
Standen 13 TQ8539
Standford 10 SU8134
Standish 36 SD5609
Standlake 18 SP3902
Standon (Hants.) 9 SU4227
Standon (Herts.) 20 TL3922
Standon (Staffs.) 32 SJ8134
Stane 50 NS8859
Stanfield 29 TF9320
Stanford (Beds.) 13 TL1238
Stanford (Kent) 13 TR1238
Stanford Bishop 24 SO6851

Stanford Bridge Syde

Stanford Bridge 24 SO 7165
Stanford Dingley 10 SU 5771
Stanford Rivers 20 TL 5301
Stanford in the Vale 18 SU 3493
Stanford le Hope 20 TQ 6882
Stanford on Avon 26 SP 5878
Stanford on Soar 34 SK 5422
Stanford on Teme 24 SO 7065
Stanghow 42 NZ 6715
Stanhoe 28 TF 8036
Stanhope 41 NY 9939
Stanion 27 SP 9187
Stanley (Derby.) 33 SK 4140
Stanley (Durham) 47 NZ 1953
Stanley (Staffs.) 33 SJ 9252
Stanley (Tays.) 56 NO 1033
Stanley (W Yorks.) 38 SE 3422
Stanmer 12 TQ 3309
Stanmore (Berks.) 10 SU 4778
Stanmore (Gtr London) 19 TQ 1692
Stannington (Northum.) 47 NZ 2179
Stannington (S Yorks.) 33 SK 2988
Stansbatch 23 SO 3461
Stansfield 20 TL 7852
Stanstead 20 TL 8449
Stanstead Abbots 20 TL 3811
Stansted 12 TQ 6062
Stansted Mountfitchet 20 TL 5124
Stanton (Glos.) 25 SP 0634
Stanton (Northum.) 47 NZ 1390
Stanton (Staffs.) 33 SK 1246
Stanton (Suff.) 29 TL 9673
Stanton Drew 17 ST 5963
Stanton Fitzwarren 17 SU 1790
Stanton Harcourt 18 SP 4105
Stanton Hill 34 SK 4860
Stanton Lacey 24 SO 4978
Stanton Long 24 SO 5690
Stanton Prior 17 ST 6762
Stanton St. Bernard 17 SU 0962
Stanton St. John 18 SP 5709
Stanton St. Quintin 17 ST 9079
Stanton Street 29 TL 9566
Stanton Wick 17 ST 6162
Stanton by Bridge 33 SK 3627
Stanton by Dale 34 SK 4637
Stanton in Peak 33 SK 2464
Stanton on the Wolds 34 SK 6330
Stanton under Bardon 26 SK 4610
Stanton upon Hine Heath 32 SJ 5624
Stanwardine in the Fields 32 SJ 4124
Stanway (Essex) 21 TL 9324
Stanway (Glos.) 25 SP 0532
Stanwell 11 TQ 0574
Stanwell Moor 11 TQ 0474
Stanwick 27 SP 9871
Stanydale 63 HU 2850
Stape 43 SE 7993
Stapehill 8 SU 0500
Stapeley 32 SJ 6749
Staple 13 TR 2756
Staple Cross 12 TQ 7822
Staple Fitzpaine 7 ST 2618
Staple Hill 7 ST 2416
Staplefield 11 TQ 2728
Stapleford (Cambs.) 20 TL 4751
Stapleford (Herts.) 20 TL 3117
Stapleford (Leic.) 34 SK 8018
Stapleford (Lincs.) 34 SK 8757
Stapleford (Notts.) 34 SK 4837
Stapleford (Wilts.) 8 SU 0637
Stapleford Abbots 20 TQ 5096
Stapleford Tawney 20 TQ 5098
Staplegrove 7 ST 2126
Staplehurst 12 TQ 7843
Staplers 9 SZ 5189
Stapleton (Avon) 17 ST 6175
Stapleton (Cumbr.) 46 NY 5071
Stapleton (Here. and Worc.) 23 SO 3265
Stapleton (Leic.) 26 SP 4398
Stapleton (N Yorks.) 42 NZ 2612
Stapleton (Salop) 24 SJ 4604
Stapleton (Somer.) 7 ST 4621
Stapley 7 ST 1813
Staploe 27 TL 1460
Star (Dyfed) 14 SN 2435
Star (Fife.) 57 NO 3103
Star (Somer.) 16 ST 4358
Starbotton 41 SD 9574
Starcross 5 SX 9781
Starston 29 TM 2384
Startforth 41 NZ 0416
Startley 17 ST 9482
Stathe 7 ST 3728
Stathern 34 SK 7731
Station Town 42 NZ 4036
Staughton Highway 27 TL 1364
Staunton (Glos.) 16 SO 5412
Staunton (Glos.) 17 SO 7929
Staunton on Arrow 24 SO 3660
Staunton on Wye 24 SO 3645
Staveley (Cumbr.) 40 SD 3786
Staveley (Cumbr.) 40 SD 4698
Staveley (Derby.) 33 SK 4374
Staveley (N Yorks.) 38 SE 3662
Staverton (Devon.) 5 SX 7964
Staverton (Glos.) 17 SO 9823
Staverton (Northants.) 26 SP 5461
Staverton (Wilts.) 17 ST 8560
Stawell 7 ST 3638
Staxigoe 67 ND 3852
Staxton 43 TA 0179
Staylittle 22 SN 8892
Staythorpe 34 SK 7554
Stean 41 SE 0873
Stearsby 38 SE 6171
Steart 7 ST 2745
Stebbing 20 TL 6624
Stedham 11 SU 8622
Steele Road 46 NY 5292
Steen's Bridge 24 SO 5457
Steep 10 SU 7525
Steeple (Dorset) 8 SY 9080
Steeple (Essex) 21 TL 9030
Steeple Ashton 17 ST 9056
Steeple Aston 18 SP 4725
Steeple Barton 18 SP 4424
Steeple Bumpstead 20 TL 6741
Steeple Claydon 18 SP 7027
Steeple Gidding 27 TL 1381
Steeple Langford 8 SU 0337
Steeple Morden 27 TL 2842
Steeton 37 SE 0344
Steinmanhill 62 NJ 7642
Stelling Minnis 13 TR 1446
Stemster 67 ND 1862
Stenalees 3 SX 0157
Stenhousemuir 50 NS 8682
Stenness 63 HU 2176
Stenton 52 NT 6274
Steppingley 19 TL 0135
Stepps 50 NS 6668
Sternfield 21 TM 3861
Stert 17 SU 0259
Stetchworth 20 TL 6458
Stevenage 19 TL 2325
Stevenston 49 NS 2642
Steventon (Hants.) 10 SU 5547
Steventon (Oxon.) 18 SU 4691
Stevington 27 SP 9853
Stewartby 27 TL 0242
Stewarton 50 NS 4246
Stewton 35 TF 3687
Steyning 11 TQ 1711
Steynton 14 SM 9108
Stibb 4 SS 2210
Stibb Cross 4 SS 4314
Stibb Green 10 SU 2262
Stibbard 29 TF 9828
Stibbington 27 TL 0898
Stichill 52 NT 7138
Sticker 2 SW 9750
Stickford 35 TF 3560
Sticklepath 5 SX 6394
Stickney 35 TF 3456
Stiffkey 29 TF 9743
Stifford's Bridge 24 SO 7348
Stilligarry 63 NF 7638
Stillingfleet 38 SE 5940
Stillington (Cleve, Durham) 42 NZ 3723
Stillington (N Yorks.) 38 SE 5867
Stilton 27 TL 1689
Stinchcombe 17 ST 7298
Stinsford 8 SY 7191
Stirchley 24 SJ 6906
Stirling 50 NS 7993
Stisted 20 TL 8024
Stithians 2 SW 7336
Stivichall 26 SP 3376
Stixwould 35 TF 1765
Stoak 32 SJ 4273
Stobieside 50 NS 6239
Stobo 51 NT 1837
Stoborough 8 SY 9286
Stoborough Green 8 SY 9184
Stock 20 TQ 6998
Stock Green 25 SO 9859
Stock Wood 25 SP 0058
Stockbridge 9 SU 3535
Stockbriggs 50 NS 7936
Stockbury 13 TQ 8461
Stockcross 10 SU 4368
Stockdalewath 46 NY 3845
Stockerston 27 SP 8397
Stocking Pelham 20 TL 4529
Stockingford 26 SP 3391
Stockinish 63 NG 1391
Stockland 7 ST 2404
Stockland Bristol 7 ST 2443
Stockleigh English 5 SS 8406
Stockleigh Pomeroy 5 SS 8703
Stockley 17 SU 0067
Stockport 33 SJ 8989
Stocksbridge 37 SK 2798
Stocksfield 47 NZ 0561
Stockton (Here. and Worc.) 24 SO 5161
Stockton (Norf.) 29 TM 3894
Stockton (Salop) 24 SO 7299
Stockton (Warw.) 26 SP 4363
Stockton (Wilts.) 8 ST 9738
Stockton Heath 32 SJ 6185
Stockton on Teme 24 SO 7167
Stockton on the Forest 38 SE 6556
Stockton-on-Tees 42 NZ 4419
Stockwith 34 SK 7994
Stodmarsh 13 TR 2160
Stody 29 TG 0535
Stoer 64 NC 0428
Stoford (Somer.) 7 ST 5613
Stoford (Wilts.) 8 SU 0835
Stogumber 7 ST 0937
Stogursey 7 ST 2042
Stoke (Devon.) 4 SS 2324
Stoke (Hants.) 10 SU 4051
Stoke (Hants.) 10 SU 7202
Stoke (Kent) 12 TQ 8275
Stoke Abbott 7 ST 4500
Stoke Albany 26 SP 8088
Stoke Ash 29 TM 1170
Stoke Bardolph 34 SK 6441
Stoke Bliss 24 SO 6562
Stoke Bruerne 26 SP 7450
Stoke Canon 5 SX 9397
Stoke Charity 10 SU 4839
Stoke Climsland 4 SX 3574
Stoke D'Abernon 11 TQ 1259
Stoke Doyle 27 TL 0286
Stoke Dry 27 SP 8597
Stoke Ferry 28 TF 7000
Stoke Fleming 5 SX 8648
Stoke Gabriel 5 SX 8457
Stoke Gifford 17 ST 6280
Stoke Golding 26 SP 3997
Stoke Goldington 27 SP 8348
Stoke Hammond 19 SP 8829
Stoke Holy Cross 29 TG 2301
Stoke Lacy 24 SO 6149
Stoke Lyne 18 SP 5628
Stoke Mandeville 19 SP 8310
Stoke Newington 20 TQ 3286
Stoke Orchard 17 SO 9128
Stoke Poges 19 SU 9884
Stoke Prior (Here. and Worc.) 24 SO 5256
Stoke Prior (Here. and Worc.) 25 SO 9467
Stoke Rivers 6 SS 6335
Stoke Rochford 34 SK 9127
Stoke Row 18 SU 6883
Stoke St. Gregory 7 ST 3426
Stoke St. Mary 7 ST 2622
Stoke St. Michael 8 ST 6646
Stoke St. Milborough 24 SO 5682
Stoke Talmage 18 SU 6799
Stoke Trister 8 ST 7328
Stoke by Clare 20 TL 7443
Stoke sub Hamdon 7 ST 4747
Stoke upon Tern 32 SJ 6327
Stoke-by-Nayland 21 TL 9836
Stoke-on-Trent 33 SJ 8745
Stokeford 8 SY 8787
Stokeham 34 SK 7876
Stokeinteignhead 5 SX 9170
Stokenchurch 18 SU 7596
Stokenham 5 SX 8042
Stokes Bay 9 SZ 5897
Stokesay 24 SO 4381
Stokesby 29 TG 4310
Stokesley 42 NZ 5208
Stolford 7 ST 2245
Ston Easton 17 ST 6253
Stondon Massey 20 TL 5800
Stone (Bucks.) 18 SP 7812
Stone (Glos.) 17 ST 6895
Stone (Here. and Worc.) 25 SO 8675
Stone (Kent) 12 TQ 5774
Stone (Kent) 13 TQ 9427
Stone (Staffs.) 33 SJ 9034
Stone Allerton 7 ST 3950
Stone Cross 12 TQ 6104
Stone House (Cumbr.) 41 SD 7785
Stonebroom 33 SK 4159
Stonefield 50 NS 6957
Stonegate 12 TQ 6628
Stonegate Crofts 62 NK 0339
Stonegrave 42 SE 6577
Stonehaugh 46 NY 7976
Stonehaven 57 NO 8685
Stonehouse (Glos.) 17 SO 8005
Stonehouse (Northum.) 46 NY 6958
Stonehouse (Strath.) 50 NS 7546
Stoneleigh 26 SP 3272
Stonely 27 TL 1067
Stones Green 21 TM 1626
Stonesby 34 SK 8224
Stonesfield 18 SP 3917
Stoney Cross 9 SU 2511
Stoney Middleton 33 SK 2275
Stoney Stanton 26 SP 4894
Stoney Stratton 8 ST 6539
Stoney Stretton 24 SJ 3809
Stoneybridge 63 NF 7433
Stoneyburn 51 NS 9762
Stoneygate 26 SK 6102
Stoneyhills 21 TQ 9497
Stoneykirk 44 NX 0853
Stoneywood 62 NJ 8910
Stonganess 63 HP 5402
Stonham Aspal 21 TM 1359
Stonnall 25 SK 0603
Stonor 18 SU 7388
Stonton Wyville 26 SP 7395
Stony Stratford 26 SP 7840
Stonybreck 63 HU 2071
Stoodleigh 5 SS 9218
Stopham 11 TQ 0219
Stopsley 19 TL 1023
Storeton 32 SJ 3084
Stornoway 63 NB 4333
Storridge 24 SO 7448
Storrington 11 TQ 0814
Storth 40 SD 4780
Stotfold 19 TL 2136
Stottesdon 24 SO 6782
Stoughton (Leic.) 26 SK 6402
Stoughton (Surrey) 11 SU 9851
Stoughton (W Susx) 10 SU 8011
Stoul 58 NM 7594
Stoulton 25 SO 9049
Stour Provost 8 ST 7921
Stour Row 8 ST 8220
Stourbridge 25 SO 8984
Stourhead 8 ST 7734
Stourpaine 8 ST 8509
Stourport on Severn 25 SO 8171
Stourton (Here. and Worc.) 25 SO 8585
Stourton (Warw.) 18 SP 2936
Stourton (Wilts.) 8 ST 7733
Stourton Caundle 8 ST 7114
Stove 63 HY 6036
Stoven 29 TM 4481
Stow (Borders) 52 NT 4644
Stow (Lincs.) 34 SK 8781
Stow Bardolph 28 TF 6205
Stow Bedon 29 TL 9596
Stow Longa 27 TL 1171
Stow Maries 20 TQ 8399
Stow cum Quy 28 TL 5260
Stow-on-the-Wold 17 SP 1925
Stowbridge 28 TF 6007
Stowe (Salop) 23 SO 3173
Stowe (Staffs.) 33 SK 0027
Stowell 8 ST 6822
Stowford 4 SX 4386
Stowlangtoft 29 TL 9568
Stowmarket 21 TM 0458
Stowting 13 TR 1241
Stowupland 29 TM 0659
Straad 49 NS 0462
Strachan 62 NO 6792
Strachur 55 NN 0901
Stradbroke 29 TM 2373
Stradishall 20 TL 7452
Stradsett 28 TF 6605
Stragglethorpe 34 SK 9152
Straiton (Lothian) 51 NT 2766
Straiton (Strath.) 44 NS 3804
Straloch (Grampn.) 62 NJ 8621
Straloch (Tays.) 56 NO 0463
Stramshall 33 SK 0735
Strands 40 NY 1204
Stranraer 44 NX 0660
Strata Florida 22 SN 7465
Stratfield Mortimer 10 SU 6764
Stratfield Saye 10 SU 6961
Stratfield Turgis 10 SU 6959
Stratford St. Andrew 29 TM 3560
Stratford St. Mary 21 TM 0434
Stratford Tony 8 SU 0926
Stratford-upon-Avon 26 SP 2055
Strath Fleet 66 NC 6702
Strath Gairloch 64 NG 7977
Strathan (Highld.) 64 NC 0821
Strathan (Highld.) 59 NM 9891
Strathaven 50 NS 7044
Strathblane (Central) 50 NS 5679
Strathcarron (Highld.) 59 NG 9442
Strathconon 60 NH 4055
Strathdon 61 NJ 3513
Strathkanaird (Highld.) 66 NC 1501
Strathkinness 57 NO 4516
Strathmiglo 56 NO 2109
Strathpeffer 60 NH 4858
Strathwhillan 49 NS 0235
Strathy 67 NC 8465
Strathyre 55 NN 5617
Stratton (Corn.) 4 SS 2306
Stratton (Dorset) 8 SY 6593
Stratton (Glos.) 17 SP 0103
Stratton Audley 18 SP 6026
Stratton St. Margaret 17 SU 1787
Stratton St. Michael 29 TM 2093
Stratton Strawless 29 TG 2220
Stratton-on-the-Fosse 8 ST 6550
Stravithie 57 NO 5311
Streat 12 TQ 3515
Streatham 11 TQ 2972
Streatley (Beds.) 19 TL 0728
Streatley (Berks.) 18 SU 5980
Street (Lancs.) 36 SD 5252
Street (N Yorks.) 43 NZ 7304
Street (Somer.) 7 ST 4836
Street End 10 SZ 8599
Streethay 25 SK 1410
Streetly 25 SP 0898
Strefford 24 SO 4485
Strensall 38 SE 6360
Strensham 25 SO 9040
Stretcholt 7 ST 2943
Strete 5 SX 8447
Stretford 32 SJ 7894
Stretford Court 24 SO 4455
Strethall 20 TL 4939
Stretham 28 TL 5174
Strettington 11 SU 8807
Stretton (Ches.) 32 SJ 4452
Stretton (Ches.) 32 SJ 6182
Stretton (Derby.) 33 SK 3961
Stretton (Leic.) 34 SK 9415
Stretton (Staffs.) 25 SJ 8811
Stretton (Staffs.) 33 SK 2526
Stretton Grandison 24 SO 6344
Stretton Heath 24 SJ 3610
Stretton Westwood 24 SO 5998
Stretton en le Field 26 SK 3012
Stretton on Fosse 18 SP 2238
Stretton under Fosse 26 SP 4581
Stretton-on-Dunsmore 26 SP 4072
Strichen 62 NJ 9455
Stringston 7 ST 1742
Strixton 27 SP 9061
Stroat 17 ST 5798
Stromeferry 59 NG 8634
Stromemore 59 NG 8635
Stromness (Orkney) 63 HY 2509
Stronachlachar 55 NN 4010
Stronchrubie 66 NC 2419
Strond 63 NG 0384
Strone (Highld.) 60 NH 5228
Strone (Strath.) 49 NS 1880
Stronenaba 55 NN 2084
Stronmilchan 55 NN 1528
Strontian 54 NM 8161
Strood 12 TQ 7369
Stroud (Glos.) 17 SO 8504
Stroud (Hants.) 10 SU 7223
Struan 58 NG 3438
Strubby 35 TF 4582
Struen Station 56 NN 8065
Strumpshaw 29 TG 3507
Strutherhill 50 NS 7650
Struy 60 NH 4039
Stuartfield 62 NJ 9745
Stubbington 9 SU 5503
Stubbins 37 SD 7918
Stubhampton 8 ST 9113
Stubton 34 SK 8748
Stuckgowan 55 NN 3202
Stuckton 8 SU 1613
Studham 19 TL 0215
Studland 8 SZ 0382
Studley (Oxon.) 18 SP 5912
Studley (Warw.) 25 SP 0763
Studley (Wilts.) 17 ST 9671
Studley Roger 38 SE 2970
Stump Cross 20 TL 5044
Stuntney 28 TL 5578
Sturbridge 32 SJ 8330
Sturmer 20 TL 6944
Sturminster Common 8 ST 7812
Sturminster Marshall 8 SY 9499
Sturminster Newton 8 ST 7813
Sturry 13 TR 1760
Sturton by Stow 34 SK 8980
Sturton le Steeple 34 SK 7884
Stuston 29 TM 1378
Stutton (N Yorks.) 38 SE 4741
Stutton (Suff.) 21 TM 1434
Stwekley 19 SP 8525
Styal 32 SJ 8383
Suckley 24 SO 7151
Sudborough 27 SP 9682
Sudbourne 21 TM 4153
Sudbrook 16 ST 5087
Sudbrooke 34 TF 0276
Sudbury (Derby.) 33 SK 1631
Sudbury (Suff.) 21 TL 8741
Suddie 60 NH 6654
Sudgrove 17 SO 9307
Suffield 29 TG 2332
Sugnall 32 SJ 7930
Sulby 43 SC 3994
Sulgrave 26 SP 5545
Sulham 10 SU 6474
Sulhamstead 10 SU 6368
Sullington 11 TQ 0913
Sullom 63 HU 3573
Sully 16 ST 1568
Sumburgh 63 HU 4009
Summer Bridge 37 SE 1962
Summercourt 2 SW 8856
Summerleaze 16 ST 4284
Summerseat 37 SD 7914
Summit 37 SD 9418
Sunadale 49 NR 8145
Sunbury 11 TQ 1069
Sunderland (Cumbr.) 40 NY 1735
Sunderland (Tyne and Wear) 47 NZ 3957
Sunderland Bridge 42 NZ 2637
Sunderland Point 36 SD 4255
Sundhope 51 NT 3324
Sundon Park 19 TL 0525
Sundridge 12 TQ 4854
Sunk Island 39 TA 2619
Sunningdale 11 SU 9567
Sunninghill 11 SU 9367
Sunningwell 18 SP 4900
Sunniside (Durham) 42 NZ 1438
Sunniside (Tyne and Wear) 47 NZ 2159
Sunny Bank 40 SD 2992
Sunnylaw 56 NS 7998
Sunnyside 12 TQ 3937
Surbiton 11 TQ 1867
Surfleet 35 TF 2528
Surfleet Seas End 35 TF 2628
Surlingham 29 TG 3106
Sustead 29 TG 1837
Susworth 39 SE 8302
Sutcombe 4 SS 3411
Suton 29 TM 0999
Sutterton 35 TF 2835
Sutton (Beds.) 27 TL 2247
Sutton (Cambs.) 27 TL 0998
Sutton (Cambs.) 27 TL 4479
Sutton (Gtr London) 11 TQ 2463
Sutton (Kent) 13 TR 3349
Sutton (Norf.) 29 TG 3823
Sutton (Notts.) 34 SK 6784
Sutton (Notts.) 34 SK 7637
Sutton (Oxon.) 18 SP 4106
Sutton (Salop) 32 SJ 6631
Sutton (Salop) 24 SO 5082
Sutton (Salop) 24 SO 7286
Sutton (Staffs.) 32 SJ 7622
Sutton (Suff.) 21 TM 3046
Sutton (Surrey) 11 TQ 1046
Sutton (W Susx) 11 SU 9715
Sutton Bassett 26 SP 7790
Sutton Benger 17 ST 9478
Sutton Bonington 34 SK 5025
Sutton Bridge 28 TF 4821
Sutton Cheney 26 SK 4100
Sutton Coldfield 25 SP 1296
Sutton Courtenay 18 SU 5093
Sutton Crosses 35 TF 4321
Sutton Grange 42 SE 2874
Sutton Howgrave 42 SE 3179
Sutton Lane Ends 33 SJ 9270
Sutton Leach 32 SJ 5393
Sutton Maddock 24 SJ 7201
Sutton Mallet 7 ST 3736
Sutton Mandeville 8 ST 9828
Sutton Montis 8 ST 6224
Sutton Scotney 10 SU 4539
Sutton St. Edmund 27 TF 3613
Sutton St. James 35 TG 3918
Sutton St. Nicholas 24 SO 5345
Sutton Valence 12 TQ 8148
Sutton Veny 8 ST 9041
Sutton Waldron 8 ST 8615
Sutton Weaver 32 SJ 5479
Sutton at Hone 12 TQ 5570
Sutton in Ashfield 34 SK 5058
Sutton on Sea 35 TF 5282
Sutton on Trent 34 SK 7965
Sutton on the Hill 33 SK 2333
Sutton upon Derwent 38 SE 7046
Sutton-in-Craven 37 SE 0044
Sutton-on-Hull 39 TA 1132
Sutton-on-the-Forest 38 SE 5864
Sutton-under-Brailes 18 SP 2937
Sutton-under-Whitestonecliffe 42 SE 4882
Swaby 35 TF 3877
Swadlincote 33 SK 3019
Swaffham 28 TF 8109
Swaffham Bulbeck 28 TL 5562
Swaffham Prior 28 TL 5764
Swafield 29 TG 2832
Swainby 42 NZ 4701
Swainshill 24 SO 4641
Swainsthorpe 29 TG 2101
Swainswick 17 ST 7568
Swalcliffe 18 SP 3738
Swalecliffe 13 TR 1367
Swallow 39 TA 1703
Swallowcliffe 8 ST 9626
Swallowfield 10 SU 7264
Swanage 8 SZ 0278
Swanbourne 18 SP 8027
Swanibost 63 NB 5162
Swanland 39 SE 9927
Swanley 12 TQ 5168
Swanmore 9 SU 5815
Swannay 63 HY 2929
Swannington (Leic.) 33 SK 4116
Swannington (Norf.) 29 TG 1319
Swanscombe 12 TQ 6074
Swansea 15 SS 6593
Swanton Abbot 29 TG 2625
Swanton Morley 29 TG 0117
Swanton Novers 29 TG 0132
Swanwick (Derby.) 33 SK 4053
Swanwick (Hants.) 9 SU 5109
Swarby 35 TF 0440
Swardeston 29 TG 2002
Swarkestone 33 SK 3728
Swarland 47 NU 1601
Swarland Estate 47 NU 1603
Swaton 35 TF 1337
Swavesey 27 TL 3669
Sway 9 SZ 2798
Swayfield 34 SK 9822
Swaythling 9 SU 4315
Swefling 29 TM 3463
Swepstone 26 SK 3610
Swerford 18 SP 3731
Swettenham 32 SJ 8067
Swilland 21 TM 1853
Swillington 38 SE 3830
Swimbridge 6 SS 6230
Swinbrook 18 SP 2812
Swinderby 34 SK 8662
Swindon (Glos.) 17 SO 9325
Swindon (Staffs.) 25 SO 8690
Swindon (Wilts.) 17 SU 1484
Swine 39 TA 1335
Swinefleet 38 SE 7621
Swineshead (Beds.) 27 TL 0565
Swineshead (Lincs.) 35 TF 2340
Swineshead Bridge 35 TF 2142
Swiney 67 ND 2335
Swinford (Leic.) 26 SP 5679
Swinford (Oxon.) 18 SP 4408
Swingfield Minnis 13 TR 2142
Swinhill 50 NS 7748
Swinhoe 53 NU 2028
Swinhope 35 TF 2196
Swinister 63 HU 4371
Swinithwaite 41 SE 0489
Swinscoe 33 SK 1347
Swinside Hall 53 NT 7216
Swinstead 34 TF 0122
Swinton (Borders) 53 NT 8447
Swinton (Gtr Mches.) 37 SD 7701
Swinton (N Yorks.) 42 SE 2179
Swinton (N Yorks.) 43 SE 7573
Swinton (S Yorks.) 38 SK 4499
Swintonmill 53 NT 8145
Swithland 26 SK 5413
Swordale 65 NH 5765
Swordland 59 NM 7891
Swordly 66 NC 7363
Sworton Heath 32 SJ 6784
Swyddffynnon 22 SN 6966
Swynnerton 33 SJ 8435
Swyre 7 SY 5288
Syde 17 SO 9411

Sydenham Torroble

Sydenham (Gtr London) 12 TQ 3571
Sydenham (Oxon.) 18 SP 7301
Sydenham Damerel 4 SX 4075
Syderstone 28 TF 8332
Sydling St. Nicholas 8 SY 6399
Sydmonton 10 SU 4857
Syerston 34 SK 7447
Syke 37 SD 8915
Sykehouse 38 SE 6216
Sykes 36 SD 6251
Sylen 15 SN 5107
Symbister 63 HU 5362
Symington (Strath.) 50 NS 3831
Symington (Strath.) 51 NS 9935
Symondsbury 7 SY 4493
Synod Inn 22 SN 4054
Syre 66 NC 6843
Syreford 17 SP 0320
Syresham 26 SP 6241
Syston (Leic.) 26 SK 6211
Syston (Lincs.) 34 SK 9240
Sytchampton 25 SO 8466
Sywell 26 SP 8267

Tackley 18 SP 4720
Tacolneston 29 TM 1395
Tadcaster 38 SE 4843
Tadden 8 ST 9801
Taddington (Derby) 33 SK 1471
Tadley 10 SU 6060
Tadlow 27 TL 2847
Tadmarton 26 SP 3937
Tadworth 11 TQ 2356
Tafarn-y-Gelyn 31 SJ 1861
Tafarnaubach 16 SO 1110
Taff's Well 16 ST 1283
Tafolog 22 SH 8909
Tafolwern 22 SH 8902
Tai'r Bull 16 SN 9926
Tai'r-lon 30 SH 4450
Tai-bach (Clwyd) 31 SJ 1528
Taibach (W Glam.) 15 SS 7789
Tain (Highld.) 67 ND 2266
Tain (Highld.) 65 NH 7782
Takeley 20 TL 5521
Tal-y-Bont (Gwyn.) 31 SH 7668
Tal-y-bont (Gwyn.) 30 SH 5921
Tal-y-cafn 31 SH 7971
Tal-y-llyn (Gwyn.) 22 SH 7109
Tal-y-llyn (Powys) 16 SO 1127
Talachddu 23 SO 0733
Talacre 31 SJ 1083
Talaton 7 SY 0699
Talbenny 14 SM 8412
Talerddig 22 SH 9300
Talgarreg 22 SN 4251
Talgarth 23 SO 1534
Taliesin 22 SN 6591
Talisker 58 NG 3230
Talke 32 SJ 8253
Talkin 46 NY 5557
Talladale 64 NG 9270
Tallentire 40 NY 1035
Talley 15 SN 6332
Tallington 27 TF 0908
Talmine 66 NC 5862
Talog 14 SN 3325
Talsarn 22 SN 5456
Talsarnau 30 SH 6135
Talskiddy 2 SW 9165
Talwrn 30 SH 4876
Talybont (Dyfed) 22 SN 6589
Talybont (Powys) 16 SO 1122
Talysarn 30 SH 4852
Talywern 22 SH 8200
Tamerton Foliot 4 SX 4761
Tamworth 26 SK 2004
Tan-y-fron 31 SH 9564
Tan-y-groes 14 SN 2849
Tandridge 12 TQ 3750
Tanfield 47 NZ 1855
Tangley 10 SU 3352
Tangmere 11 SU 9006
Tangusdale 63 NF 6500
Tangwick 63 HU 2277
Tangy Loch 48 NR 6927
Tankerness 63 HY 5007
Tankersley 38 SK 3499
Tannach 67 ND 3247
Tannadice 57 NO 4758
Tannington 29 TM 2467
Tansley 33 SK 3259
Tansor 27 TL 0590
Tantobie 47 NZ 1754
Tanton 42 NZ 5210
Tanworth in Arden 25 SP 1170
Tanygrisiau 30 SH 6845
Tapeley 6 SS 4729
Taplow 19 SU 9182
Tarbert (Harris) 63 NB 1500
Tarbert (Jura) 48 NR 6082
Tarbert (Strath.) 49 NR 8668
Tarbet (Highld.) 66 NC 1648
Tarbet (Highld.) 59 NM 7992
Tarbet (Strath.) 55 NN 3104
Tarbock Green 32 SJ 4687
Tarbolton 50 NS 4327
Tarbrax 51 NT 0255
Tardebigge 25 SO 9969
Tarfside 57 NO 4979
Tarland 61 NJ 4804
Tarleton 36 SD 4420
Tarlscough 36 SD 4313
Tarlton 17 ST 9599
Tarnbrook 36 SD 5855
Tarporley 32 SJ 5562
Tarr 7 ST 1030
Tarrant Crawford 8 ST 9203
Tarrant Gunville 8 ST 9212
Tarrant Hinton 8 ST 9310
Tarrant Keynston 8 ST 9204
Tarrant Launceston 8 ST 9409
Tarrant Monkton 8 ST 9408
Tarrant Rawston 8 ST 9306
Tarrant Rushton 8 ST 9305
Tarring Neville 12 TQ 4404
Tarrington 24 SO 6140
Tarsappie 56 NO 1220
Tarskavaig 58 NG 5810
Tarves 62 NJ 8631
Tarvin 32 SJ 4867
Tasburgh 29 TM 2096
Tasley 24 SO 6994
Taston 18 SP 3521
Tatenhill 33 SK 2022
Tatham 41 SD 6069
Tathwell 35 TF 3282
Tatsfield 12 TQ 4156
Tattenhall 32 SJ 4858
Tatterford 28 TF 8628
Tattersett 28 TF 8429
Tattershall 35 TF 2157
Tattershall Bridge 35 TF 1956
Tattershall Thorpe 35 TF 2159
Tattingstone 21 TM 1337
Taunton 7 ST 2324
Taverham 29 TG 1513
Tavernspite 14 SN 1812
Tavistock 4 SX 4774
Taw green 5 SX 6497
Tawstock 6 SS 5529
Taxal 33 SK 0079
Tayinloan 48 NR 6945
Taynish 48 NR 7283
Taynton (Glos.) 17 SO 7221
Taynton (Oxon.) 18 SP 2313
Taynuilt 55 NN 0031
Tayport 57 NO 4528
Tayvallich 48 NR 7386
Tealby 35 TF 1590
Tean 2 SV 9016
Teangue 58 NG 6609
Tebay 41 NY 6104
Tebworth 19 SP 9926
Tedburn St. Mary 5 SX 8194
Teddington (Glos.) 25 SO 9632
Teddington (Gtr London) 11 TQ 1671
Tedstone Delamere 24 SO 6958
Tedstone Wafre 24 SO 6759
Teesside 42 NZ 5020
Teeton 26 SP 6970
Teffont Evias 8 ST 9831
Teffont Magna 8 ST 9832
Tegryn 14 SN 2233
Teigh 34 SK 8616
Teigngrace 5 SX 8474
Teignmouth 5 SX 9473
Telford 24 SJ 6909
Tellisford 17 ST 8055
Telscombe 12 TQ 4003
Templand 45 NY 0886
Temple (Corn.) 4 SX 1473
Temple (Lothian) 51 NT 3158
Temple (Strath.) 50 NS 5469
Temple Bar 22 SN 5354
Temple Bruer 34 TF 0053
Temple Cloud 17 ST 6157
Temple Ewell 13 TR 2844
Temple Grafton 25 SP 1254
Temple Guiting 17 SP 0928
Temple Hirst 38 SE 6025
Temple Normanton 33 SK 4167
Temple Sowerby 41 NY 6127
Templecombe 8 ST 7022
Templeton (Devon.) 5 SS 8813
Templeton (Dyfed) 14 SN 1111
Tempsford 27 TL 1653
Ten Mile Bank 28 TL 6097
Tenbury Wells 24 SO 5968
Tenby 14 SN 1300
Tendring 21 TM 1424
Tenston 63 HY 2716
Tenterden 13 TQ 8833
Terling 20 TL 7715
Ternhill 32 SJ 6332
Terregles 45 NX 9377
Terrington 38 SE 6670
Terrington St. Clement 28 TF 5520
Terrington St. John 28 TF 5416
Teston 12 TQ 7053
Testwood 9 SU 3514
Tetbury 17 ST 8993
Tetbury Upton 17 ST 8795
Tetchill 32 SJ 3832
Tetcott 4 SX 3396
Tetford 35 TF 3374
Tetney 39 TA 3101
Tetney Lock 39 TA 3402
Tetsworth 18 SP 6802
Tettenhall 25 SJ 8801
Teversal 34 SK 4661
Teversham 20 TL 4958
Teviothead 46 NT 4005
Tewin 19 TL 2714
Tewkesbury 25 SO 8933
Texa 48 NR 3943
Teynham 13 TQ 9663
Thakeham 11 TQ 1017
Thame 18 SP 7006
Thames Ditton 11 TQ 1567
Thames Haven 20 TQ 7581
Thaneston 57 NO 6375
Thanington 13 TR 1356
Thankerton 51 NS 9737
Tharston 29 TM 1894
Thatcham 10 SU 5167
Thatto Heath 32 SJ 5093
Thaxted 20 TL 6131
The Bryn 16 SO 3309
The Den 49 NS 3251
Theakston 42 SE 3085
Thealby 39 SE 8917
Theale (Berks.) 10 SU 6371
Theale (Somer.) 7 ST 4646
Thearne 39 TA 0736
Theberton 29 TM 4365
Theddingworth 26 SP 6685
Theddlethorpe All Saints 35 TF 4688
Theddlethorpe St. Helen 35 TF 4788
Thelbridge Barton 5 SS 7812
Thelnetham 29 TM 0178
Thelwall 32 SJ 6587
Themelthorpe 29 TG 0524
Thenford 26 SP 5141
Therfield 20 TL 3337
Thetford 28 TL 8783
Theydon Bois 20 TQ 4598
Thickwood 17 ST 8272
Thimbleby (Linc.) 35 TF 2369
Thimbleby (N Yorks.) 42 SE 4495
Thirkleby 42 SE 4778
Thirlby 42 SE 4884
Thirlestane 52 NT 5647
Thirn 42 SE 2185
Thirsk 42 SE 4282
Thistleton 34 SK 9118
Thistley Green 28 TL 6776
Thixendale 39 SE 8461
Thockrington 47 NY 9579
Tholomas Drove 27 TF 4006
Tholthorpe 38 SE 4766
Thomas Chapel 14 SN 1008
Thomastown 61 NJ 5737
Thompson 29 TL 9296
Thomshill 61 NJ 2157
Thong 12 TQ 6770
Thoralby 41 SE 0086
Thoresby 34 SK 6371
Thoresway 35 TF 1696
Thorganby (Lincs.) 35 TF 2097
Thorganby (N Yorks.) 38 SE 6841
Thorgill 43 SE 7096
Thorington 29 TM 4274
Thorington Street 21 TM 0135
Thorlby 37 SD 9652
Thorley 20 TL 4719
Thormanby 42 SE 4974
Thornaby-on-Tees 42 NZ 4518
Thornage 29 TG 0436
Thornborough (Bucks.) 26 SP 7433
Thornborough (N Yorks.) 42 SE 2979
Thornbury (Avon) 17 ST 6390
Thornbury (Devon.) 4 SS 4008
Thornbury (Here and Worc.) 24 SO 6159
Thornby 26 SP 6675
Thorncliff 33 SK 0158
Thorncombe 7 ST 3703
Thorncombe Street 11 TQ 0042
Thorndon 29 TM 1469
Thorne 38 SE 6813
Thorne St. Margaret 7 ST 0920
Thorner 38 SE 3740
Thorney (Cambs.) 27 TF 2804
Thorney (Notts.) 34 SK 8572
Thorney Hill 8 SZ 2099
Thorney Island 10 SU 7503
Thornfalcon 7 ST 2723
Thornford 8 ST 6103
Thorngumbald 39 TA 2026
Thornham 28 TF 7343
Thornham Magna 29 TM 1071
Thornham Parva 29 TM 1072
Thornhaugh 27 TF 0600
Thornhill (Central) 56 NS 6699
Thornhill (Derby.) 33 SK 1983
Thornhill (Dump. and Galwy.) 45 NX 8795
Thornhill (Hants.) 9 SU 4612
Thornhill (Mid Glam.) 16 ST 1584
Thornhill (W Yorks.) 37 SE 2418
Thornicombe 8 ST 8703
Thornley (Durham) 41 NZ 1137
Thornley (Durham) 42 NZ 3639
Thornliebank 50 NS 5459
Thorns 20 TL 7455
Thornthwaite (Cumbr.) 40 NY 2225
Thornthwaite (N Yorks.) 37 SE 1858
Thornton (Bucks.) 18 SP 7535
Thornton (Fife.) 51 NT 2897
Thornton (Humbs.) 38 SE 7545
Thornton (Lancs.) 36 SD 3342
Thornton (Leic.) 26 SK 4607
Thornton (Lincs.) 35 TF 2467
Thornton (Mers.) 36 SD 3300
Thornton (Northum.) 53 NT 9547
Thornton (Tays.) 57 NO 3946
Thornton (W Yorks.) 37 SE 1032
Thornton Curtis 39 TA 0817
Thornton Dale 43 SE 8383
Thornton Hough 32 SJ 3080
Thornton Rust 41 SD 9788
Thornton Steward 42 SE 1787
Thornton Watlass 42 SE 2385
Thornton le Moor (Lincs.) 35 TF 0496
Thornton-in-Craven 37 SD 9048
Thornton-le-Beans 42 SE 3990
Thornton-le-Clay 38 SE 6875
Thornton-le-Moor (N Yorks.) 42 SE 3988
Thornton-le-Moors 32 SJ 4474
Thorntonhall 50 NS 5955
Thorntonloch 53 NT 7574
Thorntonpark 53 NT 9448
Thornwood Common 20 TL 4705
Thoroton 34 SK 7642
Thorp Arch 38 SE 4346
Thorpe (Derby.) 33 SK 1550
Thorpe (Lincs.) 35 TF 4982
Thorpe (N Yorks.) 37 SE 0161
Thorpe (Norf) 29 TM 4398
Thorpe (Notts.) 34 SK 7649
Thorpe (Surrey) 11 TQ 0268
Thorpe Abbotts 29 TM 1979
Thorpe Acre 34 SK 5120
Thorpe Arnold 34 SK 7620
Thorpe Audlin 38 SE 4715
Thorpe Bassett 43 SE 8573
Thorpe Bay 21 TQ 9284
Thorpe Constantine 26 SK 2608
Thorpe End Garden Village 29 TG 2811
Thorpe Green 21 TL 9354
Thorpe Hesley 33 SK 3796
Thorpe Langton 26 SP 7492
Thorpe Larches 42 NZ 3862
Thorpe Malsor 27 SP 8379
Thorpe Mandeville 26 SP 5345
Thorpe Market 29 TG 2436
Thorpe Morieux 21 TL 9453
Thorpe Salvin 34 SK 5281
Thorpe Satchville 26 SK 7311
Thorpe St. Andrew 29 TG 2609
Thorpe St. Peter 35 TF 4861
Thorpe Thewless 42 NZ 4023
Thorpe Underwood 38 SE 4658
Thorpe Waterville 27 TL 0281
Thorpe Willoughby 38 SE 5731
Thorpe by Water 27 SP 8996
Thorpe in Balne 38 SE 5910
Thorpe in the Fallows 34 SK 9080
Thorpe on the Hill 34 SK 9065
Thorpe-le-Soken 21 TM 1822
Thorpeness 21 TM 4759
Thorrington 21 TM 0920
Thorverton 5 SS 9202
Thrandeston 29 TM 1176
Thrapston 27 SP 9978
Threapland 41 SD 9860
Threapwood 32 SJ 4345
Three Bridges 11 TQ 2837
Three Cocks 23 SO 1737
Three Crosses 15 SS 5794
Three Holes 28 TF 5000
Three Leg Cross 12 TQ 6831
Three Legged Cross (Dorset) 8 SU 0806
Three Mile Cross 10 SU 7168
Threekingham 35 TF 0836
Threlkeld 40 NY 3225
Threshfield 37 SD 9963
Thrigby 29 TG 4512
Thringarth 41 NY 9323
Thringstone 33 SK 4217
Thrintoft 42 SE 3293
Thriplow 20 TL 4446
Throcking 20 TL 3330
Throckley 47 NZ 1567
Throckmorton 25 SO 9749
Throphill 47 NZ 1385
Thropton 47 NU 0202
Throwleigh 5 SX 6690
Throwley 13 TQ 9955
Thrumpton 34 SK 5131
Thrumster 67 ND 3345
Thrunton 53 NU 0810
Thrupp (Glos.) 17 SO 8603
Thrupp (Oxon.) 18 SP 4715
Thrushelton 4 SX 4487
Thrushgill 36 SD 6462
Thrussington 34 SK 6416
Thruxton (Hants.) 10 SU 2845
Thruxton (Here. and Worc.) 24 SO 4334
Thrybergh 34 SK 4694
Thundersley 20 TQ 7788
Thurcaston 26 SK 5610
Thurcroft 34 SK 4988
Thurgarton (Norf.) 29 TG 1835
Thurgarton (Notts.) 34 SK 6949
Thurgoland 38 SE 2801
Thurlaston (Leic.) 26 SP 5099
Thurlaston (Warw.) 26 SP 4671
Thurlby (Lincs.) 34 SK 9061
Thurlby (Lincs.) 35 TF 1017
Thurleigh 27 TL 0558
Thurlestone 5 SX 6742
Thurlow 20 TL 6750
Thurloxton 7 ST 2729
Thurlstone 37 SE 2303
Thurlton 29 TM 4198
Thurmaston 26 SK 6109
Thurnby 26 SK 6404
Thurne 29 TG 4015
Thurnham (Kent) 12 TQ 8057
Thurnham (Lancs.) 36 SD 4554
Thurning (Norf.) 29 TG 0729
Thurning (Northants.) 27 TL 0883
Thurnscoe 38 SE 4605
Thursby 46 NY 3250
Thursford 29 TF 9833
Thursley 11 SU 9039
Thurso 67 ND 1168
Thurstaston 31 SJ 2483
Thurston 29 TL 9365
Thurstonfield 46 NY 3156
Thurstonland 37 SE 1610
Thurton 29 TG 3200
Thurvaston 33 SK 2437
Thuxton 29 TG 0307
Thwaite (N Yorks.) 41 SD 8998
Thwaite (Suff.) 29 TM 1168
Thwaite St. Mary 29 TM 3395
Thwing 39 TA 0570
Tibbermore 56 NO 0523
Tibberton (Glos.) 17 SO 7521
Tibberton (Here. and Worc.) 25 SO 9054
Tibberton (Salop) 32 SJ 6720
Tibbie Shiels Inn 51 NT 2320
Tibenham 29 TM 1389
Tibshelf 33 SK 4360
Tibthorpe 39 SE 9555
Ticehurst 12 TQ 6930
Tichborne 9 SU 5630
Tickencote 27 SK 9809
Tickenham 16 ST 4571
Tickhill 34 SK 5993
Ticklerton 24 SO 4890
Ticknall 33 SK 3524
Tickton 39 TA 0641
Tidcombe 10 SU 2858
Tiddington (Oxon.) 18 SP 6404
Tiddington (Warw.) 26 SP 2256
Tidebrook 12 TQ 6130
Tideford 4 SX 3459
Tidenham 16 ST 5596
Tideswell 33 SK 1575
Tidmarsh 10 SU 6374
Tidmington 18 SP 2538
Tidpit 8 SU 0718
Tiers Cross 14 SM 9010
Tiffield 26 SP 6951
Tifty 62 NJ 7740
Tigerton 57 NO 5364
Tigharry 63 NF 7171
Tighnabruaich 49 NR 9772
Tighnafiline 64 NG 8789
Tigley 5 SX 7560
Tilbrook 27 TL 0769
Tilbury 12 TQ 6376
Tile Cross 25 SP 1687
Tile Hill 26 SP 2777
Tilehurst 10 SU 6673
Tilford 11 SU 8743
Tillathrowie 61 NJ 4634
Tillicoultry 50 NS 9197
Tillingham 21 TL 9903
Tillington (Here. and Worc.) 24 SO 4645
Tillington (W Susx.) 11 SU 9621
Tillington Common 24 SO 4546
Tillyarblet 57 NO 5267
Tillycorthie 62 NJ 9123
Tillyfourie 62 NJ 6412
Tillygarmond 62 NO 6393
Tillygreig 62 NJ 8823
Tilmanstone 13 TR 3051
Tilney All Saints 28 TF 5618
Tilney High End 28 TF 5617
Tilney St. Lawrence 28 TF 5414
Tilshead 8 SU 0347
Tilstock 32 SJ 5337
Tilston 32 SJ 4551
Tilstone Fearnall 32 SJ 5660
Tilsworth 19 SP 9724
Tilton on the Hill 26 SK 7405
Timberland 35 TF 1158
Timbersbrook 33 SJ 8962
Timberscombe 6 SS 9542
Timble 37 SE 1752
Timperley 32 SJ 7988
Timsbury (Avon) 17 ST 6658
Timsbury (Hants.) 9 SU 3424
Timworth Green 28 TL 8669
Tincleton 8 SY 7691
Tindale 46 NY 6159
Tingewick 18 SP 6533
Tingley 38 SE 2826
Tingrith 19 TL 0032
Tinhay 4 SX 4085
Tinshill 37 SE 2540
Tinsley 33 SK 3990
Tintagel 3 SX 0588
Tintern Parva 16 SO 5200
Tintinhull 7 ST 5019
Tintwistle 37 SK 0297
Tinwald 45 NY 0081
Tinwell 27 TF 0006
Tipperty 62 NJ 9627
Tipton 25 SO 9592
Tipton St. John 7 SY 0991
Tiptree 21 TL 8916
Tir-y-mynach 23 SH 9302
Tirabad 22 SN 8741
Tirley 17 SO 8328
Tirphil 16 SO 1303
Tirril 40 NY 5026
Tisbury 8 ST 9429
Tissington 33 SK 1752
Titchberry 4 SS 2427
Titchfield 9 SU 5305
Titchmarsh 27 TL 0279
Titchwell 28 TF 7543
Tithby 34 SK 6936
Titley 23 SO 3260
Titlington 53 NU 1015
Tittensor 33 SJ 8738
Tittleshall 28 TF 8920
Tiverton (Ches.) 32 SJ 5560
Tiverton (Devon.) 5 SS 9512
Tivetshall St. Margaret 29 TM 1787
Tivetshall St. Mary 29 TM 1686
Tixall 33 SJ 9722
Tixover 27 SK 9700
Toab 63 HU 3811
Tobermory 54 NM 5055
Toberonochy 54 NM 7408
Tobson 63 NB 1438
Tocher 62 NJ 6932
Tockenham 17 SU 0379
Tockenham Wick 17 SU 0381
Tockholes 36 SD 6623
Tockington 17 ST 6186
Tockwith 38 SE 4652
Todber 8 ST 7919
Toddington (Beds.) 19 TL 0129
Toddington (Glos.) 25 SP 0432
Todenham 18 SP 2436
Todhills 46 NY 3663
Todmorden 37 SD 9324
Todwick 34 SK 4984
Toft (Cambs.) 20 TL 3655
Toft (Ches.) 32 SJ 7676
Toft (Lincs.) 35 TF 0617
Toft Monks 29 TM 4295
Toft next Newton 35 TF 0488
Toftrees 28 TF 8927
Toftwood 29 TF 9811
Togston 47 NU 2401
Tokavaig 58 NG 6012
Tokers Green 10 SU 7077
Toll of Birness 62 NK 0034
Tolland 7 ST 1032
Tollard Royal 8 ST 9417
Toller Fratrum 7 SY 5797
Toller Porcorum 7 SY 5697
Tollerton (N Yorks.) 38 SE 5164
Tollerton (Notts.) 34 SK 6134
Tollesbury 21 TL 9510
Tolleshunt D'Arcy 21 TL 9312
Tolleshunt Major 21 TL 9011
Tolob 63 HU 3811
Tolpuddle 8 SY 7994
Tolstachaolais 63 NB 1938
Tolworth 11 TQ 1965
Tomatin 60 NH 8028
Tombreck 60 NH 6934
Tomdoun 59 NH 1501
Tomich (Highld.) 59 NH 3127
Tomich (Highld.) 60 NH 5348
Tomich (Highld.) 65 NH 7071
Tomintoul (Grampn.) 61 NJ 1618
Tomintoul (Gramps.) 61 NO 1490
Tomnavoulin 61 NJ 2026
Ton 16 SO 3301
Tonbridge 12 TQ 5845
Tondu 15 SS 8984
Tong (Isle of Lewis) 63 NB 4436
Tong (Salop) 24 SJ 7907
Tonge 33 SK 4123
Tongham 11 SU 8848
Tongland 45 NX 6953
Tongue 66 NC 5957
Tongwynlais 15 ST 1581
Tonna 15 SS 7798
Tonwell 20 TL 3317
Tonypandy 15 SS 9992
Tonyrefail 16 ST 0188
Toot Baldon 18 SP 5600
Toot Hill (Essex) 20 TL 5102
Toot Hill (Hants.) 9 SU 3718
Topcliffe 42 SE 3976
Topcroft 29 TM 2693
Topcroft Street 29 TM 2692
Toppesfield 20 TL 7337
Toppings 36 SD 7213
Topsham 5 SX 9788
Torbay 5 SX 8962
Torbeg 49 NR 8929
Torbryan 5 SX 8266
Torcastle 55 NN 1378
Torcross 5 SX 8242
Tore 60 NH 6052
Torhousemuir 44 NX 3957
Torksey 34 SK 8378
Torlum (Benbecula) 63 NF 7850
Torlundy 55 NN 1477
Tormarton 17 ST 7678
Tormitchell 44 NX 2394
Tormore 49 NR 8932
Tormsdale 67 ND 1350
Tornagrain 60 NH 7649
Tornahaish 61 NJ 2908
Tornaveen 62 NJ 6106
Torness 60 NH 5727
Torpenhow 40 NY 2039
Torphichen 51 NS 9672
Torphins 62 NJ 6202
Torpoint 4 SX 4355
Torquay 5 SX 9164
Torquhan 52 NT 4447
Torran (Raasay) 58 NG 5949
Torran (Strath.) 54 NM 8704
Torrance 50 NS 6174
Torridon 59 NG 9055
Torrin 58 NG 5720
Torrisdale 66 NC 6761
Torrish 67 NC 9718
Torrisholme 36 SD 4464
Torroble 66 NC 5904

Torry
Wainhouse Corner

Torry (Grampn.) 61 NJ4339
Torry (Grampn.) 62 NJ9404
Torryburn 51 NT0286
Torrylin 49 NR9621
Torterston 62 NK0747
Torthorwald 45 NY0378
Tortington 11 TQ0005
Tortworth 17 ST6992
Torvaig 58 NG4944
Torver 40 SD2894
Torwood 50 NS8484
Torworth 34 SK6586
Toscaig 58 NG7138
Toseland 27 TL2362
Tosside 37 SD7655
Tostock 29 TL9563
Totaig 58 NG2050
Tote 58 NG4149
Totegan 67 NC8268
Totland 9 SZ3286
Totley 33 SK3179
Totnes 5 SX8060
Toton 34 SK5034
Totscore 58 NG3866
Tottenham 20 TQ3491
Tottenhill 28 TF6310
Totteridge 19 TQ2494
Totternhoe 19 SP9921
Tottington 37 SD7712
Totton 9 SU3513
Tournaig 64 NG8783
Toux (Grampn.) 61 NJ5458
Toux (Grampn.) 62 NJ9850
Tovil 12 TQ7554
Tow Law 41 NZ1139
Toward 49 NS1368
Towcester 26 SP6948
Towednack 2 SW4838
Tower Hamlets 20 TQ3582
Towersey 18 SP7305
Towie 61 NJ4412
Towiemore 61 NJ3945
Town End (Cambs.) 27 TL4195
Town End (Cumbr.) 40 SD4483
Town Street 28 TL7786
Town Yetholm 53 NT8228
Townend (Strath.) 50 NS4076
Townhead 45 NX6946
Townhead of Greenlaw 45 NX7465
Townhill 51 NT1089
Townshend 2 SW5932
Towthorpe 38 SE6258
Towton 38 SE4839
Towyn (Clwyd) 31 SH9779
Towyn (Gwyn.) 22 SH5800
Toy's Hill 12 TQ4751
Toynton All Saints 35 TF3964
Toynton Fen Side 35 TF3961
Toynton St. Peter 35 TF4063
Trabboch 50 NS4321
Trabbochburn 50 NS4621
Traboe 2 SW7421
Tradespark (Highld.) 60 NH8656
Tradespark (Orkney) 63 HY4408
Trafford Park 37 SJ7996
Trallong 15 SW9629
Tranent 52 NT4072
Trantlemore 67 NC8853
Tranwell 47 NZ1883
Trapp 15 SN6519
Traprain 52 NT5975
Traquair 51 NT3334
Trawden 37 SD9138
Trawsfynydd 30 SH7035
Tre'r-ddol 22 SN6592
Tre-ddiog 14 SM8928
Tre-groes 22 SN4044
Trealaw 16 SS9992
Treales 36 SD4432
Trearddur Bay 30 SH2478
Treaslane 58 NG3953
Trebartha 4 SX2677
Trebarwith 3 SX0585
Trebetherick 2 SW9377
Treborough 7 ST0036
Trebudannon 2 SW8961
Treburley 4 SX3477
Trecastle 15 SN8729
Trecwyn 14 SM9632
Trecynon 16 SN9903
Tredavoe 2 SW4528
Tredegar 16 SO1409
Tredington 26 SP2543
Tredinnick 2 SW9270
Tredomen 23 SO1231
Tredunnock 16 ST3795
Treen 2 SW3923
Treeton 34 SK4387
Trefdraeth 30 SH4070
Trefecca 23 SO1431
Trefeglwys 23 SN9690
Trefenter 22 SN6068
Treffgarne 14 SM9523
Treffynnon 14 SM8428
Trefil 16 SO1212
Trefilan 22 SN5457
Trefnannau 31 SJ2015
Trefnant 31 SJ0570
Trefonen 31 SJ2526
Trefor 30 SH3779
Trefriw 31 SH7763
Tregadillett 4 SX2983
Tregaian 30 SH4579
Tregare 16 SO4110
Tregaron 22 SN6759
Tregarth 30 SH6067
Tregeare 4 SX2486
Tregeiriog 31 SJ1733
Tregele 30 SH3592
Tregidden 2 SW7523
Treglemais 14 SM8229
Tregole 4 SX1998
Tregonetha 2 SW9563
Tregony 2 SW9244
Tregoyd 23 SO1937
Tregurrian 2 SW8465
Tregynon 23 SO0999
Trehafod 16 ST0491
Treharris 16 ST1097
Treherbert 15 SS9398
Trelawnyd 31 SJ0879
Trelech 14 SN2830
Trelech a'r Betws 14 SN3026
Treleddyd-fawr 14 SM7528
Trelewis 16 ST1197
Trelights 3 SW9879
Trelill 3 SX0477
Trelleck 16 SO5005
Trelleck Grange 16 SO4901
Trelogan 31 SJ1180
Trelystan 23 SJ2603
Tremadog 30 SH5640
Tremail 4 SX1686
Tremain 14 SN2348
Tremaine 4 SX2388
Tremar 4 SX2568
Trematon 4 SX3959
Tremeirchion 31 SJ0773
Trenance 2 SW8567
Trenarren 3 SX0348
Trench 24 SJ6913
Treneglos 4 SX2088
Trenewan 4 SX1753
Trent 8 ST5918
Trentham 33 SJ8640
Trentishoe 6 SS6448
Treoes 15 SS9478
Treorchy 15 SS9596
Tresaith 14 SN2751
Trescott 25 SO8497
Trescowe 2 SW5731
Tresham 17 ST7991
Tresillian 2 SW8646
Tresinwen 14 SM9040
Tresmeer 4 SX2387
Tressait 56 NN8160
Tresta (Fetlar) 63 HU6190
Tresta (Shetld.) 63 HU3650
Treswell 34 SK7779
Trethurgy 3 SX0355
Tretio 14 SM7829
Tretire 16 SO5124
Tretower 16 SO1821
Treuddyn 31 SJ2458
Trevalga 3 SX0889
Trevanson 2 SW9772
Trevarren 2 SW9160
Trevarrick 2 SW9843
Trevellas 2 SW7452
Treverva 2 SW7631
Trevethin 16 SO2802
Trevigro 4 SX3369
Trevine 14 SM8432
Treviscoe 2 SW9455
Trevone 2 SW8975
Trevor 30 SH3746
Trewarmett 3 SX0686
Trewarthenick 2 SW9044
Trewassa 4 SX1486
Trewellard 2 SW3733
Trewen 4 SX2583
Trewidland 4 SX2560
Trewint 4 SX1897
Trewithian 2 SW8737
Trewoon 3 SW9952
Treyford 10 SU8218
Trickett's Cross 8 SU0801
Trimdon 42 NZ3634
Trimdon Colliery 42 NZ3835
Trimdon Grange 42 NZ3735
Trimingham 29 TG2738
Trimley 21 TM2736
Trimley Heath 21 TM2737
Trimpley 24 SO7978
Trimsaran 15 SN4504
Trimstone 6 SS5043
Trinant 16 SO2000
Tring 19 SP9211
Trinity 57 NO6061
Trislaig 55 NN0874
Trispen 2 SW8450
Tritlington 47 NZ2092
Trochrie 56 NN9740
Troedyraur 22 SN3245
Troedyrhiw 16 SO0702
Trofarth 31 SH8571
Troon (Corn.) 2 SW6638
Troon (Strath.) 49 NS3230
Troston 28 TL8972
Trottiscliffe 12 TQ6460
Trotton 10 SU8322
Troutbeck 40 NY4103
Troutbeck Bridge 40 NY4000
Trow Green 17 SO5706
Trowbridge 17 ST8557
Trowle Common 17 ST8358
Trows 52 NT6932
Trowse Newton 29 TG2406
Trudoxhill 8 ST7443
Trull 7 ST2122
Trumisgarry 63 NF8674
Trumpan 58 NG2261
Trumpet 24 SO6539
Trumpington 20 TL4455
Trunch 29 TG2834
Truro 2 SW8244
Trusham 5 SX8582
Trusley 33 SK2535
Trusthorpe 35 TF5183
Trysull 25 SO8494
Tubney 18 SU4498
Tuckenhay 5 SX8156
Tuddenham (Suff.) 28 TL7371
Tuddenham (Suff.) 21 TM1948
Tudeley 12 TQ6245
Tudhoe 42 NZ2635
Tudweiloig 30 SH2336
Tuffley 17 SO8315
Tugby 26 SK7601
Tugford 24 SO5587
Tullibody 50 NS8595
Tullich (Highld.) 65 NH8576
Tullich (Strath.) 55 NN0815
Tullich Muir 65 NH7373
Tulliemet 56 NN9952
Tulloch (Grampn.) 57 NO7671
Tulloch (Highld.) 65 NH6192
Tullochgorm 49 NR9695
Tulloes 57 NO5145
Tullybannocher 56 NN7521
Tullyfergus 56 NO2149
Tullynessle 61 NJ5519
Tumble 15 SN5411
Tumby 35 TF2359
Tumby Woodside 35 TF2657
Tummel Bridge 56 NN7659
Tunstall (Humbs.) 39 TA3032
Tunstall (Kent) 13 TQ8961
Tunstall (Lancs.) 41 SD6073
Tunstall (N Yorks.) 42 SE2195
Tunstall (Norf.) 29 TG4107
Tunstall (Staffs.) 33 SJ8551
Tunstall (Suff.) 21 TM3655
Tunstead 29 TG3022
Tunworth 10 SU6748
Tupsley 24 SO5340
Tur Langton 26 SP7194
Turgis Green 10 SU6959
Turin 57 NO5352
Turkdean 17 SP1017
Turnastone 24 SO3536
Turnberry 44 NS2005
Turnditch 33 SK2946
Turner's Hill 12 TQ3435
Turners Puddle 8 SY8293
Turnworth 8 ST8107
Turriff 62 NJ7249
Turton Bottoms 36 SD7315
Turvey 27 SP9452
Turville 18 SU7691
Turville Heath 18 SU7391
Turweston 18 SP6037
Tushingham cum Grindley 12 SJ5246
Tutbury 33 SK2129
Tutnall 25 SO9870
Tutshill 16 ST5394
Tuttington 29 TG2227
Tuxford 34 SK7370
Twatt (Orkney) 63 HY2624
Twatt (Shetld.) 63 HU3252
Twechar 50 NS6975
Tweedmouth 53 NT9952
Tweedsmuir 51 NT1024
Twelveheads 2 SW7642
Twenty 35 TF1520
Twerton 17 ST7263
Twickenham 11 TQ1473
Twigworth 17 SO8421
Twineham 11 TQ2519
Twinhoe 17 ST7359
Twinstead 21 TL8637
Twiss Green 32 SJ6595
Twitchen (Devon.) 6 SS7830
Twitchen (Salop) 24 SO3679
Two Bridges 5 SX6075
Two Dales 33 SK2762
Two Gates 26 SK2101
Twycross 26 SK3305
Twyford (Berks.) 10 SU7975
Twyford (Bucks.) 18 SP6626
Twyford (Hants.) 9 SU4724
Twyford (Leics.) 26 SK7210
Twyford (Norf.) 29 TG0124
Twyford Common 24 SO5135
Twyn-y-Sheriff 16 SO4005
Twynholm 45 NX6654
Twyning 25 SO8936
Twyning Green 25 SO9037
Twynllanan 15 SN7524
Twywell 27 SP9578
Ty'n-dwr 31 SJ2342
Ty'n-y-groes 31 SH7771
Ty-hen 30 SH1731
Ty-mawr 31 SH9047
Ty-nant (Clwyd) 31 SH9944
Ty-nant (Gwyn.) 31 SH9026
Tyberton 24 SO3739
Tyburn 25 SP1490
Tycroes 15 SN6010
Tycrwyn 31 SJ1018
Tydd Gote 35 TF4518
Tydd St. Giles 35 TF4216
Tydd St. Mary 35 TF4418
Tyldesley 36 SD6902
Tyler Hill 13 TR1460
Tylers Green 19 SU9094
Tylorstown 16 ST0195
Tylwch 23 SN9780
Tyn-y-ffridd 31 SJ1230
Tyn-y-graig 23 SO0149
Tyndrum 55 NN3330
Tyneham 8 SY8880
Tynehead 51 NT3959
Tynemouth (Tyne and Wear) 47 NZ3468
Tynewydd 15 SS9399
Tyninghame 52 NT6179
Tynribbie 55 NM9446
Tynron 45 NX8093
Tyringham 27 SP8547
Tythegston 15 SS8578
Tytherington (Avon) 17 ST6788
Tytherington (Ches.) 33 SJ9175
Tytherington (Somer.) 8 ST7744
Tytherington (Wilts.) 8 ST9140
Tytherleigh 7 ST3203
Tywardreath 3 SX0854
Tywyn (Gwyn) 31 SH7878
Tywyn Trewan 30 SH3175

Uachdar 63 NF7955
Ubbeston Green 29 TM3271
Ubley 16 ST5257
Uckerby 42 NZ2402
Uckfield 12 TQ4721
Uckington 17 SO9224
Uddingston 50 NS6960
Uddington 50 NS8633
Udimore 13 TQ8718
Udny Green 62 NJ8726
Udstonhead 50 NS7047
Uffcott 17 SU1277
Uffculme 7 ST0612
Uffington (Lincs.) 27 TF0608
Uffington (Oxon.) 18 SU3089
Uffington (Salop) 24 SJ5313
Ufford (Northants.) 27 TF0904
Ufford (Suff.) 21 TM2953
Ufton 26 SP3762
Ufton Nervet 10 SU6367
Ugborough 5 SX6755
Uggeshall 29 TM4580
Ugglesbarnby 43 NZ8707
Ugley 20 TL5128
Ugley Green 20 TL5227
Ugthorpe 43 NZ7911
Uig (Isle of Lewis) 63 NB0534
Uig (Isle of Skye) 58 NG1952
Uig (Isle of Skye) 58 NH3963
Uigshader 58 NG4246
Uisken 54 NM3819
Ulbster 67 ND3241
Ulceby (Humbs.) 39 TA1014
Ulceby (Lincs.) 35 TF4272
Ulcombe 13 TQ8449
Uldale 40 NY2536
Uley 17 ST7898
Ulgham 47 NZ2392
Ullapool 64 NH1294
Ullenhall 25 SP1267
Ullenwood 17 SO9416
Ulleskelf 38 SE5140
Ullesthorpe 26 SP5087
Ulley 34 SK4687
Ullingswick 24 SO5950
Ullinish 58 NG3237
Ullock 40 NY0724
Ulpha 40 SD1993
Ulrome 39 TA1656
Ulsta 63 HU4680
Ulverston 40 SD2878
Ulzieside 50 NS7708
Umberleigh 6 SS6023
Unapool 66 NC2333
Under River 12 TQ5552
Underbarrow 40 SD4692
Underhoull 63 HP5704
Underwood 34 SK4750
Undy 16 ST4386
Unifirth 63 HU2856
Union Cottage 62 NO8290
Union Mills 43 SC3578
Unstone 33 SK3777
Up Cerne 8 ST6502
Up Exe 5 SS9302
Up Hatherley 17 SO9120
Up Hill (Kent) 13 TR2140
Up Holland 36 SD5105
Up Nately 10 SU6951
Up Somborne 9 SU3932
Up Sydling 8 ST6201
Upavon 17 SU1354
Upchurch 13 TQ8467
Upcott 23 SO3250
Upend 20 TL7058
Uphall 51 NT0571
Upham (Devon.) 5 SS8808
Upham (Hants.) 9 SU5320
Uphill (Avon) 16 ST3158
Uplawmoor 50 NS4355
Upleadon 17 SO7527
Upleatham 42 NZ6319
Uplees 13 TQ9964
Uplowman 7 ST0115
Uplyme 7 SY3293
Upminster 20 TQ5686
Upnor 12 TQ7470
Upottery 7 ST2007
Uppark 10 SU7717
Upper Affcot 24 SO4486
Upper Ardchronie 65 NH6188
Upper Arley 24 SO7680
Upper Astrop 18 SP5137
Upper Basildon 10 SU5976
Upper Beeding 11 TQ1910
Upper Benefield 27 SP9789
Upper Boddington 26 SP4853
Upper Borth 22 SN6088
Upper Breinton 24 SO4640
Upper Broughton 34 SK6826
Upper Brow Top 36 SD5258
Upper Bucklebury 10 SU5368
Upper Caldecote 27 TL1645
Upper Chapel 23 SO0040
Upper Chute 10 SU2953
Upper Clatford 10 SU3543
Upper Clynnog 30 SH4746
Upper Cokeham 11 TQ1605
Upper Coll 63 NB4539
Upper Cwmtwrch 15 SN7611
Upper Dallachy 61 NJ3662
Upper Dean 27 TL0467
Upper Denby 37 SE2207
Upper Derraid 61 NJ0233
Upper Dicker 12 TQ5510
Upper Elkstone 33 SK0559
Upper End 33 SK0876
Upper Ethie 65 NH7663
Upper Farringdon 10 SU7135
Upper Framilode 17 SO7510
Upper Froyle 10 SU7542
Upper Gravenhurst 19 TL1136
Upper Green 10 SU3663
Upper Hackney 33 SK2961
Upper Hale 10 SU8448
Upper Hambleton 27 SK8907
Upper Hardres Court 13 TR1550
Upper Hartfield 12 TQ4634
Upper Heath 24 SO5685
Upper Helmsley 38 SE6956
Upper Heyford (Oxon.) 18 SP4926
Upper Hill 24 SO4753
Upper Hopton 37 SE1918
Upper Hulme 33 SK0160
Upper Inglesham 18 SU2096
Upper Killay 15 SS5892
Upper Knockando 61 NJ1843
Upper Lambourn 18 SU3180
Upper Langwith 34 SK5169
Upper Lochton 62 NO6997
Upper Longdon 33 SK0614
Upper Lydbrook 17 SO6015
Upper Maes-coed 23 SO3335
Upper Minety 17 SU0091
Upper North Dean 19 SU8598
Upper Poppleton 38 SE5554
Upper Quinton 25 SP1746
Upper Sanday 63 HY5303
Upper Sapey 24 SO6863
Upper Scoulag 49 NS1059
Upper Seagry 17 ST9580
Upper Shelton 27 SP9943
Upper Sheringham 29 TG1441
Upper Skelmorlie 49 NS1968
Upper Slaughter 17 SP1523
Upper Soudley 17 SO6610
Upper Stondon 19 TL1535
Upper Stowe 26 SP6456
Upper Street (Hants.) 8 SU1418
Upper Street (Norf.) 29 TG3516
Upper Sundon 19 TL0527
Upper Swell 17 SP1726
Upper Tasburgh 29 TM2095
Upper Tean 33 SK0139
Upper Tillyrie 56 NO1006
Upper Tooting 11 TQ2772
Upper Town (Avon) 16 ST5265
Upper Tysoe 26 SP3343
Upper Upham 10 SU2277
Upper Wardington 26 SP4946
Upper Weald 18 SP8037
Upper Weedon 26 SP6258
Upper Wield 10 SU6238
Upper Winchendon 18 SP7414
Upper Woodford 8 SU1237
Uppermill 37 SD9906
Upperthong 37 SE1208
Upperton 11 SU9522
Uppertown (Stroma) 67 ND3576
Uppingham 27 SP8699
Uppington 24 SJ5909
Upsall 42 SE4587
Upshire 20 TL4100
Upstreet 13 TR2262
Upton (Berks.) 11 SU9879
Upton (Bucks.) 18 SP7711
Upton (Cambs.) 27 TL1778
Upton (Cambs.) 27 TF1000
Upton (Ches.) 32 SJ4069
Upton (Dorset) 8 SY9893
Upton (Hants.) 10 SU3555
Upton (Hants.) 9 SU3716
Upton (Lincs.) 34 SK8686
Upton (Mers.) 31 SJ2687
Upton (Norf.) 29 TG3912
Upton (Northants.) 26 SP7160
Upton (Notts.) 34 SK7354
Upton (Notts.) 34 SK7476
Upton (Oxon.) 18 SU5186
Upton (Somer.) 7 SS9928
Upton (W Yorks.) 38 SE4713
Upton Bishop 17 SO6427
Upton Cheyney 17 ST6969
Upton Cressett 24 SO6592
Upton Cross 4 SX2872
Upton Grey 10 SU6948
Upton Hellions 5 SS8303
Upton Lovell 8 ST9440
Upton Magna 24 SJ5512
Upton Noble 8 ST7139
Upton Pyne 5 SX9197
Upton Scudamore 8 ST8647
Upton Snodsbury 25 SO9454
Upton St. Leonards 17 SO8615
Upton Warren 25 SO9267
Upton upon Severn 25 SO8540
Upwaltham 11 SU9413
Upware 28 TL5370
Upwell 28 TF5002
Upwey 8 SY6684
Upwood 27 TL2582
Uradale 63 HU4137
Urafirth 63 HU3078
Urchal 60 NH7544
Urchany 60 NH8849
Urchfont 17 SU0356
Urdimarsh 24 SO5249
Ure 63 HU2180
Urgha 63 NG1799
Urishay Common 23 SO3137
Urlay Nook 42 NZ4014
Urmston 32 SJ7695
Urquhart 61 NJ2863
Urra 42 NZ5702
Urray 60 NH5053
Urswick 40 SD2674
Ushaw Moor 47 NZ2342
Usk 16 SO3701
Usselby 35 TF0993
Utley 37 SE0542
Uton 5 SX8298
Utterby 35 TF3093
Uttoxeter 33 SK0933
Uwch-mynydd (Gwyn.) 30 SH6419
Uwchmynydd (Gwyn.) 30 SH1425
Uxbridge 19 TQ0583
Uyeasound (Unst) 63 HP5901
Uzmaston 14 SM9714

Valley 30 SH2979
Valleyfield 51 NT0086
Valsgarth 63 HP6413
Valtos (Island of Skye) 58 NG5163
Valtos (Isle of Lewis) 63 NB0936
Vange 20 TQ7287
Vardre 15 SN6902
Varteg 16 SO2506
Vatten 58 NG2843
Vaul 48 NM0448
Vauld, The 24 SO5349
Vaynel Hall 30 SH5369
Vaynor 16 SO0410
Veensgarth 63 HU4244
Velindre (Dyfed) 14 SN1039
Velindre (Dyfed) 22 SN3538
Velindre (Powys) 23 SO1836
Veness (Eday) 63 HY5729
Venn Ottery 7 SY0791
Vennington 23 SJ3309
Ventnor 9 SZ5677
Vernham Dean 10 SU3356
Vernham Street 10 SU3457
Vernolds Common 24 SO4780
Verwig 14 SN1849
Verwood 8 SU0908
Veryan 2 SW9139
Vicarage 7 SY2088
Vickerstown 36 SD1868
Victoria 3 SW9961
Vidlin 63 HU4766
Viewpark 50 NS7161
Villavin 4 SS5816
Vine's Cross 12 TQ5917
Vinehall Street 12 TQ7520
Virginia Water 11 SU9967
Virginstow 4 SX3792
Vobster 8 ST7048
Voe (Shetld.) 63 HU4062
Vowchurch 24 SO3636
Voxter 63 HU3769
Voy 63 HY2515

Wackerfield 42 NZ1522
Wacton 29 TM1891
Wadborough 25 SO8947
Waddesdon 18 SP7416
Waddingham 34 SK9896
Waddington (Lancs.) 36 SD7243
Waddington (Lincs.) 34 SK9764
Wadebridge 3 SW9972
Wadeford 7 ST3110
Wadenhoe 27 TL0083
Wadesmill 20 TL3517
Wadhurst 12 TQ6431
Wadshelf 33 SK3171
Wadworth 34 SK5697
Waen Fach 31 SJ2017
Wainfleet All Saints 35 TF4959
Wainfleet Bank 35 TF4759
Wainhouse Corner 4 SX1895

Wainscott

Weston under Penyard

Wainscott 12 TQ7471
Wainstalls 37 SE0428
Waitby 41 NY7507
Wakefield 38 SE3320
Wakerley 27 SP9599
Wakes Colne 21 TL8928
Walberswick 29 TM4974
Walberton 11 SU9705
Walcot (Lincs.) 35 TF0535
Walcot (Lincs.) 35 TF1256
Walcot (Salop) 24 SJ5912
Walcot (Salop) 23 SO3485
Walcot (Warw.) 25 SP1258
Walcote 26 SP5683
Walcott (Norf.) 29 TG3632
Walden 41 SE0082
Walden Head 41 SD9880
Walden Stubbs 38 SE5516
Walderslade 12 TQ7563
Walderton 10 SU7910
Walditch 7 SY4892
Waldridge 47 NZ2549
Waldringfield 21 TM2744
Waldron 12 TQ5419
Wales 34 SK4782
Walesby (Lincs.) 35 TF1392
Walesby (Notts.) 34 SK6870
Walford (Here. and Worc.) 24 SO3872
Walford (Here. and Worc.) 17 SO5820
Walford (Salop) 32 SJ4320
Walgherton 32 SJ6948
Walgrave 26 SP8071
Walk Mill 37 SD8629
Walkden 36 SD7303
Walker 47 NZ2864
Walker Fold 36 SD6742
Walker's Green 24 SO5248
Walkerburn 51 NT3637
Walkeringham 34 SK7692
Walkerith 34 SK7892
Walkern 19 TL2926
Walkerton 56 NO2301
Walkhampton 4 SX5369
Walkington 39 SE9936
Wall (Northum.) 47 NY9168
Wall (Staffs.) 25 SK0906
Wall Bank 24 SO5092
Wallacetown 49 NS3422
Wallasey 31 SJ2992
Wallend 13 TQ8775
Walling Fen 39 SE8829
Wallingford 18 SU6089
Wallington (Gtr London) 11 TQ2863
Wallington (Hants.) 9 SU5806
Wallington (Herts.) 19 TL2933
Wallis 14 SN0125
Walliswood 11 TQ1138
Walls 63 HU2449
Wallsend 47 NZ2766
Wallyford 51 NT3671
Walmer 13 TR3750
Walmer Bridge 36 SD4724
Walmersley 37 SD8013
Walmley 25 SP1393
Walpole 29 TM3674
Walpole Highway 28 TF5113
Walpole St. Andrew 28 TF5017
Walpole St. Peter 28 TF5016
Walsall 25 SP0198
Walsall Wood 25 SK0403
Walsden 37 SD9322
Walsgrave on Sowe 26 SP3781
Walsham le Willows 29 TM0071
Walsoken 28 TF4710
Walston 51 NT0545
Walterstone 16 SO3425
Waltham (Humbs.) 39 TA2503
Waltham (Kent) 13 TR1148
Waltham Abbey 20 TL3800
Waltham Chase 9 SU5614
Waltham St. Lawrence 10 SU8276
Waltham on the Wolds 34 SK8025
Walthamstow 20 TQ3788
Walton (Bucks) 27 SP8936
Walton (Cumbr.) 46 NY5264
Walton (Derby.) 33 SK3569
Walton (Leic.) 26 SP5987
Walton (Powys) 23 SO2559
Walton (Salop) 32 SJ5818
Walton (Somer.) 7 ST4636
Walton (Suff.) 21 TM2935
Walton (W Yorks.) 38 SE3516
Walton (W Yorks.) 38 SE4447
Walton (Warw.) 26 SP2853
Walton Cardiff 25 SO9032
Walton East 14 SN0123
Walton West 14 SM8713
Walton on the Hill (Surrey) 11 TQ2255
Walton on the Naze 21 TM2521
Walton on the Wolds 34 SK5919
Walton-in-Gordano 16 ST4273
Walton-le-Dale 36 SD5627
Walton-on-Thames 11 TQ1066
Walton-on-Trent 33 SK2118
Walton-on-the-Hill (Staffs.) 33 SJ9520
Walworth 42 NZ2218
Walwyn's Castle 14 SM8711
Wambrook 7 ST2907
Wanborough 18 SU2082
Wandsworth 11 TQ2673
Wangford 29 TM4679
Wanlip 26 SK5910
Wanlockhead 50 NS8712
Wansford (Cambs.) 27 TL0799
Wansford (Humbs.) 39 TA0656
Wanstead 20 TQ4087
Wanstrow 8 ST7141
Wanswell 17 SO6801
Wantage 18 SU4087
Wapley 17 ST7179
Wappenbury 26 SP3769
Wappenham 26 SP6245
Warbister 63 HY3933
Warbleton 12 TQ6018
Warborough 18 SU6093
Warboys 27 TL3080
Warbstow 4 SX2090
Warburton 32 SJ7089
Warcop 41 NY7415
Ward Green 29 TM0564
Warden 13 TR0271
Wardington 26 SP4946
Wardlaw Hill 50 NS6822
Wardle (Ches.) 32 SJ6057
Wardle (Gtr Mches.) 37 SD9116
Wardley 27 SK8300
Wardlow 33 SK1874
Wardy Hill 28 TL4782
Ware 20 TL3614
Wareham 8 SY9287
Warehorne 13 TQ9832
Waren Mill 53 NU1534
Warenford 53 NU1328
Warenton 53 NU1030
Wareside 20 TL3915
Waresley 27 TL2454
Warfield 11 SU8872
Wargrave 10 SU7878
Warham All Saints 29 TF9441
Warham St. Mary 29 TF9441
Wark (Northum.) 53 NT8238
Wark (Northum.) 47 NY8576
Warkleigh 6 SS6422
Warkton 27 SP8980
Warkworth 47 NU2406
Warlaby 42 SE3591
Warland 37 SD9419
Warleggan 4 SX1569
Warley 25 SP0086
Warlingham 12 TQ3658
Warmfield 38 SE3720
Warmingham 32 SJ7161
Warmington (Northants.) 27 TL0791
Warmington (Warw.) 26 SP4147
Warminster 8 ST8644
Warmsworth 38 SE5400
Warmwell 8 SY7585
Warndon 25 SO8856
Warnford 9 SU6223
Warnham 11 TQ1633
Warninglid 11 TQ2526
Warren (Ches.) 33 SJ8870
Warren (Dyfed) 14 SR9397
Warren Row 18 SU8180
Warren Street 13 TQ9253
Warrington (Bucks.) 27 SP8954
Warrington (Ches.) 32 SJ6088
Warsash 9 SU4905
Warslow 33 SK0858
Warsop 34 SK5667
Warter 39 SE8750
Warthill 38 SE6755
Wartling 12 TQ6509
Wartnaby 34 SK7123
Warton (Lancs) 36 SD4028
Warton (Lancs.) 40 SD4972
Warton (Northum) 47 NU0002
Warton (Warw) 26 SK2803
Warwick (Cumbr.) 46 NY4656
Warwick (Warw.) 26 SP2865
Warwick Bridge 46 NY4756
Washaway 3 SX0369
Washbourne 5 SX7954
Washfield 5 SS9315
Washfold 41 NZ0502
Washford 7 ST0441
Washford Pyne 5 SS8111
Washingborough 34 TF0170
Washington (Tyne and Wear) 47 NZ3356
Washington (W Susx) 11 TQ1212
Wasing 10 SU5764
Waskerley 47 NZ0545
Wasperton 26 SP2659
Wass 42 SE5579
Watchet 7 ST0743
Watchfield (Oxon.) 18 SU2490
Watchfield (Somer.) 7 ST3446
Watchgate 40 SD5399
Water 37 SD8425
Water End (Herts.) 19 TL0310
Water End (Herts.) 19 TL2304
Water Meetings 51 NS9513
Water Newton 27 TL1097
Water Orton 25 SP1791
Water Stratford 18 SP6534
Water Yeat 40 SD2889
Waterbeach 28 TL4965
Waterbeck 46 NY2477
Waterden 28 TF8835
Waterfall 33 SK0851
Waterfoot (Lancs.) 37 SD8321
Waterfoot (Strath.) 50 NS5654
Waterford 20 TL3114
Waterhead (Cumbr.) 40 NY3703
Waterhead (Strath.) 50 NS5411
Waterheads 51 NT2451
Waterhouses (Durham) 47 NZ1841
Waterhouses (Staffs.) 33 SK0850
Wateringbury 12 TQ6853
Wateringhouse 63 ND3090
Waterloo (Dorset) 8 SZ0194
Waterloo (Mers.) 36 SJ3297
Waterloo (Norf.) 29 TG2219
Waterloo (Strath.) 50 NS8153
Waterloo (Tays.) 56 NO0636
Waterlooville 9 SU6809
Watermillock 40 NY4322
Waterperry 18 SP6206
Waterrow 7 ST0525
Waters Upton 32 SJ6319
Watersfield 11 TQ0115
Waterside (Strath.) 50 NS4308
Waterside (Strath.) 50 NS4843
Waterside (Strath.) 50 NS5160
Waterside (Strath.) 50 NS6773
Waterstock 18 SP6305
Waterston 14 SM9306
Watford (Herts.) 19 TQ1196
Watford (Northants.) 26 SP6069
Wath (N Yorks.) 42 SE3277
Wath (N. Yorks.) 37 SE1467
Wath Upon Dearne 38 SE4300
Watlington (Norf.) 28 TF6211
Watlington (Oxon.) 18 SU6994
Watnall Chaworth 34 SK4946
Watten 67 ND2454
Wattisfield 29 TM0174
Wattisham 21 TM0151
Watton (Humbs.) 39 TA0150
Watton (Norf.) 28 TF9100
Watton-at-Stone 20 TL3019
Wattston 50 NS7770
Wattstown 15 ST0194
Waunarlwydd 15 SS6095
Waunfawr 30 SH5259
Wavendon 19 SP9137
Waverton (Ches.) 32 SJ4663
Waverton (Cumbr.) 46 NY2247
Wawne 39 TA0836
Waxham 29 TG4326
Waxholme 39 TA3229
Way Village 5 SS8810
Wayford 7 ST4006
Wealdstone 19 TQ1689
Weare 16 ST4152
Weare Giffard 6 SS4721
Weasenham All Saints 28 TF8421
Weasenham St. Peter 28 TF8522
Weaverham 32 SJ6173
Weaverthorpe 39 SE9670
Webheath 25 SP0266
Weddington 26 SP3693
Wedhampton 17 SU0557
Wedmore 7 ST4347
Wednesbury 25 SP0095
Wednesfield 25 SJ9400
Weedon 18 SP8118
Weedon Bec 26 SP6259
Weedon Lois 26 SP6047
Weeford 25 SK1404
Week 5 SS7316
Week St. Mary 4 SX2397
Weekley 27 SP8880
Weeley 21 TM1422
Weeley Heath 21 TM1520
Weem 56 NN8449
Weeping Cross 33 SJ9421
Weeting 28 TL7788
Weeton (Lancs.) 36 SD3834
Weeton (W Yorks.) 38 SE2846
Weir 37 SD8724
Welbeck Colliery Village 34 SK5869
Welborne 29 TG0610
Welbourn 34 SK9654
Welburn 38 SE7168
Welbury 42 NZ3902
Welby 34 SK9738
Welches Dam 28 TL4786
Welcombe 4 SS2218
Weldon 27 SP9289
Welford (Berks.) 10 SU4073
Welford (Northants.) 26 SP6480
Welford-on-Avon 25 SP1552
Welham 26 SP7692
Welham Green 19 TL2305
Well (Hants.) 10 SU7646
Well (Lincs.) 35 TF4473
Well (N Yorks.) 42 SE2682
Well Hill (Kent) 12 TQ4963
Welland 24 SO7940
Wellesbourne 26 SP2755
Welling 12 TQ4575
Wellingborough 27 SP8968
Wellingham 28 TF8722
Wellingore 34 SK9856
Wellington (Here. and Worc.) 24 SO4948
Wellington (Salop) 24 SJ6411
Wellington (Somer.) 7 ST1320
Wellington Heath 24 SO7140
Wellow (Avon) 17 ST7358
Wellow (I. of W.) 9 SZ3887
Wellow (Notts.) 34 SK6666
Wells 7 ST5445
Wells of Ythan 62 NJ6338
Wells-Next-The-Sea 28 TF9143
Wellsborough 26 SK3602
Wellwood 51 NT0888
Welney 28 TL5294
Welsh Bicknor 17 SO5917
Welsh End 32 SJ5035
Welsh Frankton 32 SJ3633
Welsh Hook 14 SM9327
Welsh Newton 16 SO4918
Welsh St. Donats 16 ST0276
Welshampton 32 SJ4334
Welshpool (Trallwng) 23 SJ2207
Welton (Cumbr.) 46 NY3544
Welton (Humbs.) 39 SE9527
Welton (Lincs.) 34 TF0079
Welton (Northants.) 26 SP5865
Welton le Marsh 35 TF4768
Welton le Wold 35 TF2787
Welwick 39 TA3421
Welwyn 19 TL2316
Welwyn Garden City 19 TL2412
Wem 32 SJ5129
Wembdon 7 ST2837
Wembley 19 TQ1985
Wembury 4 SX5148
Wembworthy 5 SS6609
Wemyss Bay 49 NS1869
Wenallt 31 SH9842
Wendens Ambo 20 TL5136
Wendlebury 18 SP5519
Wendling 29 TF9213
Wendover 19 SP8708
Wendron 2 SW6731
Wendy 20 TL3247
Wenhaston 29 TM4275
Wennington (Cambs.) 27 TL2379
Wennington (Essex) 20 TQ5381
Wennington (Lancs.) 36 SD6169
Wensley (Derby) 33 SK2661
Wensley (N Yorks) 41 SE0989
Wentbridge 38 SE4817
Wentnor 24 SO3892
Wentworth (Cambs.) 28 TL4878
Wentworth (S Yorks.) 38 SK3898
Wenvoe 16 ST1272
Weobley 24 SO4051
Weobley Marsh 24 SO4151
Wereham 28 TF6801
Wergs 25 SJ8601
Wernrheolydd 16 SO3913
Werrington (Cambs.) 27 TF1703
Werrington (Devon.) 4 SX3287
Werrington (Staffs.) 33 SJ9647
Wervin 32 SJ4171
Wesham 36 SD4132
Wessington 33 SK3757
West Acre 28 TF7715
West Allerdean 53 NT9646
West Alvington 5 SX7243
West Anstey 6 SS8527
West Ashby 35 TF2672
West Ashling 10 SU8007
West Ashton 17 ST8755
West Auckland 42 NZ1826
West Bagborough 7 ST1633
West Barns 52 NT6578
West Barsham 28 TF9033
West Bay 7 SY4690
West Beckham 29 TG1339
West Bergholt 21 TL9527
West Bexington 7 SY5386
West Bilney 28 TF7115
West Blatchington 11 TQ2706
West Bradenham 29 TF9209
West Bradford 36 SD7444
West Bradley 7 ST5536
West Bretton 38 SE2813
West Bridgford 34 SK5837
West Bromwich 25 SP0091
West Buckland (Devon) 6 SS6510
West Buckland (Somer.) 7 ST1720
West Burrafirth 63 HU2557
West Burton (N Yorks) 41 SE0186
West Burton (W Susx) 11 TQ0014
West Caister 29 TG5011
West Calder 51 NT0163
West Camel 7 ST5724
West Challow 18 SU3688
West Charleton 5 SX7542
West Chelborough 7 ST5405
West Chevington 47 NZ2279
West Chiltington 11 TQ0918
West Clandon 11 TQ0452
West Cliffe 13 TR3445
West Coker 7 ST5113
West Compton (Dorset) 7 SY5694
West Compton (Somer.) 8 ST5942
West Cross 15 SS6189
West Curry 4 SX2893
West Curthwaite 46 NY3248
West Dean (W Susx) 10 SU8512
West Dean (Wilts.) 9 SU2526
West Deeping 27 TF1009
West Derby 32 SJ3993
West Dereham 28 TF6500
West Ditchburn 53 NU1320
West Down (Devon) 6 SS5142
West Down (Wilts) 8 SU0548
West Drayton (Gtr London) 11 TQ0679
West Drayton (Notts.) 34 SK7074
West End (Avon) 16 ST4469
West End (Beds.) 27 SP9853
West End (Hants) 9 SU4614
West End (Herts.) 20 TL3306
West End (N Yorks.) 37 SE1457
West End (Norf.) 29 TG4911
West End (Oxon.) 18 SP4204
West End (Surrey) 11 SU9461
West End Green 10 SU6661
West Farleigh 12 TQ7152
West Felton 32 SJ3425
West Firle 12 TQ4707
West Geirnish 63 NF7741
West Ginge 18 SU4386
West Grafton 10 SU2460
West Green 10 SU7456
West Grimstead 8 SU2026
West Grinstead 11 TQ1721
West Haddlesey 38 SE5526
West Haddon 26 SP6371
West Hagbourne 18 SU5187
West Hallam 33 SK4341
West Halton 39 SE9020
West Ham (Gtr London) 20 TQ4081
West Handley 33 SK3977
West Hanney 18 SU4092
West Hanningfield 20 TQ7399
West Hardwick 38 SE4118
West Harnham 8 SU1229
West Harptree 16 ST5556
West Hatch 7 ST2820
West Heath 10 SU8556
West Helmsdale 67 ND0114
West Hendred 18 SU4488
West Heslerton 43 SE9175
West Hill 7 SY0694
West Hoathly 12 TQ3632
West Holme 8 SY8885
West Horndon 20 TQ6288
West Horrington 7 ST5747
West Horsley 11 TQ0753
West Hougham 13 TR2640
West Humble 11 TQ1652
West Hyde 19 TQ0391
West Ilsley 18 SU4682
West Itchenor 10 SU7900
West Kennet 17 SU1167
West Kilbride 49 NS2048
West Kingsdown 12 TQ5762
West Kington 17 ST8077
West Kirby 31 SJ2168
West Knighton 8 SY7387
West Knoyle 8 ST8532
West Langdon 13 TR3247
West Langwell 66 NC6909
West Lavington (W Susx.) 11 SU8920
West Lavington (Wilts.) 17 SU0052
West Layton 42 NZ1409
West Leake 34 SK5226
West Lexham 28 TF8417
West Lilling 38 SE6465
West Linton (Borders) 51 NT1551
West Littleton 17 ST7575
West Looe 4 SX2553
West Lulworth 8 SY8280
West Lutton 39 SE9269
West Lynn 28 TF6120
West Mains 51 NS9550
West Malling 12 TQ6857
West Malvern 24 SO7646
West Marden 10 SU7613
West Markham 34 SK7272
West Marton 37 SD8850
West Meon 9 SU6424
West Mersea 21 TM0112
West Milton 7 SY5096
West Monkton 7 ST2528
West Moors 8 SU0802
West Muir (Tays.) 57 NO5661
West Newton (Norf.) 28 TF6972
West Norwood 12 TQ3171
West Ogwell 5 SX8170
West Overton 17 SU1367
West Parley 8 SZ0997
West Peaston 52 NT4265
West Peckham 12 TQ6452
West Pennard 7 ST5438
West Pentire 2 SW7760
West Putford 4 SS3515
West Quantoxhead 7 ST1141
West Rainton 47 NZ3246
West Rasen 35 TF0589
West Raynham 28 TF8725
West Row 28 TL6775
West Rudham 28 TF8127
West Runton 29 TG1842
West Saltoun 52 NT4667
West Sandwick 63 HU4488
West Scrafton 41 SE0783
West Stafford 8 SY7289
West Stoke 10 SU8208
West Stonesdale 41 NY8802
West Stoughton 7 ST4149
West Stour 8 ST7822
West Stourmouth 13 TR2562
West Stow 28 TL8170
West Stowell 17 SU1362
West Street 13 TQ9054
West Tanfield 42 SE2778
West Tarbert 49 NR8467
West Thorney 10 SU7602
West Thurrock 12 TQ5877
West Tilbury 12 TQ6677
West Tisted 9 SU6429
West Tofts 56 NO1134
West Torrington 35 TF1381
West Town 16 ST4767
West Tytherley 9 SU2730
West Tytherton 17 ST9474
West Walton 28 TF4713
West Walton Highway 28 TF4912
West Wellow 9 SU2818
West Wemyss 51 NT3294
West Wick (Avon) 16 ST3661
West Wickham (Cambs.) 20 TL6149
West Wickham (Gtr. London) 12 TQ3866
West Winch 28 TF6316
West Wittering 10 SZ7999
West Witton 41 SE0688
West Woodburn 47 NY8986
West Woodhay 10 SU3962
West Woodlands 8 ST7743
West Worldham 9 SU7436
West Wratting 20 TL6052
West Wycombe 19 SU8394
West Yell 63 HU4582
Westbere 13 TR1961
Westbourne (Dorset) 8 SZ0690
Westbourne (W Susx.) 10 SU7507
Westbury 36 SD3731
Westbury (Salop) 24 SJ3509
Westbury (Wilts.) 8 ST8751
Westbury Leigh 8 ST8649
Westbury-on-Severn 17 SO7114
Westbury-sub-Mendip 7 ST5049
Westcliff-on-Sea 21 TQ8685
Westcombe 8 ST6739
Westcote 18 SP2120
Westcott (Bucks.) 18 SP7117
Westcott (Devon) 7 ST0104
Westcott (Surrey) 11 TQ1348
Westcott Barton 18 SP4224
Westdean (E Susx) 12 TV5299
Wester Clynekirton 67 NC8906
Wester Culbeuchly Crofts 62 NJ6562
Wester Denoon 57 NO3543
Wester Fintray 62 NJ8116
Wester Gruinards 65 NH5292
Wester Lonvine 65 NH7172
Wester Skeld 63 HU2943
Wester Teaninich 65 NH6267
Wester Wick 63 HU2842
Westerdale (Highld.) 67 ND1251
Westerdale (N Yorks.) 42 NZ6605
Westerdale Moor 42 NZ6502
Westerfield (Shetld.) 63 HU3551
Westerfield (Suff.) 21 TM1747
Westergate 11 SU9305
Westerham 12 TQ4454
Westerleigh 17 ST6979
Westerton 57 NO6654
Westfield (Caithness) 67 ND0564
Westfield (E Susx.) 12 TQ8115
Westfield (Lothian) 51 NS9372
Westfield (Norf.) 29 TF9909
Westgate (Durham) 41 NY9038
Westgate (Humbs.) 38 SE7707
Westgate (Norf.) 29 TF9740
Westgate on Sea 13 TR3270
Westhall (Cumbr.) 46 NY5667
Westhall (Suff.) 29 TM4280
Westham (E Susx.) 12 TQ6404
Westham (Somer.) 7 ST4046
Westhampnett 11 SU8706
Westhay 7 ST4342
Westhead 36 SD4407
Westhide 24 SO5844
Westhope (Here. and Worc.) 25 SO4651
Westhope (Salop) 24 SO4786
Westhorpe (Lincs.) 35 TF2131
Westhorpe (Suff.) 29 TM0469
Westhoughton 36 SD6505
Westhouse 41 SD6673
Westhouses 33 SK4257
Westing 63 HP5705
Westlake 5 SX6253
Westleigh (Devon) 6 SS4628
Westleigh (Devon) 7 ST0517
Westleton 29 TM4469
Westley (Salop) 24 SJ3507
Westley (Suff.) 28 TL8264
Westley Waterless 20 TL6256
Westlington 18 SP7610
Westlinton (Cumbr.) 46 NY3964
Westmarsh 13 TR2761
Westmeston 12 TQ3313
Westmill 20 TL3627
Westmuir (Tays.) 57 NO3652
Westness (Rousay) 63 HY3829
Westnewton (Cumbr.) 45 NY1344
Weston (Avon) 17 ST7266
Weston (Berks.) 10 SU3973
Weston (Ches.) 32 SJ5080
Weston (Ches.) 32 SJ7252
Weston (Dorset) 8 SY6870
Weston (Hants.) 10 SU7221
Weston (Herts.) 19 TL2630
Weston (Lincs.) 35 TF2925
Weston (Northants.) 26 SP5847
Weston (Notts.) 34 SK7767
Weston (Salop) 32 SJ5628
Weston (Salop) 24 SO5993
Weston (Staffs.) 33 SJ9727
Weston (W Yorks.) 37 SE1747
Weston Beggard 24 SO5841
Weston Colville 20 TL6153
Weston Favel 26 SP7862
Weston Green 20 TL6252
Weston Heath 24 SJ7813
Weston Hills 35 TF2821
Weston Jones 32 SJ7524
Weston Longville 29 TG1116
Weston Lullingfields 32 SJ4224
Weston Patrick 10 SU6946
Weston Rhyn 31 SJ2835
Weston Subedge 25 SP1240
Weston Turville 19 SP8511
Weston Underwood (Bucks.) 27 SP8650
Weston Underwood (Derby) 33 SK2942
Weston by Welland 26 SP7791
Weston under Penyard 17 SO6323

Weston under Wetherley Wool

Weston under Wetherley 26 SP3569
Weston-in-Gordano 16 ST4474
Weston-on-Trent 33 SK4027
Weston-on-the-Green 18 SP5318
Weston-super-Mare 16 ST3261
Weston-under-Lizard 24 SJ8010
Westoning 19 TL0332
Westonzoyland 7 ST3534
Westow 38 SE7565
Westport 7 ST3819
Westrigg 50 NS9067
Westruther 52 NT6349
Westry 27 TL3998
Westward 46 NY2744
Westward Ho! 6 SS4329
Westwell (Kent) 13 TQ9947
Westwell (Oxon) 18 SP2210
Westwell Leacon 13 TQ9647
Westwick (Cambs.) 27 TL4265
Westwick (Norf.) 29 TG2727
Westwood (Devon.) 7 SY0199
Westwood (Wilts.) 17 ST8158
Westwoodside 38 SK7499
Wetheral 46 NY4654
Wetherby 38 SE4048
Wetherden 29 TM0062
Wetheringsett 29 TM1266
Wethersfield 20 TL7131
Wethersta 63 HU3565
Wetherup Street 29 TM1464
Wetley Rocks 33 SJ9649
Wettenhall 32 SJ6261
Wetton 33 SK1055
Wetwang 39 SE9359
Wetwood 32 SJ7733
Wexcombe 10 SU2758
Weybourne 29 TG1143
Weybread 29 TM2480
Weybridge 11 TQ0764
Weydale 67 ND1464
Weyhill 10 SU3146
Weymouth 8 SY6778
Whaddon (Bucks.) 18 SP8034
Whaddon (Cambs.) 20 TL3546
Whaddon (Glos.) 17 SO8313
Whaddon (Wilts.) 8 SU1926
Whale 40 NY5221
Whaley 34 SK5171
Whaley Bridge 33 SK0181
Whaligoe 67 ND3240
Whalley 36 SD7335
Whalton 47 NZ1281
Wham 37 SD7762
Whaplode 35 TF3224
Whaplode Drove 27 TF3113
Whaplode Fen 35 TF3220
Wharfe 37 SD7869
Wharles 36 SD4435
Wharncliffe Side 33 SK2994
Wharram le Street 39 SE8666
Wharton (Ches.) 32 SJ6666
Wharton (Here. and Worc.) 24 SO5055
Whaston 42 NZ1406
Whatcombe 8 ST8301
Whatcote 26 SP2944
Whatfield 21 TM0246
Whatley 8 ST7347
Whatlington 12 TQ7618
Whatstandwell 33 SK3354
Whatton 24 SK7439
Whauphill 44 NX4049
Whaw 41 NY9804
Wheatacre 29 TM4594
Wheathampstead 19 TL1713
Wheatley (Hants.) 10 SU7840
Wheatley (Notts) 34 SK7685
Wheatley (Oxon) 18 SP5905
Wheatley Hill 42 NZ3839
Wheatley Lane 37 SD8337
Wheaton Aston 25 SJ8412
Wheatsheaf 32 SJ3253
Wheddon Cross 6 SS9238
Wheedlemont 61 NJ4726
Wheelerstreet 11 SU9440
Wheelock 32 SJ7458
Wheelton 36 SD6021
Wheldrake 28 SE6744
Whelford 17 SU1698
Whelpley Hill 10 TL0004
Whenby 38 SE6369
Whepstead 20 TL8358
Wherstead 21 TM1540
Wherwell 10 SU3840
Wheston 33 SK1376
Whetsted 12 TQ6546
Whetstone 26 SP5597
Whicham 40 SD1382
Whichford 18 SP3134
Whickham 47 NZ2061
Whiddon Down 5 SX6992
Whigstreet 57 NO4844
Whilton 26 SP6364
Whim 51 NT2153
Whimple 7 SY0497
Whimpwell Green 29 TG3829
Whinburgh 29 TG0009
Whinnyfold 62 NK0733
Whippingham 9 SZ5193
Whipsnade 19 TL0117
Whipton 5 SX9493
Whissendine 34 SK8214
Whissonsett 28 TF9123
Whistley Green 10 SU7974
Whiston (Mers.) 32 SJ4791
Whiston (Northants.) 27 SP8560
Whiston (S Yorks.) 34 SK4489
Whiston (Staffs.) 25 SJ8914
Whiston (Staffs.) 33 SK0347
Whitbeck 40 SD1184
Whitbourne 24 SO7156
Whitburn (Lothian) 51 NS9464
Whitburn (Tyne and Wear) 47 NZ4061
Whitby (Ches.) 32 SJ4075
Whitby (N Yorks.) 43 NZ8911
Whitchurch (Avon) 17 ST6167
Whitchurch (Bucks.) 18 SP8020
Whitchurch (Devon) 4 SX4972
Whitchurch (Dyfed) 14 SM8025
Whitchurch (Hants.) 10 SU4648
Whitchurch (Here. and Worc.) 16 SO5417
Whitchurch (Oxon) 10 SU6377
Whitchurch (S Glam) 16 ST1680
Whitchurch (Salop) 32 SJ5441
Whitchurch Canonicorum 7 SY3995
Whitcott Keysett 23 SO2782
White Chapel 36 SD5542
White Coppice 36 SD6119
White Court 20 TL7421
White Lackington 8 SY7198
White Ladies Aston 25 SO9252
White Notley 20 TL7818
White Roding 20 TL5613
White Waltham 10 SU8577
Whitebrook 16 SO5306
Whitecairns 62 NJ9218
Whitechurch 14 SN1436
Whitecraig (Lothian) 51 NT3570
Whitecroft 17 SO6106
Whitecross 51 NS9676
Whiteface 65 NH7189
Whitefield (Gtr Mches.) 37 SD8005
Whitefield (Tays) 56 NO1734
Whiteford 62 NJ7126
Whitehall 63 HY6528
Whitehaven 40 NX9718
Whitehill (Hants.) 10 SU7934
Whitehill (Strath.) 49 NS2656
Whitehills 62 NJ6565
Whitehouse (Grampn.) 62 NJ6214
Whitehouse (Strath) 49 NR8161
Whitekirk 52 NT5981
Whiteley Village 11 TQ0962
Whitemans Green 12 TQ3025
Whitemire 60 NH9854
Whitemoor 2 SW9757
Whiteparish 9 SU2423
Whiterashes 62 NJ8523
Whiterow 67 ND3548
Whiteshill 17 SO8307
Whiteside (Lothian) 51 NS9667
Whitesmith 12 TQ5214
Whitestaunton 7 ST2810
Whitestone 6 SX8694
Whiteway 17 SO9110
Whitewell 36 SD6546
Whitewreath 61 NJ2356
Whitfield (Avon) 17 ST6791
Whitfield (Kent) 13 TR3146
Whitfield (Northants) 26 SP6039
Whitfield (Northum) 46 NY7758
Whitford 31 SJ1477
Whitgift 39 SE8022
Whitgreave 33 SJ8928
Whithorn 44 NX4440
Whiting Bay (Island of Arran) 49 NS0425
Whitington 28 TL7199
Whitland 14 SN1916
Whitletts 50 NS3622
Whitley (Berks) 10 SU7170
Whitley (Ches.) 32 SJ6178
Whitley (N Yorks) 38 SE5521
Whitley Bay 47 NZ3577
Whitley Chapel 47 NY9257
Whitley Row 12 TQ5052
Whitlock's End 25 SP1076
Whitminster 17 SO7708
Whitmore 32 SJ8041
Whitnage 7 ST0215
Whitnash 26 SP3263
Whitney 23 SO2647
Whitrigg (Cumbr.) 40 NY2038
Whitrigg (Cumbr.) 46 NY2257
Whitsbury 8 SU1218
Whitsome 53 NT8650
Whitson 16 ST3783
Whitstable 13 TR1166
Whitstone 4 SX2698
Whittingham 53 NU0611
Whittingslow 24 SO4288
Whittington (Derby) 33 SK3975
Whittington (Glos.) 17 SP0120
Whittington (Here. and Worc.) 25 SO8582
Whittington (Here. and Worc.) 25 SO8752
Whittington (Lancs.) 41 SD5976
Whittington (Salop) 32 SJ3230
Whittington (Staffs.) 25 SK1508
Whittle-le-Woods 36 SD5822
Whittlebury 26 SP6943
Whittlesey 27 TL2797
Whittlesford 20 TL4748
Whitton (Clev.) 42 NZ3822
Whitton (Humbs.) 39 SE9034
Whitton (Northum.) 47 NU0501
Whitton (Powys) 23 SO2667
Whitton (Salop) 24 SO5772
Whitton (Suff.) 21 TM1447
Whittonditch 10 SU2872
Whittonstall 47 NZ0757
Whitwell (Derby.) 34 SK5276
Whitwell (Herts.) 19 TL1821
Whitwell (I of W.) 9 SZ5277
Whitwell (Leic.) 27 SK9208
Whitwell (N Yorks.) 42 SE2899
Whitwell-on-the-Hill 38 SE7265
Whitwick 34 SK4316
Whitwood 38 SE4124
Whitworth 37 SD8818
Whixall 32 SJ5034
Whixley 38 SE4457
Whorlton (Durham) 41 NZ1014
Whorlton (N Yorks.) 42 NZ4802
Whygate 46 NY7675
Whyle 24 SO5560
Whyteleafe 12 TQ3358
Wibdon 17 ST5797
Wibtoft 26 SP4787
Wichenford 24 SO7860
Wichling 13 TQ9256
Wick (Avon) 17 ST6972
Wick (Dorset) 8 SZ1591
Wick (Here. and Worc.) 25 SO9645
Wick (Highld.) 67 ND3650
Wick (S Glam.) 15 SS9272
Wick (Shetld.) 63 HU4439
Wick (W Susx) 11 TQ0203
Wick (Wilts.) 8 SU1621
Wick Rissington 17 SP1821
Wick St. Lawrence 16 ST3665
Wicken (Cambs.) 28 TL5770
Wicken (Northants.) 26 SP7439
Wicken Bonhunt 20 TL5033
Wickenby 35 TF0882
Wickersley 34 SK4891
Wickford 20 TQ7593
Wickham (Berks.) 10 SU3971
Wickham (Hants.) 9 SU5711
Wickham Bishops 20 TL8412
Wickham Market 21 TM3056
Wickham Skeith 29 TM0969
Wickham St. Paul 20 TL8336
Wickham Street (Suff.) 20 TL7554
Wickham Street (Suff.) 29 TM0869
Wickhambreaux 13 TR2158
Wickhambrook 20 TL7454
Wickhamford 25 SP0642
Wickhampton 29 TG4205
Wickmere 29 TG1633
Wickwar 17 ST7288
Widdington 20 TL5331
Widdrington 47 NZ2595
Wide Open 47 NZ2472
Widecombe in the Moor 5 SX7176
Widewall 63 NB4391
Widford (Essex) 20 TL6905
Widford (Herts.) 20 TL4115
Widmerpool 34 SK6327
Widnes 32 SJ5185
Wigan 36 SD5805
Wiggaton 7 SY1093
Wiggenhall St. Germans 28 TF5914
Wiggenhall St. Mary Magdalen 28 TF5911
Wiggenhall St. Mary the Virgin 28 TF5814
Wigginton (Herts.) 19 SP9410
Wigginton (N Yorks.) 38 SE5958
Wigginton (Oxon.) 18 SP3833
Wigginton (Staffs.) 26 SK2106
Wigglesworth 37 SD8056
Wiggonby 46 NY2953
Wiggonholt 11 TQ0616
Wighill 38 SE4746
Wighton 29 TF9339
Wigmore (Here. and Worc.) 24 SO4169
Wigmore (Kent) 12 TQ8063
Wigsley 34 SK8570
Wigsthorpe 27 TL0482
Wigston 26 SP6099
Wigtoft 35 TF2636
Wigton 46 NY2548
Wigtown 44 NX4355
Wigtwizzle 33 SK2495
Wilbarston 26 SP8188
Wilberfoss 38 SE7350
Wilburton 28 TL4875
Wilby (Norf.) 29 TM0389
Wilby (Northants.) 27 SP8666
Wilby (Suff.) 29 TM2472
Wilcot 17 SU1461
Wildboarclough 33 SJ9868
Wilden 27 TL0955
Wildhern 10 SU3550
Wildsworth 39 SK8097
Wilford 34 SK5637
Wilkesley 32 SJ6241
Wilkhaven 65 NH9486
Wilkieston 51 NT1168
Willand 5 ST0310
Willaston (Ches.) 32 SJ3277
Willaston (Ches.) 32 SJ6752
Willen 27 SP8741
Willenhall (W Mids.) 25 SO9698
Willenhall (W Mids.) 26 SP3676
Willerby (Humbs.) 39 TA0230
Willerby (N Yorks.) 43 TA0079
Willersey 25 SP1039
Willersley 23 SO3147
Willesborough 13 TR0441
Willesden 19 TQ2284
Willett 7 ST1033
Willey (Salop) 24 SO6799
Willey (Warw.) 26 SP4984
Williamscot 26 SP4745
Willian 19 TL2230
Willimontswick 46 NY7763
Willingale 20 TL5907
Willingdon 12 TQ5902
Willingham (Cambs) 27 TL4070
Willingham by Stow 34 SK8784
Willington (Beds.) 27 TL1150
Willington (Derby.) 33 SK2928
Willington (Durham) 42 NZ1935
Willington (Tyne and Wear) 47 NZ3167
Willington (Warw.) 18 SP2638
Willington Corner 32 SJ5367
Willitoft 38 SE7434
Williton 7 ST0740
Willoughby (Lincs.) 35 TF4772
Willoughby (Warw.) 26 SP5167
Willoughby Waterleys 26 SP5792
Willoughby-on-the-Wolds 34 SK6325
Willoughton 34 SK9293
Wilmcote 25 SP1658
Wilmington (Devon.) 7 SY2199
Wilmington (E Susx) 12 TQ5404
Wilmington (Kent) 12 TQ5372
Wilmslow 33 SJ8480
Wilnecote 26 SK2201
Wilpshire 36 SD6832
Wilsden 37 SE0935
Wilsford (Lincs.) 34 TF0043
Wilsford (Wilts.) 17 SU1057
Wilsford (Wilts.) 8 SU1339
Wilshamstead 27 TL0643
Wilsill 37 SE1864
Wilson 33 SK4024
Wilsthorpe 27 TF0913
Wilstone 19 SP9014
Wilton (Borders) 52 NT4914
Wilton (Cleve.) 42 NZ5819
Wilton (N Yorks.) 43 SE8582
Wilton (Wilts.) 8 SU0931
Wilton (Wilts.) 10 SU2661
Wimbish 20 TL5936
Wimbish Green 20 TL6035
Wimbledon 11 TQ2470
Wimbledon Park 11 TQ2472
Wimblington 27 TL4192
Wimborne Minster 8 SZ0199
Wimborne St. Giles 8 SU0212
Wimbotsham 28 TF6205
Wimpstone 26 SP2148
Wincanton 8 ST7128
Wincham 32 SJ6675
Winchburgh 51 NT0874
Winchcombe 17 SP0228
Winchelsea 13 TQ9017
Winchelsea Beach 13 TQ9115
Winchester 9 SU4829
Winchfield 10 SU7654
Winchmore Hill (Bucks.) 19 SU9394
Winchmore Hill (Gtr London) 20 TQ3195
Wincle 33 SJ9565
Windermere (Cumbr.) 40 SD4198
Winderton 26 SP3240
Windlesham 11 SU9363
Windley 33 SK3045
Windmill Hill (E Susx) 12 TQ6412
Windmill Hill (Somer.) 7 ST3116
Windrush 17 SP1913
Windsor 11 SU9676
Windygates 57 NO3400
Wineham 11 TQ2320
Winestead 39 TA2924
Winfarthing 29 TM1085
Winford 16 ST5364
Winforton 23 SO2947
Winfrith Newburgh 8 SY8084
Wing (Bucks.) 19 SP8822
Wing (Leic.) 27 SK8903
Wingate (Durham) 42 NZ4036
Wingates (Gtr Mches.) 36 SD6507
Wingates (Northum.) 47 NZ0995
Wingerworth 33 SK3867
Wingfield (Beds.) 19 SP9926
Wingfield (Suff.) 29 TM2276
Wingfield (Wilts.) 17 ST8256
Wingham 13 TR2457
Wingrave 19 SP8719
Winkburn 34 SK7158
Winkfield 11 SU9072
Winkfield Row 11 SU9071
Winkhill 33 SK0651
Winkleigh 5 SS6308
Winksley 37 SE2471
Winless 67 ND3054
Winmarleigh 36 SD4748
Winnersh 10 SU7870
Winscales 40 NY0226
Winscombe 16 ST4157
Winsford (Ches.) 32 SJ6566
Winsford (Somer.) 6 SS9034
Winsham 7 ST3706
Winshill 33 SK2623
Winskill 41 NY5835
Winslade 10 SU6547
Winsley 17 ST7960
Winslow 18 SP7627
Winson 17 SP0908
Winster (Cumbr.) 40 SD4193
Winster (Derby.) 33 SK2460
Winston (Durham) 42 NZ1416
Winston (Suff.) 29 TM1861
Winstone 17 SO9609
Winswell 4 SS4913
Winterborne (Avon) 17 ST6480
Winterborne Clenston 8 ST8302
Winterborne Herringston 8 SY6887
Winterborne Houghton 8 ST8104
Winterborne Kingston 8 SY8697
Winterborne Monkton (Dorset) 8 SY6787
Winterborne Stickland 8 ST8304
Winterborne Whitechurch 8 SY8399
Winterborne Zelston 8 SY8997
Winterbourne Abbas 8 SY6190
Winterbourne Bassett 17 SU1074
Winterbourne Dauntsey 8 SU1734
Winterbourne Earls 8 SU1633
Winterbourne Gunner 8 SU1735
Winterbourne Monkton (Wilts.) 17 SU0972
Winterbourne Steepleton 8 SY6289
Winterbourne Stoke 8 SU0740
Winterburn 37 SD9358
Winteringham 39 SE9222
Winterley 32 SJ7457
Wintersett 38 SE3815
Winterslow 9 SU2232
Winterton 39 SE9218
Winterton-on-Sea 29 TG4919
Winthorpe (Lincs.) 35 TF5665
Winthorpe (Notts.) 34 SK8156
Winton (Cumbr.) 41 NY7810
Winton (Dorset) 8 SZ0894
Wintringham 43 SE8873
Winwick (Cambs.) 27 TL1080
Winwick (Ches.) 32 SJ6092
Winwick (Northants.) 26 SP6273
Wirksworth 33 SK2854
Wirswall 32 SJ5444
Wisbech 27 TF4609
Wisbech St. Mary 27 TF4208
Wisborough Green 11 TQ0526
Wiseton 34 SK7189
Wishaw (Strath.) 50 NS7954
Wishaw (Warw.) 25 SP1794
Wispington 35 TF2071
Wissett 29 TM3679
Wistanstow 24 SO4385
Wistanswick 32 SJ6629
Wistaston 32 SJ6853
Wiston (Dyfed) 14 SN0218
Wiston (Strath.) 51 NS9531
Wiston (W Susx) 11 TQ1512
Wistow (Cambs.) 27 TL2781
Wistow (N Yorks.) 38 SE5835
Wiswell 36 SD7437
Witcham 28 TL4680
Witchampton 8 ST9806
Witchford 28 TL5078
Witham 20 TL8114
Witham Friary 8 ST7440
Witham on the Hill 35 TF0516
Witherenden Hill 12 TQ6426
Witheridge 5 SS8014
Witherley 26 SP3297
Withern 35 TF4382
Withernsea 39 TA3328
Withernwick 39 TA1940
Withersdale Street 29 TM2781
Withersfield 20 TL6547
Witherslack 40 SD4384
Withiel 3 SW9965
Withiel Florey 7 SS9832
Withington (Ches.) 32 SJ8170
Withington (Glos.) 17 SP0315
Withington (Gtr Mches.) 32 SJ8392
Withington (Here. and Worc.) 24 SO5643
Withington (Salop) 24 SJ5713
Withleigh 5 SS9012
Withnell 35 SD6322
Withybrook 26 SP4384
Withycombe 7 ST0141
Withyham 12 TQ4935
Withypool 6 SS8435
Witley 11 SU9439
Witnesham 21 TM1850
Witney 18 SP3509
Wittering 27 TF0502
Wittersham 13 TQ8927
Witton 29 TG3331
Witton Gilbert 47 NZ2345
Witton Park 42 NZ1730
Witton le Wear 42 NZ1431
Wiveliscombe 7 ST0827
Wivelsfield 12 TQ3420
Wivelsfield Green 12 TQ3519
Wivenhoe 21 TM0321
Wivenhoe Cross 21 TM0423
Wiveton 29 TG0343
Wix 21 TM1628
Wixford 25 SP0854
Wixoe 20 TL7142
Woburn 19 SP9433
Woburn Sands 19 SP9235
Wokefield Park 10 SU6765
Woking 11 TQ0058
Wokingham 10 SU8068
Wold Newton (Humbs.) 43 TA0473
Wold Newton (Humbs.) 35 TF2496
Woldingham 12 TQ3755
Wolf's Castle 14 SM9627
Wolferlow 24 SO6661
Wolferton 28 TF6528
Wolfhill 56 NO1533
Wolfsdale 14 SM9321
Woll 52 NI4622
Wollaston (Northants.) 27 SP9062
Wollaston (Salop) 23 SJ3212
Wollerton 32 SJ6229
Wolsingham 41 NZ0737
Wolston 26 SP4175
Wolvercote 18 SP4809
Wolverhampton 25 SO9198
Wolverley (Here. and Worc.) 25 SO8279
Wolverley (Salop) 32 SJ4631
Wolverton (Bucks.) 26 SP8141
Wolverton (Hants.) 10 SU5557
Wolverton (Warw.) 26 SP2062
Wolvey 26 SP4387
Wolviston 42 NZ4525
Wombleton 42 SE6683
Wombourne 25 SO8793
Wombwell 38 SE3902
Womenswold 13 TR2250
Womersley 38 SE5319
Wonastow 16 SO4811
Wonersh 11 TQ0145
Wonston 10 SU4739
Wooburn 19 SU9187
Wooburn Green 19 SU9188
Wood Dalling 29 TG0927
Wood End (Herts.) 20 TL3225
Wood End (Warw.) 25 SP1071
Wood End (Warw.) 26 SP2498
Wood Enderby 35 TF2764
Wood Green (Gtr London) 20 TQ3191
Wood Hayes 25 SJ9501
Wood Norton 29 TG0128
Wood Street 11 SU9551
Wood Walton 27 TL2180
Wood Wick 63 HY3923
Woodbastwick 29 TG3315
Woodbeck 34 SK7777
Woodborough (Notts.) 34 SK6347
Woodborough (Wilts.) 17 SU1059
Woodbridge 21 TM2749
Woodbury 7 SY0087
Woodbury Salterton 7 SY0189
Woodchester 17 SO8302
Woodchurch 13 TQ9434
Woodcote (Oxon.) 18 SU6481
Woodcote (Salop) 32 SJ7715
Woodcroft 16 ST5495
Woodditton 20 TL6559
Woodeaton 18 SP5311
Woodend (Cumbr.) 40 SD1696
Woodend (Northants.) 26 SP6149
Woodend (W Susx) 11 SU8108
Woodfalls 8 SU1920
Woodford (Corn.) 4 SS2113
Woodford (Gtr Mches.) 33 SJ8982
Woodford (Northants.) 27 SP9676
Woodford (Wilts.) 8 SU1136
Woodford Bridge 20 TQ4291
Woodford Green 20 TQ4192
Woodford Halse 26 SP5452
Woodgate (Here. and Worc.) 25 SO9666
Woodgate (Norf.) 29 TG0215
Woodgate (W Mids.) 25 SO9982
Woodgate (W Susx) 11 SU9304
Woodgreen (Hants.) 8 SU1717
Woodhale 41 SE0279
Woodhall 41 SD9790
Woodhall Spa 35 TF1963
Woodham 11 TQ0261
Woodham Ferrers 20 TQ7999
Woodham Mortimer 20 TL8205
Woodham Walter 20 TL8006
Woodhaven 57 NO4127
Woodhead (Grampn.) 62 NJ7938
Woodhead (Grampn.) 62 NJ9061
Woodhill 24 SO7384
Woodhorn 47 NZ2988
Woodhouse (Leic.) 34 SK5315
Woodhouse (S Yorks.) 33 SK4184
Woodhouse Eaves 34 SK5214
Woodhouselee 51 NT2364
Woodhurst 27 TL3176
Woodingdean 12 TQ3605
Woodland (Devon) 5 SX7968
Woodland (Durham) 41 NZ0726
Woodlands (Dorset) 8 SU0508
Woodlands (Grampn.) 62 NO7895
Woodlands (Hants.) 9 SU3111
Woodlands Park 11 SU8578
Woodleigh 5 SX7348
Woodlesford 38 SE3629
Woodley 10 SU7973
Woodmancote (Glos.) 17 SP0008
Woodmancote (W Susx) 11 SU7707
Woodmancott 10 SU5642
Woodmansey 39 TA0537
Woodmansterne 11 TQ2760
Woodminton 8 SU0122
Woodnesborough 13 TR3156
Woodnewton 27 TL0394
Woodplumpton 36 SD4934
Woodrising 29 TF9803
Woodseaves (Salop) 32 SJ6830
Woodseaves (Staffs.) 32 SJ7925
Woodsend 10 SU2275
Woodsetts 34 SK5483
Woodsford 8 SY7690
Woodside (Berks.) 11 SU9371
Woodside (Herts.) 19 TL2506
Woodside (Tays.) 56 NO2037
Woodstock 18 SP4416
Woodthorpe (Derby.) 34 SK4574
Woodthorpe (Leic.) 34 SK5417
Woodton 29 TM2894
Woodtown 6 SS4926
Woodville 33 SK3119
Woodyates 8 SU0219
Woofferton 24 SO5168
Wookey 7 ST5145
Wookey Hole 7 ST5347
Wool 8 SY8486

Woolacombe — Zennor

Name	Page	Grid
Woolacombe	6	SS 4543
Woolaston	17	ST 5999
Woolavington	7	ST 3441
Woolbeding	11	SU 8722
Wooler	53	NT 9928
Woolfardisworthy (Devon)	6	SS 3321
Woolfardisworthy (Devon)	5	SS 8208
Woolfords Cottages	51	NT 0057
Woolhampton	10	SU 5766
Woolhope	24	SO 6135
Woollage Green	13	TR 2449
Woolland	8	ST 7706
Woolley (Cambs.)	27	TL 1474
Woolley (W Yorks.)	38	SE 3113
Woolmer Green	19	TL 2518
Woolpit	29	TL 9762
Woolscott	26	SP 4968
Woolstaston	24	SO 4498
Woolsthorpe	34	SK 8334
Woolston (Ches.)	32	SJ 6589
Woolston (Hants.)	9	SU 4410
Woolston (Salop)	32	SJ 3224
Woolston (Salop)	24	SO 4287
Woolstone (Bucks.)	19	SP 8738
Woolstone (Oxon.)	18	SU 2987
Woolton	32	SJ 4286
Woolton Hill	10	SU 4261
Woolverstone	21	TM 1838
Woolverton	17	ST 7853
Woolwich	12	TQ 4478
Wooperton	53	NU 0420
Woore	32	SJ 7242
Wootton (Beds.)	27	TL 0045
Wootton (Hants.)	9	SZ 2498
Wootton (Humbs.)	39	TA 0815
Wootton (Kent)	13	TR 2246
Wootton (Northants.)	26	SP 7656
Wootton (Oxon.)	18	SP 4319
Wootton (Oxon.)	18	SP 4701
Wootton (Staffs.)	32	SJ 8227
Wootton (Staffs.)	33	SK 1045
Wootton Bassett	17	SU 0682
Wootton Bridge	9	SZ 5491
Wootton Common	9	SZ 5390
Wootton Courtenay	6	SS 9343
Wootton Fitzpaine	7	SY 3695
Wootton Rivers	17	SU 1962
Wootton St. Lawrence	10	SU 5953
Wootton Wawen	25	SP 1563
Worcester	25	SO 8555
Worcester Park	11	TQ 2266
Wordsley	25	SO 8887
Worfield	24	SO 7595
Workington	40	NX 9928
Worksop	34	SK 5879
Worlaby	39	TA 0113
World's End (Berks.)	10	SU 4876
World's End (Clwyd)	32	SJ 2347
Worle	16	ST 3562
Worleston	32	SJ 6856
Worlingham	29	TM 4489
Worlington (Devon.)	5	SS 7713
Worlington (Suff.)	28	TL 6973
Worlingworth	29	TM 1699
Wormbridge	24	SO 4230
Wormegay	28	TF 6611
Wormelow Tump	24	SO 4930
Wormhill	33	SK 1274
Wormiehills	57	NO 6239
Wormingford	21	TL 9332
Worminghall	18	SP 6408
Wormington	25	SP 0336
Worminster	7	ST 5742
Wormit	57	NO 3925
Wormleighton	26	SP 4453
Wormley	20	TL 3605
Wormshill	13	TQ 8857
Wormsley	24	SO 4248
Worplesdon	11	SU 9753
Worrall	33	SK 3092
Worsbrough	38	SE 3503
Worsley	36	SD 7400
Worstead	29	TG 3026
Worsthorne	37	SD 8732
Worston	37	SD 7642
Worth (Kent)	13	TR 3356
Worth (W Susx)	12	TQ 3036
Worth Abbey	12	TQ 3134
Worth Matravers	8	SY 9777
Wortham	29	TM 0777
Worthen	23	SJ 3204
Worthenbury	32	SJ 4146
Worthing (Norf.)	29	TF 9919
Worthing (W Susx)	11	TQ 1402
Worthington	33	SK 4020
Wortley	38	SK 3099
Worton	17	ST 9757
Wortwell	29	TM 2784
Wotherton	23	SJ 2800
Wotton	11	TQ 1348
Wotton Under Edge	17	ST 7593
Wotton Underwood	18	SP 6815
Woughton on the Green	19	SP 8737
Wouldham	12	TQ 7164
Wrabness	21	TM 1731
Wragby	35	TF 1378
Wramplingham	29	TG 1106
Wrangle	35	TF 4250
Wrangway	7	ST 1217
Wrantage	7	ST 3022
Wrawby	39	TA 0108
Wraxall (Avon)	16	ST 4872
Wraxall (Somer.)	8	ST 5936
Wray	36	SD 6067
Wraysbury	11	TQ 0173
Wrea Green	36	SD 3931
Wreay (Cumbr.)	46	NY 4349
Wreay (Cumbr.)	10	NY 4423
Wrekenton	47	NZ 2758
Wrelton	43	SE 7686
Wrenbury	32	SJ 5947
Wreningham	29	TM 1699
Wrentham	29	TM 4982
Wressle	38	SE 7031
Wrestlingworth	27	TL 2547
Wretton	28	TF 6800
Wrexham	32	SJ 3349
Wribbenhall	24	SO 7975
Wrightington Bar	36	SD 5313
Wrinehall	32	SJ 7546
Wrington	16	ST 4662
Writtle	20	TL 6606
Wrockwardine	24	SJ 6212
Wroot	38	SE 7102
Wrotham	12	TQ 6159
Wrotham Heath	12	TQ 6258
Wroughton	17	SU 1480
Wroxall (I. of W.)	9	SZ 5579
Wroxall (Warw.)	26	SP 2271
Wroxeter	24	SJ 5608
Wroxham	29	TG 3017
Wroxton	26	SP 4141
Wyaston	33	SK 1842
Wyberton	35	TF 3240
Wyboston	27	TL 1656
Wybunbury	32	SJ 6949
Wych Cross	12	TQ 4231
Wychbold	25	SO 9166
Wyche	24	SO 7643
Wyck	10	SU 7539
Wycombe Marsh	19	SU 8992
Wyddial	20	TL 3731
Wyke (Dorset)	8	ST 7926
Wyke (Salop)	24	SJ 6402
Wyke (W Yorks.)	37	SE 1526
Wyke Regis	8	SY 6677
Wyke, The (Salop)	24	SJ 7306
Wykeham (N Yorks.)	39	SE 8175
Wykeham (N Yorks.)	43	SE 9683
Wyken	32	SJ 3925
Wylam	47	NZ 1164
Wylde Green	25	SP 1293
Wylye	8	SU 0037
Wymering	9	SU 6405
Wymeswold	34	SK 6023
Wymington	27	SP 9564
Wymondham (Leic.)	34	SK 8518
Wymondham (Norf.)	29	TG 1101
Wymondley	19	TL 2128
Wyndburgh Hill	46	NT 5504
Wyndham	15	SS 9391
Wynford Eagle	8	SY 5895
Wyre Piddle	25	SO 9647
Wysall	34	SK 6027
Wythall	25	SP 0775
Wytham	10	SP 4708
Wyverstone	29	TM 0468
Wyverstone Street	29	TM 0367
Y Fan	23	SN 9487
Y Rhiw	30	SH 2228
Yaddlethorpe	39	SE 8806
Yafford	9	SZ 4581
Yafforth	42	SE 3494
Yalding	12	TQ 7050
Yanworth	17	SP 0713
Yapham	38	SE 7851
Yapton	11	SU 9703
Yarburgh	35	TF 3493
Yarcombe	7	ST 2408
Yardley	26	SP 1385
Yardley Gobion	26	SP 7644
Yardley Hastings	27	SP 8656
Yardro	23	SO 2258
Yarkhill	24	SO 6042
Yarlet	33	SJ 9129
Yarlington	8	ST 6529
Yarm	42	NZ 4111
Yarmouth	9	SZ 3589
Yarnfield	33	SJ 8632
Yarnscombe	6	SS 5523
Yarnton	18	SP 4711
Yarpole	24	SO 4665
Yarrow	51	NT 3527
Yarrow Feus	51	NT 3325
Yarsop	24	SO 4047
Yarwell	27	TL 0697
Yate	17	ST 7082
Yateley	10	SU 8160
Yatesbury	17	SU 0671
Yattendon	10	SU 5474
Yatton (Avon)	16	ST 4265
Yatton (Here. and Worc.)	24	SO 4367
Yatton (Here. and Worc.)	24	SO 6330
Yatton Keynell	17	ST 8676
Yaverland	9	SZ 6185
Yaxham	29	TG 0010
Yaxley (Cambs.)	27	TL 1892
Yaxley (Suff.)	29	TM 1173
Yazor	24	SO 4046
Yeading	19	TQ 1182
Yeadon	37	SE 2040
Yealand Conyers	40	SD 5074
Yealand Redmayne	40	SD 5075
Yealmpton	4	SX 5751
Yearsley	42	SE 5874
Yeaton	32	SJ 4319
Yeaveley	33	SK 1840
Yedingham	43	SE 8979
Yelford	18	SP 3504
Yelling	27	TL 2562
Yelvertoft	26	SP 5975
Yelverton (Devon)	4	SX 5267
Yelverton (Norf.)	29	TG 2901
Yenston	8	ST 7120
Yeoford	5	SX 7898
Yeolmbridge	4	SX 3187
Yeovil	7	ST 5515
Yeovil Marsh	7	ST 5418
Yeovilton	7	ST 5422
Yerbeston	14	SN 0609
Yesnaby	63	OY 2215
Yetlington	53	NU 0209
Yetminster	8	ST 5910
Yettington	7	SY 0585
Yetts o' Muckhart	56	NO 0001
Yielden	27	TL 0167
Yieldshields	50	NS 8750
Yiewsley	19	TQ 0680
Ynysboeth	16	ST 0696
Ynysddu	16	ST 1892
Ynyshir	16	ST 0292
Ynyslas	22	SN 6092
Ynysybwl	16	ST 0594
Yockenthwaite	41	SD 9079
Yockleton	24	SJ 3910
Yokefleet	39	SE 8124
Yoker	50	NS 5168
Yonder Bognie	62	NJ 5946
York	38	SE 6052
Yorkletts	13	TR 0963
Yorkley	17	SO 6306
Yorton	32	SJ 4923
Youlgreave	33	SK 2164
Youlstone	4	SS 2715
Youlthorpe	38	SE 7655
Youlton	38	SE 4863
Young's End	20	TL 7319
Yoxall	33	SK 1419
Yoxford	29	TM 3968
Ysbyty Ifan	31	SH 8448
Ysbyty Ystwyth	22	SN 7371
Ysceifiog	31	SJ 1571
Ysgubor-y-coed	22	SN 6895
Ystalyfera	15	SN 7608
Ystrad	16	SS 9796
Ystrad Aeron	22	SN 5256
Ystrad Meurig	22	SN 7067
Ystrad-Mynach	16	ST 1493
Ystradfelte	15	SN 9313
Ystradffin	15	SN 7846
Ystradgynlais	15	SN 7910
Ystradowen (Dyfed)	15	SN 7512
Ystradowen (S Glam.)	16	SS 0177
Ythanbank	62	NJ 9034
Ythsie	62	NJ 8830
Zeal Monachorum	5	SS 7103
Zeals	8	ST 7731
Zelah	2	SW 8051
Zennor	2	SW 4538